D0820153

THE ENDLESS CITY

The Urban Age Project by the London School of Economics and Deutsche Bank's Alfred Herrhausen Society

Edited by Ricky Burdett and Deyan Sudjic

ESS CITY

INTRODUCTION

CITIES

*A statistical analysis of the
six Urban Age cities*

ISSUES

INTERVENTIONS

*An exploration of 20 projects
demonstrating new urban thinking
in the six Urban Age cities*

POSITIONS

INDEX

FOREWORD

In the beginning was the city …

We do not know when a surplus of food first allowed the establishment of a community based on the division of labour in a large, self-contained settlement. Exactly when the first city came into being lies hidden in the depths of history. The early cities that have been discovered by archaeologists show signs of already being fully developed. There seems to be hardly any difference between the problems they experienced and those of today's big cities – waste disposal, drinking-water supply, epidemics, traffic noise, street fights after sports events, environmental pollution … Ancient Rome could be recognized from afar by its pall of smoke.

The city is an expression of the 'human quality', like writing and religion. Civil liberty, science and the rule of law arose in cities. It was here that the foundations for modern states were laid. Compared with cities, nation states are 'young' enterprises that have yet to prove their viability.

Cities have always had a magnetic pull. Even in their early days, they had to surround themselves with walls for protection against immigration. Anyone not living in the city felt like a second-class citizen. This is how it was in ancient Rome, where wars were even waged over citizenship. People living in cities have always enjoyed more freedom and possibilities for development than those living outside them.

Since the advent of written records, we know that it has been customary to hold cities responsible for all human errors and corruption. Babylon, ancient Rome, Paris and New York, for instance, all became symbols of disastrous development. Sodom and Gomorrah were destroyed, yet today cities can be found all over the world. Despite their biblical condemnation they have remained a model of successful urban development: for over 5,000 years people have been streaming into cities in the hope of finding freedom and a better future. New York, Shanghai, Johannesburg, Mexico City, São Paulo and Mumbai have come to represent a promise of salvation for many people – they are places full of hope. In 50 years' time, more than 75 per cent of the world's population will live in cities; at that point national governments in the capitals will no longer be safe from urban populations if they fail to keep their cities' promises. Demonstrations and burning barricades in Paris, for example, have often proved more effective than the National Assembly's democratically approved decisions. Such events can quickly turn a mayor into a powerful opponent of the government. This is the reason that the British and French governments hesitated for years before finally allowing London and Paris to have their own lord mayors. Behind this attitude there may be an unarticulated fear that whoever controls the biggest city also controls the country.

All problems become more concentrated in the close confines of urban areas, yet cities are poised for unlimited growth. Today there is not enough energy and water for everyone, and in many places security is only available to those who can pay for it. If a city's economic strength starts to wane – if it migrates to other, more attractive, cities – the country will become poor. If cities become ungovernable due to their sheer size, new secondary powers will start to emerge that could ignite a general and apparently aimless revolution.

Failing cities lead to failing states. If inhabitants start to fence themselves inside a city, this is already a sign of declining government-controlled order. If the governability of cities, their plans and their architects cannot successfully adjust to the changing conditions of the twenty-first century, there is a risk that urban culture, and with it the nation state, will die out in the wilderness of future mega-cities. The superficially fantastic new megacities seem to have embraced unrestricted growth, but where are the extra supplies of energy and food to come from to safeguard that growth? How much environmental destruction can they withstand?

Cities are the great common task of all nation states. They are threatened by scarce resources, environmental problems, new diseases, uncontrolled growth and migration, and by the ethnic and religious conflicts stemming from the despair of disappointed immigrants. In 2020 a predicted 1.4 billion people will be living in slums. How can this be reconciled with an intended future of prosperity and positive human interaction? If we want the city to remain the driving force behind human development, we must reinvent it now; otherwise there is the risk that it will become the final stage of human civilization in the twenty-first century.

The Urban Age project of the London School of Economics and Deutsche Bank's Alfred Herrhausen Society is a long-term investigation into the future of the city. Our first analyses led to sceptical optimism. In spring 2004 Richard Sennett invited me to a conference of European mayors, which was a decisive trigger for the Alfred Herrhausen Society's involvement in this topic. In a discussion with Ricky Burdett, what was initially an idea focused only on Europe became a major global project, but without the faith of Deutsche Bank's CEO Dr Josef Ackermann, as well as his generous support and advice, the Urban Age programme could not have come into being. I would like to take this opportunity to express a special thanks to him and to Deutsche Bank.

Wolfgang Nowak is Managing Director of the Alfred Herrhausen Society, the International Forum of Deutsche Bank

THE URBAN AGE PROJECT

Ricky Burdett and Philipp Rode

As a project, the Urban Age started surreptitiously in early 2004, when the LSE Cities Programme brought together mayors from European and American cities to discuss the links between physical form and social well-being. We realized at that point that the big questions facing cities were clear – globalization, immigration, jobs, social exclusion, sustainability – but that many people running cities did not have the answers. Given that more than half the world's population is now living in cities – a number that is likely to reach 75 per cent by 2050, while it was only 10 per cent in 1900 – these urban questions have become truly global ones, with significant consequences for the future of our planet. Behind the dramatic statistics lie very different visceral realities that link urban form to urban society, shaped by the homogenizing impact of global flows of capital, people and energy. And each city form – compact, high-rise, low-rise, hyper-dense, sprawling, dispersed, polycentric, geometric, organic or informal – brings with it its own set of social, economic and environmental consequences. These are the issues that lie behind mankind's first Urban Age.

It was during a brief conversation with Wolfgang Nowak – the head of Deutsche Bank's Alfred Herrhausen Society – that the Urban Age project began to take shape as a worldwide series of conferences investigating the future of cities. Three years on, after six conferences in six world cities, the Urban Age has moved from a loose association of urban experts to a more formal network of city leaders, academics, designers and professionals – from a group of urban nomads to an urban tribe, as Saskia Sassen has described it. By analysing, experiencing and debating the complex urban experiences of New York City, Shanghai, London, Mexico City, Johannesburg and Berlin, we have structured a framework of interdisciplinary inquiry that allows us to draw lessons from, rather than recommend standard solutions, to the problems associated with the emerging world of mega-cities. Reflecting the intellectual mission of the LSE Cities Programme, at the core of this inquiry lies a shared belief that the future well-being of our cities lies in a more profound understanding of the links between the built environment – housing, buildings, transport, infrastructure, streets and public spaces – and the social, economic and political processes that give rise to them. The Urban Age is, in effect, an exploration of the connections between urban form and urban society, translating a conventionally constrained two-dimensional discourse into a three-dimensional dialogue. In this it recognizes the insights of Jane Jacobs, one of the greatest urbanists of the twentieth century, that 'the look of things and the way they work are inextricably bound together'.

10%
of the world's population lived in cities in 1900

50%
live in cities today

75%
is an estimate for the year 2050

The Urban Age was designed to influence the next generation of urban leaders. The reason for this is simple. Urban policymakers still struggle to balance the escalation of public and private investment in cities with more sustainable forms of urban development. Questions regarding the size, speed of growth, shape and spatial distributions of densities, land uses and morphologically differentiated areas of the city have become increasingly complex and politicized. The design of the built environment, the distribution of urban density, and their impacts on social inclusion and quality of life are at the forefront of political discussions in cities across the globe. More often than not, traditional models of urban growth and theories of city form fail to explain the dynamics now evident in both the networked global city, which thrives as a new economic centrality in the world system, and in the megacity, which faces severe pressures generated by its own relentless growth. Moreover, these contemporary stylized paradigms seem to confound themselves in the cities of the developed North and the developing South, of the individualist West and the more group-oriented East. A set of common challenges face New York City and London, but also Mexico City and Johannesburg or the rapidly growing Shanghai. The development patterns of these cities generate important conceptual and practical questions that prompt us to rethink basic notions of urbanity and cityness.

A Sounding Board for Cities

It is for this reason that the format of the Urban Age inquiry has been experimental and iterative. The conferences took place three times a year, from February 2005 in New York City to the final Urban Summit in Berlin in November 2006, with a smaller one-off event on German cities held in the formerly East German shrinking city of Halle in the summer of 2006. Each conference lasted for two days, with an invited audience of between 100 and 150 people drawn from the city's political, development, academic and design communities. Each conference was small enough to allow for discursive sessions among all participants and large enough to incorporate many opinions and backgrounds. During the preparation lead-in time, the Urban Age team carried out research on key local themes and identified partner institutions – research centres and city authorities – which helped shape the content and audiences of the individual events. The outcome of this research formed the basis of illustrated conference Newspapers, containing diagrams, graphs and texts, which were distributed to all participants in advance of each conference. Many of these diagrams have been refined and reworked for this publication, providing an authoritative comparative database on the spatial and social DNA of these six Urban Age cities.

Rather than issuing full transcripts, each conference was followed up by a Bulletin summarizing the more substantive contributions and including a series of salient quotes from key speakers and participants, giving a flavour of the differing dimensions of the debate within each city. In addition, some of the academic experts were commissioned to write a reflection, presenting their personal perspective on local economic development, transport policies and public safety within each of the six Urban Age cities. Most of this material, conference presentations and audio files, as well as photographs and visual data, is available on the comprehensive Urban Age website, which has served as the main platform for the dissemination of information to a wider audience of city scholars and practitioners (see www.urban-age.net).

About 20 travelling experts, drawn from the International Advisory Committee chaired by Richard Sennett and Deyan Sudjic, were invited to give presentations alongside recognized local players, representing some of the major institutions of city life – from mayors, governors and policymakers, to experts in the local urban economy, culture, transport and design. Local speakers and experts were drawn from the city under investigation as well as from the wider geographical region. Together with the international experts, they provided a sounding board on the core issues facing each Urban Age city. To maximize the potential for exchange, the conference rooms were laid out in a U-shaped format – encouraging eye-contact – with more formal 15-minute presentations followed by 5-minute responses providing an opportunity for a wider debate and participation from the invited audience. Presentations utilized knowledge gained from lessons learned on the ground and were followed by short statements and an open discussion on how policy is responding to the dominant urban trends in each city.

A key objective of the Urban Age conference series was to identify the trends and policies that are failing to respond to local needs, resulting in the continued propagation of dysfunctional urban areas across the globe. In addition to the academic experts, a group of urban practitioners, comprising politicians, architects and engineers, were actively involved at each conference, supporting and challenging the notions put forth by the academics and local participants. Tours of each city's diverse conditions and regular social events played a significant role in reinforcing links between the Urban Age experts and local participants, with high-level political representation at formal dinners – including the President of Mexico, the Chancellor of Germany and key government ministers.

Reflecting the interdisciplinary mission of the Urban Age to investigate work, mobility, housing and public life in cities, each conference was broken down into dedicated sessions on the four key areas of investigation: the changing nature of work and its impact on the physical form of the city; the effects of mobility and transport systems on social cohesion and economic viability; how the design of housing and neighbourhoods affects local communities and urban integration; and how the public life and urban spaces of the city foster or impede tolerance and conflict among the different constituencies.

While each conference followed a standard structure, the family of urban experts and cognizance of urban issues grew and changed as we moved from venue to venue. Key cross-cutting themes included investment and economic development, planning and legal structures, sustainability and energy consumption, and political economy and networking cities. How cities are governed, by whom and for whom, became a major theme from the very first conference in New York City, where the apparent atrophy of its Mass Transit Authority was more clearly associated with the deficiencies of the decision-making system – the MTA is controlled by the State of New York and not the Mayor of New York City – than with lack of investment or ambition to improve public services. By contrast, the fast turnaround of the fortunes of London's public transport system since 2000 – with the adoption of the controversial but successful Congestion Charge and increased investment in bus- and rail-based systems – has more to do with the new Mayor of London's role as the Chairman of Transport for London, than a sudden discovery that public transport matters. Similarly, the mismatch between political boundaries and the need for effective urban governance were rendered palpable in Mexico City, when it became clear during the conference that the Mayor of Mexico City DF (the historic core of this vast expanding city, inhabited by less than half of the nearly 20 million people of the wider city, the rest occupying the sprawling informal suburbs of the State of Mexico) and the Governor of the State of Mexico did not cooperate in any form of political institution that allowed them to tackle the city's severe problems of public transport, housing, pollution or infrastructure. This was, therefore, a matter of the architecture of decision-making rather than a matter of architecture.

Vertical Ghettos and the Death of Downtown

Of the six cities visited, Mexico City best epitomizes the tensions between spatial and social order. Its endless low-rise spread, with 60 per cent of its nearly 20 million inhabitants living in illegal and informal housing, conceals a fast-developing landscape of difference exacerbated by the dominance of the car in a city where petrol is cheaper than mineral water. Investment in two-tier motorways, rather than the type of sustainable public transport that has so successfully transformed Bogotá or Curitiba, is pulling the city even further apart, lengthening commuting times for its workers and pushing the poor to the far fringes of this seemingly limitless city. Here, the rich seek protection in golf-course residential typologies within armed and gated communities, or in the emerging vertical ghettos of Santa Fe, with their shimmering high-rises overlooking the organic but well-established shanty towns, where the vibrant informal sector constitutes 60 per cent of the city's economy. Despite the high quality of the city's early-twentieth-century well-planned, compact neighbourhoods of Condesa and Roma, architects and planners are struggling to convince their civic leaders that intensification of the city's central districts is the solution to its massive infrastructure deficiencies – poor public transport, lack of water, crumbling terrain and limited open space – while the absence of any form of growth boundary or development control outside its legal boundaries makes any attempt at city planning meaningless. Yet architecture and urban design are still managing to play significant social roles. Even the controversial private-sector-led regeneration of the recently abandoned Centro Histórico, with street improvements, pedestrianization and city-centre housing, reflects the impact the built environment can have on the image and identity of a city struggling to establish its credentials as a democratic and economically thriving city in a period of intense political and economic change. Having perhaps reached a natural limit to its horizontal expansion, Mexico City needs to untangle its messy governance structures and recognize that a parallel policy of region-wide growth containment, coupled with a re-densification of its more central neighbourhoods and extensive rail-based public transport, is the only way to respond to the city's seemingly intractable spatial problems.

The civic leaders of Johannesburg face similar but more extreme challenges in tackling the radical demise of its downtown area. Home to the city's major financial institutions until the end of apartheid in 1994, the gritty central district of Hillbrow has since become a no-go area to black and white residents alike. At night the downtown area is eerie, the flickering lights of makeshift kitchens in multi-storey apartments indicating the presence of a new, disenfranchised urban underclass. The effect of this transformation has been profoundly spatial. A large percentage of the city's business institutions have moved out – recently completed hotels and office blocks remain empty or boarded up – to the anodyne suburban centres of Sandton and Rosebank, surrounded by a fast-expanding sea of walled shopping centres and gated residential communities, inhabited by white families and the emerging class of economically empowered blacks. Soweto and Alexandra, formerly segregated black townships with single-storey shacks or two-storey homes laid out on a regular grid, remain physically, if not politically, segregated. There is little or no public transport except the unreliable and expensive communal taxi service that constitutes the only

NEW YORK CITY/LONDON
GLOBAL CAPITALS IN COMPETITION

Although defined by similar parameters –
around 8 million residents and comparable
demographic and economic profiles – New York
City occupies half the space of London, one of
the developed world's most dispersed cities.

JOHANNESBURG/SHANGHAI
TWO KINDS OF TRANSFORMATION

The transformation of post-apartheid Johannesburg
is a less conspicuous and slower process than
Shanghai's explosive urbanization. While the latter
grows upwards with thousands of new office and
residential towers, Johannesburg's expansion
outwards is evident in a 'doughnut effect' of people
abandoning the city centre for high-security
residential enclaves.

MEXICO CITY/BERLIN
POPULATION EXTREMES

Mexico City is the first city, after Tokyo, to reach a population of more than 20 million, while Berlin's overall population has stagnated for years. Mexico City's sprawl stretches endlessly to the horizon; Berlin is a dense compact city with traditional perimeter housing and formal urban layout.

lifeline to jobs. In a region that will become one of the most populous in Africa – the twelfth largest in the world by 2050, despite the effects of the HIV/AIDS epidemic and an average life expectancy of 52 – and has set itself the target of becoming a global city region, Johannesburg's 3-million-plus population is growing at a significant pace. This is creating a physical landscape that monumentalizes separation over inclusion – behind gates, cameras and barbed wire – in which public space fails to perform its democratic potential as a place of interaction and tolerance, and where a non-existent public-transport system reduces the possibility of economic progress. As a new generation of civic leaders begins to tackle these complex urban questions, only 12 years after the birth of a new South Africa, Johannesburg is in a position to redirect its considerable economic power towards the construction of a more compact and integrated environment. It can achieve this through policies and actions that prioritize public transport and investment in the centre, retro-fit its disenfranchised communities with social spaces and facilities, contain the proliferation of out-of-town shopping malls and gated communities. All this will prepare the ground for the new phase of development that will inevitably follow as the region continues to expand.

Like all the other cities of the Urban Age, with the exception of Berlin, New York is growing once again, having experienced and recovered from a period of relative conflict, crime and economic decline. Today, the densest city in the United States is building on its melting-pot status as the only American majority-minority city, where over half of the 8 million people living in its five boroughs are of non-white, non-Hispanic origin. Its compact urban core – with residential blocks arranged along a tight and regular urban grid, and active street frontages lined by shops – has demonstrated resilience, accommodating waves of colonization by different ethnic groups, artists and cultural entrepreneurs, and varying forms of economic activity, from garment sweatshops to corporate headquarters, underscoring the importance of built form in sustaining cycles of urban change. Despite the growth in business and services, New York's less-affluent residents still suffer from an acute shortage of affordable housing, high levels of crime and poor inner-city schools in one of the world's richest cities, where the average GDP per person is US$40,000. The sheer density of the city and its physical distribution between the Hudson and East rivers supports one of the most efficient public-transit systems in the world, used by over half the population to go to work (in Los Angeles it is only 7 per cent). Despite huge investment in its transport system over the last decades – over US$68 billion – the city of New York suffers from a flawed system of governance, resulting in poor strategic coordination, best illustrated perhaps by the ongoing Ground Zero debacle. Together with a string of new housing projects on the edges of Manhattan, Brooklyn, Queens and The Bronx, a series of linear parks and open spaces are being developed on derelict industrial sites, creating the potential of a Blue Belt around Manhattan and providing an urban lung for its high-density residents. While this large-scale, private-sector urban retro-fitting initiative responds to overheated market demands, it risks fuelling an inevitable process of gentrification of the next generation of target areas, which, without the appropriate policies to determine the social mix of people and uses, or public investment in facilities and open spaces, could end up with environments that lack the vibrancy and urbanity of the city's diverse neighbourhoods.

Leaving New York in a snowstorm after a 4-hour taxi ride to JFK airport and taking the 430 km/h, 8-minute Magnetic Levitation (Maglev) train journey from Shanghai airport to the centre is bracing at many levels. New York feels delicate, even fragile, in contrast to the heroic scale and pace of change in China's febrile mercantile city – where over 5,000 towers more than 8 storeys high have been built within 25 years. The raised Maglev monorail flies over a landscape of endless duplications of similar-looking gated communities (regimented apartment blocks neatly aligned at equal distances), vast billboards advertising the very same real-estate opportunities, and isolated reflecting-glass skyscrapers, all part of Shanghai's urban experiment-in-the-making in a city of over 18 million people. The drivers behind this hyper-scale residential development are not only the high levels of in-migration, typical of so many cities of the global South, but also the overpowering demand by the city's residents, especially its emerging professional class, for more space and facilities inside their homes. Only 15 years ago, the average space available to a single person in Shanghai was 6 square metres, roughly the size of small car. Today, that figure has at least doubled, fuelling the housing boom that marks the skyline, and, more significantly, its negative impact on the public realm, the ground level in every corner of the city. The decision to accommodate growth by building high, with isolated point blocks surrounded by car ramps and empty open space, is damaging the subtle urban grain of a city of immense character and dynamic street life. Shanghai's city planners are aware that in the pursuit of economic progress, mistakes are being made that at some point in the future will need to be corrected. Forced relocation of inner-city dwellers (to remote high-rise estates), the banning of bicycles and motorcycles on selected streets (because they cause congestion), the construction of more elevated motorways (to supposedly relieve congestion) and the cynical appropriation of prime sites by corporate behemoths (especially along the Hung Po River), are indicators of an unsustainable development pattern balanced by significant public investment in the underground system, with the addition of 218 km (the equivalent of over half of New York City's entire network) in the years to come. The much-celebrated plan for 11 new satellite towns on the fringes of Shanghai's vast metropolitan area, each themed according to national flavours – the German Town, the Italian Town, the Scandinavian Town, and so on – has been quietly abandoned in favour of a more pragmatic response to the needs of a rampant real-estate sector. This is just one of the many ambiguities of this independent socialist city, which has recently witnessed the effect of Beijing-directed Communist Party purges among its ruling elite.

London is also juggling with the interplay of private interests and public intervention, as it once again faces a period of intense growth after decades of decline. While a mere 500,000 people will be added to London's current total of 7.5 million by 2015 – a modest figure in comparison to the growth rates of Shanghai or Mexico City – most new Londoners will be from outside the UK, many of them from the enlarged European Union, attracted by 400,000 new jobs in the city's strong service and business sectors. One of the first decisions taken by the new Mayor of London in 2001, itself a new institution in the history of governance of this 2,000-year-old city, was to accommodate all growth within the city's existing boundary – the so-called Green Belt. The combination of a demographic and economic growth, a strong property market and the availability of brownfield sites – ex-industrial areas, old railway-goods yards, redundant gas and electricity depots – has started an unprecedented process of urban retro-fitting that is transforming the image as well as the reality of living and working in London. Clusters of high-rise buildings are springing up around existing and new business and transport hubs, while the townscape of the Thames is filling up with a new generation of office and residential structures that add little to the urban quality or grain of the city, re-emphasizing the lasting value of London's traditional stock of terraced housing, which, like Berlin's perimeter housing

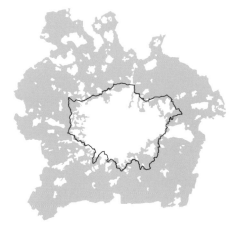

GREEN BELT

In London, the political decision has been made to accommodate future growth within existing boundaries (black contour), protecting regional open spaces (green belt).

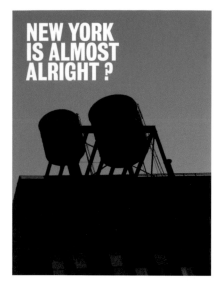

NEW YORK
IS ALMOST
ALRIGHT ?

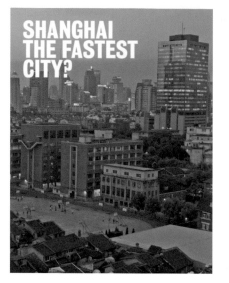

SHANGHAI
THE FASTEST
CITY?

LONDON
EUROPE'S
GLOBAL CITY?

MEXICO CITY
GROWTH
AT THE LIMIT?

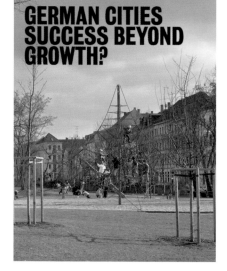

GERMAN CITIES
SUCCESS BEYOND
GROWTH?

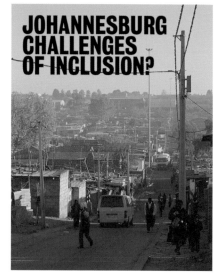

JOHANNESBURG
CHALLENGES
OF INCLUSION?

BERLIN
AN URBAN
EXPERIMENT?

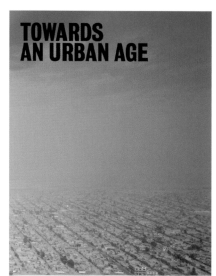

TOWARDS
AN URBAN AGE

or New York's apartment blocks, has demonstrated enormous capacity for change and adaptation as the city undergoes cycles of economic, social and cultural change. London still has one of the oldest and most expensive underground systems in the world, about to undergo a massive facelift through a controversial public-private finance initiative that will affect travel in London for decades. To protect Londoners from spiralling prices (according to investment bank UBS, London in 2006 is the world's most expensive city) there is a requirement that up to 50 per cent of any new housing project must consist of affordable housing, not only for families on waiting lists but also for key workers such as fire fighters, nurses and police officers who are otherwise being progressively priced out of the market. The reality in many of London's inner-city areas is still bleak. More than half of all children live in poverty (52 per cent), and across the city 85,000 children live in temporary housing, many in the 150,000 officially overcrowded households. The new generation of housing typologies currently being designed for London's new communities – with a large concentration in the Thames Gateway in the ex-Docklands area – has the potential to relieve pressure on housing demand, but risks polarizing the relatively diffuse distribution of wealth in London that determines its diverse character.

'Poor but sexy' is how Berlin's Mayor Klaus Wowereit charmingly defended his city at the final conference, the Urban Age Summit, which brought together over 300 participants, including Chancellor Merkel, from the German capital and other Urban Age cities. This statement struck a chord among the city's new residents and taxpayers – many of them young, adventurous and bohemian – coming as it did just as the German national government refused to take on the responsibility for the capital's state of near-bankruptcy. Some of Germany's leading opinion-makers talked seriously about the potential of Berlin to become a special economic zone, where a particular fiscal regime is needed to revive the city's stagnant economy now that the money has run out for new museums, opera houses and theatres. For the outsider, the concept of Berlin as poor is difficult to reconcile with the all-encompassing lustre of newness that defines the reborn centre on both sides of the former Wall, from the glazed halls of the Hauptbahnhof, Berlin's brand-new railway station, to the glitzy sheen of so many of the city's newest monuments clustered around Potsdamer Platz and Unter den Linden, the effortless efficiency of the S/U-Bahn and tram-based public transport system, to the generosity of the Tiergarten, Berlin's vast and manicured green urban lung. Even the quality of the municipal paving is of a much higher standard than anything to be found in the central districts of London, New York or Tokyo. Yet its reputation as sexy seems well deserved, given the high birth rate of its residents (more children are born in Berlin's neighbourhood of Prenzlauer Berg than in any other German city), the pervasiveness of its café culture and the promiscuous metropolitan intensity of the night life. However, the statistics confirm the other side of the story. The misleading predictions of a steep population increase after reunification – when the city instead experienced a minor population loss and a high population churn, which has seen one half of Berliners moving out and being replaced in the last 10 years – reflect the reality of a city with few jobs, high unemployment and low wages. Today, 16 years after reunification, there are only a handful of corporate global headquarters compared to Frankfurt, New York or London. Despite this, the city has demonstrated a resilience in the face of economic gloom, based – to a degree – on the spatial quality of its distinctive urban form, composed of perimeter blocks with generous courtyards and tree-lined avenues. Building on its legendary spirit of freedom and open culture, the city is now attracting artists, writers, musicians and creative types who settle – legally or illegally – in redundant warehouses-cum-studios or make the most of large sunlit 200-square-metre apartments, often at less than EURO 500 (US$675) a month. Berlin, ultimately, is a city that is unlikely to regain its central role in the German economy, but is trying to make the most of its locus at the heart of a European city network and its highly adaptable urban and architectural form.

Accommodating Differences

So what are the lessons, after two years of investigation, that emerge from these cities? In their own specific ways all six Urban Age cities respond to the generic challenges and opportunities of globalization, immigration, jobs, social exclusion and sustainability that we confronted, with our city mayors, at the beginning of this urban journey. The positive impacts of globalization on local economic development are palpable, but so are their negative physical effects on income disparity, social exclusion and an increasingly ghettoized landscape of rich and poor – behind barbed wire, security walls or cul-de-sac layouts. Immigration is, in many ways, the lifeblood of emerging global cities such as Shanghai, Mexico City or Johannesburg, but the spatial distribution of new arrivals, in remote locations starved of the most basic facilities and infrastructure (schools, sewers and transport), creates environments that fail to build on the very strength of cities, as described by Richard Sennett, as places where 'urban life becomes a source of mutual strength rather than a source of mutual estrangement and civic bitterness'.

Older cities like New York, Berlin and London, which have accumulated difference over time, have developed resilient urban structures that accommodate social difference both within their overall dense but distributed urban structures and in the design of the building blocks of urban form – the housing typology. The Berlin perimeter block, the London terraced house or the New York grid with its mixed-use, multi-storey buildings and active street frontages, have successfully adapted to cycles of social and economic change without setting in stone the temporary (albeit sudden and dramatic) shifts in economic and political life that are currently affecting Shanghai, Mexico City and Johannesburg. It is here that the next generation of city leaders can make a difference, by reversing the trend of increasing fragmentation and discontinuity in favour of more integrated urban structures that build on the local DNA of each city form.

At the metropolitan and regional scale, it is clear that more compact urban development provides the only sustainable answer to global urban growth. This is true not only because less sprawl leads to a reduction in energy use and pollution – and cities contribute 75 per cent of world CO_2 emissions – but also because dense cities require less investment in public transport, infrastructure and services to make them work. The upgrading of New York's and London's ageing public-transport systems, Shanghai's investment in an extensive underground network, and the successes of Bogotá's less-onerous Transmilenio bus and cycle network all show how city governments have prioritized public transport not simply as an end in itself but as a form of social justice, providing millions of people with access to jobs and amenities.

In many ways, the emerging Urban Age agenda – in favour of the compact, mixed-use, well-connected, complex and democratic city – articulated at the conferences and in this publication, runs contrary to what is happening on the ground in the vast majority of urban areas. They are larger than anything we have seen before, and are growing at a faster pace, but the shape and the language of the emerging urban landscapes are somewhat familiar. They are, in effect, by-products of outdated western planning models predicated on separation rather than inclusion, propounding single-function zones, elevated motorways and gated communities as the answers to rapid urbanization. Despite the increasingly mature pro-city debate in the economically advanced countries of the world, we seem to have dumped these models on to the fragile urban conditions of the exploding cities of the global South.

Two years of urban travel and investigation have allowed the Urban Age to identify that beneath the skin of at least these six world cities lie deep connections between social cohesion and built form, between sustainability and density, between public transport and social justice, between public space and tolerance, and between good governance and good cities that matter to the way urban citizens live their lives. Perhaps more so than ever before, the shape of cities, how much land they occupy, how much energy they consume, how their transport infrastructure is organized and where people are housed – in remote, segregated environments behind walls or in integrated neighbourhoods close to jobs, facilities and transport – all affect the environmental, economic and social sustainability of global society. One of the overriding realizations of the Urban Age is that cities are not just concentrations of problems – which they are – but that they are also where problems can be solved.

POPULATION GROWTH

Population growth in the six Urban Age cities follows a variety of patterns. London, New York and Berlin had their period of exponential growth at the beginning of the twentieth century; Mexico City, Shanghai and Johannesburg did not start to grow at similar rates until the 1950s. By 1910, London and New York each had a total population of over 5 million and they shared a period of decline followed by growth in recent years. It was not until 1990 that the populations of Mexico City and Shanghai crossed the 15 million mark.

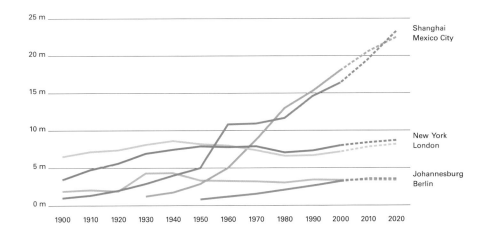

NATIONAL URBANIZATION

The United States, Britain and Germany were already largely urbanized by 1950. Since then, the proportion of their urban population has grown from between 65 and 80 per cent to levels between 80 and 90 per cent. Mexico and South Africa started with similar levels of around 43 per cent in 1950, but Mexico urbanized more rapidly and is about to pass 80 per cent within the next decade. The case of China is one of extreme change where the key phase of urbanization is a phenomenon of the present.

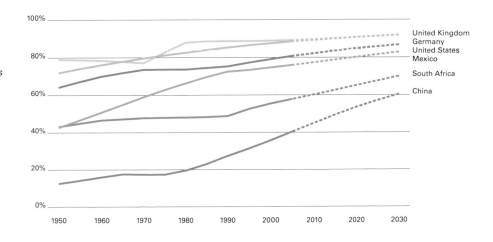

WHERE WE LIVE

The darkest shades on the map represent areas where urban populations are the most concentrated and intense. It is estimated that over 80 per cent of the Earth's land surface is affected by the human footprint.

WHERE THE BIG CITIES ARE

While every region of the world has a number
of cities with over 1 million inhabitants, a new
generation of megacities with over 10 million
people is developing across Asia and some
parts of Africa, Central and South America.

New York

Mexico City

● 1 Million

● 5 Million

● 10 Million

● 20 Million

THE SPEED OF URBAN CHANGE

The relentless pace of urban change can now be measured in many rapidly expanding cities. The number of people who will be added to each city every hour by 2015 is indicated in this map, reflecting increased migration and natural population growth. The fastest growing cities are located outside the advanced economies of the North Atlantic core, with concentrations in India, China and sub-Saharan Africa.

+12
New York

+23
Mexico City

+24
São Paulo

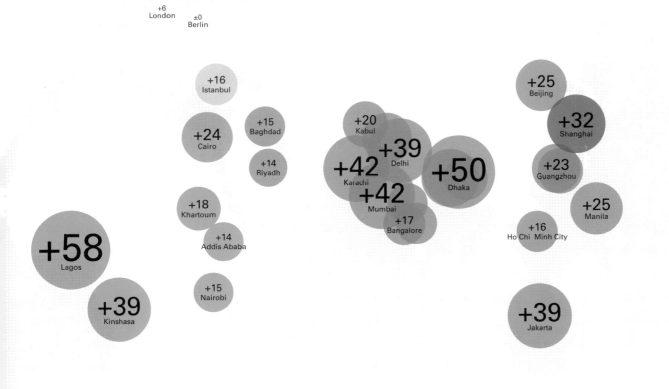

+6
London

±0
Berlin

+16
Istanbul

+15
Baghdad

+24
Cairo

+14
Riyadh

+20
Kabul

+39
Delhi

+42
Karachi

+50
Dhaka

+42
Mumbai

+17
Bangalore

+25
Beijing

+32
Shanghai

+23
Guangzhou

+25
Manila

+16
Ho Chi Minh City

+18
Khartoum

+14
Addis Ababa

+58
Lagos

+39
Kinshasa

+15
Nairobi

+39
Jakarta

+4
Johannesburg

Increased international air travel is one of the
key traces of globalization, bringing cities into
closer contact and, at the same time, highlighting differences between them.

THEORY, POLICY AND PRACTICE

Deyan Sudjic

When I began my job at the Design Museum one of the first things I did was to look back in the museum's files at the correspondence with the local authority over the grant of planning permission for our building. At the end of the 1980s, the trustees were working on a scheme to convert a two-storey Thames-side banana store, within sight of Tower Bridge and no more than 30 years old, into a three-floor museum. This was at the depths of the depression that gripped London's docklands after the shipping-container revolution had exploded with the impact of a neutron bomb, and wiped out enclosed docks the world over. When the big ships moved downriver to the container ports, the resulting cataclysm of change left behind miles of silent, empty warehouses, derelict wharves, mirror-smooth water basins undisturbed by traffic – and not much else. It was hardly the most radical of innovations in technological terms, but in many cities the container has done as much to transform the fabric of urban life as the car.

London's waterfront was all but lifeless 25 years ago. With the exception of a few artist-squatters, some scrap dealers protecting their investments with tangled coils of razor wire, and packs of feral dogs, nobody lived or worked there. On the eve of its abolition by Margaret Thatcher, the Greater London Council went as far as considering a proposal to turn the entire area into a giant park, so convinced were some of its members that there was no serious possibility of attracting employers or housing builders into the area. The message to the museum, planning its move south of the river from its original home in South Kensington, was conveyed in a letter from Southwark's planning officer. 'The Borough is not the planning authority for Shad Thames,' he wrote. The area at that time was the responsibility of the London Dockland Development Corporation, a body appointed by central government, and boycotted for a while by some left-wing councillors and activists on the grounds of its lack of democratic scrutiny. But, the letter went on, 'if we were the planning authority, we would be minded to refuse the application, on the grounds that museum use contravenes our policies on employment generation for the area'.

We are in the hands of a very different planning regime today. Culture-led regeneration is now seen as a key strategy by the planning authorities of every political stripe in almost every country – surfacing in the shape of the Guggenheim's negotiations with cities like Rio de Janeiro, and Macao, the European Capitals of Culture programme and countless lower-profile initiatives. And London, for better or worse, is currently experiencing a massive burst of investment that is transforming its physical character. In this context, the development of Tate Modern and the construction of the Millennium Bridge have been two of the more significant steps in the transformation of Southwark from run-down post-industrial wasteland into a reinvigorated urban neighbourhood. Southwark is now presented as a model of urban good practice, studied by city planners from all over the world. Twenty years ago, and with equal commitment, Southwark Council believed it had a duty to protect the way of life of its threatened communities and to create – or defend – what it saw as the kind of employment that would give them 'real' jobs.

The limitations of those policies were clear even then. Creating employment is not as straightforward as forbidding the transformation of warehouses into lofts, or building advanced factory units and simply hoping that they will find willing takers. Southwark has become a focus for new office development partly because – despite the centuries-long stigma of lying south of the River Thames – it is physically very close to the epicentre of the City of London's financial district. But it took the explosion of publicity over the opening of Tate Modern to finally secure a transformation in perceptions of the area. New residential and office developments quickly followed. Land values soared. Organic-food producers colonized the old Borough Market. Artists' studios, gourmet restaurants and fashionable bars proliferated. One of the glummer former back offices of MI6 was flattened to make way for a glassy building housing the IPC magazine conglomerate headquarters next to Tate Modern.

To some observers these are signs of success; to others they are anything but. Gentrification has always been a mixed blessing. In the crudest terms, it has never been popular among those who take a class-based view on development, and even for those who do not, there have been enough analytical studies to suggest that gentrification can be an employment killer. If Lower Manhattan's warehouses had not been re-zoned for residential use – in the process allowing owners to capitalize on the increased value of their properties by driving out the small businesses specializing in tailoring, jewellery, printing and meat packing – there would be more jobs available in the city than there are today. It was such studies that provided the theoretical underpinning for Southwark's stance. Explorations of the impact of gentrification in Manhattan have suggested that, although some streets may have been beautified and fashionable tourist attractions, coupled with a zero-tolerance policy on crime, have helped to build a service economy, it has been at the expense of traditional industrial employers. High-income newcomers bring life of a certain kind into the city. It can be argued that successful cities are the ones attractive enough to persuade the market makers, the money brokers and the corporate rainmakers to move to them. It can also be argued that their arrival serves to drive up property prices and to exclude those who grew up in them. Under the impact of global capital flows, extreme gentrification may have the effect of bringing on the characteristics of a Manhattan, in which even the wealthy have problems living comfortably when their domestic helps find it impossible to afford homes within commuting distance of their employers – London is also experiencing this phenomenon. Optimistic believers in the power of the market might claim to see in this hints of evidence of a self-limiting mechanism.

It is perhaps too early to be certain that Southwark's policies in the 1980s were entirely misguided. London's white working class still faces unemployment issues, but it is not complacency to observe that much of the growth in the population of central London has been fuelled by the entry-level jobs that it can offer migrants. In itself this fact suggests that the loss of an entire category of traditional employment with the departure of the docks did not, in the end, make much difference to the city's

SKYLINE AS BILLBOARD
Shanghai built its new financial district in
Pudong before it had the jobs to fill it. This was
planning by government decree, in collision
with an exploding market. The mayor staged
an international competition for a masterplan
for Pudong, and declared all the participants
winners, resulting in a fragmental environment
that suits the prevailing investment market.

prospects of creating jobs open to the many. Indeed, for some of Britain's more tightly
regulated competitors within the European Union, the country may have created jobs
at their expense.

The point to be made about all this is not so much whether Southwark was
doing the wrong thing or the right thing, but that, like everybody else, planners tend
to use the weapons and strategies of the last war to fight the battles of the next one.
The situation also gives pause for thought about the way in which ideas about cities
form and change. With the same impeccably worthwhile intention of creating jobs
and a better way of life for its inhabitants, two different generations of planners
proposed opposite strategies, and thus it may well be that cities are more often the
product of unintended consequences than of anything else. The Tate attracts 4 million visitors a year to its new home in Southwark, in part because the construction of
the Jubilee Line extension to the Underground brought it within easier reach. That
extension was built not as the outcome of some long-standing, carefully worked out
plan about where best to direct investment in London's transport infrastructure, but
as a knee-jerk reaction by central government to the trouble in which the huge
Canary Wharf development found itself. The Reichmann brothers' investment vehicle Olympia and York was on the edge of bankruptcy, largely due to the fact that it had
built its office towers at Canary Wharf without a mass-transit system in place to get
the bankers to their desks. The Reichmanns claimed to have found a way of avoiding
the effects of property-market downturns by spreading their risks over two continents. By working simultaneously in two very different markets, they reasoned that
even if one was in recession, the other would be at a different point in the economic
cycle. The harsh reality was that as Canary Wharf took shape, the Reichmanns found
themselves struggling in London and New York as well as Toronto, all at the same
time. The Jubilee Line extension was the Thatcher government's attempt to rescue its
friends, by giving Canary Wharf an Underground link to the outside world, and a
massive public subsidy into the bargain. Of course it was presented in rather different
terms, but the fact remains that there were large areas of south London for which a
comparable level of investment could have helped far more people get to work, and
perhaps would have done rather more for the capital's economy.

Canary Wharf itself was the product of another eruption of unintended consequences. Credit Suisse First Boston and the American developer G. Ware Travelstead
together came to understand that the tax incentives and the relaxed planning regime,
introduced by the Conservative government in the hope of attracting business parks
and light industrial sheds into dockland areas, could equally well benefit the builders
of office towers. Thus, almost absent-mindedly, London's third financial district was
created from nothing. This in turn caused a radical change in the planning regime in
the City of London. From tight control over the degree of alterations considered
permissible to existing buildings, the City turned its collection of 1960s structures
into an urban free-fire zone, triggering an epidemic of redevelopment that not only
changed the face of the city, but also pushed Canary Wharf over the brink of bankruptcy as it faced competition for tenants from a wave of much more attractively sited
new buildings. This was the no doubt entirely deliberate outcome of the City's determination to protect its heritage of more than a millennium of economic supremacy.

The Planner's Armoury

Ideas about how cities should be understood, and what steps might be taken to
address and resolve their problems, can be seen as the product of the more-or-less

Centuries old buildings are demolished at a
rapid rate to accommodate China's dramatic
upwards and outwards urbanization, creating
unexpected juxtapositions between old and
new, as in this central district of Shanghai
showing one of the few remaining Hutong
housing neighbourhoods encroached by
concrete towers.

random interactions of three somewhat disparate groups. The first of these might be
called the theorists, representing those groups of researchers who spend their working lives looking at the meaning of cities. They each have their own perspective of
course: sociological, political or economic. They may be geographers or anthropolo-
gists; they may be detached or engaged, angry or objective. But they are not the same
as the policymakers – the second strand in the three-sided perspective that shapes our
views of the city – and there is sometimes little comprehension and still less warmth
between them. The policymakers write the papers that can be used to shape the structure of city administrations. They offer the strategies that mayors need to deliver their
programmes. They look for ways to fund and implement them. They draft constitutional systems to guide the establishment of administrative and democratic systems.
One set of such policymakers would have devised the approach of the old Southwark,
with its vain attempt to cling to old-fashioned jobs, informed perhaps at second hand
by the work of researchers into the impact of gentrification and the nature of social
exclusion. Another would have prepared the blueprints for the creation of the development corporation that shouldered aside the dockland boroughs – drawing on the
experience of the English new-town administrations, the highly centralized French
code of practice, and possibly even containing a faint echo of the armoury of planning instruments, government institutions and Machiavellian tactics that Robert
Moses used to bend Manhattan to his will. Still another set of policy types would have
shaped a new set of tools intended to nudge London into its twenty-first-century
incarnation – their big-bang regeneration strategies fuelled by Olympic bids and the
introduction of intricate financial instruments with which to finance the updating of
the city's now-threadbare Victorian infrastructure. Finally, it was the policy community that was responsible for the introduction of the idea – alien to the Anglo-Saxon
at least – of a directly elected mayor.

Neither the theorists nor the policymakers share the perspective of the third
conceptual strand: the builders, the investors, the developers, the architects and the
master planners, the transport engineers – in other words, those who actually shape
the physical aspects of the city. These are the people who see themselves as involved
with the practice of city-making. These groups themselves combine many different
strands of thinking. They are driven by motivations ranging from creative self-
expression and idealism to egotism and self-interested pragmatism. Each has its own
way of working in the city and understanding its mechanisms, but the climate in
which each operates is shaped by the others, even if there is seldom any sense that they
are all part of a continuum. Ask an avant-garde architect to provide an example of
what he or she sees as a vital life-enhancing urban phenomenon, and the chances are
that what they come up with will be understood as exactly the opposite by most city
mayors. This third strand comprises the people who see the potential within mathe-
matically expressed density and zoning codes to make a profit on a piece of land, as
they did at Canary Wharf. Sometimes they are the people with the ability to create a
place of character and distinctiveness from the least promising ingredients. These are
the individuals who take pleasure in the process of design and building for its own
sake. And they are the ones who effected the rule change that gave rise to a much more
laissez-faire planning regime in the City of London in order to see off the challenge
from Canary Wharf.

If there is one key insight that above all others has driven the Urban Age project,
it is the belief that our thinking, understanding and actions about and for the city
should seek to explore a new level of maturity. In essence, it is an approach that

RECONSTRUCTING THE AESTHETICS OF THE CITY
Once the no-man's land between two divided cities, the new Potsdamer Platz and other surrounding developments overlook Peter Eisenman's memorial to the victims of the Holocaust in the heart of Berlin.

involves bringing all these strands together. If these fragmented constituencies can be encouraged to learn from and gain greater understanding of one another, they will have the chance of arriving at a more complete picture of the world in which to operate – one that offers more than each could hope to explore on its own. Attempting this convergence is no easy task, but its potential benefits are fundamental in the framing of a new approach to what the city can be. Ultimately, the point must be to allow urban theory to inform policy, and to give theory and policy the understanding of physical, spatial reality that comes from an insight into architectural space. With this conceptual underpinning, we might have a real chance of deploying a powerful new set of critical tools for addressing the future of the city.

This is by no means a simple undertaking. There are walls of complex misunderstanding constructed between theory and policy, and between them and those who see the city in spatial terms. This division is in large part the result of a turf war, underscored by the intricate social hierarchy of academic politics. Yet in this attempt to create a dialogue between communities lies our best hope of adding anything significant to the somewhat threadbare repertoire of analytical tools currently available for understanding and impacting upon the nature of the urban condition.

The city is a subject that is apparently about everything. It is about climate change and racial tolerance, social justice and economic development, culture and personal memory, national identity and civil liberty. Without some sort of focus, however, or a framework applied to the ways in which we think about it, the city is a subject so all-embracing that any discussion about it becomes a discussion about everything – and so, in the end, about nothing.

Utopian Visions and Dystopian Realities

It is chastening, but valuable, for critics to be confronted with how little they really know. Before attending the Urban Age conference in Shanghai, I had not understood that of the city's 17 million or so people, more than 3 million are illegal migrants, or that the city had levels of inequality of an order close to Manhattan's. These are impressive – or depressing – changes for the country that Mao clothed in olive drab. I knew that Johannesburg was a city shaped by apartheid, but I had not understood what it meant to try not just to deal with inequalities, but to do so against the background of a Soweto that was deliberately built to exclude the possibilities of urban life. I could not have imagined what it is like for the city's transport officials to work with a suburban rail system that saw dozens of its employees murdered last year until I met one of those officials. And until I had heard white South-African planners use the word 'comrade' to describe the black ANC councillors for whom they worked in the way that their London equivalents might use the word 'Mr', I did not really appreciate the nature of politics in that city. Probably I still don't.

The most salutary lesson from the privilege of being able to plug into the networks that shape such different cities is an understanding of – however much the urban age operates as part of a single global system, with cities acquiring the same kind of landmarks, museums, airports, motorways, and being subjected to the same quack remedies of tax incentives and marketing programmes – just how different and distinct they remain. It is also a reminder of the difference between knowing a little about a lot and taking a narrow focus on a single issue.

We do not belong to a generation with the shared faith enjoyed by the pioneer architectural modernists, when they chartered a liner to cruise the Mediterranean in agreeable comfort and drew up their vision of what the modern city ought to be in

POTENTIAL FOR DEVELOPMENT
Manhattan is built out to its edges with development proliferating in the outer boroughs. As a result, nearby areas such as the Williamsburg waterfront in Brooklyn are being purged of their manufacturing roots in favour of boxy residential towers with stunning views of New York City's skyline.

the charter of Athens. They divided their ideal city into functional zones, shaped by sunlight angles. Theirs was a generation free from the luxury of self-doubt. Ours is not, and that is why we struggle now in trying to find a renewed sense of purpose about what cities should be. We are full of doubt – or at least we should be. We are the witnesses to the many soured urban utopias invented by the architects on that liner and propagated by a political system that measured success by the number of new buildings it could deliver each month.

Politicians love cranes. They need solutions within the timeframes of elections – but there is only a limited number of problems susceptible to this kind of timescale. The result is that a constant cycle of demolition and reconstruction has come to substitute careful consideration about how to address the deeper issues of the city. In Manchester, where Engels and Ruskin reeled in horror at the impact of urbanization on just a fraction of the scale of that of the Pearl River Delta, and where the great German architect Karl Friedrich Schinkel went to learn the secrets of industrial building, areas are now visible that were originally built up in the 1880s, demolished in the 1930s, and have been built up and demolished again twice since then.

Visions for cities tend to be the creation of the boosters rather than the theorists or the policymakers. City builders have always had to be pathological optimists, if not out and out fantasists. They belong to a tradition that connects the mapmakers who parcel up areas of swampland to sell to gullible purchasers with the show-apartment builders, selling plans to investors in Shanghai who are banking on a rising market, making them a paper profit before they have even made good on their deposits.

Politicians Love Cranes

These are visions of cities as machines for making money, if not for turning the poor into the not-so-poor, which is what attracts the ambitious and the desperate to them in the first place. There are other kinds of vision that start, as so many urban visions have done, with an attempt to deal with the pathology of the city. Modernism, after all, was probably as much about notions of hygiene as anything else.

But there are other, less-tangible visions that no city can do without for long. In some cases, they are a reflection of the ways in which societies organize themselves, most clearly understood as manifestations of a cultural identity. It is only that uniquely Japanese ability to manage chaos into order, for example, that makes Tokyo so different from many poorer Asian cities with similar basic structures. Tokyo is a city without an obvious urban logic beyond the great green void of the emperor's garden at its heart. It has no rational street address or numbering system, a hugely crowded underground rail system, absurd traffic jams – and yet it is one of the most intricately and carefully organized cities in the world. In any other culture such a chaotic structure would be reflected in external, literal chaos. In Japan, apparently genetically programmed levels of social cohesion turn the same raw material that you might find in a Philippine slum into something entirely different.

A city is an *à la carte* menu – this is what distinguishes it from a village, which offers so much less in the way of choice. In the end it is the vision of what it is that gives a city a shared sense of itself. A positive vision of urbanity has to be based on ensuring that more and more customers can afford to make the choice. And there is perhaps a kind of psychological comfort to be found in the idea that a city can still be the product of vision, rather than of unintended consequences.

Those who seek to understand the contemporary city have a lot to learn from novelists and film-makers: architects and city planners are storytellers too, coming up with a narrative long before they ever build anything. They offer a story or, more often, a myth of community or of greenness, an image of modernity or of tradition. It is the literary view of the city from Dickens and Zola onwards that allows us to understand its nuances of light and shade. They help us understand the flawed but rich nature of city life that does not survive the conventional response to urban reality, which is to try to sweep the dark underbelly of the city away. To do that is to risk the collateral damage that will destroy the very qualities that make a city work. The result is to turn a city into a village, which is no place for the dispossessed and the ambitious, desperate to escape from poverty.

In London the area known as the King's Cross railway lands is a gash in the urban fabric that has not healed since the canals and railways tore into it at the start of the nineteenth century. It reflects the reality of city life in its most brutal and extreme form. Hookers and addicts share the pavements with commuters, skirting the vast swathe of canals and sheds, trapped between the Euston Road and the residential streets of Camden Town. Or at least they used to. The area is undergoing a paroxysm of development that irresistibly recalls the feverish transformation of this very piece of land portrayed by Charles Dickens in *Dombey and Son*. Dickens captured the surrealistic dislocation of houses left stranded by railway embankments, and roads that lead nowhere.

Almost the same thing is happening again. The huge glass and white steel box awkwardly tacked on to the back of Victorian St Pancras, designed to handle the high-speed rail link to Paris and Brussels, is nearing completion. It represents a construction project on a scale that matches that of the Victorians, even if it does not reflect their confidence or architectural ambition. Negotiating the area involves threading your way through new viaducts that erupt from the mud, past tower cranes, ancient warehouses and gasometers. The landscape is by turns pastoral and derelict. As it is now, King's Cross is a mud-splattered, anarchic mess that reveals the shifting tectonic plates of urban life. The new King's Cross will be a polite, comfortable place for commuters to drink milky coffee on their way from the train to the office. It is the product of a view of the city as an organism that is tractable and easy to manipulate, but it is unlikely ever to be a city in the sense that Dickens or Zola would understand.

Just as ideas about cities are based on the three groups involved respectively with theory, policy and practice, so the physical reality of a city as considered by the Urban Age is the product of an interrelated, but usually distinct, set of issues. These might be summarized as being concerned with five fundamental topics. One is public space, which is at the very heart of any definition of a city. Then there is movement in and around the city. Public space without the possibility of movement in it is like a dead butterfly in a specimen case: movement means access, which is the real issue connected with space. And space is as much about the symbolic and the theatrical as it is about the technical. It embodies not just capacity, but the mechanisms of democracy too. It is arguable that when Brazil created its new capital city, Lúcio Costa's master plan included only the appearance of democratic space, not its reality, since Brazilian urban life remained in Rio and São Paulo, rather than the great grassy mall of Brasília. Even the fig leaf of democratic space in the national capital vanished when the army took over and set up machine-gun nests outside Niemeyer's government buildings.

Another key to understanding the city lies with its neighbourhoods – the places in which its people live. And to live, and support themselves, there is the question of work. To make all this possible, there is the intangible yet vital issue of security. To make a genuinely functioning city, the people who inhabit it must feel secure.

GOVERNING GLOBAL GROWTH
The organic, cluttered environment of
Tottenham Court Road in central London reflects
the UK capital's uneven relationship with metropolitan government and the exigencies of a
global financial centre.

Security is not wholly susceptible to rational calculation. It is possible to measure security by murder rate or prison population, but in different cities the same statistics about the same issues will have entirely different consequences because they trigger different reactions among the populace.

The city is a complex interaction of issues and ambitions that are shaped by the everyday choices of its citizens as much as by their political leaders or their officials, but these are also governed by the behaviour of the marketplace. In the development of a city, the involvement of oil companies and car builders is as significant as the role of the financial institutions that make house-building possible. City development involves the law and investment regimes, as well as such apparently simple ideas as being able to take a breath of fresh air without worrying about its effects on our health or that of our children. A city is a vision as well as a mechanism, in the sense that Bogotá's bus lanes represent an ideal of easy movement for the masses, as opposed to a negative regulatory system to force through change on the owners of private cars. A city is also the product of precipitate innovation or financial instruments of the kind represented by the introduction of a residential mortgage to China in 1999, and the resulting wave of apartment building that it made possible. Given the costs and obligations that come with the privileges of urban life, however, a city is also a test of the limits of the power of persuasion as opposed to compulsion. Ultimately, a genuine city can only be about the former and not about the latter.

Low Density Urbanism

When all this has been taken into consideration, what options are left for shaping the city? In essence, perhaps, we have only two. First is the option of the high-density city. This, we tell ourselves, is the anti-suburban model, based on an ideal of diversity and inclusiveness. Those infected by the European prejudice towards cities taking a certain kind of physical form embrace this model in opposition to what they maintain, for a variety of reasons – sometimes snobbish, sometimes well-meaning – to be the shortcomings of the low-density city.

Low-density urbanism, on the other hand, is a model equated with what is considered the destructive selfishness of the gated community and the environmentally disastrous results of low-density car-orientated suburbs, which allegedly will become unsustainable long before fossil fuels run out and which do nothing to support the traditional energy and vitality of urban life. However, it could equally well be presented as a model of freedom and sturdy individual choice, in the way Frank Lloyd Wright suggested it might be when he fantasized about his ideal suburban city, Usonia. To those who promote this model, the high-density city is, despite the claims of its champions, a claustrophobic, overdeveloped and dehumanizing ant hill.

Is there nothing in between these two poles that could be used as a model for shaping the city in a constructive and positive way? Is there as yet enough understanding of the lessons taught by cities outside the traditional compounds of Europe and North America that have shaped the majority of thought about what cities can be? What can they do to manoeuvre themselves to a position where they are actually improving life for the people who flock to them – which, in the end, is the underlying justification for a city?

It is difficult to argue that we have as yet absorbed enough of the experiences of the cities of Latin America or China or India to draw on them in any practical way. We know perhaps that a vigorous mayor can pick up one or two of the technical innovations that have filtered north from Curitiba, with its dedicated bus lanes and

INFORMAL URBANISM
Mexico's expansive informal sector is visible
throughout the city centre and its periphery,
occupying street corners, entire pavements,
as well as marginal zones in residential and
commercial neighbourhoods.

pedestrian zones, its investment in schools, clinics and social centres, and its pallia-
tives for social justice that make laws seem worth obeying even for the dispossessed
and the disadvantaged. But there must be more to it than that. We need to look harder
and with clearer vision at the experiences of the informal settlements of the *favelas*
and the *barrios*, not just as urban pathologies, but for an understanding of what
Bernard Rudofsky might have described as urbanism without urbanists. The areas
designated for informal settlements are very often extremely formally organized in
their establishment.

One fashionable alternative to the duality between density and suburbia is the
embrace of chaos. It is an intellectual strategy that could be seen as an attempt to
inoculate against despair those who profess it. Instead of deploring the reality of
what is all around us, we search for the oblivion that comes from looking over the
edge to see the urban vertigo of Lagos or Shanghai. We can take in this view, and then
come away with a reinforced belief that having once acknowledged what is behind
the door we are in some sense living in the real world, even if we barricade ourselves
against it.

Is there in fact any reason to believe that there are universal solutions to the
questions that the city poses? Is it not simply naive to suggest that there is just one
kind of urbanism or urbanity? How can the aspirations and strategies appropriate to
Berlin, say, be relevant to Johannesburg? The well-meaning response to this question
is that there is a case to be made for learning from previous mistakes, and that it
outweighs the possibility of such exchanges acting as some form of hotspot for
cross-contamination.

Change is a fundamental part of the human condition, and what seems to be a
key issue about our interaction with the urban world is to avoid the creation of conditions that serve to freeze the city and cancel out the possibility of further change. The
real trouble with gentrification, just as with the creation of huge swathes of social
housing, is that it prohibits further social or physical change. The problems with the
system-built apartment blocks from the 1960s are not just the day-to-day difficulties
of housing management and maintenance. Their heavy concrete structural panels
give them the mechanics of a pack of cards, ruling out any changes in their layouts.
They cannot easily contract or expand to reflect changing household sizes.

The development practices of global capital can create analogous problems by
relying too much on oversimplified and standardized briefs. A Korean development
fund operating in Spain is going to be hard-pressed to comprehend the subtleties and
complexities of local differences. It will instead rely on a familiar and comprehensible
formula, reducing urbanism to the most banal mix of functions, tenures and financial instruments. The richer, subtler, more effective version of urbanism is the kind
that allows cities to mutate and change as time passes, rather than the type that freezes
a neighbourhood into a particular form.

It has become a commonplace to suggest that the big world cities, which have
become the links in a chain of globalization, have more in common with one another
than they do with the nation state in which they happen to find themselves or even
with the smaller cities with which they share that country. This development is
understood to have propelled them far beyond the traditional city scale, and the
dichotomy that conventionally characterizes the national context in which cities
operate, between a deprived provincial fringe and a privileged metropolitan core.
That old pattern has always driven pork-barrel politics, and has allowed small-town
politicians to argue for what they claim is a more equitable division of the spoils

LIFE IN THE MARGINS
In a city that has experienced a surge in inner-city crime and abandonment of its central districts, the inhabitants of Johannesburg have come to rely increasingly upon emerging and constantly evolving systems of commerce and communication, often informal, often stratified, to navigate their post-apartheid existence.

than a central government has to offer in terms of the location of jobs and in such infrastructure investments as the location of airports.

This strategy, however, may now be seen as self defeating. If London loses out in its attractiveness for an Indonesian corporation or a Russian oil company as a place in which to do financial business, it will not be Manchester, Edinburgh or Birmingham that becomes a viable alternative. It will be Frankfurt, Tokyo or New York. Divert investment for a new runway from Heathrow to, say, Manchester, and the beneficiary could be the German rather than the British taxpayer.

Paris's grip on the fashion world is not going to be challenged by Lyon or Marseille: it is Milan or Tokyo it has to compete with. Rather than spread investment thin, a more effective strategy may be to concentrate it where it will have the maximum impact. The world cities are disproportionately responsible for the success of national economies and thus these are the cities that matter equally disproportionately. At the same time, their social composition makes them increasingly distinct from the nation at large. London's population growth over the last decade, for example, is almost exclusively made up of people who were not born in Britain. It is this new growth, reversing decades of steady decline, coupled with the success of the Singapore and Hong Kong city states – and perhaps of the more recent emergence of the Gulf city states too – that has raised the possibility of an urban renaissance at the expense of the nation state.

It is possible to understand this either as a new phenomenon, or simply as a new version of an old one, just as it is possible to see the whole anti-globalization narrative, with its curiously irrational distaste for innocent companies such as Starbucks (who, after all, dispense coffee rather than napalm), as a contemporary twist on the same xenophobic themes that have made rural peasant communities suspicious of big-city ways throughout the centuries. What is new is the way in which more and more systems are increasingly centralized, even as we assume that the world is becoming more networked, diffuse and decentralized. Entertainment is dominated by Los Angeles to an extraordinary extent. International finance is concentrated in three cities, in which traditional locational economics still apply, despite the prophecies of those who see the city giving way to a much more diffuse form of settlement. And the form of the city can still be read in terms of building typologies required by the dominant groups within them – mainly towers for the lawyers that allow for the maximum number of corner offices and free-form blobs for the bankers who want deep-plan dealing rooms.

The city is clearly a much older creation than the nation state, with which it is now increasingly in competition for prestige and authority. It is significant that we still speak of the ancient imperial systems as 'Rome' or 'Byzantium' – cities that attempted to replicate themselves as colonial franchises, in the way that Venice did, rather than to project a larger national or trans-national identity such as America or Ottoman Turkey. It is, of course, at least arguable that contemporary America has also had its most powerful impact through a kind of colonial propagation, through its distinctive urban model of downtown skyscrapers, strip malls and edge cities.

A city is, perhaps, closer to being a self-organizing system than a more conscious artificial creation such as an entire nation, which is the product of a particular historical moment and which may yet prove to be of only transient importance. A city without a national context has to live on its wits and its energy and its ability to import human talent. It must become a machine for relentlessly converting ideas and skills into the necessities for survival and prosperity. Over time it must

continually adapt and find new ways to survive, and it must be able to switch from one technology to another to do it.

Nation states look for homogeneity – that is, after all, what they are all about. Yet the most successful cities are usually the most heterogeneous, and the most cosmopolitan. Interestingly, in this respect, it is the comparative ethnic uniformity of Tokyo that has kept it from fully transforming itself into a true world city. Despite its enthusiastic embrace of all things exotic in terms of appearance, in substance it remains essentially Japanese. The converse of this phenomenon is the suspicion with which certain cities are regarded by their hinterlands. New York is held in varying degrees of contempt or fear by much of the rest of the United States. There are no presidential votes to be had on bailing out America's big cities.

Even in the context of the United Kingdom, the differences between a capital city – which also happens to be the one true world city in Europe – and the rest of the country grows wider and wider. Londoners may have British passports, speak more or less the same language as their compatriots, and use their legal system. But London is not the same as the rest of the country. Britain's financial and creative forces are overwhelmingly concentrated on the city, to an extent that makes the rest of the country uncomfortable and alienated. Clearly it must be part of the strategy of a successful city to manage this alienation in such a way as to minimize the friction. But it is a friction that exists in everything, from the ethnic and religious composition of London set against the rest of Britain to the hugely higher cost of housing in the capital, which contributes to labour inflexibility.

It is clear that many cities are indeed the product of nation-building impulses that range all the way from Berlin's origins as a deliberate assertion of Prussian statehood in order to cement its pre-eminence over other German cities, to the establishment of Washington or Canberra as self-conscious new capitals. However, those self-conscious national creations seldom become cities of real economic power: compare the GDP of Brasília with São Paulo, or that of Ankara with Istanbul. Many cities have much older origins. London, for example, goes back 2,000 years to Roman imperialism, and predates anything that looks like the United Kingdom in its present form by several hundred years. There are streets in the City of London that have been in more-or-less continuous use for the best part of two millennia. Wood Street for example, where office buildings designed by Richard Rogers and Norman Foster now touch each other, was once the main north-south route from the Roman city to the parade ground of the fortress just beyond the city wall. And what was once the site of a temple dedicated to Mithras came to be occupied by a Christian chapel attached to the Saxon royal palace and is now the site of a prominent stone-built neo-Gothic church. The interesting question is if it is still, in any meaningful sense, the same city, even though the language spoken by its people, and their way of life, is so different, or has it reinvented itself for every new incarnation? It is possible to regard a city as a kind of machine that can be rented or leased, and offers its temporary tenants the possibility of economic growth. To function in this way, there must be something about its past and the traditions and layers of experience that serve to create a kind of urban DNA that can survive in radically different contexts.

Cities, for all their adaptability also have ways of doing things that do not change. Paris is still marked by monumental spaces and ruthless ways with planning. London and New York each have their own, rather different, urban codes that serve to underpin them through every successive incarnation. In some contexts there are signs of a dynamic of tension between pairs of cities. In the last century, Rio allowed itself to be overtaken by São Paulo, Melbourne by Sydney, San Francisco by Los Angeles.

Despite its longevity, the city has many characteristics of a far more modern entity than the nation state. In terms of human organization, as a location that attracts the brightest and the best of talents, and offers them the chance to make the most of themselves, it has never been surpassed. Provided it can stay on reasonably good terms with the rural hinterland on which it depends for water and other natural resources, and can supply the material or intellectual goods that make it a sought-after trading partner with the wider world, a city will flourish. In the West, until the late Middle Ages and the emergence of Spain, France and England as nation states, the great cities of the world had few rivals in terms of economic, cultural or political power. Even now the mayor of a city like London, with a popular mandate from a direct election, has a personal authority to which few prime ministers can aspire. And it is cities rather than countries that are the cultural powerhouses.

Nevertheless, there are those who see the city as a redundant entity, typified by the rust-belt doughnuts of the American north-east seaboard. They suggest that the place to find the maximum economic activity and growth is in what they present as another form of spatial organization – a post-urban form – the edge city, or whatever it might end up being called. This is not a city in the sense that we understand it, with pedestrian public spaces and casual interaction between strangers, but is instead an agglomeration without what might be called 'cityness'. What we do not yet know is if this is simply another form of the city, or an authentic replacement for it, or even the raw material for the original qualities of the city to reassert themselves in a new form. Let us not forget that what were once disparaged as suburbs in order to be denigrated as inferior and soulless adjuncts to real cities, have now become fully accepted as vital and urbane parts of the contemporary urban city.

The question that really needs to be explored is the nature of cohesion and urban identity. Despite how divided cities such as Beirut, Berlin or Belfast once were, the links holding a successful city together are more effective and more subtle than nationalism. The question of what actually constitutes a city goes beyond the definition of a collection of settlements that have spatial contiguity. A city depends on characteristics that make it feel like an entity to which its citizens want to belong. It offers a menu of shared experiences that go further than a national flag or a national anthem.

Cities have an ability to clone themselves as imperial systems – franchises or brands might be an appropriate way of putting it – and they are built on trade and organization. Maybe the most important difference between the city and the state is that the city is a much closer fit to social and economic imperatives than a nation state can be. Despite the efforts of the planners and the speculators and the politicians, the city is formed by the everyday reality of human experience.

THE URBANIZATION OF THE WORLD

Edward Soja and Miguel Kanai

Over the past 30 years, the world has been experiencing an unusually expansive and reconfigured form of urbanization that has defined a distinctively global urban age – one in which we can speak of both the urbanization of the entire globe and the globalization of urbanism as a way of life. This dynamic interrelationship between the urban and the global is the focus of this essay, which presents an overview of the urbanization of the world understood as the extension in the spatial reach of city-based societies, economies and cultures to every place on the planet.

We see this extended form of contemporary urbanization not just as an adjunct to the globalization process but also as its primary driving force, stimulating innovation, creativity and economic growth while at the same time intensifying social and economic inequalities and conflict filled political polarization. But as the world urbanizes, cities are being globalized. Not only is urbanization increasingly reaching everywhere, everywhere is increasingly reaching into the city, contributing to a major reconfiguration of the social and spatial structures of urbanism and creating the most economically and culturally heterogeneous cities the world has ever known.

The Urbanization of the World

There can be no doubt that more people are living in cities than ever before. Just how many is not easy to determine, because countries differ on the criteria used to define what is urban. It is now widely accepted, however, that 2006 marked a remarkable moment in the urbanization of the world. In its report, 'The State of the World's Cities', the United Nations HABITAT office made a formal pronouncement that, for the first time, the majority of the world's population – nearly 3.3 billion – now live in urban agglomerations rather than in rural areas. This urban-rural tipping-point, however, is just one measure of a much more extensive, focused and accelerating urbanization process that has been spreading over the entire Earth's surface for at least the past 30 years.[1]

The urbanization of the world has brought with it new terms to describe what were conventionally called cities and metropolitan regions. The term 'world city' emerged early in the 1960s to reflect the increasing global influences on urban life.[2] Influenced significantly by the work of Saskia Sassen in the early 1990s, the concept of the 'global city' began to be widely used for the most influential financial command centres of the global economy. More recently, the world's largest agglomerations have taken on several additional descriptions.[3] The term we will use most often is the

FEELING THE URBAN AGE

While cities are growing larger and faster
than ever before, the quality of the new urban
environment is becoming more homogeneous,
disconnected from its social and cultural
heritage, as in the Pudong business and
government district in Shanghai.

ACCELERATING THE PACE OF CHANGE

City regions of 1 million people or more multiplied in the twentieth century. Today they accommodate a total of 1 billion people, reflecting their role as centres of global flows of people, capital, culture and information. While there were only a handful of city regions of this scale up to the mid-twentieth century, the number soared to 450 by 2005.

<u>1825</u>

<u>1900</u>

1950

2005

THE WORLD'S CHANGING URBAN POPULATION

The urban centre of gravity has shifted. By 2005, 70 per cent of the urban population lived in cities in developing countries. Expected to increase to 80 per cent by 2030, this share is more than double what it was in 1950.

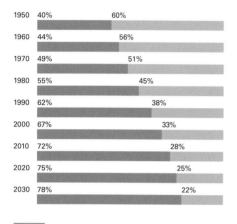

1950	40%	60%
1960	44%	56%
1970	49%	51%
1980	55%	45%
1990	62%	38%
2000	67%	33%
2010	72%	28%
2020	75%	25%
2030	78%	22%

■ Developing countries
■ Developed countries

'global city region', defined as a new metropolitan form characterized by sprawling polycentric networks of urban centres clustered around one or more 'historic' urban cores.[4] Particular emphasis is given here to 'city regions' of more than 1 million inhabitants in their contiguous urbanized area; to 'megacity regions', whose population exceeds 10 million; and to even larger emerging agglomerations that we tentatively call 'megalopolitan city regions', which can be defined by their demographic and economic magnitudes as well as quasi-continental extents.

The global imprint of these regional agglomerations and their networked extensions is vividly illustrated in the satellite picture of the 'world at night'. Punctuating this view of the world are nearly 450 city regions in the million-plus category. They occupy only a small portion of the Earth's surface, but they concentrate well over a billion residents and, almost surely, account for an even greater share of the world's built environment, economic wealth, cultural creativity and political power.[5] These million-plus city regions form the peaks of the world map of population density and stand out as the primary power points of the urban global age.

Another vivid picture of the accelerating growth in the number of million-plus city regions is presented in the series of maps on the previous double-page spread. While there were only two cities – London and Beijing – that had more than 1 million inhabitants in the early nineteenth century, 100 years later that list had expanded to 16. By 1900, London had become the first megacity region and reached the 10 million mark, which is indicated by a larger circle on the maps. The number of million-plus cities then quadrupled by 1950, with New York, Paris, Moscow, Shanghai and Tokyo added to London on the list of megacity regions. By 2000, the number of million-plus metropolitan regions soared to well over 400, and the list of megacity regions expanded to more than 20. The urbanization of the world shows every sign of continuing at an accelerating rate.[6]

Looking at the global distribution of the million-plus city regions on the 2005 map, both China (97) and India (40) have larger numbers than the United States (39). Regionally there are more million-plus city regions in Latin America and the Caribbean (57) and on the African continent (41) than in western Europe (40). This distribution accentuates all the statistical evidence indicating an unusually rapid urbanization of the world's developing countries in the past half-century. In 1950, developing countries contained slightly less than 40 per cent of the world's urban population and by 1970 they still accounted for less than 50 per cent. This figure climbs dramatically after that, so that by 2005 only 30 per cent of the world's urban dwellers are in 'developed' countries, and almost 4 out of 5 urban dwellers in the year 2030 are expected to live in developing countries. Perhaps the most rapidly urbanizing continental region has been sub-Saharan Africa, which is expected to have a larger share of the world's urban population than Europe by 2030.[7]

The evolution of megacity regions also deserves attention. By the middle of the twentieth century Greater New York City was the largest city region in the world, with a population of over 10 million. But it was soon overtaken by Greater Tokyo, which became the first city region to pass the 20 million mark at the time of Japan's high economic growth and the Tokyo Olympics in the mid 1960s. By 1985, there were still only nine megacity regions, but the list increased rapidly in the next two decades. The table on page 60 lists the 20 agglomerations over 10 million in 2005, along with the world's 10 largest city regions in 1950 and 1985. Notable from this data is the shift in the world's urban centre of gravity. In 1950, the 10 largest cities of the world included only three in what could be described then as developing countries

(Shanghai, Buenos Aires and Calcutta). In 2005, the list has expanded to eight of the top 10 (Mexico City, Mumbai, São Paulo, Delhi, Calcutta, Buenos Aires, Jakarta and Shanghai) and 15 of the total of 20 megacity regions.

Emphasizing the regional dimension of the contemporary urbanization process helps to understand better both what has been happening to the size and geographical scope of urban agglomerations as well as to their internal configuration. Over the past 30 years, the modern metropolis has been experiencing a distinctively regional urbanization process, in which urbanism as a way of life, once confined to the historic central city, has been spreading outwards, creating urban densities and new 'outer' and 'edge' cities in what were formerly suburban fringes and greenfield or rural sites. In some areas, urbanization has expanded on even larger regional scales, creating giant urban galaxies with population sizes and degrees of polycentricity far beyond anything imagined only a few decades ago. Although the rate of population growth in some of the largest megacity regions has slowed somewhat in the face of official census data, when viewed from a broader spatial perspective the world's megacity regions have continued to expand in dramatic ways. An increasing share of the world's population is now being absorbed into expanding regional networks of cities, and in some cases city regions are coalescing into even larger agglomerations in a process that can be called 'extended regional urbanization'.

Much can be learned about this extended form of regional urbanization by looking at recent developments in China, where at least three expansive megacity regions, in the Pearl River Delta and in the expanding hinterlands around Shanghai and Beijing, have been coalescing into a giant Chinese urban galaxy. Conservative estimates suggest that each of the megacity regions contains at least 40 million people, depending on how they are defined and bounded. Strong arguments can be made, however, that the actual populations are much higher.

In less than one-third of a century, China has experienced what is almost certainly the largest scale of urbanization and the most rapid rural-to-urban transition in human history. In 1970, China could be described as a country of 'limited urbanization', where less than 20 per cent of the national population lived in cities. By the early twenty-first century, the urbanization rate of China had officially reached 40 per cent – the world's average for developing countries – and it is expected to pass the 50 per cent mark within the next decade (see also Xiangming Chen's essay on contemporary Chinese urbanization, page 126–33). This would represent a net addition of around half a billion people to the Chinese urban population. Yet even these figures probably underestimate the magnitude of Chinese urbanization, especially given the country's current GDP per capita and its unusually high industrialization rate.[8]

The suspected undercounting can be attributed to several factors. There are recently urbanized areas that have not yet been reclassified from their rural designation, and there are many migrants from the countryside in cities who are still not counted as part of the urban population. Undercounting, however, is not just a problem of time-lags in the demographic measurement process; it also reflects China's policies restricting population mobility and emphasizing urbanization in the countryside. While the growth of smaller cities has been encouraged, increasing constraints were put on the concentration of the population in the largest cities in the coastal region. These interventions, however, did not stop the enormous demographic pull and economic synergism of the coastal urban cores, with the paradoxical result that the areas with the highest reported urbanization rates are also where the largest numbers of undercounted city residents are located.

	Rank	City-Region	Country	Population	Visual comparison
1950	1	New York-Newark	United States of America	12,338,000	
	2	Tokyo	Japan	11,275,000	
	3	London	United Kingdom	8,361,000	
	4	Paris	France	5,424,000	
	5	Moscow	Russian Federation	5,356,000	
	6	Shanghai	China	5,333,000	
	7	Rhein-Ruhr North	Germany	5,295,000	
	8	Buenos Aires	Argentina	5,041,000	
	9	Chicago	United States of America	4,999,000	
	10	Kolkata (Calcutta)	India	4,446,000	
	11	Osaka-Kobe	Japan	4,147,000	
	12	Los Angeles	United States of America	4,046,000	
	13	Beijing	China	3,913,000	
	14	Milan	Italy	3,633,000	
	15	Berlin	Germany	3,337,000	
	16	Philadelphia	United States of America	3,128,000	
	17	Mumbai (Bombay)	India	2,981,000	
	18	Rio de Janeiro	Brazil	2,930,000	
	19	Saint Petersburg	Russian Federation	2,903,000	
	20	Mexico City	Mexico	2,883,000	
1985	1	Tokyo	Japan	30,304,000	
	2	New York-Newark	United States of America	15,827,000	
	3	Mexico City	Mexico	14,109,000	
	4	São Paulo	Brazil	13,395,000	
	5	Shanghai	China	12,395,000	
	6	Buenos Aires	Argentina	10,538,000	
	7	Osaka-Kobe	Japan	10,350,000	
	8	Mumbai (Bombay)	India	10,341,000	
	9	Los Angeles	United States of America	10,181,000	
	10	Kolkata (Calcutta)	India	9,946,000	
	11	Beijing	China	9,797,000	
	12	Seoul	Republic of Korea	9,549,000	
	13	Paris	France	9,105,000	
	14	Rio de Janeiro	Brazil	9,086,000	
	15	Moscow	Russian Federation	8,580,000	
	16	Cairo	Egypt	8,326,000	
	17	Tianjin	China	8,132,000	
	18	London	United Kingdom	7,667,000	
	19	Chicago	United States of America	7,285,000	
	20	Metro Manila	Philippines	6,888,000	
2005	1	Tokyo	Japan	35,327,000	
	2	Mexico City	Mexico	19,013,000	
	3	New York-Newark	United States of America	18,498,000	
	4	Mumbai (Bombay)	India	18,336,000	
	5	São Paulo	Brazil	18,333,000	
	6	Delhi	India	15,334,000	
	7	Kolkata (Calcutta)	India	14,299,000	
	8	Buenos Aires	Argentina	13,349,000	
	9	Jakarta	Indonesia	13,194,000	
	10	Shanghai	China	12,665,000	
	11	Dhaka	Bangladesh	12,560,000	
	12	Los Angeles	United States of America	12,146,000	
	13	Karachi	Pakistan	11,819,000	
	14	Rio de Janeiro	Brazil	11,469,000	
	15	Osaka-Kobe	Japan	11,286,000	
	16	Cairo	Egypt	11,146,000	
	17	Lagos	Nigeria	11,135,000	
	18	Beijing	China	10,849,000	
	19	Metro Manila	Philippines	10,677,000	
	20	Moscow	Russian Federation	10,672,000	

Unauthorized and often unreported migrants are an increasing problem in the largest cities. In Shanghai alone, the so-called 'floating population' of unregistered internal migrants is estimated to be between 3 and 4 million, adding almost 20 per cent to the officially recognized population. As the economic stimulus of these large coastal agglomerations extends well into their regional hinterlands, many nearby 'rural towns' have been industrializing rapidly and mushrooming in size.[9] The population of the formerly rural township of Dongguan, near Hong Kong and Shenzhen, for example, has reached more than 5 million. These newly industrialized (and urbanized) areas and populations, not always included in overall national urbanization statistics, are a vital part of the growth of polycentric, networked and increasingly interconnected megacity regions.

The emergence of expansive megacity regions more generally and of huge urban galaxies in particular are important hallmarks of the urban global age, extending the urbanization of the world well beyond officially designated urban areas. Despite their growing importance, however, these emerging megalopolitan city regions are not yet given much attention in the urban research community, nor among policymakers and data collectors around the world. Richard Florida, known for his work on creative cities, has recently pointed out that no major global institution compiles and reports systematic data for what are perhaps the most significant territorial units of today's global economy.[10] Assisted by satellite images, Florida has prepared a preliminary and selective mapping of what he calls the 'New Megalopolises', megacity regions interconnected in vast amorphous fields. These are highly extended versions of older notions such as Patrick Geddes' 'conurbation' (1915), Jean Gottmann's 'megalopolis' (1961) and increasingly resemble the shape of Constantinos Doxiadis' 'eperopolis', literally 'continental city' in Greek (1968).

Using a slightly modified version of Florida's estimates of megalopolitan populations, three vast continental zones of macro-regional urbanization can be identified: in North-East Asia, western Europe and North America. The sub-regions comprising these three zones are listed in the table on page 63. The super continental conurbation of North-East Asia is the largest of the three, reaching over 300 million people based only on official statistics. Japan, a highly urbanized and regionally integrated country, contributes 115 million – almost half of which is concentrated around Tokyo and the narrow Kanto Plain. The megacity regions in the coastal areas of China, the Korean peninsula and Taiwan are other areas of high economic and demographic dynamism.

The transnational megalopolitan population of western Europe adds up to more than 260 million, with the largest cluster of 50 million in what Florida describes as the Euro-Lowlands, a densely urbanized region spreading across six countries and characterized by the absence of an overarching metropolitan centre such as London or Paris. Connecting with the Euro-Lowlands to the north-west is an extended Greater London, and to the south lie the Euro-Heartland and Urb-Italy, to use Florida's names. This composite arc of development, concentrated around what some have called Europe's 'Blue Banana', constitutes the continent's economic engine.

In North America, where the megalopolitan population surpasses 200 million, the older Gottmann-identified megalopolises of Bos-Wash and Chi-Pitts have been extended to include the Golden Triangle of southern Ontario and areas to the south and west in the United States. To this Atlantic-oriented zone must be added a growing Pacific Rim megalopolis stretching from Vancouver to Tijuana. At its core is the earlier California megalopolis of San-San (San Francisco-San Diego), now bulging

THE RISE OF THE MASSIVE CITY

Large-scale regional urbanization is a less well-known aspect of the contemporary urban world. City regions have unprecedented, quasi-continental sizes with major agglomerations in Europe, East Asia and North America considered the main drivers of the global economy.

outwards into Mexico and Nevada to form what some call Bajalta California.[11]

Several other megalopolitan zones can be seen taking shape around the world, adding new dimensions to the concept of extended urbanization. In Latin America, for example, Brazil's two leading city regions, São Paulo and Rio de Janeiro, have grown increasingly connected, both physically and functionally, while maintaining differentiated roles and cultural identities as well as increasing decentralization, a socio-economic polarization and territorial fragmentation.[12] A similar integration process is occurring in neighbouring Argentina between the two leading metropolitan regions of Buenos Aires and Rosario, along a 300-kilometre corridor on the lower Paraná-Río de la Plata river basin.[13] Moreover, these megacity regions can be extended further to include an incipient formation stretching across five countries, from Santiago de Chile to Belo Horizonte.

The South Asian subcontinent, certainly one of the largest zones of macro-regional urbanization in the world, also deserves special consideration. Just looking at the megacity regions of the subcontinent, the list would include Mumbai or Bombay (19.8 million), Delhi (19.7), Kolkata or Calcutta (15.6), Karachi in Pakistan (14.3) and Dhaka in Bangladesh (13.2). In addition, the city regions of Bangalore (7.1) and Hyderabad (6.7) concentrating high-tech industries, India's automotive centre of Chennai or Madras (7.7) in the south, the textile, chemical and pharmaceutical centre of Ahmedabad (5.6) in the west, and Pakistan's second urban-industrial centre of Lahore (7.5) are all on the way to becoming megacity regions.[14]

These 10 South Asian agglomerations add up to nearly 120 million already and there are at least 30 more million-plus city regions in India alone. Urban centres are expected to further integrate into synergetic megalopolitan formations with the regional infrastructure now being developed, particularly the Golden Quadrangle mega-project, a network of express motorways linking India's largest megacity regions. While much research is dedicated to the challenging problems urbanization generates in the subcontinent, Anglo-American literature has so far not engaged with processes of large-scale megalopolitan growth in India to the extent that, for example, the now burgeoning literature on urban China has. Florida does not include the subcontinent in his maps of the New Megalopolises either. How best to identify the sub-regions of this zone of accelerating urbanization, and assess its economic potential in the global economy as well as for more socially inclusive and environmentally sustainable forms of urban development, will have to await further research.

The urbanization of the world can be extended still further, beyond the almost 450 million-plus city regions and the emerging megalopolitan city regions and urban galaxies. More than ever before, it can be said that the Earth's entire surface is urbanized to some degree, from the Siberian tundra to the Brazilian rainforest to the icecap of Antarctica, perhaps even to the world's oceans and the atmosphere we breathe. Of course, this does not mean there are dense agglomerations everywhere, but the major features of urbanism as a way of life – from the play of market forces and the effect of administrative regulations, to popular cultural practices and practical geopolitics – are becoming ubiquitous. To a degree not seen before, no one on Earth is outside the sphere of influence of urban industrial capitalism.

Globalization, Urbanization, Industrialization

The extended urbanization of the world opens up new ways of understanding the globalization of capital, labour and culture, and the forces that have led to the formation of a new mode of capitalist development, variously described as post-Fordist,

Megalopolitan City Region	Population in millions
ASIA	
Greater Sapporo	4.6
Greater Tokyo	54.7
Mid-Japan	
Osaka-Nagoya	36.1
Ky-Fuko-Shima	
Fukuoka, Hiroshima, Kitakyushu	20.0
Greater Seoul	
Seoul, Busan, Daegu, Taejon, Gwangju	43.8
Greater Taipei	
Taipei-Chungli, Kaohsiung-Tainan, Taichung	16.7
Greater Beijing	
Beijing, Tianjin, Tangshan	36.5
Shang-King	
Shanghai, Nanjing, Hangzhou	50.5
Hong-Zeng	
Shenzhen, Guangzhou, Hong Kong	40.0
Total	302.9
EUROPE	
Greater Glasgow	3.8
Greater London	
London, Manchester, Liverpool, Leeds-Sheffield, Birmingham	49.1
Greater Dublin	3.5
Greater Madrid	5.8
Lis-Port	
Lisbon, Porto	9.7
Greater Paris	14.6
Euro-Lowlands	
Ruhr-Cologne, Amsterdam-Rotterdam, Brussels-Antwerp, Lille	50.0
Euro-Sunbelt	
Barcelona, Marseille, Valencia, Lyon	24.8
Euro-Heartland	
Stuttgart, Frankfurt, Mannheim	22.0
Urb-Italy	
Milan, Rome, Turin	46.9
Greater Prague	10.6
Euro-East	
Katowice, Budapest, Vienna	20.1
Total	260.9
NORTH AMERICA	
Bos-Wash	
Boston, New York, Philadelphia, Washington	54.8
Tor-Buf-Chester	
Toronto, Buffalo, Rochester, Ottawa, Montreal	20.1
Chi-Pitts	
Pittsburgh, Cleveland, Detroit, Cincinnati, Chicago, Minneapolis	45.0
Chatlanta	
Atlanta, Charlotte, Raleigh	19.6
Gulf Coast	
Houston, New Orleans	9.3
So-Flo	
Miami, Tampa, Orlando, Jacksonville	13.7
Daustin	
Dallas, San Antonio, Austin	9.1
Bajalta California	
San Francisco, Los Angeles, San Diego, Tijuana, Las Vegas, Phoenix, Mexicali	42.0
Total	213.6

flexible and information based. The spread of urbanism and the characteristics of urban industrial capitalism can be seen as the distinguishing feature of the current round of intensified globalization. Commercial capitalism was globalized centuries ago, creating mercantile world cities such as Amsterdam and London. Financial capital was diffused globally with the spread of colonialism and imperialism, centring financial power in such global command posts as London, Paris and New York. Over the past 30 years, global trade and financial flows have been expanding rapidly, but what is most new and different has been the globalization of productive or industrial capital – that is, investments in the production of goods, services and information, facilitated by the revolution in information and communications technology, and reorganized in what is now called the New Economy or flexible capitalism.[15]

Urbanization, industrialization and globalization have been intimately tied together at least since the Industrial Revolution. Few human activities gain as much from being located in dense urban agglomerations as industrial production or manufacturing. The clustering of producers and consumers in urban space gives rise to a variety of agglomeration economies, which can lead to greater productivity and technological innovation, thus creating a potential snowball effect that stimulates urban-industrial expansion. This holds true not only for making pins and needles but also for the production and exchange of information, and the development of what are now being called the creative or cultural industries. As we have rediscovered in recent years, cities in themselves, as socially constructed human habitats, generate positive forces of creativity, innovation and economic development as well as negative spill-over effects that aggravate social inequality and environmental sustainability. Studying the powerful forces that emanate from agglomeration has become the springboard for some of the most exciting research findings in contemporary urban and regional studies.[16]

Globalization and the formation of a New Economy have not been leading to a post-industrial or post-urban era, as many have claimed, but rather to a new and different round of urban industrialization that, in turn, is creating a new and different global geography of economic development. For most of the past 200 years, advanced forms of industrialization have been tightly confined geographically to the major urban centres of the advanced capitalist countries and, for much of the twentieth century, a few industrialized socialist countries. The familiar international division of labour consisting of First, Second and Third Worlds, often roughly reduced to a North-South divide, arose primarily from differences in the organizational form and level of urban industrial production and consumption.

This fairly stable geo-structural and territorial division of the world into industrialized and industrializing countries has been radically reconfigured over the past 30 years through the spread of urban industrialism into what can be called 'new industrial spaces'. Several generations of 'Asian Tigers' have created a growing list of Newly Industrialized Countries or NICs, from the early group that included Hong Kong, Taiwan, South Korea and Singapore to the most recent explosion of urban industrial production in China and India, the two most populous countries on Earth. Ireland, once the classic case of an internal colony, has become a Celtic Tiger, the richest country in Europe apart from Norway and Luxembourg, as the list of NICs continues to grow. A new global geography of industrialization has emerged in conjunction with the urbanization of the world.

New industrial spaces have also been developing within nation states, as formerly non-industrialized areas experience rapid urban industrialization. The evolving regional geography of industrial development in China is one example, the regional power shift between the so-called Frostbelt or Rustbelt and the Sunbelt in the United States is another. At the scale of the metropolitan region, many new industrial complexes have emerged in what were once suburban or rural areas. The best-known example of this metropolitan expansion of urban industrialism is probably Silicon Valley, but similar 'technopoles' and 'silicon landscapes' have been developing in many other major city regions. The decentralization of industrial geographies within metropolitan regions has thus been accompanied to varying degrees by a simultaneous recentralization, thereby intensifying the trend towards greater polycentricity.

Globally extended and reconfigured urban industrialization has generated a set of paradoxical consequences with regards to the spread of a global culture. On the one hand, the world has been experiencing an increasing social, economic and cultural homogenization, with cities beginning to look what some commentators call a Coca-colonization or McDonaldization or simply an Americanization of the world. At the same time, new patterns of differentiation and geographically uneven development are emerging, as the general processes of urban globalization take particular forms in the world's major city regions. Néstor Canclini captures such cultural hybridity and physical fragmentation in his essay on the multiple predicaments that the Latin-American megacity regions face in an age of urban globalization.

However one explains the changes mentioned above, a strong argument can be made that the differences existing 30 years ago between what could then be described as First, Second and Third World cities and urbanization processes, while not entirely disappearing, have significantly decreased, as virtually all cities are experiencing some degree of globalization. This has led to the unexpected situation in which we can learn just as much about the new urbanization processes from Mexico City, Johannesburg and Shanghai as we can from New York, London and Berlin.

The old International Division of Labour (IDL) has been significantly transformed by these simultaneous processes of global homogenization and differentiation. What was once conveniently characterized as North vs South, for example, has been broken into three continental zones focused on the three super-sized urban fields mentioned earlier. These three global core regions, North American, western European and East Asian, along with their continental spheres of influence, define a new tripartite Global Division of Labour (GDL, as global replaces international) linked within and between each zone by inter-urban networks that transcend national borders and connect in an encompassing worldwide web. Increasingly, the geographical and functional organization of the global economy has come to hinge around a new power hierarchy of financial command centres, led by the three great 'capitals of capital' London, New York and Tokyo, and buttressed by a growing number of ever more interconnected and synergetic global cities.[17]

Every one of the city regions articulates with the global cultural and political economy in different ways, creating a mixture of similarity and difference, along with a growing range of emergent hybridities and 'fusions'. Understanding how the general features of global urbanization combine with local particularities in the growing list of city regions, megacity regions and emerging megalopolitan city regions will require rigorous and comprehensive comparative analysis. Such analyses must be especially cognizant of the multiple scales at which the urbanization process is expressed: global, supranational, national, sub-national and regional, metropolitan, municipal, neighbourhood and local.[18] Recognizing the need for rigorous comparative analyses of these multi-scalar urban globalization processes, we will examine some of the major changes taking place within the world's cities and city regions.

An important starting point in looking at the changes that have taken place within urban regions over the past 30 years is what Mike Davis recently described as the mass production of slums.[19] The expansion of urban poverty has made 'extended' slums and burgeoning informal economies a distinctive feature of both the urbanization of the world and the globalization of the urban. According to the United Nations, one out of three urban dwellers – more than one billion people – live in slums. Some have put the figure even higher. The global concentration of urban poverty is the other, darker side of the growing concentration of economic wealth and political power.

Urban areas containing poorly housed and underemployed populations have been part of the industrial capitalist city from the very beginning, but never before have more people lived in urban slums than today. The largest slum populations are in the megacity regions in developing countries, in some cases accounting for more than three-quarters of all local inhabitants, but the expansion of transnational migrations has also created growing slums of what are now called the immigrant working poor in such global power centres as New York, Los Angeles and London.

A Planet of Slums

We live today in what Davis provocatively calls a 'planet of slums'. He attributes this explosion of urban poverty to an unquestioned embrace of market forces, the adoption of neo-liberal forms of local, national and supranational governance, the attendant acceptance of debilitating structural adjustment programmes imposed by the World Bank and the International Monetary Fund, reduced state responsibilities for social welfare, and the adoption of policies fostering liberalization, deregulation and decentralization of national economies. The globalization of the urban hinges around the massive expansion of slums, but it is only part of the story of urban restructuring.

Simultaneous with the growth of urban poverty has been an almost equally large expansion of the professional-managerial-executive and 'creative' class, a largely neo-liberal elite that is having a particularly influential effect on shaping the city-building process. This has led to the emergence of a new dualism in the world's major cities, quite different from the older division between industrial bourgeoisie and urban proletariat. The overseers-underclass dualism has grown in many parts of the developed world at the expense of what was, in the post-World War II decades, a burgeoning middle class. Although it is difficult to quantify, the world's megacity regions may be nearing the point where nearly one-third of the population consists of wealthy residents of guarded and gated communities, super-rich suburbs and gentrified neighbourhoods in the urban core, often starkly located next to the worst slums.

One must be careful, however, not to overemphasize or simplify this dualism. The re-stratification of urban social structures is much more complex, fragmented and multilayered. The fortunate fifth of the income distribution, for example, is probably more politically and culturally heterogeneous and unpredictable than ever before. Not only is there the traditional division between new and old wealth, the nouveau riche now symbolically attached to the neologism of yuppie, there are many variations that have developed within the upper income brackets over the past 30 years. Especially relevant to the city-building process, for example, is a growing polarity between those who 'secede' from the city and urban responsibility by moving into insular gated communities and those who commit themselves much more to urban regeneration as gentrifiers and inner-city dwellers.

Specialized ethnic niches further complicate the re-stratification of class, creating growing disparities of wealth and social mobility among immigrant populations, as well as aggravating divisions between domestic and immigrant populations of the same ethnic group. One must also be careful not to assume a withering away of the old middle class due to the growing polarization between the rich and the poor. In many ways, a new globalized middle class is being reconstituted in the world's major city regions, in between (and sometimes overlapping both) the upper 20 per cent and the lower 40 per cent of the income ladder. And it too is increasingly heterogeneous, fragmented and unpredictable in its politics.

What is perhaps most important to understand about the new urban division of labour, and also about its spatial expression, is that it is significantly different from what it was 30 years ago. There are some pervasive continuities with the past based on class, race and gender, but simply projecting past trends on to the present, without recognizing what is new and different, can lead to misunderstanding and oversimplification. Take, for example, one of the characteristic features of the new urban geography that has been emerging in many of the world's major city regions, the so-called 'hollowing out' of the historic central city core of its former domestic population. Should this be seen as a form of urban decay, signalling perhaps the declining significance of downtown nucleations in an age of the Internet and instant communications? Or is it just a product of continued suburbanization or the inevitable effect of market forces? What are the implications of decentralization and reduced inner-city densities for public policy?

One interesting case is Osaka. Once reputed to be the densest city in Japan, central Osaka is now almost devoid of a resident population, but has experienced little of the urban decay seen in the West. Its large downtown is thriving as a centre for commerce, office activities, entertainment and the creative industries. The inner ring around the centre has become increasingly dense, and suburbanization not only sprawled outwards but also densified and agglomerated as part of the vast and polycentric Mid-Japan megacity region.

Greater Los Angeles provides another model of inner-city transformation. After the Watts Riots in 1965, as many as a million and a half white and black, largely working class, residents of the inner ring surrounding downtown left the area, many settling further out in the Greater Los Angeles region. In the past four decades, however, nearly 5 million immigrants have moved into the same area. When combined with increasing suburban densities, this has transformed what was once the least densely populated major American metropolis into what is now the densest urbanized area in the United States, passing New York City's metropolitan region for the lead in 1990. At another extreme are American cities such as Detroit and St Louis, where the outflow of people and jobs has been far greater than the inflow of new migrants, reducing the total city population (but not that of the surrounding city region) to less than half its former size. Statistics showing inner-city population losses in other parts of the world, the special case of declining city populations in former East Germany and several other former-socialist countries, and some recent data indicating some population growth slowdowns or even decline in the central cities of Paris, Seoul and Manila, has led to a growing research and public policy interest on 'shrinking cities', engaging with the implications of declining urban growth-rates.[20]

It is difficult to make any generalizations about what has been happening to the older urban cores in the megacity regions of the world, for the variations are almost endless. This is one of the reasons that policy and planning for historic city centres has become so challenging and so competitive, generating whole new industries related to city-marketing and branding. Urban image-making relies on events such as international exhibitions, Olympic Games and architectural extravaganzas such as the Gehry-designed Guggenheim Museum in Bilbao. With decentralization and deregulation, every local government vies with the others to attract attention, investment and tourists. Although some lip service is often given to local problems of poverty and inequality, such competitive urban 'wars' for investment, jobs, visitors and global image have, in many cities, diverted attention from social services and community welfare, thereby aggravating the increasing economic inequalities and social polarization that has been an integral part of the new urbanization processes.

In contrast to the varying fates of central cities, there is a fairly clear general trend affecting suburbia. In many developed-world city regions, in conjunction with what Deyan Sudjic has called the rise of the '100-mile city', there has been a growing urbanization of suburbia, another of the paradoxical twists on urban globality.[21] As older inner-city areas have their former populations replaced by new immigrants, new urban growth is taking place in outer cities or edge cities, as once relatively homogeneous dormitory suburbs become cities in themselves. In many parts of former suburbia there are now more jobs than bedrooms, increasing numbers of cultural and entertainment facilities, and growing problems of crime, drugs and traffic gridlock. In many cases, the old socio-spatial dualism of urbanism and suburbanism as separate and distinct ways of life has begun to disappear, as the modern metropolis evolves into what might be called an exopolis, with the ex-signifying a growing external or outer city, as well as meaning an urban form quite different from anything known in the past.[22]

The polycentricity and complex urban networking of the megacity region reflects these changes, as city space becomes increasingly unbounded, reconfigured and rescaled. Everywhere cities are being reshaped by three interrelated forces: the globalization of capital, labour and culture; the formation of a 'new economy' variably described as flexible, global and information-intensive; and the facilitating effects of a revolution in information and communications technology. Cities are no longer spatially defined by and confined to their old metropolitan hinterlands or commuting zones, as urban economies become geographically reconfigured into multiple scales that connect the local with the global in a nesting of larger and larger nodal regions and inter-urban networks.

In this concatenation of regional scales, the globalization of the urban begins to coincide with the urbanization of the globe. Sustaining this transformative process has been an extraordinary expansion of population movements and migrations, transnational, intra-national and within the urban region itself. The nature, impact and public policy response to these mass movements of people, from global diasporas to local neighbourhood gentrification, differ greatly from place to place, but nearly everywhere they are creating what can be described as crises of governance and planning. Exploring this growing crisis of governance and planning brings us to the concluding section.

Towards a New Urban Agenda

We live in a world where nearly one in six inhabitants is a slum dweller – and the numbers are growing. One outgrowth of the discussion about the simultaneous urbanization of the globe and the globalization of the urban, is the expectation that the problems associated with urban poverty and inequality are likely to shape local and global politics in the twenty-first century more than ever before and in ways that few have anticipated. As these and other urban problems intensify, programmes dealing with them at a national scale have tended to decline nearly everywhere. This has shifted attention and hopes for the future to other scales of intervention, from the global and supranational to the regional and local.

As this rescaling of the urban action agenda progresses, it is becoming increasingly apparent that the existing governmental structures and institutions are not yet organized to deal with the new responsibilities and, in many cases, adamantly resist any changes in their authority and power. Resurgent nationalisms weaken the efforts of transnational organizations such as the United Nations or the European Union to deal with growing problems of urban poverty and social exclusion. Attempts to foster regional coordination at the sub-national and metropolitan scales are often met with localisms, as existing local governments turn instead to more entrepreneurial city-marketing strategies, competing for tourist and investment dollars.

Any attempt to create a new global action agenda for the urban age must begin with an awareness of the tensions that exist between established governmental structures and the need to find ways of strengthening more progressive forms of planning and policymaking at every geographical scale. Rather than bemoaning the difficulties of this task, however, we will identify some of the most positive developments that have been occurring in recent years with regards to the challenges and opportunities facing the city-building professions.

Urban and regional planning in the future will be increasingly shaped by new ideas about the generative effects of urban and regional economies. Prominent economists, drawing on the pioneering work of Jane Jacobs in *The Economy of Cities*, have been arguing that what can be called the stimulus of urban agglomeration is the primary cause of economic development in the world today. Dense and heterogeneous cities and city regions have become the driving forces of the global economy, generating enormous wealth as well as technological innovation and cultural creativity. Planners and policymakers are accordingly giving increasing attention to promoting efficient regional economic integration, developing clustered forms of economic activity and enhancing conditions conducive to creativity and innovation. But at the same time, urban agglomerations can also function to intensify inequalities and social polarization, as well as contributing significantly to global environmental degradation. One major challenge for the future of the city-building professions is to find ways to take advantage of the economic power of city regions and the creative capacity of dense and heterogeneous urban populations, while at the same time controlling the accompanying negative spillover effects, from widening income inequalities and global warming to increased intercultural friction and conflict. Finding an appropriate structure of local and regional governance is crucial.

As the global reaches into the urban and urbanization spreads around the globe, new movements are emerging that are likely to affect local efforts to deal with urban poverty and inequality. Struggles over environmental issues and poverty become simultaneously local, urban, metropolitan, regional, national, supranational and global issues. They include the rise of what some call global civil society, global or cosmopolitan citizenship and identity, and the global justice movement.

At the supranational regional scale, perhaps the most important counter-trend to the entrepreneurial approach to planning has been occurring within the European Union, one of the most important seedbeds for a New Regionalism – or at least the revival of the older welfare-oriented urban and regional planning that had declined significantly with the rise of neo-liberal state policies in the 1980s and the unabated market-driven globalization that has occurred ever since.

There are examples of improved metropolitan governance worldwide. The case of London deserves particular attention. Reversing the trend towards fragmentary governance and lack of explicit territorial planning, the Greater London Authority has been reinstated and now Londoners can elect a citywide mayor who will be responsible for London's sustainable development as a global city within the South-East of England, the UK and Europe. In Mexico City, where residents have also recently regained the right to vote for a municipal mayor in the Federal District, there has also been an increased cooperation between the national government, the District and the surrounding State of Mexico where more than half of the city region's population lives. In South Africa, the region of Gauteng is the first in the world to be officially described as a global city region. Increased cooperation between the Johannesburg, Tshwane (former Pretoria) and Ekurhuleni (former East Rand) metropolitan councils is leading to joint development programmes and planning frameworks that will allow the city region to attain a competitive position in the global economy while reversing the fragmentary and racially exploitative patterns of apartheid urbanism.

Not all metropolitan reforms are state initiated. In the United States, many of the metropolitan initiatives of 'growth with equity' have emerged from civil society, and particularly from coalitions of community-based and grassroots organizations that, through multiscalar organizing and coalition building, have been able to advance innovative and effective forms of community based regionalism.[23] New approaches to 'building resilient regions' have been encouraged from another nongovernmental source, the John D. and Catherine T. MacArthur Foundation, which in 2007 announced the creation of a new Research Network aimed at expanding knowledge of 'how regions shape the response to major national and demographic challenges'.

In Latin America, a wave of local democracy has also swept the region, as urban social movements have been able to enter progressive electoral coalitions gaining control of city governments.[24] Latin American cities have been producing highly innovative urban planning strategies, ranging from the low-cost and socially inclusive rapid-transit systems of Curitiba and Bogotá to the community architecture projects of Caracas, featured in Guy Battle's essay on urban sustainability.[25]

It is clear that the global urban agenda should not be understood as a single and centralized project, largely in the hands of elite institutions and empowered professionals. There are many different ways to achieve greater social and spatial justice in combination with sustained and equitable urban development, but these efforts will require working at multiple scales of governance and in increasingly eclectic conditions. For the city-building professions more generally, and architects and designers in particular, this represents a special challenge. As Rem Koolhaas argues, '[this is] the first generation of architects that has had a direct experience of working in so many different urban systems at any one time'.[26] As a result, they have the opportunity to shape realities that are attuned to both the larger imperatives of the urban global age and the localized and unique conditions of each individual city region. Especially important here is the need to reflect upon the ways form-making and site-specific physical interventions interact with the economic dynamism of urban agglomeration and its capacity to generate creativity, innovation and economic development. The interaction here must be made to work effectively in both directions.

NEW YO

37% of population foreign born compared to

0.7% in Shanghai and Mexico City

54% commute to work in less than 30 min

21m residents in the Metropolitan region

8m NYC residents

3.2m immigrants

65% of residents belong to an ethnic minority, making NYC a majority-minority city

$68bn spent on upgrading public transport in NYC since 1982

19% live below poverty line

29%
of the population was employed in manufacturing in 1964

20%
of the population was employed in manufacturing in 1980

4%
of the population was employed in manufacturing in 2005

93% jobs in the service sector

55% of New Yorkers use public transport to get to work

$1.3m for average Manhattan apartment

$225,000 for a Manhattan parking space

24,000 people/km² is the average density in Manhattan

830km² area of NYC

27,070km² area of the Metropolitan region

33% of homes are owner occupied

43m visitors in 2005

$23bn spent by visitors in 2005

14% green, open space

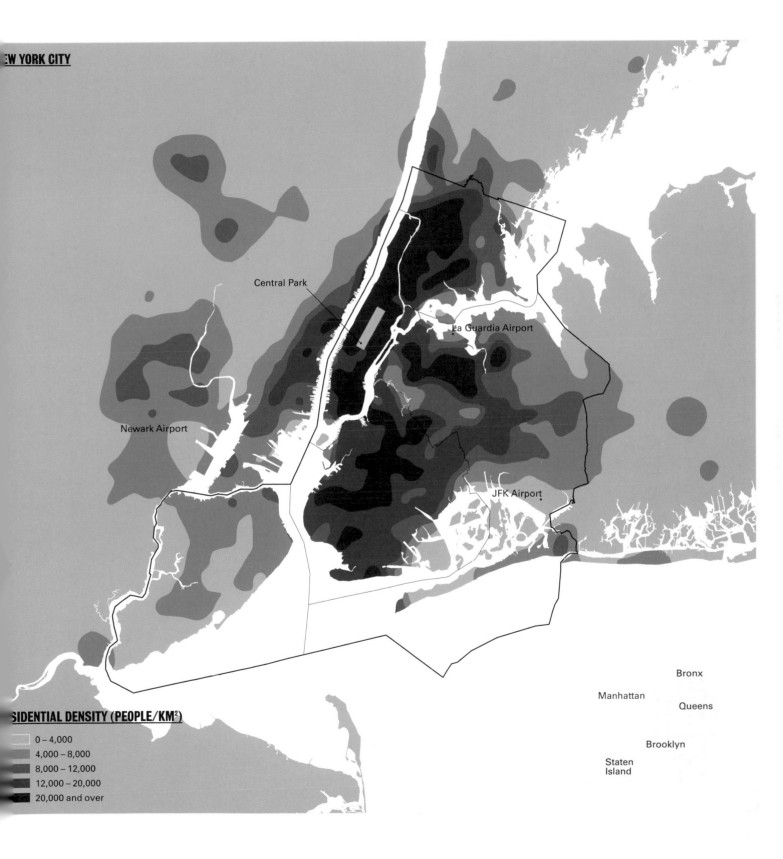

Central Park

La Guardia Airport

Newark Airport

JFK Airport

Bronx

Manhattan

Queens

Brooklyn

Staten
Island

SIDENTIAL DENSITY (PEOPLE/KM²)

	0 – 4,000
	4,000 – 8,000
	8,000 – 12,000
	12,000 – 20,000
	20,000 and over

FINDING ITS NERVE

Deyan Sudjic

BUILDING ON STREET CULTURE

A densely networked grid of streets and public transport in New York City enables a majority of the city's residents to use public transport to commute to work. With close to 40 per cent of Midtown Manhattan residents walking to work, residents in the outer boroughs, meanwhile, rely on the city's ageing subway infrastructure. During the black out of 2003, millions flooded the city's streets, relying on either walking or bus transport to get home.

New York is perhaps the most populous and certainly the most urban of America's cities. Such qualities are not universally considered as positive attributes in a country where the traditional city is regarded with a certain degree of political and popular suspicion and which is continually elaborating new forms of exurbia.

Understanding New York's very particular qualities and prospects is an essential part of coming to terms with the evolving nature of the contemporary city, as it faces up to the reality of the extraordinary size jump experienced in the later years of the twentieth century. Scores of cities now have populations far larger than entire European nations. A city with an effective population of 18 million people – now the size of both New York and London – is an entity with no historical precedent. If such a metropolitan area is to achieve the cohesion and the sense of identity that until now has been regarded as the fundamental essence of any successful city, then it must either learn from and build upon New York's experiences, or else find an alternative workable model.

Through a mix of muddle and dynamism, New York is succeeding as a city. It continually attracts new people and creates new jobs for them. It has proved itself an urban machine with an impressive capacity to turn poor migrants into citizens with at least a foothold on the ladder to prosperity. By the standards of cities like Houston or Los Angeles, it has done so with relative restraint in its use of land and natural resources. New York, at least in comparison with Houston or another city like Phoenix, is a city that has the possibility of bringing its consumption of fossil fuels used for transport within some kind of limit. It still has significant numbers of people who regularly walk to work.

From one perspective it is a city that has begun to address years of underinvestment in its infrastructure and to reclaim its marginalized neighbourhoods, even as it has had to face fiscal problems, a lack of affordable housing and a middle class under increasing stress. A contrary view would be to see New York as relying on federal and state tax subsidies, overly dependent on an excessively narrow employment base, and facing the prospect of serious difficulties meeting the financial obligations of the bond issues made to fund a huge investment in transport infrastructure. Despite the much-publicized turnaround in its fortune over the last decade, it still lacks such basic urban infrastructure as a rapid transit link to its primary airport. New York may have more pedestrians than Dallas, but it is also more polluted, faces a famine of affordable housing, dead rats in its gutters and it

may be in the midst of what is inevitably no more than a temporary lull between crime waves.

New York's experiences offer lessons both for rapidly growing cities – some positive, others cautionary – and for cities that share some of its characteristics, such as London and Berlin. London and New York are cities with striking parallels. When their metropolitan areas are taken into account, they have comparable populations, size and economic base. Both are attracting newcomers drawn from an extraordinarily widespread range of countries. In the past both have suffered from the loss of traditional industries associated with their roles as port cities. They have evolved analogous structures, at least as far as their business districts are concerned: London's West End office area parallels Midtown; the City is Wall Street; and Lower Manhattan is reflected in Canary Wharf.

The two cities have considered similar remedies for their problems, from new financial instruments to fund public transport, through various forms of tax incentives for housing and job creation, to road pricing and policing methods. It is an interplay that has produced a significant flow of key individuals between the two cities to take up senior roles in their implementation. At the same time, however, New York and London have many discontinuities. Their political systems are very different. In the ethos of each the paradox can be seen of a New York supposedly governed by market forces, actually shaped by rent control to an extent that London, with its supposedly more socialized system, has never contemplated. But a comparison of New York and London offers a rich potential source for understanding the impact of urban change, and policy and design upon it. It is an interplay that can be seen in Mayor Bloomberg's plan for New York, 'PlanNYC 2030', with its emphasis on environmental issues, traffic pricing and affordable housing apparently modelled on Livingstone's plan for London.

Cities are the economic mechanisms that create the wealth that sustains their people. But do jobs build cities or is it cities that build jobs? In other words, is it those urban qualities of a city that are within our power to change that are responsible for attracting fresh investment that brings jobs? Or is it simply the creation of jobs that brings with it all those other desirable urban qualities.

The public realm is the key aspect of contemporary life that is unique to the modern city, in which strangers can come together to share the experience of city life. But at a time of public fear of terror, how is it still possible to feel safe in the crowd?

The city may be a powerful machine for the transformation of the migrant poor into more affluent city dwellers, but to judge by the stress the middle classes find themselves under – priced out of affordable housing, concerned about public education and health systems – the city must address the squeezed middle, especially in the field of housing. Then there is the issue of movement within the city. Commuting distances, driven by the cost of housing and an imbalance between mass-transit systems and the private car, are escalating. Finding ways of reducing journey times is a vital part of improving the quality of life in a city.

All these issues spark a whole group of contingent questions – and the issues that they raise are interrelated. The result cannot be a prescriptive blueprint, advocating the low-density garden city or the high-density alternative of the past. It must go beyond such tidy-minded attempts to zone cities by functions. Its form will depend on clarity about the definition of the city and a pooled experience of its nature.

BEHIND THE BOOM

Susan Fainstein

During the first decade of the new millennium New York City suffered the worst terrorist attack in the history of the United States, teetered on the brink of economic freefall, then rebounded to maintain its place as the country's pre-eminent global city. Although in 2006 it still had not fully regained the jobs lost earlier in the decade, it was continuing on an upward trajectory that reflected its strengths in financial and business services, as well as culture, tourism, medicine and higher education. Immigrants and gentrifiers were contributing to population growth, new construction was adding tens of thousands of units to the housing stock and the government was running a fiscal surplus. The disparity between the fortunes of Manhattan and the outer boroughs had diminished, with business investment and new construction dispersing throughout the city. Racial tensions had eased as the Bloomberg administration actively sought to mitigate their causes and as immigrants blurred the divisions among whites and blacks. Thus, in the aggregate, New York perhaps never looked calmer or more prosperous.

Beneath the glamour and wealth, however, lay some uncomfortable facts. Despite New York's overall economic improvement, the proportion of the population in poverty exceeded one-fifth in 2006, a level that had not changed in five years.[1] The city lagged behind the nation in job recovery after the recession of 2001. Moreover, poverty was not restricted to the jobless but had increased among the employed to such an extent that in 2005 more than 14 per cent of working families remained below the federal poverty line.[2] Income among the bottom half of the population stagnated, while earnings soared at the top, resulting in an unprecedented extreme of income inequality. As the year 2006 ended, hedge fund managers and investment bankers were receiving astronomical bonuses on top of their regular salaries, further distorting the income distribution. The firm Goldman Sachs alone paid out US$16.5 billion in total in 2006, or US$623,418 per employee. Some of the best-paid traders received as much as US$100 million.[3] Within Manhattan, the top 20 per cent of the population had about 50 times the income of the bottom quintile.[4]

In the meantime, housing prices were skyrocketing, as the vacancy rate for rental apartments hovered close to 3 per cent. Housing scarcity and increased high-end demand meant that nearly a quarter of renters paid more than 50 per cent of their income for shelter.[5] Homelessness, while declining slightly in 2005 from the previous year, exceeded 35,000.[6] Even though the pace of new housing construction had picked up strongly, most of it was being built for the luxury market. At the same time,

THE CITY'S BACKYARD

Central Park is a defining element of New York City's urbanism with green, open space and cultural offerings including open-air theatre and music alongside the activities of runners, bicyclists and bird watchers. Yet in the mid 1970s, the park was a neglected eyesore. A group of citizens banded together to reclaim its 340 hectares for public use with the support of then mayor Ed Koch. This much publicized public-private partnership raised substantial private funds to restore this vital amenity to the public domain.

tens of thousands of units of affordable housing were leaving the protection of various rent-regulatory programmes, either because they had outlived the period of commitment required at their inception or because their present occupants no longer qualified as low-income under the city's rent-stabilization law.[7]

The Restructuring of Governance, Economy and Space

Several factors account for the changes New York has undergone since it suffered the fiscal crisis of the late 1970s. That crisis, brought on by economic recession, declining tax revenues and increasing expenditures, led to a restructuring of the city's governing institutions and policy emphases. Where previously New York had been America's most generous large city in terms of social programmes, budgetary tightening following the fiscal crisis meant that its working class and poor endured sharp cutbacks in expenditures on public health, housing and education. The city's problems at the time became redefined from poverty and neighbourhood decline to lagging economic growth and high crime rates. In response to fears of corporate flight, the Koch administration began to offer giant subsidies to property developers in the belief that the construction of modern offices could staunch the outward flow. It also provided tax breaks to firms threatening to leave New York. The rationale was that companies were leaving because doing business in the city was too expensive; thus, subsidies were necessary to bring down occupancy costs.

These initiatives continued under subsequent mayoral administrations. At the end of the 1980s, David Dinkins, New York's first African American mayor, sought to redirect public programmes towards lower-income residents, but he did not think he could afford to reverse the business-subsidy programmes of his predecessor. Moreover, because he had to deal with another recession-induced fiscal crisis, he was inhibited from new spending initiatives. Dinkins' short-lived administration was succeeded by the longer tenure of Rudolf Giuliani. He openly neglected poor neighbourhoods, cut back on housing programmes and aggravated racial tensions by excluding African-Americans from his administration; he also vocally supported the police in notorious cases of shootings of black individuals who turned out to be unarmed.

During the 1990s, Giuliani promoted vigorous anti-crime measures and was rewarded with sharply declining crime rates.[8] The perception of danger that had contributed to out-migration and neighbourhood decline diminished rapidly and continued to drop during the subsequent Bloomberg mayoralty. The image of New York as a somewhat seedy, threatening haven for the lower classes made place for the more appealing representation of it as a global city that sheltered the world's cultural and business elites.

The metropolis withstood the various shocks caused by deindustrialization, the stock-market bust of 1987, the dot.com implosion of the late 1990s and the World Trade Center attack because of an economic base that proved adaptable to changes in the world economy. Throughout the post-1970 period, the city sustained a haemorrhaging of industrial jobs, eventually causing it to lose its position as the country's largest manufacturing centre. In 1980 it looked as if New York's experience would parallel that of other old American cities, with neighbourhood abandonment and employment outflow feeding upon themselves. Few would have predicted that the trend would shortly reverse itself, albeit with a strikingly different economic base. Whereas the city had seemed to be undergoing a structural decline as a consequence of suburbanization, regional shift and infrastructural obsolescence, it bounced back in the 1980s due in part to the influx of hundreds of thousands of immigrants.

RUSH TO BUILD

Unlike the city's slow recovery following the fiscal crisis of the 1970s, the rebuilding of Ground Zero, the area in Lower Manhattan destroyed by the terrorist attacks on the World Trade Center on 9/11 in 2001, was matched by massive investment on behalf of city, state and federal agencies, which has succeeded in encouraging businesses and residents to return to the area.

During the sharp recession of the early 1990s it once more looked as if permanent structural factors would keep the city depressed, but again it revived. Then the downturn of the early part of the next decade proved less severe and more short-lived.

New York maintained its historic niche as the nation's premiere financial centre during a time when global restructuring had enormously enhanced the role of financial institutions. As new financial activities based on the trading of derivatives and private investments unmediated by the stock and bond markets burgeoned, the hedge funds and investment firms that managed these deals grew commensurately. Simultaneously, the city's position as a centre for business services was enhanced by the growing importance of activities like management consulting, advertising and corporate law.[9] In turn the changing demands for space, caused by the expansion of office-based firms and the housing needs of their well-to-do employees, fuelled massive property redevelopment within both the commercial and residential sectors.[10] The real-estate industry itself became an economic driver, as its investments resulted in spatial restructuring and brought handsome returns to participants. Former industrial sites became office and housing locations; modest housing was upgraded for high-income occupants; and partially abandoned neighbourhoods became repopulated.

Despite the heavy involvement of the city government in promoting real-estate investment, no effort at comprehensive planning guided physical development until recently. The City Planning Commission was a weak agency devoted primarily to minor zoning changes although its purview extended to land-use actions with important implications for the city's future. The principal force behind development initiatives was the Economic Development Corporation (EDC), a semi-autonomous mayoral agency unconcerned with the environmental or aesthetic impacts of property investment. City charter required review and approval of EDC's land-use proposals by local authorities, yet its operations were frequently in conjunction with New York State's Empire State Development Corporation, which, as an agency of state government, was immune from the regulations regarding citizen participation that constrained land-use initiatives of the city administration.

The EDC's efforts resulted in a patchwork of major mixed-use projects in Manhattan and Brooklyn. These included Battery Park City (BPC) in downtown Manhattan and MetroTech in central Brooklyn, both constructed during the 1980s; the renewal of Times Square in the Manhattan core, completed in the 1990s; and Columbus Circle, a huge structure also in midtown Manhattan, which opened in the 2000s. All four of these projects were reviewed under the city's land-use process and involved expensive office space for financial and business service firms; BPC included residential, recreational, retail and restaurant uses as well. MetroTech was primarily offices – the first such space produced in Brooklyn since World War I; however, the adjacent Atlantic Terminal, constructed by the same developer a few years later, housed a large shopping mall. In the new Times Square, massage parlours, adult bookstores and low-end movie theatres gave way to major entertainment corporations including the Walt Disney Company, while chain retailers took over ground-floor storefronts, and major publishing, legal and financial firms moved into four new high-rise office buildings. Columbus Center, 260,000 square metres of space built at a cost of US$1.7 billion, houses the headquarters of the Time-Warner Corporation, as well as additional office space, a luxury hotel, a shopping mall, luxury apartments, Jazz at Lincoln Center's new home and New York's most expensive restaurants.

MAJORITY–MINORITY CITY

Close to two-thirds of residents in New York City's five boroughs are part of an ethnic minority. The social cohesion among this vibrant mix of nationalities, religions and ethnicities is fostered by two major factors: the protection each group enjoys in the areas they inhabit, and the tradition of tolerance and acceptance that embrace the city's diversity.

Culture and Tourism

New York has secured its pre-eminence in the global system of cities not only through its commanding position within the flows of capital but also as a result of its cultural importance. The major broadcast television networks and many cable networks are headquartered within the city; here also are the country's most influential arts institutions – the Metropolitan Museum of Art, the Museum of Modern Art, the New York City Ballet, the Metropolitan Opera, the Broadway theatres – as well as a creative community that supports less-established venues. As measured by the location quotient, a figure that indicates the concentration of people in particular occupations compared to other metropolitan areas, New York City dominates in the fields of fashion, artistic and literary production, and multimedia design.[11] Participants in the various creative occupations intermingle at clubs and openings, cross-fertilizing each other and thereby encouraging further cultural production. The cultural-production complex attracts tourists, who are pulled by the promise of seeing culture made rather than simply copied or consumed.[12]

Tourism is a rapidly expanding sector of the city's economy, and increasing levels of both public and private investment have been promoting it. In the seven years between 1999 and 2006 the total visitor volume rose 20 per cent, and, since September 2001, international tourism surged 42 per cent to a record 7.1 million foreign visitors.[13] Thus, the drop immediately after the World Trade Center attack has been fully reversed, new hotel rooms are being added and the Jacob Javits Convention Center is being doubled in size. A synergy exists among culture, amenities enjoyed by residents, and tourism, as the huge number of visitors means that restaurants, galleries and theatres, which could not support themselves on local patronage alone, are able to survive and even flourish. Also, more tourists are visiting areas of the city outside central Manhattan. Nevertheless, the great majority of facilities and attractions remain concentrated there, and consequently the effects of tourism, for better and for worse, are largely encapsulated within the most affluent parts of the city.[14]

Housing

Incentives for the construction of affordable housing have waxed and waned until recently, peaking under Mayor Koch's 10-year housing programme during the latter part of the 1980s. At that time the city possessed a large stock of deteriorated housing ('in rem housing') that it had acquired as a consequence of tax delinquency. The rehabilitation of these units, along with new construction – much of it under the auspices of non-profit community development corporations – brought families back to the once-desolate South Bronx and improved neighbourhoods throughout the city. Housing construction and rehabilitation, however, were opportunistic, with projects sited wherever available parcels of buildings could be found. Once the in rem stock was depleted, opportunities for providing low-income housing diminished, particularly as the city's economic and population growth forced up the value of land and put an end to the landlord abandonment that had occurred during the 1970s.

Only now, under the Bloomberg administration, which took office in 2002, has there been a sustained effort towards land-use planning and a renewed emphasis on providing affordable housing. Nevertheless, while the mayor has declared a commitment to increasing the supply of affordable housing, embodied in additional incentives to private developers and allocation of public funds, the still-escalating price of land makes substantial additions to the stock extremely difficult. At the same time, housing constructed during earlier periods under various federally and

RESILIENT CITIES
As New York once again absorbs a new wave of international migration, the city is making more of its assets. Entire neighbourhoods like the Lower East Side have been transformed as illustrated by the refurbishment of an urban block on Avenue D at 10th Street, bringing private investment into a previously poor area.

state-sponsored subsidy programmes is continuously leaving the low-income pool, with the result that no net increase of affordable housing is likely. Emblematic of this trend is the recent sale for US$5.4 billion of the Stuyvesant Town/Peter Cooper Village complex by the Metropolitan Life Insurance Company (Met Life).[15] Met Life constructed the more than 11,000 apartments of Stuyvesant Town and the adjacent, somewhat more expensive, Peter Cooper Village immediately after World War II. They occupied land cleared as part of a state-sponsored slum-clearance programme, and for 60 years the development has housed an ethnically diverse, working- and middle-class population of more than 25,000 residents in a secure, well-maintained setting on Manhattan's East Side. The area in which it is located has become increasingly desirable, and now the new owners are moving as quickly as possible to push the units out of its regulated status.

Development trends in New York are thus causing the city to resemble its European counterparts, as the centre, which includes parts of Brooklyn as well as Manhattan, gentrifies. To some extent the outer boroughs, as in many European cities, consist of high-rise buildings sheltering working- and lower-middle-class households. But little is currently happening on that periphery to adequately absorb the households being relentlessly pushed out from the centre, despite a surge in new housing construction in the Bronx, Brooklyn and Queens. At the same time the suburban ring around New York remains largely unaffordable. The result is that many families are moving to exurban areas on the far edge of the metropolitan area or are doubling up with friends and relatives in the boroughs.

Population Patterns

Immigration has proved to be the main source of New York's population growth during the last two decades. Unlike Los Angeles, the only American city that exceeded it as a recipient of immigrants and where most newcomers were of Mexican and Central American origin, the immigrant stream to New York was extremely varied. According to the 2000 US Census, 36 per cent of New York's population, which reached its all-time peak of slightly over 8 million, were foreign-born. Of these, the largest group (30 per cent) came from the Caribbean, of which about one-third emigrated from the Dominican Republic. The next-largest group was Asian (24 per cent), of which close to 40 per cent were Chinese. Third were Europeans (19 per cent), with the greatest number drawn from various countries that once comprised Eastern Europe. Central America and Mexico amounted to about 9 per cent, while Africans constituted 3 per cent.

Although, as noted above, perception of racial hostility has diminished recently, racial isolation has not. Segregation has remained sharp and stable, with the African American population concentrated in Harlem (northern Manhattan), central Brooklyn and parts of the Bronx and Queens.[16] The number of blacks in the city's population has increased continuously since 1910; in 2000 persons identifying themselves as black constituted 34 per cent of the total, with significant increases since 1970 in foreign-born blacks from the Caribbean and a recent surge in immigrants from Africa. In sum, blacks still trailed whites in income by a substantial amount, with the black median only two-thirds of the white in 2000. Thus, although the city's demography is increasingly polyglot and most immigrant neighbourhoods have quite a varied ethnicity, the black-white divide remains as salient as ever. Racial segregation is reflected in low-performing schools, which are disproportionately non-white, and in the persistence of the vicious circle of racial isolation, unemployment –

BUILDING TO THE EDGE

New York's waterfront, which stretches along its five boroughs, is the site of extensive change and re-structuring. Brooklyn is experiencing the greatest pressure with previously active mercantile districts like Red Hook (below), at the mouth of the East River, becoming the focus for redevelopment. Elsewhere in Brooklyn new housing is replacing old factories and warehouses as in the neighbouring district of Williamsburg (right).

LIVING WITH DIVERSITY

One of New York City's more deprived but ethnically diverse boroughs, the Bronx, is experiencing an intense level of investment and regeneration. The Hub in the South Bronx (below and right) is now one of the largest commercial centres in the borough at the heart of a vibrant retail trade network of goods, servicing its diverse ethnic communities.

especially of African American males – and single-headed households. The current mayor has pledged himself to educational improvement and combating poverty, but the instruments at his disposal are limited, particularly given the continued commitment to deregulation and privatization.

New York's Future

New York most closely resembles London among the world's large cities. During the 1980s there was increasing convergence between these two global cities, as both were governed by conservative regimes and experienced similar economic restructuring. They continue to mirror each other in the composition of their economic base. Each has turned away from the disregard for planning that characterized their earlier governing regimes and presently they are both undertaking massive efforts at remaking their physical environments. London is building new rail connections and stimulating the development of Thames Gateway. New York is prioritizing transit improvements, including the long-deferred Second Avenue subway and a connection between the Long Island Railroad and Grand Central Station. Plans are proceeding for rebuilding the midtown West Side of Manhattan, the World Trade Center site, the East River waterfront in the three boroughs that face it and Coney Island at the far south shore of Brooklyn. Also underway is construction of baseball stadiums for both major-league teams and a basketball arena that forms a centrepiece for a massive mixed-use project in downtown Brooklyn. Both cities are witnessing the work of internationally famous architects, as Frank Gehry, Richard Rogers, Norman Foster *et al.* leave their marks upon the landscape.

The two cities diverge, however, in the type of social conflicts that they confront with their institutional structures, and the extent of their commitment to redistributive policies. While both cities attract a major flow of immigrants, difference based on national origin and religion is less salient in New York than in London. On the other hand, the black-white divide in New York results in a persistent spatial segregation of class and race that does not occur nearly as extensively in London.

The mayor of New York has much more authority than his London counterpart, while the community districts of New York have nothing approaching the powers of the borough governments of London. Both cities are hostage to national policy, but London is more directly dependent on the UK central government for funding and policy orientation than is New York. The difference between the national regimes of Labour-led Britain and the Republican-led United States is reflected in local attitudes and the tools at the disposal of local government to address issues of inequality. Thus, London now forces property developers to build a percentage of affordable housing along with market-rate units, while New York relies on incentives that stimulate only small amounts of new construction. The UK government is bolstering social services of all kinds. In contrast, New York remains committed to removing people from the welfare rolls and continues to have large numbers of medically uninsured.

In April 2007, Mayor Bloomberg announced an ambitious plan to accommodate population growth up to the year 2030.[17] Calling for the construction of 265,000 new housing units, it proposes re-zoning to allow increased densities, stipulates that a proportion of new housing be affordable, and calls for subsidies to lower housing costs. It also proposes substantial new investment in mass transit so as to improve access for households living in areas distant from the Manhattan core. The plan, which addresses numerous issues of land use, environment and infrastructure, represents the first major effort at developing a comprehensive strategy for the city's development since the 1970s. Many of its components, however, require approval by other levels of government, so far lack financing, and will depend on commitments for future mayoral administrations.

In New York, as in London, the city's role as a financial, service and cultural centre persists and provides the underpinning for its continued prosperity. Short of renewed terrorist attacks or a great plunge in financial markets, the city's enormous wealth will likely continue to accumulate. Immigration and gentrification will ensure that almost all its neighbourhoods will be lively. New York is further sustained by a vast non-profit sector that includes major institutions of higher education and elite medical centres. Its built environment reflects its role as the capital of capital, and its cultural scene will remain among the most exciting in the world. At the same time, the social distance between black and white, rich and poor shows no sign of amelioration, and the shrinking of the middle class is not abating. The development policy of the current mayoral administration primarily benefits large corporations and property companies to the detriment of small businesses, despite enormous growth in self-employment during this decade. Despite the mayor's aim to reduce poverty, policy is not moving towards direct aid to the poor. However, the primary factor in determining whether or not the public sector grapples seriously with issues of poverty and poor housing depends as much on Washington as on New York's government. In sum, then, the situation of New York City is contradictory and not easily characterized. There are opposing trends granting opportunities to many while depriving others. The rising tide is not lifting all boats, but at the same time New York's problems seem more manageable than they did during the low points that punctuated the last 40 years.

Following pages
REORIENTATING THE CITY
As more jobs and housing are created in New York City's outer boroughs, no longer does reference to 'the City' connote such a traditional Manhattan-centred view. Nonetheless, any sites that offer views of Manhattan's skyline, especially along the East River frontage (as illustrated here on axis with the Empire State Building) become hotly contested scenarios for real estate speculation.

AN URBAN AGE
IN A SUBURBAN NATION?

Bruce Katz and Andy Altman

The proposition put forward by the Urban Age project is bold and visionary: 'The late twentieth century was the age of economic globalization. The first part of the twenty-first century will be the age of the city, the "Urban Age". The design of the built environment, the distribution of urban density, and their impacts on social inclusion and quality of life, are at the forefront of political discussion in towns and cities across the globe.' Many Americans might scoff at this notion. An urban age in the land of strip malls, exit ramps and big boxes?

The American experience poses a critical question: is an urban age possible in a suburban nation? Just a decade or two ago it would have been difficult to imagine the promise of an urban age in the United States: competitive cities that create and nurture strong, resilient and adaptive economies; sustainable cities that promote accessible transport, residential and employment density and energy efficiency; inclusive cities that grow, attract and retain the middle classes and integrate individuals across racial, ethnic and class lines; and physical cities where the built environment – neighbourhood design, the architecture of private and public space – is a critical foundation of competitiveness, sustainability and inclusivity.

From its very inception, the United States has been ambivalent, if not hostile, to the city. From Thomas Jefferson's 'Pestilence City' in the eighteenth century, through the nativistic movements of the 1850s and 1890s, and Frank Lloyd Wright's 'Vanishing City' in the 1930s, to more recent futurist tracts, the city has always been perceived as dirty and unhealthy, bureaucratic and antiquated, home to people and concepts that were not quite American. As Thomas Jefferson famously wrote: 'When we get piled upon one another in large cities, as in Europe, we shall become as corrupt as Europe.'

The American story of the past 50 years has been relentlessly suburban. In region after region, the low-density dispersal of people and jobs – 'sprawl' – has dominated our physical landscape. A whole new lexicon has been created to describe America's unique contribution to human settlement: 'edge cities', 'edgeless cities', 'exurbia', 'boomburgs' and the 'exit-ramp' economy. If that was the exclusive to the United Nations, we could confine our discussion of the urban age to other parts of the globe. However, hidden beneath the story of sprawl and decentralization there is an emerging narrative about the power and potential of cities and urban places.

Firstly, broad demographic, economic, fiscal and cultural forces, far from exclusively fuelling decentralization, are increasingly promoting diversity, density and urbanity. Secondly, these forces – and a wave of urban innovation – are fuelling a visible, albeit uneven and incomplete, resurgence of American cities. Thirdly, these broad forces are also altering the shape and composition of many suburbs and forcing America to reconsider the very notion of what is urban. Finally, a note of caution: the full economic, physical and social potential of urban places in the United States – the achievement of an urban age – will not be realized unless and until cities and their suburban allies push through systemic policy reforms at the state level and develop a responsible partnership with the federal government.

The Big Picture

The United States is going through a period of rapid and complex demographic change. The country is growing by leaps and bounds – 33 million people in the past decade, 24 million in the decade before. Its growth is fuelled in part by an enormous wave of immigration. Thirty-four million, or 12 per cent, of the country's residents are foreign-born, the highest share since 1930. Immigration is essential to offsetting another major demographic trend – the ageing of the population. Like much of the industrialized West, the American population is growing older and living longer. Family structure is changing, too. Women and men are delaying marriage, having fewer children, heading smaller households.

These demographic forces are giving cities and urban places their best shot at attracting and retaining residents than at any other time since the 1950s. Cities attract immigrant families who seek communities that are tolerant and welcoming. They appeal to elderly individuals who seek places with easy access to medical services, shopping and other necessities of daily life. They draw middle-aged couples whose children have flown the nest and who are therefore open to new neighbourhoods and shorter commutes. Cities also lure young people in search of the urban lifestyles popularized on television shows like *Seinfeld*, *Sex and the City* and *Friends*.

The pace of demographic change in the United States is matched only by the intensity of economic transformation. Globalization and technological innovation are reshaping and restructuring the economy and altering what Americans do and where they do it. These forces have accelerated the shift of the economy from the manufacture of goods to the conception, design, marketing and delivery of goods, services and ideas. These forces are placing a high premium on education and skills, with communities and companies now engaging in a fierce competition for talented workers who can fuel innovation and prosperity. These forces are changing the ways in which businesses manage their disparate operations – enabling large firms to locate headquarters in one city, research and design somewhere else, have production facilities somewhere else again and back-office functions – within or outside the firm – in still other places.

As with changing demographics, the restructuring of the American economy gives cities and urban places a renewed economic function and purpose. Yes, globalization and technology do have decentralizing tendencies and have made 'Sprawl-Mart' possible. But, an economy based on knowledge bestows new importance on institutions that engender knowledge – universities, medical research centres – many of which are located in the heart of central cities and urban communities. More generally, the shift to an economy based on ideas and innovation changes the value and function of density. We now know that higher employment density and efficient transport systems contribute to labour productivity. Residential and employment density also enhances innovation. This happens partly by creating a 'quality of place'

URBAN FORM

The rapid urbanization occuring in Las Vegas, Nevada (above) coincides with construction of the MGM Project City Center in downtown Las Vegas, one of the largest privately financed developments in the United States at US$7 billion. Close to 35 million tourists every year create a stable employment base for residents contained in the sprawling outskirts of the city. Suffering from compromised air quality, scarce water resources and an intemperate and extreme climate, Las Vegas contrasts sharply with the quality of life for residents in Colorado Springs, Colorado. A former resort community, Colorado Springs boasts an eco-friendly lifestyle and urban economy now heavily dependent on the military.

IMMIGRANT VOICES
Hispanic and Asian populations in America's
cities grew by over 40 per cent during the 1990s.
In the face of national policies to restrict the
country's borders, these immigrant groups are
becoming increasingly vocal about equal rights
to employment, services and fair treatment, as
illustrated by a demonstration held in downtown
Los Angeles, one of North America's 'majority-
minority' cities (right).

that attracts knowledge workers and partly by enabling interactions and knowledge-
sharing among workers and firms, within and across industries.

Finally, the evidence shows that the urban form is not only competitively wise,
but fiscally sound. We have known for decades that compact development is more
cost-efficient – both because it lowers the cost of delivering essential government
services (police, fire, emergency medical) and because it removes the demand for
costly new infrastructure.

A Second Life for American Cities
Broad market, demographic and cultural forces – and policy innovation – have given
American cities a second life. They are growing again after decades of decline. Atlanta,
Chicago, Denver and Memphis literally 'turned around' by converting a 1980s population loss into a 1990s population gain. Immigrants are fuelling population growth
in cities and, in the process, are jumpstarting housing markets, revitalizing neighbourhoods and spurring entrepreneurial activity. The Hispanic population in the
top 100 cities grew by 43 per cent during the 1990s, or a total of 3.8 million people.
The Asian population in the top 100 cities grew by 40 per cent during the 1990s, or
1.1 million people.

Beyond demographics, cities have a strong footing in the 'ideas economy'. Some
60 per cent of jobs in America's cities fit squarely into 'new economy' categories,
compared to only 40 per cent in suburban communities. Signs of urban resurgence
abound: poverty rates declined in cities during the 1990s; the number of people living
in high-poverty neighbourhoods – and the number of high-poverty neighbourhoods – declined precipitously during the past decade; home ownership went up;
unemployment fell; the number of minority- and women-owned businesses soared.

The picture, of course, is not complete. The urban crisis in the United States is
not over. Cities still house disproportionate shares of low-income families and
cannot, by themselves, respond to the inevitable challenges of housing affordability,

healthcare and public education. Given their social and fiscal starting points, cities still struggle mightily to attract and retain middle-class families. Nor have all cities benefited equally from the advantageous turn of events. Even a casual visit to Detroit or St Louis or Camden reminds us of the devastating impact of decades of persistent poverty and institutionalized racism. But trend lines are moving in the right direction. Major forces unleashed in the last two decades are improving the economic and social potential of urban places. And, significantly, smart, innovative policies are also making a difference.

Over the past 15 years, American cities – sometimes with support from federal and state governments, often not – have begun to pursue bold, systemic, transformative strategies to unleash their potential in the marketplace and, in the words of Henry Cisneros, to 'act as instruments of social change'.

Just consider the following examples. Fifteen years ago, cities were beset by crack, gangs and disorder; since then we have witnessed a dramatic shift in policing techniques and a decline in urban crime. One cannot rebuild strong cities without safe streets. Ten years ago, David Osborne's book *Reinventing Government* was a bestseller; since then almost every city has become more efficient and consumer-friendly and, in the process, has created a climate for business and residential investment. Ten years ago Mayor Daley took over Chicago's public schools, sparking a wave of governance reform in the public-education system. Dozens of cities are experimenting with charter schools, small schools, comprehensive reading efforts – often led by individuals and constituencies outside the formal education structure. Ten years ago cities, armed with new federal investments, began to transform the worst public housing in the country; since then dozens of projects have been demolished and remade as economically integrated communities of choice and connection. Ten years ago, living downtown was still an oddity outside a few urban centres like Philadelphia, New York and Chicago; now it is a real-estate phenomenon as developers cannot move quickly enough to convert warehouses, historic structures, office buildings and even department stores to residential use.

The past decade has seen an explosion of interest in light rail and other major forms of public transit. The past decade has seen bold new efforts to return cities to their rivers and lakes – with cities like San Francisco, Milwaukee and Chattanooga tearing down or reshaping motorways that block access to the water. The past decade has seen an explosion of locally led prosperity campaigns to improve the incomes of working families through liveable wages, local- and state-earned income credits, greater access to federal work benefits and crackdowns on predatory lenders and other institutions that prey on low-income families.

What unites these efforts is their focus on transformation – of the physical, socials and economic landscapes. These are big, entrepreneurial efforts at a time when both national parties are claiming that government is the problem, not the solution. These are also efforts that celebrate the city – its fabric, diversity and complexity – and assert boldly that the cities do not need to replicate the suburbs to be competitive; rather they are competitive on their own terms.

Remaking the Suburbs

With suburbs taking on a greater share of the United States' population, they are beginning to look more and more like traditional urban areas – in population and in form. In many metropolitan areas, a substantial portion of immigrants in the past decade skipped cities and went directly to the suburbs. Racial and ethnic minorities

COMPETING CENTRALITIES
Cities located on the suburban fringe of larger metropolitan regions form an integral element to the area's overall urban vitality. Located at the northern apex of Washington DC, the downtown core of Silver Spring, Maryland was revitalized in the late 1990s with the establishment of Discovery Communications, a domestic and international media enterprise.

now make up more than a quarter of suburban populations, up from 19 per cent in 1990. The similarities between cities and older suburbs also extend to economic integration. Many suburbs built in the early or mid part of the twentieth century are home to the working poor – challenging ingrained perceptions of suburbs as isolated, wealthy enclaves. In 2005, for the first time, there were more people living below the poverty line in American suburbs overall than in central cities. Together, these trends send a clear message: these are no longer your parents' suburbs.

The older suburbs are not just important because they resemble cities in their social and economic composition; they are also population centres of great magnitude. Our calculations show that America only has 64 'older suburban' or 'first suburban' counties – places like Nassau County in Long Island, Westchester County north of New York City, and Erie County surrounding Buffalo. Incredibly, these 64 counties house over 52 million people and comprise nearly 20 per cent of the American population. That means that more than 50 per cent of the American population – a majority of the nation – lives in traditional central cities and five dozen or so urban counties. In New York the combination of the major central cities and these urban counties comprises over 70 per cent of the population.

A growing number of suburbs increasingly resemble cities in another way – their form. We see this as places like Montgomery County in Maryland develop downtown areas like Bethesda and Silver Spring that rival traditional central cities in their cultural amenities, their access to transit, their eclectic mix – often on the same site – of office, retail and residential. We see this as developers and financial institutions spend billions of dollars building or rebuilding malls – so-called 'lifestyle centres' – that resemble nothing more than a traditional main street, evidence of the market value, acceptance of and demand for urban places. Across suburbia and even exurbia we see pockets of urbanity popping up, as homebuilders and master developers, banks and real-estate agents embrace 'new urbanism' and 'smart growth' – movements that, like the wave of innovation in American cities, are only 10 years old.

As with the story of city resurgence, the story of suburban urbanization is not uniform across the nation or even within particular counties or metropolitan areas. Again, low-density sprawl still dominates the physical landscape. But it is clear that the market is increasingly emphasizing the 'urban' in 'suburban' – partly because it is told to by enlightened suburban jurisdictions and partly because it wants to, since density and urbanity pays more. The urbanization of the suburbs does not repeal capitalist instincts – it co-opts, embraces and even sanitizes them.

Urban Age Prospects for the American City
The urban age in the United States is not a foregone conclusion. Rather it will depend upon cities and suburbs making smart choices locally and then joining together collectively to push through state and ultimately federal policies that curb sprawl, promote reinvestment, and grow the middle classes.

The hard truth of the matter is that for every smart decision made locally, another miscalculated bet is made on a convention centre or a sports stadium, when we know that these facilities rarely meet their inflated expectations. The sad truth is that city after city is expending enormous energy chasing the tantalizing prize of biotech, when we know that only 10 or so metropolitan areas really have a shot at agglomeration economies that will make a discernible difference in the creation of jobs and in fiscal vitality.

CRISIS AND RECOVERY

Derelict buildings litter the urban landscape of Detroit, Michigan. After suffering a substantial loss of jobs linked to the collapsed economy of this 'Motor City', accelerated development is now helping the city to reinvent itself through waterfront investment, the creation of commercial districts and tourism despite persistent poverty and racial segregation.

The fact is that too many cities spend too much time mimicking 'magic-bullet' projects and solutions, and too little time fixing the basics – good schools, safe streets, competitive taxes, efficient services – so that markets can flourish, families can succeed and cities once again can be home to the middle classes. Yet even smart, strategic city-only solutions will not be sufficient. To achieve their true potential, urban places will need to be part of new political alignments that, in the short term, pursue structural state reforms and, in the long term, restore sanity to the federal role in American society.

Let us remind ourselves, first and foremost, of the city-shaping and family-strengthening powers of states in the American union. States set the rules and geography of governance that define local power. They set the rules of the development game that define growth patterns. They are major investors in all levels of education – primary and secondary, community colleges and public universities. With devolution, they now administer large federal block grants on transportation, workforce development, welfare and housing. And, they help set the opportunity structure for working families through large investments in healthcare and other critical supports as well as through regulation of multiple sectors and segments of the economy. Most importantly, a growing number of states are ripe for change. If American history has taught us anything, states – as laboratories of democracy, as political battlegrounds for federal presidential contests – will ultimately shape federal policies and practices for decades to come.

Let us give you a hopeful example. In 2003, the Brookings Institution published a major report in the Commonwealth of Pennsylvania that unveiled the competitive and fiscal implications of the state's main development pattern – the hollowing-out and spreading out of once-grand cities like Pittsburgh, Philadelphia, Scranton, Erie and Reading. What was also demonstrated in Pennsylvania was how sprawl was embedded and hardwired in an intricate network of state spending, tax, regulatory and administrative policies: state transport policies that allocated only 42 per cent of road and bridge spending on older urban communities, where 58 per cent of the population lives; state tax policies that leave cities stranded with tax-exempt properties and saddled with the costs of maintaining older infrastructure; state governance policies that support incredible localism among hundreds of suburban municipalities, each able to compete favourably with cities and older communities because they can benefit exclusively from job growth without taking responsibility for traffic or worker housing or poverty concentration; state building codes that make it cheaper to build new rather than renovate older properties; state housing policies that, under the guise of neighbourhood renewal, often reinforce the concentration of poverty rather than enhance access to opportunity.

What we also discovered in Pennsylvania was an urban coalition that was less than the sum of its parts. Pennsylvania, like many states, does not have a shortage of talented mayors or business owners or community, faith and civic leaders. It does not have a lack of real-estate practitioners or university presidents or heads of healthcare systems or environmentalists or conservationists. Yet these talented people are rarely organized well enough to be able to pursue structural change. City is pitted against city and urban constituencies are pitted against urban constituencies. The city/suburban divide – sometimes racial, sometimes not – is deep and pronounced. Cities and urban places, in short, have perfected the practice of city building – they are all well-versed in the 'art of the deal' – and have neglected the mechanics of coalition building – the 'art of the political'.

In the year following the release of our report, we witnessed the growth of a vibrant political coalition in Pennsylvania that has led a discussion about city revitalization, balanced growth and state competitiveness. The confluence of powerful ideas, a progressive governor (Ed Rendell, the former mayor of Philadelphia), and a vocal network of advocates has transformed state policies. The state has embraced 'fix it first' policies in transportation – stopping sprawl-inducing road projects at the fringe in order to fund infrastructure repair in the metropolitan core. It has resuscitated the State Planning Board to bring coherence to the actions of dozens of state agencies. An Interagency Land Use Team has been revitalized to better focus the state's actions and investments, and substantial new resources have been dedicated to brownfield remediation and land acquisition – illustrating the potential for common ground between old and new communities. Finally, the state has adopted bold reforms to prepare the Pennsylvania workforce for a radically different economic era. Policy fermentation has broken out all over the state. Should Pittsburgh consolidate with Allegheny County? Should metropolitan areas in the state be allowed to experiment with new taxing regimes and governance forms? Should the state's fiscal receivership law be turned into a tool for attacking the structural roots of urban decline and distress?

The important point here is that politics determine policies, and policies shape markets and growth patterns. In Pennsylvania and elsewhere, sprawl and economic and social change have left in their wake the potential for common ground between cities, older suburbs and even newer suburbs on a variety of issues – economic development, infrastructure spending, regional governance, local taxation, education and workforce, environmental protection, affordable housing.

That brings us to the 800-pound gorilla in the room – the importance, even with devolution, of the federal government. Since the early part of this decade, President Bush has tried to completely remake the fiscal and policy architecture of the United States and dramatically curtail the role and function of the federal government. With mixed results, his efforts have sought the following: dramatic reductions in housing subsidies, community development grants and investment in key infrastructure like Amtrak and transit; the crowding out of investments in working families, including healthcare, childcare, income supplements, nutrition assistance and worker training; and harmful reforms of key programmes like Medicaid and housing vouchers. The Bush administration has largely failed to enforce a whole series of laws that protect consumers and encourage investment in cities – the Community Reinvestment Act, the Fair Lending Act, the Fair Housing Act and the Home Mortgage Disclosure Act. All this has put a chill not just on city revitalization but on national prosperity, with rising deficits, rising interest rates and growing trade imbalances.

With the election of a new, more pro-urban Congress in 2006, it is likely that many of President Bush's proposed changes will be rejected and that funding for critical investments (such as public housing redevelopment) will be restored. But it is not sufficient for cities to merely rely on Congressional beneficence. They must take the offensive, re-educate policymakers about the new-found economic, environmental and social relevance of cities and urban communities, and articulate a new urban and metropolitan agenda that matches the intensity and realities of our times.

Cities must make this case, at the state and federal level, with suburban allies. Let's do the maths. Cities alone in the United States do not have the electoral weight to sway state and federal policies. But as part of new majoritarian alliances, they can begin to take back the debate and regain their power. The challenge for urban places is to go back to school on political organizing and coalition building, and create new networks of leaders and advocates across municipal jurisdictions, disciplines, racial and ethnic lines, and 'red' and 'blue' states and regions.

Messy, Conflicting Intensity

In 2030, fully half of the American built environment will have been constructed since the year 2000. The question for the nation, therefore, is not whether it grows, but how it grows, where it grows, and what it grows.

Our hypothesis today is that a distinctively American 'urban age' is possible in this suburban nation. It is possible because cities – with their density and diversity – have gained a second life in an era of demographic change and market restructuring. It is possible because many suburbs are exhibiting urban heterogeneity and embracing urban forms as a way to survive and thrive. It is possible because a new wave of policy innovation is sweeping cities and states. It is possible economically because consumers and firms are demanding it, and architects and designers and builders and financial institutions are creating it. It is even possible socially (that is, urban revitalization can promote economic integration rather than widen disparities) if a broader commitment to inclusion and advancement takes hold in the country.

The 'urban age' in America will, therefore, be complicated. It will be locally grown, not centrally planned. It will embrace, not repel, broader American themes of choice and competition. It will depend on American virtues of innovation and entrepreneurialism and risk-taking. It will challenge notions of 'city' and 'suburb'. It will stretch definitions of density to include many places that, by the standards of other countries, are not that dense. It will vary considerably across this vast and diverse nation – taking root in some places, bypassing others.

But the urban age in the United States is not a foregone conclusion. It will be heavily influenced by policy and politics. It will need to be fought for locally to ensure that market resurgence does not exacerbate racial, class and economic disparities. It will need to be fought for at the state and federal levels to ensure that higher levels of government respond to the power of new political coalitions and embrace the connection between density, competitiveness, fiscal responsibility and social inclusion.

It will not be the urban age of the twentieth century, with one single dominant city at the core of metropolitan economies; rather urbanity will peacefully coexist with low-density sprawl as part of new complex and interdependent metropolitan communities.

It will, in short, be quintessentially American – messy, conflicting, contentious, mercantile, polycentric, endlessly interesting, and alternately inspiring and appalling to the world.

GHAI

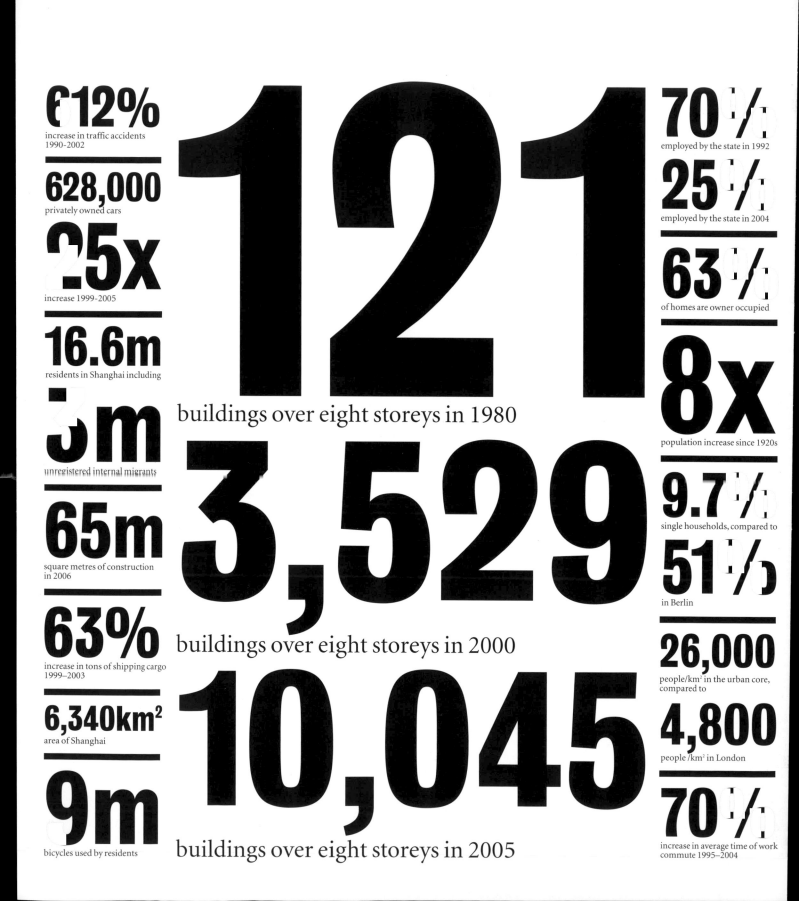

612%
increase in traffic accidents
1990-2002

628,000
privately owned cars

25x
increase 1999-2005

16.6m
residents in Shanghai including

3m
unregistered internal migrants

65m
square metres of construction
in 2006

63%
increase in tons of shipping cargo
1999–2003

6,340km²
area of Shanghai

9m
bicycles used by residents

121
buildings over eight storeys in 1980

3,529
buildings over eight storeys in 2000

10,045
buildings over eight storeys in 2005

70%
employed by the state in 1992

25%
employed by the state in 2004

63%
of homes are owner occupied

8x
population increase since 1920s

9.7%
single households, compared to

51%
in Berlin

26,000
people/km² in the urban core,
compared to

4,800
people/km² in London

70%
increase in average time of work
commute 1995–2004

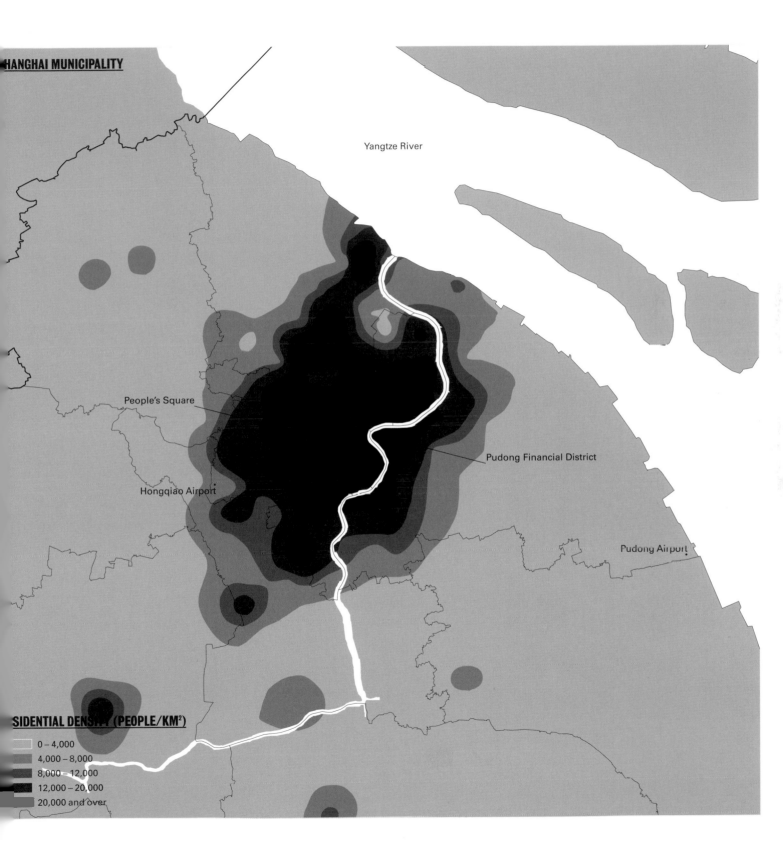

SHANGHAI MUNICIPALITY

Yangtze River

People's Square

Pudong Financial District

Hongqiao Airport

Pudong Airport

RESIDENTIAL DENSITY (PEOPLE/KM²)

0 – 4,000
4,000 – 8,000
8,000 – 12,000
12,000 – 20,000
20,000 and over

THE SPEED AND THE FRICTION

Deyan Sudjic

Fifty years ago Shanghai was an island of floodlit art deco cinemas, modern sky-scrapers and electric trams, marooned in the midst of a China that had hardly changed in 1,000 years. As the city petered out on the road to Nanjing, the neon signs and the street lights disappeared into the darkness of a medieval night. To drive across the city in those days, you needed three different driving licences to negotiate your way from the Chung Hwa Road to what was then called the Boulevard des Deux Républiques, to Edward VII Avenue and Broadway. You could have worshipped in your choice of onion-domed Russian Orthodox churches, the product of the army of White Russian refugees that sailed out of Vladivostock with the Bolsheviks on their heels. It is a history that suggests a city shaped by a mix of pragmatism, opportunism and anarchy. Shanghai was China's window on to the world, its most industrially advanced and commercially sophisticated city. And it still is, even as Beijing is working hard to re-establish pre-eminence with a building programme in the capital that is just as frenetic as Shanghai's. Shanghai's decision to hold a World Expo in 2010 is its own response to the 2008 Olympics in Beijing.

There is a tendency among western observers to look at China's two great cities, Shanghai and Beijing, as vast urban agglomerations that have broken the bounds of size and scale and thus isolated themselves from conventional urban precedents. But in terms of population size, Shanghai, with around 16.5 million people, is a city of the same order of magnitude as New York and London. The most striking differences between Shanghai, London and New York are political organization and urban culture. Shanghai is effectively a city state, with the powers of the central government at its disposal to annex satellite towns and villages and to open up territory into its direct control. We know Shanghai is big because there is no obfuscation about the difference between the city in the political sense and in wider definitions of it as an entity. But, as much as we are ready to analyse London or New York as urban regions, the perception is still shaped by political boundaries.

Shanghai, where almost one-fifth of the population is made up of temporary in-migrants from predominantly rural China, is the key city setting the pattern for the explosive urban growth in Asia. It is as much a phenomenon of our times as the equally rapid and – to its contemporaries – equally disturbing transformation of western industrial cities of the early nineteenth century. It is a phenomenon that is producing a sense of strangeness and dislocation, this time bound up with the overwhelming impact of speed. When the British happened on the Chinese walled

EXPLODING LANDSCAPES

Growing upwards and outwards at spiralling speed, Shanghai is an urban experiment in-the-making, radically altering the spatial and social experience of its 17 million city dwellers as its economy expands at the heart of China's fastest growing region.

URBAN VISIONS
The emerging Pudong Financial District on the banks of the Huang Po River has become the breeding ground of a new generation of skyscrapers and tower blocks that service Shanghai's role in the global economy. The artists' vision of the early 1990s has become a fragmented yet tangible reality in a city that confronts the formality of a centralized state with the informality of a developing nation.

settlement of Shanghai towards the end of the Opium War and fought for their right to sell the opium that they cultivated in India to the citizens of the Chinese empire, there was nothing on what is now the Pudong side of the Huangpo River. British traders – attracted by the river traffic on the Yangtze and its many tributaries linking inland China and the trade routes from Europe, the United States and later Japan – persuaded their government to insist on their unhindered access to Shanghai's port.

Fossilized through the Mao years, the Bund still looks like a hallucinogenic transplant of a European city to Asia. But Shanghai was never a traditional colony. The city was run by a series of different but parallel administrations. It was an arrangement that allowed a hybrid culture to flourish in the cracks between regimes. In parts of the city, it was never entirely clear exactly who was responsible for enforcing any kind of legal system.

The long freeze on Shanghai's development only lifted at the end of the 1980s, with the introduction of the market economy to China. In terms of physical development and planning, this triggered a great deal of research into appropriate models for Shanghai. Of course Hong Kong, with its carefully managed state land bank and the government's use of auctions to fundraise and control development, was studied with care. But so was the experience of Barcelona as it emerged from its transformation for the Olympics of 1992. Before the wave of new building really took hold, Shanghai staged an architectural competition for a redevelopment strategy that would deal with the whole Pudong area. It showed both the strengths and weaknesses of Shanghai's position. Many of the world's leading architects – Toyo Ito, Massimiliano Fuksas and Richard Rogers among them – were invited to take part. They all put forward more-or-less radical attempts at masterplanning, all of them mutually exclusive in their approach to land-use and form. The city claimed to have adopted the best features of all the competitors, and the development of a new business district in Pudong has proceeded at breakneck speed, although along lines that bear little resemblance to anything that emerged in the competition.

Shanghai has moved beyond the first rush of crude tower building, and the mood has changed. In central Shanghai, the American architects – led by John Portman – who were responsible for many of the early high-rises, have given way to a wider selection of designers who are beginning to show a more considered range of approaches. As demonstrated by the property investment in the Bund, and in some of the surviving fragments of nineteenth-century Shanghai, the city is also beginning to develop a more nuanced attitude to its own past. Under the Pearl Television Tower you find the mayor's call to his citizens to 'Rejoice in the present, while recalling the past' carved in both Chinese and English into a low granite wall. Shanghai is determined that every visitor knows all about what is going on now, and expresses this in language that seems to recall the days of the Red Guards. 'Persist in the development of Pudong without wavering until it is done' reads one giant billboard at the foot of the Pearl Television Tower. The city is busy planting trees and even the flyovers are fringed with plant boxes dangling green over the side of the road. It has installed its famous US$700 million Maglev train system to make the 40-kilometre trip to Pudong airport at an astonishing 430 km/h. And it is metamorphosing with such speed that it demolished the central railway station built as recently as 1988. The city had already outgrown it.

At the regional level, Shanghai is developing a policy for its position at the centre of the Yangtze delta. On a national level, it is competing with Hong Kong and Tokyo. It is moving beyond manufacturing to advanced service industries, as much a part of the rhetorical agenda for every ambitious city as culture-led renewal. The question facing Shanghai is whether its best model is New York, London or Tokyo – or perhaps California – as it attempts to create a balance between its suburban industrial estates and its high-rise city centre. It is still working to reduce cycling by another 25 per cent in the next five years, just as it is working to reduce population densities in the inner city, where there are still particularly crowded areas such as the Old West Gate, with people living at 76,000 per square kilometre – nearly 10 times the average density of London.

Getting to grips with a city that has been undergoing double-digit economic growth for more than a decade demands a set of conceptual tools rather different to the conventional repertoire employed by those who spend their time thinking about urban issues. The inescapable fact is speed. Shanghai is a city whose development over the last 10 years has, by any standards, been extraordinarily rapid. The descriptions accompanying comparative maps of the administrative, spatial and social characteristics of Shanghai, London and New York make for avid reading.

The story of Shanghai's speed and friction can be told in summary. Since 1990, living space per person has doubled to reach 15 square metres per resident. In the same period, the city has built 40 per cent more roads. There are nearly 2 million cars. The underground system has reached a daily capacity of 1.4 million people, and is intended to reach 5 times that figure. The city has developed an entirely new business district in Pudong in less than two decades, and it has embarked on the construction of a ring of satellite towns – designed in German, Italian, Scandinavian and Chinese urban styles. In the rush to build office towers to catch a perceived market, speed has been the determinant factor of form. Rather than give architects and engineers the time to produce considered technical solutions to optimize net-to-gross ratios, developers have demanded instant starts. Without time to make sophisticated calculations, engineers have over-specified structural cores. Buildings less than 10 years old have aged with remarkable rapidity. Some have become redundant even before they are finished.

In Shanghai, friction comes with speed. It's the kind of friction that comes as development accelerates and decelerates, the friction that fills the gap between the imperatives of what is still operating within the framework of a Marxist control-and-command economy, the actual results and often-unintended consequences. This provides an echo of the gaps between the administrations that ran the old Shanghai. The will to centralize can be perceived in the language of Shanghai's plans – not just in the huge sign that exhorts its citizens to 'Persist without wavering until it is done', but even more in what the city calls 'the six pillars'. This is not a Maoist call to arms, but a policy to build a strong economy based on cars, semiconductors, petrochemicals, trade, finance, real estate and construction.

After New York, Shanghai was the second in the Urban Age investigations of cities. It provided a chance to learn from a city in the midst of a spasm of change so violent that it questions the extent of human resilience to explore the meaning of speed and friction. It is a city moving so fast that it is possible to see the impact of theory on practice like nowhere else in the world.

CONFRONTING CHANGE

Over nine million bicycles jostle with the fast changing lifestyle of China's most cosmopolitan city. Overhauling its transport infrastructure and investing heavily in an extensive underground system, Shanghai restricts the issue of new driving licences to only 500 a day even while the number of private cars and elevated motorways has grown exponentially in the last decade.

INHABITING THE CITY OF THE FUTURE

The rush to triple the amount of individual living space in a city of 17 million people coupled with the need to accommodate new immigrants from inland China has fuelled Shanghai's seemingly irrepressible housing boom. High-density and high-rise residential towers create a form-less and austere landscape, challenging conventional notions of urbanity and continuity, as illustrated in the Huangpu District on the outskirts of Shanghai.

THE URBAN LABORATORY

Xiangming Chen

Shanghai is recognized as the most rapidly globalizing city in the world. As the first city to emerge from the modern developing world, it appears well on its way to hosting the World Expo in 2010. Shanghai's rise has caught worldwide attention. It is no surprise that the city of Chicago, led by its can-do mayor Richard M. Daley, opened its first overseas development office in Shanghai in February 2007. Anyone not already aware of the city's rising global importance received a wake-up call through the worldwide financial shockwaves unleashed when the Shanghai Stock Exchange plunged on 27 February 2007.

Shanghai has experienced the fastest economic growth of any megacity in the world since the early 1990s, averaging about 15 per cent a year. It has attracted US$120 billion in direct foreign investment since 1992, averaging well over US$10 billion annually in recent years – more than any other city, and most countries, in the world. Over the past two decades Shanghai has undergone a spatial transformation perhaps more dramatic than any other city. This spawned the mythological rumour that half of the world's cranes were working in Pudong (east of the Huangpo River) in the latter half of the 1990s. The massive build-up turned a former agricultural region of rice paddies and farmhouses, largely cut off from the rest of Shanghai, into a booming district filled with modern skyscrapers and factories, and which included the world's fastest train and its tallest hotel. Shanghai has gone through 'the greatest transformation of a piece of earth in history' according to a Baltimore-based architect who was involved in planning work on the city.[1] With a clever design another American architect, Benjamin Wood, turned a small piece of gigantic China's global city, located in an old central city neighbourhood, into Xintiandi (translated as 'New Heaven and Earth'). This has now become a top tourist destination, drawing numerous foreigners and fashionable locals to its luxury shops, outdoor cafés and trendy restaurants.

Shanghai in the Rear View Mirror

The new boom and glamour of Shanghai is, in a sense, a renaissance of the old Shanghai. A relatively small market town and a cotton-production centre throughout the seventeenth century, 200 years later it had blossomed into China's most cosmopolitan city and, by the 1920s, it had become known as 'the Paris of the East'. Shanghai then ranked as the world's sixth-largest city behind London, New York, Tokyo, Berlin and Chicago. More importantly, it had become by far the most dominant financial,

CONTRASTING REALITIES

Large sections of Shanghai's traditional low-rise housing areas – many of them lacking basic services – are being demolished as the city makes space for new structures that service the global economy and accommodate lifestyle aspirations of the newly affluent. Migrant workers across the new China advertise their services by scrawling their mobile phone numbers on construction sites.

URBAN EXTREMES

Every corner of Shanghai offers a new perspective on the pace and scale of its urban change. Bicycles are replaced by motorized vehicles and are banned from some main roads to reduce car congestion. Meanwhile, many of the city's traditional inner-city dwellers are moving into new housing blocks in the periphery, tripling the average size of a residential unit from the size of a small car, or about 4 square metres, to 16 square metres per person within a decade.

industrial, shipping and cultural centre in China. Between 1886 and around 1930, Shanghai consistently handled about half of China's foreign trade, and it absorbed 34.3 per cent of the country's total foreign investment in 1931. Between 1902 and 1904, its inhabitants accounted for 69 per cent of the market for the 529 western books translated into Chinese in China.[2] By 1933, it accounted for more than half of China's total industrial output. By 1936, the Paris of the East was host to half of the bank headquarters, bank branches and trust companies – both foreign and domestically owned – in the whole of China. But Shanghai's star dimmed from the late 1930s through to 1949, during the tumultuous years of the Chinese Communists' wars with Japan and the Nationalists.

The city was poised to rise again after the Chinese Revolution of 1949, but the central-government policy of redistributing its economic and technical resources to financing the development of poor interior cities stagnated Shanghai's growth until the late 1970s. The city turned over 350 billion Yuan (US$44 billion) in revenue to the central government between 1949 and1985 but got back only 3.5 billion Yuan (US$440 million) for building municipal infrastructures – a lopsided ratio of 100:1 in favour of the central government.[3] It languished behind the booming cities of South China such as Shenzhen and Guangzhou, which were favoured by the central government during the 1980s. The onset of the 1990s, when former Shanghai mayors Jiang Zemin and Zhu Rongji rose to power on a national level, ushered in a 'golden decade' for Shanghai. Groomed and guided by both the national and municipal governments, the city has since been steaming along an upward trajectory to becoming China's pre-eminent global city. 'The Paris of the East' of the past appears to be jumping forward to becoming 'the New York of China' of the future. That future seems not too distant for a city that is already home to the Asia headquarters of more than 150 global corporations, including General Motors and IBM.

The Shanghai 'Miracle'

The torrential growth of Shanghai during a relatively short time span amounts to a 'miracle' of global-city building. The most powerful force behind this 'miracle' was the state-led model of urbanization anchored to a specific policy of allowing a few coastal cities to experiment with leasing the rights of state-owned land to foreign investors, which emerged in the 1980s. Shanghai was one of those cities. By 2000 it had raised more than US$13 billion from leasing land for infrastructure construction and urban redevelopment. As a former mayor of Shanghai commented at the time, if the city had depended on the central government for traditional budget allocation instead of raising funds through land lease, the urban-renewal projects completed between 1990 and 2000 would have taken 100 years to complete. The US$120 billion of foreign investment it has attracted since 1992 saved it from such a protracted process. Almost 4,000 buildings with 20 or more storeys have risen in the city since the early 1990s, doubling Shanghai's own housing stock and resulting in more than twice the number of buildings in New York. The massive scale of land lease amounts to a highly rational, calculated move by the government to use its sole control over non-priced land to create a lucrative land-lease market to finance rapid urban build-up. If land lease is the defining feature of state-led urban development in Shanghai, it injects a strong dose of hybrid capitalism, relative to the 'free-market' of Hong Kong, where the government would auction valuable properties for development.

The four themes of the Urban Age project – labour and workplaces, transport and mobility, housing and urban neighbourhoods, and public life and urban space – are both more evident and more subtle in the transformed nature of Shanghai than in any other new Chinese city. The already heavily eroded state sector, which accounted for only 24.3 per cent of all employment in 2000, lost further ground with 20 per cent of all employment in 2004. In the meantime, the share of jobs in foreign-owned enterprises grew from 7 to 10 per cent, while the proportion of private- and informal-sector jobs jumped from 11.7 to 27.2 per cent.[4] Another important dimension of the state-led reorganization of Shanghai's economy is reflected in the relative decline of the manufacturing sector (from 63.8 per cent of the city's GDP in 1990 to 48.6 per cent in 2005) and the rise of the service sector (from 31.9 to 50.5 per cent). This shift from manufacturing to services reflects the state-set goal of turning Shanghai into a world-class centre of financial and advanced business services. The finance, insurance and real-estate (FIRE) sectors (key producer services in Saskia Sassen's global-city model) as a share of Shanghai's total services output rose to about 30 per cent in 2005, closing a little of the gap between Shanghai and true global cities such as New York and London. These services, however, remain functionally limited in a city that continues to be a dominant manufacturing centre in the Yangtze River Delta and in China as a whole. Aggressive as it is, the government's push for Shanghai to become a global city rubs up against the resilient dependency rooted in its industrial tradition.

The most densely populated central city area in China, parts of Shanghai's Huangpo district have a whopping 126,500 people per square kilometre, giving each person less than 8 square metres. In addition, the average house price in central Shanghai is 4 times as high as that in areas away from the centre. To reduce this density and to take advantage of the large housing-price differential, the city's municipal government has drawn up a massive plan – to be executed between 2006 and 2010 – to build 'one new city and nine new towns' with a combined population of 5.4 million, plus 60 new small towns with populations of around 50,000 each.[5] Each of the nine new towns was designed to resemble the typical city of a different European country. For example, Thames Town in Songjiang New City – about 40 kilometres south-west of central Shanghai – looks like a British village, with cobbled streets, Tudor-style houses and red telephone boxes. Since mass-transit lines do not yet link Thames Town to downtown Shanghai, it has few permanent residents and feels like a ghost town during the week. At weekends, however, couples find the town and its stranded tram a perfect backdrop for photo opportunities. While these towns will develop more connections to Shanghai, they are planned as self-sufficient satellite cities where people can live, work and shop without having to commute to central Shanghai.[6]

To allow for people to live further from the city's downtown area while still being within easy commuting distance of the centre, the Shanghai government is planning to expand the transport network – including the underground, roads, railways and a Maglev train – to the regional edges. Millions of Shanghainese may soon have to choose, if they haven't already, between moving out to the new and more spacious suburban housing or staying put in the old and crowded central-city dwellings. Those who have moved enjoy the lower mortgage payments, larger living spaces, better air quality, green parks, modern facilities and reduced noise in the suburban towns of Pudong, but they miss the familiar social networks and the shopping and transport convenience. Despite the fairly generous compensation offered by the government and/or property developers for vacating housing units slated for demolition, some residents refuse to move because they do not like the inconvenience of a long commute to and from downtown Shanghai, where the affluent families that are often their employers still reside. Others are put off by the lack of commercial facilities and social services. However, as more amenities such as shopping centres, schools and hospitals become available in the suburbs, more families are likely to relocate there. While this will reduce the high density in the city centre, it may trigger the type of suburban sprawl that characterizes so much of American metropolitan development. As the growing population pressure calls for 200,000 new housing units a year for the next 10 years to be added in Shanghai, the city looks set to spread and stretch out further sooner rather than later.

Lessons from Shanghai

The apparent role of the Chinese state in building Shanghai into a global city lends strong support to the argument that the state remains powerful rather than the suggestion that its powers are being eroded in the face of accelerated globalization and autonomous global cities. The unparalleled speed with which the transformation of Shanghai has occurred simply would not have happened elsewhere. However, is the same Chinese state capable of managing the drawbacks that go hand in hand with such rapid development? What must and could the state do to offset these negative consequences? In a democratic society there is a system of rights and a history of local participation that limits the extent to which any government can suddenly reverse course. The state's handling of the 'backlashes' of globalization and marketization in Shanghai, in contrast, continues to rely on top-down macro-control and administrative interference, although the latter approach now works less well than it has in the past, exposing the growing weakness of a still-powerful state as a global-city builder. For example, it was only after repeated administrative measures pushed down by the central government that the city's 'hot' property market slowed with a 10 per cent drop in property prices in mid 2006. But it might reflect the municipal government's push to sell more less-expensive, lower-end housing units across the city. In late 2006, the central government removed Shanghai's party secretary and a number of senior municipal government officials for misappropriating around US$400 million from municipal pension funds for property development. Rumours about factional struggles aside, this episode exemplifies the reasserted will of the central state to rein in the powerful and autonomous Shanghai leadership.

Although the local government has demonstrated some political muscle in holding off the central government's global-city building project, it faces an increasing range of local challenges, such as creating enough jobs to reduce the pressure of unemployment on social stability in China's most populous city – 17 million people including over 3 million migrants. As the mayor of Shanghai acknowledged in 2003, 'Job creation will be one of the priorities, or one of the most difficult challenges in future'. The official unemployment rate in the city has been around 5 per cent since 2003, or more than 300,000 jobless, according to the municipal government's latest statistics. It created only 100,000 new jobs in 2003 as the city's 400,000-plus job opportunities were offset by 300,000 job cuts due to the restructuring and reorganization of state-owned enterprises.[7] The shrinking formal labour market is also accompanied by a growing informal economic sector, which is gradually being recognized by the government as a timely, complementary source of jobs. While the relative size of Shanghai's informal economy is smaller than those of Mexico City and Johannesburg, its emergence and expansion marks the departure from its socialist past and the entrance into the ranks of global cities shaped by the capitalist economy.

FLOATING POPULATION
Three million people, or 20 per cent of Shanghai's residents are migrants from rural China who work in the city's booming construction sector but lack basic rights to education and social support.

DENSITY AND SCALE

The residential density of Shanghai is increasing
at the core, with taller closely packed buildings
exerting noticeable impact on the quality of
the environment. Over the last two decades the
number of buildings above eight storeys has
soared from just over 100 to 10,000.

It also exposes the state's weakness in handling its burden of economic restructuring.

The lessons from and about Shanghai revolve around the strengths and weaknesses of this method of building a dynamic global city. The government faces a dilemma in its relationship with the rapidly changing local communities, which have gained autonomy through earlier government-initiated administrative reforms. In 1996, the local government introduced reforms intended to strengthen the power of street offices in areas such as community service, education, sanitation, social security and safety, and returned 1–2 per cent of taxes for community development. Measures like this changed the street office from a weak branch of the district government to a sort of grassroots-level governance tool. The 'Shanghai Model' of community reform is characterized by the power transition from higher-level government to local level on the one hand, and the reconstructing of a local administrative system on the other. These are two related but different processes with different orientations. Any merging of these two processes could burden a local community with governmental tasks and turn it into another local administrative unit, which would lead to an expansion of existing government functions and a deviation from the essence of community building.

Finally, Shanghai teaches us something about the power of individual choices, or lack thereof, in a state-directed but increasingly independent market-driven residential housing market. As the blocks surrounding Xintiandi are torn down to make way for luxury flats and a proposed theatre district that aspires to rival New York's Broadway or London's West End, the existing low-income residents, who are largely without any choice, may have to purchase low-cost housing away from the city centre or beyond, whether their relocation compensation from the government would make the move economically feasible or not. At the same time, the new rich live downtown in luxury flats or detached villas in suburban gated compounds as elite members of a new and privileged community. Looking at the Gini index (a standard measure of income inequality with the number 1.00 representing complete inequality) for Pudong, Shanghai rose from .37 in 1994 to .45 in 2001, approximating the high level of inequality in the United States. With their wealthy status and exclusive nature, the gated communities in Shanghai differ little from their counterparts in Mexico City, Johannesburg and even in American metropolitan regions. In this regard, the city is much less a typical Chinese global city. It is simply a globalizing city on a familiar development trajectory. But it is the blazing speed of its growth and globalization in a transitional socialist system that makes it quite distinctive. This in turn renders Shanghai a live laboratory for the Urban Age project and beyond.

CHINA'S NEW REVOLUTION

Xiangming Chen

China is undergoing an urban revolution of unprecedented scale and complex dimensions. By 2015, eight years after the world's urban population has surpassed its rural population – a historic watershed crystallizing our urban age – more than half the population of China will live in urban areas. The projected urban population of 700 million is far larger than that of any country other than India. Aside from size, China's urban revolution involves dramatic and profound spatial and social transformations, creating a new type of Chinese city that departs radically from its past.

The Chinese City from Past to Present

Despite having one of the world's longest recorded civilizations, China's is largely rooted in an agricultural economy and village culture, yet there is a salient urban aspect to its history, which is punctuated by the changing fortunes of a few prominent cities. It is a little-known fact that scenic Hangzhou (near Shanghai) was one of the earliest cities in the world to reach a population of one million, which it achieved as early as the thirteenth century, when it was a lively commercial hub. Back then the city was the residence of the emperor and his courtiers. Now, the nouveau riche live there like kings. Their consumption made the city boom, and its economy has been growing at double-digit rates for 13 years. House prices in Hangzhou have tripled since 1999, approaching prices in Shanghai. Multimillion-dollar villas built around the famous West Lake sell for more than 50,000 Yuan (around US$6,000) per square metre. Guangzhou (Canton) became a bustling outpost of foreign trade in the mid-nineteenth century after it was prised open by British colonial expansion in the Far East. Today in Guangzhou, tea drinking – a Cantonese custom steeped in centuries of tradition – is giving way to a passion for coffee that has become the latest trend in the city's culinary landscape. Shanghai, which throughout the seventeenth century remained a relatively small coastal town, blossomed into China's most cosmopolitan city and by the 1930s had become known as 'the Paris of the East'. Today Shanghai is poised to become China's premiere global city of the twenty-first century. Until 1949, however, these cities stood out as 'islands' of concentrated wealth and glamour, as well as decadence and corruption, in a sea of largely impoverished rural China.

The founding of socialist China in 1949 ushered in an urban era featuring a new kind of Chinese city – the socialist city – that was shaped by ideologically driven planning into a 'producer city', as opposed to a 'consumer city'. The socialist city became the location of state-owned factories and grew into an engine of local economic

BUILDING COMPETITION

China's urban population will double in the
next decades spurred by massive projects such
as the 2008 Beijing Olympics and the 2010 Expo
in Shanghai. High profile architecture, such as
Herzog & de Meuron's Olympic Stadium, reflect
the economic and spatial restructuring of
China's most global cities.

CITIES IN A CHANGING CONTEXT
Chinese cities reflect the tensions of decades of social, economic and political change – from the rigid constraints of state socialism to highly differentiated economic terrains and changing market conditions.

development under rigid central planning. The state prevented the city from generating population growth, especially through in-migration, and the development of commercial and municipal infrastructures that normally accompany rapid industrialization. The rigid system of household registration (*hukou*) kept the rural population out of the cities, while the work-unit compounds (*danwei*) kept employees of state agencies and factories in, and treated them as collective labourers and residents based on relatively egalitarian principles and social relations. In the Chinese socialist city, a labour market did not exist and the workplace was primarily state-owned and heavily politicized. Public space became synonymous with social control which crowded out almost all private spaces. Public housing was the predominant form of residential living and was offered virtually free to reflect the artificially suppressed low wages. Cheap public transport ensured decent access to work and basic commercial services in a landscape barren of consumer and leisure facilities. Intercity mobility was highly restricted, which reinforced social control and resulted in a high level of spatial homogeneity. While the Chinese city did not live up to the expectations of the full egalitarian ideal of state socialism, this same planning uniformity proved a great leveller of the many geographic and socio-economic differences remaining from the pre-socialist era. The city remained a largely undifferentiated urban space, accommodating simple working and living conditions throughout the 1970s.

The Chinese City Transformed

China's cities began to turn away from state socialism around 1980, when the central government selected four cities (Shenzhen, Zhuhai, Shantou and Xiamen) on the south-east coast as special economic zones by granting them favourable policies and an administrative autonomy that enabled them to attract foreign investment and to experiment with market reforms. The success of targeting these few cities as a new model of decentralized and market-oriented development led the central government, in 1984, to designate 14 larger cities, including Shanghai, along the entire coastal belt as so-called 'open cities', giving them financial incentives and administrative flexibility in dealing with foreign investors and pursuing economic development. These policies began to unleash the power of an urban revolution that has transformed the Chinese city.

Exemplifying state-led urban development, the central government of China allowed a number of coastal cities to experiment with leasing the use rights of state-owned land to foreign investors in the mid and late 1980s. While this policy had a major influence on Shanghai, it also pushed the much smaller cities on or near the coast to take off. Located near Shenzhen and Hong Kong, the city of Dongguan, a formerly rural township, turned much of its rice and lychee fields into massive factory floors and became a booming manufacturing hub that stretches over 2,520 square kilometres and has more than 5 million inhabitants. By 2003, Dongguan had become China's third-ranked city in export volume, behind Shanghai and Shenzhen. With revenues from leasing valuable land for building factories, the local government funded its entire primary and secondary education at no cost to residents while enabling experimentation with free health insurance and pensions.[1]

A second factor in this process is that while industrial production has transformed many former economic backwaters like Dongguan into large-scale manufacturing centres, it is accompanied by a more differentiated labour market, a slower-growing service sector lacking municipal infrastructure and social services, and the continued dominance of the central city with some government-guided dispersal to the metropolitan fringes. A third element is that China's city growth has been fuelled by the huge influx of rural migrant workers – up to several million in booming coastal cities. Migrant workers generally face harsh working conditions and contribute to the creation of wealth and prosperity in cities, but they are subject to exclusionary government policies and end up having to eke out a meagre living from the lowest echelon of the socio-economic hierarchy and on the margins of the residential landscape. Finally, Chinese urbanization has become closely linked with globalization. Multinational corporations have not only created a great deal of factory employment and a growing number of higher-paid and knowledge-intensive research and development jobs in Beijing and Shanghai, they have also reshaped local consumption patterns by stimulating a broad desire for a globally oriented lifestyle characterized by the popularity of brand-names and luxury residential estates – a lifestyle only within reach of a relatively small and wealthy proportion of the population. Spatial and social inequalities have consequently widened considerably.

Under the interactive influence of these four forces, the Chinese city has experienced a deep transformation from its state-planned form to become a locus of increasingly differentiated economic, social and territorial conditions. First of all, the transformed city has a fundamentally restructured economic base with a differentiated labour market that simply did not exist in the socialist city. In all Chinese cities and towns, the share of employment in the state sector dropped from 70 per cent in 1992 to 25 per cent in 2004, while that of the private sector rose from 4.7 per cent to 20.8 per cent. The continued decline of state-owned industries has occurred through consolidation, mergers and acquisitions, relocations, mandatory early retirement and job cuts. As the expanding private sector has created new jobs at fairly low skill-levels, in the past decade rapid expansion of higher education – especially graduate schools – has increasingly made it more difficult for higher-degree holders to find employment than undergraduate-degree holders. Employers prefer applicants who have practical work experience over those with academic qualifications. The percentage of graduates who sign job contracts prior to graduation has dropped from 68.2 per cent to 40 per cent for graduates and from 76.7 per cent to 40.7 per cent for postgraduates in 2005 over 2003.[2] As a solution to this problem, the government is encouraging university and vocational-school graduates to find work in the countryside, which continues to send migrants into the cities.

If the restructured economic base and a dynamic labour market add major wrinkles to the transformed Chinese city, new large-scale urban design, coupled with the development of ambitious transit systems, complicates the hybrid urban space further by stretching the metropolitan boundary. Some of Beijing's 14 satellite cities will be expanded under a plan developed by the municipal government to ease overcrowding in the capital. Several satellite cities with a good geographic location, industrial foundation and inhabitable environment will accommodate as many as 500,000 residents each. They now house just over 1 million people in a combined area of 157 square kilometres. Their population density – 6,879 per square kilometre – is much lower than the 27,400 average in the downtown area. The capital's deteriorating environment and chronic traffic problems – brought on by economic development – are the primary reasons why the municipal government is pushing the plans to take shape in time for the opening of the Summer Olympic Games in August 2008.

Another salient feature of the transformed Chinese city is a more differentiated residential landscape created by advanced house privatization. By the end of 2005, private house ownership in China's coastal cities had reached 82 per cent, which is

Previous pages
FAST CITIES

The construction of the Jin Mao tower in Shanghai's Pudong financial centre is symptomatic of the speed of urbanization across China. Building quality is often sacrificed to meet the vertiginous speed of construction programmes, with bold visions quickly rendered obsolete by a process of rapid change.

higher than in countries such as the United States (68 per cent), the United Kingdom (67 per cent) and Germany (only 42 per cent).[3] This high private-ownership rate has become a major factor in dictating housing supply and demand, which hampers the government's efforts to curb rising house prices. The central government first introduced cooling measures in 2005, but the market showed few signs of slowing down, especially in the rapidly developing coastal cities. Further measures were introduced in May 2006. These included raising down-payments on loans for luxury homes from 20 to 30 per cent, taxing proceeds from homes resold within five years instead of two as previously, and the refusal to grant bank loans to developers unless they invest at least 35 per cent of the project costs from their own capital. The government also introduced rules to increase low-cost housing, requiring developers to designate 70 per cent of the units in a property project to apartments of a maximum of 90 square metres. However, a Ministry of Construction survey found that the average size of new flats in 16 main cities in the first half of 2006 was more than 120 square metres, much larger than an ordinary household could afford. Another survey found that 70 per cent of China's urban residents could not afford to buy a new apartment based on average house prices in east China.[4] Despite the continued demand for new housing due to projected population growth in China's cities, market- and profit-driven property developers will continue to build more luxury homes and avoid having to put up low-cost housing, thus reinforcing the disparities based on the discrepancy between supply and demand and affordability.

Contributing to social and spatial inequalities in the transformed city is the massive influx of rural migrants in China's cities, which host approximately 120 million rural workers today, and the figure is likely to reach 300 million by 2020. Adding this to the projected 700 million urbanites, by 2015 these numbers are likely to raise the real, not official, urban population to about 1 billion. Migrant workers have contributed 16 per cent of China's GDP growth over the past 20 years, especially in such industries as construction, manufacturing, commerce, catering and environment cleaning, according to a new report released by UNESCO.[5] However, migrant workers have faced discriminating treatment by some local authorities and employers. In 2004 alone, unpaid wages for migrant workers totalled an estimated 20 billion Yuan (US$2.5 billion); total unpaid wages have amounted to around 100 billion Yuan (US$12.5 billion) over the last few years. In Beijing, up to 3 billion Yuan (US$375 million) was owed to 700,000 rural migrant labourers working on construction sites in 2004.[6] To redress this glaring problem, partly exposed by the media, in early 2006 the Chinese government issued a series of decrees to guarantee all-round protection of migrant worker's legitimate rights and interests, including their rights to on-time payment, social insurance and education for their children. However, incompatible government policies have worked at cross-purposes concerning the interests and rights of migrants. The majority of the approximately 400,000 migrant children in Beijing attend the 300 or so private schools located on the metropolitan fringes, which are organized by migrants themselves and NGOs, because most of them cannot afford to pay the fees and transport costs associated with attending state schools in the city. Yet some of these private schools are being closed down by the municipal government on the basis that they are not up to the official educational standards.

Tough Challenges for the Transformed City
Is the Chinese city so much transformed that it has totally replaced the socialist city of the recent past? The answer would appear to be 'yes' in light of rapid economic

growth, huge wealth creation, more mobility and choices, and housing improvement on the one hand, and growing unemployment, traffic congestion, high property prices and, above all, socio-economic and spatial inequalities on the other. The most obvious solution seems to be targeted interventions by the dominant one-party state.

The national state, having decentralized decision-making to sub-national and local governments over the last two decades, finds it increasingly difficult to deal with the more autonomous cities via the traditional means of macro-regulation and intervention. This comes up against China's budget law, which allows the government to spend the extra-budgetary income without the approval of the generally rubber-stamping legislature. As a result, when governments at all levels work out their budgets, they often deliberately underestimate their revenues so that they have some 'extra money' to spend at the end of the fiscal year.

The central government 'forced' a slowdown of urban fixed-asset investment, including real estate, from 24.2 per cent in the third quarter of 2006, compared with the historic high of 31.9 per cent in the second quarter, through tighter land controls and lending, and a higher threshold for market access. However, the interests and priorities of the central versus municipal governments have diverged widely. The central government is concerned with macro-issues such as inflation and other symptoms of overheating, while local governments prioritize growth because it means more jobs and less risk of social unrest, as well as political careers through reward-promotions. The inability of the Chinese state to fully reassert itself is closely connected with the fact that China's economic development is becoming increasingly local-government led. Local governments are essentially businesses competing among themselves to maximize GDP, forcing maximized revenues through multiple channels to maintain high property prices, motorway tolls and sales taxes. More revenue allows local governments to make more fixed investments to boost GDP further and pursue illusory prosperity through the construction of large-scale 'image projects'.

Some targeted measures by the central government, however, are still capable of influencing local development. By requiring developers to return land left idle for more than two years after acquisition of the lease, by threatening to prosecute developers who manipulate market prices as well as information, and by banning sales of government-owned land for detached houses, the national government makes local governments responsible for controlling property prices. While this contributed to a relatively small decline in the average sales price of properties in Shanghai in early 2006, it reflected the municipal government's big push to sell greater numbers of less-expensive, lower-end housing units across the city.

If the Chinese city has been largely transformed by the new and powerful model of local government-led economic development, it poses strong challenges to the national state to rebalance a delicate relationship between the relative interests at central and local levels. While too much autonomy on the part of cities leads to runaway growth and high levels of inequality – triggering fragmentation and social discontent that could destabilize the centre – trying to rein in cities threatens positive local-development initiatives. The central and local governments could join in reverting to the socialist means of redistribution such as taxation, financial transference, social security, or even direct subsidies to assist the marginal and vulnerable poor and unemployed. However, despite the challenges of dealing with growing inequality and other problems already entrenched in the transformed city, it is too late to turn back the clock to the more egalitarian and controlled socialist city, regardless of its legacies.

DON

£4
cost of single trip on London underground

£0.09
for an equivalent journey in Mexico City

4,795
people/km² is the average density in London

7.5m
residents in Greater London

19m
residents in the South-East of England

38%
green, open space

14x
more per capita than in Mexico City

511,000
new residents and

636,000
new jobs expected by 2016

50%
increase bus journeys since 1985

38%
of new residents in 1992 were foreign born

40%
of new residents in 1997 were foreign born

56%
of new residents in 2001 were foreign born

1,600km²
area of Greater London

28,000km²
area of the South-East of England

91%
employed in service sector

£320,000
average house price, an increase of

52.6%
since 2002

500,000
security cameras

27%
of population foreign born, more than

3x
the national average

£22,000
Gross City Product per capita

18%
of United Kingdom's GDP contributed by London

59%
homes are owner-occupied

Heathrow Airport

Trafalgar Square

Canary Wharf

SIDENTIAL DENSITY (PEOPLE/KM²)

- 0 – 4,000
- 4,000 – 8,000
- 8,000 – 12,000
- 12,000 – 20,000
- 20,000 and over

GOVERNING THE
UNGOVERNABLE

Deyan Sudjic

The single most arresting fact about London is that it is growing. After decades in which, like in every other major European and North American city, it was haemorrhaging people – the victim of the hollowing-out doughnut effect – London has turned around. The forecasts now point to a sustained and substantial population increase, much of it through migration. Something remarkable has happened here. A combination of an ageing population beginning to understand that the only source of the young and able-bodied needed to care for the baby boomers in their declining years – and to pay the contributions needed to fund their pensions – is from the outside, and of the booming opportunities for the highly skilled in everything from banking to the art market, have between them transformed the character of the city and its prospects. The transformation is both reflected in, and in part the product of, a transformed system of city government for London.

In 2005, London's only remaining evening newspaper carried a front-page story to the effect that the first directly elected mayor in the city's history, Ken Livingstone, was so exercised by the thought of his legacy that he intended to run for office for two more terms in order to preside over the opening ceremonies for the 2012 Olympics. The story does not have to be literally true to pose real questions about the impact of the singularly un-British approach to local government that Livingstone represents. After two or more decades of drift and ambiguity, London as an urban entity now has a clear focus of power. This development is the most startling product of Tony Blair's local-government reforms. They were intended to change the face of every big city in the country, but London is the one success story of a reform programme that has failed to take root elsewhere. It should have been the most difficult and the most unmanageable, yet it has turned out to be the city in which a change of government, or rather the introduction of a government, has had the most clear-cut impact.

Despite his incendiary past as a self-styled man of the left, Livingstone is clearly now modelling himself on a combination of big-city American mayors of the stamp of Fiorello La Guardia, Ed Koch and Rudy Giuliani, with a touch of the imperial style of François Mitterrand thrown in, rather than the more restrained tradition of municipal public service. It is inconceivable that a Labour traditionalist would earmark GB£100,000 from the Greater London Authority's budget to spend on fighting a public inquiry to defend his personal choice of sculptor for a singularly lifeless tribute to Nelson Mandela destined for Trafalgar Square. Nor would such a figure ever have claimed that it was his duty as mayor to lead, rather than to listen, a destiny

CONCENTRATION OF POWER

Since Ken Livingstone was elected as London's first executive mayor in 2000, he has pushed through policies that bolster its role as a global capital by promoting higher density development across the city. The results are evident in clusters of new offices around the Square Mile, the self governing financial hub of the City of London.

manifest in his decisions on everything from questions of aesthetics to the extension of the congestion charging zone westwards. Yet Livingstone has done all these things. The intriguing question posed by his highly personal, interventionist style of shaping London in his own image is personified at the most superficial level by the affair of the Mandela statue, and in a much more far-reaching way by the eruption of a wall of skyscrapers, which have been breaching the 305-metre barrier along Bishopsgate, encouraged by Livingstone's enthusiasm for creating Europe's first skyline to aspire to the model of Shanghai rather than Manhattan. How much is the jaw-dropping scale of the capital's once-in-a-century transformation the product of the imposition of a single guiding vision, or would it have taken place without it?

London has tended to shrug off attempts to tame and direct its growth ever since its townsfolk ignored the attempts of Tudor monarchs to prevent the expansion of suburbs outside its city walls, and refused to accept Christopher Wren's master plan for reconstruction after the Great Fire of 1666. The city's rush westwards was given a massive – and entirely unintended – boost by the random creation of a heavy-bomber aerodrome at Heathrow, which later became Europe's largest airport. And the Great Lurch East of the 1990s, represented by the eruption of the Canary Wharf financial centre from the site of a derelict banana warehouse, was equally accidental. It was the product of the market taking ruthless advantage of a set of tax incentives and planning relaxations that were intended to have the quite different effect of encouraging the growth of small business in the area.

If one believes that London is a gently anarchic city that has always grown haphazardly in fits and starts, and it is that quality that lies behind its long-term robust good health, then the interventionism proposed by Livingstone is either irrelevant or even counterproductive. In fact, the mayor has produced a blueprint for future development that is as prescriptive as anything London has experienced in the past. It remains to be seen how effective it will be. Certainly London has had large-scale urban visions in the past. It was Nash's London that was heroic enough to inspire Napoleon III to remodel Paris, just as it was the London Underground that once set the pace for the Paris Metro. The Barbican, London Wall and Paternoster Square were all products of carefully considered planning strategies, at least two of which have subsequently been expunged.

But in the last quarter of a century, London has stopped believing that such strategies are possible, which is what makes Livingstone's blueprints for the city's physical and transport policy seem so strikingly different from past reforms. For London, it is the legacy issues that are really what the Olympics are all about. Learning from Barcelona's experiences, Livingstone is planning to use the Games for the catalytic effect that they will have on London's bleak eastern fringes. The Olympics will be focused on Newham and Stratford to help kick-start London's eastwards growth, in an attempt to find somewhere to put the extra 800,000 Londoners that Livingstone is predicting will need to be housed in the next two decades. Development will be concentrated on Stratford, which will get the stadium, the pool, an aerodrome, a hockey stadium and four indoor arenas, and the 17,000-bed Olympic Village; the Lower Lea Valley will be the site of the smaller venues. The scale of the project is massive, amounting to the total re-engineering of East London. Initial estimates of the cost started at GB£2 billion (US$4 billion), By the time work started in 2007, they had reached GB£9 billion (US$18 billion).

Nor are these the only major developments under way in the city. The area around King's Cross is just beginning to take in the scale of the transformation about

ROOM FOR EXPANSION

The Thames Gateway is Europe's largest regeneration corridor, expanding on both sides of the sinuous and tidal river as it opens eastwards towards the North Sea. Once home to London's major port and industrial activities, the area suffered economic and social decline with the closure of the docks in the 1980s. Occupying a zone twice as large as the city of Amsterdam, the Thames Gateway has the potential to accommodate hundreds of thousands of new homes to absorb a projected population increase of 500,000 by 2016.

to overtake it. The new St Pancras station, designed to handle traffic on the high-speed link to Paris and Brussels, is just the first step. The huge glass and white steel box awkwardly tacked on to the back of Victorian St Pancras will soon form just part of a sprawling development on the site of the railway and canal lands. As one developer labours on a masterplan for a project that will match Canary Wharf in scale, another has already opportunistically swooped in to take advantage of the possibilities offered by a shift in perceptions of the area that has started to take place. This is no longer an area dominated by the drug and sex trade. *The Guardian* newspaper will be moving into offices here. At White City, a gap in the city's fabric for most of a century is being filled by a giant shopping complex. South of the Thames, at Elephant & Castle, the comprehensive approach to planning of the 1960s is being unpicked on a massive scale.

This shift is producing qualitative as well as quantitative changes. For the rest of the world it provides a unique opportunity to see the tensions and fault lines between planning and market forces, between a centralized vision and laissez-faire. For Londoners it is a giddying, dizzying ride, which places them in the uncertain territory of a metropolis in the midst of the kind of change it has not seen for a century.

THE CAPITAL OF SUBURBIA

Ricky Burdett

London is facing an unprecedented period of growth and change in the twenty-first century. Covering over 1,500 square kilometres, its population of 7.5 million is relatively thinly spread, with a gross population density of 4,795 people per square kilometre, making it less dense than other world cities such as New York, Paris or Tokyo. Its political structure is also comparatively fragmented, with 33 local authorities within the Greater London Authority's (GLA) boundary that is the responsibility of the 'new' executive mayor of London, Ken Livingstone, who took office – for the first time in London's 2,000-year history – in 2000 and again in 2004. In contrast, New York, with a similar population size, occupies half the footprint of London, yet is made up of only five boroughs controlled by a mayor with strong executive powers. Like New York, London sits in a wider metropolitan city region covering the southeast of England of 19 million people, many of whom commute to London daily.

Several hundred years after its establishment as a mercantile centre within the walls of ancient Roman Londinium, the City of London still commands London's fortunes, regardless of its concentration into the 'Square Mile' of intense financial and commercial activity that drives the UK economy. It is due largely to the City's performance that London has just surpassed New York as the world's leading financial centre – according to a PriceWaterhouseCoopers report it became the most expensive city on Earth in 2007 – and its growing economy will bring 400,000 new jobs and 500,000 new residents by 2016. Many of these new arrivals are young and foreign, continuing a 10-year run in which more than 95 per cent of immigrants to London were born outside the United Kingdom. While New York remains the world's only 'majority-minority' megacity – with more than 65 per cent of residents from non-American backgrounds – London is catching up due to the influx of immigrants from the recently expanded European Union, including strong representation from Poland and other ex-Eastern European nations. Adding to the internationalization of the city will be the 2012 Olympics – an opportunity to regenerate a large swathe of East London – and the completion of the high-speed rail link to what is still charmingly referred to as 'The Continent', linking London to Paris or Brussels in two and a quarter hours, and from there to Europe's extensive high-speed rail network. All this offers a rare opportunity for London to reinvent itself as a model of sustainable urban living. Or, this growth could simply add fuel to an overburdened public-transport system, severe deprivation and social exclusion, elements that reflect the other face of this world city.

Nottingham

Norwich

Leicester

Birmingham

Northampton

Ipswich

Luton Airport

Stansted Airport

Oxford

Dover

Gatwick Airport

Southampton

Brighton

Bournemouth

WORKFORCE COMMUTING TO LONDON

3% to 5%

5% to 8%

8% to 15%

15% to 25%

25% and higher

EXTENDING THE CAPITAL CITY

Greater London sits at the heart of a wider met-ropolitan region – the South-East of England – that is home to over 19 million people, many of whom commute on a daily basis to work in the capital. The average length of these commut-ing patterns (left) reflects the extensive nature of its suburban and regional rail network. With an economy equal to that of Switzerland or Saudi Arabia, London contributes nearly 20 per cent of the UK's national GDP while housing just over 10 per cent of the entire population. The updated rail link through the Channel Tunnel will link Paris and Brussels to central London in less than three hours, enhancing its position as Europe's only global city (above).

Mapping London: Fragmentation and Urban Sprawl

To understand London's potential as a sustainable city, one needs to grasp its spatial and socioeconomic character. An aerial photograph of London reveals its peculiar, organic urban structure. Acres of typical two- and three-storey terraced housing stretch outwards from the city centre for more than 30 kilometres in each direction. Large sections of central London are defined by the eighteenth- and nineteenth-century estates of the great aristocratic families – the Bedford Estate, the Grosvenor Estate and the Queen's own Crown Estate – which cover the city's most valuable real estate with elegant streets and squares, much of it in white-stuccoed 'upstairs-downstairs' housing stock. Pockets of taller buildings (not really skyscrapers by international standards) mark the city's old and new financial centres, clustering around the City of London – with Norman Foster's distinctive curved 'Gherkin' at the epicentre of a new generation of highly sculpted vertical monuments – and Canary Wharf, marked by an ever-growing series of undistinguished corporate boxes. It may be growing at a snail's pace compared with Shanghai, but the skyline of traditional London is changing, especially along the River Thames, as developers make the most of this sustained economic boom and legislative laissez-faire.

A network of local centres – London's distinctive urban villages with higher densities and clusters of public buildings – is distributed along the city's radial arter-ies and around public-transport hubs. Hampstead, Chelsea, Greenwich, Chiswick, Stratford, Stoke Newington and Wimbledon are the local realities of a polycentric city. The dispersed urban form is punctuated by large green parks and the distinctive curved outline of the River Thames snaking its way from Heathrow in the west to the Thames Estuary in the east, becoming vast and tidal as it reaches the North Sea.

A parallel image, mapping London's social deprivation (indexing levels of unemployment, education and social security), tells a similarly fragmented story. Pockets of 'poverty' are scattered across inner London, often at close quarters with the highest concentrations of wealth, especially in Camden, Kensington and Fulham. Most of outer suburban London is relatively comfortable and stable, reversing the social map of many other European cities, including Paris and Milan, where wealth is concentrated in the centre and minorities are relegated to the periphery. Despite years of investment in some of the poorer areas, strong corridors of deprivation remain in South London and large sections of East London, especially in the redundant dock-lands which, until the 1970s and 1980s, employed the bulk of workers who supported this once-mercantile city. Unexpectedly perhaps, the map of ethnic minorities tells a rather different story, with an even more scattered distribution of London's populous Asian, Caribbean, Irish, Chinese and other immigrant communities that in fact do not reflect social deprivation but instead capture the diverse and open feel of so many of London's neighbourhoods, lacking the sense of 'ghettoization' of the Bronx or Harlem in New York, where race and poverty are more closely equated.

Beyond its perimeter, the Green Belt, Patrick Abercrombie's inspired planning policy implemented in the 1943 'Greater London Plan', acts as a large open lung that contains and embraces this vast metropolis. But within the city's boundaries, especially to the east of the centre, large expanses of ex-industrial land – literally brownfield sites – expand for kilometres on both sides of the river along the so-called Thames Gateway, forming one of Europe's greatest areas of potential expansion and regeneration. This has been designated one of the UK's housing growth areas, and is set to accommodate more than 200,000 new homes over the next 15 to 20 years. The mayor, central government and local authorities are working together to create

A COLLECTION OF URBAN VILLAGES

Reflecting its DNA as an organic, urban structure, London is a multi-centred city with many
local hubs that form the focus of diverse residential communities. Fuelled by international migration – over 90 per cent of the city's new residents
since 1991 were born outside the UK – an intense
street culture of markets, cafes and commercial
activities sustains the heart of many of London's
villages and local centres, such as Broadway
market in East London.

sustainable urban communities, rather than dormitory suburbs, but London still
needs to invest more in its transport and social infrastructure before diverse, well-
connected and compact urban neighbourhoods can be delivered. Located at a critical
point in the wider Thames Gateway, the London 2012 Olympics and the investments
that come with it will play an important role in unlocking the potential of this vast
urban wasteland on the front door – when viewed from the east – of this world city.

The Public and Private Faces of London

While London has just 12 per cent of the UK's population, it accounts for 18 per cent
of the country's total output. It acts as an international gateway to the rest of the
UK economy, making a net contribution to the Exchequer of GB£12.8 billion
(US$25.6 billion) per year, and supports an estimated 4 million jobs across the coun-
try. A recent study by the national government confirms that its productivity is closer
to United States than UK levels. Surprisingly perhaps, London's creative industries —
advertising, media, fashion and design – now provide even more jobs (over 500,000)
than financial services. London today has a young and growing population. It is an
ethnically and culturally diverse city that has become a top global tourist destination,
hosting more than 24 million visitors per year.

Yet behind the affluence hides a high level of public squalor. London exhibits
joblessness and deprivation on a much larger scale than other parts of the UK and
is home to 13 of the 20 most deprived wards in the country. Many of these are located
in relatively central and eastern areas, sitting cheek-by-jowl with the greatest concentrations of wealth in the world. The short walk from the glittering office blocks in
the City of London to the deprived neighbourhoods of Hackney and Tower Hamlets
reveals the physical reality of this inequality. The decaying buildings, litter-strewn
streets and abandoned spaces of unloved housing estates graphically illustrate the
statistics that lie behind one of the world's modern global capitals: 43 per cent of children in inner London live in poverty; its population suffers from the second-highest
unemployment rate in England; unemployment for black and ethnic groups, which
make up nearly one-third of London's population, is running at more than double
the national average. A recent spate of gun-related murders among South London's
youth gangs reflects the intensity of the problem.

Resolving these profound social and economic problems is a major challenge
for London and its political leaders. The mayor's 'London Plan' goes some way
towards setting targets for the provision of affordable housing and promoting social
inclusion. Today, any new residential project has to deliver up to 50 per cent affordable housing in order to receive planning permission – a pragmatic response to the
high-value residential property market that is beginning to deliver housing for 'key
workers' like police officers, nurses and fire fighters, as well as deprived families and
immigrants. The actual percentage of social housing provided in individual projects
is a subject of negotiation between the mayor, the local authority and the developer,
and varies from location to location across London.

Taking the moral high-ground and showing national governments what cities
can do – building on the campaign launched by 22 of the world's largest cities – the
mayor of London has decided to tackle the challenges of climate change head on,
taking advantage of increased planning powers he has recently received from central
government. He has committed himself to a substantial revision of the 'London Plan'
to reduce carbon-dioxide emissions by 60 per cent by 2050, focusing on the city's
housing stock, which accounts for nearly 40 per cent of emissions today. All new

housing and commercial developments must adhere to higher environmental standards and there is an ambitious plan to retro-fit all existing social housing stock with improved insulation and energy-conservation measures. While London cannot on its own deal with the massive amount of CO_2 emissions generated by air travel to and from its five airports, there is a plan to invest heavily in combined cooling-heating and power-energy supply, and large-scale renewable-power generation in London. The question is whether the mayor has sufficient powers to implement these laudable objectives, but he has advanced the debate on climate-change issues, challenging city leaders to take a proactive role in the face of inactive national governments.

London has an extensive, well-distributed but relatively old public-transport infrastructure. More than 3 million people a day – roughly the same number of people who use the entire national rail network – use London Underground. This constitutes 37 per cent of the population. More than 5.4 million people use the city's bus network each day, and the number is growing, especially since the improvements made with the introduction of the Congestion Charge. But overcrowding and unreliability on commuter rail routes is still matched by chronic and widespread traffic congestion. The success of the Congestion Charge, which has reduced car use in the city centre by 20 per cent, is encouraging, and the effects of the extension to include parts of central west London are still unknown. Central government concedes that the transport system in London is 'by no means all bad but it is showing its age'.

In its Business Plan, Transport for London – the mayor's transport agency – has identified that the main threats to London's growth are rising cost pressures due to a prolonged failure to invest in the city's infrastructure and public services in the context of population and employment growth. London's office accommodation is among the most expensive in the world. Average housing costs – at around GB£320,000 (US$640,000) per typical unit – are almost double the national average. The greatest demand for homes will be in Inner London, with lower- and middle-class income groups drawn to housing further out. This could lead to the creation of a 'ghettoized' city, with pockets of rich and poor neighbourhoods, rather than the greater diversity and social mix that has served London so well for centuries.

Survival and Expansion

The creation of compact, mixed-used neighbourhoods, well-served by public transport, is critical to London's survival as a fair and balanced city. This was the core argument of the Urban Task Force. London's need for new housing is an opportunity to get things right. If the city's growth is to be accommodated in an economically efficient and sustainable way, it must optimize use of its available land space. In line with the government's commitment to 'urban renaissance', the mayor has given a strong lead by ensuring that future growth is accommodated within London's existing boundaries. But while central government and the mayor have identified the Thames Gateway as a key area of expansion, the development cannot take place without investment in the necessary transport infrastructure to make it viable. This is why so much effort is being put into lobbying for the Crossrail line, an East–West fast rail service that would connect one international hub (Heathrow, the world's busiest airport) to another (Stratford International Rail Station) in less than 20 minutes – a journey that takes well over an an hour today.

Perhaps the greatest opportunity of all is presented by regeneration of the Lower Lea Valley – the site of London's 2012 Olympics. This long, narrow strip of 600 hectares of low-grade industrial land, cut off by road and rail from its surroundings,

ADDRESSING DIVERSITY
While not achieving New York's status as a 'majority-minority' city, London's ethnic populations make up nearly a third of the total. New immigrants from the wider European Union and Africa have settled in the capital alongside more established immigrant communities from former colonies such as India, Pakistan, Bangladesh and in the Caribbean.

OLYMPIC OPPORTUNITIES

Available land, improved public transport and investment are driving developments east of the centre along the River Thames as the economy and population grow. The 2012 Olympics is being designed to transform a largely underused area of the Lower Lea Valley (above) into a new urban quarter, centred around Stratford International railway station and a major urban park.

is relatively close to London's emerging business centre at Canary Wharf and straddles the new Stratford International Rail Station. It benefits from a large expanse of water and green areas, stretching along the Lea River towards the Thames. Relatively well-served by existing rail, underground services and the proposed extensions of the Docklands Light Railway, the area's accessibility would be enhanced by the arrival of Crossrail but provides a viable investment opportunity for ambitious developers. An international design team – including Foreign Office Architects, EDAW and Allies & Morrison – is now working on the Olympic and post-Olympic Legacy scenarios that will bring about substantial investment and change in an area that is, in effect, on the fringes of inner London. There is the opportunity here for a new piece of London, with up to 30,000 new households set in an environment of parks, trees and water that will benefit existing and new communities – not a housing ghetto for young urban professionals.

The nature and structure of public space is also changing in London, in line with the shifting demographic and national profiles, with many more young people and foreigners on the streets, and retailers ready to cash in on the creation of new opportunities for commercial activity. The modern cappuccino culture reflects not only the pervasive presence of a younger and more international population, but also a new attitude to London's 'old' public realm. Historically, London's public spaces have been residential squares or larger parks. The city's current imagination of public realm encompasses spaces that are less green and more densely occupied – a shift in lifestyle that is both threatening and enriching. The downside is the pervasive consumerism that nullifies street culture; the upside is the recognition that the quality of the public realm – paving, lighting, street furniture and landscaping – does indeed matter, and that we begin to take pride in how our city looks and feels after years of neglect.

Trafalgar Square must be the flagship of this newfound attitude. Somerset House, Tate Modern's Turbine Hall, the renovated South Bank and the King's Road are others. Trafalgar Square had become a racetrack, with three lanes of traffic whizzing round the 'heart of the capital', where Londoners have traditionally met to celebrate, commiserate and protest. Only four years ago, it was difficult to reach the heart of the Square, a perception reinforced by the statistic that in 1997 less than 10 per cent of users were Londoners. The simple acts of reuniting one side of Trafalgar Square to the National Gallery and opening a grand staircase to the north, has redefined the sense of both enclosure and permeability to one of London's iconic urban landmarks. Today, tourists and Londoners alike use the space as a stage-set of theatre and reality. Regardless of the, at times, overly aggressive programming of events, Trafalgar Square does perform an important function in the public life of the capital – and all this without the overpowering presence of retail.

While the tension between inner-city residents and night-time revellers seems to have attained equilibrium in the streets of Barcelona, Amsterdam or Manhattan, London is still struggling to balance this equation. The City of Westminster famously reversed its decision to pedestrianize a large part of Soho because of the noise and disruption it caused to the local residents (i.e. voters), including acres of rubbish from heaving restaurants and bars. As inner-city regeneration grows increasingly reliant on the mantra of mixed-use development, its combination of different and often incompatible activities can engender conflict and fuel a sense of increasing social exclusion.

As ever, in this profoundly mercantile city, private investors have got there first. In the eighteenth and nineteenth centuries, London's developers created beautiful

DISPERSED AND ORGANIC

London's built form is less unified than that of other capitals such as Paris or Berlin, reflecting the fragmented nature of its planning history and governance structure. At the centre of this panorama of South London, the bulk of the former Battersea Power Station stands empty surrounded by various nineteenth- and twentieth-century housing typologies.

and sustainable set-pieces of urban design: the great squares and streets of Bloomsbury, Belgravia or Bedford Park. In the 1980s, Canary Wharf took the bold step of investing in high-quality open spaces for privileged users in what was then an unknown location. This has paid off handsomely. Retail developers have taken note – the remodelling of Elephant & Castle will replace an enclosed shopping centre with a traditional grid of streets and interstitial landscaped public spaces. Broadgate, Paddington Basin and More London vie to create the city's slickest and most-controlled environments as unique selling points of these emerging commercial districts.

One pressing question is if, and how, London can leverage private funding for public-realm projects without relinquishing control to private interests. The Elephant & Castle scheme illustrates the challenge of revamping a space's negative image while preserving its character and generating benefits for local stakeholders.

The promotional rhetoric of projects at Stratford City, Elephant & Castle, King's Cross and White City privileges the design of their spaces over their buildings, underscoring the significance of public space in realizing the commercial potential of regeneration. While this signals a newfound engagement with the civic, the increasing privatization of the 'public' realm raises questions about whether and how London's public spaces can create the spontaneous possibilities of truly urban places and still continue to be spaces where, as Richard Sennett puts it, you feel safe 'lost in a crowd'.

It is indicative that London has never really had a 'plan'. Christopher Wren's hurried attempts to redraw London in grand baroque style after the Great Fire of 1666 failed, and the City of London was rebuilt more or less as it was overnight. Only the Green Belt has held strong, and it is not by chance that the current mayor has based his 'London Plan' on generic concepts and aspirations rather than detailed spatial visions. Much of what we see today along the vibrant corridor of the Thames in central London cannot be traced back to any planning documentation. The revival of the South Bank as London's cultural quarter, the construction of the Millennium Bridge and the rediscovery of the Thames waterfront owe more, perhaps, to the decision by the Tate Gallery to occupy an empty power station at Bankside than they do to the vision of any of the city planners. Five million people a year in an area that was unknown to visitors and most Londoners before 2000 has transformed Southwark and Bermondsey (with the help of the Jubilee Line) into hotspots of urban activity and real-estate opportunity. It is here, not in the wealthy Square Mile, that Renzo Piano is building London's tallest and newest skyscraper.

The irony is that despite its reputation as liveable, though expensive, London is known among experts as 'the ungovernable city', where private interests still prevail within a staunchly democratic decision-making structure. Nonetheless, London today still acts as inspiration to many city leaders across the world. This is partly because of its history – it was, after all, the first modern 'megacity' fuelled by the Industrial Revolution that formulated the first modern forms of city government – and partly because of the novelty of its new governance structures, pioneering policies and its growing reputation as a 'happening' city. London is certainly moving forwards with greater awareness of its own political, social, economic and environmental potential than it was a decade ago. But, perhaps uniquely for a world city, it has the capacity and potential to absorb growth and change in a sustainable way, working with the organic grain of its urban fabric, building on its traditions as one of the world's greatest humanist cities.

TOWARDS A EUROPE OF CITIES

Tony Travers

Urban policy has become a key sphere of government in most European countries. The idea that state intervention can be used to change the way cities develop has taken root relatively quickly. The need for intervention has intensified as economic and social need has affected developed economies the world over. Of the six global regions visited by the Urban Age, it is within the ex-industrial areas of Europe that the need for action has been greatest.

Since the early 1960s, many major cities in Britain, Germany, France and Italy have faced massive industrial and physical change. More recently, the emerging economies of the former Soviet Bloc, notably Poland, the Czech Republic and Hungary, have faced similar challenges. The key problems that have occurred are: rapid deindustrialization; a growing mismatch between the skills demanded by new industries and those available within the workforce; changes in attitudes towards government; and middle-class flight from cities and environmental degradation, particularly in older urban areas.

A number of these problems are interrelated. Most obviously, deindustrialization often leads to structural unemployment and urban dereliction. Moreover, the growth of 'globalization' can be seen as a key cause of the rapid industrial change that has triggered some (though not all) of the problems faced by older cities. The UK, which was the first country to industrialize and which has, since the early 1980s, adopted a flexible approach to economic change, has probably faced greater challenges than most other countries.

Thus, cities such as Liverpool, Manchester, Glasgow, Newcastle upon Tyne, Birmingham and Sheffield – concentrated within a relatively small geographical area of the UK – suffered significant deindustrialization in the years from the late 1970s to the mid 1990s. However, cities in France (e.g. Lille, Marseille), Germany (e.g. Leipzig, Berlin, the Rhine-Ruhr area), Spain (e.g. Barcelona, Bilbao) and even Sweden (Gothenburg) have faced the same problems. As the globalized competition for industrial and low value-added process activities continues to evolve, the need for urban policy will migrate to other urban (and some rural) areas.

Degeneration and Counter-Urbanization

The first modern efforts to tackle urban regeneration occurred in Britain during the late 1970s. In 1977, a consultative paper on inner-city policy was published by the (then Labour) government. This described the type of problem that had seriously eroded the economic competitiveness and quality of life of many inner urban areas.[1] The Urban Programme was initiated in an effort to provide specific grant funding for local authorities wishing to tackle housing, economic regeneration and skills issues.

However, the radical economic policies of Margaret Thatcher's government, particularly between 1979 and 1987, accelerated the economic and social changes affecting British cities. Subsidies were withdrawn from loss-making industries such as coal-mining, steel-making and car production, leading to a rise in unemployment and reduced economic activity in many parts of urban England, Scotland and Wales. Both the scale of the adjustment and its social impacts were profound. The Conservative government, like its Labour predecessor, realized that new kinds of intervention would be needed to revive the economies of areas where old industries had disappeared. Development corporations were set up in the dockland areas of London and Liverpool. Tax breaks were given to businesses within so-called 'enterprise zones'. But the scale of necessary regeneration continued to grow, and by the late 1980s it was vastly greater than it had been just a decade before. Population and economic activity had drained out of a range of Britain's older cities, leaving a rump of poverty and hollowed-out centres.

Even London was not protected from the decline and counter-urbanization of the 1970s and 1980s. The city's population, which had reached over 8.5 million in the 1940s, dropped as low as 6.7 million by 1986. Official projections suggested such decline was likely to continue. London docks were abandoned and much of the inner east part of the capital was suffering from high, structural unemployment. Moreover, there was a clear and growing divide between the affluent, often in suburban and rural areas, and the poor, generally trapped in declining inner cities. Civil unrest affected places such as Brixton (London), Toxteth (Liverpool) and the St Paul's district of Bristol.

British metropolitan areas appeared to be following the baleful example of a number of their American counterparts, with hollowed-out centres surrounded by 'white-flight' edge cities. Political leadership in Liverpool, Sheffield and parts of London was seen (notably by the Thatcher government) as extremist and incompetent.[2] On one occasion councils in Lambeth and Liverpool refused to set a local tax, leading to legal proceedings against the councillors concerned. Local taxation was 'capped'. The relationship between Thatcher's radical centre-right government and many parts of local government was aggressive and difficult.

Other countries in Europe and North America experienced similar deindustrialization impacts to those found in Britain – though often not so suddenly. The impact in places such as Sheffield, Glasgow and Liverpool was more immediate than in, for example, Gothenburg, Lille or Bilbao, though it was not dissimilar from what had occurred in Detroit or Pittsburgh. Such rapid change, in a country with broadly social-democratic traditions such as Britain, triggered the development of a series of policy responses at national and local levels. Policies of this kind are now commonplace throughout Europe.

The City Challenge

John Major's government developed a number of targeted grants between 1990 and 1997 that were designed to incentivize local government and other institutions to work together in the provision of partnership-based solutions to interconnected problems such as poor housing, crime, low skills and urban dereliction. 'City Challenge' was the best-known of these resource streams. The Major government

CREATIVE RECYCLING

Over the last decade many European cities have re-evaluated their urban assets, creatively adapting redundant industrial and manufacturing areas to other uses – including culture and recreation. The Ruhr Valley in Germany has successfully dealt with a massive scale of economic and political restructuring by transforming its former steel and coal mills into parks with leisure activities, as the one designed by Latz and Partners.

accepted that the rapid economic and social changes of previous decades had left British cities with serious problems. Ministers were appointed to oversee policies in particular areas of the country. In 1994, government regional offices were created, including one for London. Relative peace and harmony replaced the all-out urban warfare of the Thatcher years.

By the time Labour took office in 1997, the Conservatives had delivered much improvement and regeneration to British cities. Housing had been changed significantly by the selling-off of many publicly-owned homes, the transfer of many others to not-for-profit 'social landlords' and substantial reinvestment in remaining local-authority stock. Serious efforts had been put in place to re-skill the labour force, particularly in areas where economic change had been great. British government and European Community resources had been used to start the rebuilding of the city centres of Manchester, Birmingham, Liverpool and Glasgow.

London had seen the development of Canary Wharf as part of the city's wider Docklands redevelopment. A major Canadian developer, Olympia & York, created plans for an entire new business centre to the east of the City of London. The Thatcher government was sufficiently enthusiastic about the scale of this project to agree to extend the underground rail system from central London to Canary Wharf – in addition to the Docklands Light Railway, which had already been built to link Bank station to the development. Once the Underground had been extended, Canary Wharf and its surrounding area was able to develop into a business district to rival the West End and the City. In the longer term, the success of this development has made it possible for governments to envisage further major developments in London's East End.

Tony Blair's Labour government, which had its political roots in urban Britain, further developed the policies put in place in the previous two decades. An Urban Task Force was appointed, chaired by architect Lord (Richard) Rogers. It reported in 1999, suggesting a number of possible improvements to policy, including a greater role for good design, better urban transport and the need for higher population densities within cities.[3] Subsequently, the government published a white paper outlining its response to Rogers.

Labour's decade in office led to an array of initiatives designed to improve cities and the quality of life of their inhabitants. Grant streams with names such as Neighbourhood Renewal Fund, Education Action Zones, Community Empowerment Funds and Neighbourhood Management Pathfinders were made available for local authorities and their partners through an array of bidding initiatives.[4] Indeed, urban regeneration and housing improvement have become fully fledged industries in their own right within Britain, embracing the public, private and not-for-profit sectors.

In all cities, including the capital, there were spectacular pockets of decay. Liverpool, Manchester and Newcastle upon Tyne in particular faced the need to maintain or improve public services against a backdrop of falling populations. Although the 1990s had seen a modest revival in the fortunes of most older city centres, the surrounding ring of inner city and suburbs often continued to decline. The population drift from cities to rural areas, which had been taking place for several decades, slowed down in the 1990s and 2000s, but by no means stopped altogether.

The Age of Partnerships
Arts-based regeneration was added to the mix of urban funding schemes the Blair government had inherited from the Conservatives. Lottery-funded projects such as

TOWARDS AN URBAN RENAISSANCE

British cities had suffered severe decline in the late twentieth century, losing up to 30 per cent of their populations. The pro-city policies initiated in early years of the twenty-first century have promoted a turn-around in the fortunes of ex-industrial cities like Manchester, Leeds and Birmingham, where new buildings like Future Systems' iconic Selfridges Department Store have signalled renewed confidence in regional economies and the role of provincial urban centres.

Tate Modern (London), The Lowry (Salford) and the Baltic Flour Mill (Gateshead) provided examples of culture-led redevelopment of the kind that had been pioneered in cities such as Barcelona and Bilbao. Lottery-funded theatres, galleries and minor local improvements became widespread symbols of regeneration during the early years of the Blair government. Some of these schemes were hugely successful. Almost all of them sought to improve the design quality of their urban environments.

Other cultural and leisure developments included the New Art Gallery opened in Walsall and the Sage (a centre for music and the performing arts) in Gateshead. In Birmingham a new, architecturally exotic, Selfridges store entered the urban fabric. Most of these projects were important as visible features of the new, post-industrial, economies that British cities were developing.

After a decade in power, the Labour government came to the conclusion that there needed to be fewer initiatives and grant streams.[5] Local Strategic Partnerships (LSPs) were introduced, to bring together councils and other local partners in an attempt to deliver consistent and effective services. Resources for LSPs were to be provided through Local Area Agreements (LAAs), which involved pooling several different central-government grants. Plans for the future include creating single budgets for many other streams of public funding within local areas.

The idea of Metropolitan Area Agreements – through which authorities could work together in formal arrangements at the city-regional level – was also outlined in the 2006 local government white paper.[6] City authorities were to be encouraged to form joint boards to provide services such as transport, skills training and regeneration across metropolitan areas in the hope that cities throughout England could follow the example of London, which had enjoyed city-region government since 2000.

Tony Blair's government had introduced a directly elected mayor and assembly in London. This new institution had responsibility for most transport modes and also for aspects of economic development, policing and the fire service. The mayor was also required to publish a spatial-development strategy, which became known as the 'London Plan'. Ken Livingstone (elected mayor in 2000 and 2004) used this plan to increase the density of the city's development and to encourage the use of public transport and thus reduce energy use. The mayor also planned to tilt the development of the city from west to east, notably through his decision to champion the holding of the 2012 Olympic Games in London.

The Revival of the European City

By 2007, urban policy and regeneration in British cities has moved on significantly from the tentative steps taken back in the late 1970s and early 1980s. Many of the previously derelict ex-industrial areas of cities such as Glasgow, Manchester, Liverpool, Newcastle and London Docklands have re-emerged as sparkling new urban communities. Residential and commercial high-rise buildings are being constructed in virtually all the larger cities as city leaders seek to signal the radical nature of the changes that have occurred.

Broadly similar trends can be seen in many other cities that had suffered from sharp industrial decline during the 1960s and 1970s. European centres as diverse as Marseille, Lyon, Gothenburg, Naples and Berlin redeveloped themselves in the wake of the decline of traditional industrial sectors. Barcelona, in particular, was seen as having created a new and stylish role for itself, complete with Olympic Games, metro and redeveloped waterfront. Elsewhere in Spain, Bilbao's Guggenheim Museum became the acme of culturally led urban regeneration.

It is still impossible to judge whether the resources, initiatives and innovations that have targeted urban regeneration in Britain, Spain, France, Germany and other European cities have finally rekindled the dynamism that created them in the first place. Affluence and cheap transport have allowed people to live outside urban centres while still participating in the global economy. The sprawl of many new cities, particularly in the United States, suggests that car-borne commuting has not yet stopped growing. Low-cost airlines make the long-distance separation of work and living possible. Despite concerns about the environment and the use of natural resources, there is only limited evidence of effective government action to require people to live in more densely packed and efficient urban areas.

Public concerns about land-use policies and the consumption of natural resources, coupled with efforts to reduce environmental pollution, may yet provide an effective stimulus for the wholesale regeneration and repopulation of cities. Alternatively, it is possible people will continue to drift out of urban areas into suburbs and rural areas. Public policies towards the taxation of fuel and aviation will probably be the key determinants of how land use evolves in developed societies.

Britain remains one of the most densely populated countries in the world. It has one 'global' city and several other major conurbations. Population projections show the UK's population rising – due to in-migration – over the next 20 to 30 years. Economic growth has been relatively strong for more than 15 years and shows little sign of abating. Moreover, such growth has been concentrated in the south-east part of the country, though with significant constraints on the use of 'green' land. London's population has grown from 6.7 million to 7.5 million within 20 years. This number is projected to rise to over 8 million by 2015.

Other British cities are now seeing the emergence of immigration-led population increases, so it is possible that they, too, will begin to see their populations rising more quickly in the coming decade. Rising populations and increases in the numbers employed ought to guarantee the conditions that would allow regeneration to be sustained. If cities can capture the tax benefits of economic growth, they could then reinvest in their own development.

Government understanding of urban policy has become significantly more sophisticated during the decades since deindustrialization began to erode the economies and social structures of British and European cities. But it remains unclear as to precisely which interventions deliver particular objectives. The process of intervention and investment, while evidently successful in many places, does not work everywhere. A continuous challenge for the future will be to increase the success-rate of urban-regeneration policy.

THE EUROPEAN CITY MODEL

Joan Clos

It is difficult to speak of a standard European model of the city when taking into account the diversity of the continent's cities, especially in terms of their respective traditions, whether Anglo-Saxon, Central European, Nordic or Mediterranean. Nonetheless, it is possible to extract a set of common characteristics that are present in all these cities and which define a similar way of understanding them.

The normative European city is a dense, compact area grouped around a core rather than sprawling like American cities; this preserves the integrity and coherence of its open spaces. When dense enough it favours mobility on foot or public transport and it is able to avoid an excessive level of greenfield development. In such a city a host of various activities occur in the same place, combining residence, work and leisure to create a diverse and complex urban lifestyle. It is home to people from a substantial mix of social backgrounds, reducing the tendency towards ghettos caused by income, origin or race and encouraging social integration. Public areas are places of peaceful, enriching coexistence. The mobility of residents is not entirely dependent on cars, and public transport plays a major role. Public transport needs a high concentration of people, and public areas call for a variety of uses. All these features and characteristics are interdependent, and all play a part in shaping the city.

This form of city construction originated in part from the city's maturity and size when the Industrial Revolution began, when private vehicles first made an appearance and when homes lay cheek-by-jowl with factories. It was accustomed to compact, high-density lifestyles, either within city walls or surrounding districts. Activities were mixed and took place in areas marked by streets or public squares.

At the start of the twentieth century, economic activity became more specialized, especially in industry and transport. The demand for quality housing and improved living conditions in the city prompted public-health officials and modern architects to try and regenerate the city. Such regeneration, however, was often carried out with considerable respect to the existing city fabric, and zoning redirected new economic and residential uses towards the suburbs. Consequently, the compactness of the core was preserved. However, the city witnessed spatial segregation of activities and sometimes a reduction of densities in the new growth areas.

The other major factor behind the transformation of cities in the twentieth century was the private vehicle, which offered a new freedom and efficiency. Growth areas in European cities were built around car use. However, old city centres were ill-equipped for this new traffic. Consequently they encountered major problems when trying to make cars the universal means of transport as American cities had done. Due to the compactness and density of European cities, public transport had to play a vital role to ensure the city's function.

Segregation and Specialization

The original city still exists, and is now the heart of a new European city, thanks to its capacity to transform itself, integrate economic and social changes and rebuild what war had thoroughly destroyed. This is a complicated, yet necessary, internal transformation and public authorities have been deeply involved in the process. This can be seen in the remodelling of the old Paris by Haussmann or the opening of the Via Laietana in Barcelona, for example. Of course, it is not true to say that all European cities reflect these characteristics. In many cases they show opposite trends, especially when they have undergone expansion and transformation in the latter half of the twentieth century. Some cities are paradigms of the European model and yet combine compactness with dispersion, as is the case of the Metropolitan Area of Barcelona.

Social segregation and specialization in production are spontaneous trends brought about by individuals, groups and sectors with a view to improving efficiency. This gives rise to spatial segregation, which is supported by people simply expecting the car to solve all their mobility problems. In the long run, this zoned approach to the city, which for a certain time was useful for production, generally brings about strong restrictions to the economic and social efficiency. Accordingly, different models of organization must be sought.

In the twenty-first century, the internationalization of socio-economic relations and the growth of the knowledge economy are influencing the European city in a number of ways. Industrial manufacturing activity is losing its specific weight in the economy, particularly in Europe and other parts of the developed world. This is due to the relocation of production and to the declining use of human labour in the manufacturing process. Classic industrial specialization will no longer play a major part in shaping the city, but creative synergy in all spheres of services and production activity requiring high levels of knowledge will find a better setting in this complex – but not necessarily standardized – city. In this sense, the characteristic traits of the European city can be considered efficient in terms of advanced economic development. It should also be pointed out that the compact, integrated city is friendlier to its surroundings, offering coherence and diversity as well as environmental benefits (conservation of energy, water, air).

From the standpoint of positive coexistence in the city, experience shows that solutions that create ghettos, while apparently straightforward and reassuring in the short-term, may sow the seeds of far-reaching conflicts, whereas integrating solutions, although more complicated, better contribute to establishing and enriching long-term coexistence.

Nevertheless, it is necessary to avoid the unconsidered and standardized repetition of these characteristics. We must not forget that some of the features we now value – such as density without quality urban design and with a mix of incompatible uses – have led in the past to situations of deep crisis in the city, and could do so again in the future.

It is therefore necessary to 'reinvent' older European cities on the basis of their experiences of urban transformation. Their continuing capacity for transformation, by preserving their assets while simultaneously rectifying failures, will make it possible to rebuild cities that can look to the future with optimism.

INTENSITY AND PUBLIC LIFE

The compact urban form typical of so many European cities provides a sustainable model for the twenty-first century that supports the complexity of public life. Barcelona's investment in public spaces, building on the tradition of Las Ramblas in the heart of its medieval district, has helped the city regenerate its dense inner core, attracting new residents and businesses that have contributed to the success of the Barcelona 'model'.

60% of construction is done by the informal sector

397 cars/1,000 people, compared to

38 in Shanghai

8.7m residents in the Federal District

19m in the Metropolitan zone

2h 30min avg. daily commute, compared to

1h 24min in London

55% of journeys by minibus or collective taxis

50,000 minibuses

76% of Mexico's population live in urban areas

0.4m people lived in the Metropolitan zone in 1900

3.1m people lived in the Metropolitan zone in 1950

19m people lived in the Metropolitan zone in 2000

7.5% land used for recreation in the Metropolitan zone

3.7 average number of people living in a household

25,000 informal street vendors

5,877 people/km² is the average residential density of the Federal District

200km length of underground system, compared to

408km in London

76% owner-occupied housing in the Federal District

1,484 km² area of the Federal District

4,979km² area of the Metropolitan zone

22% of Mexico's GDP is contributed by Mexico City

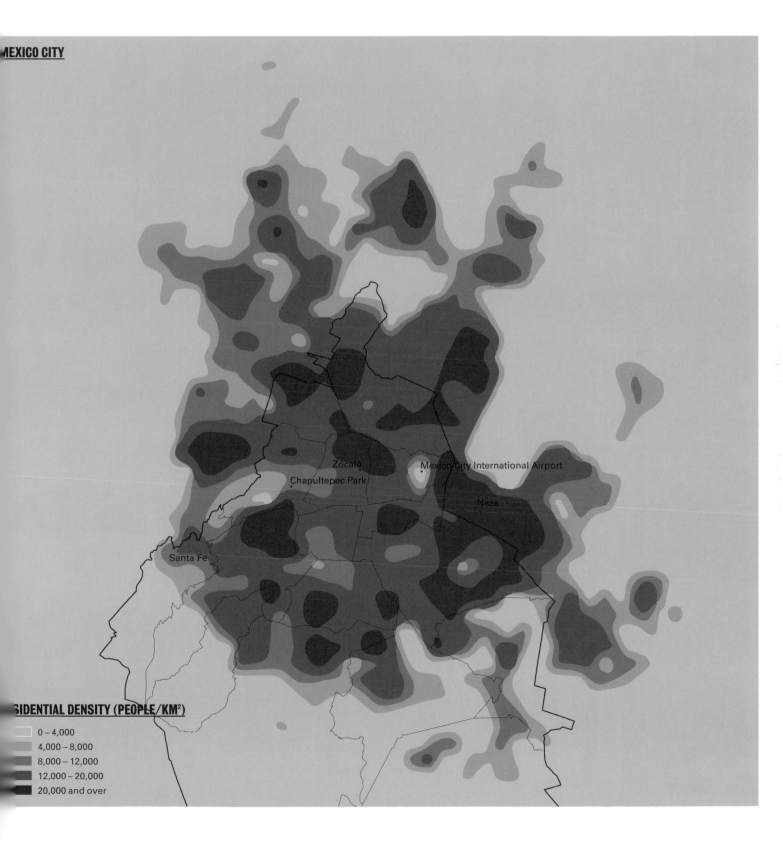

Zócalo

Chapultepec Park

Mexico City International Airport

Neza

Santa Fe

RESIDENTIAL DENSITY (PEOPLE/KM²)

- 0 – 4,000
- 4,000 – 8,000
- 8,000 – 12,000
- 12,000 – 20,000
- 20,000 and over

BACK FROM THE BRINK

Deyan Sudjic

Mexico is the city that was always spoken of as if it was one day going to be the biggest settlement on the planet. It was probably the first of the twentieth century's monster cities to make an impression on the wider world, portrayed as an unstoppable eruption of humanity swamping the landscape to touch the horizon in all directions. In the 1970s, predictions were made that it was well on the way to becoming a megalopolis of 30 million people or more. As it turned out, that has not happened. The population of the city centre is static, and some of its denser historic areas have been in decline – an issue addressed by the city in the formation of a special trust to encourage investment and development. What growth there is now concentrates in the urban sprawl beyond city limits in the administrative control of the state of Mexico. The lower-middle class is moving out into areas where gated communities are not just for the privileged.

Certainly Mexico City grew quickly from the 1940s, when it began to lose its former incarnation as the Garden of Eden, blessed with a near-perfect climate, reminiscent of the golden age of Los Angeles, but shaped physically by the remains of its Aztec and its Spanish past as represented by flower-studded baroque courtyards, the presence of the surrounding mountains, and the famous lake. The photochemical smog that accompanied its discovery of the motor car, through the medium of the locally produced Volkswagens that once monopolized its streets, made that growth look particularly threatening. The toxic haze was not helped by Mexico City's extreme altitude and its mountains, two elements that conspire to entrap the city's pollution in the brown cloud that seems to thicken under the wings of descending aircraft.

Certainly Mexico is huge – 19 million or so people now live in the Federal District of the city itself and the urbanized sprawl around it. But that is a close match for Shanghai, New York and London when their respective city regions are taken into account. These three all have their own disparities in wealth, but Mexico's seem more violent and more entrenched, and it does not have the pervasive impact brought about by 50 years of Mao and Marx to suppress the sometimes chaotic lawlessness of the country that China has.

There are street children and kidnappings and water shortages in Mexico, as well as a sewage system at the limits of its original design life. But Mexico never became the horror story that it sometimes threatened. For a start, its growth has started to taper off, almost to the point that one could consider the idea that growth might be self-limiting. Its reputation may also have had something to do with its accessibility and its proximity to the United States, and thus its visibility. For those with a taste for the dizzying sense of staring into the urban abyss, Mexico City is a lot more convenient to get to than Lagos or Tehran, Dhaka or Cairo.

Mexico has had more to contend with than the explosive growth of the flight of the dispossessed from the countryside. It has a fractured government system to deal with, divided between the surrounding municipalities of the State of Mexico and the Federal District – a territory that was tightly controlled by the federal government in the same way that Washington was before it acquired a mayor. Until very recently the two administrations failed to reach a shared view of what the place needed to function properly. And to complicate matters further, the whole country is still dealing with a gradual reawakening of national democratic politics. In particular Mexico City has experienced the impact of a left-leaning mayor, Andrés Manuel López Obrador, who faced removal from office before he stepped down to run for president in the national elections staged in the summer of 2006.

Obrador's five-year track record says a lot about the nature of the city. Mexico City has within it the elements of a global city, the visible impacts of a global system, both negative and positive. It has slick business parks and boutique hotels, and it is losing industrial jobs to China and to the NAFTA factories on the American border. An overvalued peso is not helping. But it is also a city in which what could be seen as pre-modern conditions still prevail in certain aspects of civic life. It displays the chronic symptoms of uneven development in its lurch towards the global economy. It is a city in which illegal land sales blight development in some areas, and in which the informal economy constitutes far more than the all-pervasive street traders and the 120,000 taxis.

Obrador's two most visible legacies to the city reflect the extremes of Mexican life. On the one hand he has introduced dedicated bus lanes, modelled on the precedents of Bogotá and Curitiba, which have transformed public transport in the city. On the other, his personal grand project, the massive and quixotic plan to create a double-decker urban motorway, the Segundo Piso, asks more questions than it answers. It is enormously expensive, yet it appears to benefit only the relatively wealthy car-owning residents of the areas through which it passes – in a city in which commutes of three hours are forced on the maids who work for the rich, but live in far-distant *barrios*. It was a curious choice of project for a left-leaning mayor. But then this is already a city full of unintended outcomes. When the city tried to restrict car use by introducing odd and even number plate only days, the response of the rich was of course to buy a second car. And visually the tangle of concrete column threads on top of existing surface roads is already a lurid scar on the landscape of the city.

It seems that many of Mexico City's infrastructure systems have failed to address the implications of rapid growth and change. It has a metro system that was its pride and joy when Mexico hosted the Olympics in 1968, an event that marked the country's attempts to present itself as a modern state. The metro was state-of-the-art when it was built, but has failed to adapt to its changing environment and the city has outgrown it. It has a historic city centre that was losing population to more salubrious suburbs even before the impact of the earthquake. It has a pattern that seems to recall that of Los Angeles: a downtown that faced becoming irrelevant; a deprived east, a rich west. Mexico has been growing chaotically for long enough to have already revealed the limits of modernization.

RAPID GROWTH

The Zócalo (top), Mexico City's locus of political power and public protest, lies at the heart of the Centro Historico – an area that has seen substantial population decline despite the city's horizontal expansion that accommodates over 20 million residents. Much of this informal urban growth is fuelled by the private motorcar, with a high percentage of the city's budget invested in controversial projects like the Segundo Piso (above), a double-decker urban motorway serving Mexico City's rich suburbs.

AFTER THE EXPLOSION

José Castillo

Crisis and megacity are the two derogatory terms most used to describe the urban circumstances of Mexico City over the past 50 years. They relate to a century-long symmetrical mirror of conditions, demographic as well as economic, that best explain the 'boom and bust' cycles of development of this ever-growing metropolis and its spatial and social effects.

This is a city that in the 1940s – at the onset of modernization – had 1.6 million inhabitants, had expanded to 5 million in 1960, and that is currently close to 20 million, spread over an area of 1,400 square kilometres. The seemingly uncontrolled population growth, coupled with cyclical economic downturns coinciding with political change, forms the perfect background to understanding the paradoxical perseverance of Mexico City. This history of failures and excesses, and the way they have played out in the built environment and its social organization, has granted Mexico City an unparalleled legitimacy in global urban discussions.

For 25 years Mexico City has captured worldwide interest as the ever-present, ever-growing, ever-developing megacity. This eternal condition of megacityness, of being on the edge of either disaster or survival, has historically configured the local mindsets, its collective consciousness, its urban policies and its political agendas. It has shaped an attitude within the city's decision-making bodies and the planning processes that is reactive at best – ingrained with pessimism and suspicion over any effort to engage with the city in a productive or appreciative way.

A City in Crisis

The use of the term megacity, introduced by Janice Perlman and used by the United Nations since the late 1970s, implied much more than just a quantitative aspect, applied to urban agglomerations of more than 10 million inhabitants. The expression carried beleaguered associations with the most negative and problematic traits inherent in cities. The complexity of agglomerations and critical mass we see today as full of potential was at the time perceived as a problem that could not easily be addressed. Urban research carried out during the 1970s and 1980s was centred on discussions of 'ideal city size' and urban primacy with regards to national development.

Throughout that time Mexico City represented a perfect case study for the discourse on the crisis of cities. Although other 'world cities', including New York and London, were facing problems of their own – fiscal pressures, dismal infrastructure, bad city management and dubious political representation – it was Mexico City that

Previous pages
ENDLESS CITY
Low-rise informal settlements in Mexico City eat into the high altitude plateau that sits between volcanoes and mountain ridges. The combination of geographic conditions, extensive sprawl and car dependency has a damaging impact on air quality, with exhaust emissions and industry-generated pollution trapped above the vast metropolitan area.

THE FORMAL VERSION
Mexico City's mass-produced and anonymous urban landscapes, such as this housing project in Ecataepec, take the shape of informal settlements or low-income sprawl, and compete for limited resources such as water and electricity.

was considered the prime example with the most extreme manifestation of this new urban phenomenon.

In his 1984 book *The World of Cities*, the British urban theorist Peter Hall called Mexico City 'the ultimate world city: ultimate in size, ultimate in population, ultimate in threat of paralysis and disintegration, ultimate in the problems it presents …' In a similar fashion, a landmark article on the cover of *Time* magazine in 1984 – 'A proud capital's distress' – proclaimed Mexico City the worst-case scenario of cities, representing everything that was wrong with them in general. This view took hold to such an extent that five years later *Time* described the city as 'the anteroom for an ecological Hiroshima' and an 'urban gas chamber'. It was certainly not an optimistic (or fair) viewpoint, even by American journalistic standards. And yet, at the same time, that 1984 article contained a subtext hinting that maybe Mexico City could offer the world a lesson, albeit a grim one.

The 1980s inaugurated an absolute blurring of the distinction between perceptions and actual experiences within the city: rumours became facts and vice versa, and exaggerations became the norm. To paraphrase Carlos Monsiváis, the prominent Mexican writer and chronicler, the citizens of Mexico City became chauvinistic about (their own) catastrophe.

In order to assess the issues relevant to the city today, it is necessary to revisit past perceptions of Mexico City from abroad and within, including how its identity has been constructed as a global phenomenon over the past 25 years. Taking a critical viewpoint on some of the assessments put forward in relation to the events, facts and perceptions of this time affords the possibility of constructing not so much a revision of history, but rather a productive understanding of how a city can come to terms with its short- and long-term future.

The first aspect to take to task is the way in which demographics operate in the context of cities. The growth rates seen in Mexico City during the twentieth century – with a population that doubled in size every 10 years – were quite remarkable. One of the central tenets of 'megacityness' is indeed constructed around population size. The 1980s census showed Mexico City as the largest agglomeration in the world and the forecast by the United Nations for its population size at the turn of the century was 26 million, while the city's own estimates were 36 million. The birth rate in 1970 was 4.26 per cent. Nowadays, with a population of 19 million and a birth rate of 2.06 per cent, we can conclude that Malthusian demographics are not the best basis for the formulation of urban policies. Even now, discussion on the city's growth is not about size itself but the ways in which more sustainable growth can be accommodated.

In the 1984 *Time* article, Mexico City was portrayed as a disaster in progress. Overcrowding, poverty, pollution and corruption seemed to be the four horsemen of the apocalyptic megacity of the 1980s. Catastrophic and exaggerated as this may sound today, a number of events that affected Mexico City in that decade were instrumental in shaping specific negative attitudes towards it. Some of these were economic in nature, some political, some of them natural disasters, some environmental crises. But their combination forged a cocktail that eventually allowed for political change, social mobilization and environmental awareness without which an understanding of the city today would not be possible. The period between 1981 and 1988 became for Mexico City what the summer of 1977 had been for New York City, characterized by impending fiscal crisis, failing infrastructure, fear and insecurity.

Environmental crises and urban catastrophes have been key to the understanding of Mexico City ever since its founding at the centre of a series of shallow lakes by

INFORMALITY AND CULTURAL IDENTITY
Much of Mexico City's informal development
sustains highly complex and established social
and cultural networks, with religious shrines and
icons scattered across the public spaces of the
city's self-determined neighbourhoods.

the Aztecs in 1325. In 1629, the great flood of Mexico City took the lives of 30,000 citizens, and the city remained partially flooded for five years. By 1634, its population had decreased to 400 families. Even the King of Spain, Philip IV, suggested that the city be moved to higher grounds between Tacuba and Tacubaya, an area close to the current Chapultepec Park, Polanco and Lomas de Chapultepec. The option was discarded for economic reasons, since at the time it was less expensive to drain Texcoco Lake, the largest of the original five in the Valley of Mexico, than to move the capital a few kilometres west. This decision has proven to be problematic given the centuries-old battle against water that persists to this day. In many respects, the key issues faced by Mexico City are what British sociologist Anthony Giddens, in discussing risk in contemporary societies, would call manufactured risks, resulting from the pressures on the social and natural structures of the city by the processes of urbanization and modernization.

Without resorting to an overarching theory of urban catastrophe, it seems relevant to reconsider three key events that took place during the 1980s, each of which was instrumental in forging the material history of a city in the decade that followed.

On 5 April 1981, the largest open air dump site of Mexico City, located in Santa Cruz Meyehualco, Iztapalapa, in the south-eastern section of the city, burned for eight days and eight nights, covering the city with a huge cloud of toxic smoke. This toxic airborne event, not unlike the one in Don DeLillo's novel *White Noise*, transformed the life of citizens, exposing them for the first time to the term 'environmental contingency', which would be used daily over the next 10 years. The incident combined the nature of air pollution with the problems of an unsound waste-management policy. In addition, it exposed the corruption and mob-like practices implicit in urban services and infrastructure management.

Only three years later, on 19 November 1984, a liquid petroleum gas distribution centre belonging to the state-owned oil company PEMEX exploded in San Juanico, Ecatepec, on the northern periphery of Mexico City. The explosion occurred very early on the Monday morning of a long holiday weekend and killed more than 500 people. The distribution centre was surrounded – without even the smallest nod to security – by informal settlements, and wreckage from the gas tanks was found thousands of metres from its original position. The combination of irresponsible practices, corruption, ageing infrastructure and lax security caused an inferno rarely encountered in urban environments. Just as the film *Los Olvidados* by Luis Buñuel had exposed the 'misery belts' that existed on the outskirts of Mexico City in the 1950s, San Juanico uncovered the relationship between the poverty-ridden suburbs and their susceptibility to both natural and manmade disasters.

Less than a year later Mexico City was exposed to the most significant natural disaster in its history – or at least the worst since the seventeenth century floodings. On 19 September 1985, at 7.19 a.m. Mexico City was hit by a powerful earthquake registering 8.1 on the Richter scale, with an aftershock 36 hours later. It levelled thousands of dwellings, destroyed 400 mid-rise buildings and killed an unknown number of people. The official estimates were 5,000, but this seems unconvincing given the prevailing censorship at the time. More careful analysis in the years that followed put the death toll closer to 35,000. President Miguel de la Madrid initially refused international aid, stating that Mexico was capable enough – and proud enough – to pull through on its own. The days and months that followed saw the birth of civil society: citizens taking control in times of difficulty reflecting the total lack of government effectiveness in dealing with an unforeseen urban crisis.

WATER AS THE LIFEBLOOD OF THE CITY

A system of interconnected lakes originally occupied a large part of what is now Mexico City. Yet, where water was once abundant, now it is scarce. A system of aquifers extracts water more than twice as fast as it is replenished, despite a rainfall comparable to New York City and London. The city's water management policies and practices grossly underserve a significant portion of the population, with informal and low-income communities on the eastern edge of the city particularly vulnerable to the city's looming water shortage.

REDEFINING MARKET REALITIES

With 60 per cent of jobs in the informal sector, the unemployment rate for the city is not readily understood. Goods are sold and services offered outside traditional market economies, with an impressively efficient recycling of everyday items such as shoes, clothing, and household goods. The vendors lining the sidewalk adjacent to the Cathedral in the Zócalo (above) present formal signage to advertise their trades to passers-by.

Both Carlos Monsiváis and Elena Poniatowska have written accurate descriptive chronicles of how the earthquake of 1985 represented a turning-point in all forms of social organization and resistance to the political status quo. Afterwards, the seeds of democracy were firmly planted (or at least revamped for the first time since the 1968 violent student clamp-down) by 'grassroots' efforts, which likewise transformed the media and its relationship with power.

Although very different in their causes and their effects, the three disasters radically altered both the physical form of the city and the way we think about infrastructure, the environment and security. The open-air dump of Santa Cruz Meyehualco was closed in 1982 and the only current landfill, Bordo Poniente, operates in parallel with 13 rubbish-treatment plants that process 12,000 tonnes of rubbish a day. The way the city deals with solid waste nowadays is certainly more sophisticated, environmentally friendly and territorially sound than before. The gas explosion in San Juanico forced new regulations with regards to infrastructural works and their relationship to residential neighbourhoods, but also raised awareness about urban misery. The 1985 earthquake was influential in more aspects of urban life and form than any other event in the previous 50 years, spawning new building regulations, opening up spaces in the urban tissue, shifting the patterns of growth and density, and, most importantly, creating a social and civic consciousness that informed a more democratic and liberal urban citizen.

A MegaCity in the Making

For many years the media were either subjected to the authoritarian regime's censorship or were themselves instruments of the regime. During the opening of the 1986 World Cup in the Azteca Stadium, then President Miguel de la Madrid was booed by 115,000 voices; the government-controlled television stations responsible for broadcast of the event edited the sound feed for foreign television to avoid embarrassment – a predictable eventuality for this burgeoning democracy.

The printed and electronic press now enjoys a critical attitude towards government and private powers, and has helped to establish an urban agenda of reform, through insights as well as by connecting public issues and demands with government actions. *Reforma*, *La Jornada* and *El Universal* are newspapers with a strong local agenda, communicating the effects of specific policies and conditions through comparative knowledge of other cities, by exposing corruption and ineffective practices, and by taking politicians to task on campaign promises. Radio and television play a similarly steering role with programmes that are crucial for the rapport between an audience of citizens, government officials and policymakers. Public debates, surveys and opinion polls have become daily tools to test the relevance of ideas and are used to great effect.

Over the past 25 years, Mexico City has not only changed, but a different kind of citizenship has also been constructed through the extension of democratic life from electoral processes to all aspects of urban living. While public rallies and pickets are still an important part of social-political negotiation processes, these have been complemented with other mechanisms that connect citizens to their authorities.

Two additional circumstances are crucial to understanding the development of Mexico City during the 1980s. These are the recurrent economic and financial crises that frame the 12 years from 1982 to 1994 and the contested presidential elections of 1988, when President Carlos Salinas captured the presidency amid widespread allegations of fraud. It was no surprise that Mexico City was the first large city in the country to challenge the monolithic power of the PRI, Mexico's leading Institutional Revolutionary Party, which saw senators, representatives, most local congressmen and, since 1997, the mayor elected from oppositional parties over the last 15 years.

The second change was a clear transformation of macro- and micro-economic conditions in the country as a whole, very much evident in the city itself. The shift of economic activities to the service sector, the slimming-down of the bureaucracy and its processes of decentralization, and most of all the control of hyperinflation rates of 100 per cent in the 1980s, all gave rise to a decade of moderate growth and single-digit inflation. The exception was the 1994 crisis, which proved levels of interaction within the global economy that differed greatly from the 1982 crisis. It took only a few days for the American government to come to the rescue of the Mexican economy, an understandable reaction given the countries' mutual economic dependency. In a sense, the 1980s proved to be the formative years for a megacity in the making, although pollution, corruption, extreme poverty and uncontrolled growth seem now rather like urban legends played out in the media with exaggeration, not quite delivering their self-fulfilling prophecies, nor completely disappearing from the urban agenda.

A whole new range of issues and conditions have surfaced that are currently affecting urban form and urban life. The single-most relevant issue on the urban agenda today is fear. While it could be argued that the most severe perceived lack of security was during the mid 1990s, the recurrent talk of fear and the actual persistence of distinct forms of organized crime and violence have had immeasurable impact on attitudes towards the city. During the 1980s the focus was on abuses by the police and politicians; insecurity was a tool and an effect of an authoritarian regime, with crime deeply ingrained in the political system.

Between 1984 and 1988, close to 50 journalists were killed for exposing corruption at city and national levels. Manuel Buendía, one of the most prominent and critical journalists in the early 1980s, was publicly shot on Insurgentes Avenue; a former top-ranking federal police officer and then PRI candidate to Congress was convicted and sentenced for the crime. During the mid 1990s a highly visible series of violent burglaries, hijackings and murders contributed significantly to the rise of gated communities, the privatization of public life, the ubiquity of security guards and a pervasive fear that guided the thread of urban life. This metropolization of crime cut across geographies and social divides, with the tactics of protection playing out at both ends of the social spectrum. Recent political imperatives of the newly elected federal and local administrations are attempting to reconcile issues of insecurity and crime. In Mexico City, the result has been evictions and eminent claims on properties used by drug and smuggling cartels. Whether these new policies will make the city safer or jeopardize civil liberties (or result in revisions of the judiciary system) is yet to be seen, but it shows a refreshing attitude to confronting citizens' concerns, even if attitudes guided by control and fear of the 'other' persist in the way housing, workspaces and public areas are conceived.

In the face of this continued polarization of society, the geographies of leisure and consumption have changed too: they have shifted from Zona Rosa to Polanco, and from Reforma to Santa Fe, offering as a result similarities between city-centre and upscale neighbourhoods that explain the global, cosmopolitan allure of Mexico City. Although none of these changes has been able to bridge the social disparities that define the country as a whole, they do offer a paradigm for appreciating Mexico City's multiple and remarkable urban transformations. Shaped by multi-centred growth

ECONOMIC POWERHOUSE

Mexico City contributes close to one third of the country's GDP. Concentrating 42 per cent of producer services and 59 per cent of the financial sector in all of Mexico, these activities are contained within discrete and dispersed commercial buildings throughout the city, as illustrated by a typical multi-use building in the mid-twentieth-century neighbourhood of Condesa.

FEAR AND PUBLIC LIFE

A persistent culture of fear and insecurity pervades the urban realities of life in Mexico City. This pushes social life into interior spaces, private homes or secure malls. Large sections of the Centro Historico (above) and new suburban centres are heavily guarded by the police and private security firms creating an atmosphere of tension in the public spaces of the city.

and incremental actions in individual neighbourhoods, the new image of Mexico City counters the perception of the monolithic block where either survival or perdition engulfs the entire megacity.

Transport and Housing: Policy in Practice

Transportation and mobility, and their impact on the quality of life, have also conceptually changed. The prevailing attitude of the 1980s was that air pollution was the most crucial issue to be addressed through policy, changing patterns of behaviour, environmental consciousness and civic awareness. The development of cleaner fuels, combined with stricter regulations for car manufacturers, tougher annual inspections, as well as the implementation of a 'day without a car' programme, were instrumental actions. And although in the first years of the 'day without a car' programme, the rule of unintended consequences took effect when many wealthier people bypassed the system by simply buying another car, notably increasing the sales of private cars in the city. Yet things have started to change.

What air pollution represented in the 1980s and early 1990s, congestion has come to represent in the first decade of the twenty-first century. The realization that the city can come to a halt is actually transforming attitudes towards car use and the possibilities of public transportation. The recent Metrobús project, a dedicated bus-lane system modelled after the Bogotá and Curitiba examples, is a perfect case study of how best practices from other cities can be implemented and do make a difference.

It is paradoxical that the other landmark transportation project of the past six years has been a system of elevated motorways built exclusively for private car use, a schizophrenia not uncommon in government policy due to the political benefits of such simple (if absurd) projects. The recent administration of Mayor Marcelo Ebrard has stopped the development of this wasteful project to embrace instead investment in public transport such as new Metrobús routes and a new underground line. In addition, the use of bicycles as a means of transport is being fostered through the improvement of dedicated bicycle lanes and the raising of civic awareness of commuters. Although these changes seem more symbolic than substantial, one hopes that these paradigm shifts can extend to other forms of sustainable development.

Meanwhile, a continuous grey carpet of low-rise sprawl extends to the horizon of the megacity. The huge growth of these peripheries during the 1960s, 1970s and 1980s, mostly through informal urbanization, was the result of disjointed policies and plans between the Federal District and the State of Mexico, between transportation planning and housing policies, and between private developers and the state. And although the previous decades' housing policies have now been turned on their head, current housing provisions have little to do with publicly-funded, architect-designed housing for the nuclear family. Instead, financial incentives have been favoured that allow home-owners to improve their houses and secure a mortgage to buy a new property. This has resulted in a higher demand for housing, which has led to a densification of central districts, even when these policies are not coordinated with initiatives such as transportation, economic development or open space.

Bando Dos, a regulation fostering growth and densification in the central neighbourhoods of the city while prohibiting it in the peripheries, is the perfect example of sensible urban policy with poor implementation. While it is more than desirable to densify, it is crucial to understand how the social values and profits (economic and otherwise) involved are captured by the different stakeholders. Six years of the programme have proven that the main beneficiaries are landowners and developers, who enjoy increased land values that subvert the original purpose of the programme to create affordable housing for a target population instead of the middle classes. In addition, the lack of political will to coordinate urban policies with the State of Mexico, on whose peripheries almost half the city's population lives, means that the effectiveness of the programme has been limited.

The peripheries – areas that fall somewhere between models of development in the shanty towns of the developing world and the traditional American suburb – are the materialization of a two-fold process. On the one hand we witness the dominant model of informal urbanization in areas such as Neza, Ecatepec and Valle de Chalco. Their development operates outside the legal, regulatory and professional framework and is the result of different forms of occupation such as squatting, illegal sales and subdivisions of under-serviced land. Alternatively, we can see a more recent phenomenon, characterized by the large-scale transformation of rural tracts of land into developer-driven housing in places such as Iztapaluca to the east and Tecamac to the north. These two processes inform each other and prove symbiotic rather than oppositional. Although it would seem that informal housing strives to be 'formalized' through the provision of services and infrastructure, what is less acknowledged is that formal housing transforms through use, growth and programmes, in the end acquiring the very same messiness and 'paralegality' of informality.

In the past five years however, informal growth has been challenged by a more accelerated pace of formal housing production with changes in housing finance and construction. Implemented since the early 1990s, these changes allow for larger land appropriations on sites that were once communal, and more effective policies ensuring housing delivery. In recent years, total annual housing production from the formal sector (provided by the state as well as private developers) has been close to 105,000 units a year, with a comparable number of units provided through the informal sector. And yet this housing growth is focused in peripheries that are moving further outwards to the north and east of Mexico City and that cannot keep pace with population growth. A case in point is the fast expansion of the Iztapaluca municipality, the population of which has tripled, from less than 200,000 to more than 600,000, in the last 10 years alone.

The impact of formal developments in places such as Iztapaluca is enormous. The sheer size of development sites is increasing due to the fact that private interests can now purchase in larger and larger parcels land that was previously communally owned. The result in some of these planned neighbourhoods is the emergence of large amounts of units overnight, with recent developments of up to 13,000 units. This housing stock is usually built by a single developer, and in many cases designed by a single architect, with very little state intervention.

There are a number of paradoxes in this model of development. The settlements are characterized by large-scale interventions, but one cannot fail to be amazed at the limited amount of planning. In effect, the larger the settlement, the less planning there seems to be. These developments are becoming, by design or by accident, large gated communities in which homogeneous streets, repetitive rows of houses and a prevalence of cul de sacs have become the prevailing urban strategy. Planning is limited to the layout of a street grid, and the maximization of saleable land through the repetition of a very limited number of housing typologies. There is no zoning, no planning for educational, commercial or civic uses, a very limited approach to public space, no relation to metropolitan transport infrastructure, and, most importantly, no room for growth and transformation. Urbanity is collapsed to the simple construction of housing, not neighbourhoods.

The apparently homogenous developments with a specific low- and middle-income iconography of 'garage, two-storey house, elevated water-tank home' does transform over time due to mechanisms of subversion, negotiation and resistance to the rules that codify urban life in these communities. Adaptation becomes a mechanism for survival. These transformations thus operate in limbo between illegality and rule of law. They challenge preconceptions of zoning, of progressive growth, of fear, privacy and domesticity.

Urban Governance

These phenomena have contributed to a radical change in urban politics and city management over the past 20 years, with the city becoming simultaneously more democratic, more effective and certainly more accountable. From 1928 to 1997, the Federal District had no independent rights and became a centralized, managed entity under federal power. The mayor, or *regente*, was hand-picked by the president and the 16 *delegaciones* or precincts had *delegados* hand-picked by the mayor, without a city council to offer the necessary supervision or framework of accountability. The mayors ranged from political heavyweights to close friends of the president, and prior to 1988 not a single one of them was a Mexico City native. The political structure was organized around issues of political and social control, caving in only when necessary and managing dissent in the same fashion as the PRI ruled the country as a whole.

INERTIA AND ADAPTABILITY
A substantial portion of the growth of Mexico City occurs outside of the boundaries of the Federal District, determined by makeshift adaptations on behalf of a majority of the population's poor communities. The creative adaptation of informal housing units (top) and the ad-hoc harnessing of local electricity supplies (bottom) demonstrate a degree of resilience in the face of unreliable provision of public services, infrastructure and regulation.

In 1997 the first elections for a mayor and for a local legislative body in over 80 years took place. The PRD, the left-wing party, had ruled the Federal District for almost 10 years by then, but with surprisingly different agendas and policies than the more recent ones. If caution and passivity characterized Lázaro Cárdenas' tenure, Lopez Obrador, the mayor from 2000 to 2005, engaged in a series of extremely polemical infrastructural works, characterized by the elevated motorway projects and without any interest in dialogue with other spheres of government. The lack of interest in continuing this form of public work by the new mayor Marcelo Ebrard is good news for urban planning and promises more sound transportation policies for the future. His administration offers a more complex but comprehensive understanding of the way the city works.

What urban governance has ignored in the past century is that most of the growth of Mexico City is occurring in the State of Mexico, outside the city's political boundaries. In reality, the elected mayor of the Federal District only governs half the city's voters, and if one takes into account all 79 executive bodies at the three levels of government, this could be a recipe for disaster. The important advances in coordinating a common agenda between the Federal District and the State of Mexico with support from the federal government offer hope, as they are taking place at decision-making, implementation and funding levels.

So what are we to make of a post-crisis, post-megacity global agglomeration? Is it possible to extract 'grim' lessons from Mexico City? And if so, which would they be? Most importantly, is it possible to imagine a conceptual model for Mexico City beyond megacityness and crisis, beyond the usual deficiency of resource-allocation, clumsy management and extreme poverty, which can produce an urban environment that can be sustainable in the long-term?

While the lack of urban projects and the virtual invisibility of planning policies is yet to be addressed, one has to acknowledge that the past 25 years have proven that pessimism as a framework for urban policy decisions has its limitations. It can be argued that 'quality of life' has been transformed by more informed and incremental decisions, whereby the partial successes in lowering the level of air pollution, recent shifts towards more sustainable transportation policies, the acknowledgement of integrated urban-planning decisions that take into account housing location as much as workspaces or public spaces, are all testimony to an improvement in the learning curve about the potential for megacityness.

Mexico City is brandishing a new optimism that seems poised to embrace the imperative to be not only more equitable and efficient, but also a more competitive and alluring global urban economy. Monsiváis' 'Chauvinism of the Catastrophe' will most certainly evolve into a wider understanding of Mexico City – in spite of its ever-present paradoxes – as the space of potentials.

MAKESHIFT GLOBALIZATION

Néstor Canclini

URBAN CONCENTRATIONS

As Latin American cities continue to constitute a substantial share of their national GDP, exploding populations in capital cities such as São Paulo are employed in an ever-expanding informal economy. The Avenida São João is one of the central arteries of Brazil's economic powerhouse.

It has been stated that Latin American cities oscillate between European urban models and conflictive processes that are closer to those of cities in the United States. How accurate is this pendulum imagery? What are the specific dilemmas facing Latin America's largest urban agglomerations? An investigation of Mexico City offers insight into this inquiry and allows lines with other metropolises on the continent.

A comparison of cities in Europe, the United States and Latin America provides a useful understanding of the internal differences within each city and how the local, the national and the global interact and generate specificities for each case. In the United States many cities have become what Amalia Signorelli calls 'constellations of ghettos, both of misery and of luxury, segregated from each other, yet (they may be) connected through independent channels to national circuits of political, economic and cultural integration', which are often managed by 'command centres which need not locate within any specific city'.

Europe and Latin American cities that have been built upon European – especially Spanish and Portuguese – urban models have performed modernizing functions, integrating both foreign immigrants and migrants from other parts of the country. Apart from the existence of wealthy and poor neighbourhoods situated in the centre and the periphery, these cities fostered the coexistence of different ethnic groups. Over the past two decades, the growth of insecurity and fear in almost every large Latin American city has led to the entrenchment of the wealthy in gated communities and de-territorialized security systems, which mirror the land uses and fragmentary interactions of the North American model.

The Internationalization of Cities in Latin America

Several Latin American cities experienced an early phase of cosmopolitanism. Buenos Aires, Lima and Mexico, as well as other colonial settlements, functioned as regional capitals with articulated links with Spain. This supranational interaction persisted even after the various independence processes and the emergence of modern nations. In the early twentieth century the large city-ports opened up and became entities wherein local traditions merged with the cultural repertoires of the metropolitan centres with which they maintained trading ties: cities on the Atlantic such as Buenos Aires, Caracas, La Habana and Rio de Janeiro with Spain, France and the United Kingdom (Habana and Rio also experienced a rich interaction with Africa); Lima, Panamá and other cities on the Pacific with the United States and Asia.

This early stage of globalization followed the colonial or imperial logic that favoured ties with a single core. Until the mid-twentieth century the structure and meaning of life in such Latin American urbanities were conditioned above all by their role as the political, economic and cultural centres of each nation.

Despite this, what makes Mexico City (like São Paulo) a global city is not its primary status within the region, nor its connections with a national urban system, but rather its critical nodal position within economic and communication networks of a global span. Although the population of Mexico City increased from 185,000 to over 3 million between the mid-nineteenth century and 1940, its urban layout maintained the basic square pattern established in the sixteenth century by the Spanish conquistadors. Fifty years ago, city life took place in a clearly demarcated territory holding a geographic, political and cultural nucleus within the historical centre, which comprised buildings remaining from the colonial era, those from the nineteenth century and some archaeological sites that are still evocative of the pre-Hispanic past. Today, however, urban vistas merge monuments with advertisements; the solemn aesthetics of cultural heritage stand side by side with the ephemeral discourses of commercial messages and political campaigning.

The Industrial City and Metropolitan Growth

As in other Latin American cities, the modern urban experience that defines the Mexican capital began to take shape in 1940 with the industrialization processes engendered therein, the massive migration from across the country, and the expansion rate of the urban sprawl. In the Federal District of Mexico and its metropolitan area, the population shifted from 1.64 million inhabitants in 1940 to over 19 million today. Such rapid demographic growth erased the district's layout as it merged with its surrounding municipalities to become a metropolitan conurbation. From the mid-twentieth century onwards, the *delegaciones* located in the city centre registered negative population growth, while the largest demographic increases took place in the surrounding ring and the 29 metropolitan municipalities in the states of Mexico and Morelos.

The effects of these changes on social interactions and cultural development can be broadly categorized into three key transformations: the experience of the urban unfathomable; the territorial imbalances that characterize the localized cultural offerings in the city; and the development of cultural industries that stimulate forms of social communication mediated by telecommunications.

The 'unfathomable' refers to the problems faced by the residents of a megacity in making sense of the heterogeneous multitude of zones, neighbourhoods, journeys and experiences offered by the urban ensemble. The urbanized area of Mexico City expanded from 120 square kilometres in 1940 to the 1,700 square kilometres of the Metropolitan Zone today. This area's population equals the sum of 16 out of the 32 Mexican states, and is roughly comparable to the population of the whole of Central America, demonstrating a diversity of ethnic groups, lifestyles, and production and consumption activities similar to those of the five countries in the American subcontinent. In this context, 'city-continent' may well be seen as an alternative definition of the megalopolis. The multicultural nature of the Mexican capital encompasses more than 30 indigenous languages as well as some from Europe. Such diversity may be enriching, but it can also give rise to distorted stereotypes. Studies of social imaginations on the city show that – concerning traffic congestion, pollution and urban violence – the mainstream perceives the structural explanations of social science as too far removed and would rather focus on identifying specific culprits: too many migrants, political protests, street vendors or police corruption. The inability to conceive of the urban agglomerate in its entirety is further evidenced by the localized character of almost all social movement and its low capacity to influence, which articulates an integrated vision of the reorientation of metropolitan public policies. Rapid population growth and urban disorder render the megalopolis a city of internal miscommunication.

Cultural Consumption and Communication

Because urban expansion was not paralleled by the rise of a new cultural infrastructure, from the mid-twentieth century onwards the cultural offerings in Mexico City (theatres, concert halls, bookshops) were concentrated in a triangle that extends from the historical centre to Chapultepec that resolves towards the south at the Ciudad Universitaria. The period also witnessed the expansion of intangible media, mainly radio, television and mobile phones. The latest polls on cultural consumption in Mexico City indicate that 97 per cent of households own at least one television and one radio set, 74 per cent own VCR equipment, and that there are more mobile phones than land lines. While forms of entertainment that require on-site attendance are highly clustered, the messages of electronic media are distributed more equally throughout the entire urban space. A trend emerges to simply use the city as a workplace or as medium to get to work. Attendance of cultural and recreational events in public places decreases as the mainstream retreats to lifestyles in which culture is consumed at home. The reinvention of social and cultural ties by radio, television and the Internet is believed to make up for the disconnection between residents of the megalopolis that territorial dispersion had brought about.

Polls show that six of the most common leisure activities enjoyed by residents of Mexico City occur within the house: watching television, reading the newspaper, resting, listening to music, spending time with family and working out. With the exception of exercise, which may entail jogging around the streets or going to the gym, and family life, which could include going for walks or other outings, people in the Mexican capital seem to avoid public life in the city. On weekdays, no more than 6 per cent of the population engage in activities that require contact with the city – visiting friends, shopping, dining out and attending the cinema or theatre. On weekends, this figure climbs to 30 per cent. Mediated information and entertainment prevail over local engagement.

Cultural representation and urban imagination are constructed, most of all, through the agendas promoted by media. In Mexico City, as in Bogotá, Caracas and São Paulo, media circuits have become more important than traditional places in the transmission of information about urban life. In some cases they provide new modes of gathering and recognition, from communication through radio and television – i.e. participatory programmes with 'call-ins' – to meetings in commercial centres that have come to replace the old spaces of wandering and encounter. Many of these cultural options have the capacity to link large parts of the population with macro-urban experiences and with those of other countries, which in turn changes the perception of the city as public space. Such media do not only favour a more fluid interaction between the capital and national life, they also open it up to transnational goods and messages. The megalopolis becomes a place where information, international spectacles, branches of large-scale retailers from abroad, are concentrated in managerial control centres, actual innovations and globalized imaginations.

DESIGNING SOCIAL DIVERSITY

The challenges of accommodating the increasing gap between rich and poor in Latin American cities is brought into sharp relief by the juxtaposition of a new residential complex with the Favela Paraisópolis in São Paulo, where private pools on individual balconies look out over a neighbouring slum deprived of water and sewers.

The Global City?

The Mexican capital is endowed with a vast cultural supply that places it in an internationally competitive position. The city's communications systems, entertainment and versatile service industries provide international electronic connections even if conditions of efficiency and security in the city are highly deficient. Entrepreneurs and government officials have expressed their concerns about the heightened insecurity and the slow pace of traffic – it now takes residents around two hours to make a trip that should take only 30 minutes, severely impacting productivity. It is estimated that 20 million work hours are lost daily due to the congestion generated by more than 3 million vehicles circulating in the metropolitan area.

The rapid growth of Mexico City in the past 50 years, as in São Paulo, Caracas and Lima, is due to the massive migration of Mexicans hoping to reap the benefits of industrialization. With the external liberalization of the Mexican economy, the city is now entering a phase of deindustrialization and the most dynamic growth sectors are expected to relate to transnational services. The Federal District and its metropolitan periphery have become one of the world's 20 urban megacentres, with the greatest links to global networks of management, innovation and commercialization. A clear example of this shift is found in the 8 square kilometres of Santa Fe dedicated to the offices of Hewlett Packard, Mercedes Benz, Chubb Insurance, Televisa and other corporations, as well as shopping centres and upmarket housing complexes. The shift is also confirmed by the revitalization of the Paseo de la Reforma, Polanco, Insurgentes and Periférico Sur, the mushrooming of 29 commercial mega-malls, the presence of new international hotels, the modernization of telecommunications and satellite connections, and the diffusion of information services, cable and digital television.

The shrinking ability of the globalized city to benefit the vast marginal zones of exclusion has turned Mexico City's metropolitan area into the region responsible for the highest expulsion rate of Mexicans to the United States. Dualist frameworks of intervention for urban regeneration and expansion plans have benefited only limited enclaves, such as the Historic Centre, Reforma-Polanco and Santa Fe, segregating the rest of the population and creating a rift between the globalizing 'utopia' and the historical city. Global service nodes attempt to isolate themselves from traditional sectors, from informal or marginal economic activities, from deficient urban services, from the frustrations of the unemployed and from the fears of insecurity.

The duality between the global city and the insecure local city of the margins may ultimately prevent Mexico City from being perceived as an attractive location by those that bind global networks and attain more balanced and sustainable internal development. One of the strategic tasks for cultural policy in this megalopolis is articulating its historical heritage and local traditions alongside modern developments to improve the competitiveness of the megacity in the global economy. Mexico City also needs a strategy of redistributing cultural resources in urban space in order to facilitate intercultural communication through media policies that consider the diverse socio-cultural needs of the population rather than being limited to the expansion of media clienteles.

Until majorities are included in a coherent modernization project, insecurity will pervade all sectors of society, air pollution will dominate and informal policies will assert their influence on the gestures of modernity. These and other signs indicate that urban duality fails. What predominates today is a conflictive intersection between the different cities of Mexico City.

JOHANN

FOURWAYS GARDENS
*Secure
your lifestyle!*

Steve Hodgson
083 290 0687
www.gps4ways.co.za

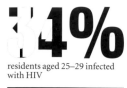**34%**
residents aged 25–29 infected with HIV

150%
increase of office space in Sandton, outside the city centre 1997–2004

**22.7%**
aged 14 or younger

3.2m
residents in Johannesburg

8.8m
residents in Gauteng province

1/3
of all journeys by foot

1,960
people/km² is the average residential density in Johannesburg

**31%**
of the population is unemployed, an increase of

**65%**
between 1996–2001

69%
of office space was in the Central Business District in 1990

30%
of office space was in the Central Business District in 2000

22%
of office space was in the Central Business District in 2005

1,600 km²
area of Johannesburg

17,000km²
area of Gauteng province

**17%**
of South Africa's GDP is contributed by Johannesburg

**6.7%**
of population foreign born

4%
of the population reach the age of 65

600
gated communities, enforced by

1,100
checkpoints

**18.74%**
households without any income

**24.1%**
live below the poverty line

29
average age of male resident

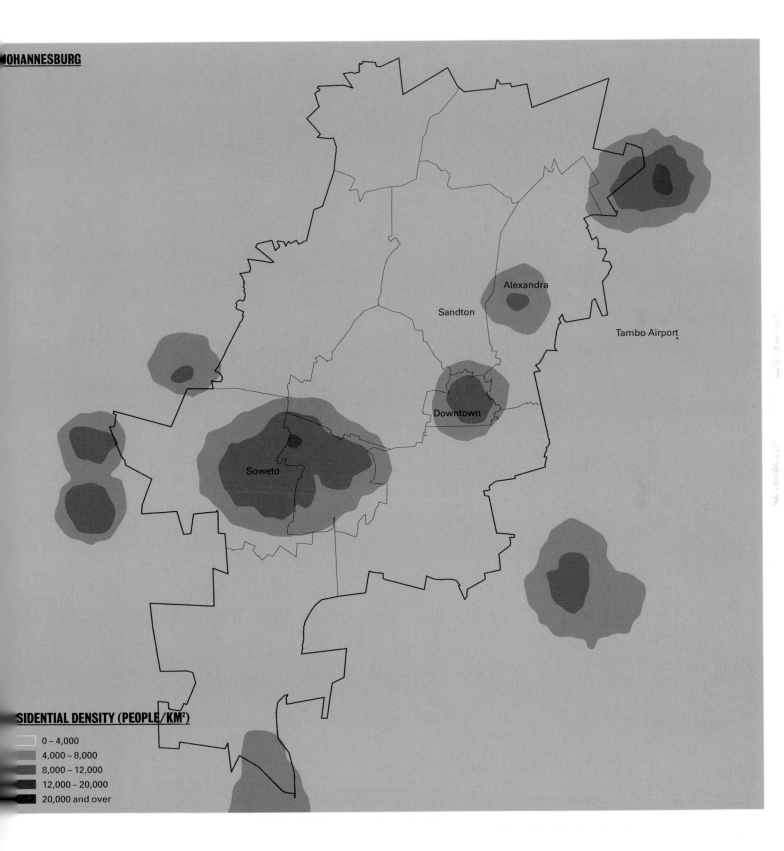

JOHANNESBURG

Alexandra

Sandton

Tambo Airport

Downtown

Soweto

RESIDENTIAL DENSITY (PEOPLE/KM²)

- 0 – 4,000
- 4,000 – 8,000
- 8,000 – 12,000
- 12,000 – 20,000
- 20,000 and over

THE VIEW FROM OUTSIDE

Deyan Sudjic

Johannesburg, like Melbourne or San Francisco born a generation or two before it, is a city that erupted into existence out of a spasm of explosive growth. In all three cities, rapid urbanization was triggered by the rush to exploit the discovery of large deposits of gold. Like Melbourne, Johannesburg became an instant metropolis towards the end of the nineteenth century, crystallizing from a mining camp into a city of stone and stucco. It imported electric trams and trolleybuses, dance halls and department stores in a matter of decades. Of course, Johannesburg had more gold, and therefore more need of rather more mining labour than the other two cities. It attracted the ambitious and the dispossessed from around the world: Russian Jews fleeing persecution; indentured Chinese labourers (65,000 of them were shipped in and then out again when they were considered surplus to requirements); Indians moved in from Natal as well as Africans – pass laws permitting.

Unlike Melbourne and San Francisco, however, Johannesburg grew up on the edge of the goldfields. And, in contrast to its coastal counterparts, it is a mile above sea level. Johannesburg has lost the trams that still grace Melbourne and San Francisco. These trams have been replaced by swarms of microbuses that put it closer to Mexico City or Moscow in its ethos. The surviving public-transport system is regarded with such anxiety by Johannesburg's citizens than nobody who can afford a car would even consider using it. But its shared roots with its American and Australian counterparts are still recognizable. That is, perhaps, what makes it a subject of such fascination to those who observe the evolution of cities from the relative comfort of western Europe.

Johannesburg is the product of a set of circumstances that are highly specific to Africa. It was born out of the conflict between Afrikanerdom and a British empire engaged in the last thrashings of its final bout of expansionism. It was shaped by the cruel restrictions of the apartheid regime, as well as by the dreams of modernity of the post-war years, that brought about some distinctive inversions of urban norms. But it is also a kind of laboratory for projecting urban phenomena to their extremes.

The apartheid regime deliberately planned for low density in black areas, as an instrument of social control. Soweto, for example, was built on the model of an English garden city and has only densified through multiple occupancy. Higher densities were reserved for the more affluent whites in the inner ring, living in Brazilian-inspired high-rises. Now the city has become a honey pot for a new kind of Africa, drawing in-migrants, legal and otherwise, from all over the continent. The whites have consolidated in the northern suburbs. In fact the pre- and post-apartheid city does not represent as entirely sharp a break as it might seem. There was a gradual relaxation of the racial controls on black urban settlement before majority rule, and the patterns of change echo those of other cities.

The city forms part of a complex urban hierarchy that reflects South Africa's origins as the union of a range of once-individual states – a country with its parliament in Cape Town, the executive based in Pretoria, which is now close to the edge of the Johannesburg conurbation, and a supreme court in Bloemfontein.

Johannesburg grew rapidly as a commercial, banking city, an upstart challenger that quickly overtook the older, more genteel Cape Town. To some, the city is in itself a mark of colonialism in an Africa of nomadic movement. Certainly it attempted to exclude black people from citizenship for half a century. One reflection of South Africa's post-apartheid constitutional settlement is the way in which Johannesburg has constantly drawn and redrawn its political boundaries during the last decade. It has allowed it to incorporate suburbs with an ease that Los Angeles would certainly envy. It has also seen local boundaries within the city reshaped, initially along radial lines to ensure an income and racial balance within each unit. These boundaries have now been superseded with an entirely different structure. Soweto itself was incorporated within the city boundaries only four years ago.

Its population now counts around 3 million, with the infrastructure and the skyscrapers of the first world, in which can be seen a degree of hollowing out and suburban flight that matches any American city. But the process has been given an accelerated twist by an epidemic of violent crime and by the rapid changes resulting from the creation of a black managerial class since the ANC came to power. The starkest symbolic move in this process was the departure of the stock exchange for the white northern suburbs. The last four-star hotel in the city centre closed years ago.

Johannesburg is a city in which the malls and gated communities typically associated with southern California have been given their most baroque – even Tuscan – expression, in deference to the style of choice of the developers. They have turned the northern edge city of Sandton into an alternative to the city centre that has been abandoned by all but the most determined of banks and mining conglomerates. Sandton is growing as quickly and is as affluent as any American sunbelt city. In some ways, Johannesburg's gated settlements, literal re-creations of medieval walled cities, could be seen not as a reflection of American suburbs, but as predictions for what they may one day be like.

CONFLICTING REALITIES

Johannesburg claims the status as Africa's premiere metropolis, transforming what was an all-white apartheid city of approximately 250,000 people into a teeming urban conglomeration of 3.25 million in little more than 10 years. Fortified shopping districts in neo-Tuscan style (bottom) and heavily guarded residential enclaves constitute the new reality of this growing African city as its struggles to establish its own identity (top).

The prospect of the skyscrapers of the central business district being taken over by Nigerian traders, and hemmed in by street markets selling magic and bush meat, and of formerly affluent white suburbs being turned into no-go areas, can at times seem like a real-life version of J. G. Ballard's dystopias. Indeed, there is something about the mood of the skyline of downtown Johannesburg that suggests Shanghai's art deco Bund, marooned in Mao's China.

The reality is that Johannesburg is facing many of the same issues as peers in the United States and Europe. In addition to these, however, it has to deal with the prospect of a tragic drop in population, caused by the appalling mortality of HIV/AIDS and tuberculosis. The death rate among young adults is a phenomenon causing the city to urgently address the need to protect the property rights of child heads of households.

Johannesburg has the economic potential to address the challenges it faces, and to share its wealth with a wider section of the community. Its attempts at urban

A WHIRLWIND OF CHANGE

The Nelson Mandela statue in Sandton's new public square – Johannesburg's alternative city centre in the northern suburbs – reflects the pace and change of a city where the physical landscape encapsulates the tensions and opportunities of South Africa's new political and structural realities.

regeneration have already started to take effect. By directing government jobs to the city centre, blight is being reversed. Retail is beginning to come back into the centre and the new constitutional court, weighted with resonance, has been built on the site of an apartheid-era prison in the stigmatized Hillbrow area.

One continual refrain that sounds eerily familiar in Europe is Johannesburg's determination to present itself as Africa's 'world-class' metropolis. The very words are a betrayal of a certain level of anxiety. Despite its dominant position as Africa's industrial and financial powerhouse, with 45 million or so citizens South Africa looks modest in comparison to the continent's real giant, Nigeria, which has a population of 100 million. In fact, Johannesburg may one day find itself being measured against Nigeria's former capital, Lagos. To that end, South Africa is putting great store on symbolic markers, in particular the 2010 Football World Cup, for which Johannesburg will be one of the centrepieces. The city is working on a series of large-scale investments in the build up to this event, of which Gautrain, linking the city's downtown to the airport and Pretoria, is the most ambitious.

On a global scale, Johannesburg's population is still relatively modest. But it has been through a whirlwind of change in its shape and structure, the outcome of which is still far from clear. In Johannesburg, the threats facing all cities are present in their starkest, bleakest form, but it is also a place filled with a vitality that rivals all others.

RECOVERING FROM APARTHEID

Lindsay Bremner

As one approaches Johannesburg from its recently renamed Oliver Tambo (formerly Johannesburg) International Airport, one gets a first and spectacular view of the city cradled between two parallel ridges, its cluster of high-rise buildings held comfortably in a protective earth bowl, as if they had always been there. The airport highway undulates gently, maintaining a linear focus on this distant view, until it reaches a complicated tangle of intersecting motorways. Here the city disappears, and one girdles metropolitan Johannesburg to arrive at one's destination, no doubt, in a suburban location. The city anticipated will have been reduced to a visual icon of the city it once was. The narrative of this journey is, in many ways, the narrative of the city.

From its origins, when gold was discovered in 1886 in the east-to-west ridges that structure its landscape, Johannesburg was tied to its geology, its fortunes to the booms and slumps of the gold-mining industry. Early miners found gold close to the surface. When these outcrops were exhausted, shafts were sunk and deep level mining began. The subterranean landscape was surveyed and mapped. Mining headgear, ore dumps, battery stamps, reduction works, slimes dams and railway lines traced this underground geography on to the surface of the earth. Ridges and valleys were translated into a churning metallurgical landscape. Syndicates, consolidations and new financial institutions sprang up to bankroll mining operations.

The grid of the city was laid out on a triangular piece of land between farm portions. Mining compounds, municipal locations and slum yards spread around its edges. It soon became one of the world's richest and most rapidly growing centres, attracting a global network of interest and capital. From its inception, Johannesburg was constructed in the image of western modernity. Its building boom prior to the turn of the twentieth century drew on the style of fin de siècle Vienna, while the boom following the Anglo-Boer War (1899–1902) produced monumental Edwardian buildings, consolidating the relationship between the gold-mining industry and the British homeland.[1] The 1930s depression saw the abandonment of the gold standard and foreign capital flood into the country. This transformed Johannesburg into a little New York.[2] By 1936, at the time of the British Empire Exhibition in Johannesburg, *The Times* described the city as the 'largest and most densely populated European city in Africa' with 'fascinating shops and smartly dressed shoppers'.[3] It claimed for itself the status of 'the Empire's great gold centre'.[4]

In *The Origins of Totalitarianism* (1951), however, Hannah Arendt revealed that many of the immigrants to South Africa in the late nineteenth century belonged to

THE CHALLENGES OF INCLUSION

More than a decade after the end of apartheid Johannesburg's central districts have suffered from the 'doughnut effect', with people moving away from a crime-ridden core to new suburban districts such as Sandton (above). Soulless but safe commercial and housing clusters accommodate Johannesburg's emerging white and black middle classes, while the former townships of Alexandra (opposite) and Soweto remain poorly served by public transport and basic services.

a class of people who were unemployed and redundant in their countries of origin. The goldfields were a useful destination after their expulsion from the metropolitan centre. Early on, they provided the human labour for digging gold, but were soon replaced by the black men who flocked to the mines from South Africa's neighbours and rural areas. Black life in Johannesburg was directly related to this industrial utility. It was both indispensable and expendable. Its experience of the modern was one of precariousness, exploitation and humiliation. It was organized, through the biopolitics of race, to facilitate and legitimize its usage, to allow it to be lavishly spent.

Bare Life: Spatial Planning and Segregation

The site of this transformation of life into what Giorgio Agamben calls 'bare life' was the black township – a space conceived by planners and architects from models, images and procedures of modernity, in particular those of nineteenth-century English reformers Robert Owen and Ebenezer Howard.[5] The introverted 'neighbourhood unit' or 'urban village', in which housing units face inwards towards communal facilities embedded at their geographic centres, with internal movement oriented towards these to 'stimulate social cohesion and a sense of community', provided the model for early urban slum-clearance programmes.[6] The wartime government transformed this planned neighbourhood approach into a distinctly South African discourse. Coherent residential communities separated by green belts with carefully planned employment sites and transport between were presented as technological solutions to the problems of cities.[7]

These themes came together in apartheid's primary spatial-planning instrument, the Group Areas Act of 1950. Under this legislation, each race group was consolidated into its own residential area. Each consolidated area was to be self-governed and as functionally independent of other areas as possible. Each area was separated from others, preferably by natural barriers (ridges or rivers) or by motorways, railways or a buffer zone of open space. In moving to and from work, no race group was permitted to cross the residential area of another. A centralized production and exchange facility (a central business district) accommodated white-administered civic, commercial and financial functions.

The unravelling of this schizophrenic model of urban life, as well as the city's growing reputation as Africa's premiere metropolis, has transformed what was an all-white apartheid city of approximately 250,000 people into a teeming urban conglomeration of 3.25 million in little more than 10 years.

The city began to reposition itself in the new international division of labour in the mid 1990s by reinventing itself as a 'world-class African City'. Industry was being reoriented to high-tech sectors and service activities, to winning new markets, attracting foreign capital and gaining access to new capital flows.[8] This was accompanied by a spatial re-centring, driven primarily by political, marketing and real-estate imperatives, from the modernist core to the erzatz corporate sprawl of Sandton, now at the heart of its financial and corporate life and its cultural imaginary.

Sandton came into existence in the early twentieth century as a site of country estates and recreational activity for wealthy Johannesburgers. It was proclaimed a city in 1969. Identified with wealth and leisure, its middle-class lifestyle attracted property developers in unprecedented numbers. They clustered around what is now known as Nelson Mandela Square, designed as a copy of the piazza in Siena, Italy. It is here that the infrastructures of the 'African world-class city' have been built – corporate head offices, the Johannesburg stock exchange (relocated from the city centre),

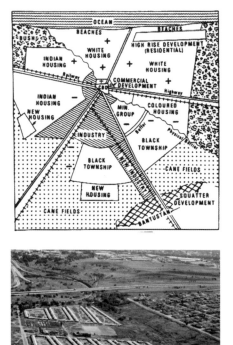

THE LANDSCAPE OF APARTHEID

The spatial segregation of racial groups into distinct residential areas separated by natural barriers, motorways or buffer zones was the primary spatial-planning instrument of the apartheid government of the 1950s (top and bottom).

banking headquarters, international financial houses, hotels, shopping complexes and a conference centre. A high-speed train will soon link it directly to the airport.

A mere 3 kilometres away lies the black ghetto of Alexandra, an area of 7.6 square kilometres housing 350,000 people (at between 45,000 and 81,000 people per square kilometre).[9] Sandton, on the other hand, houses 160,000 at between 0 and 1,500 per square kilometre. With an average age of 23 and unemployment of 32 per cent (officially) or 60 per cent (unofficially), it is clear that Alexandra's proximity to the glamour zone of the post-gold city has not resulted in its integration into the urban economy. In 2001, a Presidential Lead project was launched by President Thabo Mbeki and 1.7 billion rand (US$25 million) of central-government funding was invested into its recuperation. So far this has shown only limited results.

Growth from the Ashes of Apartheid

Living in Johannesburg today is a vast experiment in how to inhabit apartheid's ruins. Its former central business district and surrounding residential neighbourhoods were subject to mass abandonment in the 1980s and early 1990s, as business and property owners relocated to suburban nodes.[10] While these relocations can be attributed to many factors, (infrastructure requirements, convenience, corporate restructuring, prestige, racist assumptions about property values) a clear picture of capital flight from the city emerges.

City government, through the Johannesburg Development Agency, has poured considerable resources into managing the public space of this ruined city, often portrayed as out of control and dangerous. In a number of instances, architecture and urban design have been called on as instruments of urban and social warfare to tabulate, regularize and formalize this public space, underpinned by modernist notions of a relationship between physical order, urban management and social stability.

For instance, Metro Mall, an inner-city transportation interchange, provides ranks for buses and taxis and serves an estimated 100,000 commuters per day. It attempts to rein in the city's anarchic taxi industry and to regularize street trading. A variety of trading spaces accommodate 800 traders, as well as management offices and facilities for taxi and hawker associations. Despite its regulatory underpinnings, this building indicates a significant shift in approach to dealing with public buildings. Most importantly, it acknowledges the street as public space and generates street life on the city's edges and its interior corridors. Dignified entrances confer a sense of arrival to those entering; robust materials confront the demands of heavy use.

Faraday Market, on the southern side of the city adjacent to an underground railway station, similarly accommodates ranks and loading platforms for taxis. Offloading, storage and selling spaces for traditional herbs and medicines (many in reused sheds), consulting rooms for traditional healers and taxi association offices all filter commuters into the city. Unlike at Metro Mall, with its thoroughly urban typologies, at Faraday rural and urban types are overlaid in programmatic, spatial and iconographic repertoires.

South Africa in general and Johannesburg in particular now occupy increasing prominence in the continental economy. Johannesburg attracts people from all over the globe, as in its origins. Multinationals use the city as a springboard for their African operations; transcontinental traders and cross-border shoppers circulate in migratory cycles of various durations; others fleeing persecution or impoverishment seek asylum in the city. In the popular imagination, portions of it are now a little Lagos, Kinshasa, Mogadishu, Karachi or Beijing.

SPACE AND EXCLUSION

A city that understands the intimate relationship between social exclusion and spatial design, Johannesburg is experimenting with new forms of urban design that promote social inclusion. Metro Mall (top and bottom) is one of a series of positive interventions with shops and facilities around the city's intensely used 'taxi ranks' – transport hubs for thousands of microbuses that form the city's rudimentary public transport system for the majority of the black population.

REGENERATION AS HOPE

In the face of violent inner city decline, Johannesburg has pioneered a number of residential, cultural and transport initiatives that are beginning to show signs of a sustained urban regeneration. The Brickfields project has brought a mix of much-needed affordable and private housing in the downtown area, going against the grain of so much of Johannesburg's unsustainable suburban expansion.

The inner-city neighbourhoods of Hillbrow, Joubert Park, Berea and Yeoville – constructed speculatively in the 1950s as points of entry for European immigrants recruited by the South African government – now serve as arrival halls for many of these migrant groups. As in many other post-colonial cities in Africa, these parts of Johannesburg are characterized not only by ruination, but also by what A. M. Simone has called 'highly urbanized social infrastructures' – mechanisms through which people cobble together provisional, often illicit livelihoods, through cooperation, flexibility and evasion. These deploy new spatial and material strategies that have reinvented the city's modernist landscape – people inhabit the rooftops of apartment buildings, ground floors extend to the street edge in makeshift structures, a parking garage becomes a church, large inner-city hotels function as bases for cross-border shoppers, the Mimosa is home to the foot soldiers of the Ibo-controlled drug trade.

The city has been transformed into a fluid, dynamic, rhizomatic space, a particularly African form of the modern that western urban-management practices, town-planning codes and administrative systems seem unable to make sense of. For what has emerged is a form of urbanity in which entanglements, hybrids, incessant mobility and constant adaptation are not obstacles to modern life, but the very modalities through which it is lived.

The Wealth Divide

Post-race society has inaugurated new modalities for the acquisition of wealth. Black Economic Empowerment (BEE) legislation, aimed at the transfer of economic power into black hands, has realigned the economy. Acquisitions, mergers and buy-outs have transferred formerly white or foreign-owned companies into the ownership and control of black entrepreneurs. A new black elite has emerged of super-rich proportions, mostly close to the ruling party, and new meanings to the concepts of money and work have been produced.

This class, of the instantly and spectacularly rich, has acquired its wealth not by way of effort or productive work, but through political networks, alliances and largesse. New wealth is not earned; it is not even acquired; it is conferred. It has no meaning other than by being spent and displayed. Habits of lavish spending on the body (food, drink, gym memberships, hair, nails, clothes, handbags, mobile telephones, etc.), cars (BMWs, Mercedes-Benzs, SUVs) and houses and their interiors (furniture, fabrics, fittings, decorations) have fuelled, or rather reinvented, a lifestyle that uses up, discards and moves on – centred on objects, display and masquerade.

Architecture offers enormous possibilities to construct the public theatres of consumption and display – the shopping centres, casinos, homes, clubs, bars, restaurants and gyms, in and through which wealth and its signifiers circulate; architecture which is commercial, stylized, saturated with images and surface appearances.

An example is Melrose Arch, a secured suburban precinct for living, working and playing (penthouses, offices, restaurants, health clubs) adjacent to the motorway between Johannesburg and Pretoria. Its buildings are arranged around a public square recalling the layout of an eighteenth-century European town. Its architectural styles form an eclectic assortment of borrowed images – Hundertwasser drawings, Buenos Aires modernism, Potsdamer Platz-tableaux that style consumption with elegance and sophistication by alluding to imaginary elsewheres. Montecasino is another example – a gambling citadel, named after the famous Benedictine monastery bombed by the Allies in World War II. Built in the image of a tumbledown Tuscan village, its fake facades hide 2,300 square metres of 'shoppertainment' –

a hotel, shops, movie houses, a theatre and a vast gambling floor studded with black-jack tables and artificial trees. It is one of the 10 most lucrative casinos in the world, and the centre of Johannesburg's new middle-class world.

These places serve a number of purposes. Johannesburg never was a symbolic or a civic totality – this was denied it by the politics of race. The theatrical spectacles of the Tuscan village or the European town offer opportunities to forget the racial city and recompose the present by gazing into a magical mirror of a frozen and imaginary past. This effaces the 'nascent democratic public sphere' by reducing it to sites dominated by private interest and consumer choice.[11] They surrender the urban entirely to the logic of the commodity form, of organizing desire and provoking fantasy.

Even the inner city, subject to a number of regeneration drives since 1994, is currently being 'revitalized' according to this logic. Only partially useful to new capital as rentable space, it has been put to the profitable use of producing consumers. For instance, a derelict, seven-storey office block next to the Nelson Mandela Bridge in Braamfontein, draped in advertising since 2003 has, in three years, rewarded its owner six times over. Far more lucrative and far less troublesome than recommissioning and letting, this has become a widely used model of urban regeneration, producing a kind of 'post-architectural' city-in-the-making.

Commodity relations saturate everyday life in Johannesburg, even for the poorest of the poor. For those unable to access the glamorous, hedonistic lifestyles of football, *kwaito* or television stars seen nightly on television through talent, patronage or largesse, other possibilities exist. Criminal activity offers a way of acquiring the cars, designer clothes and women that turn its perpetrators into objects of attraction in their own communities. 'If I steal a car and drive to a party with my girlfriend, everybody will say, "What a car he's driving," and every girl will wish to be in love with me,' said one young man interviewed in research conducted by the Centre for the Study of Violence and Reconciliation.[12]

In the face of extremely high levels of violent crime, the city has battened itself down. Fences, palisades, walls, gates, private security guards, cameras and other sophisticated security technologies have transformed the city into bristling electro-magnetic fields and carved new frontiers into it. New development takes place rapidly and almost without exception in gated, walled compounds. Erratic and highly individualized, this logic of defensiveness reinforces apartheid geographies and defers the possibility of anything remotely resembling a coherent city emerging.

To conclude, Johannesburg, from its early incarnation as a tented mining camp, to its consolidation as a colonial town in the image of the metropolitan centre, to the divisive instruments of apartheid that organized it for 50 years, to its current transformation into Africa's pre-eminent metropolis, has, since its inception, been a site where the logics of modern city-making have been at work. Its *tabula rasa* beginnings and globally significant stakes have produced an intense form of urban modernity in Africa, a continent that has otherwise been seen as signifying the limits or failure of the modern project. While not arguing for the exceptionalism of Johannesburg, it does occupy a privileged position in the history of global modern urbanity. I do not suggest, as Rem Koolhaas has with Lagos, that Johannesburg is a kind of urban *noir* – a chaotic and terrifying future to which all cities are headed. Instead, I suggest that just as London, Paris, New York or Tokyo can be studied as modern cities, so can Johannesburg. And that a refusal to condemn it to an 'outside-of-the-modern' permits us to enhance our understanding of modernity itself.

PARALLEL LIVES
The post-apartheid landscape of new housing in Johannesburg is creating a discontinuous environment of inward-looking enclaves surrounded by walls and security fences and guarded gates.

Following page
MANAGING MIGRATION
Much of Johannesburg's spiralling urban growth has come from illegal immigrants from other African states like Nigeria, who are often deported back to their country of origin from this detention centre.

AFRICAN URBANISM

Caroline Kihato

'I was born in the street. I was born in the slum, raised in the slum. In the valley of Mathare[1] … we have no water, no sanitation, we use "flying toilets" – a paper bag which we throw in the river …The other day I went to a friend's house for a party but it turned out to be a funeral … I learn a lot, I see a lot and then I can appreciate life. Most of the inspiration I get for the songs I write is what I see. When you have to survive some situation, creativity comes to you.'[2]

African cities are a conundrum. As these excerpts of voices of young hip-hop slum residents in Nairobi reveal, African urban experiences defy easy characterization. They are at once spaces of opulence and abject poverty, connectivity to global circuits and spaces of marginalization, despair and enormous creativity. They shape and are shaped by layers of history, culture and ideology, making a simplistic rendition of them impossible, or at least likely to be inaccurate. There are no simple policy solutions to the challenges facing African cities, nor can they be easily salvaged from Afro-pessimist discourses – however unhelpful these may be analytically. Rather, one must question the conceptual frameworks used to discuss urban Africa, and to some extent cities in the global south generally. Current notions have obscured a deeper understanding of urbanization processes in developing contexts. Moreover, the conceptual blinders turned towards African cities have consequences, not only for urbanism across the continent, but also for understanding urbanization in the twenty-first century. In this era, cities such as Mumbai, Lagos, São Paulo and Johannesburg play a significant role in shaping the global future for the majority of the world's residents. The often-superficial understanding of urbanization processes attributes to them a singular linear character. This results in a depiction of the urban age as a phenomenon with a universal set of qualities, which manifest themselves uniformly across varied contexts. Indeed, the experiences of African cities illustrates that urbanization processes are just as varied as cities are diverse. Cities across the globe follow a range of historical trajectories, and as such Lubumbashi is no less a city than Mumbai or Toronto.

The Unending Urban Crisis

Much of the literature on African cities depicts them as spaces that are in perpetual crisis, plagued by corruption, disease and poverty. They have been perceived as 'helpless wastelands of horror, corruption and incurable diseases'.[3] So stark are portrayals of an African urban crisis that mainstream urban literature writes of African cities as if they are 'diseases to be cured'.[4] This crisis emanates from viewing contemporary African cities through lenses that privilege formal institutions, and gauge a city's success by the extent to which these institutions work. The language and frames of analysis of discourses on 'good governance', 'decentralization', 'democracy', 'development' and 'service delivery' focus almost exclusively on how governments and civil-society institutions can be re-engineered to address the problems that ostensibly symbolize the African city. Embedded in this perspective is the assumption that cities can be shaped and populations manipulated in order to direct their future. For this to be done, cities must be 'knowable and governable' and have the institutional and analytical tools to achieve this end.[5]

It is not surprising then that much of government policy in African cities aims at formalizing and regulating the city, putting all its spaces within the gaze and reach of the state. From the bulldozing of slum areas and the removal of street hawkers to the building of markets, and low-cost housing, state interventions betray a disquiet about the spaces the state is unable to see or regulate. In cities where the majority of the population live, socialize and eke out a living outside state regulation in informal economies, these efforts have seemed rather like rearranging the deckchairs of the Titanic while it is sinking. Simone's work in three African cities – Pikine Dakar (Senegal), Douala (Cameroon) and Winterveld Johannesburg (South Africa) – demonstrates that the everyday activities of urban dwellers exist in parallel worlds from organized local institutions such as local authorities and civil society organizations.[6] He argues that these activities are governed by logics that defy the predictability of formal institutional and associational life. Rather, urban life seems embedded in ephemeral, fluid and invisible social interactions that hold greater significance for ordinary people than the organized formal structured realm:

'For many urban residents, life is reduced to a state of emergency. What this means is that there is a rupture in the organization of the present. Normal approaches are insufficient. What has transpired in the past threatens the sustenance of well-being at the same time as it has provided an inadequate supply of resources in order to deal with this threat.'[7]

In a richly textured analysis of Ojuelegba, a busy junction in Lagos, Yusuf and Weates offer an alternative view of conceptualizing and understanding everyday life in the city. They show that local myths and belief systems provide a valid and well-reasoned explanation for social action and interaction. For them, the apparent irrationality and disorganization that Ojuelegba represents to some is in fact no less rational or organized than, for example, downtown Paris or New York. By descending from 'a map-centric to a granular perspective', they convincingly show the power that mythical spirits have in shaping social interaction and daily experiences in contemporary urban spaces.[8] Using the symbolism of Esu Elegbara, the guardian of the crossroads, a trickster, after whom Ojuelegba is named, they reveal the hidden rationality that governs and shapes urban experiences at this junction, which has resisted any form of planning and organization. Indeed, 'Esu proffers an alternative form of rationality for them, indicating a different model of existential health and navigation through the world'.[9] These analyses not only escape the vilifying language often used to describe and understand urban Africa, they also legitimize African urban trajectories as important in their own right. In doing this, they challenge notions of a singular urbanization process and acknowledge that they are diverse. Most importantly, they develop conceptual frameworks that make sense of urban Africa on its own terms, and not in the image of an urban reality constructed elsewhere.

SEEKING IDENTITY
Grafitti on a broken storefront in Johannesburg's Faraday Market area captures the dilemmas of establishing an urban identity to rapidly growing African cities.

Cities of a Lesser God?

Overturning notions of a single urban age or urban condition is not an easy task. Finding new languages and conceptual tools for making sense of urban realities in Africa is made all the more difficult by the inherent location of the analysis in a Eurocentric teleology. Part of the language of an African urban crisis emanates from a western linear perception of how cities ought to evolve and develop. In these discourses, all that separates African cities from cities in the West is time – homogeneous time, utopian and un-ruptured by the specificities and agency of locality. Homogeneous time 'linearly connects past, present and future' and the history of the world is one history, a meta-narrative that links the world through time and space:

'Such a conception of the politics requires an understanding of the world as one, so that a common activity called politics can be seen to be going on everywhere. One should note that time in this conception easily translates into space, so that we should speak here of the time-space of modernity.'[10]

Africa's urban history is thus inevitable and the passing of time will deliver the continent to a future that mirrors a western idea of how things ought to be. In other words, the evolution of all cities inevitably follows a single trajectory, based on that of the West – shifting from pre-modern to modern, pre-capitalist to capitalist, from underdeveloped to developed. In critiquing these linear historical methods of writing Africa, Mamdani points to the fallacy of what he terms a 'history by analogy' by asking 'but can a student, for example, be understood as not yet a teacher?'[11] It is the same myth that led Hegel to state that Africa is a continent without history.

'It [Africa] is no historical part of the World; it has no movement or development to exhibit. Historical movements in it – that is in its northern part – belong to the Asiatic or European World'.[12]

Africa's apparent silence in history implies a lack of agency in determining its own destiny. By de-historicizing the continent, African urban spaces are denied any role in defining their own forms of urbanism or developing their own conceptual tools for better understanding their characteristics. Indeed, African urbanites are at best passive spectators of their own fate, unable to change an inevitable destiny.

This linearity also unwittingly creates hierarchies of experiences that have an impact on the theorization of urban Africa. New York, London and Paris represent the 'real' urban experience, while Lubumbashi, Lagos and Johannesburg represent somewhat deviant, if inauthentic cities. These labels and categories would be innocuous were it not for the theoretical implications they have on our understanding of urbanization processes, both in Africa and across the globe. The centring of the western urban experience has meant that it provides the theoretical foundations for understanding the urban condition everywhere. In other words, Western cities possess the analytical and theoretical content that informs the discourses on urbanization not only in the West, but in cities across the globe. Cities in the global South, therefore, are at most understudies possessing no original history or authentic future.[13] This is often evident in the way debates on urbanization quickly descend into binary oppositions – 'developed' versus 'developing' cities, 'formal' versus 'informal' urbanization, 'global' versus 'local' cities. The latter terms not only have a lesser social status but are also theoretically inferior to their more 'advanced' counterparts. This implies that the condition of formality gives value and content to the informal in ways that undermine any true analysis or understanding of the informal on its own terms. Indeed, the lesser forms of urbanization can only be given analytical content by their lead twin. They are incapable of producing any conceptual insights that are

UNDERSTANDING THE AFRICAN CITY

Like other major cities in one of the world's most rapidly urbanizing continents, Lagos is a site of opportunity, growth and mobility that connects its residents both to the global networks and to spaces of marginalization.

automatically universally applicable. These linear modes of writing history not only lead to conclusions of Africa's deviancy, but more inimically, rid the continent of its own analytical content or value.

Seeking New Languages

Urbanizing Africans see the cities in which they live as sites of opportunity, growth and mobility. While there are risks and frustrations in these cities – as there are in cities throughout the world – those who choose to live there do so in the hope of fulfilling their ambitions of personal development, escaping patriarchy and accessing global networks. For many, the city symbolizes possibility, dreams that can come true, desires that can be fulfilled and hope that things will get better. The words of Zakah, a hip-hop artist born in a slum in Nairobi, not only assert an urban identity, but also portray agency even amid squalor and poverty: '[T]hey [tourists] think there are only zebras and lions. But when they come here I think they'll see we're doing something international. People everywhere are going to feel us because our skills are real.'

Planners and analysts need to stop considering African cities as spaces that are not yet fully evolved, but as important sites for theorizing and understanding Africa as part of the world. This involves reversing their marginalization in urban discourses and asserting them at the centre of analysis and theorization. The challenge for African urbanists is to find new languages, methodologies and conceptual tools for understanding African cities as an analytical category in their own right, not just as a deviant form of existence. This would require breaking free of the tradition that uses western cities as reference points. Universalizing the characteristics of such cities and proclaiming them as applicable and desirable everywhere rids African urban spaces of their own history and agency in shaping city form. For those people whose history and identity are intricately intertwined with the continent's cities, this is not just a moral obligation but a deeply rewarding and enriching one as well.

3.4m
residents in Berlin

4.4m
residents in the Metropolitan region

50.7%
one person households

890km²
area of Berlin

5,370km²
area of the Metropolitan region

78.5
average life expectancy

35.6%
green, open space

6%
of the population in East Berlin is foreign born, compared to

13%
in West Berlin

3,810
people/km² is the average density

21.6%
employed in financial and business services

50%
of land occupied by buildings in inner Berlin in 1940 was destroyed by WWII

23%
of land occupied by buildings in 1940 was destroyed by subsequent planning decisions

56%
of land occupied by buildings in 2001 was built 1953–2001

40 m²
average living space, compared to

16m²
in Shanghai

35%
journeys made by bike or on foot

1.1m
bus passengers per day

19%
of the population is unemployed

34.6%
of buildings in 2002 were built before 1918

€23,000
Gross City Product per capita in 2005

88%
homes are rented, compared to

41%
homes rented in London

30,600
net migration increase 2000-2005

40,870
net migration decrease 1994-1999

Tegel Airport

Brandenburg Gate

Alexander Platz

Schoenefeld Airport

SIDENTIAL DENSITY (PEOPLE/KM²)

0 – 4,000
4,000 – 8,000
8,000 – 12,000
12,000 – 20,000
20,000 and over

LOOKING FOR A NEW FUTURE

Deyan Sudjic

After leading the world for many years as an advanced industrial economy, Germany is now offering the rest of Europe an accelerated insight into what life is going to be like with an ageing population, a falling birth-rate and a society in which too few active young people are prepared to carry the burden of social responsibility forced on them by demographics.

What was once East Germany has lost almost 1.5 million of its inhabitants since the reunification of 1990. That drop means that 16 per cent of all homes in the Eastern *Länder* are either abandoned or unoccupied. House prices in these areas have fallen by 30 per cent in five years. Compared with Britain, where home-ownership levels are almost 3 out of 4 households, just 10 per cent of housing is privately owned in Berlin – half that of Hamburg and Munich. In some areas the population drop has been even more vertiginous. The new cities built by the German Democratic Republic (GDR) in the 1950s to serve its chemical industries have lost as much as one in three of their populations in the last decade. It is a decline rapid enough to threaten disaster. Some settlements can no longer sustain pressure in their water mains, sewage systems no longer have the critical mass to function properly and the survivors are too scattered for public transport to be sustainable.

But Germany is not a country prepared to sit back and see all this just happen. It is doing what it can to shape its future, including a massive investment in transport infrastructure. More downbeat is a necessary willingness to embark on a costly programme of housing demolition, with a view to concentrating the remaining population in a more sustainable pattern.

This is a far cry from the euphoria of 1990. What was meant to be a huge expansion in West German prosperity eastwards has turned into an exercise in managed retrenchment – albeit a fascinating one. Despite this, Germany is still a society that is ready to contemplate large plans, even if it lacks a single dominant city - a surprising fact given its status as the most populous state in Europe.

There has been a series of ill-fated attempts to turn Berlin – the most likely candidate for the role of a German Paris or London – into a genuine metropolis. Albert Speer and Adolf Hitler set out to build Germania, doubling Berlin's population and equipping it with the stone monuments that would reinforce its claims to the spotlight by sheer force of malignant will. Whether such an entity could ever have been understood as a genuine city, which is above all else a settlement dedicated to making the random interactions of life possible, is open to doubt. Reunification briefly provided another glimpse of a new version of Berlin as a world city. It was another chance for a fresh start. And as if to demonstrate that property development has always been fuelled by the culture of irrational exuberance, as much as by cold calculation, the boldness of reunification resulted in the construction of a city that failed to reflect the realities of Germany's actual urban structure – a network of cities, rather than one dominant city on the French or British model. But while the world's attention was focused on the extraordinary transformation of Berlin's old centre from a fortified wasteland on the periphery of two cities that never spoke to each other into a single entity, the real transformation in Germany was the rise and rise of Munich and the eclipse of Frankfurt's dreams of becoming a world financial centre that would equal London. It is a shift that can be measured in the passenger numbers passing through the expanding Munich airport, and in the emerging network of ICE trains that has made Frankfurt the root of a Y-shaped pattern. In fact, despite the impression that Berlin is the focus of Germany's most serious property bust, with 1.75 million square metres of empty office space (9.7 per cent of the total), it is close to the European average while Frankfurt, with a vacancy rate of 17.2 per cent, is much more challenged.

An equally persistent theme as that of the quest for the metropolis has been the hope that Germany does not need one and the belief that it should learn to make the most of what it has. The evidence would suggest that it has indeed done so. As Europe's leading exporter, economic growth is concentrated in Germany's urban areas. The country's 10 biggest cities account for 20 per cent of the economy's GDP while accommodating only 13 per cent of the population. Moreover, the number of new jobs created in these cities is higher, with a growth-rate of 3.1 per cent a year, compared with a national average of 1.1 per cent. Half of all the new jobs generated in Germany in 2005 were in its 10 largest cities.

Germany has invested heavily in its transport infrastructure, which combined with a new tax on fuel and energy stopped the longstanding growth in car mileage. Railways have seen an average annual growth rate of 3 to 4 per cent, helped by 215 new high-speed trains linking the major cities. Despite this, there is no question but that the old East is economically troubled, and despite the massive investment in infrastructure, the situations in the two halves of the country are very different. With 18.8 per cent of the workforce in the East out of a job in 2005, things are almost twice as bad as they are in the West.

The impact this is having in eastern areas of Germany is significant. Berlin, if it is not going to be London or Paris, does seem to have identified a role for itself as a creative centre, on a grander scale, continuing the role of the pre-reunification Kreuzberg as a Bohemian enclave. 'Poor but sexy', in the words of its mayor. Dresden also seems to have found a new role, by reconstructing its baroque past. But for Halle, looking back to the legacy of Josef Haydn, its most famous son, may not be enough to give it a future.

Despite the attractions of cheap accommodation, which has allowed creative communities to flourish in Berlin and other depressed but grandly proportioned cities, and the basis of an already fixed economic future, the other cities of eastern Germany do not yet have the cultural base to follow in Berlin's footsteps. With only 1.9 per cent of the population in the East born outside Germany compared with 10.6 per cent in the West, the statistics suggest that the East is still a long way from producing a genuinely cosmopolitan urban culture. It would also suggest that despite the prejudices of right-wing extremists, a strong migrant community is clear evidence of a city's economic health.

UPGRADING THE CITY
Berlin continues to make substantial investment in its urban infrastructure in anticipation of new residents seeking a high quality of life. Neighbourhoods such as Mitte (above) are particular magnets, providing ample space for new residents. Yet, although over 1.5 million people (half the overall population) have moved to Berlin since 1995, an approximately equal number have left in the same period.

THE STUNTED METROPOLIS

Franziska Eichstädt-Bohlig

CITY CULTURE

Berlin's ability to attract young people and artists
to live in the city reflects the low housing costs
generated by a stagnant economy. The sense
of tranquil energy of this bohemian city approxi-
mates a relaxed urban utopia with makeshift
beaches and boat parties on the River Spree
animating the river front.

Why is Berlin so hip? Why does its late-nineteenth-century Prussian severity attract
people from all over the world? Can such a poor and economically disadvantaged
place really become a cosmopolitan city? Isn't explosive boom the elixir for each
and every metropolis?

Berlin, like all formerly East German cities, is structurally weak. Years of zero
growth and little hope of a more dynamic near future is as typical here as it is in
Leipzig, Dresden, Erfurt, Halle, Magdeburg or Rostock. All these cities have a large
number of empty flats, shops and offices, and much disused industrial land that
cannot easily be reoccupied. Instead of the traditional housing shortage, for the first
time in history there is an abundance of space.

It was almost a shockwave of deindustrialization that came over the cities of
the former German Democratic Republic (GDR) in the aftermath of reunification.
The old island of West Berlin already had only a slim, artificially maintained economy. The industrial enterprises of East Berlin were shut down with the introduction
of the Deutschmark. Globalization led to further job losses. Step by step, companies
transferred production from high-wage Germany to Eastern Europe or the Far East.

For a few years the euphoria of unification brought a lot of highly subsidized
real-estate investment, but this was not accompanied by lasting economic power.
The government's relocation to the new capital of Berlin was – and still is – the
strongest push for the city's economic invigoration, but at the price of the dislocation
of as many jobs as the move brought with it. The hoped-for increase in population
has failed to materialize.

Berlin, housing Siemens, Borsig and AEG, once enjoyed a global reputation
as a manufacturing city but now has fewer than 100,000 industrial employees. Apart
from the state-owned railway, no company of any significance keeps its headquarters
in Berlin. The GDP of Germany's capital and largest city represents a low share of the
country's as a whole. Unemployment is at 19 per cent and refuses to abate. Incomes
are lower than the national average. The city is up to its ears in debt. In comparison
with London or Paris it is pitifully poor.

Yet the city sparkles with life. Berlin is an expert in the art of living and surviving. It attracts creative and unconventional people from East and West, and increasingly from all over the world. The growth factor in this city is creativity, albeit on a
low-budget level. There are several reasons for this. In the first place, Berlin offers
enough inner-city space for creative living and working on little money. Young

people hungry for adventure have taken over old, disused factories in the centre of Berlin. Legally or illegally they have settled into the city's many empty shops and buildings and brought them back to a life of morbid charm or modern elegance. With great cunning and tenacity they have made centres of art and creativity out of deserted factories and other buildings: KunstWerke, Sophiensäle, Kulturbrauerei, Pfefferberg, Tacheles and others. These initiatives are not limited to Berlin. In Leipzig a gigantic cotton mill has become a cultural and artistic factory, and even in the small town of Dessau a group of young people is renovating and fitting out an enormous old brewery with elan.

The quality of life in Berlin is high, yet affordable. Decades of social-democratic city politics, with a highly subsidized programme of urban renewal and a good infrastructure, have contributed to this. The legacy of socialism can be seen in inner-city nursery schools, playgrounds and sports fields. Much urban investment was in fact made with a growing population in mind. As this has not come about there is now competition for children among kindergartens and schools, particularly in middle-class districts.

Traffic is decreasing because of poverty, unemployment and rising petrol prices. Today Berlin has only 320 cars per 1,000 inhabitants. Even though this is still too many to keep the Green Party happy, it is once again a pleasure to stroll about the city streets. Life here is not only affordable; compared with many other large cities it is remarkably good. You can bring up your children here, even in trendy districts like Prenzlauer Berg. Having children is 'in' once again as the scene gets older.

It is not only the urban space and affordable quality of life that make Berlin so attractive; there is also a very important intangible dimension. It is above all the 'clash of civilizations' between the past 'actually existing socialism' of the GDR and present real capitalism that is so compelling. Berlin, Leipzig or Halle are challenging themselves to take up what is left of this history and turn it into a new future. They are offering themselves as a school for structuring globalization in close contact with worldwide social and political change.

Of course the majority of people do not want this; they want to be left in peace. In Berlin there is an old West Berlin and a modernized, but mentally just as old East Berlin. Both have adapted to the changes – passively and in sufferance – only as far as absolutely necessary. This is also the case in other structurally weak cities, which are characterized by much passivity and resignation. But the future-oriented, creative people who have made new lives here outside the conventional rules, and found the necessary urban space and like-minded friends, are also opening new doors for the city and its cultural and economic identity. Media, IT and advertising, art and music, fashion and design have become an important core of Berlin's new economic life, and will hopefully continue to grow. For there is no way back to the old industrial society. Berlin needs to reinvent itself as a society of knowledge and creativity.

IMPROVISATION AT THE CORE
Over 100,000 buildings dispersed across Berlin remain empty. Taken over by artists and other new residents for informal and often temporary uses, the generous stock of vacant buildings corresponds to equally low rents and a productive culture of makeshift urbanism, as can be seen in the Tacheles building above.

1940–1945: WAR DAMAGE (BLUE)

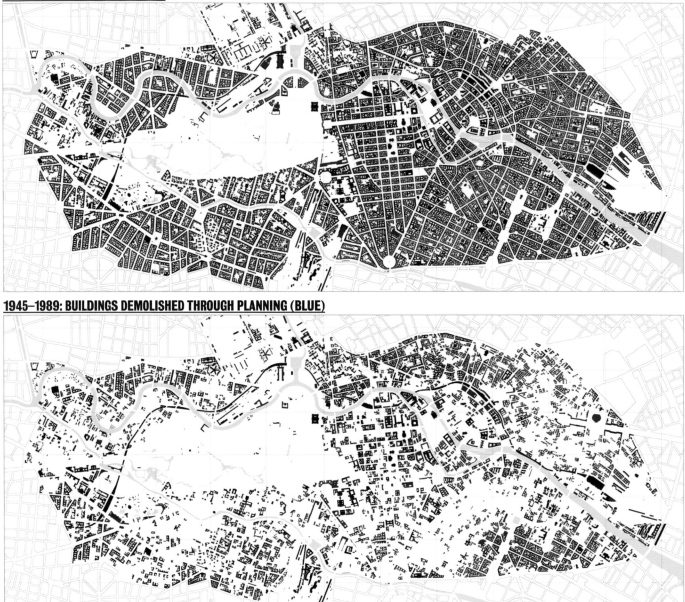

1945–1989: BUILDINGS DEMOLISHED THROUGH PLANNING (BLUE)

THE CITY REMADE

Although massive destruction of Berlin's building stock occurred during World War II, an aggressive planning policy following reconstruction systematically tore down a significant portion of buildings to make way for a uniform development. Almost 60 per cent of the city has been rebuilt, modelled largely on typologies evoking the historical city. The 1940–1945 map (above) indicates the destruction caused during World War II; the 1945–1989 map (below) shows the demolition by subsequent planning decree; the 1940–2001 shows the combined loss of pre-1940 stock through war damage and demolition through planning (opposite top); the 1940–2010 map (opposite below) shows the unparalleled total new construction from 1940 to 2010 indicated in red.

1940–2001: TOTAL OF BUILDINGS DEMOLISHED THROUGH WAR AND PLANNING (BLUE)

1940–2010: TOTAL NEW BUILDINGS AND INTERVENTIONS (RED)

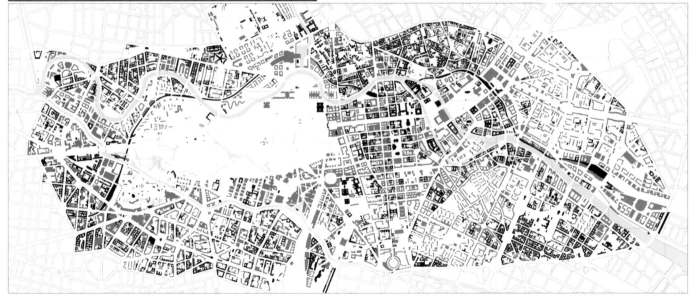

THE GERMAN SYSTEM

Dieter Läpple

Germany is currently rediscovering the city. The stories of decline and crisis that have long dominated discourse on cities in Germany are beginning to be superseded by more positive attention. Nevertheless, German cities are still facing many issues: mass unemployment, erosion of their fiscal basis and – particularly in some cities of the former East Germany – urban shrinkage.

The problems of population decline and job losses have been ongoing for some decades. An apparently unstoppable peripheral migration was turning the city system into an increasingly polycentric urban landscape. Accelerated economic and social changes have resulted in a persistent form of mass unemployment concentrated in the cities. In the last two decades, developments in the German labour market have apparently led not just to increased social inequalities, but also to the permanent exclusion of some social groups from regular gainful employment and consequently from active participation in social, cultural and political life.

From 1980 onwards unemployment escalated in all larger West German cities, and initially presented a polarization between the North German and the South German city-regions. In the unification boom between 1989 and 1992 unemployment was temporarily reduced, but this upturn proved to be a flash in the pan. Since 1992 the overall unemployment rate has once more increased, with its most dramatic effects in East German cities. The development in cities in unified Germany shows

URBAN UNEMPLOYMENT

Persistent unemployment is a major problem for most cities in Germany. The rise in unemployment rates since the early 1990s is defined by significant regional variation across different parts of the country.

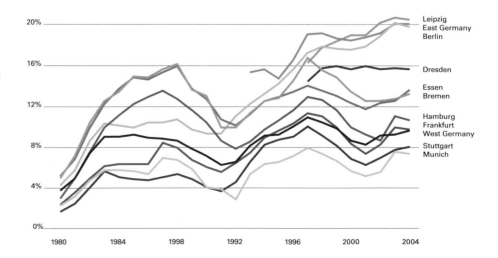

Leipzig
East Germany
Berlin

Dresden

Essen
Bremen

Hamburg
Frankfurt
West Germany

Stuttgart
Munich

20%

16%

12%

8%

4%

0%

1980   1984   1998   1992   1996   2000   2004

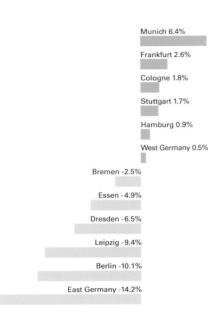

Munich 6.4%

Frankfurt 2.6%

Cologne 1.8%

Stuttgart 1.7%

Hamburg 0.9%

West Germany 0.5%

Bremen -2.5%

Essen -4.9%

Dresden -6.5%

Leipzig -9.4%

Berlin -10.1%

East Germany -14.2%

EMPLOYMENT LEVELS

Urban employment between 1997 and 2004
shows a highly uneven distribution across
Germany. Cities with globally competitive
sectors such as Munich and Frankfurt have
benefited the most, while those in decaying
industrial areas such as the Ruhr and most of
East Germany have been adversely affected.

a very distinct East-West divide, which overshadows that which still exists between the North and the South.

The social consequences of two and a half decades of sustained mass unemployment can be seen not only in its current high levels, but also in its consolidation into permanence and its selective spatial concentration in cities. This has led to the coexistence of growing and shrinking city neighbourhoods, as well as an increasing socio-spatial polarization and segregation within cities. City areas have evolved in which, over time, the social problems intensify with unemployment. City neighbourhoods have therefore become the central problem and operation areas of urban planning in recent years.[1]

In the public debate, mass unemployment is most closely linked with globalization, which has been blamed for the export of jobs, or more specifically the displacement of jobs through cheap international competition. However, a closer inspection of the development of the West German job market shows that the significant increase in unemployment since 1980 is paradoxically not linked with a decline in job vacancies but rather with an increase – albeit a minor one. Despite globalization, employment opportunities have increased in West Germany; at the same time factors such as immigration and a rise in the numbers of female workers have led to a larger workforce. New jobs mainly arose in the service sector, for which those ejected from the manufacturing industry were unsuited. Consequently, these jobs were primarily taken by those new to the labour market and unemployment increased, or rather consolidated itself at a high level.

Empirical studies show that the current labour-market problems in Germany are caused by a lack of employment dynamic in economic sectors not oriented to the world market and not exposed to international competition. In these 'sheltered' sectors a possible extension of employment is blocked – especially for the less qualified – through the institutional framework of the labour market. Ongoing mass unemployment is therefore a complex result of economic-technological change (accelerated through globalization), a crisis of the national labour-regulation system, an insufficient education and qualification system, as well as deep-rooted changes in society.

The intensified problem of the labour market in former East German cities has its historical roots in the system problems experienced during the era of the German Democratic Republic (GDR), exacerbated by the abrupt transformation during unification and the strong decline of the population through the emigration of the young, qualified work force to the western *Bundesländer*.[2] The outcome was an extensive erosion of the economic basis of East German cities.

It is indisputable that as a result of structural change linked with new forms of globalization and the emergence of information technologies, German cities have largely lost their role as privileged centres of manufacturing employment. However, this structural change manifested itself not only in an elaborate deindustrialization process, it has also led to new and crucial development opportunities for cities. As the traditional industrial systems – based on economies of scale of large factories and office towers – were transformed, new forms of knowledge economy emerged. These are based on intellectual work, human creativity, social interaction and networking, and above all they have a great affinity with urban locations. As a result of this shift from an industrial to a knowledge- and culture-based economy, a new urban dynamic has emerged – especially in the large West German urban regions of Munich, Frankfurt, Cologne and Hamburg. However, there are also losers among the cities in West Germany that depended traditionally on manufacturing, such as the cities in the

Ruhr region, and above all East German cities whose economic basis, following a phase of far-reaching deindustrialization, is only now slowly consolidating.

The transformation from an industrial to a knowledge-based economy coincides with a clear polarization of city development, which is marked through a coincidence of growth and shrinkage. Although not all cities could benefit from the new economic dynamism, overall cities are becoming increasingly significant as centres of work: 'Half of all metropolises recorded over the period 1997 to 2004 an increase in workplace centrality, only a fourth a decrease.'[3]

The polarization of city development is also visible in the development of the population. Shrinking cities are mainly concentrated in the East and growing cities in the West. However, the population development in East German cities is also beginning to show a reversal of trend. After the West German core cities achieved once again a positive migration balance in 1999, East German core cities also saw a positive migration balance in 2002. Simultaneously, the migration dynamic in East German fringes decreased (see figure below). In East German cities such as Leipzig, Dresden and Berlin the population has only recently begun to increase again.

It can therefore be concluded that the transformation from an industrial to a knowledge-based economy has established conditions for a new economic dynamic in German cities and city-regions. At the same time, the labour market has become more uncertain. Permanent full-time positions will soon be the exception rather than the norm. Through the increased employment of women and the erosion of the societal time structure, the familiar everyday life in suburban areas – with long commuting distances and times – will become ever-more complicated. Against this background many are rediscovering the advantages of the city. The city offers not only a wider supply of employment opportunities, but also multiple services and opportunities in situ, which makes the everyday organization in the new world of work easier. This means that the city wins in attractiveness not only as workplace, but also as a place of residence.

A New Form of Urban Centrality

The urban system in Germany, as in many other countries, shows that globalization and digitalization do not result in a decline or disintegration of cities, as predicted by many experts, but rather to a re-evaluation of the city and new urban dynamics. The decrease in transport and communication costs, and the high mobility of goods,

URBAN MIGRATION TRENDS

In the beginning of the twenty-first century, Germany's tendency to suburbanization appears to be reverted. The graph indicates the migration balance per 1,000 inhabitants, with urban cores once again showing positive net migration rates slightly higher than those on the fringe. Re-urbanization is fuelled by cities' renewed economic dynamism and attractiveness to a diversifying population.

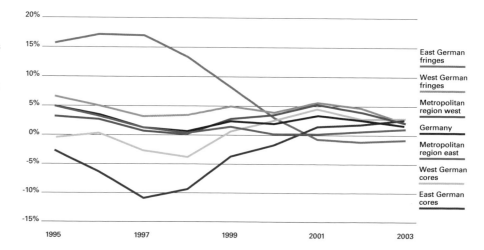

East German fringes
West German fringes
Metropolitan region west
Germany
Metropolitan region east
West German cores
East German cores

information and people do not lead in themselves to a diffusion of resources and power. On the contrary, as the fluidity of goods and information increases, the advantages of scale effects and especially the advantages of agglomeration economies are strengthened.[4] The specific features of this general trend arise from the shift from an industrial to a knowledge-based economy. In this context the new urban dynamics – which are a manifestation of the reinforcement of agglomeration economies – are submitted to a double selectivity.

The cities that mainly profit from this new urban dynamic are those that, as a result of historical development, possess good conditions for a knowledge-based service economy. This form of selectivity is summarized by the American urban economist Ed Glaeser: 'The key to urban success or failure in today's economy is simple: high-skill cities prosper; low-skill ones stagnate or decline.'[5] In the context of German urban development this can be seen in the polarization between the shrinking industrial cities in the Ruhr region and dynamic service metropolises such as Munich or Frankfurt. There is, however, a further selectivity, which can be characterized by the process of metropolization. Besides the skill level of the urban workforce, the size of cities matters. It is mainly the service metropolises, with their large labour markets, especially the highly qualified, that benefit from the new urban dynamics. With the transition to a knowledge economy, intellectual labour and creativity are becoming the key production factors; as a consequence, urban labour markets increasingly function as 'urban magnets' that attract companies and qualified professionals. Companies look at the availability of a qualified labour force in their choice of locations and qualified professionals look for places with a high variety of employment possibilities and urban living conditions.

'Large labour markets also encourage what economists call the coordination of labour: a big city makes it much easier for worker and entrepreneur to find a niche.'[6] The larger and more diverse the labour market, the easier it is for workers to find the right job for the right career, and the easier it is for entrepreneurs to find the right workers for a production of complex and rapidly changing products or services. In the words of Pierre Velz: 'The size of labour markets is probably the main competitive advantage of cities.'[7] The function of metropolitan regions as labour-market hubs activates dynamics between supply and demand, where dense labour markets become a framework for common learning and the creation of specialized pools of knowledge and skills. So skill level and size of cities form a positive feedback which is a driving force for the rise of a new form of urban centrality.

The best-known appearance of the new urban centrality is the global city. As presented convincingly by Saskia Sassen in many publications, the new type of global city takes on a strategic role in the globalized economy: the control, integration and management functions of global value chains are concentrated in the global cities.[8] At the same time, global cities are central production sites and transnational market places for high-quality, knowledge-based services. Following Saskia Sassen: 'Economic globalization and telecommunication have contributed to produce a spatiality for the urban which pivots both on cross-border networks and on territorial locations with massive concentrations of resources.'[9]

While in many countries one dominant global city has emerged, Germany has no veritable global city. Instead it has a multi-polar system that forms the historical basis for the development and profiling of metropolitan functions. One could say that in Germany the new urban centrality takes the form of a process of metropolization. Instead of the emergence of a single global city in Germany we are confronted with a network of complementary metropolitan regions that forms an interlinked nexus for the spatially distributed metropolitan functions.[10] As a result of this development, metropolitan regions such as Munich, Frankfurt (Rhine-Main), Hamburg, Cologne/Düsseldorf (Rhine) as well as Stuttgart have benefited most from the new urban dynamic.[11]

An Export Champion Without a Global City?

Germany has held the position of 'export world champion' for many years and has been exceptional with regards to the integration of its economy into the world market. So how can the absence of a real German global city be explained? How can we elucidate the contradiction between the key position of Germany in the global economy and the 'secondary importance' of German cities in the global network?

Germany was – to borrow Helmuth Plessner's term – a 'belated nation'.[12] It comprised numerous small states, princedoms and free cities, and only gained a common capital city in 1871 with the founding of the Prussian-German Empire. Berlin became the seat of government and, over the following decades – promoted by the Prussian and especially the centralized Nazi state – Germany's dominant metropolis, although it never achieved the centrality of London or Paris. The historical catastrophes of the Nazi regime and World War II brought about the collapse of the German Empire and Germany's subsequent division into four occupied zones. This in turn led to the division of Germany, the division of the German city system and the division of the city of Berlin. East Berlin became the capital of East Germany and West Berlin had to survive as an island surrounded by East Germany. In the process, the central metropolitan role of Berlin was dismantled. Many companies moved away from the divided, politically unstable Berlin to West German regional metropolises such as Frankfurt, Hamburg, Munich, Cologne, Düsseldorf and Stuttgart.

The new Bank of German States (*Bank Deutscher Länder*) – predecessor of the Deutsche Bundesbank – was founded in Frankfurt in the American occupation zone after the closure of the Reichsbank in Berlin. As a consequence, the Deutsche Bank and the Dresdner Bank moved their headquarters to Frankfurt. At the same time, the American occupation government decided to develop Frankfurt airport to become the central airbase of the US Air Force in Germany. Frankfurt's functions as a key gateway and an international financial centre were a direct result of these decisions. Similar historical decisions led to the specialization of other cities: Siemens' move from Berlin to Munich, together with the subsequent concentration of the German defence and aircraft industries in this city-region, established it as Germany's high-tech metropolis. Insurance companies of national importance were moved from Berlin to Munich and Cologne. Hamburg inherited Berlin's national primacy in the news and media sector. The liberal British licensing policy led to the emergence of the NWDR (later NDR) as a pioneering institution among the regional broadcasting corporations in Germany and a whole body of small independent studios dealing with film dubbing and production. The combination of liberalization and denazification on the part of the British occupation authorities fostered the rise of a very successful print-media cluster in Hamburg, insofar as they granted newspaper licences to Germans of political integrity, such as Rudolf Augstein (*Der Spiegel*), Axel Springer (*Die Welt*) and Gerd Buderius (*Die Zeit*). Finally, with the creation of the German Federal Republic (Bundes Republik Deutschland – BRD) in 1949, the seat of the federal government and the federal administration was moved from Berlin to Bonn.

The alternating centrality within the German city system can be seen in the

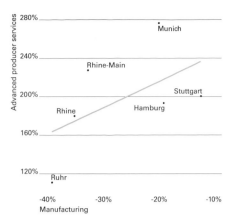

MANUFACTURING AND SERVICES

Although manufacturing has contracted in every city as the service sector expands, the positive correlation from 1980 to 2001 in regional growth rates between advanced producer services and resilient urban manufacturing is defined by a relationship more complex than that of pure substitution.

figure on page 238, which is based upon a study by Hans Blotewogel.[13] In 1939 the German city system had a clear hierarchy, with Berlin at the top. After a clear gap regional metropolises followed: Hamburg, Munich, Stuttgart, Frankfurt, Cologne, Leipzig, Dresden and Breslau (today's Wreclaw). In the schematic hierarchical profile for the year 1939 a clear West-East difference is also recognizable in the structure of the city system: in the West (left from Berlin) it shows a much denser and multilayered city network than in the East, where few great centres dominate.[14] The collapse of the German Empire in 1945 led to a deep-rooted transformation of the German city system. The illustration on centrality for the year 1970 shows the divided Berlin, which forfeited its central role. On the right side is the city system of the GDR with East Berlin and the regional metropolises Leipzig and Dresden. The spatially isolated West Berlin is equivalent in its centrality to the West German regional metropolises Hamburg, Frankfurt and Munich.

The diagram for the year 1995 shows the urban system after the German unification. Although the government resides in Berlin again and also exhibits the greatest centrality, it does not show a clear hierarchy with one dominating city, but rather a multi-polar network of six or eight metropolises. It is highly unlikely that Berlin will regain its former central economic role again.

The Diversity of Urbanization

This historical sketch implicitly classifies Germany's urban network as a deviant or even deficient case in the hierarchy of the global urban system. Can Germany really be reduced to a special deficient case? An alternative explanation can be found in the discussion on national varieties of capitalism.[15] If it is true that modern capitalism is not a homogeneous entity, but that different models of capitalism have formed themselves under different historical conditions so that today we are confronted with divergent capitalisms, then it is not unlikely that these different models have correspondingly divergent patterns of urbanization.

The 'belated' industrial nation of Germany had already developed an alternative to the liberal production system at the end of the nineteenth century. This can be characterized as a form of regulated, corporate market economy.[16] The economic historian Werner Abelshauser gives reasons for the emergence of the specific German production regime, with its welfare state, market-oriented and interventionist components mainly the reactions to the economic backwardness of Germany compared to the dominating economic power of England: 'Germany, the belated industrial nation, was forced to face up to the economic and social structural changes of the late nineteenth century, wanted to overtake the leading industrial power, without being able to catch up in detail with its progress to date. It was the challenge of economic backwardness therefore, which led in numerous areas to the development of effective institutions.'[17] Germany's backwardness may have been a handicap in some ways, but it also offered opportunities. Above all, institutions for the protection of long-term economic and social interests – for example, in the modern welfare state, the transfer of technologies and education, cartel systems or political economic interventions – were more easily established than short-term, individual economic interests, because industrial citizenship still had a relatively limited political influence.

The emergence of the German production model was linked with the development and proliferation of a interregional network of industrial districts. In the process of Germany's industrialization it has developed 'more than elsewhere, numerous significant regional industrial districts of the economy … which represent

EMPLOYMENT IN CENTRAL PLACE FUNCTION IN THOUSANDS

1939

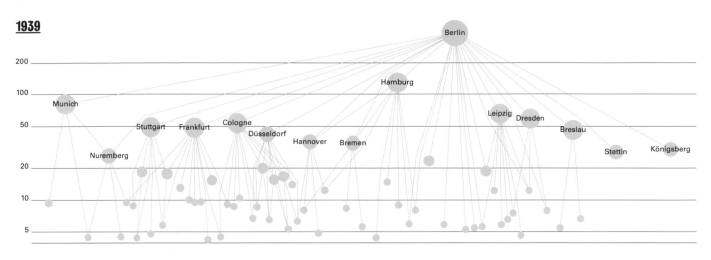

1970

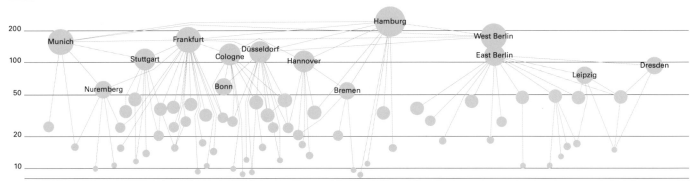

1995

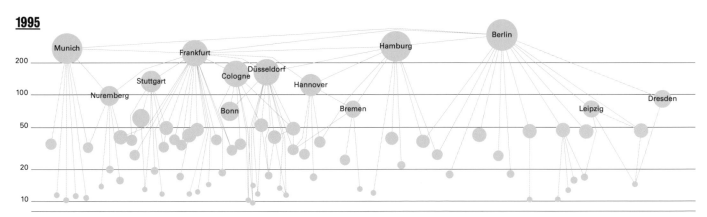

*Employment in branches of the tertiary sector with central
place function reduced by an estimated ration of employment
oriented towards self-supply of the cities population

integrated industrial regions each with specific specializations and comparative institutional advantages.'[18] The emergence of new institutions thus occurred in combination with the development of industrial regions at both regional and local levels.

This model of a corporate market economy and the distinct federal structure of the German state formed the basis for the economic and social system of West Germany after the devastation of World War II. It is likely that Germany has formed not only an alternative model of production, but also an alternative and effective model of urbanization. This model is characterized by its poly-centrality and its conditioning by the tradition of industrial districts as described by Abelshauser. According to him, these districts form 'the backbone of the German export industries because in the course of the twentieth century they had not only accumulated an attractive "industrial culture", but they must also clearly carry lower transaction costs as a result of an historically grown, trust-endowed institutional framework and therefore enjoyed distinct advantages over other regions.'[19]

Urban Employment Dynamics

Due to their specific manufacturing tradition, German companies concentrated on high-quality, customer-oriented niche products as an alternative to mass-produced products and global price competition.[20] With this highly diversified, export-oriented, high-quality manufacturing network, Germany established itself in the upper niches of the world market. This characteristically German production model and strategy led to the phenomenon of the regional service and manufacturing nexus. The globalization push in the 1980s and 1990s led, in Anglo-Saxon countries, to a strong geographical dispersal of manufacturing functions on a global scale – an important factor in the growth of strategic service functions in global cities. In contrast, the German development dynamics were based on the interconnection of knowledge-intensive manufacturing activities and advanced, knowledge-based producer services that manifested themselves in a regional service and industry nexus as well as regional service-manufacturing links.

Pioneering studies on the regional service-manufacturing links in West Germany have confirmed a strong correlation between employment in the two areas. They found that city-regions in which service-sector employment had increased also showed extraordinary growth rates in manufacturing employment – and vice versa. In other words, new service jobs have been created most notably in regions in which knowledge-intensive services and knowledge-intensive industries interact.[21]

In their empirical study on urban employment dynamics in Germany, Dietmar Darthe and Günther Schmidt come to the following conclusion: 'For economic and innovative strengths of a location, the intensity between knowledge-intensive industry and service branches is of paramount importance. In an ideal case this collaboration leads to the emergence of service-manufacturing districts, i.e. to innovative regional clusters of knowledge-intensive manufacturing and knowledge-intensive service branches …'[22]

The connection between the employment dynamic of advanced producer services and manufacturing in some German metropolitan regions for the period 1980 to 2001 is illustrated on page 241. Despite a strong deindustrialization during this period, a positive correlation can be seen. Conspicuous is the above-average growth rate for the Munich region in advanced producer services. It is particularly strong in technical services and still possesses a competitive core of high-tech manufacturing. The Ruhr region can in some ways be seen as a counterpoint to

Munich. In this low-performing region the link between manufacturing and services takes the form of a 'negative spiral'. The above-average deindustrialization, caused by the collapse of the mining and steel industries, reflects the below-average development of advanced producer services. The Rhine-Main region around Frankfurt shows high performance in the advanced producer services and relatively low performance in manufacturing; the strong, globally oriented financial services here are to a great extent detached from the industrial basis of the region.

Since the mid 1990s the relationship between manufacturing and services seems to have become more disconnected.[23] This supports the argument that the urban service economy is becoming increasingly independent from the industrial development of a region. There are indications that globalization and the shift from an industrial to a knowledge-based economy weaken the spatial ties between manufacturing production and services, especially knowledge-intensive services which interact more and more globally. Does this shift demonstrate a move by the German city towards the Anglo-Saxon model?

Just as there are significant reasons for the 'persistence of many capitalisms', there are also good arguments for a continuity of a specific pattern of urbanization.[24] First of all, the relationship between the development of manufacturing and services has not actually broken down – it has simply become more dispersed. Nevertheless, in most metropolitan regions there is still a competitive core of knowledge-intensive industries – which are crucial for a sustainable urban economy. Secondly, the different metropolises developed their specialist service-sector expertise in line with their traditional manufacturing expertise. Most of the specialized services are deeply grounded in the specific economic tradition of the city or the city-region.

The dynamics of globalization tend to weaken or even to dissolve the spatial ties between manufacturing production and services – knowledge-based services increasingly cater to a global market and service-production sites become integrated with cross-border networks. However, the current globalized competition also causes – as Pierre Veltz points out – 'the shift from a price-based competition to a more complex pattern, where quality, diversity and innovation, for goods and services, are becoming key factors of economic survival, and the traditional difference between price-based competition and differentiation is getting less and less clear, except for small niches'.[25] Faced with this new global competition, the possibility of reshaping networks of actors and value chains rapidly and efficiently becomes a key challenge. This challenge might function as a counterforce to the weakening of links between manufacturing production and knowledge-based services in the metropolitan economy. It might foster – besides forms of ongoing disconnection – new forms of re-connection between services and manufacturing functions.

Metropolization and Specialization

A very specific feature of the German metropolitan system is its complementary functional specialization. The division of labour between different city-regions has, since the 1980s, shown a new profiling through the emergence of specific clusters of knowledge-based services. In Germany metropolitan functions are not concentrated in a single global city but spatially distributed over different metropolitan regions. In this sense the process of metropolization is directly linked with a process of functional specialization.

The figures opposite demonstrate this process of increasing specialization. Their empirical basis is the calculation of 'location quotients' as a measure for the

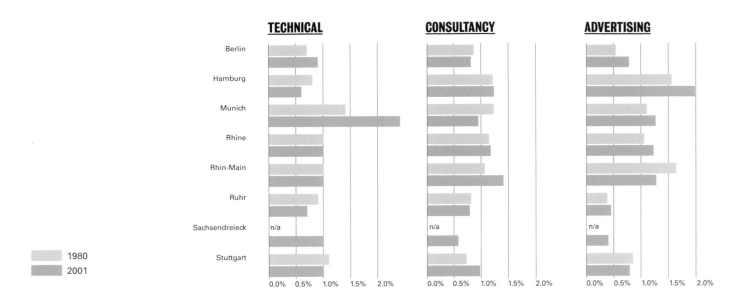

	TECHNICAL	CONSULTANCY	ADVERTISING
Berlin			
Hamburg			
Munich			
Rhine			
Rhin-Main			
Ruhr			
Sachsendreieck	n/a	n/a	n/a
Stuttgart			

1980
2001

0.0% 0.5% 1.0% 1.5% 2.0%

LOCATING DYNAMIC SECTORS

The location of major economic sectors reflects the polycentric character of Germany's metropolitan network. The graphs represent the location in 1980 and 2001 of technical services (left), knowledge-based economic sectors such as consultancy, including accountancy (middle), and advertising (right).

degree of specialization of a region in a specific economic branch. The spatial reference base for the calculation of the location quotient is the totality of the observed metropolitan regions. It thus allows a ranking of the regions for the respective years of the calculation.[26]

The left figure above shows the ranking for technical services. For 1980 it still shows a relatively balanced picture with Munich, Stuttgart and Rhine-Main as group leaders. In the period until 2001, Munich breaks away to take up a clear lead. Sachsendreieck surprisingly takes second position. Munich, Germany's high-tech industry region, is unchallenged among the German metropolitan regions as the centre of the knowledge-based technological services.

The middle figure above shows the development of the specialization in the areas of consultancy, including accountancy (knowledge-based economic services). Here too, in 1980 there is still a relatively balanced structure with a very broad leading group led by Munich. In the period until 2001 a major change occurs. By 2001 Rhine-Main and Hamburg take the lead and Munich falls back. The strong position of Rhine-Main in economic services is strongly linked to Frankfurt's dominant role as an international finance centre. It has been assumed that there are diverse interactions between the economic and finance services. The strong position of Hamburg in this area is probably connected with Hamburg's central role as a trade and international commerce centre, which again is marked through its tradition as a seaport.

The right figure above shows the ranking for 'advertising', an important part of the culture-based creative services. In 1980 there was already a clear specialization in this area, with Rhine-Main and Hamburg in the higher ranks. By 2001 Hamburg had clearly become the centre of this economy. In the 1980s advertising was still strongly connected with the economic services; therefore Frankfurt/Rhine-Main still held leading positions.[27] Hamburg's ascent was considerably favoured through the potential of its media clusters. An important economic impulse resulted from the privatization of television.

These figures illustrate an increasing specialization of the German metropolitan regions, in particular clusters of knowledge- and cultural-based services and the emergence of a complementary division of labour. These functional specialization processes are linked with both increasing forms of disembedding and the fostering

GLOBAL ECONOMIC SUPREMACY

Germany's largest cities are part of multi-tiered economic networks, showing strong functional relations with smaller domestic centres as well as European and global nodes. While lacking an overarching 'global city', Germany has numerous metropolitan centres with high levels of specialization.

of new forms of re-embedding of the transregional and global market-oriented services into the production context of the respective urban economies. The specific mode of operation of these 'post-Fordist' labour markets mould to a large extent, mutually reinforcing processes of metropolization and specialization.

A Multi-tiered Network of Cities

In order to clarify the German city system and the specific role of the network of complementary metropolitan regions, we have focused on the city, city-regions and national levels. However, the analysis of global cities or globalized city-regions like this should take a global rather than a national perspective. As Saskia Sassen points out, a global city is by definition part of a cross-border network. Therefore we should finally engage with the question of the transnational interdependence of the German metropolitan region.

Given the strong orientation of the German economy towards the global economy and the significantly advanced European economic integration, it is obvious that the German urban system is highly open and connected to both the European and global networks of cities. However, the German metropolitan regions take in a particular 'cross-section' position between the global and the national economic systems with their particular institutions, organizational forms and infrastructural transport and communication supplies.[28]

There are only a few substantiated empirical analyses of the inter-urban and transnational relationships of German metropolitan regions.[29] Through the analysis of location networks of knowledge-intensive services, Fischer et al. examined in the context of the Globalization and World Cities Study Group and Network (GaWC), how and to what degree the metropolitan region Rhine-Main is tied into the international World City Network. They concluded that on an international level the strongest connections exist with London, Paris and New York.[30] However, an above-average connection can also be seen with East Asian cities like Hong Kong, Beijing, Shanghai and Tokyo.[31] Within the German city system, Frankfurt/Rhine-Main is

EMPLOYMENT IN CENTRAL PLACE FUNCTION IN THOUSANDS

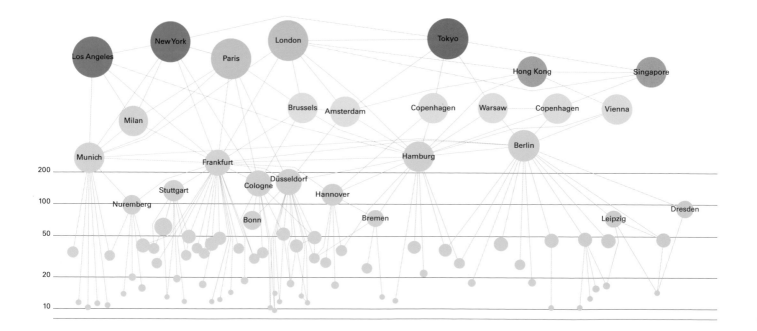

connected particularly intensively with Berlin, Munich, Hamburg, Düsseldorf, Stuttgart and Cologne.[32]

The inter-urban and transnational relationships of interdependencies are always marked by both competition and cooperation. London and Frankfurt are competitors, especially since the establishment of the European Central Bank in Frankfurt, but they also have mutually cooperative relationships. Generally one can establish that each German metropolis can only advance its capacity and innovativeness within its framework of specialization with the help of effective national and transnational networks and forms of cooperation. There are very close forms of collaboration between the advertising economy of Hamburg and those of London, Paris, Vienna, New York and Hong Kong. Munich, with its businesses in the research and development sector, has very developed forms of cooperation with the technology regions of Grenoble, Boston or Silicon Valley, as well as with the global cities London, New York and Tokyo.

In this sense the German metropolitan regions are in many ways tied into a multi-tiered network. In the figure on page 242 the national hierarchy profile of the German city system, as illustrated by Blotevogel for 1995 (see the figure on page 238), is supplemented by an heuristic sketch of transnational relationships of interdependencies and collaborations. This figures illustrates the multiple ways in which the German metropolitan regions are embedded in global, European and national and regional relationships.

Observing the German city and metropolitan system from the perspective of its integration in these multi-tiered networks, the absence of a German city high up in the hierarchy of global cities must not necessarily be seen as a deficit. The multiple levels of integration of the German metropolitan system result in a high capacity for performance and innovation, but also a great flexibility and adaptability. Therefore, the German metropolitan system could prove to be a valid alternative to the highly centralized model of the global city of the future.

UNDERSTANDING THE CITY

The relationship between the physical structure of cities and the social and economic lives of their residents is captured by this selection of variables, providing an overview of the DNA of the six Urban Age cities. By comparing the population of each city to its average density and the levels of water or energy each resident consumes, these variables give an indication of how populations are concentrated and how cities makes use of their resources. The dramatic variation in socio-economic well-being, purchasing power and sense of security is captured by other parameters that describe variations in crime, cost of housing and travel – reflecting differing dynamics between each city and its national and regional economy.

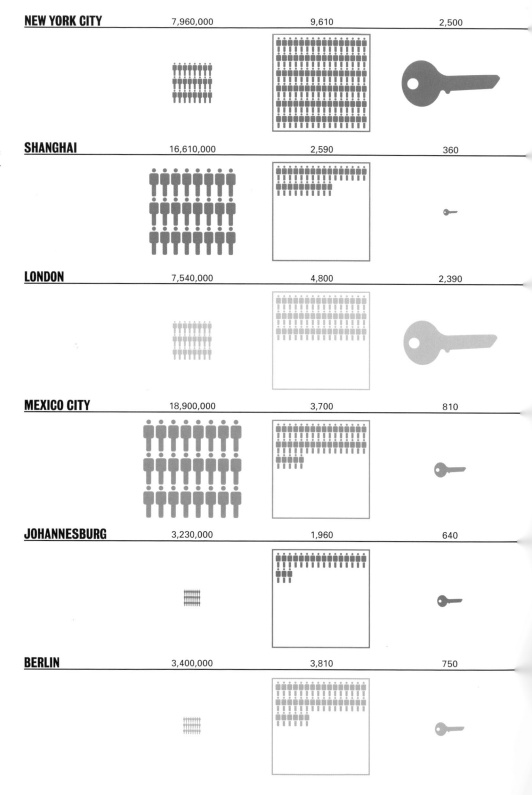

	SIZE Population	**DENSITY** Average density people/km²	**HOUSING** Average rent per month in US$
NEW YORK CITY	7,960,000	9,610	2,500
SHANGHAI	16,610,000	2,590	360
LONDON	7,540,000	4,800	2,390
MEXICO CITY	18,900,000	3,700	810
JOHANNESBURG	3,230,000	1,960	640
BERLIN	3,400,000	3,810	750

INCOME	WEALTH	TRAVEL	CRIME	ENERGY	WATER	AGE
GDP per capita in US$	Working time required in minutes to buy 1 kg of bread	Average cost of public transport ticket in US$	Murder rate per 100,000 inhabitants	kWh per capita per annum	Litres per capita per day	Average age
58,700	16	2.0	6.7	63,000	500	35.8
6,900	35	0.5	1.5	5,600	1,860	37.7
38,400	5	2.7	2.1	20,500	160	36.5
16,400	53	0.2	17.6	1,800	360	29
5,100	12	1.2	18.9	5,600	380	29.1
28,300	10	2.5	1.4	21,600	160	42.2

THE ECONOMY OF CITIES

The distribution of employment by sector in the Urban Age cities shows the extent to which cities have changed into service-based economies. In all of the cities, the service sector employs more than half of the urban labour force. This transition appears the most far reaching in New York City and London where less than 10 per cent of the urban labour force is engaged in industrial activities. Yet, cities are far from becoming mono-cultural 'office economies'; in fact, financial and business services are the main employment category only in London. Even in New York, it is 'other services' that make up almost half of the city's employment base. This broad category includes a diverse range of urban activities including personal, social, health, educational and entertainment services. All of these niche activities require specialized work places from which they can contribute most efficiently to the urban economy. The reduced share of urban manufacturing does not diminish the importance of this sector within urban production complexes supporting leading sectors of a city's economy. Moreover, Shanghai, one of the fastest growing urban economies in the world, retains an important manufacturing base. Shanghai's various industries employ up to a third of the city's labour force, making it one of the pillars of this rapidly expanding global economic node.

NEW YORK CITY

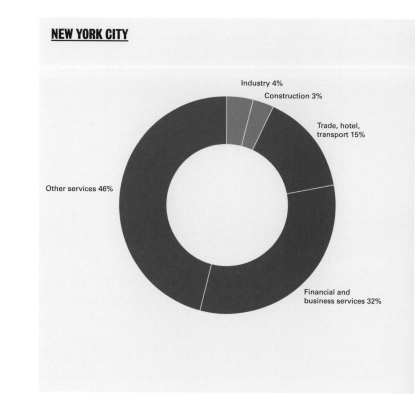

Industry 4%
Construction 3%
Trade, hotel, transport 15%
Other services 46%
Financial and business services 32%

MEXICO CITY

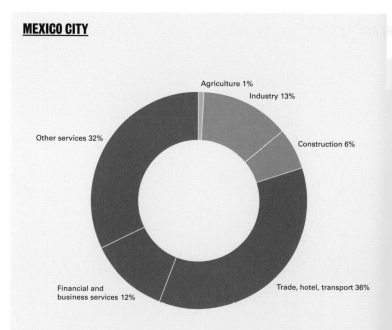

Agriculture 1%
Industry 13%
Construction 6%
Other services 32%
Financial and business services 12%
Trade, hotel, transport 36%

SHANGHAI

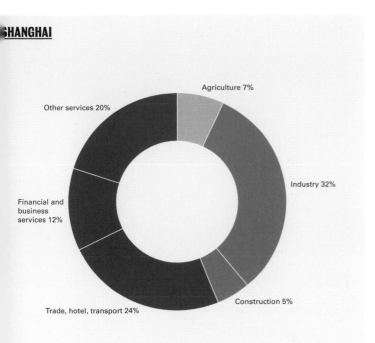

Agriculture 7%

Other services 20%

Industry 32%

Financial and business services 12%

Trade, hotel, transport 24%

Construction 5%

LONDON

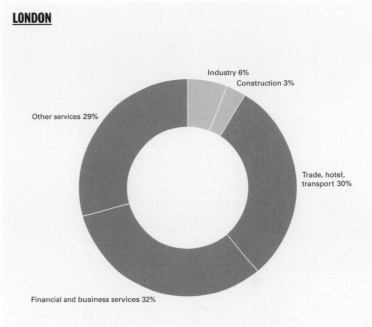

Industry 6%

Construction 3%

Other services 29%

Trade, hotel, transport 30%

Financial and business services 32%

JOHANNESBURG

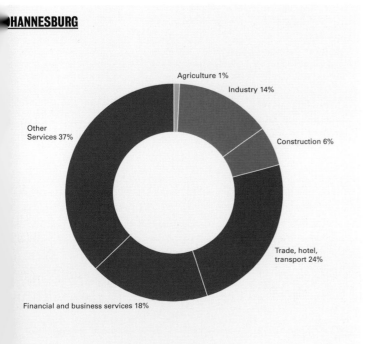

Agriculture 1%

Industry 14%

Other Services 37%

Construction 6%

Trade, hotel, transport 24%

Financial and business services 18%

BERLIN

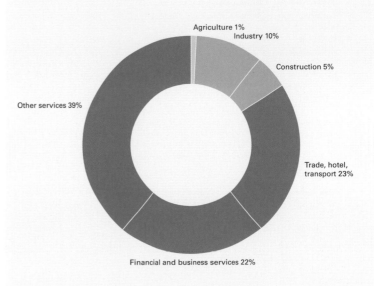

Agriculture 1%

Industry 10%

Construction 5%

Other services 39%

Trade, hotel, transport 23%

Financial and business services 22%

GOVERNING THE NEW METROPOLIS

The territorial reach and administrative infrastructure of the six Urban Age cities varies significantly, impacting strongly on how they are governed and able to respond to the process of urban change. The diagrams illustrate how traditional city boundaries have been overtaken by population growth spilling out into the surrounding city-regions, an emerging characteristic of the twenty-first century city. Mexico City, for example, has outgrown the confines of the Federal District, expanding well into the neighbouring State of Mexico and creating an administrative disjunction between where people live and who determines their future. Berlin, too, has experienced more rapid growth in its metropolitan hinterland than in its urban core. Like New York City, London is now controlled by a single municipal entity – the Greater London Authority – but is surrounded by the Green Belt that successfully limits urban growth. Johannesburg's population of 3.2 million occupies the same footprint as London's nearly 8 million inhabitants and sits within the Gauteng Province, one of Africa's most rapidly developing urban regions. Shanghai constitutes an exception, with its Municipality operating as a city-state with over 6,300 square kilometres and more than 16.6 million inhabitants.

Metropolitan region
——————— City boundary
——————— Administrative unit boundaries

NEW YORK METROPOLITAN REGION
21,200,000 people
NEW YORK CITY: 5 BOROUGHS
7,960,000 people

MEXICO CITY METROPOLITAN REGION
18,900,000 people
MEXICO CITY: 16 DELEGACIONES
8,720,000 people

SOUTH-EAST OF ENGLAND

19,030,000 people

LONDON: 33 BOROUGHS

7,540,000 people

UTENG PROVINCE

60,000 people

HANNESBURG: 11 REGIONS

30,000 people

BERLIN METROPOLITAN REGION

4,390,000 people

BERLIN: 12 BEZIRKE

3,400,000 people

DENSITY AND URBANITY

The world cities studied by the Urban Age present divergent distributions of urban density, land-use arrangements and growth models. The highest gross residential density peak is reached in some central city neighbourhoods of Shanghai, which accommodate over 90,000 people per square kilometre. Overall, Shanghai and New York City are the densest cities in the group – the low average density of Shanghai is simply a result of its vast administrative area that includes a significant amount of open space. Mexico City does not reach Manhattan-like peaks in its centre and maintains a more homogeneous high density throughout its entire urban area. The two European cities, London and Berlin, demonstrate a more even spread of residential density across the geographical surface. Johannesburg, on the other hand, shows an even more fragmented and disjointed distribution, reflecting the higher densities of former black townships and the dramatic loss of residents in the downtown area. Each city's density model covers an area of 100 x 100 km.

On the diagrams:
Central area: average within central area of 10 km radius
Administrative boundary: average within administrative boundary

NEW YORK CITY

Central area 15,361 people/km²
Administrative boundary 9,600 people/km²
Peak 53,000 people/km²

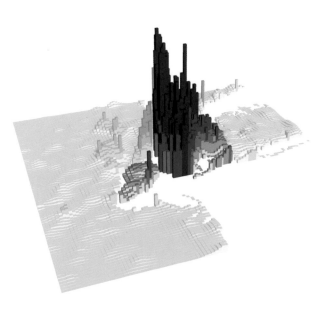

MEXICO CITY

Central area 12,541 people/km²
Administrative boundary 5,880 people/km²
Peak 48,300 people/km²

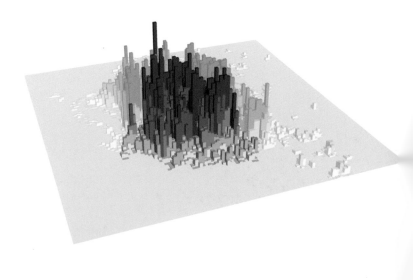

SHANGHAI

Central area 24,673 people/km²
Administrative boundary 2,590 people/km²
Peak 96,200 people/km²

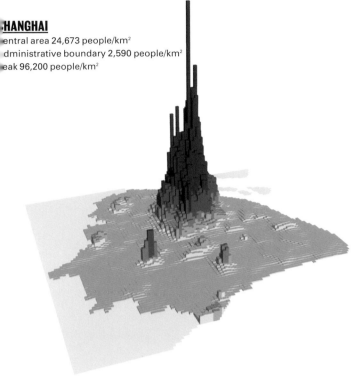

LONDON

Central area 7,805 people/km²
Administrative boundary 4,800 people/km²
Peak 17,200 people/km²

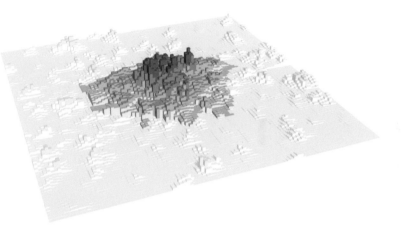

JOHANNESBURG

Central area 2,270 people/km²
Administrative boundary 1,960 people/km²
Peak 38,500 people/km²

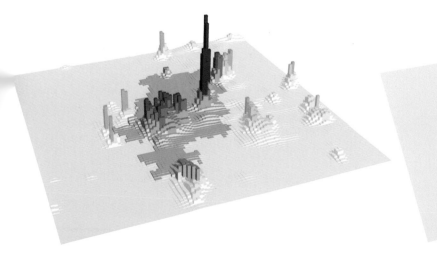

BERLIN

Central area 7,124 people/km²
Administrative boundary 3,810 people/km²
Peak 21,700 people/km²

ACCOMMODATING DIFFERENCE

Avoiding social exclusion is one of the biggest challenges for contemporary cities as economic growth enhances social inequality. Concentrations of social disadvantage assume different geographical patterns in different places. Exclusion is evident in decayed inner cities, as well as some areas of central, East and South London, with more affluent people concentrated around the periphery, while in New York City the poor are concentrated in the outer boroughs of Queens, Brooklyn and the Bronx. Many cities relegate their disadvantaged populations to underserved metropolitan peripheries. This is the case in Shanghai and Mexico City. A combination of both patterns appears in Berlin and Johannesburg: the spatial patterns of social disadvantage also reflect their singular development histories and recent transformations.

Level of relative social disadvantage

Privileged
Average
Disadvantaged
Severely disadvantaged
——————— City boundaries
——————— Municipal districts

NEW YORK CITY

Central Park

MEXICO CITY

Zócalo

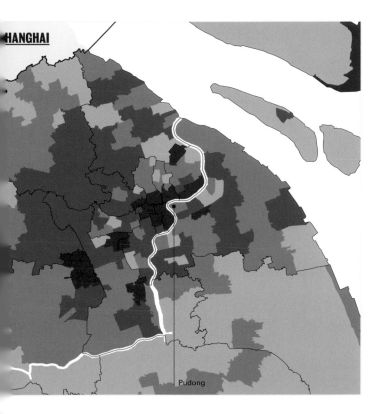

SHANGHAI

Pudong

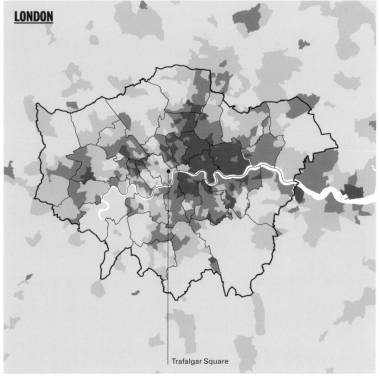

LONDON

Trafalgar Square

JOHANNESBURG

Downtown

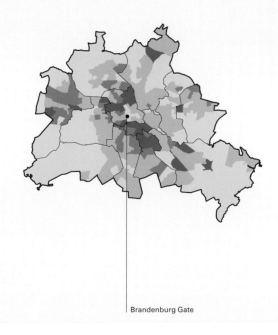

BERLIN

Brandenburg Gate

LIVING WITH CHILDREN

The ability of cities to accommodate young people and families is an important factor in determining their long-term economic and social sustainability. For this reason, city leaders are beginning to focus policies on improving the quality of inner-city schools as well as the provision of social facilities for young people in traditional urban cores. With the single exception of the increasing attraction of central Berlin for young couples with children, many western cities reflect an established trend where families move out of the city centre in search of more space and higher quality environments.

New York City's Manhattan stands out as a relative child-free zone, as do many parts of central London, while outer boroughs and suburban areas accommodate a greater percentage of families with children. Shanghai and Johannesburg also illustrate the effects of fertility rates, which are generally low in the former and differentiated by racial groups in the latter.

Percentage of population of 19 years or younger

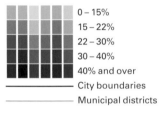

0 – 15%
15 – 22%
22 – 30%
30 – 40%
40% and over
——————— City boundaries
——————— Municipal districts

NEW YORK CITY

Central Park

MEXICO CITY

Zócalo

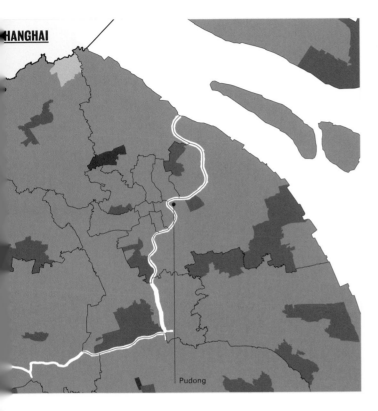

SHANGHAI

Pudong

LONDON

Trafalgar Square

JOHANNESBURG

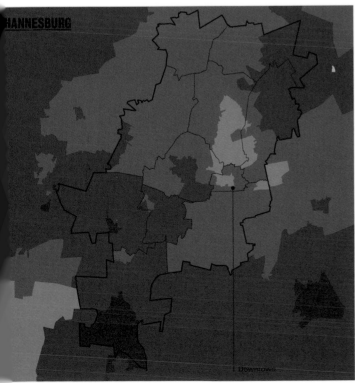

Downtown

BERLIN

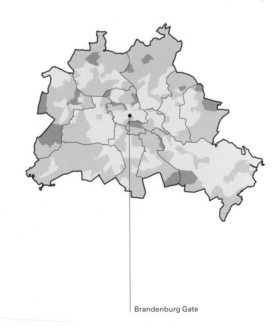

Brandenburg Gate

FINDING WORK

Cities are the powerhouses of the global economy and respond to changing needs in the formal and informal employment sectors. The ability to accommodate urban change and economic restructuring is a sign of resilience that determines their potential to succeed or fail as places where people have access to jobs and wealth. The six Urban Age cities demonstrate a very varied distribution of jobs across their urban terrains, with unemployment often connected to areas of relative social exclusion and urban decay. London, Berlin and Shanghai present high unemployment rates in their older industrial cores, while the problem is more acute in peripheral areas of Johannesburg to which the African population used to be confined. Both economic restructuring and residential segregation explain New York's complex patterns. Unemployment is rather hidden in Mexico City, given the large informal economy where many workers have refuge, albeit in much less stable and socially vulnerable conditions.

Unemployment

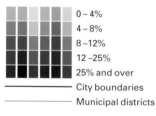

	0 – 4%
	4 – 8%
	8 –12%
	12 –25%
	25% and over
————	City boundaries
————	Municipal districts

NEW YORK CITY

Central Park

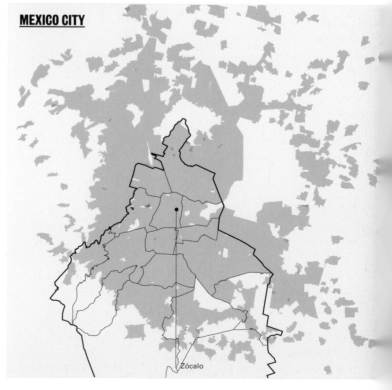

MEXICO CITY

Zócalo

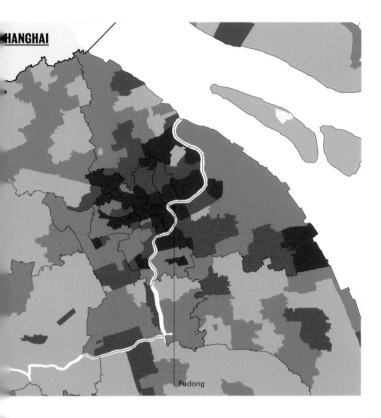

SHANGHAI

Pudong

LONDON

Trafalgar Square

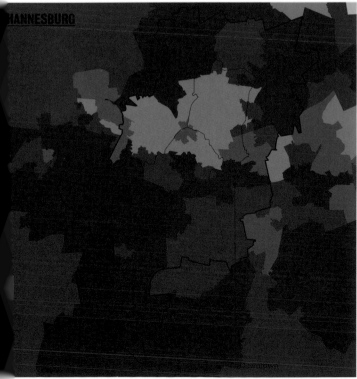

JOHANNESBURG

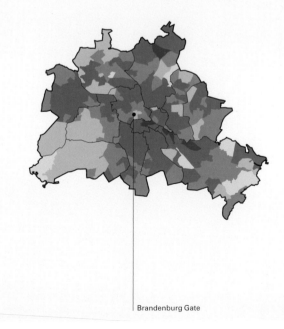

BERLIN

Brandenburg Gate

MOVING IN THE CITY

Transport infrastructure and mobility patterns in the six Urban Age cities offer a striking illustration of specific geographic, historic and political conditions. Mature cities like New York City, London and Berlin are characterized by an extensive urban rail system, relying on a network of regional rail and good connections to intercity rail. In Shanghai, Mexico City and Johannesburg, exponential growth and infrastructure building came much later. Mexico City began construction of its underground in the late 1960s and now operates a 200-km-long network. Despite its reliability and efficiency, it is used by only 14 per cent of the population with minibus services accounting for more than half of all trips. Johannesburg has no underground system and most of its 120-km surface rail serves only older areas, while the majority of new affluent developments rely on private cars. The 12,500 privately run mini-taxis are used for 20 per cent of all trips to work, with 40 per cent still done by foot. Shanghai's system is 65 km long with another 10 lines, totalling 218 km, under construction to keep up with the 23 per cent of daily trips to work using rail, metro or bus.

—————————— Inter-city rail

—————————— Rail

—————————— Underground/subway

-------------------- Planned extensions

UNDERGROUND/SUBWAY LENGTH

New York City 390 km

Shanghai 148 km

London 408 km

Mexico City 200 km

Johannesburg 0 km

Berlin 144 km

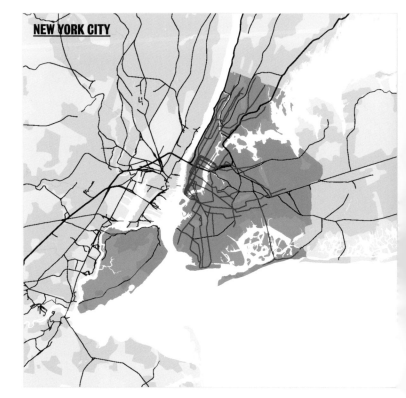

NEW YORK CITY

MEXICO CITY

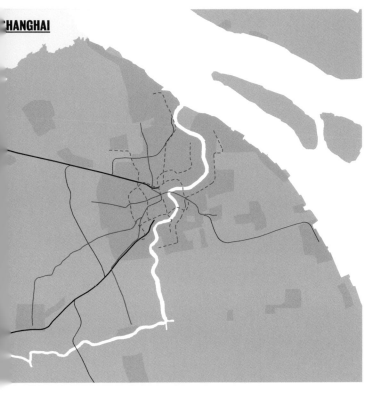

SHANGHAI

LONDON

JOHANNESBURG

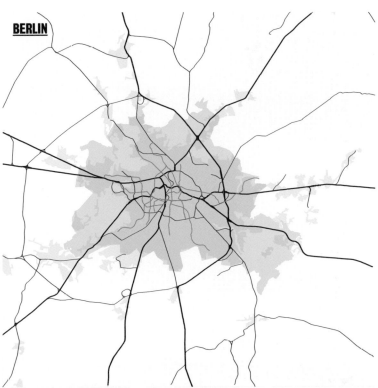

BERLIN

HOW PEOPLE MOVE

These diagrams illustrate how people get to work in the six Urban Age cities. Over 50 per cent of New Yorkers use public transport – bus, tram and subway – while around 30 per cent of Londoners use its extensive underground and bus system, close to the 27 per cent of all Berliners. Cycling is still prevalent in Shanghai, although many bicycles are being replaced by cars. Despite their lower economic profiles, Johannesburg and Mexico City display different patterns of public transport use, with a significant proportion of lower-income groups left with no other way of getting to work than on foot in Johannesburg. At the opposite end of the economic scale, 40 per cent of midtown residents in New York's Manhattan walk to work and over 90 per cent of affluent business workers use public transport to go to London's financial hub.

CAR OWNERSHIP (PER 1,000)

New York City 210

Shanghai 38

London 341

Mexico City 383

Johannesburg 183

Berlin 361

ROAD FATALITIES (PER 100,000)

New York City 4.1

Shanghai 2.5

London 2.9

Mexico City 28.7

Johannesburg 25.5

Berlin 2.0

NEW YORK CITY

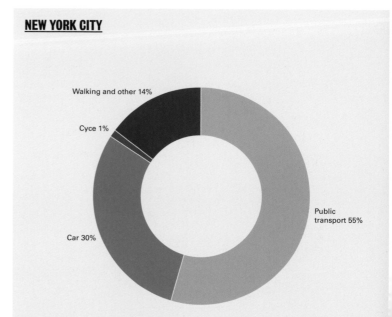

Walking and other 14%

Cyce 1%

Car 30%

Public transport 55%

MEXICO CITY

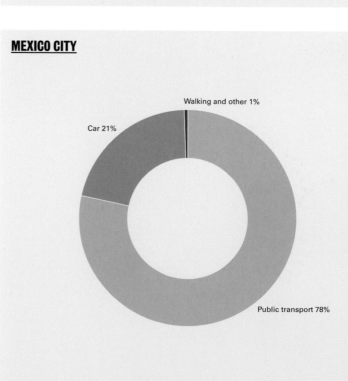

Walking and other 1%

Car 21%

Public transport 78%

SHANGHAI

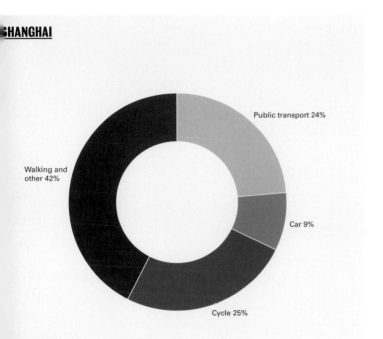

Public transport 24%

Car 9%

Cycle 25%

Walking and other 42%

LONDON

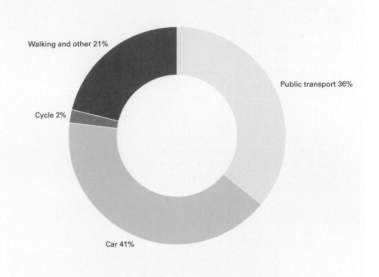

Walking and other 21%

Public transport 36%

Cycle 2%

Car 41%

JOHANNESBURG

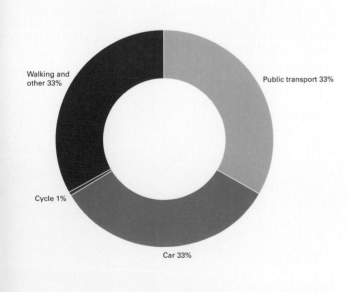

Public transport 33%

Walking and other 33%

Cycle 1%

Car 33%

BERLIN

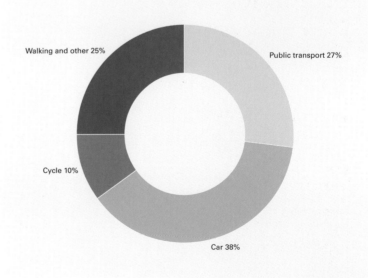

Walking and other 25%

Public transport 27%

Cycle 10%

Car 38%

DIVERSITY IN NEW YORK CITY AND LONDON

New York City and London are both highly
diverse and multi-cultural: people from all over
the world have settled there, and have transformed the ethnic composition and economic
resilience of these cities. New York City is one
of the few 'majority-minority' metropolises of
the United States and London is called 'the first
post-national city' in the UK. Both cities show
enclaves of ethnic concentration, but in New
York City these areas are also associated with
pockets of social deprivation creating a greater
sense of 'ghettoisation'. In London, which has
recently experienced an influx of immigrants
from the wider European community, the correlation is more diffuse with many Asian communities dispersed across more affluent areas of
the capital.

Percentage of population from ethnic minorities

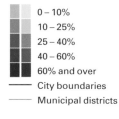

0 – 10%
10 – 25%
25 – 40%
40 – 60%
60% and over
—— City boundaries
—— Municipal districts

NEW YORK CITY

Central Park

LONDON

Trafalgar Square

TRANSPORT IN NEW YORK CITY AND LONDON

New York achieved its initial metropolitan development relying on a comprehensive public transport system that allowed a large part of the population to reach employment clusters in the city's centre. To some extent this has also been the case in London. Both cities now have extensive public transport networks, on which millions of commuters rely daily. The use of public transport decreases as one moves away from the urban core. Providing sustainable transport solutions to the ever-expanding functional area in each city is one of the biggest challenges in the twenty-first century.

Percentage of population travelling to work by public transport

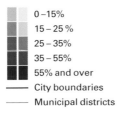

- 0 –15%
- 15 – 25 %
- 25 – 35%
- 35 – 55%
- 55% and over
- —— City boundaries
- —— Municipal districts

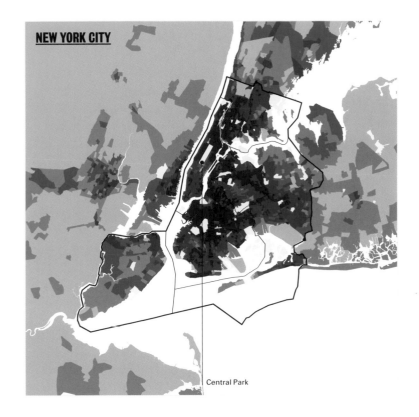

NEW YORK CITY

Central Park

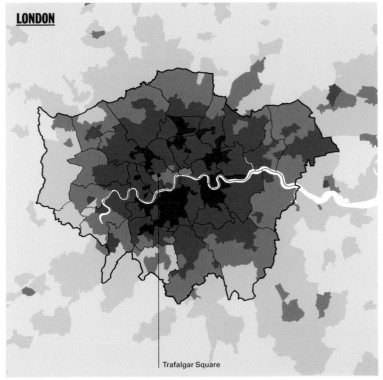

LONDON

Trafalgar Square

URBAN GRAIN

The arrangement of buildings, streets and open spaces defines the urban grain and character of a city. By showing the buildings in black and the open spaces in grey – all at the same scale of 1 square kilometre – the figure-ground images of distinct urban neighbourhoods in each of the Urban Age cities reveal different spatial characteristics and social dynamics at street level. The dense, continuous grid of New York City's East Village or informal settlements in Mexico City's north-eastern neighbourhoods contrasts dramatically with the relative sparseness in the barren landscape of Shanghai's Hongkoo district. Johannesburg's more dispersed residential neighbourhoods, often surrounded by high-security fences and walls, lack the sense of continuity of the resilient Notting Hill area in West London or the tightly packed perimeter housing block of central Berlin. In the following pages, aerial views of the six Urban Age cities – also shown at the same scale of 1:15,000 – re-emphasize the variety of morphological character that accounts for the diverse urban experiences offered by New York City, Shanghai, London, Mexico City, Johannesburg and Berlin.

NEW YORK CITY, EAST VILLAGE

MEXICO CITY, GUSTAVO A. MADERO DELEGACION

SHANGHAI, HONGKOO DISTRICT

LONDON, NOTTING HILL

JOHANNESBURG, SANDTON

BERLIN, PRENZLAUER BERG

SEEING LIKE A CITY

Saskia Sassen

Periods of rapid transition make change visible. The speed of change itself makes novel patterns legible. When the object of study is cities, or more generally urban regions, legibility is even more pronounced – the material reality of buildings, transport systems, and other components of spatial organization are on the surface, so to speak. When rapid transformation occurs simultaneously in several cities or urban regions with at least some comparable conditions, what also becomes visible is the variability of spatial outcomes that may result from similar novel dynamics.

In its trek across six global cities, the Urban Age team brought to the fore this mix of shared underlying dynamics and variable spatial forms. Firstly, all six cities have seen increases in density, but the spatial forms through which density functions vary sharply across these cities. The elusive quality we in the West have come to call urbanity might well be present with its own specific features, even when unrecognizable to our limited gaze. The notion of 'cityness' is one way of unpacking that category and allowing for far greater variations in what constitutes urbanity. Seen this way, cityness is a critical feature, even though some of the forms such cityness assumes are almost illegible to the foreigner. This opens up a whole field for research and interpretation, and invites us to reposition western notions of urbanity. Thirdly, the question of economic informality assumed a whole new set of meanings and contents. While present in all, the juxtaposing of New York and London with Mexico City and Johannesburg allowed us to see the emergence of a new type of informal economy, which is nevertheless often obscured by the vastness and continuity of older informal economies, particularly in the cases of Mexico City and Johannesburg. In Shanghai and Berlin, on the other hand, informality has taken on expanded meanings, moving into highly creative professional activities in highly visible ways.

Lastly, and perhaps as elusive as the question of cityness, we identified two contradictory dynamics in the relation between underlying economic dynamics, and spatial forms and physical typologies. On the one hand, similar underlying economic dynamics across these cities materialize through different geographical patterns and built environments. Given similar underlying dynamics, the morphological variation of these cities highlights the diverse constraints that shape the territorialization of global dynamics across different cities and urban regions. This finding contests the common notion that differences in spatial form suggest different economies or, more typically, different stages of economic development, with the geographically dispersed and multipolar region of Los Angeles often seen as the new spatial form.

On the other hand, we found that similar spatial forms and built environments can house different economic activities, when such activities are viewed as a way of capturing specialization and differences. Other than Berlin, all the Urban Age cities have major financial exchanges and financial centres with densely built environments, yet they often differ widely in their financial practice and global financial circuits.

These four major trends became legible largely through the combination of our rapid progress across these six cities and the specialized knowledge of each city's expert community of researchers and practitioners. It is this mix of mobility and depth that differentiates the Urban Age from other urban research projects.

Economic Topography

The typical account of economic globalization emphasizes hypermobility, global communications and the neutralization of place and distance. The global economy is taken as a given, arising out of the power of transnational corporations and global communications technologies. But if we focus on the fact that power and communications capacities need to be produced, implemented, managed, we begin to introduce a range of place-bound dimensions that vary between locations. In short, we begin to recover the possibility that cities matter to the global economy. Instead of power and communication capacities per se, the emphasis shifts to the practices that constitute what we call 'economic globalization' and 'global control': the work of producing and reproducing, the organization and management of global economies and markets. Such work is easily overlooked in accounts centred on the hypermobility of capital and the power of transnational corporations. This does not deny that hypermobility and power are critical, but rather it brings to the fore the fact that many of the resources necessary for global economic activities are not hyper-mobile and are, indeed, deeply embedded in place, notably in global cities.

The vast new economic topography being implemented through electronic space is one moment, one fragment, of a vast economic chain that is in part embedded in non-electronic spaces. There is no fully dematerialized firm or industry. Even the most advanced information industries, such as finance, are installed only partly in electronic space; this is also true of industries that make digital products such as software. The growing digitization of economic activities has not eliminated the need for major international business and financial centres and all the material resources they concentrate, from state-of-the-art telematics infrastructure to brain talent.

Globalization can be deconstructed in terms of the strategic sites where global processes and the linkages that bind them materialize. Among these sites are export-processing zones, offshore banking centres and, on a far more complex level, global cities. Together these sites generate a specific geography of globalization and make it clear that it is not a planetary event, nor does it resemble an expanding oil slick. It is a lumpy geography. It is a geography that has changed over the last few centuries and especially the last few decades, and has included diverse types of sites. Mines, plantations and merchant markets have been sites in the world economy for millennia. And so have cities. Today that geography has come to include electronic space.

Once we bring place and work into analyses of the global economy – particularly as these are constituted in major cities (rather than in coffee plantations, for example) – we begin to see the multiplicity of economies and work cultures in which the global information economy is embedded (see pages 248–9). Even the most global and advanced firms and financial exchanges need cleaners, lorry drivers, secretaries. This brings into the picture the neighbourhooods in which the workers live, whether

THE URBAN ECONOMIC CHAIN
Fragments of informal economic exchange in cities have an extensive impact on the livelihood of residents across all spectrums of the urban food chain, as evidenced by the street beggar exploiting the stationary traffic on one of Shanghai's new urban motorways.

MONGREL CITIES

The imagined city pictured above is constituted
by a pastiche of elements imported from urban
landscapes around the globe. This twenty-first
century form is defined by iconic structures
littered across a high-density sprawl contained
only by the natural landscape.

high-income professionals or migrant workers. The construction workers in downtown Shanghai and the cleaners on Wall Street belong to advanced economic sectors. Much of this is missed when we focus on hypermobile electronic financial networks or on global commodity markets.

What feeds this expanding urban footprint of global capital, including its electronic components, is the fact that global markets and global firms need central places in which to conduct the most complex work of globalization. Firms that can function in electronic networks also need a vast physical infrastructure for connectivity – the capacity for global communication is different from the material conditions that make this possible. Focusing on cities allows us to specify a geography of strategic places on a global scale – places bound to one another by the dynamics of economic globalization. It amounts to a new geography of centrality. Together, the cities that constitute this geography function as a socio-technical infrastructure for a new global political economy, but also for new cultural and social spaces.

One of the questions this raises is whether this new transnational geography is also the space for new transnational politics by traditionally disadvantaged and isolated actors. This geography is dominated by flows of capital, services, information, goods and the new transnational professionals. But it also contains a broad array of workers and work cultures, including types that despite appearances belong to globalized advanced sectors. The global economy is the workplace not only for high-level professionals but also for a growing number of disadvantaged employees – factory workers in export processing zones in the vast manufacturing fields around Shanghai and Hong Kong, garment sweatshop workers in London and New York, traders from Nigeria in the central marketplace in downtown Johannesburg, poor foreign students in Berlin – doing all kinds of informal professional work for global firms.

Armed with statistics about how each of our cities fits into the circuits of global firms and global markets, the urban landscapes of each should be read through these lenses. Particular processes, built environments and spatial forms in each city *are* the concrete and localized channels through which globalization exists and functions. Density is a marker of the business centres of all our cities, but its spatial forms and locations can vary sharply: Johannesburg and Mexico City's central spaces are increasingly housed in edge cities and not necessarily high-rise buildings. New York, London and Shanghai build up their centres and they do so with corporate towers. Within these distinct spatial forms there is homogenizing of the built environment's visual order, especially in state-of-the-art office districts and in luxury commercial and residential spaces. What inhabits those homogenized state-of-the-art built office districts can vary greatly to the point that these districts could be seen as akin to a new type of infrastructure for the new corporate advanced economy: we are seeing a repositioning of the meaning of built environments.

Centres and Margins

Cities have long been at the intersection of multiple worldwide circuits. Fernand Braudel has given us one of the most detailed accounts of fifteenth- and sixteenth-century European world cities and their networks. What began to change in the 1980s was their proliferation and their increasingly complex organizational and financial frameworks. It is the new challenge of coordinating, managing and servicing these increasingly complex, specialized and vast economic circuits that has made cities strategic.

Perhaps one of the great ironies of our global digital age is that it has produced not only massive dispersal but also extreme concentrations of top-level resources in a limited number of places. Indeed, the organizational side of today's global economy is located, and continuously reinvented, in what has become a network of about 40 major and lesser global cities. These need to be distinguished from the hundreds of cities located on often just a few global circuits: while these cities are articulated with the global economy they lack the mix of resources that enables them to manage and service the global operations of firms and markets.

To understand the nature of the relationship between cities and the global economy, it helps to specify the multiple global circuits through which cities are connecting across borders. Particular networks link particular groups of cities. This allows us to recover details about the diverse roles of cities in the global economy. Some of these intercity geographies are thick and highly visible – the flows of professionals, tourists, artists and migrants between specific groups of cities (see pages 30–1). Others are thin and barely visible – the highly specialized electronic financial trading networks that connect particular cities, depending on the type of instrument involved. Somewhere in the middle are global commodity chains for diverse products and exporting and importing hubs.

These circuits are multidirectional and crisscross the world, feeding into intercity geographies with both expected and unexpected strategic nodes. For instance, if we consider the leading global markets for trading financial instruments on commodities, we see that New York dominates coffee and London dominates platinum, but Shanghai, a far less powerful financial centre, now dominates copper. Cities located on global circuits, whether few or many, become part of distinct and often highly specialized intercity geographies. Thus, in tracking the global circuits of gold as a financial instrument, London, New York, Chicago and Zurich dominate. In tracking the direct trading in the metal, Johannesburg becomes a critical node on the map.

This networked system also feeds unnecessary mobilities, because the intermediary economy of specialized services thrives on mobilities, whether they are useful or not. Thus in 2004, the UK exported 10,200 tonnes of milk and cream to France, and imported 9,900 tonnes of the same dairy goods from France; it also exported 1,500 tonnes of fresh potatoes to Germany, and imported 1,500 tonnes of the same product from the same country.

New York and London are clearly part of a global geography of growing numbers and diversity of circuits. These powerful global intercity networks bind them to Tokyo, Paris, Frankfurt, Zurich, Amsterdam, Toronto, Los Angeles, Sydney and Hong Kong, among others. But this global geography also now includes cities such as Mumbai, Shanghai, Bangkok, Taipei, São Paulo, Mexico City and Johannesburg. Shanghai is at the intersection of major global manufacturing, trading and real-estate development circuits. Johannesburg is at the heart of long-standing intercity networks centred not only on the trade in gold and diamonds, but also on new types of tourism, such as the so-called cosmetic-surgery safaries, the mix of novel circuits connected to the upcoming Football World Cup it is hosting, and the informal cross-border sub-Saharan trading and manufacturing networks. The intensity of transactions among diverse groupings of cities through the financial markets, trade in goods and services, and investment has increased sharply, and so have the orders of magnitude involved. But cultural transactions – biennales, travelling exhibitions – and global tourism also feed these intercity networks.

There is a growing inequality between the concentration of strategic resources and activities in these cities compared to others in the same countries. Alongside these new global and regional hierarchies of cities is a vast territory that has become increasingly peripheral and progressively excluded from the major economic processes that are seen as fuelling growth in the new global economy. Formerly important manufacturing centres and port cities have lost functions and are in decline, not only in less developed countries but also in the most advanced economies. Some ports become global and state-of-the-art specialized service economies, while others become obsolete. The United States and Germany have seen many cities shrink or simply die in older industrial areas even as other small cities are undergoing a diluted and mostly national version of the processes we find in global cities – they are becoming part of larger intercity geographies. Most significant here is the distinctive German urban system, balanced and multi-polar, as well as the effort of smaller cities to become part of larger inter-urban networks. There are foundational structural trends that make cities, both large and small, key cogs in the service economy. What assumes extreme global forms in global cities takes on more domestic and softer forms in at least some smaller cities, such as Halle.

In brief, the growth of a global economy has contributed to a new geography of centrality. It assumes many forms and operates in many arenas, from the distribution of telecommunications facilities to the structure of the economy and of employment. Global cities accumulate immense concentrations of economic power while cities that were once major manufacturing centres decline. But inside global cities we also see sharper spatio-social segmentations.

Messy, Anarchic and Expensive

Why do powerful and wealthy global firms that can buy all the available communication technologies, and that operate partly in electronic networks, need to be located in cities – always somewhat messy, anarchic, mixed and expensive places? The more globalized and electronic the operations of these firms, the more central functions become complex and charged with risk and uncertainties. As managing and servicing the global operations of a firm becomes more burdened with incomplete knowledge and uncertain global market conditions, complex cities become valuable for mixing different types of talents and sources of knowledge. They are the Silicon Valleys for producing knowledge and innovations: the whole is more than the sum of the top-level firms and professionals located in the city. As discussed in more detail in *Cities in a World Economy*, the global city is a space for interaction effects, fuzzy-logic effects, unexpected datums that fill a piece of the puzzle.

The massive trends towards the spatial dispersal of economic activities at the metropolitan, national and global levels commonly associated with globalization have contributed to a demand for new forms of territorial centralization of top-level management and control operations. The spatial dispersal of economic activity made possible by telematics would contribute to an expansion of central functions if this dispersal were to take place under the continuing concentration in control, ownership and profit appropriation that characterizes the current economic system.

There is evidence that the spatial organization of a growing number of firms and economic sectors contains moments of both agglomeration and dispersal at a regional, national or global level. Agglomeration might vary sharply in content and in the specifics of the corresponding spatial form – this can be seen in the different architectures of density across London's financial centre, Mexico City's Santa Fe office district and the newly developed business district of Pudong in Shanghai. A focus on the presence of such translocal chains of operations helps situate the specifics of a city,

SHIFTING GEOGRAPHIES
The Santa Fe office district (top) was created on the site of a former dump in Mexico City's far western edge. Concentrating office towers, residential complexes and shopping in one urban nucleus, the area remains underserved by critical infrastructure. Like the Pudong business district in Shanghai (bottom), it represents one of the great ironies of our digital global age by producing dispersal from the city centre while also agglomerating ever-expanding economic resources from international financial firms as well as regional offices.

a metro area or an urban region in a far broader systemic dynamic. Shanghai is both a space for dispersing operations for non-Chinese financial and manufacturing firms, and a space for agglomerating headquarter functions of Chinese firms. Johannesburg shows up prominently among the dozens of cities where the leading global service firms have dispersed their operations, but it also has the highest concentration of headquarters for South African firms and for foreign firms dealing in gold and diamonds.

This coexistence of dispersal and density also contests the common notion that spatial dispersal is the new, post-modern urban form, capturing novel economic and cultural dynamics. In that view, epitomized by the Los Angeles region, agglomeration and spatial density belong to an older economic phase – that of the modern city. However, by visualizing different density distributions, the Urban Age project has produced important data in this regard. These show that while all the Urban Age cities have high levels of density, diverse formats shape this density across cities.

In my own research I found that for the most globalized and innovative firms agglomeration was fed by the global dispersal of many of their operations. The more globalized and thus geographically dispersed a firm's operations, the more likely the presence of agglomeration economies in particular moments (the production of top-level headquarter functions) of that firm's chain of operations.

It is the most specialized functions of the most globalized firms that are subject to the highest agglomeration economies. The complexity of the functions that need to be produced, the uncertainty of the markets in which such firms are involved and the growing importance of speed in all these transactions is a mix of conditions that constitutes a new logic for agglomeration; it is not the logic posited in older models, where weight and distance are seen to shape agglomeration outcomes. The mix of firms, talents and expertise in a broad range of specialized fields makes a certain type of dense environment function as a strategic knowledge economy wherein the whole is more than the sum of its parts.

Understanding the Urban Landscape
The recurrence of this combination of activities in global cities feeds particular types of visual orders evident in at least some parts of each of the Urban Age cities. This in turn feeds into an understanding of contemporary urbanization as marked by a homogenizing of the urban landscape, especially in global cities, with their intense and rapid urban reconstruction.

But this homogenizing of the economic urban landscape obscures the diversity of economic trajectories through which cities and regions become globalized. A focus on homogenized landscapes easily slides into a second, possibly spurious, inference that similar visual landscapes contain similar economies. These homogenized built environments may be a function of convergences in architectural and urban-design practice, but not necessarily of economies.

Both propositions (that similar visual landscapes are indicators of similar economic histories and similar presents) may indeed capture various situations, but they fail to capture the specific conditions at work in each global city, and, in fact, render them invisible. Hence we cannot assume that such inferences from the visual order always hold. This raises questions about the common perception of the Los Angeles model – with its low density and multipolarity – as representing the new urban spatial form arising out of what are today's new dynamics.

The Urban Age's research on the diverse spatial forms that density assumes in the six cities was what led me to question the prevailing homogenization and convergence theories. One aspect of such an inquiry is to establish the particular specialized sectors that might inhabit that homogenized landscape. An easy starting assumption was that even though Shanghai, London and Chicago use some of the same architects – each with a strong identifiable style – this does not necessarily mean that the economic activities that inhabit those buildings, or that bring foreign investors through those airports, are going to be the same.

The different economic history of each place – self-evident in all the Urban Age cities – feeds into their current economies in ways that have been obscured by some of the indicators we use; one result of this is that similar-looking office districts, airports and infrastructures in part house very different specialized economies as well as the similar, standardized components evident in all advanced urban service economies. This reinforces the point about the partial disembedding of the economies of global cities from the larger national economy, and the fact that there is a specialized division of functions across global cities that is critical to the global economy.

Under these conditions, the state-of-the-art built environments that characterize all these cities are more akin to an infrastructure *for* advanced urban economies. This repositions the meaning of these new kinds of built environments, often referred to as the hyperspace of global business. We are then dealing with homogenized state-of-the-art infrastructures in these cities, rather than necessarily homogenized economies. This qualifies the notion that globalization leads to economic homogenization, at least in part. There is a kind of convergence at an abstract systemic level, but at the concrete, material interface of the urban, the actual content of the specialized services that inhabit the built environment can vary greatly.

There is an important background trend evident in all reasonably working economies that feeds the homogenized urban environment – the growing service intensity in the organization of all economic sectors, including standardized and often non-globalized sectors. Whether in mining, agriculture, manufacturing or service industries such as transport and health, more firms are buying more corporate services. Some of this translates into a growing demand for services produced in global cities; but much of it translates into a demand for such services – although in a less complex version – in regional centres and smaller cities. The growth in demand for producer services is then a structural feature of advanced market economies. Globalization brings to this trend a sharp increase in the demand for complexity and diversity of professional knowledge. The growth of this intermediate economy across diverse urban areas amounts to a kind of structural convergence that explains emergent spatial patterns even when the sectors thus serviced are radically different.

This convergence filters through spatial organization and the visual order. It accounts for patterns in cities small and large – notably the rise of young, professional urbanites associated with high-income gentrification and growth of the cultural sector. A mining firm, a transport firm and a software firm all need to buy legal and accounting services. To some extent these may be produced in the same city and similar built environments, even though they are feeding very different economic sectors. Very old economy sectors, such as transport and mining, are also feeding this growth.

What then makes for a city's specialized difference in a globalizing world that standardizes state-of-the-art infrastructures and built environments? It was my detailed knowledge of Chicago that allowed me to explore them in depth. What I found for Chicago is likely to hold, under its own specificities, for each Urban Age city. The differences between London and New York as financial centres has already

FORMAL AND INFORMAL ECONOMIES
Shanghai, like other Urban Age cities, displays a
flexible approach to urban labour markets, with
highly formalized forms of work in the health
sector (above) which contrast and co-habit with
the vast informal sector of the city's economy.

been mentioned, but what makes the case of Chicago – and thereby such cities as Shanghai and São Paulo – interesting is the switch from a heavy industrial economic history into a specialized knowledge economy of advanced corporate services. It is a far more dramatic change than that of London or New York, with their long histories as financial and trading centres.

It is common to see Chicago as a latecomer to global-city status because of its agro-industrial past. Why did it happen so late – almost 15 years later than New York and London? In fact, Chicago's knowledge economy developed in response to the particular needs of its agro-industrial regional economy. This is most visible in its pre-eminence as a futures market historically built on the need for buyers and sellers of agricultural products and cattle to guess what prices would work once harvests were in and cattle ready for slaughter. But this past economic history also underlies other highly specialized components of its global-city functions. The complexity, scale and international character of its agro-industrial past required highly specialized financial, accounting and legal expertise – quite different from that required to handle the sectors in which New York specialized: service exports, finance on trade and finance on finance.

The specialized economic histories of major cities and urban regions matter in today's global economy because there is a networked division of functions. This fact is easily obscured by the common emphasis on intercity competition and the standardization (no matter how good the architecture) of built environments. Because financial, legal and accounting experts in Chicago had to address the needs of the agro-industrial complex, the city today has a specialized advantage in producing certain types of financial, legal and accounting instruments; the same thing has occurred in Shanghai and, to some extent, Mexico City. For this specialized advantage to occur, however, the past knowledge must be repositioned in a different set of economic circuits. The expertise must be disembedded from an (agro-)industrial economy and re-embedded in a knowledge economy – one in which expertise can increasingly be commodified, function as a key input and thereby constitute a new immaterial good in a knowledge economy. Having a past as a major agro-industrial complex makes that switch more difficult than a past as a trading and financial centre. This partly explains Chicago's 'lateness' in bringing about that switch. That change is not simply a matter of overcoming that past, however. It requires a new organizing logic that can revalue the capabilities developed in an earlier era. It took work to make the switch. A more general logic is at work here – one that assumes specific forms in many different institutional settings, including the political and the social, a notion I have further developed in *Territory, Authority, Rights: From Medieval to Global Assemblages*.

Recovering the specialized advantage of a city's economic history also highlights a key quality about cities that derive their significance from their location in global networks rather than simply their position in a hierarchy. Two cities as diverse as Berlin and Johannesburg, for example, have such specialized functions. To recover this particular specialized advantage, one akin to a positional good, there needs to be empirical research about the intersections of regional locations and functional activities. This quality also points to the fact that 'the' global network comprises multiple, often specialized networks. I have found this to be the case with financial markets: once we disaggregate the global capital market into its multiple specialized financial markets, it becomes clear that there are several specific networks of cities in play. A city like Chicago dominates some of these financial circuits but is a fairly minor player in others. This opens up a whole research agenda that goes beyond city

Dhobi Ghat is Asia's largest open air launderette, representing an infrastructure of highly skilled jobs servicing multiple economic sectors, including the hotel industry. Washing is done by hand in concrete sinks, then hung out to dry in the open air. Despite its high visibility in a central location near Mumbai's city centre and it being a major tourist destination, the jobs contained within it are not formally recognized as part of the global economic system.

rankings. The aim is to recover the more complex city networks that are a strategic infrastructure for the global operations of markets and firms, and on which a variety of other types of actors and networks can build, such as global civil society actors, alternative cultural circuits and transnational migration networks, even as these also build their own distinct city networks.

Place and Production in the Global Economy

I have conceptualized global cities as production sites for today's leading economic sectors. My purpose in emphasizing production or work-processes is to recover the infrastructure of activities, firms and jobs – from trucking to technical repair and cleaning – that are necessary to run the advanced corporate economy, but are never recognized as such. Specialized corporate industries are typically conceptualized in terms of the hypermobility of their outputs and the high levels of expertise of their professionals. The full work-process that includes non-expert jobs and diverse infrastructures is left out. A detailed analysis of advanced service-based urban economies shows that there is a need for the firms, sectors and workers which may appear as though they have little connection to an urban economy dominated by finance and specialized services. In fact, they fulfil a series of functions that are integral to that economy, but they do so under conditions of social, income-related and often racial/ethnic segmentation.

We found geographies of centrality and marginality. They may be less visible in Berlin and Shanghai than in New York City and Johannesburg, but they still exist. The downtowns of cities and business centres receive massive investments in real estate and telecommunications, with Shanghai the most extreme instance. The new 'centres' at the edge of the city come a close second – notably Johannesburg's Sandton and Mexico City's Santa Fe. At the same time, low-income urban and metropolitan areas are starved of resources, with New York City's ghetto areas in Brooklyn and the many shanty towns in Mexico City two brutal instances. These spatial outcomes are partly fed by the socio-economic dynamics that produce an extremely high-paid professional stratum of workers and firms and an extremely low-paid and unprotected stratum of marginally surviving, often informal, firms and workers. What distinguishes the current global urban era is that a good share of both types of workers and firms are part of the new advanced urban economy.

In the day-to-day work of the leading services complex, a large share of the jobs involved is low paid and manual, many held by women and immigrants. Although these workers and jobs are never represented as part of the global economy, they are a key element of the infrastructure of jobs involved in running and implementing the global economic system. The top end of the corporate economy – the towers that project engineering expertise, precision, 'techne' – is far easier to recognize as necessary for an advanced economic system. We see here a valuing dynamic that has widened the gulf between the devalorized and the valorized, indeed overvalorized, sectors of the economy.

Making Legible the Obscure

Economic globalization, then, needs to be understood in its multiple localizations, rather than simply in terms of the broad, overarching macro-level processes that dominate the mainstream account. Further, we need to understand that some of these localizations are not recognized as contributing to the global economy.

The city makes legible what other settings obscure. For instance, the mainstream account about globalization recognizes that there is a transnational professional workforce and that this feeds into the highly internationalized business environments in global cities. What has not been recognized is the possibility that we are seeing an internationalized labour market for low-wage manual and service workers, or that there is an internationalized business environment, albeit through small firms, in many immigrant communities. These processes continue to be couched in terms of immigration, a narrative rooted in an earlier period. One of the many contributions that Urban Age has made to understanding how the global and major urban economies function is to make visible this diversity of economies and labour markets.

The Urban Age cities are seeing an expansion of low-wage jobs that do not fit the traditional understanding of globalization, yet are part of it. Because many of the jobs are done by the growing populations of migrants, they become somehow invisible. There is here a rupture of the traditional dynamic whereby membership in leading economic sectors enables the formation of strong organized labour movements. Women and immigrants emerge as the labour supply that facilitates the imposition of low wages and powerlessness under conditions of high demand in high-growth sectors. It breaks the historic nexus that would have led to empowering workers. Cities have long housed inequality, but today a new type of inequality sits alongside traditional forms. Homelessness has long been part of cities, but where it was once largely confined to single men – so-called hobos – it has expanded to encompass whole families, with children making up the majority of homeless people in large cities. These social and spatial inequalities assume their most visible form in global cities.

Another localization rarely associated with globalization is informalization. This reintroduces the community and the household as an important economic space in global cities of the highly developed countries. Informalization in this setting can be seen as the low-cost – and often feminized – equivalent of deregulation at the top of the system. As with deregulation, informalization introduces flexibility, reduces the 'burdens' of regulation and lowers costs – in this case, especially the costs of labour. Informalization in the major cities of highly developed countries can be seen as a downgrading of a variety of activities for which there is an effective demand in these cities, but also as a devaluing and an adding to enormous competition, especially given low start-up costs and the lack of alternative forms of employment. Going informal is one way of producing and distributing goods and services at a lower cost and with greater flexibility. This further devalues these types of activities. Immigrants and women are important actors in the new informal economies of these cities. They absorb the costs of informalizing these activities. Many of the expanding informal economies evident in the Urban Age cities are part of the advanced urban economy, whether in the global North or South. It is easy to think of informalization as anomalous, as belonging to an older order – but in fact it is part of advanced capitalism.

Informality assumes a whole range of new meanings in this context, offering a growing range of practices – economic, artistic, professional – in these cities. While informality can be a form of injustice and powerlessness, it can also enable new economies – of survival and also of creativity. Many entrepreneurs start informally because it allows a more experimental form of business. In all the Urban Age cities – from Mexico to Berlin – the informal economy is not only expanding, it is also diversifying. There are informal architectural projects in Mexico City and in Berlin, informal art spaces in Johannesburg and London, informal professional services, from design to software development, in Shanghai and New York City.

The New Politics

What makes the localization of these processes strategic, even though they mostly involve powerless and often invisible workers, is the valorization of new forms of global corporate capital defining these cities. Typically, analyses about the globalization of the economy privilege the reconstitution of capital as a global actor and emphasize the vanguard character of this reconstitution. At the same time, such analyses remain silent about the globalization of a sector of labour. Those analyses overlook the transnationalizing of identities and loyalties among various population segments that explicitly reject the imagined community of the nation. With this come new solidarities and notions of membership. Major cities have emerged as strategic sites for both, and thus they become sites for new types of political operations.

The global character of major cities lies not only in their telecommunication infrastructure and global firms, but also in the many different cultural environments in which these workers exist. It is no longer appropriate to think of global cities simply in terms of the corporate towers and corporate culture at their centres. Today's global cities contain conditions for the making of post-colonial histories.

All the Urban Age cities concentrate diversity. Their spaces are inscribed with the dominant corporate culture but also with a multiplicity of other cultures and identities. The slippage is evident: the dominant culture can encompass only part of the city. And while corporate power inscribes these cultures and identities with 'otherness', thereby devaluing them, they are present everywhere. For example, through immigration a proliferation of originally highly localized cultures have made themselves felt in New York, London and Berlin, cities whose elites consider themselves 'cosmopolitan', or transcending any locality. Yet these elites may have trouble seeing immigrant communities as contributing to the cityness they regard so highly. An immense array of cultures from around the world, each rooted in a particular country or village, are now reterritorialized in a few single places, such as New York, Los Angeles, Paris, London and most recently Tokyo. Against this context, immigration and ethnicity are too often defined as 'otherness'. When understood as a set of processes by which global elements are localized, international labour markets are constituted and cultures are deterritorialized, putting them centre-stage along with the internationalization of capital as a fundamental aspect of globalization today.

Cities have long been able to accommodate mixes of elements. Alexandria had its Greek, Latin, Jewish and Egyptian quarters two millennia ago. London had Lombard Street in the twelfth century. Today's global cities are mongrel cities. The immensity of diversity and how it feeds different experiences of cityness is an overwhelming factor. No generalization can capture this.

The internationalization of New York is highly visible, even Wall Street and Midtown, traversed as they are by professionals from all over the world. This lies at the heart of the city's urbanity. The internationalization of Shanghai is far less visible to the Western eye, beyond the evidently foreign workforce, but it is there, in the millions of migrants from China's many old nations. London's internationalization is deep and old, but less legible than New York's. It is particularized in ways that make it part of familiar 'English' urbanity. The harshness and tensions so evident in New York are barely detectable in London. Johannesburg is a major magnet for traders from sub-Saharan Africa, its diversity made in the central market of the old downtown. Its internationalization is now surging, often with the violence that marks beginnings, conditions as much a part of globalization as are firms and finance.

Finally, the centrality of place in a context of global processes engenders a transnational economic and political opening in the formation of new claims for rights to place and belonging. The city has emerged as a site for new claims: by global capital that uses the city as an 'organizational commodity' but also by disadvantaged sectors of the population taking the same internationalized presence as capital.

The linkage of people to territory in global cities is far less likely to be intermediated by the national state or 'national culture'. There is a loosening of identities from traditional sources such as the nation or the village. This unmooring of identity formation engenders new notions of community of membership and of entitlement. Yet another way of thinking about the political implications of this strategic transnational space is the formation of new claims on that space. Has economic globalization at least partly shaped the formation of claims? There are indeed major new actors making claims on these cities, notably foreign firms that have become increasingly entitled to do business through progressive deregulation of national economies, and the large increase over the last decade in international businesspeople. These are among the new 'city users'. They have profoundly marked the urban landscape. Perhaps at the other extreme are those who use urban political violence to make their claims on the city – claims that lack the de facto legitimacy enjoyed by the new city users. These are made by actors struggling for recognition and entitlement to their rights to the city.

There is something to be captured here – a distinction between powerlessness and a condition of being an actor or political subject even though one lacks power. I use the term 'presence' to name this condition. In the context of a strategic space such as the global city, the types of disadvantaged people described here are not simply marginal; they acquire presence in a broader political process that escapes the boundaries of the formal polity. This presence signals the possibility of a politics. What this politics will be will depend on the specific projects and practices of various communities. In so far as the sense of membership of these communities is not subsumed under the national, it may well signal the possibility of a transnational politics centred in concrete localities.

THE OPEN CITY

Richard Sennett

STREET CULTURE

Manahattan's Lower East Side is experiencing a decade-long transformation of its low-rise density and unexpected mix of urban life with new luxury towers dotting its skyline. Jewish, Italian and, more recently, Chinese immigrants defined various ground floor uses of the area's six-storey walk-up residential buildings, yet this vital and unregulated urban atmosphere is now being appropriated by the affluent young who are reprogramming the storefront spaces into cafes, nightclubs and fashion boutiques, pricing out the very people who made the area so attractive and informal, and fracturing the area's heterogeneous social elements.

The cities everyone wants to live in should be clean and safe, possess efficient public services, be supported by a dynamic economy, provide cultural stimulation, and also do their best to heal society's divisions of race, class and ethnicity. These are not the cities we live in. They fail on all these counts due to government policy, irreparable social ills and economic forces beyond local control. The city is not its own master. Still, something has gone wrong – radically wrong – in our perception of what a city should be. We need to imagine just what a clean, safe, efficient, dynamic, stimulating, just city would look like concretely; we need those images to confront critically our masters with what they should be doing – and precisely this critical imagination of the city is weak. This weakness is a particularly *modern* problem: the art of designing cities declined drastically in the middle of the twentieth century. In saying this, I am propounding a paradox, for today's planner has an arsenal of technological tools – from lighting to bridging and tunnelling to materials for buildings – that urbanists even 100 years ago could not begin to imagine. We have more resources to use than ever before, but we simply do not use them creatively.

This paradox can be traced to one big fault. That fault is over-determination, both of the city's visual forms and its social functions. The technologies that make experiment possible have been subordinated to a regime of power that wants order and control. Worldwide, urbanists anticipated the 'control freakery' of New Labour by a good half-century; in the grip of rigid images and precise delineations, the urban imagination lost vitality. In particular, what is missing in modern urbanism is a sense of time – not time looking backwards nostalgically but forward-looking time: the city understood as process, its imagery changing through use, an urban imagination image formed by anticipation, welcoming surprise. A portent of this freezing of the imagination appeared in Le Corbusier's 'Plan Voisin' for Paris in the mid 1920s. The architect conceived of replacing a large swath of the historic centre of Paris with uniform, X-shaped buildings; public life on the ground plane of the street would be eliminated; the use of all buildings would be coordinated by a single master plan. Not only is Le Corbusier's architecture a kind of industrial manufacture of buildings, he has tried to destroy just those social elements of the city that produce change in time, by eliminating unregulated life on the ground plane; people live and work, in isolation, higher up.

This dystopia became reality in various ways. The Plan's building type shaped public housing from Chicago to Moscow in the form of housing estates for the poor

that came to resemble warehouses. Le Corbusier's intended destruction of vibrant street life was realized in suburban growth for the middle classes, with the replacement of high streets by mono-function shopping malls, by gated communities, by schools and hospitals built as isolated campuses. The proliferation of zoning regulations in the twentieth century is unprecedented in the history of urban design, and this dissemination of rules and bureaucratic regulations has disabled local innovation and growth. It has frozen the city in time.

The Closed System and the Brittle City

The result of over-determination is what could be called the Brittle City. Modern urban environments decay much more quickly than urban fabric inherited from the past. As uses change, buildings are now destroyed rather than adapted; indeed, the over-specification of form and function makes the modern urban environment peculiarly susceptible to decay. The average lifespan of new public housing in Britain is now 40 years; that of new skyscrapers in New York is 35 years.

It might seem that the Brittle City would in fact stimulate urban growth, with the new sweeping away the old more rapidly, but again the facts argue against this. In the United States, people flee decaying suburbs rather than reinvest in them. In Britain and on the European continent, as in America, 'renewing' the inner city usually means displacing the people who live there. 'Growth' in an urban environment is a more complicated phenomenon than simple replacement of what existed before; growth requires a dialogue between past and present. It is a matter of evolution rather than erasure. This principle is as true socially as it is architecturally. The bonds of community cannot be conjured up in an instant, with a stroke of the planner's pen; they too require time to develop. Today's ways of building cities – segregating functions, homogenizing populations, pre-empting through zoning and regulation of the meaning of place – fail to provide communities the time and space needed for growth. The Brittle City is a symptom. It represents a view of society itself as a closed system. The closed system is a concept that dogged state socialism throughout the twentieth century as much as it shaped bureaucratic capitalism. This view of society has two essential attributes: equilibrium and integration.

The closed system ruled by equilibrium derives from a pre-Keynesian idea of how markets work. It supposes something like a bottom line in which income and expenses balance. State planning, information feedback loops and internal markets are meant to ensure that programmes do not 'over-commit', do not 'suck resources into a black hole' – such is the language of recent reforms of the health service, familiar again to urban planners in the ways infrastructure resources for transport are allocated. The limits on doing any one thing really well are set by the fear of neglecting other tasks. In a closed system, a little bit of everything happens all at once. A closed system is also meant to be an integrated system. Ideally, every part of the system has a place in an overall design; the consequence of that ideal is to reject experiences that stand out because they contest or are disorienting. Things that 'don't fit' are diminished in value.

The emphasis on integration puts an obvious bar on experiment. As the inventor of the computer icon, John Seely Brown, once remarked, every technological advance poses at the moment of its birth a threat of disruption and dysfunction to a larger system. The same threatening exceptions occur in the urban environment, threats that modern city planning has tried to forestall by accumulating a mountain of rules defining historical, architectural, economic and social context – 'context' being a polite but potent word in repressing anything that does not fit in, ensuring that nothing sticks out, offends or challenges. Thus, the sins of equilibrium and integration bedevil coherence, for planners of education as much as planners of cities, as planning sins have crossed the line between state capitalism and state socialism. The closed system thus betrays the twentieth-century bureaucrat's horror of disorder.

The social contrast to the closed system is not the free market, nor is a place ruled by developers the alternative to the Brittle City. That opposition is in fact not what it seems. The cunning of neo-liberalism in general, and of Thatcherism in particular, was to speak the language of freedom while manipulating closed bureaucratic systems for private gain by an elite. Equally, in my experience as a planner, those developers in London, as in New York, who complain most loudly about zoning restrictions are all too adept in using these rules at the expense of communities. The contrast to the closed system lies in a different kind of social system, not in brute private enterprise but rather in a social system that is open rather than closed.

The idea of an open city is not my own: credit for it belongs to the great urbanist Jane Jacobs, in the course of arguing against the urban vision of Le Corbusier. She tried to understand what results when places become both dense and diverse, as in packed streets or squares, their functions both public and private; out of such conditions comes the unexpected encounter, the chance discovery, the innovation. Her view, reflected in the *bon mot* of William Empson, was that 'the arts result from overcrowding'. Jacobs sought to define particular strategies for urban development once a city is freed of the constraints of either equilibrium or integration. These include encouraging quirky, jerry-built adaptations or additions to existing buildings, encouraging uses of public spaces that do not fit neatly together, such as putting an AIDS hospice square in the middle of a shopping street.

In Jacobs' view, big capitalism and powerful developers tend to favour homogeneity, determinate, predictable and balanced in form. The role of the radical planner, therefore, is to champion dissonance, as she declares: 'If density and diversity give life, the life they breed is disorderly'. The open city feels like Naples, the closed city feels like Frankfurt.

Recently, in re-reading Jacobs' work, I have detected glints of something lurking beneath the stark contrast evident in her enmity to the closed system and her advocacy of complexity, diversity and dissonance. If she is the urban anarchist she is often claimed to be, then she is an anarchist of a peculiar sort, her spiritual ties closer to Edmund Burke than to Emma Goldman. She believes that in an open city, as in the natural world, social and visual forms mutate through chance variation; people can best absorb, participate and adapt to change if it happens step-by-lived-step. This is evolutionary urban time – the slow time needed for an urban culture to take root, then to foster, then to absorb chance and change. It is why Naples, Cairo or New York's lower East Side, though resource-poor, still 'work' in the sense that people care deeply about where they live. People 'live into' these places, like nesting. Time breeds that attachment to place.

I have wondered what kinds of visual forms might promote this experience of time. Can these attachments be designed by architects? Which designs might abet social relationships that endure through being given the opportunity to evolve and mutate? The visual structuring of evolutionary time is a systematic property of the open city, which has three important systematic elements: passage territories; incomplete form; and development narratives.

Passage Territories

The experience of passing through different territories of the city is significant, both because that act of passage is how we know the city as a whole, and also because planners and architects have difficulties designing the experience of passage. Walls, for example, seem to be structures inhibiting passage yet they are an integral part of the open city, and there are ways in which the edges of urban territory function like walls.

The wall would seem an unlikely choice for an open city – it is an urban construction which literally closes in that city. Until the invention of artillery, people sheltered behind walls when attacked; the gates in walls also served to regulate commerce coming into cities, often the places where taxes were collected. Massive medieval walls, such as those surviving in Aix-en-Provence or in Rome, furnish a perhaps misleading general picture; ancient Greek walls were lower and thinner. But we also mis-imagine how those medieval walls functioned. Although they enclosed the city, they also served as sites for unregulated development therein. Houses were built on both sides of medieval town walls; informal markets selling black-market or untaxed goods sprung up and nestled against them; it was the zone of the wall towards which heretics, foreign exiles and other misfits gravitated, far from the controls of the centre. They were spaces that would have attracted the anarchic Jane Jacobs. But they were also sites that might have suited her organic temperament. These walls functioned much like cell membranes, both porous and resistant. That dual quality of the membrane is, I believe, an important principle for visualizing more modern living urban forms. Whenever we construct a barrier, we have to equally make the barrier porous; the distinction between inside and outside has to be breachable, if not ambiguous.

The usual contemporary use of plate glass for walls does not do this. It is true that on the ground plane you see what is inside the building, but you cannot touch, smell or hear anything within. The plates are usually rigidly fixed so that there is only one, regulated, entrance. The result is that nothing much develops on either side of these transparent walls, as in Mies van der Rohe's Seagram Building in New York or Norman Foster's new London City Hall – there is dead space on both sides of the wall and life in the building does accumulate there. By contrast, the nineteenth-century architect Louis Sullivan used much more primitive forms of plate glass more flexibly, as invitations to gather, to enter a building or to dwell at its edge; his plate-glass panels function as porous walls. This contrast in plate-glass design highlights one current failure of imagination in using a modern material to sociable effect. The idea of a cellular wall, which is both resistant and porous, can be extended from single buildings to the zones in which the different communities of a city meet.

Incomplete Form

A discussion of walls and borders leads to a second systematic characteristic of the open city: incomplete form. Incompleteness may seem the enemy of structure, but this is not the case. The designer needs to create physical forms of a particular sort, 'incomplete' in a special way. When we design a street, for instance, so that buildings are set back from a street wall, the space left open in front is not truly public space. Instead, the building has been withdrawn from the street with people walking by tending to avoid these recessed spaces. It is better planning if the building is brought forward, into the context of other buildings. Although the building will become part of the urban fabric, some of its volumetric elements will be incompletely disclosed. There is incompleteness in the perception of what the object is.

THE DEMOCRATIC POTENTIAL
OF URBAN SPACE

Porous and incomplete open spaces at the
heart of cities like Johannesburg (top left) and
Mexico City (top right) provide opportunities
for democratic engagement. Highly designed
environments like People's Square in Shanghai
(bottom left) and the open space in front of City
Hall in London (bottom right) reduce the democratic potential of civic space.

Incompleteness of form extends to the very context of buildings themselves. In classical Rome, Hadrian's Pantheon coexisted with the less-distinguished buildings that surrounded it in the urban fabric, though Hadrian's architects conceived the Pantheon as a self-referential object. The same coexistence is evident in many other architectural monuments: St Paul's Cathedral in London, Rockefeller Center in New York, the Insitut du Monde Arabe in Paris – all great works of architecture that stimulate building around themselves. It is the fact of that stimulation, rather than the fact the buildings are of lesser quality, that counts in urban terms. The existence of one building encourages growth of buildings around it, with the buildings acquiring specifical urban value through their relationship to one another; in time they become incomplete forms when considered by themselves.

Incomplete form is most of all a kind of creative credo. In the plastic arts it is conveyed in sculpture purposely left unfinished; in poetry it is conveyed in, to use Wallace Stevens' phrase, the 'engineering of the fragment'. The architect Peter Eisenman has sought to evoke something of the same credo in the term 'light architecture', meaning an architecture planned so that it can be added to, or more importantly revised internally in the course of time as the needs of habitation change. This credo opposes the simple idea of replacement of form that characterizes the Brittle City, but it is a demanding opposition – as can be seen when trying to convert office blocks to residential buildings, for example.

Development Narratives

Our work as urbanists aims to shape the narratives of urban development, focusing on the stages in which a particular project unfolds. Specifically, we try to understand what elements should happen first and what the consequences of this initial move will be. Rather than a lock-step march towards achieving a single end, we look at the different and conflicting possibilities at each stage. Keeping these possibilities intact and leaving conflict in play opens up the design system. We claim no originality for this approach. If a novelist were to announce at the start of the plot what the characters will become and what the story means, we would immediately close the book. All good narrative has the property of exploring the unforeseen, of discovery; the novelist's art is to shape the process of that exploration. The urban designer's art is akin. In summary, we can define an open system as one in which growth admits conflict and dissonance. This definition is at the heart of Darwin's understanding of evolution; rather than the survival of the fittest (or the most beautiful), he emphasized the process of growth as a continual struggle between equilibrium and disequilibrium; an environment rigid in form and static in programme is doomed; biodiversity instead gives the natural world the resources to change. That ecological vision makes equal sense of human settlements, but it is not the vision that guided twentieth-century state planning. Neither state capitalism nor state socialism embraced growth in the sense Darwin understood, in environments that permitted interaction among organisms with different functions, endowed with different powers.

Democratic Space

When the city operates as an open system – incorporating porosity of territory, narrative indeterminacy and incomplete form – it becomes democratic not in a legal sense, but as physical experience. In the past, thinking about democracy focused on issues of formal governance; today it focuses on citizenship and issues of participation which have everything to do with the physical city and its design. For example, in the ancient *polis*, the Athenians put the semicircular theatre to political use. This architectural form provided good acoustics and a clear view of speakers in debates; moreover, it made possible the perception of other people's responses during debates. In modern times we have no similar model of democratic space – certainly no clear imagination of an urban democratic space. John Locke defined democracy in terms of a body of laws that could be practised anywhere. Democracy in the eyes of Thomas Jefferson was inimical to life in cities; he thought the spaces it required could be no larger than a village and his view has persisted. Throughout the nineteenth and twentieth centuries, champions of democratic practices have identified them with small, local communities, face-to-face relationships. Today's city is big, filled with migrants and ethnic diversities, in which people belong to many different kinds of community through their work, families, consumption habits and leisure pursuits. For cities like London and New York, becoming global in scale, the problem of citizen participation is how people can feel connected to others, when, necessarily, they cannot know them. Democratic space means creating a forum for these strangers to interact.

In London, a good example of how this can occur is the creation of a connection between St Paul's Cathedral and Tate Modern, spanned by the Millennium Bridge. Though highly defined, the corridor is not a closed form; along both the south and north banks of the Thames it is regenerating lateral buildings unrelated to its own purposes and design. And almost immediately upon opening, this corridor has stimulated informal mixings and connections among people walking the span within its confines, prompting an ease among strangers – the foundation for a truly modern sense of 'us'. This is democratic space. The problem participation cities face today is how to create, in less ceremonial spaces, the same sense of relatedness among strangers. It is a problem in the design of public spaces, hospitals, urban schools, big office complexes, the renewal of high streets, and most particularly the places where the work of government is done. How can such places be opened up? How can the divide between inside and outside be bridged? How can design generate new growth? How can visual form invite engagement and identification? These are the pressing questions that urban design must address in the urban age.

ENGAGEMENT AND IDENTIFICATION

The Millennium Bridge in London, connecting the financial centre of the Square Mile with the long neglected South Bank, has successfully performed as a democratic space by promoting a sense of relatedness among strangers.

DESIGNING GOVERNMENT

Gerald Frug

WHO DECIDES?

The ability of city governments to determine the future of major public services – including schools, inward investment and public transport – is critical to their long-term success. New York City's extensive transport system is heavily used by the majority of its residents – with over 500,000 commuters a day using Penn Street Station, spilling onto 34th Street – yet, the budget and policy of the Mass Transit Authority is determined hundreds of miles away in the state capital of Albany.

No city is able to do whatever it pleases. Cities can exercise power only within the legal frameworks that others have established for them. These legal frameworks are created either by national governments (as in the United Kingdom, China, Mexico and South Africa) or by sub-national governments (such as the *Länder* in Germany and the states in the United States). National or sub-national governments decide whether city governments are elected or appointed. They dictate whether cities can act independently or only with express approval from a higher government. They specify which governmental services will be provided locally and which will be provided by others. They define city fiscal authority and determine the extent of city power to regulate land-use development within their boundaries. And they decide where those boundaries are. These legal rules have a major influence on both the experience of city life and the practice of local self-government.

There are a variety of ways in which national and sub-national governments can empower and disempower cities. This can be seen simply by examining the legal structure of New York, London, Shanghai, Mexico City, Johannesburg and Berlin. There are many differences in the legal systems that frame the power of these cities, but four key issues relate in particular to the cities of the Urban Age project: the fragmentation of the metropolitan areas in which the cities are located; the organization of the cities themselves as vehicles for the provision of governmental services; the impact of the concept of being a 'global' city on city decision-making; and the role of privatization in city planning and service delivery.

Regional Fragmentation

The national governments of the United Kingdom, China and Mexico, and the state government of New York City have determined the extent to which the metropolitan regions that surround their major cities are fragmented and the impact of this fragmentation on the possibility of regional planning. Both the national and provincial governments have a role in these decisions in South Africa and Germany. One way they have done so is by deciding the location of the city borders (see pages 250–1). Central governments in all six countries have, over time, expanded the boundaries of their major cities . The current boundaries of the City of New York were established in 1898, when the State of New York consolidated what is now Manhattan and the Bronx with Brooklyn and other nearby areas. Parliament's definition of London has increased its jurisdictional area from one defined as within a 26-kilometre radius

of Charing Cross to the present boundaries of the Greater London Authority, encompassing around 1,600 square kilometres. In a mere dozen years (1986 to 1998), China enlarged Shanghai's urban area from 375 to 3,200 square kilometres. The Mexican national government has redefined the borders of Mexico City – the Federal District – many times, resulting in it growing 10 times larger than it was originally. In the 1920s, the Greater Berlin Act combined dozens of smaller cities and villages into a significantly expanded city, and South Africa similarly created the current borders of the City of Johannesburg out of widely disparate white suburbs and black townships in 1995.

Yet none of these cities is large enough to encompass its entire region, and none is ever likely to do so. For many reasons, including central-government policies fostering the creation of new towns outside the borders of major cities, urbanization has extended far beyond the growth of their official boundaries. Sometimes, more people live in the surrounding areas than in the cities themselves. Equally importantly, central governments have divided the surrounding areas into a multitude of different jurisdictions. This fragmentation frustrates regional planning, because there is no adequate mechanism through which to coordinate the policies of the major cities with those of their suburbs.

The six cities do not suffer from this jurisdictional fragmentation and urban sprawl to the same degree. While the borders of London, Shanghai and Johannesburg do not encompass their entire region, the Greater London Authority, the Shanghai Municipal Government and the City of Johannesburg are able to plan for an area that makes considerable sense. The same cannot be said for New York City, Berlin or Mexico City. The New York Regional Planning Association's definition of the core area of the New York City region includes independent cities not only in New York State but also in New Jersey. Berlin is completely surrounded by the state of Brandenburg, where suburbanization is taking place. And the population of Mexico City is almost equally divided between the jurisdiction of the Federal District and the nearby suburbs located in the adjacent State of Mexico. Recognizing this problem, the Federal District has begun a process of intergovernmental cooperation with the State of Mexico by reinvigorating the Comisión Ejecutiva de Coordination Metropolitana. These efforts are still in their early stages. Still, given these recent developments in Mexico City – and the fact that Berlin continues to house most of its region's population – New York is currently the city least able to engage in planning for its immediate geographic area.

To enable regional planning, national or sub-national governments everywhere must redesign governmental structures. Not everyone emphasizes the need for this kind of institutional reform. Instead, there is a great deal of loose talk these days in urban circles about how the region is already the 'real' city. Cities no longer matter, it is often said, because the region operates economically in a way that disregards city boundaries. It is not that important that businesses and commuters disregard city boundaries in their daily decision-making if there is no institution or other mechanism empowered to engage in regional planning and policymaking. If no regional political organization exists that can react to and help direct private decisions, the fragmented municipal governments – along with the national or state governments – will make the necessary policy decisions. It is not true, therefore, that the growth of metropolitan regions and their economic interpenetration have made the borders of the major cities irrelevant. Quite the contrary: city borders remain decisive in the design of metropolitan policy.

WHO CONTROLS?

The population of Greater Mexico City (the *Zona Metropolitana*) is roughly equally divided between the 16 *delegaciones* (districts) of the Federal District and the 58 adjacent municipalities of the State of Mexico. Boundaries between the two entities blur, yet intense political divisions between the Governor of the State of Mexico and the Mayor of Mexico City have historically crippled the greater region's ability to provide infrastructure and services for an exploding population.

Progress on fostering regional planning does not require the creation of a regional government. Of course, such an additional level of government is an option, and some national governments around the world have established them. But it is not the only option, and it has considerable disadvantages. Creating another layer of centralized government with power to supervise local ones can generate considerable confusion about the allocation of responsibility among the multiple levels of supervising governments. Moreover, for a long time local governments have struggled to gain the authority they have now attained, and they often oppose suggestions that will limit their authority. As a result, political opposition to an additional layer of government is often intense.

Instead of establishing a new level of government, the national (or sub-national) government might decide it would make more sense to organize an institution that would bring all the relevant local governments together into an inter-local decision-making body. It can invest this newly created inter-local body with authority to plan for the region and, at the same time, design the decision-making process to maximize the chances for agreement rather than impasse. The Comisión Ejecutiva de Coordination Metropolitana in Mexico is not a full implementation of this alternative structure, but it could be a step towards creating one. The Comisión Ejecutiva is a cooperative undertaking between only two parties – the Federal District and the State of Mexico. In other metropolitan areas, the design of the proper inter-jurisdictional framework would be much more complicated. Moreover, the Comisión Ejecutiva has not been granted its own decision-making authority or the power to raise revenue. But, like future organizations elsewhere, it could be given these powers. In all six countries, central governments can create such an inter-local institution. Doing so would not establish a level of government separate from the municipalities. The municipalities themselves, acting together, would be the decision-making body; collectively they would be able to determined how to exercise their newly granted prerogatives. Regionalism could thus become a vehicle for increasing local power rather than limiting it.

The Organization of Cities

This regional perspective leads many people to insist that public officials and urban theorists should focus only on regions. Because the populations of all six cities represent only a fraction of their metropolitan areas – so the argument goes – the cities themselves are too small to be effective. But these cities can also be considered too large. Berlin and Johannesburg have more than 3 million people; London, New York and Mexico City have more than twice that; Shanghai in turn is twice as big again. Perhaps, then, to make local democracy meaningful, cities need to do more than simply connect to other cities within their region. City-government power should also be subdivided into components so that local residents can effectively make their views known.

The establishment of this kind of subdivision of city government and the need for regional thinking are not unrelated. The empowerment of a region with millions (in Shanghai tens of millions) of people would not allow for meaningful democratic participation by local citizens. But the current boundaries of the principal cities are also inadequate to this task. In contrast, sub-city governments can enable citizen participation in the daily governmental decision-making that affects their lives. Of course, this kind of democratic structure is not accepted as a value in all six cities. Indeed, it is controversial everywhere. Moreover, working out the details of this structure is no easy matter. Nevertheless, it might make sense both to establish district governments within the city and to coordinate their decisions – and the decisions of the cities as a whole – with those of the region. Neither centralization nor fragmentation seems a good way to make public policy.

National or state governments in five of the six countries have recognized the need for some kind of governmental subdivision within their major cities. London, Shanghai, Mexico City, Johannesburg and Berlin all have sub-city governments, although these governments wield very different powers. London has 32 elected borough governments (as well as a financial district in the City of London). These governments are responsible for much of the local government authority exercised within the boundaries of the Greater London Authority. Their tasks range from delivering important services to making planning decisions. Although the Greater London Authority itself has considerable planning authority and controls much of the city's transportation infrastructure, parliament has given it only a very limited ability to intervene into borough affairs. Shanghai is divided into 19 sub-units (18 districts and 1 county), and these sub-local governments, each with its own mayor, also exercise important authority. Unlike in London, however, the Shanghai Municipal Government has significant control over the actions of these district authorities. The Federal District in Mexico is divided into 16 *delagaciones* and, since 2000, the leadership of each has been elected by their residents. As in Shanghai, the government of the Federal District has considerable power over the decisions made by these neighbourhood governments. Johannesburg is divided into 11 regions (currently being reduced to 7) that are responsible, under the control of the city government,for important city services. Berlin is divided into 12 *Bezirke* (reduced from 23 in 2001), each of which has an elected council and a mayor. The district mayors form the Council of Mayors, which advises the governing Senate of Berlin, but district policies remain subject to control by the citywide government.

Once again, New York City is an exception to the pattern found elsewhere. Although it is divided into five boroughs, these have been stripped of most of their authority. In fact, they never had the kind of decentralized power exercized by the London boroughs, the Shanghai districts, or the Mexico City *delagaciones*. Instead, after the creation of New York City in 1898, the borough presidents were members of a citywide government body, called the Board of Estimate, which had an important role in land-use decisions. The population of the boroughs varied widely, however, and in 1989 the United States Supreme Court ruled that the Board of Estimate's structure, which granted equal weight to the votes of each borough president, was an unconstitutional violation of the democratic principle of one person, one vote. As a result, the Board of Estimate was abolished. Borough presidents were also once able to nominate members of the New York City Board of Education, but that too was abolished in 2002. As a result, the boroughs currently have little authority, leaving New York City as the most centralized of the six municipal governments. This does not mean that the New York City government controls all governmental decision-making within the city's boundaries. The state government – and, even more directly, state-created public authorities – exercise considerable power. The power allocated to neighbourhoods, however, is very limited.

The variety of sub-city governmental structures within the six cities demonstrates that there is a considerable range of options for establishing a district-based internal organization of city government. London is illustrative of the power of neighbourhood governments and New York is illustrative of their powerlessness.

WHO GOVERNS?

The offices of the municipal goverments under the direction of the mayors of Berlin (top), Shanghai (middle) and New York City (bottom) wield enormous control over the development of their cities. And although the Berlin mayor is selected by the city parliament, and not elected like the mayors of New York City and Shanghai, the city-state condition of Berlin also provides a hefty budget with which to administer change. In contrast, the two-track government system of Shanghai compromises its mayor's authority, yet still offers a great deal of local control on land use and planning decisions.

Shanghai, Mexico City, Berlin and Johannesburg present alternative ways of ensuring local decision-making power while, at the same time, enabling citywide supervision over the exercise of that power. Other possibilities are also available. Central governments might create a citywide institution that brings together the sub-city governments and empowers them collectively to make citywide decisions. This structure could be similar to the intercity regional organization outlined above for the region as a whole. If it were so designed, decision-making would be organized from the bottom up, beginning with the district and ending with the region. None of the six cities is currently organized in this way. The London Assembly, one of the institutions that constitute the Greater London Authority, has a related but quite different structure. The boroughs themselves are not represented in the Assembly. Instead, election districts for some members of the Assembly combine boroughs into larger subcomponents of the city, while other members are elected at large. Moreover, the Assembly has very limited powers; the powers of the Greater London Authority are principally lodged in the mayor.

Command Centre for the World

So far New York City has stood out from the other five cities. It is the one least connected to its region and least organized into effective sub-components. It also stands out in another way: together with London, it is the quintessential global city. Admittedly, what it means to be a global city is a matter of controversy. I use the term here simply as a short-hand reference to Saskia Sassen's definition of the concept, as outlined in her book *The Global City: New York, London, Tokyo*. She defines global cities as command centres for the world economy and, more specifically, as key locations for finance and related service firms. How does one understand the impact of their global-city status on the power of New York and London? More precisely, what is the role of the city government in producing, or at least furthering, their role as global cities? The answer to this kind of inquiry is by no means clear, despite the fact that the desire to be a global city dominates the consciousness of officials in both cities. It dominates the consciousness of the Shanghai Municipal Government and the City of Johannesburg as well. Although its role in Mexico City and Berlin is more contentious, it is significant there too.

There is little doubt that government officials in all six cities now seek to promote their global-city status. The substantial government-induced investment in the Santa Fe neighbourhood of the Federal District is illustrative of this effort in Mexico City. The results are even more dramatic elsewhere. The Canary Wharf and Thames Gateway in London and the Brooklyn Waterfront and World Trade Center site in New York City are prominent, but are not the only examples in these cities. Johannesburg has shifted high-end business to the 'northern suburbs' (actually part of the city) of Rosebank, Hyde Park and Sandton. Berlin is building a new 'City of Science, Business and Media' – Berlin Adlershof – in the south-eastern part of town. Shanghai is perhaps the most striking illustration of all: the astonishing government-led transformation of the city in the last 15 years, including the creation of the Pudong business area, is one of the most dramatic city-development projects in the world. Although the role of governmental action in these transformations varies from city to city, government has played a role everywhere. Globalization is not some mysterious outside force imposed on unwilling cities. Cities are working hard to advance their global status.

But nowhere does government act alone. Instead, the effort to become a global city, or to enhance that position once achieved, has generally relied on what are commonly called public-private partnerships. The strongest role for a city government in these partnerships is exercised in Shanghai. Doug Guthrie's recent book, *China and Globalization: The Social, Economic, and Political Transformation of Chinese Society* (published in 2006), describes the way in which the Shanghai Municipal Government has guided the development decisions that have transformed the city. For example, it owns all real estate within the city; it leases it, under long-term leases, to private interests. The contracts between the government and the private sector thus frame the way that Shanghai is developing.

London, New York, Mexico City, Johannesburg and Berlin have exercised governmental power to pursue a globalization agenda as well – ranging from providing tax incentives to acquiring land through eminent domain to offering permits to specific developments. All these projects illustrate this governmental role. But the other city governments do not have the power exercisable by the Shanghai Municipal Government. Under the existing centrally established rules that frame city power, these municipal governments adopt a more distanced relationship with the private-development projects in their city. They seek to encourage and direct private decision-making but, unlike in Shanghai, they do not become partners in the development itself. Even so, their power to promote their global-city role is substantial. It is important to recognize, however, that none of the six cities, including Shanghai, can easily slow down the globalization process, or redirect city policy from such a goal. As elsewhere, a national agenda is the primary ingredient in policymaking.

A governmental embrace of globalization has a profound effect on the allocation of public resources and the nature of city life. As Guido Martinotti has argued, a focus on attracting international business – through office-building construction, the establishment of secure residential neighbourhoods, the support for upscale shopping malls and the like – shifts city-government policy from its traditional focus on providing services to residents. Many of those who take advantage of the new business neighbourhoods are not city residents; they are international business people who come and go, moving from city to city. Many city residents, on the other hand, have no connection to the global business network or even to the neighbourhoods in which it is located. Yet traditional city services (education, sanitation, housing, police) have to compete for resources against those seeking to support the global-city policy from a limited budget. Admittedly, a global-city strategy also requires a large support network of low-wage workers, and cities therefore seek to attract – and do attract – many poor residents to undertake the required tasks. The most striking example of this aspect of globalization is the floating population in Shanghai. Estimated to be between 4 and 5 million people, these workers from neighbouring provinces do much of the construction work on the new high-rise Shanghai, but they are denied many city services. Similarly, although some of the new immigrants in London, New York and Berlin, like some of the participants in the informal economy in Mexico City and Johannesburg, provide support for global business, many of them are left out of this part of the city and its economy. As a result, they struggle to live in a city not focused on them as principal generators of economic vitality or as a priority for city development.

The State Bows Out

The public-private partnerships that dominate efforts to promote global-city status are just one example of the trend towards privatization in all six cities. State-created public corporations – quangos, as they are called in the United Kingdom – are another example. The Empire State Development Corporation, one such state-created entity, has played a significant role in the economic development of New York City. Like other public authorities, it is established and controlled by the state, not the city. Moreover, it is organized like a corporation, run by a governing board of directors that is neither elected nor otherwise directly accountable to the public.

Another aspect of privatization is the outright conveyance of property to the private sector. Canary Wharf in London is a prominent example of this phenomenon. According to its website: 'In December 1995 Canary Wharf was purchased by a consortium of international property investors led by Mr. Paul Reichmann and including HRH Prince Al Waleed bin Talal bin Abdulaziz Al Saud, CNA Financial Corp, which is 83 per cent owned by Loews Corporation, Franklin Mutual Series Fund and affiliates of Republic New York Corporation. Canary Wharf Group plc is a publicly listed company on the London Stock Exchange.'

Who Are the Stakeholders Now?

Perhaps the most significant illustration of the trend towards privatization is current emphasis on 'governance', rather than government, as the vehicle for public policy decision-making. What is new in this new vocabulary is not that government is working with the private sector to accomplish its objectives. Government has always depended on the private sector to support its aspirations, particularly depending on it as a source of revenue and investment. What is new is that government no longer feels capable of being the decision-maker. It now needs to come to a consensus with others – with corporations, interest groups, communities, stakeholders.

Who are these people? Who *is* a stakeholder? Which corporations and interest groups are entitled to participate in urban governance? Who is included in the concept of community? It is important to recognize that there is no uncontroversial answer to any of these questions. It is also important to recognize that none of these institutions and groups are citizens. Only individuals, only human beings – not institutions and groups – can be citizens; only individuals can vote. Institutions and groups, however, can share decision-making power. That is, they can become stakeholders, participate in governance, and be appointed to the boards of urban-development corporations. This kind of public-private merger is taking place on a large scale in the United Kingdom, the United States and elsewhere around the world.

The emphasis on governance and the focus on being a global city reinforce each other. Governance imagines 'stakeholders' being 'at the table', working with city officials and others to formulate policy through consensus. It is unimaginable that representatives of global business enterprises will be excluded from such a meeting. However, it is quite imaginable that there will be no one there from the floating population, the informal economy, or representing the poor newcomers who have recently immigrated from another country. Moreover, if the city officials, also at the table, are themselves seeking to promote globalization, a consensus with those in the room may not be that difficult to achieve. There is likely to be disagreement over particulars, but the overall direction of policy can easily be considered uncontroversial – indeed, to be a worldwide phenomenon that no one in the room could conceivably resist.

The trend towards privatization – and, particularly, the current emphasis on governance, rather than government – leads us back to the topics raised at the beginning: regional and sub-city governmental structures. My discussion of regional planning and of sub-city democracy focused on the nature and power of government institutions, not on privatization or public-private structures of governance.

Strengthening both regional planning mechanisms and the internal structure of city government is therefore important not simply for their own sakes. Making government work better and making it more responsive to its citizens strengthens the role of government as it seeks to develop a 'partnership' with private and non-profit institutions. Government provides a source of legitimacy that the other partners do not have. That source of legitimacy is democratic self-government.

Of course, there are ways to foster democratic self-government other than through strengthening regional planning and sub-city institutions. New York City can be singled out once again, but this time it should be praised for its long history of democratic organization. London first elected a mayor through a citywide vote in 2000, as part of the establishment of the Greater London Authority. Mexico City's Federal District first elected a mayor in 1997, having been run for most of the twentieth century by appointed officials. Other cities select their mayors through a parliamentary system rather than by a direct popular vote. Berlin's mayor (like its governing Senate) is elected by the city's House of Representatives, and Johannesburg's mayor is elected in a similar manner by the city council. Shanghai's mayor is not chosen by competitive elections; although he is elected by the Shanghai Municipal People's Congress, he is effectively selected by national officials. Shanghai is by no means unique in having its mayor chosen by and responsible to the national leadership. And London and Mexico City are not unusual in having only recently adopted citywide elections for their mayors. But New York City has had an elected mayor since 1834, and the vitality of its democratic organization is built on much more than its long and contentious history of electing its top official. The city's population is organized and active, and the mayor, like the governor of the State of New York, needs to be responsive to its views. It is not unusual for the government's projects – such as the football stadium proposed for the west side of Manhattan in 2005 and heartily endorsed by the mayor – to be stopped by popular pressure.

Still, even in New York City, one can strengthen the institutions of democracy. Creating regional and sub-city structures is one way of doing so. These innovations can improve the functioning of established democracies and help promote democracy where it does not now exist. Moreover, a change in the current method of governing cities can have an impact not only on government but on governance – on the role of democracy in the world's major cities. If public-private partnerships are the wave of the future – at least, the wave of the near future – it is important to reinvigorate the 'public' half of the arrangement.

POLITICS, POWER, CITIES

Enrique Peñalosa

The definition of a good city lies in the realm of ideology. There is not a scientifically or technically correct or incorrect way of making a city. Defining what makes a good city is more a matter of heart and soul than of engineering. It is more akin to an art than to a science. Yet, despite the subjective nature of urbanism, a government must adopt a vision and promote it, make decisions, build, define rules and enforce them – it must not only envision but also enact the city. If a good city is society's collective work of art, then its government acts as the piece's conductor and often its composer as well.

In *The End of History*, Francis Fukuyama argues that liberal democracy represents the 'end point of man's ideological evolution'. We live at a time in which Adam Smith's market reigns triumphant, the tenet that each person seeking his or her own benefit as freely as possible yields the most benefit to society is widely accepted as the principle on which society should be organized. Any governmental intervention is regarded as suspicious. By its very nature, urbanism cannot go along with that; it is highly interventionist. City creation or urbanism is thus based on an anachronism: governmental intervention. Urbanism has to do with community and society decisions, enforced through some form of government. It is not possible to leave the responsibility of urban design to private entrepreneurs. It is not possible to leave it up to them as to whether there should be pavements or how wide they should be, how high buildings should be, whether there should be parks and if yes, where or how big they should be, and whether there should be a mixture of residential and commercial buildings. The fact that government intervention is essential, together with the reality that there are multiple possible designs for a city, makes urbanism one of the few remaining realms of ideology.

Private Interests and Public Good

In actual urban environments, Adam Smith's notion that individuals seeking their own benefit brings about the best for society as a whole is not always valid. Individual rationality often does not coincide with society's rationality. An entrepreneur may want to build a high-rise building in the midst of a three-storey townhouse neighbourhood; it is a logical individual decision to drive to work in the comfort of one's private car, yet if all the residents of a large city were to do that it would end in a traffic jam and the quality of urban life would be negatively affected. Should the owner of rural land near a city be allowed to do whatever he wants with it, including, for

THE POWER TO CHANGE

The city of Bogotá has been able to dignify many
of the rapidly growing informal neighbourhoods
with initiatives that have improved the quality
of public space and services at the heart of the
poorest areas in this rapidly expanding city of
7 million people.

INVESTING IN THE PUBLIC REALM

Successive mayors of Bogotá, including Enrique Peñalosa, have been responsible for the transformation of its urban landscape. Key realizations include the highly efficient Transmilenio bus system connecting the suburbs to the city centre with dedicated bus lanes (top left and top right); the creation of children's nurseries, schools and libraries (bottom right) which have improved school attendance and literacy levels; and the creation of hundreds of new parks as well as one of the most extensive cycle networks – *ciclorias* – in the world.

example, building a low-density gated community, far from the reach of public transport? How should scarce road space be distributed between pedestrians, bicycles, buses and cars? It would seem that public transport should be given priority over private cars in the allocation of road space, if democracy and the public good are to prevail.

A government has many roles, but to try and construct equality is a fundamental one under democratic rule. For legitimacy to exist in a society, citizens must perceive that a fundamental objective of their state is to generate inclusion and some form of equality. With the collapse of communism, many thought equality as an issue was a thing of the past. But it has too long a history to disappear so easily. Western civilization's roots in Greece, Rome and Judaeo-Christianity cannot disengage from equality. Most social struggles and conflicts over the past 300 years were born out of a desire for equality. It has been said that the eighteenth century saw the struggle for and conquest of equality in civil rights; in the nineteenth century the focus shifted to equality of political rights; and in the twentieth century it moved to equality of social and economic rights. With the fall of communism and the general acceptance of market mechanisms and private property as the best way to manage most of society's assets, the possibility of seeking income equality virtually disappeared, even in the realm of ideology. That does not mean, however, that equality as a social goal is dead.

So, what kind of equality is the goal of today's post-communist society? There are at least two types we can realistically strive for in our time: the first is equality in quality of life, particularly for children. All children should have the same opportunities to develop their potential and be happy, have access to green spaces and play areas, to libraries and waterfronts. The second kind of equality – which is still within our reach and indeed a democratic mandate – is to make truly effective the principle that the public good must prevail over private interest. The first article in every constitution stipulates that all citizens are equal before the law. Consequently, some state explicitly that the public good must prevail over private interest. Every democratic government must have this as its guiding principle. In cities the interests of a few individuals often conflicts with those of the community as a whole. It is the role of politics and governmental institutions to manage those conflicts and find ways of promoting inclusion and social justice.

When a society lacks legitimacy, citizens do not feel bound to obey its laws, even less to denounce those who break them. There is a sense that society is not morally qualified to punish those who break the law. Legitimacy is a subjective concept, related to how much citizens perceive their social organization, their state, to be fair and just. Legitimacy is neither correlated to measurements of economic, social nor political development. Rather it is the citizens' perception of how much their dignity and well-being is a priority to their state, what priority equality and justice are really given in their society, and the truth of the tenet that all citizens are equal before the law and therefore that the public good prevails over private interest.

According to the United Nations, there will be nearly 2 billion new inhabitants in cities in developing countries over the next 40 years. Yet the growth of those cities will be more than proportional to their population growth for the following reasons: households will have fewer members and thus more dwellings will be needed for the same amount of people; more economic development means that institutional buildings – those other than housing – take up a larger share of city space; people demand larger homes as their incomes grow. It is in cities in developing countries that many of the core urban and environmental challenges are concentrated in this century.

CONGESTED TERRITORIES

The aerial view of Caracas reflects the spatial predicaments of many Latin American cities. Towers of varying scale are juxtaposed to the interventions of transport engineers, while over a million people live in unplanned *barrios* without access to basic services or infrastructure (far left of the photograph).

And issues of equality and inclusion are particularly relevant there, as their societies are highly unequal. Inequality and exclusion can be even more painful than poverty, but the way we create and organize cities may be a powerful instrument in constructing equality and social justice.

Equalizing Factors: Public Space

Public space dedicated to pedestrians can be an equalizer – a means to a more inclusive society. In public space people meet as equals, stripped bare of their social hierarchies. During work time the highest executive and the lowest-ranking employee may be equally satisfied or dissatisfied; in public space they both meet colleagues and do their jobs. It is only during leisure time that an abyss separates their quality of life. The upper-income executive goes home to a large house, probably with a garden, has access to sports clubs, country houses, restaurants, expensive cultural activities and trips abroad. The low-income person and his or her children live in a very small dwelling and the only alternative to television for spending their leisure time is public space accessible for pedestrians. Pavements, bicycle lanes, plazas, parks, promenades, waterfronts and public sports facilities show respect for human dignity and begin at least to compensate for inequality in other realms.

Access to green spaces may be the most formidable barrier to inclusion, not only now but also into the future. Until recently, few people believed the poor would own refrigerators, ordinary telephones, much less mobile ones, colour televisions, washing machines or sophisticated hi-fi systems, all of which are rapidly becoming common household items, even in lower-income homes in developing countries. Over the next few decades, lower-income citizens will all have access to computers and a wide array of electronic equipment. What they will not have is access to green spaces and sports facilities – unless governments act today. Open spaces are precious because neglecting to acquire and secure them today is not something that can be remedied easily in the future. It would be extremely difficult to purchase and demolish hundreds of buildings in order to create green spaces. And lacking such spaces severely affects quality

UBIQUITOUS SPRAWL

The artificial environment designed around
manicured lawns and cul-de-sac enclaves has
become the trademark of the emerging middle
classes in cities around the world. This new and
expanding neighbourhood in Bogotá creates
a physical context that lacks the continuity and
complexity of many traditional city forms.

of life, inclusion and, as a result, the legitimacy of social organization. Beyond the basic public pedestrian space, which should be found throughout the city, a good city should have at least one, and ideally several, 'grand' public spaces. That is to say, spaces of such quality that even the wealthiest members of society cannot avoid frequenting them.

Waterfronts are unique resources, which enhance the well-being of those who are able to enjoy them. If the public good is to prevail, access to all waterfronts must be open to all citizens. In urban areas waterfronts must have infrastructure to facilitate their enjoyment, such as promenades, pathways and benches. Private, and thus exclusive waterfronts, particularly in and near urban areas, are evidence of a lack of democracy and ineffective government.

Most cities in developing countries do not have adequate pavements – those that are at least wide enough for two wheelchairs to pass or move alongside each other, with ramps at crossings. Often there are no pavements at all, or they are occupied by parked cars. Cars parked on pavements and parking bays carved where there should be pavements are symbols of a democratic deficit and a lack of respect for human dignity. It shows that the needs of citizens with a car are considered more carefully than those of people who walk. A quality pavement shows respect for pedestrians, who make up the majority of the population.

A protected bicycle lane may be politically irrelevant in Holland, but in a city in a developing country it is a powerful symbol, showing that a citizen on a US$30 bicycle is as important as one in a US$30,000 car. A protected bicycle lane along every street is not a cute architectural fixture, but a basic democratic right – unless one believes that only those with access to a car have a right to safe mobility. Quality pavements and bicycle lanes show respect for human dignity, regardless of the level of economic development of a society. Many citizens in economically advanced societies cannot drive, because they are too young or too old, or because they have some kind of disability. A democratic city must be designed for the most vulnerable of its members.

In most countries today environmental impact studies are required by law before any infrastructure project can be approved. International agencies such as the World Bank also require such studies for projects they finance. These are positive advances in protecting waterways, plants and animals. However, these concerns do not seem to stretch to people. Developing countries' citizens who drive private cars and have political influence are often very sensitive to environmental issues, but they show a lack of similar concern for the living conditions of the poor. Even roads that are more used by pedestrians and cyclists than by cars rarely have an integrated pedestrian and bicycle infrastructure. Just as environmental impact studies are mandatory, 'human impact' studies should be required for all infrastructure projects. There are thousands of kilometres of drainage canals in cities in developing countries. If pedestrian infrastructures had been built alongside them as a result of 'human impact' requirements, extensive pedestrian networks would have been created.

The slums that abound in most developing country cities are also evidence of lack of democracy. Even when there is abundant land suitable for urbanization, the poor are forced to locate on steep slopes prone to landslides and other risks, or on low lands, which are often flooded – sometimes annually. Although over time poor neighbourhoods may solve the worst flooding risks and end up getting water supplies, sewage and other basic necessities, they are never cured of their lack of public space. Sometimes those neighbourhoods do not even have streets.

That such *favelas*, *bidonvilles*, *tugurios* happen in Rio, Mumbai, Bogotá, Caracas,

Jakarta and Nairobi, among many other cities in developing countries, shows that it is not simply a matter of poor governments. There is a systemic problem with the very social organization of urbanization. The fact that once people are able to obtain a piece of land, they are able to muster the resources to build their houses is a very clear indication that access to land is the root of the problem. Private property and the market do not work well in the case of land surrounding growing cities. They work with computers or tomatoes: when prices are above costs, supply increases and prices are driven down. That does not happen with land around cities: prices can go up indefinitely, yet the supply of land accessible for transport, jobs, schools and water supply, will stay fixed.

Governments must manage land around growing cities closely, either by creating large land banks or by controlling supply and prices. Ideally, to become urbanized land should be acquired by governments at rural prices, well ahead of its development. Communist countries such as China and Vietnam, where land belongs to the state, should have the ideal conditions for quality urban design. Unfortunately in such countries, where land is publicly owned and the land control required to achieve quality cities should in theory not be an issue, urban land-management often leaves much to be desired. Lack of solid municipal fiscal structures means that land is sold without sufficient thought of preserving some of it for parks and other facilities accessible to pedestrians.

The Failure of Democracy

It is with regards to transport that governments have most dramatically failed to comply with democratic principles in cities in developing countries. There is a fight for the scarce road space between cars and public transport, pedestrians and cyclists; and there is a battle for public funds between car owners demanding more road infrastructure and lower-income citizens demanding schools, sewage systems, housing, parks and other basic infrastructures (see pages 260–3). The minority car owners usually command the most political clout and thus direct public investment to road infrastructure aimed at reducing peak-hour traffic jams, leaving the needs of the poor unattended. Moreover, both urban and rural roads ignore or take poor care of pedestrians' and cyclists' infrastructure needs.

There is no 'natural' level of car use in a city – it is defined and determined by its government. Mature city governments such as those of Paris, New York, Tokyo, Berlin or London, explicitly or implicitly defined long ago that regardless of traffic conditions no more road infrastructure would be built in their core areas. Resources would be concentrated on public transport. If governments in Manhattan or Paris had built more and bigger roads, there would be increased car use in those cities. On the other hand, if these governments had built fewer or smaller roads, car use would have decreased there. In summary, it is the amount of infrastructure available for cars that determines the level of car use.

The governments of less-advanced cities are reluctant to make the inevitable decision: no more road infrastructure in the built city, regardless of traffic jams; resources will be concentrated not on more or bigger roads but on creating, expanding and improving public transport. From then on, car use must be restricted explicitly through means such as number plate-based use restrictions, tolls, parking limitations; or implicitly, through traffic. Many advanced cities have seen famous citizens battle against urban motorway projects. One of most high-profile is Jane Jacobs' fight against the Lower Manhattan cross-town expressway. In most advanced cities today 'transport policy' really means finding ways of achieving lower levels of car use and a higher share for public transport, cycling and walking in overall mobility. In cities in developing countries 'transport policy' still largely means the opposite: how to facilitate more car use. In societies in developing countries, where less than 50 per cent of households do not have a car, having one is held as a visible certificate of belonging to society's higher echelons. Upper-income people in less-developed and highly unequal societies tend to see using public transport alongside lower-income citizens as an affront to their position in society. Although they gladly use public transport when they travel to more advanced countries, they rarely go near it in their own.

Despite such difficult political contexts, a government that cares about quality of urban life and democracy has to progressively veer away from trying to reduce traffic jams through investments in new or bigger roads, and instead concentrate on creating or improving mass-transit and pedestrian and bicycle facilities. This is partly because a city that makes too much room for fast-moving cars becomes less humane and loses quality of life, but also because road-infrastructure investments aimed at alleviating traffic jams, primarily benefiting higher-income citizens, redirects public funds away from schools, parks, housing and many other needs. The most vulnerable members of society, such as the poor, the elderly, children and disabled citizens, are not normally conscious of their interests and rights and do not have much political influence. A democratic government must act as their proxy and confront powerful minorities on their behalf. It must present and explain its vision so as to convince even upper-income groups that car-use restriction benefits them as well in the longer term. But in the end it must wield its decision-making power in order to implement its vision regardless of political costs.

The Wealth Divide

A frequent source of inequality is the division of cities or metropolitan areas into several, sometimes dozens, of municipalities. Almost inevitably, wealthier citizens cluster in a few of those, while the poor end up elsewhere. Unfettered market forces create a situation in which expensive neighbourhoods for wealthier citizens attract similar high-income developments around them. Land around high-income developments tends to be expensive and normally low-income neighbourhoods will not be established there. The reverse is true too: a high-income housing development will not usually be developed next to a low-income one. The case of lower-income Washington DC surrounded by higher-income Maryland and Virginia municipalities is only one of thousands of examples to be found all over the world. And unlike Washington DC, other lower-income municipalities do not have the American federal government within their territory to plead to when in need.

A healthy, large city will have both low- and high-income groups. Higher-income groups provide tax funds to tend to the needs of lower-income groups. They pay high taxes and often do not even use many services provided by the city: they use private healthcare services and their children go to private nurseries and private schools. Municipalities with lower-income citizens have a greater need of social services provided by government, yet no possibility to muster the necessary funds to provide them. Inequality ensues. Blunt extraction of funds from wealthier municipalities in order to transfer them to lower-income ones does not solve the problem: it has been found that those who spend funds not generated by themselves tend to do so inefficiently. To make matters worse, poorer citizens with lower levels of education tend to be easy prey to demagogues and corrupt politicians.

While there may be historical reasons for the existence of several municipalities within one city, once they are part of a large, modern metropolitan area there is little justification for them. Most citizens cross municipal borders unaware of their boundaries, except of course when the absurdity of such political subdivision is so extreme that public transport has to turn back at the border of the municipality, as happens in São Paulo. Long-term planning also becomes complicated when such subdivisions exist. Even the construction of a critical road artery or railway line becomes problematic. When different political parties control different municipalities, more problems arise, as has been the case in Mexico City. Bureaucratic expenses of many small municipalities are higher than those of one large one, and often the level of professional competence is lower within the smaller municipalities.

For these reasons Canada has merged nearly 1,000 municipalities over the last decade, achieving more social justice, lower bureaucratic expenses and better long-term planning. In Johannesburg several municipalities were also merged after the end of the apartheid regime, to achieve greater equity. Municipalities with higher-income citizens tend to oppose these mergers, as some of their funds will subsequently have to be redistributed to lower-income areas. Many small-town politicians also oppose them as they may end up in an unelectable position, or simply because they prefer to be, as the saying goes, the head of a mouse rather than the tail of a lion.

Government Responses to Social Inequalities

Innovations are always difficult to implement. The status quo starts with a majority support, while ideas for change start with only a minority behind them. Even a politician, who earns the majority's support and is elected to government, has to confront difficulties if he or she wants to implement change. Effective government institutions are needed in order to convert a vision for a city into reality. What role should national or regional governments have in a city? It is necessary to have a clear definition of responsibilities at each level and adequate financial resources to assume them. Citizen participation is an important ingredient in an advanced democracy, but in very participatory local constituencies, such as those in Switzerland or New England in the United States, it is difficult for more centralized government bodies to lead the promotion and implementation of innovations. Change may take longer, but there is a guarantee that the public good will direct public decisions. In cities in developing countries, where the poor are too busy surviving to participate much in government decisions and often do not even have time to be informed about them, it is the role of government to represent them, to ensure that decisions lead to greater equality and justice and not to the contrary. It is a difficult task, because those benefited are often not conscious of the battles engaged in for their sake while those affected do take offence. Interest groups are usually better informed and more participative, even vociferous, than society at large. If government is to act in a democratic manner it must assume those battles and their political costs.

Government must act on behalf of the majority and also of the most vulnerable members of society, but it must also act on behalf of future generations. It is desirable, for example, to acquire rural land surrounding the city, voluntarily or if necessary through eminent domain (the seizure of private property for public use, with appropriate compensation), in order to preserve it for future urban development or parks. There is a conflict between funds required to tend present and pressing needs and a responsibility towards the future. Solutions to some present needs can sometimes be postponed, but land that is not acquired and preserved today is lost

THE CITY AS A SPACE OF CONFLICT
Prior to its use for recreation, this marginal
space in Caracas was the site of continued
violence, the red circles on the wall denoting
the residue of gun shots.

for ever, while land acquired and saved for future parks will yield happiness to many generations to come.

It is not possible for governments to provide all citizens with individual goods such as electronic equipment or clothes, yet it is possible to provide quality public goods and services: schools, libraries, transport and green space. Moreover, once citizens achieve a certain income level, it is easier to increase well-being through public goods than through private goods: through a concert hall, a green area, a waterfront. To get a 20-kilometre-long pedestrian street less than four blocks away from home can increase most people's quality of life more than increases in income. Taxes sometimes make it possible to increase not only society's well-being but also that of the individual taxpayer through a transfer from the consumption of private goods to that of public goods.

Satisfaction is not the opposite of dissatisfaction. If we open the water tap and no water comes out, it causes dissatisfaction. Yet to open the tap and get water does not exactly leave us ecstatic. Lacking what is deemed essential causes dissatisfaction, yet having it does not provide much satisfaction. Those apparently less-indispensable public goods provide the most satisfaction. Government must therefore be imaginative and take risks. For example, quality public pedestrian space is not a dire need, yet it provides much satisfaction. And its capacity to provide pleasure never wears out.

Inequality permeates everything around us so pervasively that it is difficult to differentiate between what is inevitable and that which could be altered. It seems that the social changes achieved by the French Revolution were obvious, almost natural, since the injustices redressed were so flagrant. However, such injustices were not even evident before that moment in time. Hundreds of years had gone by, in which grotesque privileges for the nobility and abuses of common citizens had been considered normal. In the same way, we are often not aware of the many examples by which the public good does not prevail over private interest. Investments in flyovers to minimize traffic jams for upper-income groups seem normal. The poor in the same city might lack schools, basic sanitation and sometimes even clean water, while private waterfronts, pavement-less streets and urban roads abound. If we were truly rigorous in applying the prevalence of the public good, cities in developing countries would ban private cars during peak hours. Only a minority would be affected. Most people's travel would take less time and there would be less air pollution; less road building and maintenance would free public funds for provisions for lower-income majorities.

Most public policy discussions and decisions, such as those relating to macroeconomics, are very short-lived. Even the most transcendental political events often do not affect people's lives as much as they are thought to. At the risk of appearing sacrilegious, it is for example irrelevant for the way people live today whether most countries' revolutions or wars of independence occurred 100 years earlier or later than they actually did. Instead, the way cities are built determines to a large degree the quality of life of their citizens for hundreds of years into the future.

The task is not simply to create a city that functions efficiently. It is to create an environment where the majority of people can be as happy as possible. Happiness is difficult to define and impossible to measure, but it is ultimately what all efforts, collective or individual, are about. Developing countries are unlikely to reach today's advanced countries' income per capita for many decades, maybe even centuries. But they have the opportunity to learn from the successes and failures of advanced countries in order to create different, better cities, which means above all cities propitious to happiness.

The Ideal City

Over the last 40 years the environment has become an issue of deep concern to all societies. So much so that today any 10-year-old anywhere in the world is worried about tropical forests and the survival of whales and mountain gorillas. Curiously, a similar interest in the human environment has not yet arisen. We are far from having a shared vision of an ideal human environment. It is said that world sustainability will depend to a large degree on what will happen in cities, particularly in fast-growing cities in developing countries. Yet, what is a sustainable city?

What is the most sustainable environment for a Galapagos Iguana or cave bird? It seems to be that which allows each animal to most fully develop and be able to realize its potential. Realization of one's potential is very close to the definition of happiness. Therefore it could be said that the most sustainable environment for an animal is that which is most propitious for its happiness. In the same way, the most sustainable city is, before anything else, the one most propitious to human happiness. And although human happiness has many definitions and requirements, in terms of habitat it demands elements such as being able to walk and play; having contact with nature such as found in parks, trails and waterfronts; being able to see and be with people; and feeling included and not inferior.

So far urban quality of life has been referred to in relation to issues such as equality and happiness. But there is another aspect to consider – a country's competitiveness in the information age will depend largely on the quality of life in its cities. Whereas land was the source of wealth and power in agricultural societies, capital fulfilled the role of land in the industrial stage. In today's post-industrial society the source of wealth is creativity and knowledge, be it that of a film director, a scientist or an engineer. While land and capital have an intrinsic value, creativity and knowledge are attached to individuals. It is they who create wealth. In the Middle Ages neighbours had to be conquered in order to acquire their wealth-generating land. Until recently industrial societies proffered subsidies to attract wealth-generating industries and capital investment; now it is necessary to create environments to which wealth-creating people are attracted. Often people are willing to accept lower real incomes as long as they live in a better city. And of course higher pay is demanded when a job requires living in an undesirable city. More important than tax rates or port infrastructure, urban quality of life can be the most valued competitive factor in the new economy.

IN SEARCH OF AUTHENTICITY

Rem Koolhaas

We are living in the waning hours of the mythology of the architect. This is an exciting but also a very complicated situation to manage. By definition, the architect is an agent of change. Since the beginning of my involvement with the profession, I have been shocked that there was no register or repertoire that allowed us to merely look, merely observe and also to decide to abstain from any activity. Architecture can never be passive and there is a strong intolerance for our profession when we cannot provide any answers – and perhaps worse, when we do not even claim any answers.

In my career I have tried to unilaterally sidestep that pressure, and to follow a journalistic intent in documenting the city and its current evolution. This has very often been interpreted as a kind of heartless cynicism. I would argue that this kind of perceived cynicism, when confronted with almost documentary evidence of how the city is evolving before our very eyes, suggests a structural issue in architecture and of observation in architecture. Somehow we conceive of ourselves as those who only act and definitely not those who see. Faced with this huge tsunami of unknown urban substance, the most important thing that architects can do is to write new theory.

This is probably a very unfashionable position. Nevertheless, it is quite shocking that since Jane Jacobs, and since the Venturis' *Learning from Las Vegas* (1972) and my own *Delirious New York* (1978), there has been hardly any theoretical description of the city by architects – of how it performs and how it should perform. The current malaise, the dearth of new ideas and the recycling of old ones, is partly to do with that situation. It is a pity, because for the first time in the East we are facing new potentials, while in the West we have a public sector that, after decades of feeble activity, seems to have found a new confidence in handling and managing the private sector.

In London, for example, after years of caving in, the public sector has almost aggressively taken the initiative and has proved successful in imposing that initiative. Our absence of manifestos, or absence of being able to claim a degree of 'newness', is dangerous. If we cannot produce new theory – and it is undeniably not an easy task – we could at least find new words. I noticed how Saskia Sassen introduced the word 'cityness' and how that word, even if it is pretty ungainly, has immediately been picked up. This shows there is a huge eagerness and a huge need for new words. If we find new words there is a hope of producing a framework of understanding. Without a framework any means of instrumentality are futile.

I used to be almost contemptuous of architecture myself, and on a rhetorical level I have done a lot to question its kind of plausibility. Recently I have become more

NEW REALITIES

The cultural, economic and social conditions of
the new generation of African cities – illustrated
by Alexandra in Johannesburg – are challenging
the theoretical and technical skills of the design
professions engaged in re-shaping their future.

TWO KINDS OF CITY

The future development of cities around the world faces conditions of unique specificity and generic similarity. The massive scale of urban growth in Lagos (top) challenges all perceived notions of public space while the speed of change in relatively affluent but centralized Asian cities like Shanghai (bottom) generates highly debased forms of modernity.

impressed again with architecture. Unlike many other fields, architecture at least has a kind of depth of memory, and in its very awkwardness and chaotic multifaceted nature – dealing with economics, politics, aesthetics, civilization – it maintains at least a sympathetic and sometimes impressive ambition to connect the dots.

I would like to say something about people in our position – those who are not a typical segment of the architecture population, who are condemned to so-called stardom. This has the perverse tendency of removing us from relevant issues of architecture. I am dying to work in a neighbourhood. I would love to do social housing. I would be interested in working for people with disabilities. But in the current configuration of the architectural profession this is unthinkable, despite sometimes passionate attempts. This removal from issues of relevance starts perhaps with our removal from the local context – rather than working on what we know, we systematically have to project ourselves into the unknown. In the best cases we do this with integrity, by trying to learn about the conditions in which we work. In the worst cases we simply project our own footprint and stamp it on again and again. For me this became a huge obstacle, which is why I went to Africa: to show that I had a heart.

Richard Sennett has introduced the terms 'gentrification' and 'gentility' and 'civility' in many of the Urban Age conversations. For me the real issue is that of authenticity. The tragedy is that the architectural profession is constituted in such a way that it can only remove what was there: i.e. it can only remove authenticity. I have an intuition – or perhaps an optimism – that in the near future the most important growth in cities and the most important aspect of cities that represents a serious shift, will be that they will no longer be places of affluence, but rather places of poverty or perhaps poorness. It is exactly in this poorness that we may be able to find subtler ways of intervening.

I would, therefore, like to discuss the developing world – because if we continue to describe the world where most urban development currently takes place as developing, then we should call ourselves finished in the developed world, done. There has in fact been some evidence of this. The issues presented by New York and London are at this point really about how to maintain very ancient and very large cities. This can only be looked at in the context of other urban and mass-urban development as they have been evolving in both the very poor parts of Africa and in the increasingly affluent parts of East Asia.

It is dangerous to discuss the world, and therefore the urban condition, in a specific situation as though there is a relative similarity between conditions around the world. There is, for instance, the question of literacy – vast numbers of new urban inhabitants are illiterate and are therefore doomed to participate in the condition of the city in a different way. While we agonize over public space in the western world, in developing cities such as Lagos, public space is not an issue, and I believe that public space is a dominant experience of the city. Every square metre is used most intensely for both private and public life, and there is almost a merging of the two. It is rarely possible to witness a larger intensity of urban interaction than in these really poor conditions.

We are confronted with another irony – and potential tragedy – in the richer south Asian conditions. This can be seen in China, for example, where the state is not entirely committed to the market economy and therefore still has the potential to generate large and collective entities (and therefore another kind of city). The situation results in highly debased forms of urban modernity and a consistent import of western precedents, which is not really very useful.

The words 'memory' and 'public space' are almost coincidental. Currently we have a very tortured relationship with that coincidence, particularly in the West. Our anxiety – about the past, about memory – is in direct proportion to our success in destroying it. This is exemplified in Hitler's former headquarters at the Berchtesgaden in Germany, which has recently been turned into a wellness centre. A western culture that makes such drastic and thoughtless site and function transformations, driven by the private sector, is seriously dysfunctional in its defence of what is public. It shows a tendency towards indulgence in vast projects of artificial memory that often occur at the expense of the original memory. The Berlin Wall is another staggering example: a monument itself would have shown louder and harder what the former tragedy had been on this site. Instead it has literally been dismantled and replaced by a series of more professional memory fabricators that now dedicate vast territories to a memory that could have been kept in its original form. It is a cliché that public space is not what it once was, that it has increasingly been contained. Less evident is the fact that we allow ourselves to be lulled into a false privacy, in which privacy is in fact traded for security, where we become willing participants in a regime of constant surveillance. We live on a curious diet of harmlessness alternating with catastrophe.

The greatest concern in all this is the complacency of the design activity field and its inability to conceive of any form of resistance. There is an incredible proliferation of new firms that are not quite design firms, but which specialize in the design of public space. These companies advertise and define themselves using words such as 'audacity', 'vivacity', 'elasticity'. A new kind of rhetoric is noticeable everywhere. The word 'gentrification', which only a decade ago had a negative connotation, has now become positive. In this gentrification, urban life has been reduced to four sectors: film screenings, music, shopping and fashion. We have therefore seen a kind of systematic laundering of authentic conditions in urban life in the name of those four categories. Increasingly, the design of our public space has become a hyper-nostalgic celebration, another form of absolute denial. It has become a celebration of its absence. On the one hand we have a kind of faux-republican style of rapid emblems of former civility. On the other is an over-scripted labyrinth of infotainment. We are all complicit in an operation in which public-private partnerships and high-tech policing continue to not only generate massive gentrification but also to a situation that could be recapitulated as gentility or death.

That is the ultimate outcome of this form of urbanization. The irony is that many of the regions now urbanizing are tropical. In the marketing machine their tropicality will be countered by air-conditioning, not by regime change, which will make all these imaginary utopias largely irrelevant. The outside is evacuated, the inside conditioned and the public turns into a captive audience. I have listened with appreciation to inventories of architectural studies that could be mobilized in these circumstances and that could provide alternatives, but I have experienced too often the problem by which the need for speed will be used against these alternatives, which will be labelled as experimental and untested and therefore, in the current market economy, as irrelevant. What may be the most exciting potential of the Urban Age project is that we are discussing a city like New York at the exact moment of its disappearance. We therefore need to shift the light on to ourselves – not to look back at what we have, but at what we might have again.

This text is based on the author's participation at the Urban Age conference in New York, February 2005.

THE PARTICULAR AND THE GENERIC

Jacques Herzog and Pierre de Meuron

CITIES IN FLUX

Launched by the opening of its ports in 1842 to western influence, Shanghai was until World War II a divided city with foreign zones under extraterritorial administration. The evolution of this 'Paris of the Orient', with its strategic location as the gateway to China's most affluent region, brings a steady influx of foreign investment and architecture as well as 3 million internal migrants without basic rights.

At some point it had all been decided: history was finished. Reality was an illusion, a fiction, a simulation. Cities were interchangeable, a blind, indistinguishable backdrop for the one remaining urban activity – shopping. We thought virtualization and simulation would rob cities of their souls, would suck them up in a kind of body snatching. End of history. Eternal life. But the bodysnatching has only occurred in the minds of one generation of thinkers and urbanists. What has actually happened? Nature has made a comeback. Terrorism has returned. History is beyond extinction, beyond control. Reality has suddenly become real again – and finite.

Terrorism is not an illusion; it is not a simulation. It has a very real impact on cities and city dwellers. The real damage may be patched up, but the aftershocks keep coming. The source of the shock is combated homoeopathically, as it were, by using the same means. Suddenly terrorism is omnipresent, real and mentally, on the streets and in people's minds. The vulnerable beauty of American cities appears more radiant and seductive than ever before, but they have now acquired the museum-like aura of something that has survived. The American city has become an urban model from times gone by.

On Sunday, 27 September 2003, much of Italy's power supply collapsed.[1] Out of nowhere Rome experienced a *notte nera*. That very night was meant to be a *notte bianca*, a white night of brightly illuminated museums. Nature, in all its sublime rawness, quite literally reappeared overnight – a menacing force that people had been lulled into believing was under control.

These menacing forces do not flare up on remote uninhabited islands; they concentrate on the city, as platform and stage, and throw it entirely off balance, forcing upon it a painful confrontation with its own historical transience and vulnerability. Cities have always been subject to immanent, existential threats: sieges, conflagration, famine, rape, the plague, earthquakes, raids, floods, gangs, unemployment, outages, Mafia. Every city grows and takes shape in relation to its own specific scenario of menace, which has emerged in the course of its history and coerced it into an unmistakable and inescapable pattern. Cities are specific because they are confronted with specific threats and they show a concrete, physical response to them. Cities are unfathomable – a trait that explains their distinctiveness. It also explains the difficulty of describing cities, of making plans for them or confining them to theories.

Not one city has ever succeeded in liberating itself from the real, simulated and cultivated bonds of its local context in order to reinvent itself. Not even after real and

radical catastrophes. On the contrary: the reconstruction of Germany's cities after the war aptly illustrates how much the (ideal) picture that cities had of themselves varied, leading to equally varied scenarios of reconstruction. These variations were greater than those that characterized the many centuries prior to the bombs that reduced them all to uniform rubble, and they have become still more marked today, even putting their stamp on newly emergent neighbourhoods by means of simulation.

Take Frankfurt and Munich. The former is a city of burghers, of *citoyens*, who have consistently taken the initiative in using their city as a platform for trade, business and urban services. The latter is a city of princely traditions, with a royal line that modelled itself in the eighteenth and nineteenth centuries after its Italian counterparts and essentially re-created a piece of Italy on German soil. Post-war Frankfurt chose to start with a *tabula rasa* and opted for a vertical skyline; Munich remained loyal to the royal court imagery and followed a path of reconstruction.

Frankfurt's *tabula rasa* and Munich's historical simulation are expressions of cultural and cultivated difference, as if the bombing had brought to light a specific urban character which had hitherto lain dormant. And what might be said about Rotterdam or Beirut or Jerusalem in this respect? Every city cultivates and internalizes defence mechanisms against the deposits of real and imagined threats that have accumulated through time. Baudrillard has put it this way: for want of a real catastrophe, one must resort to simulation to induce equally great or even greater catastrophes.

Nuclear-proof shelters sprawling through Switzerland's underground like an invisible replica of above-ground civilization are a characteristically Swiss form of urbanism, possible only in a country where the withdrawal mentality and the need for security have acquired an almost hysterical reality. Mass evacuation, gas-alarm practice, barricades, terror and anti-terror, Mafia and anti-Mafia – common to all these defence strategies and scenarios is their indisputably specific modification of cities. Preventative or corrective intervention makes concrete and sustained inroads on the reality of urban development, resulting in a kind of substratum. This substratum is not apparent and sometimes not even visible because it is not simply a folkloristic detail. On the contrary, it has a profound, formative and programmatic effect on the artificial and natural topography of cities.

This does not make cities increasingly uniform, general or even faceless. The opposite occurs: it makes them even more distinctive. A self-referential focus in cities leads to growing immersion in their own world. They become specific, like a singular species, with all the attendant fascination, as well as the unbearable and inevitable self-absorption and idiosyncrasy – a phenomenon that applies to all cities. It describes their ugliness and their beauty, their culture, subculture and lack of culture, their rise and decline, their real catastrophes and threats as well as their simulation and substitution – the inevitability and finiteness of cities.

There Are Only Cities

'Finite City' sounds tautological and misleading because it takes to task the apostles of an imminent culture of immortality. 'Real City' is ambiguous, especially since we are interested only in the physical reality of the city and do not, under any circumstances, want to open the Pandora's box of a discourse on reality. Nor does 'Specific City' fit the bill, unless the specifics target the mental morphologies and transformations that are causing cities to become increasingly wrapped up in themselves. Could it possibly be the 'Idiomorphic City' or the 'Idiosyncratic City'? Or even the 'Idiotic City',

DISTINCTIVENESS OF CITIES

As the financial and transport centre of Germany, Frankfurt (top) is home to the European Central Bank and the Frankfurt Stock Exchange, making it the third largest financial centre in Europe after London and Paris. Its profile of contemporary commerical architecture contrasts sharply with Munich (bottom), the third largest city in Germany after Berlin and Hamburg. The abundance of baroque and neo-classical buildings provide poignant reference to Munich's royal past.

because we are incapable of grasping this most complex and interesting of all things ever created by human hand? The ideal city abdicated ages ago, including Aldo Rossi's 'Rational City' or Rem Koolhaas's 'Generic City' or Venturi's 'Strip', not to mention Le Corbusier's 'Ville Radieuse'. All these attempts to describe the city, to comprehend and reinvent it, were not only necessary – they made sense. But today they leave us cold as they do not relate to us, because they refer to a world that is no longer ours. The time has come to relinquish our longing for labels, to abandon manifestos and theories. They do not hit the mark; they simply brand the author for life. There are no theories of cities; there are only cities.

All cities have one thing in common: their decline and ultimate disappearance. This one factor unmistakably shared by all cities paradoxically fosters the potential for fundamental difference. This difference no longer rests on the efforts of city planners. If today's planners want to contribute to the transformation of cities, they will have to become accomplices and confidantes of the potential of threat. In even more pointed terms, they should adopt the single-mindedness and accuracy of the terrorists. Their work will have to be unprejudiced, a blank sheet, devoid of theory and – to repeat – fathomless. It will have to address the physical, built reality of the city, where the life of the city is as unmistakably manifest as climate fluctuations are on the drilling cores of polar scientists. Only there – in the physical body of the city – can we also discover the neuralgic spots that Barthes called the *punctum* in respect of the photograph and Baudrillard 'worthwhile targets' in respect of the Twin Towers.

When these Towers were struck with the precision of a surgical operation, the bumbling helplessness of contemporary urban construction was instantly made manifest. Hardly ever do urban projects truly impact and change cities; they serve only to preserve the status quo. They merely multiply what is already there. City building does not begin with Barthe's *punctum* and it does not seek the most worthwhile targets; it takes action wherever a plot of land happens to be or become available. Even so, there are Twin Towers in every city and their destruction affects urban dwellers everywhere. Terrorists see the destruction of symbols; urban dwellers see a massive attack on their neighbourhoods and their homes. The specific, the unique, that which distinguishes us from others, the indestructible have proved vulnerable: we have to protect ourselves again and again. But how? The best protection would be to aspire to 'indistinguishability', the 'Indistinguishable City'. And that is the greatest illusion of all.

Originally written as an introduction to research on Naples, Paris, San Francisco, St Petersburg, the Canary Islands and Basel, and an urbanistic study on Switzerland, ETH Studio Basel – Contemporary City Institute, 2003.

THE DEATH AND LIFE
OF THE URBAN OFFICE

Frank Duffy

The archetypal twentieth-century city is North American in origin, technology and values. The test of a real city was a skyline dominated by high-rise office buildings clustered downtown in a central business district. A less-conspicuous but equally characteristic feature of many cities, as they developed in the latter part of the last century, was an outer ring of suburban business parks where often even more office workers congregated than in the central business district. Worldwide office workers in city centres had to rely on massive, old, sometimes creaking public-transport systems designed to cope with sharp morning and evening peak loads. Suburban offices also generated huge peaks in demand for commuter access every morning and every evening of the working week but via two even greedier consumers of time, space and energy – the automobile and the motorway.

That the office building should generally have been taken for granted as an important and continuing component of urban form is hardly remarkable given that such a large proportion of the workforce in developed economies – as much as 50 per cent – is engaged in some form of office work. However, there is reason to believe that demand for office space has already peaked, certainly in the two conventional forms and locations identified above. More significantly, because the nature of office work is now changing rapidly, the typology of conventional office buildings, both high-rise and low-rise, has become less reliable as a guide to future development. The accommodation of office activities is becoming a far more fluid and mutable phenomenon than many architects, developers and investors believe, so strongly are they conditioned by the past.

Even within the limits of the Urban Age experience, it has been possible to observe a wide range of divergence from this model. There are important differences in the way that the office function has developed in urban and architectural terms in the six cities, differences that are related to historical as well as to economic, political and cultural factors. A growing awareness of these parallel physical and social differences has stimulated the formulation of three principal questions. Is the bipolar distribution of office work, the sharp separation of living and working, and the daily commute the inevitable, single, ultimate destiny of all cities? Are there alternative models of the relationship between office work, city structure and the working population that may become even more plausible and legitimate given what appears to be the emergence of very different work patterns and lifestyles? If so, how broad is the range of possible urban and architectural forms that we should anticipate?

These questions are given an even sharper and more urgent edge by two contemporary phenomena: the astonishing worldwide explosion in the power, reliability and ubiquity of electronic technology over the last two decades, and the related rapid growth of the knowledge economy. Given such epochal changes, the continuing dominance of the conventional North American models of both the city and the office cannot necessarily continue to be taken universally for granted in the twenty-first century – especially as the North American city and the North American office building are the products of a particular work culture related to a pre-knowledge economy, a specific episode in economic history and a special approach to the governance of cities.

Missing the Point

It is not only in the United States that far too much is taken for granted by urban planners and architects about offices and office work. Paradoxically, in a period in which technological and social changes have never been faster or more far-reaching, fundamental questions about the future of the workplace are rarely addressed seriously by architects and urbanists anywhere.

The scale of the changes that are taking place in this decade in the world of work is enormous. What we are experiencing is more fundamental than anything that has happened since the early years of the Industrial Revolution.[1] It is not just our physical working environment that is changing, but also our temporal environment – the way in which we structure the use of time. A similar shift happened 200 years ago when the ancient agrarian way of life based upon the calendar of slowly changing seasons and of holy days regulated by the phases of the moon was rapidly superseded by an industrialized concept of time. When country folk migrated from the hills and the fields to work in mills in the valleys they made a bargain to exchange the open fields for the factory. Industrial workers, except those lucky enough to have peripatetic jobs, were bound by two entirely new conditions for getting work done: the twin imperatives of synchrony (having to work together in large numbers at the same time, often in shifts) and collocation (having to work together in the same place, as prisoners of the loom, the furnace or the coal face). Given the limited technology of the industrial age, few other choices existed.

Today the sociological implications of technological change are completely different – more forgiving in some ways, in other ways even more tyrannical. Field workers had their winter sleep. Even factory workers had their holidays and days of rest. Ubiquitous technology, exemplified by the already commonplace Blackberry, offers knowledge workers unprecedented freedom of movement and a completely open-ended choice of locations and times to carry out at least some of their work. However, the very utility and attractiveness of such devices make many office workers feel that it is their duty to be accessible from any direction at any time of the day or night, weekday or weekend. And yet, through massive inertia, the anachronistic temporal and spatial logic of the Industrial Revolution continues to be the norm in urban and office design. Office workers remain physically and culturally trapped in their cubicles like Dilbert in Scott Adams' heart-breaking cartoons, based on his experience working for Pacific Bell, or like Ricky Gervais within his office in the equally upsetting contemporary British television series, *The Office*. Despite a rapidly changing context, the vast majority of contemporary cities and offices show little evidence of an intelligent response to these challenges, either by celebrating new freedoms or, more importantly, by attempting to find new ways to alleviate new problems.

The Politics of Planning

The principal challenge in the design of twenty-first-century urban and office space is not creating new kinds of physical working environments to make the best possible use of the new, mobile technology. It is the much more difficult task of creating new, more civilized conventions in the use of time to tame intrusive technology and prevent it from destroying us and our social relations.

Obviously these are cultural, political and ethical matters. The design of workplaces is a subset of the design of cities, and the design of cities is itself a subset of politics. Understanding the cultural conventions upon which urban and office design has been based in the past is an essential first step to agreeing the conventions upon which the design of the twenty-first-century city and office building should be based. In an increasingly electronic world, many office-based enterprises have already discovered that the problem-solving potential of both virtual and physical realms is roughly equivalent. It is commonplace for managers today to have an equal choice when addressing a complex, open-ended, intellectual or business problem, involving several disciplines and necessitating the bringing together of parties that are widely separated geographically. They are free to proceed in one or other of two very different ways: either by arranging a series of face-to-face meetings or by being completely reliant on electronic communications. The consequence of this simple, day-to-day, technological choice is that urban designers and architects must be prepared to face up to the possibility that within the next decade a completely virtual environment might well have become sufficient for their clients to carry out all their knowledge work. In other words, the null hypothesis that designers are impelled to test today is the powerful argument that place will soon no longer be necessary. The mental exercise of justifying the value that physical places and real spaces add to knowledge work is not just a technical matter but also an ethical necessity. The future of the professions that provide places depends upon such a justification. Without it urban design and architecture will have no intellectual credibility.

Neither spatial nor temporal conventions invent themselves. They are cultural constructs for which urban designers and architects are ultimately responsible. The only way to reinvent the workplace – and ultimately the city – is for designers to be granted the intellectual firepower to persuade their clients to reject the outmoded formulae that have determined the shape of cities and buildings in the past. They must demonstrate that the way things used to be done is no longer good enough for tomorrow. More optimistically, it is obvious that the changes taking place today in the workplace give urban designers and architects an unparalleled opportunity to justify not only their jobs but also the essential value of place. However, to design workplaces and cities that are appropriate to the continuously emerging technology and economy of the twenty-first century, it is necessary to go back to first principles.

Is Shanghai the New Chicago?

Chicago towards the end of the nineteenth century was a city of prodigious growth and unstoppable energy. A small band of supremely talented architects and engineers invented the skyscraper to accommodate new entrepreneurial activities while simultaneously multiplying the value of land. Within the Chicago Loop these high-rise buildings were serviced by an integrated logistical infrastructure running beneath the city streets. Urbanistically and architecturally few previous innovations had been so ambitious, innovative and complete.

A European architect visiting the city 100 years ago would have been struck by

MOBILE LABORATORIES
The design of office space is increasingly challenged to keep pace with today's itinerant work styles. Mobile technology enables round-the-clock productivity with transactions occurring outside of the formal office environment. Likewise, the expanding service sector demands constant access to information and communication with clients, as well as work environments requiring interaction among various segmented departments.

three things.[2] The first would have been the radical novelty of constructional technique; secondly, the ruthless disregard for architectural precedents of any kind. Thirdly, had he been curious and intelligent enough to enquire, he would have been amazed by the application of commercial and industrial logic to architecture, not just in the way that Chicago's buildings were designed and constructed but also in terms of the processes by which they were financed, marketed, fitted out and, above all, used.[3] It was not by accident or zeitgeist that Chicago exhibited the prototype of vertical skyline that is still regarded by many as proof of the modernity of cities. David Burnham, Louis Sullivan, Frank Lloyd Wright and other supremely talented architects were certainly lucky to be in the right place at the right time, when the Midwest was being opened up by the railroad as the factory and bread basket of the world amid the extremely favourable context of the burgeoning post-Civil War American economy. These architects made their own luck by applying architectural and engineering imagination of the highest order to exploit an unprecedented concatenation of economic, social and technological opportunities. It was not precedent that shaped Chicago. The city's architects invented the twentieth-century city out of nothing but sheer imagination and originality. They designed from urbanistic and architectural first principles in a time, very much like the present, characterized by rapid technological, commercial and social change.

In comparison, the processes through which the new Shanghai is being built today, while hugely impressive economically, seem architecturally and urbanistically both retrospective and chaotic. High-rise office buildings and motorway systems are being taken off the North American shelf rather than being rethought in architectural, constructional or urbanistic terms in ways that are appropriate to the conditions of the dynamic, emerging Chinese economy. In terms of the office as a building type, there is very little evidence in Shanghai of anything like the same order of innovation or depth of understanding of the place of the office building within a modern economy that was the chief characteristic of the late-nineteenth-century office-building boom in Chicago. More worryingly, there is no evidence of any imaginative interest in how office work and the city are likely to change as a result of the increasing power of information technology.

Shanghai has not yet been innovative. North American and, to a much lesser extent, European models of office buildings are being replicated with enormous energy to accommodate generalized office work of a conventional, unambitious and old-fashioned kind. Even the quantity of space being built in Shanghai is probably too much – although the city is starting from a very low base. Measurements from all over the world demonstrate that office space is one of the least well-used of all business resources, being more than half empty most of the working day.[4] Why should the actual use of office space in Shanghai today be any different, especially given the time- and space-annihilating potential of information technology? Who in Shanghai is worrying about the amount, type and quality of office space that is really needed and at what cost and for whose benefit? Who is fighting for the quality of the public realm, the space between buildings? Should decisions about such matters be left to developers whose motives, with rare exceptions, are driven entirely by supply-side considerations and whose practical understanding of accommodating the organizational and technological changes that their tenants are experiencing is notoriously defective?

There is at least a partial excuse for Shanghai's conservatism in office design and acceptance of its complete divorce from advanced thinking about the nature of cities. The contemporary American office – the dominant model for the rebuilding of

Shanghai – demonstrates a shadow of the confidence and professionalism of office design in New York City and Chicago 30 years ago. It is a ghost of the explosion of innovation in those cities 100 years ago. Exhaustion and entropy have become the norm. The great tradition of Yankee invention has been overtaken by repetition and cost-cutting. Tenant demand has been swamped by supply-side considerations that are wrongly assumed to drive office development. Formulaic solutions are everywhere; fresh thinking nowhere. It is extremely unfortunate that Shanghai appears to lack the critical apparatus in its governance that would help the city understand why the architectural and urbanistic tradition that is shaping its workplaces today is exhausted and inappropriate for accommodating the emerging knowledge economy. The city's future is being compromised by an intellectually bankrupt and office typology that is in terminal decline.

The European Alternative

North American office design, while certainly the most dominant tradition, was by no means the only way in which office buildings were procured, designed, constructed and managed in the twentieth century.

To arrive from London in New York City or Chicago in the 1960s was to experience the American office as the confident, sophisticated, glittering image of American economic self-confidence at its imperial peak.[5] In New York City, Lever House (SOM, 1954), the Seagram Building (Mies van der Rohe and Philip Johnson, 1958) and the Ford Foundation (Roche Dinkeloo, 1963–8) are magnificent architectural manifestations of commercial culture. In Chicago, the Inland Steel building (SOM, 1958) with its detached core and column-free floor plate is to this day a wonder of scientific constructional technique. Within the Loop remain the grand nineteenth-century prototypes epitomized by the Reliance Building (Burnham and Root, 1895). Less visible but even more impressive was the highly professional North American system of delivery of office buildings, in which the division of labour between specialists – developers, brokers, architects, space planners, interior designers and many different sorts of engineers – was at that time unparalleled in Europe.

And yet it was in war-damaged northern Europe in the late 1950s that the first serious challenges to the North American model of the office began to emerge. The first manifestation was *Bürolandschaft*, usually translated as 'office landscaping', a free form of open planning very different to the orthogonal grids that still dominate North American office design.[6] In office landscaping, in theory at least, relationships within the workplace were based on the measurement of the internal flow of information. Implicit in office landscaping was the idea that the form of the building should be derived not from external, real-estate considerations but from internal patterns of communication. However, the landscaped office was overtaken within a decade by another, less functional but far more powerful imperative: that the form of the office should be based on democratic ideals – to play down hierarchy and to protect the rights of the individual office worker.

Bürolandschaft office buildings were generally low-rise, characterized by large open-plan floor plates and sometimes by a fluid, free form of architecture that deliberately indicated they were shaped from within rather than by the external, exchange-driven priorities of real estate. The shape of the offices that quickly superseded *Bürolandschaft* throughout northern Europe in the 1970s was the opposite: narrow, linear buildings, in which all occupants were provided with their own independent room with direct daylight and aspect. Such was the democratic ideal driving these designs that almost everyone was given an individual office and every such room was the same size. The building that marked the transition from office landscaping to social-democratic office architecture is Centraal Beheer in Apeldoorn (Herman Hertzberger, 1970–2) – an heroic attempt to use robust but highly penetrable interior architecture to reconcile the managerial advantages of open planning with local autonomy for individuals and small groups. This part of Hertzberger's experiment was never replicated. However, he was also attempting to turn the office building into a miniature city, full of streets and squares and places to meet. This idea has flourished and is exemplified by the sophisticated office complexes designed by the Norwegian architect Neils Torp (SAS Stockholm, 1987, and BA Heathrow, 1995) and by hundreds of similar buildings throughout Scandinavia, Germany and the Netherlands.

THREE TYPES OF OFFICE
The Taylorist office (top), the Social-Democratic office (middle) and Networked office (bottom).

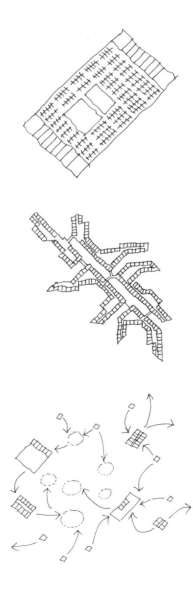

Three Types of Office

Despite the risk of a gross oversimplification of a complex topic, it may be helpful to distinguish three main streams in the development of the office building in the twentieth century.

The Taylorist Office

These offices were shaped by the huge, if indirect, influence of Frederick Taylor – the inventor of 'Scientific Management' – and his followers on office culture, technology and design. Taylor's most important contribution to industry was his insistence on the importance of systematic study of the human factor in industrial processes. Implicit in his programme was that the generalized observations of scientists and trained observers were a better guide to increasing productivity than trusting the craft skills, discretion and judgement of individual workers. The dark side of what has come to be called 'Taylorism' was a tendency to deskill and dehumanize labour – an accusation frequently made about Henry Ford, who applied Taylor's principles to the production line. Gilbreth and others were quick to apply Taylor's somewhat mechanistic, top-down managerial ideas to office work with enormous and lasting consequences in the characteristically hierarchical, rigid and repetitive but highly efficient design of the North American office.[7]

The Social-Democratic Office

The strong northern European reaction described above to the Taylorist office was driven by a widespread concern that the identity and well-being of individual office workers should be more important than simple measures of productivity. The social and political context of post-fascist northern Europe, and the reaction to what was widely considered the unchecked capitalism of North America, led to highly cellular office buildings in which the dominant idea was less the facilitation of communication than the protection of the rights of individual workers. These rights, reinforced by democratically constituted Workers' Councils, ensure that every office worker at every level should have an equal share of environmental benefits – privacy, enclosure, fresh air, external views, social facilities, etc. The architectural consequence is a complete reversal of the Taylorist proposition – office buildings that are democratic rather than controlled from high up, in which individual choice is given greater priority than military-style allocation. Social-democratic buildings tend to be purpose-built, not developer-led. They are low-rise rather than high-rise. They provide shallow, complex, uneconomical office space rather than cheap, deep,

THE OFFICE BUILDING AS ICON

The Seagram building in New York's midtown Manhattan, designed by Mies van der Rohe in 1968, has become an icon of Taylorist interior design and rigorous formality of both its office culture and architectural language.

efficient floor plates. The overriding priority is the welfare of staff rather than cutting costs.

The Networked Office

Networked offices began to emerge in the 1990s as a direct consequence of the revolution in information technology.[8] The fundamental difference between this type and the Taylorist and the social-democratic office is that since robust, reliable, ubiquitous information technology is taken for granted, the relationship between people and their workplaces and between people and their use of time, has changed fundamentally. United by the Internet, knowledge work can be carried out by any combination of people occupying 'any place, any time'. Clients, large and small, are reinventing their processes – not least their use of office space – to take global advantage of technological development. For architects the implications are enormous, suggesting the redesign of workplaces for people who are mobile, both within and outside the office. For urbanists the consequences are even greater: rethinking the basic infrastructure of cities that has long been predicated on the five-day week, the working day and the assumed sharp separation of home from workplace. The convenience and attractiveness of virtuality mean that the usefulness of real places and the functionality of real cities need to be justified by what they offer for the future rather than what they have always been. The challenge for both urban planners and architects is no longer the design of individual buildings but the invention, often on a global scale, of a combination of real places and virtual networks to accommodate highly mobile and demanding knowledge workers who prefer to come together physically only when face-to-face interaction can add obvious value to their work.

Who is Afraid of the Taylorist Office?

Why is the Taylorist model of the office still so dominant globally when the fundamental conditions that have underpinned its success for so long are being challenged in at least two principal ways – firstly, by the northern European emphasis on the importance of the rights of individual office workers and secondly by the new spatial and temporal freedoms that networked knowledge workers are learning to take for granted? The easy answer is inertia. The real reason lies deeper: a reluctance among urban designers and architects, often obsessed with formal considerations, to imaginatively address the political, cultural and design implications of the processes through which office buildings are funded, promoted, procured, constructed, leased and occupied. These processes should not be regarded as givens but as matters of choice full of consequences for architectural form and urban structure.

The Taylorist office is the construct of a very specific supply chain – an investor-funded and developer-led process leading to highly standardized office space that is cheap to build and easy to lease. Fundamentally the process is exchange-driven and is as Taylorist in its values as the form of the buildings themselves. That this process is not neutral but has long-term aesthetic consequences becomes very clear when comparing the magnificence of the office buildings in New York City and Chicago of the 1960s, when the Taylorist logic still had some validity, with the deteriorated quality of most office buildings in these cities today. Entropy is the inevitable consequence of decades of cost-cutting to the exclusion of value adding. Cost-cutting is the inherent weakness of a dehumanized, degraded, unthinking version of the Taylorist process.

Similarly the social-democratic office is not just the result of the political influence of the Workers' Councils – important as they have been – but also of a more

THE OFFICE BUILDING AS PLACE
Herman Hertzberger's design for the Centraal Beheer office (top and middle) in Apeldoorn, the Netherlands (1972) was modelled on the company's ethos that prioritized individual and informal contact within a highly professional atmosphere. These design principles are carried through in Niels Torp's design for the BBC Media Centre in White City, London (2004), which is based on an organic plan designed to promote a less hierarchical office culture (bottom).

complex set of factors including a very different supply chain characteristic of northern Europe, especially Germany. This supply chain, unlike the Taylorist model, favours purpose-built, highly specific office buildings that are intended for long-term ownership by the companies that occupy them. Many of these are privately or family owned rather than quoted on the stock market. The architectural consequence is buildings that are purpose-built and much more influenced by specific user considerations than institutionally owned, developer-driven offices. There is no doubt that some of the highest-quality working environments in the world have been created in this way. However, the social-democratic process has three serious – perhaps fatal – weaknesses: high costs and inefficiencies are tolerated; elevated user expectations, often enshrined in building regulations, have become anachronistic as life and work styles change; and finally, too much emphasis on individual work has resulted in over-privatized environments and the relative neglect of the potential of the office to facilitate the collective exchange and development of ideas – now critical in the knowledge economy. Inertia thus afflicts the social-democratic office well as the Taylorist office.

The networked office has its own specific process of procurement. Networked businesses tend to have very short time horizons because they are designed to respond to rapid change. Their concept of the ideal office is similar to a hotel – the provision of a series of services supplied on demand and paid for by the hour, the day or the week rather than by square metre per year, like the Taylorist office, or owned outright as the social-democratic office typically is. One important consequence is that networked organizations are much more interested in space in relation to output. They are prepared to measure the value added by each design feature or service. Most importantly, because of the very nature of networked organizations, the design features and services they demand are likely to be as much related to collective, social, knowledge-building activities as they are to the accommodation of solitary work.

It is too early to predict what the weaknesses of the networked office will be. One encouraging feature is that the concept of continuous feedback is inherent in the process – particularly appropriate as the changes involved in adopting new, more mobile ways of working are so profound that managing cultural change has to be taken very seriously.

The Six Cities Compared
Compared with this neat typology, the ways in which office space is provided in the six Urban Age cities in reality is much more complex and varies enormously.

On the fashionable western edge of Mexico City lies Santa Fe, a development obviously intended for the international business community with glassy, international office buildings, shopping mall and well-guarded housing for the rich. Boundaries are everywhere – even street trading is sanitized. Nothing happens by accident; everything is planned. On the eastern side of the city can be witnessed the opposite phenomenon: the enormous community of Neza where, every year, hundreds of thousands of immigrants arrive in buses and on foot from the country to establish themselves and their families in the big city. Neza provides the simplest and most basic of infrastructures. Everything else is down to an essentially open-ended and networked community that appears to be succeeding in establishing a lively economy out of literally nothing. In the historic centre of the city, near the Zócalo, there is evidence of attempts to reuse old buildings for new enterprises in order to vitalize the community and the economy.

The environment of Johannesburg is even more contrasted and extreme. Much of the city centre, which looks from a distance like the downtown of a Midwestern city, has been abandoned by much of the business community. Big office buildings have been taken over illegally by migrant workers. The city streets have become one big market. Attempts are being made by the remaining large corporations and the city to revive, or at least stabilize, the centre, but it is clear that most new entrepreneurial activity of the conventional modern sort has retreated to walled and guarded suburban communities like Sandton. On the outskirts is another legacy of apartheid – vast dormitories like Soweto, a monument to a less voluntary form of division, representing the dire consequences of a regime that adopted a form of planning based on racial segregation and a crazy, reciprocal logic of top-down allocation. Despite this fractured legacy, post-apartheid Johannesburg is now governed as one city rather than as a series of divided communities.

Shanghai is vast, dynamic and perplexing. A huge model of the city is displayed to impress visitors with the seething building activity both in the city centre and in the ring of new towns springing up, including the ecological community Dongtan. Quite what the plan is in economic terms is difficult to fathom, except that there seem to be no limits to entrepreneurial activity either in the office or the housing market. As described earlier the dominant model for new office buildings is very large, ambitious, high-rise, standalone structures, some of which are designed by prestigious, western architectural practices – literally with no questions asked. While the longer-term utility of these buildings is highly questionable, frenetic economic activity continues all around. Meanwhile the modest but charming fabric of the old city, with a few notable, refurbished exceptions, is being swept away ruthlessly. What is lacking from the knowledge economy's perspective is the provision and management of spaces for discourse and exchange within office buildings, and the protection of accessible public and semi-public spaces *between* office buildings.

Berlin is a city with very few high-rise office buildings. The model chosen for the commercial redevelopment of the huge bomb-damaged gap in the middle of the city to the east of the Brandenburg Gate is self-consciously European – sober buildings of a standard height, which are attractively ambiguous in their use: some offices, some housing, some hotels, some retail – very much the relatively dense, even pattern of old Berlin. Berlin does not have the dynamic of growth seen in the five other Urban Age cities. But it is clear that as the city overcomes the division created by the wall, an extremely useful and unplanned informal resource for the development of creative enterprises as part of the knowledge economy is the large stock of centrally located, redundant industrial buildings. Such buildings are plentiful on both banks of the River Spree, symbolically straddling the wall. They are available, relatively cheap and susceptible to mixed use.

London's office stock has changed substantially in the last three decades. From having some of the worst developer office buildings in any city – the legacy of an under-funded and unimaginative, developer-led rebuilding programme in the 1950s and 1960s – the city was shocked into modernization of its office stock by the deregulation and opening up to foreign competition of the financial services industry and the related revolution in information technology. A similar and parallel process on the outskirts turned industrial estates into business parks for high-tech firms. Meanwhile, whole areas of the formerly decayed fabric of the inner city, such as Covent Garden and Soho, now accommodate a host of relatively small media and advertising companies. Most recently, hedge funds, wanting to distinguish themselves from the rest of the financial-services industry, have colonized Mayfair. Canary Wharf and Broadgate were substantial and, at the time, highly necessary office developments. Their downside, given the rapidly developing knowledge economy, is that they are expensive, hermetic and impossible to change. While other large developments are under construction, the clue to London's continuing success is not so much the provision of large new office buildings but more their juxtaposition, given the complex and village-like nature of the city's fabric, to smaller and cheaper business and other premises.

In many ways New York City is similar to London, although increasingly conservative architecturally in the last 30 years. What still makes Manhattan work is its compactness, the efficiency of the subway system and the mix of large, robust and still relatively new office buildings. Because of the compactness and density of the city core, these more conventional offices are never very far away from semi-redundant, basically well-built industrial and retail space, still available relatively cheaply and highly attractive to newer, smaller enterprises. Manhattan is above all a dense, mixed-use city, compact and easily navigable, with lots of accommodation of all kinds including many centrally located apartments. New York City has always been and continues to be good at accommodating change – despite the narrow focus and conservatism of its new-build development and real-estate community. Across the East River, in Williamsburg, and across the Hudson in Hoboken, for example, are vast resources of redundant industrial space and developable lots astonishingly close to Manhattan.

Given the vastness and complexity of urban phenomena this analysis is necessarily superficial. However, it is clear that in all six Urban Age cities there is a massive mismatch between the simple, single-use, segregated office buildings that developers like to supply and the infinitely more subtle and shifting patterns of demand for the wide range of workspaces that are already required at all levels and prices in both developing and developed economies.

The Contribution of Place

Two things are already clear from these six Urban Age case studies. The first is that large concentrations of top-quality office space in highly segregated zones are vulnerable at the best of times, but are becoming particularly dangerous in a period when a step change is being made towards networked ways of working that are far removed both from the organizational cultures based on command and control characteristic of the North American office and from the hyper-democratic individualism that has shaped the northern European office since the 1970s. The second is that cities are fortunate if a large amount of cheaper mixed-use space, available to a wide variety of tenants at variable rates and on different terms, is closely juxtaposed to the more expensive space that still suits larger, well-established enterprises. What is necessary for the economy of cities does not appear to be attractive to developers who like to keep things simple.

What is also clear from the case studies is that cities are increasingly vital for the development of the knowledge economy. Considering the function of office work, in all its complexity, as a subset of city life, the six cities provide plenty of evidence of the value of the concentration of activities. However, it would be dangerous to assume that the concentration of office work in cities will be unaffected by the increasing power, reliability and ubiquity of information technology.

The case for the value of place as opposed to the convenience of the virtual realm still needs to be made. Virtuality will certainly change the ways in which we use space and time. The rigid diurnal and weekly temporal structure of the Taylorist and the social-democratic offices is likely to be undermined by the freedom offered by new ways of working. But, face-to-face contacts, however intermittent and irregular, are likely to be valued much more in the knowledge economy.

What place offers and will continue to offer is a level of meaning and vitality built into streets and squares, rooms and anterooms, that the virtual world cannot rival. Place is essential for making possible the phenomenon of serendipity, encounters between people and groups that occur in more or less accidental but nevertheless semi-planned ways. Place generates a tension and a spontaneity of response that is difficult to replicate in the virtual world. Place supports discourse because it is harder for people to hide, making both contradiction and agreement more likely. Cities should be thought of as multiple layers and concentrations of networks, both face to face and virtual. The most successful and intellectually fertile cities are the ones, like London and New York City, where the greatest number of networks are concentrated at high density in a relatively small area, so that there is the highest probability of overlap and leakage from one network to another and hence the greatest potential for stimulus and cross-fertilization.

Mapping the way in which knowledge-based organizations work gives a carto-graphic insight into the complex and interlocking social and intellectual matrices of, for instance, law, medicine, engineering or architecture. What makes these professions relevant to this discussion is that they are both pre- and post-Taylorist in their operations – more networked, more social, more interdependent, more open-ended, more confrontational and more permeable within and between themselves than corporate enterprises. Professional practices are independent and highly competitive, but they take for granted constant collaboration across business boundaries. They operate fluidly in and from multiple locations, depending upon finely calculated serendipity to maintain open-ended contacts – in courts, university lecture halls and clubs. Professionals work in their own offices and homes but also more socially in restaurants and coffee houses, even in busy streets – in exactly the same way as intellectuals operated in eighteenth-century Paris and London.

What cities also provide is memory and association – a rich and complex language that transcends more elementary forms of communication. Open-ended discourse is built into urban spaces, which is neither contradicted nor replaced but rather enhanced by the accessibility of electronic networks. Concentration of access to people and knowledge of every kind is what makes cities work. The beauty of using the city as an image of the new office is that the city is large and complex enough to accommodate movement and change, permeable boundaries, multiple uses, multiple constituencies, endless complementarities between the physical and the virtual.

Diversity is Everything

So, is the bipolar distribution of office work, the sharp separation of living and working and the daily commute the inevitable, single, ultimate destiny of all cities? The diversity of the six cities studied in the first phase of the Urban Age project is a useful contradiction of the Taylorist and social-democratic myths that limit our imaginative grasp of how life is lived today and even more of how we will live our lives tomorrow.

Are there other models of the relationship between office work, city structure and the working population that may become even more plausible and legitimate, given what appears to be the emergence of very different work patterns and life styles? The principal task of urban designers and architects is to imagine and legitimize diversity and to convey to clients, politicians and the general public a sense of the richness of choice that the freedoms provided by information technology can bring to society in the knowledge economy. The worst thing we can do is to attempt to force the new economy into buildings designed to reinforce outmoded ideologies.

How wide is the range of possible alternative urban and architectural forms we can anticipate? The potential range is enormous – diversity is everything. Four ideas come to mind immediately. First, the articulation of a much wider range of types of urban space that would transcend the arid public-private dichotomy that impoverishes contemporary urban discourse. Second, the invention of building forms that would be capable of accommodating a much wider range of uses over time than our contemporary vocabulary of single-use building types. Third, more rational and sustainable transport that would avoid our present dependence on over-centralized and peak-dominated systems. Fourth, the acceptance of new conventions in the use of time that would help people to better manage the unwanted intrusiveness that is the chief vice of information technology, the chief virtue of which is to make so many other things possible.

Finally, the price of breaking old bad habits in architecture and urbanism is not just to imagine what the new urban realm will be like physically, but also to be clever enough to realize how poisonous outmoded processes for financing, procuring and delivering workplaces are, whether Taylorist or social-democratic. Both value systems are irrelevant to the future city. To deliver the new world of the knowledge economy we have to invent new ways of allowing people to procure the future city without contaminating it with the past.

HOW ROADS KILL CITIES

Hermann Knoflacher, Philipp Rode and Geetam Tiwari

If we want to understand transport in cities, we have to understand human behaviour in the urban environment. No society can exist without the movement of people, goods and information. This is generally regarded as a requirement for evolution, be it through the facilitation of trade or, most importantly, for human interaction. Modern transport collapses distances between locations and should, in principle, be equally available to everyone. But transport is often treated as an end in itself. It offers the most direct evidence of technical progress. It is taken as an aspirational reflection of lifestyle, a physical representation of political achievements. It is the *raison d'être* for the world's most powerful industrial sector. Transport is one of the most highly contested areas of development.

From Space for Movement to the Movement of Space

Urban settlements developed around places that allowed people to meet, exchange ideas and live in safe and secure surroundings. Networks of private and public streets formed the arena for movement and were developed in accordance with the needs of their pedestrian users. Typically, not more than ten per cent of the city's surface was used for movement; this required people to live close to where they worked.

The situation changed significantly during the nineteenth century, when street-cars became widespread throughout the industrial world. Higher speeds supported by mechanized transport were introduced to the same networks that had mainly been used by pedestrians up to that time. With an increase in speed came an increased risk of accidents and the need for a new hierarchy in the use of existing networks. The faster modes of transport were given priority and pedestrian movement was limited.

However, public transport, including commuter and metro rail networks, still played a complementary role to the pedestrian city and generally reinforced its structures. It served longer distances in a wider network of urban connections at extremely high efficiency levels with regards to space and energy consumption. The introduction of mechanized public transport also maintained the need for social interaction as people continued to travel collectively. As a transport system with a high degree of control, public transport further allowed for integration with the overall planning of urban structure when, for example, decisions on locations of stops and stations had to be made.

Shortly after the turn of the twentieth century the presence of the car – both moving and stationary – became more and more intrusive in the public realm.

入場券36・37・43・44号機 →
定期券発売機29・30・31号機 →
Suica.イオカード発売機27・28号機 →
Suicaチャージは27・28・34～52号機 →

FULL SERVICE

Tokyo's Metro system is the world's largest and most extensive. The first line opened in 1927 during the city's rapid urbanization, followed by substantial expansion in the mid-1950s. Organic and incremental growth of the system has happened since, helping to make Tokyo a full-service global city and the most populous metropolitan area in the world, with a metro system used by over 80 per cent of its population to get to work.

Pedestrian movement was legally restricted to pavements, if not banned altogether in certain areas. Owning and driving a car became a symbol of freedom of movement, constrained only by the lack of space within city centres. But car drivers found places to live and work outside the traditional city borders, and this allowed them to significantly increase their average amount of personal living space.

Over the last half of the twentieth century this had a dramatic effect on the urban structure of cities in the industrialized world. Space-consuming traffic moved economic, cultural and leisure activities away from urban centres and transformed the cities into agglomerations – an effect that has become known as urban sprawl.

City-making in the twentieth century was dominated by a single paradigm: optimizing conditions for the movement of cars. Large areas in and around the city were tarmacked for motorways and parking while pedestrian space was reduced to a minimum. 'Transport' in its original sense lost its meaning and car traffic flows became the dominant parameter for planners and decision-makers. The free movement of cars was given priority over the quality of urban life.

Optimizing traffic flows meant not only dedicating large amounts of space to the high-speed movement of machines, often occupied by a single individual, but also adopting urban design solutions that corresponded to the new requirements of speed – linear, monotonous structures lacking design quality or sympathy with the human scale. Paradoxically, in cities built around cars and their movement, efficient access to urban space was often drastically reduced. Cars require significantly more space than other transport modes. On average, cars take up about 170 square metres per passenger at 50 kilometres per hour, as opposed to a tram which needs 2 square metres per passenger. In addition, because of the systemic character of car traffic, roads act as major barriers in cities. This is exemplified by the well-researched fact that increasing traffic flows significantly reduce the social interaction of residents living on opposite sides of the same street.

Human Behaviour in an Artificial Environment

For thousand of years, cities developed based on the 8 per cent of muscle energy available in the human body for low-speed pedestrian mobility. With the introduction of the steam engine and the invention of railways, more people were able to be transported over longer distances. This did not relieve them from their social obligations, however. Public transport is a socially agreeable kind of mechanical transport; it encourages people to act socially.

As cars became available in greater numbers, a significant change occurred in human behaviour. When urban space became dominated by car drivers moving at high speeds, society seemed willing to accept it, and when parked cars in public spaces started to suppress other human activities, it was regarded as a parking problem rather than a car problem. As a consequence, proposed solutions prioritized the need for parking and parking fees were not even remotely close to the real market prices of an equivalent amount of public space. In most cities around the world, car users still receive a substantial subsidy from their city councils, reaching up to EURO300 (US$400) per month in some European cities. Car-focused thinking has changed social values.

The effects of car use on urban life have been well documented: public space has become a dangerous territory, particularly for vulnerable street users such as children and the elderly; air and noise pollution threatens the city's eco-system. The spatial requirements of car mobility have become the greatest challenge for a dense and

CHANGING TRANSPORT CULTURES
In 2003, the Shanghai government announced a ban on bicycles from all major roads. At the time, there were over 9 million bicycles in circulation, increasing at a rate of 1 million each year. Although a cycle lane network was subsequently planned, the city maintains that the ban will help ease Shanghai's choking traffic congestion.

complex urban form. It is in the latter context that Richard Sennett referred to the paradox that 'individualized spaces provide less scope for individual experience'. The additional cost of motorization also includes the feeling of increased insecurity in cities. When public space was converted into carriageways for mechanical transport modes, the windows of the surrounding buildings – what Jane Jacobs called 'the eyes on the street' – disappeared. Public space often became a socially uncontrolled environment full of risks and dangers.

Over the last 200 years, too many transport and urban planners have ignored most of these issues while technicians, engineers and architects worked in isolation, without taking into account society's wider goals. They have optimized single elements such as vehicles, roadbeds and alignments, public transport and buildings while treating them as separate, isolated areas. This fragmented approach ignored larger developments and has placed the future of cities seriously at risk.

The Paradigm Shift

These failures have encouraged society at large to return to the fundamental questions about the nature of urban life. What are the essential qualities of our cities, what is the benefit of their proximity, and what are the appropriate transport solutions to achieve them?

This debate has made enormous progress and has resulted in extensive urban regeneration efforts in cities around the world. The latest transport revolution, based on communication and information technology has turned out to actually support the authentic character of the city. The advantages of reduced commuting times and the reduction in money spent on travelling is as critical in the developing world as the benefits associated with urban living for the more individualistic and atomized societies in the global North. Both require a compact city built at a human scale that allows for extensive interaction, complexity and public life. The question about the 'right' transport solution for our cities can be extrapolated as one about the city and its form, and leads ultimately to the question of how we want to live together. Reframing the key question leads to a greater understanding of the impact of land use and rehabilitates the concept of dense urban environments with public transport as their backbones. It acknowledges that there is a threshold level of car use beyond which cities are at risk of not functioning properly; it puts pedestrian-friendly environments at the top of the agenda, and regards walking and cycling as serious contributions to urban mobility.

The mature cities investigated by Urban Age – New York City, London and Berlin – include many examples of this paradigm shift. London is currently implementing its 100 public spaces programme, its number of cyclists has doubled within the last five years and the city's Congestion Charge has reduced car use in the centre by 20 per cent, helping to fund the 40 per cent increase in bus use since 2001. New York City has made an enormous effort to upgrade its public-transport system by investing more than US$68 billion since 1982 and has seen a 13 per cent decline in car-ownership levels between 1990 and 2003. In Berlin, almost one-third of all journeys are made on foot or by bicycle, and since 1990 its public-transport infrastructure has been upgraded in anticipation of an additional 1 million inhabitants with its S-Bahn, tram and regional rail network. The city has also been active in promoting car sharing and multimodal transport (see page 464).

It must be emphasized that these innovations were initially introduced by smaller cities, mainly in continental Europe. Barcelona, Copenhagen and Vienna informed

METROPOLITAN SCHIZOPHRENIA

Following a report by the United Nations in the early 1990s that identified Mexico City as having the most polluted air on the planet, attempts to curb car emissions included a ban on private car use on alternating days of the week. The ban had the unintended consequence of actually increasing car ownership as the wealthy purchased additional cars to avoid the restriction. Subsequently, the Segundo Piso – the second floor elevated motorway – was constructed to alleviate traffic on the city's main arteries, further accommodating the almost 95 per cent of private vehicles used by less than 20 per cent of the population on the city's streets.

public space strategies in London; Zurich and Karlsruhe were highly influential in the rehabilitation of tram services as a mode of public transport in Berlin and around the world; Amsterdam and Freiburg generally pushed the agenda for urban cycling. However, despite these shifts, the status quo in these three Urban Age cities is still one of dominating car use at the metropolitan level. The overall rise in energy consumption for transport is best illustrated by a steep increase of sport utility vehicles (SUVs), even within city centres.

On the other hand, developments in rapidly expanding cities investigated by Urban Age – Shanghai, Mexico City and Johannesburg – follow a distinctively different pattern. A vast majority of the population has long been, and still is, dependent on walking, cycling and public transport, the latter mainly provided by the informal sector. Access to private cars is still the preserve of a relatively small minority. Historically these three cities have been different in many respects. Shanghai invested heavily in its cycling infrastructure until the mid 1980s and it was only with the opening up of China's economy that major changes in government policy were brought about. The central government in Beijing, having declared car production a pillar industry, is critical to understanding city-level transport strategies that favour elevated motorways, satellite towns and mono-functional districts while putting human-scale transport infrastructure on the back burner. Shanghai is successful in attracting more car use; it doubled between 1995 and 2004, leading to a similar multiplication in average commuting distances. In the same period, the city's official policy to reduce cycling led to a drop from almost 40 per cent to 25 per cent of all journeys. Similar decisions were taken in Mexico City, where 50,000 minibuses and microbuses handle the majority of trips, although 40 per cent of the city's transport budget between 2000 and 2006 was spent on its Segundo Piso, an elevated motorway used by less than 1 per cent of residents.

Johannesburg's public space has been taken over by traffic – a fact shockingly illustrated by its accident statistics of 25 fatalities per 100,000 inhabitants per annum, compared to 3 in London. The city seems to have abandoned large areas and surrendered itself to the pursuit of safe and private environments of shopping malls. The marginalization and containment planned under apartheid have been perpetuated in the post-apartheid era. The percentage of stranded people who have more than a 30-minute walk to work, often under dangerous circumstances, because they are unable to afford any form of public transport, has increased. Forty-six per cent of households are spending more than 10 per cent of their income on daily commuting. The main public-transport provision, the city's minibus taxis, receives no operating subsidy while the provincial government is planning to invest the equivalent of US$2.7 billion in a rapid-rail project.

Car-based solutions still dominate transport agendas in the three rapidly expanding cities, mimicking policy goals on sustainability, resource management and social inclusion. Fortunately, land-use patterns in relation to transport are scrutinized with increasing sharpness. In Mexico City, informal settlements such as Ciuadad Neza have been upgraded with public funding, transforming the squatter settlement into a vibrant community of 1.5 million people. There is a healthy mix of housing and workplaces, and a large number of businesses provide nearly 65 per cent of jobs to local residents. Aiming for more inner-city housing, Mexico City has also implemented Bando Dos, a policy requiring higher density and restricting new housing in the outer districts. In Johannesburg, the debate about transport and accessibility focuses on the problems arising from the deliberately low-density levels of the apartheid city: this has led to first attempts for densification in townships like Soweto.

Over the last decade there have been serious efforts in all six cities to bring land use and transport strategies closer together. However, despite investments and expertise, the process of moving towards more sustainable urban structures in which movement is based on public transport and pedestrian mobility has been rather slow. If cities in the future will have to rely on sustainable transport, they need to move rapidly towards understanding the forces that promote traditional car use with its vast need for space, particularly through parking.

Where to Go from Here?

We need to work out what forms of local government and what kinds of technology can create the public-transport systems needed to save rapidly expanding cities from simply adopting western models. We need to understand what forces are required to break the path of car dependencies in the mature Urban Age cities to shift towards sustainable mobility in the near future. Revisiting the transport options of cities such as New York City, London or Berlin is necessary in rethinking the western model of urban development that on a daily basis produces irreversible mistakes in rapidly expanding cities around the world.

New York City and London are fairly similar cities and they offer a wide range of possible scenarios that other cities – not only in advanced economies – can choose from. The strength of North America's largest metropolis, New York City, is Manhattan. This dense, mixed-use island is home to 1.5 million residents and more than 2 million workplaces while being well connected with all parts of the city through an efficient, sustainable and cost-effective subway system. However, car traffic still dominates the surface. Many streets in Manhattan could easily be redesigned to benefit pedestrians, while the subway would guarantee the required accessibility for a vibrant and economically viable urban environment. Together with the introduction of state-of-the-art surface transport including trams and low-floor buses as well as convenient and safe cycle routes, a policy shift in this direction would be one of the many great opportunities following the widely debated introduction of a Manhattan-wide road-user charge. Removing the existing motorway that runs along the East River will offer enormous opportunities for leisure, recreational and civic activities while simultaneously opening up the waterfront to all citizens. The current experiences with waterfront redevelopment along Manhattan's West Side as well as along the East River in Brooklyn will further strengthen this case. Regional rail – challenged by governmental structures in the tri-state area – further offers the possibility for a variety of critical improvements: a good start would be a truly regional service, which does not have to terminate according to administrative boundaries.

Developments in London in the past five years have been quite the opposite. The city – although structurally disadvantaged by average residential density levels that are half those of New York City's – has become an internationally recognized innovator for urban transport. The establishment of the Greater London Authority in 2000 gave critical decision-making power on urban transport to the mayor of London, allowing for a fundamental change in transport practice. Transport for London, established by the mayor, includes planning and operations of most transport modes in one agency and reports directly to the GLA. This allows transport to be integrated in the strategic planning for the city. Traffic congestion has been tackled by actively reducing car use through the introduction of the Congestion Charge. Since its launch in February 2003, the charging zone has been expanded and the change has been increased. As a result, car use during charge hours has dropped by 20 per cent (about 80,000 cars), reducing congestion and improving the efficiency of all surface transport. The charge generates net-revenues of GB£120 million (US$240 million) a year, mainly used for the city's bus system, which has seen the fastest growth rate since the 1940s – a 40 per cent increase of bus use since 2000. The actively promoted modal change of surface transport has further allowed for new redistributions of public space. Traffic lanes are converted to bus and cycling lanes or streets are entirely redesigned to benefit pedestrians. Four tram schemes are currently under examination, one of which, Cross River Tram, would run directly through central London on dedicated lanes. The city also promotes cycling and has achieved unprecedented growth rates in this area recently.

It remains to be seen whether New York City will make use of the structural advantages of its dense, mixed-use urban typologies. Both New York and London are currently failing to achieve a more holistic integration of land use and transport policy. In particular, the growth of workplaces in the most central locations actively promoted by new single-use building projects often lack a wider vision of city access. Where possible transport solutions should include mixed-use developments, bringing working and living closer together and reducing the overall need for travel.

It is in this context that the professional crisis of transport planning needs to be understood. It is a crisis that differs from that of urbanism. The transport-planning profession struggles with the fact that fundamentally it is more a political than a technical subject. The second challenge results from an excessively narrow focus, which should be on the organization of movement and space, not just on movement.

Despite its difficulties, it is the professional community that has advocated the most innovative urban transport solutions for more than 30 years before they were finally implemented. It was strong political leadership that installed Bogotá's rapid bus system and cycle network, London's Congestion Charge and Berlin's multimodal transport approach. Ultimately, the future focus has to be the integration of land use and transport strategies and the relationship between connecting places while at the same time creating locations.

INFORMALITY AND ITS DISCONTENTS

Geetam Tiwari

CITIES AS ORGANIC SYSTEMS

The public spaces of the city are the sites for exchange of goods and transactions that sustain urban economies throughout the world, epitomized by the street market in São Paulo.

Is 'informality' an imposed definition? Informality has been defined in many ways. It is outside that which is official or legal or planned, but it is certainly not a synonym for criminality, which is simply illegal. Squatter settlements all over the world are called informal settlements because they are not part of official plans. Robert Neuwirth has recently, in his book *Shadow Cities: a billion squatters, a new urban world*, described the squatter as a new migrant to the city, who builds a shelter with his own hands on land that does not belong to him. Nearly 1 billion people who live in squatter settlements are those who came to the city in search of jobs, needed a place to live and, not being able to afford anything on the private market, built for themselves on land that was not their own. These informal settlements create a huge hidden economy – an unofficial system of squatter landlords and squatter tenants, squatter merchants and squatter consumers, squatter builders and squatter labourers, squatter investors and squatter brokers. The builders of informal housing are the largest builders of housing in the world – and they are creating the cities of tomorrow. The conventional definition of informal – unofficial, illegal or unplanned – denies people jobs in their home areas and homes in the areas they seek jobs. Another form of squatting is when the most powerful section of society occupies land that does not belong to it and indulges in unlawful activities for the accumulation of wealth. Clearly, distinctions must be made between activities that evolve for the generation of economic resources, modalities for housing provision, 'unlawful' activities by powerful sections of the society for economic and other gains, and squatting by people who cannot survive otherwise.

Traditionally cities depended on the division of labour. Human-scale settlements were planned for places where everything from small-scale transactions to wholesale business activities could occur. Has the scale changed because of the speed of movement that is possible today? The shift in geographical scale has also brought about changes in the degree of heterogeneity in socio-economic conditions and in the needs of citizens. Cities are organic systems. People with varied skills – from low levels to highly qualified professionals – find opportunities in cities. It is a common sight outside shopping malls or commercial centres in Delhi, Mumbai, Mexico City or Bangkok to find vendors selling a range of products: from food to small handicrafts to mobile-phone cards. Formal planning techniques are not adequate to respond to the dynamism that cities display. In fact, how well a city performs in terms of economic (GDP), social (crime rate) or quality-of-life indicators for all its citizens

URBAN VENDING

Informality defines the urban landscape of particular global cities, with street vendors occupying interstitial nodes that are either unanticipated or undetermined by urban designers and city regulators. The quesadilla maker finds space on a Santa Fe street corner (bottom) with city officials permitting the provision of cheap and diverse domestic conveniences by the estimated 25,000 individuals fuelling Mexico City's informal economy. An even greater tolerance is given to the estimated 50,000 street vendors in Shanghai (top), with a flexible regulation policy passed in early 2007 that grants 'formal permission' to vendors operating without a license.

is dependent upon the heterogeneous employment opportunities available to all its citizens. Often the area planned as space for the circulation of pedestrians is occupied by the aforementioned vendors, since there is no space planned for such activities. Street vendors stand around bus stops and serve the waiting commuters. Since road design does not include spaces for vendors, they therefore occupy the areas meant for either moving vehicles or pedestrians. In many Indian cities public land around planned residential or commercial areas is occupied by people who cannot afford any planned housing. For these people, living near employment opportunities – where they survive in self-constructed housing – is a necessity.

The formal plans for commercial activities, transport services or residential areas do not consider the variety of needs that exist in cities. This is why, when hawkers appear around planned developments such as Santa Fe in Mexico City, the police force has to be deployed to evict them. Similarly, planners and officials in many of these cities try to 'reclaim' public spaces by forcibly evicting the street vendors. If planners accept the heterogeneous labour market and hence the need for planning heterogeneous housing, public spaces and mobility solutions, the management of informal processes in urban spaces may improve. The present understanding or definition of informality denies the existence of a symbiotic relationship in a differentiated labour market. The result of treating the informal as problematic comes at a high social cost. People move to cities to improve their quality of life. However, since the informal settlements are outside the plans and the law, their citizens have limited access to education and other opportunities, resulting in lower social mobility.

The benefits of recognizing the contributions of informal housing and informal processes, and of integrating them within official policies, have been documented in all parts of the world. In Mexico City thousands of houses built in districts like Ciuadad Neza were considered *asentamientos irregulares* (informal settlements) or *asentamientos paracaidistas* (parasitic settlements). However, since official policies have started to support them and investments in upgrading the infrastructure have been made, the settlement that started as traditional squatters has been transformed into a vibrant city of 1.5 million people. A large number of businesses have been set up within the settlement, providing nearly 65 per cent of their jobs to the residents. Policymakers seem to be oblivious to the positive impact of street vendors on the social life of a city. The availability of work options on the street provides a positive outlet for employment and opportunities for earning an honest living to a large section of the population, which might be poor but which has highly developed entrepreneurial skills. Their presence keeps streets relatively crime-free and safer for women, children and older people. Cities that have a large number of street vendors seem to be far safer than those that do not.

In her detailed study *Street Foods: Urban Food and Employment in Developing Countries*, Irene Tinker documents the important role vendors selling food play on the streets of eight cities in Asia and Africa. The study found that street foods are frequently cheaper than home-prepared foods, especially when time spent shopping and cooking is factored in. This is important, as lower-income groups spend 50 to 80 per cent of their household budget on food. As our cities become larger and more congested, people spend more time travelling and eat out more often. Street vendors make it possible for the poorer sections of society to obtain nutritious food at affordable prices. This study showed that cheap cooked meals served by vendors represented outstanding bargains and that more expensive meals sold in restaurants were not proportionately more nutritional. A surprising finding from Pune (India) was that the cheapest street meals, cooked by the poorest vendors under the worst conditions, were equally or less contaminated with bacteria than samples taken from restaurants. The author concludes that, 'It is creditable on the part of women street food vendors who sell food in such degraded environments [...] that the quality of the food they sell is less unsatisfactory than that sold in restaurants'.

To permit the vending at logical places and to plan spaces for it requires a careful understanding of the dynamics and requirements of street vendors. Bicycles, pedestrians and bus traffic attract street vendors. Often side roads and footpaths are occupied by people selling food, drinks and other articles that are in demand by road users. Vendors often locate themselves at places that are natural markets for them. A careful analysis of the location of vendors, their numbers at each location and the type of services provided clearly shows that they are needed, since they work under completely 'free-market' principles. If their services were not required at those locations, they would have no incentive to be there. Road and city authorities, however, view their existence as illegal. Often, an argument is advanced that road capacity is reduced by the presence of street vendors and hawkers. If we apply the same principle that is used in the design of the road environment for motorized traffic, especially private cars, then vendors have a valid and legal place in the road environment. Motorway design manuals recommend frequency and design of service areas for motorized vehicles. Street vendors and hawkers serve the same function for pedestrians, cyclists and bus users. Pedestrians need cobblers on the road to have their footwear fixed, just as much as car owners need tyre-repair shops. Cyclists need to have their tyres, chains and pedals fixed. All commuters need cold drinks, snacks and other services on the roadside. These services have to be available at frequent intervals, otherwise walking or cycling would become impossible, especially in summer. As long as our urban roads are used by these various sections of society, street vendors will remain inevitable.

Undoubtedly, the growth of future cities depends upon how well we are able to plan for the 'unplanned'. The generic theme evolving from Asia, Latin America and Africa is that as cities expand, the 'informal' sector grows faster than the 'formal' sector. This means that our plans will need paradigmatic change to deal with the heterogeneous housing and mobility needs of growing city populations. We will have to plan spaces for activities that cannot always be well-defined and predicted. It is better to plan for what is inevitable than to turn a blind eye to the future.

CONFRONTING FEAR

Sophie Body-Gendrot

SITES OF CONFLICT

The imposition of order by private individuals is a means by which to judge public disorder. The public's attempt to secure private space in New Orleans in 2005 took over the role vacated by the police and other formal security mechanisms in the aftermath of Hurricane Katrina. The chaos in the city and the forced abandonment of homes meant that citizens had to protect their goods and private property individually, with public notices on the exterior of houses to deter looters and other offenders.

For many societies safety has become a worthy premium. Amplified media coverage on the tiniest incidents, an overabundance of information concerning safety risks and the readily available advice of experts in the growing safety industry in turn create urban fear and fuel the demand for more protection. But why does this endemic 'unsafety' of our times – what Zygmunt Bauman calls *Unsicherheit* and which could also be translated as insecurity or uncertainty – manifest itself as feelings of urban fear rather than as other forms of social anxiety?[1] Is city life condemned to be overshadowed by unexpected urban violence and its avoidance?

Throughout the centuries, urban historians in Europe have tracked the specific links between the notion of urban fear and certain places and categories of people. French medieval historian Lucien Febvre posits that people in cities have always lived with fear: of starvation, disease, nature, external enemies, thieves, etc. Michel de Montaigne observed that what he feared most was fear itself. Other influential authors, such as Thomas Hobbes, Charles de Montesquieu, Alexis de Tocqueville and Hannah Arendt, problematize the political instrumentalization of fear.[2] The notion of fear makes it easier to govern people and enables the mobilization of law-abiding citizens against specific targets. Consequently, it legitimizes spontaneous social separatism. According to some observers, rumours and collective contamination, a general lack of bearings and what one might label an ontological disenchantment with modernity lead individuals to feeling isolated and powerless when confronting larger problems. While governments claim an increasingly effective monopoly of 'legitimate force' (or is it 'legitimate violence'?) to maintain internal order, there is a general distrust, more pronounced in Europe than anywhere else, of the protective role attributed to the welfare state.

The metropolises of the south are not immune either. Looking at central Johannesburg, Caroline Kihato decries that, for a majority of those living in the city the few safety measures taken to make everyday urban life sustainable just look like rearranging the chairs on a sinking ship. Enrique Peñalosa, the former mayor of Bogotá, Colombia, rightly points out that in metropolises where poverty is rampant, institutions find themselves lacking in moral authority to punish criminals. The lack of state power thus becomes a disaster, and self-help is applied by the affluent as well as by the poorer residents to secure order in their daily routines.[3] Some collectives produce their own norms: for example, through gated communities with their own guards and cameras. In poor areas, too, residents put up razor wire on fences, and

gangs create defensible space within their turfs. As a poet once remarked: 'Man sticks to what he is and dreads to lose even this. Fear and hope move along, together. To lose hope is to lose all fear. Then, there is nothing left to dread.'[4]

Issues of safety and unsafety raise deep and complex questions. What resources do cities have to deal with major risks and threats in current times of global uncertainty? How do cities transmit a sense of order to their residents as well as to the hyper-mobile actors on whom they increasingly depend? Can and should order be co-produced by institutions, private entrepreneurs and citizens? If so, what shape should this co-production take? My argument here relies upon the idea that only more inclusive cities can eradicate both the actual lethal threats and the various forms of urban fear continuously instrumentalized by the media and self-serving politicians. It is indeed my view that social order and disorder are deeply intertwined. What needs to be examined is the emergence of stable/unstable city spaces in the context of urban change and global flux. Police maps and spatial representations of crime hotspots need to be contextualized with the links and boundaries between diverse groups of people (differentiated by income, ethnicity, gender, age, culture, status and lifestyles) in the public spaces of the city and the physical juxtapositions and interconnections of buildings and spaces, the urban landscape and its built structures.[5] Only then will we be able to see the complex urban landscape of safety/unsafety in a way that goes further than the separation between law-abiding citizens at one end and criminals at the other. Norms and rules may actually be emphasizing the fractal character that global networks impinge on contemporary cities.

Feelings of unsafety and impressions of disorder cannot be dissociated from issues of representation. What is often called urban violence, in reality frequently refers to 'dis-order', patterns of antisocial behaviour or incivilities (throwing rubbish out of the window, urinating in lifts, spitting on the street, writing graffiti on the walls, making noise during the night, loitering in public housing entrance halls, on roofs or in basements). These patterns of behaviour, which are not necessary illegal (i.e. the law does not forbid people to live on the streets) are often associated with a youth culture insensitive to order. They may be revealing an adversarial social assimilation, a desire not to conform to the social norms of the 'law-abiders'. But urban violence may also betray a growing distantiation of individuals within what used to be idealized as homogeneous, 'socially integrated' societies.

Paris Did not Burn

Let us take the case of the French 'riots' in November 2005. Fire on television screens raises the audience's anticipation: viewers want entertainment – torched cars and burnt-out buses catch their imagination. In an era of (relative) peace for many viewers, other people's problems are magnified under the media's scrutiny, in this case exemplified by *Newsweek's* sensationalist headline 'Paris is burning'. In Paris itself, the reality was less epic and yielded an impression of *déjà vu*. Despite the headlines, the city was not burning and the incidents were far from turning into a Jihad-led revolt. Disruptions of order by a few dozen youths occurred in a few streets surrounding housing estates, and never for more than four consecutive nights. At one point, the police prefect of Seine St Denis forbade the sale of gas canisters to youngsters, just as the prohibition to sell alcohol in Marseille during the World Football Cup was implemented to prevent British hooligans ending up in fights with their French counterparts. The majority of the so-called 'sensitive' neighbourhoods did not experience any outbursts. These incidents were not 'riots'. What the minority of mobilized young men wanted was to express their pain, their anger and, most of all, to be seen on television and to become 'visible' – after all television idolizes anti-heroes. But they had no message, no potential for negotiation, no ambitious goals, unlike the Black Panthers or even the Bloods and Crips in Los Angeles. Acting out after a very emotional incident, in which two youths had been accidentally electrocuted, there was a reaction. It was an understandable reaction given the contingent of police errors made, the poor relations between youths and the police in the concerned areas and the reduced funding for mediating community organizations over the last four years. Many adults and professionals in these areas had actually anticipated events like these. Some isolated individuals took advantage of the urban chaos to exert their personal revenge: those who had been fired vandalized the buildings of their former employers or a sports centre, or a car-rental place.[6] Others burnt their ex-girlfriend's or a hostile neighbour's car. Someone even burnt his father's car by mistake. These forms of 'crumbly' violence – no deaths, unlike the LA riots – are the most difficult to control. They need fast and tailor-made responses that the upper echelons of the bureaucratic state are unable to provide. But how come that such low-intensity disorders gain so much media attention?

By acting on the *banlieues*, the French state tries to regain the authority it has lost in numerous areas, including the global/European economic sphere. Pressures to intervene also arose from the perception of a seemingly endless massive urbanization process, the collapse of shared collective norms in multicultural urban areas characterized by their anonymity, segregation and global insecurity about jobs. In short, there seems to be a lack of choices without risks and uncertainty about the rules of the game. In the autumn of 2006, on the eve of a major presidential election, 85 per cent of the French admitted that insecurity was their first concern. This figure is to be taken seriously: insecurity has played a pivotal political role in the past, especially when French people voted for a far-right candidate as their second choice in the first round of the presidential elections in 2002. In Dutch and Scandinavian cities, the fear of radicalized Muslim immigrants itself has brought about a change in formerly tolerant societies. Consequently, in numerous European countries, presidents, prime ministers, political candidates and high-ranking civil servants make opportunistic uses of 'urban fear' in their campaigns and discourses. At the Urban Age summit in Berlin, Chancellor Angela Merkel advocated a zero-tolerance approach, which she described as 'elementary'. In a similar vein, in autumn 2006 the presidential candidate for the left in France, Ségolène Royal, supported the idea of calling for the army to take care of juvenile repeat offenders.

Living Apart

The symbolic and material flight from the city has always been part of the American urban culture, but fear and danger play an increasingly central role in the construction of such anti-urbanism. However, fear is not an objective, quantifiable phenomenon. It relies to a large extent on subjective experiences and perceptions; and, in a sense, fear can become a self-fulfilling prophecy. Fear is generated by stereotypes relative to deprivation and the possibility of losing one's possessions. It emerges out of the notion of 'otherness' – those who are not 'us' are perceived as potential enemies or at least as suspects. Likewise, danger is not an objective condition. Anything can be a risk; but not all risks are equal, neither are they all interpreted as dangers.[7] Indeed, the representation of danger relies on social (between individuals, cultures, groups, nations) and spatial (between centres and peripheries) boundaries, as well as on notions of otherness such as the infiltrated enemy, the alien and the subversive. Particularly since the eruption of external attacks in the urban fabric of New York City on 11 September 2001, specialists have argued for the necessity of rethinking security in cities and of incorporating new, indeterminate dangers in the usual registers of risks now faced by urban dwellers. Uncertain times demand an unconventional analysis, they claim. However, in London and in Madrid it became evident that attacks could also come from home-grown terrorists, and that securing space would lead to the intensification of surveillance as well as an imposed order that affects the lives of ordinary people. The aftermath of these attacks helped highlight what was really happening.[8]

For potential dangers to be minimized or neutralized, preventative actions must be taken. Yet one may wonder whether the 'orderly' responses taken actually produce misplaced hopes. Technologies are indeed limited in terms of our capacity to use them . How can we distinguish friend from foe in the context of indetermination and risk? What do we actually mean by surveillance? What are its main characteristics? Are techniques categorizing groups 'at-risk' more complex now, as they combine military and policing methods with the marketing and efficiency of large corporations?

Spatially, forms of enclosure are considered a possible answer. The building of walls has surged, between and among groups with crime-prevention and surveillance schemes thriving. CCTV cameras abound. As a result 'public space' becomes less public, as free access and use grow more limited. Mobility is restricted by various constraints and security guards, especially for people who are treated as suspects, not for what they do but for what they are. The boundaries dividing the private from the public sectors are more blurred in the de-territorialized spaces of transnational capital. Public authorities welcome the new rules because the private provision of certain services such as security alleviates public expenditure. Globalization, deregulation and privatization have thus become key components in the commercialization of public space. The irony is that while there is so much talk going on about the aesthetics of public space, the market introduces constant surveillance in the name of the common good, while citizens are hardly alarmed by the consequences of such shifts.

That such measures of 'protection' are welcomed by city residents can be explained by the lack of local social ties – residents frequently do not know who their neighbours are – and by the increasingly complex diversity of major cities. In London, for example, there are at least 250 different languages spoken in schools. In spaces of flux, people cannot intervene efficiently to redress collective harm, and the city as a whole becomes more vulnerable and less socially efficient. Even though architects and planners perform miracles in terms of prestigious, intelligent buildings, well-designed plazas and well-oiled public-transport networks, what they have to offer will not be picked up by investors, employers, employees, tourists and residents in general if crime and subsequently fear stigmatize the sites they have created. City residents and users will avoid specific modes of public transport. If they feel insufficiently protected by law-enforcers and that their grievances are being ignored, they might eventually form militias. Safety and order thus appear as colossal stakes for the powers that be: social corrosion breaks the thin threads of the city's social fabric, slowly here, rapidly there. These are lethal threats to cities.

How to Confront Fear

It is our task as urban scholars to deconstruct such elusive terms as unsafety, urban violence, disorder, community and 'sensitization to violence'. It cannot be denied that

SITES OF VIOLENCE

Violence and terror take various forms in the urban landscape: incited from within, as in the French 'riots' (top) or externally, as the 9/11 terrorist attack in New York City (middle). These recent forms of urban violence crowd assumptions about public safety, and lead to extreme measures of protection. In London, 500,000 security cameras combined with police officers and barriers (bottom) protect public space, with sentences of 3 to 5 years for offenders convicted of stealing a mobile phone from a fellow citizen.

crime and terrorism are urban threats in our time. There is a before and after 9/11, with global repercussions. Yet the answer to fear is not to escape from the city, buy a gun and shelter in a gated community. It is an illusion to think that families, their children, and their grandchildren can live safely for ever after in a bunker, dismissing the outside world. Because the city is a historical construct, what they miss is the overlapping and intersecting urbanisms, each representing different historical moments and existing simultaneously.[9] Parks, riversides, shopping centres, museums and shared collective moments of celebration illustrate the vitality of cities. Fears and rumours about crime that undermine the use of public space should be selected, confronted and addressed in public debate. The debate about sprawl is open: according to Anne Power and Richard Rogers, the harm it produces to the city should be officially acknowledged and higher taxes should be implemented for those whose lifestyle destroys the urban core.[10]

Norbert Elias has argued that a 'civilizing process' has put an end to the masses' tendency to seek justice for themselves, and that urban safety has subsequently been delegated to professionals and specialized institutions.[11] It should be clear, however, that it is not only the role of the police to pacify society and combat delinquency; it is a multi dimensional problem that should be tackled with multi dimensional solutions. In the wake of Hurricane Katrina in New Orleans in August 2005, when violent gangs started to roam the streets at night and murders and rapes occurred, half of the local police force defected. The National Guard was called in to restore order. In November 2006, one year after the incidents in the *banlieues* of French cities, more than a dozen policemen are injured daily while working in 'no-go' areas. In such environments, notions of community and public space alone are not synonymous with social integration.[12]

Policing should be carried out by consent and respecting common law traditions, as Sir Robert Peel advocated in 1829: 'The primary objectives of an efficient police are the prevention of crime and the preservation of public tranquillity.' He added that the police are the public and the public are the police.[13] To use Jane Jacobs' more contemporary phrasing, citizens can indeed be the eyes and ears of the street, and the public peace on our streets is primarily kept by an intricate, almost unconscious network of voluntary controls and standards among the people themselves, cooperating with community policemen. In London, for example, teams of 6 policemen patrol 630 wards across the city 'on their feet'. Their task is to get closer to the community, find out what residents want and simply be there.   In a sense, the British police is far ahead of other institutions in the co-production of solutions.

Such an approach reconciles basic police work and specialized counterterrorism. Rhetorically and hierarchically, the war on terror has displaced former wars on crime and on drugs in cities like London and New York. Nevertheless, it remains very complex to extract information from terrorist networks. A small group of 10 people may accumulate 860 different identities, 2,500 SIM cards, etc. It is only by cooperating with communities that information might begin to trickle upwards.[14] Local law-enforcers need to display an 'entrenched realism', talk to moderate as well as to radical community and religious leaders, use cameras and other technical resources, and rely on their know-how. When searching a building or observing street action, they may confront youth gangs, drug dealers, organized criminals or potential terrorists. Both intelligent counterterrorism and ward policing rely on an excellent knowledge of cities and their social environments. If terrorist networks are indeed globalized, they will hit strategic sites, symbols and buildings of highly localized function. It is therefore legitimate to rely as much on local expertise as on new technologies, even if many of the local measures arguably aim at soothing public opinion rather than at impeding further attack.

The issue, then, is one of communication – between police patrols operating at street level, intelligence services using surveillance techniques (including customs and immigration services), Internet analysts, terrorist judges and others – and the avoidance of vertical hierarchization in the transmission of knowledge in favour of constructive partnerships. This is not an easy task. Major cities need to win over bureaucratic habits of distrust in order to protect their populations and their assets without jeopardizing citizens' civil liberties. It is in the mayors' interest to strengthen trust and thus safety, emphasizing consensus and commonalities, and to stimulate people to stay rather than leave their cities. It follows that more secure yet diverse populations can then bond and make links with various parts of the city and beyond.

Safe Cities, Resilient Cities

The notion of public space goes hand in hand with social citizenship, of a social contract transcending individuals and linking them via an unspoken agreement on common principles. Public spaces appear then as 'the primary sites of public culture' without which democracy is severely harmed.[15] The political meaning of public space – as areas to which citizens relate and where they transcend their differences – can be extremely powerful. It goes back to the Greek *polis*, to the foundation of authority by the Romans, to the birthplace of communal liberties in the Middle Ages, and to a regulator of territorial conflicts without wars developed since the Renaissance.[16]

Historical accounts offer examples of individuals and groups resisting, refusing to succumb to moral panic and acting in positive ways to perceived dangers in times of risk and uncertainty. The behaviour of Londoners after the Blitz during World War II – with a death toll of 60,000 – is a good example. Londoners refer to events like this and to the IRA bombings in order to downplay current threats in the urban context. During World War II, numerous Americans were involved in civilian defence. The sophisticated know-how that was developed was so extensive that in some places post-9/11 looks like a copy and paste of previous urban behaviours.

Many people living in cities refuse to dramatize risks. Challenged by global trends, cities such as New York tend to intensify their essence and be more themselves than ever, in a realistic form of utopia. In that sense, the term 'crisis' is to be interpreted in its etymological meaning, as a search for solutions. The reaction of citizens refusing to yield to fear is striking. It was known all over the world that just one day after 7 July 2005 Londoners had chosen to resume their daily routines, to move on and use the buses and the underground again. A vast majority of New Yorkers had chosen to do exactly that after 9/11 and so had the Madrileños after 11 March 2004. Londoners did so again in August 2006 after the threats targeting Heathrow airport.

The range of people who are humbly trying to get along well with one another in their neighbourhoods, despite the Babel tower that globalization produces, is very visible. People can join each other and co-produce solutions, despite their differences. Against a background of crime, fear and indeterminate dangers from unknown enemies, the continuous concentration of diverse people in dense cities sends a clear message of resilience, and trust in their institutions' efficacy and their own civic capacities. Concerning threats of terrorism, recent surveys show that 60 per cent or more Americans have done nothing to change their modes of living or their mobility after 9/11. The same numbers are found in surveys of Londoners.

The key question is whether people are adaptable enough to get on with their lives under almost any threat, or whether certain threats deeply unsettle populations? These are questions that urban planners need to bear in mind when they envisage the future spaces of cities. People can make sense of bombs and of suicide-bombers, they are aware of what violence can do and why certain targets are chosen. People can handle their fears. They do so by acquiring the necessary skills. They are selective in their fear of certain risks (like SARS or the transportation of toxic wastes when the risks of being hit are negligible) and they ignore others (fear of road accidents, for instance), which allows them to get on and to exert some control over their lives. The more complex question relates to the persistent dangers in low-income, marginalized urban communities.

Understanding Turf

Social unrest is generated by spaces that appear isolated from the rest of the city. Social differences are embodied in spatial struggles, in atomized simultaneous forms of mobilization claiming exclusive use of space. Who has control over the processes of socio-spatial change in neighbourhoods? Can architects and planners contribute to creating a sense of security in disadvantaged areas? Do they have a role, perhaps comparable to that of community-based organizations, in improving the quality of their environments and the safety of the people inhabiting them? Can they help these people take charge of the public space that surrounds them via design and expertise, bringing them a sense of 'delight' rather than submitting them to sterile plazas and security devices? In other words, is participatory design to be advocated?

One of the great tasks of urban design lies in creating spaces that do not foreground fear. Solutions are complex and tailor-made for each city. Sometimes the negotiations over 'turf' ownership are strenuous and costly, but they do happen. One of the solutions comes from the people themselves. The advice from some public-housing residents, such as the elderly or women, as well as the information circulating on web logs, reveals the tactics deployed to avoid danger linked to empty space, parking lots, public transport, certain times of the day and night. In poorer immigrant neighbourhoods, girls will take certain routes in order to avoid trouble. They manage risk themselves. Some of them transform their appearance according to context. This highlights an obvious lack of equality for all in the city and these inequalities characterize the issue of safety.

The destruction of public-housing buildings is one possible solution. It intends to yield space for more affluent groups and to promote 'social mixing'. Yet this solution is controversial and always causes pain. Threatened by urban removal, people suffering from various forms of disadvantage compete in the recognition of their state of deprivation and their immediate and recognizable needs. For instance, in the Val Fourré neighbourhood of Mantes-la-Jolie in the Île-de-France region, massive public-housing projects were built in the 1960s, based on the utopian idea of the skilled worker living next door to the young executive. The structures became dysfunctional after the two oil crises of the 1970s, subsequent budget cuts in state programmes and the introduction of a law promoting home ownership. The most upwardly mobile tenants moved out and poorer families replaced them. French rural migrant families and immigrant families from North Africa were never taught how to live in an urban environment. From 1992 onwards, the destruction of six high-rise towers allowed the construction of a shopping centre, a park, smaller affordable homes, and a huge leisure centre, all intended to act as magnets to transform

Val Fourré. Will this solution eventually produce public tranquillity? The renewed public space could welcome various generations, genders and diverse categories of users. Such was the goal of planner Michel Ricard, who thought that public spaces could help a city find its own order and life. It is important to create streets, plazas, parks and gardens for those who work, relax and live there. Residents should be proud of their public spaces, which contribute to their feeling of collective belonging. A planner should establish various hierarchies with the public spaces he envisages and offer some sense between them.[17] Yet if the population is not stabilized and if the neighbourhood continues to function exclusively as an entry point for poorer rural families from the developing world, the future will remain unclear.

Other examples highlighted by the Urban Age experience yield the same questions. In Mexico City, the improvements made to Chapultepec Park are good news. Partly financed by the million-plus residents each giving one peso, the intervention is based on the utopian vision of parks as a means to coalesce a great variety of visitors at the same time and in the same space. The designers aimed for a social cohesion transcending class divisions, and relied on the universal needs for peace, entertainment and recreation within cities. Every weekend, 17,000 users mix and mingle in the park without fear. Micro-control systems are at work: security guards make sure the processes that organize movement smoothly are respected. They act invisibly. They interpret situations, make sense of them. They represent, in summary, an alternative to CCTV cameras and high-end surveillance technologies. Across town and far from the city's centre, the FARO cultural complex (see page 446) is a lesson in optimism – a piece of public space created in a place where none existed before. In the years to come, however, the institutional capacity to get the different levels of government – from the local to the national – to act together and build on these experiences for the benefit of the larger populations in Mexico City is yet to be tested.

With the precautions owed to the difference in political regime and social history, Shanghai and other large Chinese cities reveal that new neighbourhoods, though often built on the space of which the old populations have been brutally deprived, are not only made of buildings but also of a whole complex of public services and spaces where citizenship can express itself.

Another example comes from New York City, where activities that take place in functional buildings such as courts of justice or multi-use public schools, infuse their surrounding neighbourhoods with vibrancy. Some years ago the city planned a police academy as a high-rise tower block in the Melrose area of the Bronx. The residents suggested a horizontal facility as an alternative, which would require police trainees to move from one building to the other, on their way to the cafeteria or to the sports centre. These moves would activate the street, they said, creating random encounters between the police trainees and the residents. The residents also wanted to be able to exert surveillance from their windows on the small park that was to be created, a measure which has become a routine element of crime-prevention schemes.

Establishing an open marketplace or a recreation centre, favouring new, informal economies, gives way, as observed by Saskia Sassen, to an intersection of differences that produces something new – 'a structuring sort of logic, a dash of anarchy, inefficiency, disorder [and] because in that possibility lies this making, such intersections can be productive'.[18] Richard Sennett has painted a devastating picture of the effects of rendering city place 'logical', 'functional' or 'legible' for the good of the people. Such predictable planning deprives residents of the opportunity for negotiation and of their problem-solving know-how. 'The prime secret of a "good

OPEN SPACE AS SOCIAL CONDENSOR

Green open spaces, especially in high-density, compact cities, have the potential to act as places of tolerance and civic engagement. Despite the success of Chapultapec Park (above) – Latin America's largest park visited by over 15 million people a year – green open space remains a scarcity with only 5.3 square metres per person in Mexico City, 14 times less than London.

city" is the chance it offers people to take responsibility for their act "in a historical unpredictable society", rather than "in a dream world of harmony and predetermined order". Men can never become "good" simply by following the good orders or good plan of someone else'. 'Only such people could face up to the fact of their responsibility who would have mastered the difficult art of acting under conditions of ambivalence and uncertainty, born of difference and variety,' Bauman observes. Mature people need the unknown and would feel incomplete without a certain anarchy in their lives and without the love of the otherness among them.[19]

The Secrets of the Good City

Baudelaire wrote that 'the shape of a city changes faster, alas, than the heart of a mortal man'. It is not going to be easy then to find a flexible agenda, trace a tentative roadmap, duplicate what works, and to imagine new forms of compact cities. Cities have resources to confront threats. At the periphery of successful neighbourhoods, architects, planners, local authorities and other professionals involved know that it takes time, patience, imagination, skills and resources to bring areas back to life, but it does happen. Inclusive, unexpected spaces send out powerful message. Each 'solution' for change reveals a mixture of various imaginations, voices, expertises, trust and political will. Sense and meaning can fill public space through culturally conscious city governance and a civically conscious design, thus enhancing specificity and a sense of identity. Specific demands from a population can lead to better governance and to partnerships between city inhabitants and public and private agents – bus drivers, street cleaners, car-park attendants, caretakers, street-level bureaucrats – who already contribute to a sense of safety by their very presence. Trust between citizens and these more or less visible alchemists give each user (resident, commuter, investor) the sense of belonging to a shared urban space, which can become synonymous with the absence of threat.

One may feel safe within a crowd when demonstrating on large avenues of Mexico City, Bogotá or Rio de Janeiro, as diverse as that city may be, and despite their negative image. This lesson is drawn from the various mega-cities studied throughout the Urban Age project. The question that comes to mind concerns the exceptional character of such urban innovations. How often can large-scale or small-scale experiments be launched with success? And why? And should they be duplicated? How can trust and consent to change be expected in times of high uncertainty?

In the North, like the South, the flux of order and disorder produces change. Coalitions of various groups and community organizations connect people and eventually achieve urban cohesion. Reformers meet and generate resistance to ad hoc concerns in the public realm and a range of ordinary people engage (or disengage) in actions that link different groups leading to change. Increasingly diverse types of 'right to the city' movements, such as bus riders' coalitions, are copied from city to city. In Mexico City, 6,000 grass-roots organizations act as a catalyst for each other.

Civic mobilization does not occur overnight – it takes time and effort to build trust and commitment. When considering time, are Mexico City and Johannesburg moving too slowly? Is Shanghai moving too fast? Some may think so, but so many positive changes have already occurred that it would be unfair not to weigh all elements on the scale. After all, from a democratic viewpoint, Johannesburg is only 12 years old, and governance processes are not linear. Reforms happen, they happen in cycles, their effects wane, and then political will, control and commitment are needed again. The vitality and inventiveness of the informal sector force analysts to look for new paradigms and new tools to make sense of the processes at work.

The truly great public spaces of New York, Paris, Madrid, London and other cities convey a feeling of safety among a crowd of strangers. Indeed, they generate a sense of belonging to a wider political community through an architecture of sympathy. Ongoing mutations are not necessarily synonymous with a bleak future. The diversity and density of neighbourhoods leads to the discovery of the excess energy of youth, the wealth of cultures and of generations, the concentration of potential innovations, the imagination, the skills deployed. The urban age of the twenty-first century carries with it the blurred, the incomplete, the unforeseen, which, instead of generating fear, should be perceived as a new urban beginning.

AT HOME IN THE CITY

Anne Power

Cities have always been at the centre of human progress and invention – even very elementary ancient civilizations worked out ways of gathering people together and then pursued development, typically around a collection of built structures and social nuclei.[1] Out of that emerged unbelievably complex social and physical structures – what we now call cities. However, there has been a constant tension between the manmade nature of cities and the natural environment on which they depend. This makes cities difficult to classify as habitats that are part of the natural world, akin to anthills or beehives. This tension between what is manmade and environmentally harmful in cities, and their intrinsic dependence on the natural environment has caused some of the biggest problems facing the contemporary city. These issues may be addressed in part by gaining a greater understanding of how residential densification might make cities both better places to live, through a focus on the urban neighbourhood, as well as more sustainable for the wider natural environment on which they rely. The examples discussed here are drawn from recent urbanization experiences in the United Kingdom, but they carry wider implications for an age of rapid global urbanization and environmental urgencies.

Buildings produce 50 per cent of all the carbon emitted in the United Kingdom, and cities represent by far the largest collection of buildings and infrastructure. Energy consumption and environmental impact are therefore implicit in the nature of cities, as is the huge waste production that accompanies them. Without cities, carbon emissions would not arise at their current intensity and scale. Urban systems that support buildings and infrastructure – transport, trade, production, services, culture – likewise rely on buildings, materials and the energy they consume. Because cities create most of the wealth of modern society, we sometimes forget the vast through-puts on which they rely. On the other hand, the concentration of buildings in cities makes jobs, schools, transport and other services more accessible and more shared. It should be possible, as a result of collective provision, to make cities less energy intensive than their surroundings. However, the exact opposite is true at present.

Urban Sprawl and Neighbourhood Decline

We are living on an urbanizing globe, as an increasingly urban species that has been on the march for a very long time. The relentlessness of urban change has been driven by two main factors. Problems characterized by shortages of land, food and water supply, desertification and population growth have created 'push' factors that make

HOME RULE

Close to 40 per cent of all homes across London are owner occupied, with the average price for a home recently topping GB£320,000, an increase of over 50 per cent between 2002 and 2007 alone. In the face of this upwards trend, a policy guideline from Mayor Livingstone requires that up to 50 per cent of all new residential housing be within the means of lower- or middle-income residents, creating a larger pool of affordable housing with special benefits for keyworkers like nurses, fire fighters and police officers.

it impossible for the rural environment to sustain the populations it once could. At the same time there are massive 'pull' factors, mainly the attractions of cities, such as (perceived) freedom, wealth, opportunity and security. An interesting consequence of the greater freedom, wealth and opportunity that cities offer is that those in more developed countries are dispersing. As countries become richer and continue to urbanize, cities spread out, and this is the point at which the real environmental damage begins. Cities already rely on a huge land area, many multiples of their own footprints, but there is a balance that can be overstepped. London, for example, requires 293 times its own land surface area – more than the whole area of Britain – to sustain its huge consumption of energy and resources. This is partly based on Britain's colonial roots and historic, as well as modern, trading relations. But land is also a critical factor, for cities cannot survive without viable land.

The complex interdependencies between urbanized areas and their environments suggest that cities, with their vast agglomerations of power, activity and consumption, are ill understood, and that we are barely managing them. On the other hand, history shows that cities are adept at pulling back from the brink. So we may change the way we behave and still solve problems as urban pressures grow.

One factor that drives the outward movement of urban dwellers is that households tend to become smaller as populations become richer. As a result households multiply even in areas with low population growth and, in effect, three times as much land is required to house the same number of people. Simultaneously, as standards rise, people want more space per household – they need room for their cars and other modern conveniences. Density of households thus falls alongside a growth in their number. The density of people plummets and the distance between them grows.

The phenomenon of urban sprawl brings with it deep neighbourhood polarization and social problems. The fabric of cities – the buildings that are the creation of man in a natural environment – suffers wear and tear. If they are old terraced houses, they become leaky, and if they are modern concrete blocks, they become rain-streaked and grime-laden, with cold communal areas that allow in the damp and drive out the warmth. Ultimately, this decline in city fabric causes more people to move away.

We are witnessing a constant urban ebb and flow, with a moving outwards of those who are better off and a holding back of those who cannot afford to move, accompanied by a movement inwards of poor people who have no alternative living choices. Often migrants fill the spaces – in the case of the UK they came at first from rural areas, then later from Commonwealth countries, and today they are drawn from many different places, including former Eastern Europe. This sifting process fuels the decline of inner areas: slow decay, poorer populations, areas becoming unfashionable and attracting fewer people. If it is a pressured city, and if reinvestment leads to 'gentrification' and upgrading for the better-off, then this decline may be halted and then reversed but this often occurs with high social costs.

About two-thirds of the UK is losing population from older urban areas, and the inner cities are losing people faster than anywhere else. Schools, shops and transport deplete because they cannot be sustained when the local population shrinks and their incomes fall. This increases suburban housing demand, even when there are enough existing homes in central cities. In northern England, where there is a large surplus of housing, and in the Midlands, where there is a smaller surplus, there is still a big demand for new homes in outer suburban areas. Stoke-on-Trent, for instance, plans to demolish 14,000 terraced properties, which are said to be 'unsustainable', and to build the same number of new houses on green fields around the edge of the city. Newcastle has similar strategies. The greater the emphasis on the building of suburban housing, the more the decay of existing areas deepens. If their urban economy is already fragile, this can lead to breakdown.[2]

At reasonably high density, problems in cities are visible enough to demand attention. With low density, spread over distant suburbs, there is a danger that social and ethnic separation, over-reliance on cars and overuse of land cumulatively overtake us. While suburbanization lulls the more affluent into comfortable complacency, the resulting inequality and polarization threatens overall social stability. Ultimately this could lead to cities becoming unmanageable.

Alternatives to Waste

Density is a critical factor in the viability of cities, irrespective of their nation's level of development. Until very recently, density was both a result of the wealth of cities and the cause of it. Density generates urban exchanges and services. In 1900 the average urban density in the UK was about 2,500 homes per square kilometre, leading to a ratio of about 150,000 people per square kilometre. A strong community spirit was necessarily linked to these densities. By 2005, however, the average density was below 35 homes, or around 8,000 people per square kilometre – the minimum density level necessary to support a local school, a frequent bus service or local shops is established at 5,000 homes per square kilometre. Even in London, where the average density is 4,500 homes per square kilometre, there are many areas – particularly eastwards into the Thames Gateway – where the population is spread too thinly to support essential services.[3]

During the period of intense urbanization, it seemed acceptable to spread outwards – until we began to face energy problems, congestion and bottlenecks in the land supply, to the point where it has become impossible to sustain current land-use patterns. Despite the UK Treasury's intention to meet the building targets of the 2004 Barker 'Review of Housing Supply in the South-East', these targets will be impossible to meet under present scenarios. The Eastern Region Water Authority and the Environment Agency have confirmed that the intended quota of homes for the region is unattainable because of water problems. Higher density within the existing urban framework of London is therefore inevitable, and not impossible. Study of the Thames Gateway showed that all the housing the government wanted for the area could fit in the existing, relatively low-density part of the Thames Gateway within East London. This covers only a fraction of the total area.

Comparisons of land-use patterns across the world show that Europe uses on average 0.06 square kilometres per person to sustain current levels of consumption, whereas the United States uses 0.09 square kilometres per person and Bangladesh 0.002 square kilometres per person. In order to curb the problems caused by urban sprawl, we need to shrink our land use to one-third of today's levels. Cities must provide homes, a quality environment and quality services to retain the people currently moving out. It is often the case that the best-quality, most attractive homes are old and so the building blocks for renewal are the neighbourhoods dominated by older homes. The traditional approach of tearing down bad housing and replacing it with new, better housing is not an economical option because it is energy intensive, waste-producing and socially polarizing. The alternative, necessarily used in less developed countries, is 'slum upgrading' and infill development. This has proved much more successful, and has worked well in parts of London, the most built-up city in the UK.

One of the main problems with urban and neighbourhood renewal is that it can promote the take-over by wealthier people of older, poorer housing with the aim of renovation, commonly referred to as 'gentrification'. If poorer people can remain in a neighbourhood despite the improvements being made to surrounding empty homes, poorer communities will start to recover. This approach also maximizes the value of underused neighbourhoods. As cities lose population, some low-level gentrification is desirable in order to encourage people to stay: people with jobs, who are ambitious for the city, who demand and are able to organize better services – teachers, health workers and shopkeepers. As long as an adequate supply of affordable housing is maintained, renovating formerly poor housing and attracting wealthier residents is primarily beneficial.

It has been argued that having wealthy people in poor areas – as is the case in much of Inner London – is polarizing in itself. But these mixed communities are a lot better for the area than having only rich people and alienating the poor, or having only poor people and collapsing services. The big urban challenge is to do what Jane Jacobs argued for – to improve cities within their existing frame without causing the balance to tip from being mixed communities to elite ones. We have to find ways of making existing homes work harder for us.

At least 70 per cent of the homes we will have in 2050 already exist – and this ratio applies not only to the UK but across Europe. Since homes account for 27 per cent of carbon emissions, and are dependent on the other buildings that together emit half of all our carbon, we have no choice but to address the associated environmental concerns by tackling existing homes in existing neighbourhoods. Although the average home is extremely inefficient and a new home is definitely more energy efficient – in its use but not with regards to the energy it takes to build it – existing homes can potentially be upgraded very easily to save at least half of their energy use.

Tackling Urban Renewal from Within

In thinking about how to tackle the problem of renewal, urban neighbourhoods can be divided into three categories. The top 10 per cent comprises a small group of 'self-regenerating' neighbourhoods, based on high wealth and high-quality collective conditions and services. In London, Kensington or perhaps Mayfair epitomize this class of 'self-regenerating' neighbourhood. In Paris, the 16th Arrondissement or the Bois de Boulogne would be part of this class. The second group, covering up to 70 per cent of neighbourhoods, can be identified as 'wear-and-tear' neighbourhoods. These are the areas that gradually decline as the infrastructure slowly wears out. Unless there is positive reinvestment, they will eventually become poor and run-down. Inner cities, inner and some outer suburbs all over the UK are classic examples of this group. At the bottom end of the three categories is the 20 per cent of neighbourhoods that comprise both declining private and social housing; these are 'collapsing' due to the weight of social and physical problems, combined with a lack of adequate reinvestment needed to counter this.

Self-regenerating neighbourhoods continue to be attractive places to live and they invariably have high density precisely because of their popularity. They require a high level of services, some of which are paid for by the rest of the city, including the constant in-migration of cheap labour, dependent on the collapsing neighbourhoods for low-cost housing, schools and cheap retail. Self-regenerating neighbourhoods also rely on the 'free' wider infrastructure of the city, including roads, transport links, parks, etc. West London has twice the number of parks that East London has, for example, and parks in the west are almost always supervised while those in the east are often not. Self-regenerating neighbourhoods consume vast resources, particularly through the size of the homes and the space around them. But, because they drive the power and wealth creation of the city, they are supported by tacit agreement.

In wear-and-tear neighbourhoods, 70 per cent of people live in their own homes and drive private cars. But families tend to move in search of more space and a better quality of life, so they become the 'sprawl promoters', albeit inadvertently. There are disincentives to stay where they are, such as the 17.5 per cent tax (VAT) on all repair and renovation work, the fact that urban services such as schools are of poorer quality, and urban costs such as transport are higher, as is urban crime. The wear-and-tear neighbourhoods are in danger of reaching the point of collapse as working people seek better opportunities for their children – often further out of the city – as their neighbourhoods decline. The newer, outer neighbourhoods in turn decay through a similar process.

The third group – the areas that are in danger of collapse – house our 'urban saviours'. They are home to low-income workers, single-parent families, migrants and minorities. They also shelter disproportionate numbers of people experiencing real social difficulties. Concentrating problems in poor areas is a common solution to wider social problems, but it places additional strain on already pressured communities. However, there seem to be few alternatives – high- and medium-value areas are unwilling to accept this social burden. Collapsing areas are thus the very areas that rescue the neediest casualties of city competition. Collapsing neighbourhoods depend heavily on public services, which they also help provide. They are used by the wider city as a 'dump' for the problems it does not want and as a resource for the low-paid workers it needs. These areas often have deeply damaged environments. East London, for example, is covered with giant electric pylons. Burying the pylons was not considered necessary because the area only housed city workers when it was built. The government recently announced that it cannot afford to bury the pylons in Thames Gateway, except those on the site earmarked for the 2012 Olympics.

Poorer areas may have negative impacts on the city, despite the fact that they simultaneously provide an invaluable service. The reinvestment costs to bring them to a reasonable standard are way beyond the means of the people who live there. Yet in urban and house-building terms the costs are relatively modest, especially when compared with building new homes. It would cost somewhere between GB£10,000 (US$20,000) and GB£30,000 (US$60,000) to renovate and upgrade each home. Renewal is less expensive, yet also more complex, because it involves working around people already settled in an area with buildings in place. Yet we have no choice but to upgrade collapsing neighbourhoods in a crowded country that is short of affordable housing. Various government programmes, such as Decent Homes, reflect this ambition, but the incentives are still lacking.

Renewing Neighbourhoods by Increasing Density

In order to fund the move in favour of existing communities, it will be necessary to start charging the true costs of building on the urban edge. To cut carbon use by 60 per cent, existing houses and neighbourhoods – which make up the vast majority of all homes and communities – must be renewed. There is agreement between top architects, such as Norman Foster and Richard Rogers, and leading engineering firms, such as Arup, that it is relatively easy to halve current energy use in existing buildings. The estimated total cost to upgrade the whole stock of 22 million homes

RETRO-FITTING CITIES
Evidence of 'self-generating' neighbourhoods includes the introduction of new architectural styles abutting London's many Victorian and Georgian houses. These new builds generally employ sustainable materials and construction techniques in keeping with an increasing awareness about environmental responsibility.

URBAN ACUPUNCTURE
Post-Franco Barcelona was incrementally transformed prior to hosting the 1992 Olympics through the creation of a series of urban interventions that included open spaces and parks built on top of underground parking facilities throughout the 1980s. The regeneration of dense inner-city areas like El Raval in the historic core of Barcelona has attracted more residents and young people to the heart of the city.

to 'excellent' efficiency standards, is around GB£200 billion (US$400 billion) – half the Treasury's annual budget. Obviously such costs would need to be spread over time, but the goal could be achieved over a 20-year period by diverting the Treasury's indirect subsidy of GB£35,000 (US$70,000) to each new-build home. If the cost of the new infrastructure and the environmental impact of new homes was charged to the developers – a plan currently under discussion – then that charge could upgrade three existing homes to high energy-efficiency standards for every new home built. Land value multiplies through development, by a factor of five to ten in low-value areas, and a factor of thousands in parts of the South-East. In 1999, the Urban Task Force, chaired by Richard Rogers, recommended such an environmental impact charge, and the proposals in the Barker Review for a 'development' levy echo the need for an environmental and infrastructure charge.

Renewing existing homes and communities would increase the population density of built-up areas, lead to greater social integration, reduce land use, energy consumption and transport needs, and generate greater urban viability. It would maximize the value of the existing infrastructure, which would be a huge cost saving. It would renew existing neighbourhoods by attracting new resources and renovating buildings while reducing energy use and waste. It would revalue existing older property. This would in turn attract investors to small abandoned sites, scattered liberally within existing neighbourhoods and encourage high-density infill development, leading to more mixed communities and better services.

In London, where there is little choice and a major affordability crisis, density is increasing without too much effort. The mayor has now asked all London boroughs to undertake capacity studies, not for the hundreds of bigger sites that are well-plotted, but for the sites of half an acre or less, where perhaps four, ten or even twenty flats could be built, and through which projected housing demand in London could be met or even exceeded. There are over a quarter of a million of these sites, offering the capacity to add all the extra homes we need within the existing urban framework for the foreseeable future.

In the UK – and many other parts of the world – all space is now contested. The need for planning is itself wedded to the idea of making a social compact about how people live together on a crowded island. The contested spaces of cities actually work through managing proximity on a fast-changing and increasingly mobile globe. One of the reasons that people spread out from cities yet still remain attached to them for work, culture, social life and economic growth is the tension between freedom and constraint. It is one of the reasons why people still adhere to the idea of community. City communities require close, but 'soft' as well as 'hard', management.

Can Cities be Sustainable?

There are some amazing examples of urban renewal. Barcelona won back its position as a thriving city through an open spaces plan – a kind of post-Franco gift to the people of Catalonia. The city authorities set about creating open spaces, however small, in 140 neighbourhoods throughout the densest city in Europe, involving both residents and urban designers. By 1984 they had created so many attractive neighbourhood spaces, with so much support from the citizens of Barcelona, that they were able to back a very persuasive bid for the Olympics. It is one of the few Olympic bids – if not the only one – that returned profitability and positive assets to the host city.

In Curitiba, Brazil, the authorities took a distinctive approach that has become a global model for urban transport and sustainability. The mayor decided to turn main access roads to the centre into express bus-only routes, creating traffic-calm pedestrian spaces in the core. Cars would no longer be necessary, thanks to a complex local bus network linking all neighbourhoods with the main express bus routes. A unified bus fare ensured that the poorest people living in shanty towns on the edge of the city, often workers providing essential services, could get into the city for the same price as richer people living much nearer the centre. The environmental and social improvements in Curitiba ran in parallel. In Copenhagen too, one-third of all people go to work by bicycle, and 25 per cent of the city's and the country's energy comes from windmills. Copenhagen has worked on this agenda for 25 years, holding the number of cars in the city stable and stimulating walking and cycling.

Even London, for all its problems, has transformed its centre through the Congestion Charge, taming traffic, doubling the level of cycling and expanding bus use by 40 per cent since 2000 (see page 442). Manchester, the urban pit of the country for many years, has turned its industrial heritage into World Heritage. But it also discovered that becoming the greenest city in the country is emblematic of the future. With the most intensely depleted inner city and the largest supply of brownfield sites, it is overtaking Birmingham as the leading core city in recovery.

An Urbanizing Globe

At the moment, natural capital is neglected or under-costed as a result of poorer countries of the world selling their environmental capital too cheaply with European and American urban and suburban dwellers consuming it at a rate that far exceeds the planet's carrying capacity. The developed world will not survive the level of migration that will result from the unfair trading of natural capital between poor and rich countries. Professor Sir Partha Dasgupta of Cambridge University argues that we cannot continue to over-consume in the urbanized West the natural capital that belongs to all, without unravelling social and environmental conditions across the world. We all depend on sharing natural capital. Dire environmental consequences are forecast for poorer countries that are already experiencing serious migration from environmentally stressed areas. Deforestation, soil depletion, drought and desertification are just some creeping indicators of this global disaster.

We do not protest at knocking down houses and using the old, baked bricks for underlying roads; yet crunching up baked bricks for hard core is a tragic waste of the intense heat that went into producing those bricks and homes. Most bricks still have hundreds of life-years in them. This means we have to change the way we think about recycling and renewing. If we can recycle plastic bags, we can surely recycle homes. In an urban world, it makes sense to reuse everything possible that we have already put into urban building – principally by restoring and renewing the buildings.

Urbanization is continuing apace; all attempts to prevent or slow the growth in the world's cities have failed. Therefore, recycling our cities is crucial, given their environmental impact and their ultimate dependence on nature. We have a long way to go, but there is a growing awareness of the need to put the urban environment right for the sake of our social as well as physical survival.

TOWARDS A CARBON NEUTRAL LONDON

Nicky Gavron

SUSTAINABLE OBJECTIVES

With over 75 per cent of the world's energy consumed by buildings and transport, cities will play an increasingly significant role in tackling Climate Change. The City of London, the UK capital's financial centre, is a model of public transport efficiency with over 95 per cent of all commuters using rail, bus or the underground to get to work.

Sustainability is about integrating economic, social and environmental factors. That is why climate change is the most pressing issue facing our generation, confirmed by the four recent reports of the United Nations Intergovernmental Panel on Climate Change and by the Stern Review on the Economics of Climate Change.

The climate change we are experiencing now is the result of greenhouse-gas emissions in the 1950s. Back then, we used as much oil in a year as we do now in six weeks. There are still four and a half decades of emissions in the system to impact on our climate over the next 30 to 40 years, and we are still pumping more and more CO_2 into the atmosphere. Scientific evidence shows we probably have less than ten years before we reach the tipping point and trigger runaway climate change. We have to start making deep cuts in emissions – right now – and sustain those cuts over the long term. That is why Ken Livingstone, Mayor of London, and I have made tackling climate change our political priority.

Part of the Problem and All of the Solution

The battle against climate change will be won or lost in cities. In the pre-industrial era only a tiny proportion of people lived in cities. Today the population of urban areas is growing rapidly, especially in the megacities with more than ten million population. In 1975 there were five cities in this group. By 2015 there will be 26, with 22 of them in the developing world.[1] This megacity growth is taking place in a period of major economic and technological change, dominated by the emerging global economy, a revolution in information technologies and increasing emphasis on market-based decision-making. Overall, by 2050, 75 per cent of the world's population is likely to live in cities, and half already does.

Even now cities and urban areas are the main cause of climate change. With modern urban lifestyles, city dwellers use vast quantities of energy, mostly derived from fossil fuels. Cities cover about 2 per cent of the Earth's surface but account for around 75 per cent of the world's energy demand and produce 80 per cent of the CO_2 and other greenhouse-gas emissionscaused by human activity.[2] If we do not reverse the emission trend in cities we will not save the planet.

Cities are also highly vulnerable to the impacts of climate change, including warm wet winters, hot dry summers, more frequent storms and floods, droughts, heat-island effects in downtown areas and photochemical smogs.

FLOOD PLAINS
London is vulnerable to flooding from the tidal Thames, its tributaries, surface water flooding from heavy rain and overflowing sewers. The darkly shaded area on the map shows the at risk areas without defences. The Thames Barrier, the main flood defence protecting London against the tides had to be closed more than 100 times since 1982, with the frequency of occurences increasing.

More significantly, many cities are situated along coasts and estuaries. They face the most serious impact of rising sea levels. A rise of three or four metres, for example, would permanently incapacitate much of London's communications and environmental infrastructure and drown large parts of its central area. This prospect is given credibility by James Hansen of NASA's Goddard Institute, who has recently predicted that sea levels may rise by several metres by 2100, not the 60-centimetre maximum previously forecast.[3]

So, cities have a responsibility for climate change, the motivation to do something about it, but they also have huge opportunities. Globally, municipal authorities regulate and manage land use and transport systems. To a greater or lesser degree they control the environmental infrastructure such as water, waste and sewage. They own and operate buildings and vehicle fleets, and they have huge purchasing power. They promote economic development and have a vital role in forming partnerships with the private sector to engage corporate and business leadership. Municipal governments can promote local initiatives, motivate and build community consensus and lead by example.

Cities are the places in which the agglomeration of high-level, knowledge-based economic activities concentrate. Both in developed and developing countries, they generate a large part of their country's GDP. Five US cities – New York City, Los Angeles, Chicago, Boston and Philadelphia – would, together, make the world's fourth largest economy. São Paulo is home to about 10 per cent of the Brazilian population but it produces 40 per cent of national wealth. It can be argued that cities and not nations are the engines of development.

Moreover, cities make highly efficient use of many resources such as energy, water and land. Their population concentration and activities mean people can share transport, environmental and social infrastructure. Some simplistic numbers make the point. London emits 8 per cent of the UK's CO_2. It is home to about 12 per cent of the population and produces 20 per cent of national GDP. A study undertaken by GLA economists in 2005 showed the following comparisons between London and other English regions:[4]
– It consumed less electricity per GB£1 million gross value added;
– It produced less waste per capita;
– It consumed less water per GB£1 of gross value added;
– It produced less CO_2 per capita and per GB£1 gross value added from transport;
– It produced about a quarter of CO_2 per GB£1 billion gross value added from commerce and industry;
– It purchased less than half the gas per GB£1 billion gross value added for domestic and commercial use.

This validates the argument that many of the world's most difficult and complex environmental challenges can be addressed and solved by cities.[5] They have the potential to be efficient and act quickly. The conclusion to be drawn is that while national governments are crucial for negotiating international agreements, setting frameworks and standards, and for fiscal and financial incentives, when itcomes to tackling climate change, it is cities that must take centre stage.

London Government – Building in Sustainability

London had been laying the foundations for its sustainable future since the 1980s. After the abolition of the Greater London Council in 1986, the London Planning Advisory Committee (LPAC), made up of representatives from all the

London boroughs, kept strategic planning on the agenda. I was deputy chair and Labour leader from 1990 and chaired the committee from 1994 to 2000. During that time we undertook studies that laid the foundations for subsequent GLA policies and, through the Labour Group, shaped the GLA itself.

The research we commissioned included the original World City study. This clarified that London is one of the three genuine world cities, along with New York and Tokyo. Other research and policy projects were strongly influenced by the Rio Earth Summit in 1992. That kick-started our thinking about how to apply the principles of sustainable development in London and the parallel concern about climate change. The highly influential Housing Capacity and Sustainable Residential Quality studies were both incorporated into the government's seminal report, 'Towards an Urban Renaissance'.

LPAC's Traffic Reduction Strategy for London was formulated with road-user charging being introduced in 2003 as its centrepiece. We worked closely with London First, representing big business in London, which endorsed the findings. Both LPAC and London First participated in the ROCOL (Review of Charging Options for London) working party in 1998–9. It was largely due to the LPAC Traffic Reduction Strategy that the power to establish and operate road-user charging was included in the 1999 Greater London Authority Act.

A package of these and other policy and research projects – the 'LPAC legacy' – was handed over to the mayor in 2000. The LPAC Labour Group was heavily involved in the debate that defined the scope, style and functions of the GLA. One of my motivations for coming into politics was to see London government restored, so from 1990 onwards, the LPAC Labour Group and I – joined by the Association of London Government in 1994 – hammered out a plan for the kind of strategic authority London needed. We concluded that the new authority needed to be small, unequivocally strategic and focused, and not at all like traditional British local government. That is exactly what we got.

The GLA was set up as a new brand of political leadership to streamline decision-making. It is led by a directly elected, strong executive mayor. The mayor's authority is based on the mandate from the whole of Greater London. His influence is enormous. Only the president of France has a bigger direct electorate than the London mayor. However, in contrast to many mayors, especially in North America, the powers and resources of this office in London are limited. The Mayor of New York, for example, has a budget that is several times larger than that of the Mayor of London's and he has many more levers to pull.

The GLA is best described as a co-ordinating and directing 'strategic' authority, with integration running right through it. Planning apart, the GLA does not deliver services itself. It sets policies, targets and budgets for its executive group of four functional bodies: Transport for London, the London Development Agency, the Metropolitan Police Authority, and Fire and Emergency Planning. It works through a combination of powers, influence and persuasion, involving a series of partnerships with the London boroughs and other public, private and voluntary interests. Central to climate change are the London Energy Partnership, the London Climate Change Adaptation Partnership and the London Hydrogen Partnership, which aims to deliver the hydrogen economy for London. The second key element of the GLA is the 25-member elected assembly, set up to scrutinize everything the mayor does.

The GLA Act itself is imaginative, giving us the three pillars of sustainable

LONDON: OVERALL CO₂ EMISSIONS

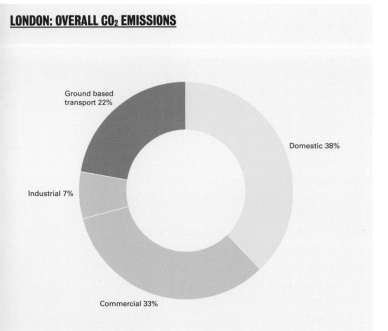

Ground based transport 22%

Domestic 38%

Industrial 7%

Commercial 33%

LONDON: DOMESTIC SECTOR CO₂ EMISSIONS

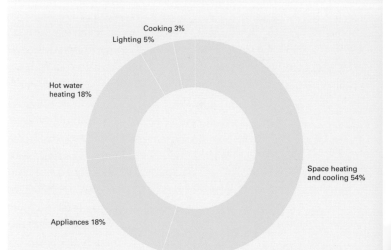

Cooking 3%

Lighting 5%

Hot water heating 18%

Space heating and cooling 54%

Appliances 18%

LONDON: INDUSTRIAL & COMMERCIAL SECTORS CO₂ EMISSIONS

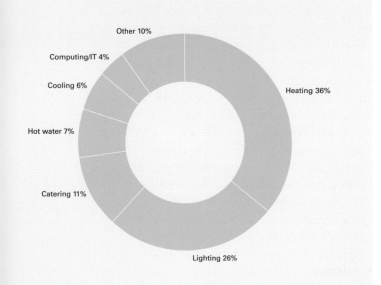

Other 10%

Computing/IT 4%

Cooling 6%

Hot water 7%

Catering 11%

Heating 36%

Lighting 26%

LONDON: GROUND BASED TRANSPORT SECTOR CO₂ EMISSIONS

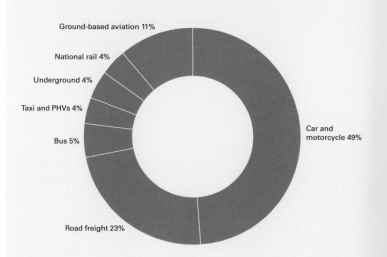

Ground-based aviation 11%

National rail 4%

Underground 4%

Taxi and PHVs 4%

Bus 5%

Car and motorcycle 49%

Road freight 23%

LONDON'S CO₂ EMISSIONS

The UK ranks eighth in worldwide carbon dioxide emissions, with London contributing 8 per cent of the country's whole (or 11 per cent including aviation to and from airports in London). Within the domestic sector (top right) heating and cooling account for more than half of emissions, making it a central element in the Green Homes Programme to provide heavily subsidized insulation, as well as general advice on energy savings. By comparison, the industrial and commerical sectors (bottom left) attribute over one quarter of emissions to lighting. Private cars and motorcycles, meanwhile, contribute half of the 22 per cent attributable to the transport sector (bottom right).

development as our principal purposes. To paraphrase, these are to promote the economic and social development of London and Londoners, and the environmental improvement of Greater London. We have to balance these over time and have regard for the health of Londoners, equality of opportunity and London's contribution to sustainable development in the UK.[6]

In 2000 we inherited a city that had seen rapid growth in population and in jobs – both projected to continue – and with a huge backlog of investment in its transport, housing and other social and environmental infrastructure. The air quality was worse than in any other European capital except Athens. In the mayor's own words, London was 'the dirty old man of Europe'.

The kind of fundamental changes we wanted for London needed a clear vision and direction. One of the first things the mayor and I decided in July 2000 was to adopt a comprehensive vision to develop London as an exemplary sustainable world city based on three interwoven themes:
— Strong, diverse long-term economic growth;
— Social inclusivity to give all Londoners the opportunity to share in London's future success;
— Fundamental improvements in London's environment and use of resources.[7]

A series of integrated strategies, eight specified in the 1999 Act and others essential to fulfilling our principal purposes, are how we articulate this vision and make sustainable development our organizing principle. These include strategies on Transport, Economic Development, Waste, Air Pollution, Noise, Energy, Water and the Spatial Development Strategy, otherwise known as the 'London Plan', which we decided should be the 'plan of plans'. The mayor's main hands-on function is strategic planning. Other strategies are implemented by our functional bodies and by the whole range of public, private and community interests that make up London.

In 2005 the government recognized that, after five years, it was time to reassess the powers and responsibilities of the GLA. The outcome of 18 months of discussion and negotiation is condensed into the new GLA Act.[8]

Much of my effort has been focused on securing a specific 'duty' to take action to tackle climate change as a headline responsibility, binding on current and future mayors. This is delivered through two new statutory strategies on climate change, one on Mitigation and Energy and the second on Climate Change Adaptation. Other proposals include additions to the mayor's planning powers, which allow the mayor to direct changes to the preparation of borough development plans and new powers to enable the mayor to 'call in' and determine strategic planning applications. Both these enable more rigorous delivery of the climate-change agenda though the planning system.

The 1999 Act gave the mayor no specific role in housing. That is changing. The mayor has already taken over responsibility for the former London Housing Board. The GLA Act requires the mayor to publish a statutory London Housing Strategy and a Strategic Housing Investment Plan. The Act also devolves responsibility for the broad allocation of the Regional Housing Pot to the mayor, who has made it plain that money will only be available for social housing schemes that have low or zero carbon emissions.

Towards a Low-Carbon London

It is paradoxical that had we invested in the environmental infrastructure in the

1990s, it would not have been low carbon. Delay has been a virtue in that science has shown us that every aspect of sustainable development must now be low-carbon development. It is a measure of how seriously we take tackling climate change that we have brought many of our strategies and other initiatives together in our Climate Change Action Plan, published in February 2007 and well before our new duty to prepare a Climate Change and Energy Strategy and a Climate Change Adaptation Strategy was formalized.[9]

London produced 44 million tonnes of CO_2 in 2006, excluding civil aviation. If we make no changes, our CO_2 emissions will reach 51 million tonnes by 2025. In 2004 we established targets in our Energy Strategy to achieve a 30 per cent reduction in CO_2 levels by 2025. This is actually pretty challenging given London's continued population and employment growth. However, it is now clear that a 30 per cent reduction is not enough to prevent catastrophic climate change. Therefore, in order to keep up with the science, we have had to update our targets. The Action Plan sets us the ambitious target to cut London's CO_2 emissions by 60 per cent from 1990 levels by 2025 – rather than the government's target of 2050. To put this in context, it means a 4 per cent reduction in London's CO_2 emissions year on year until 2025. London can achieve 30 per cent without any additional help, but to reach 60 per cent requires additional support from the government. This includes carbon pricing, investment in research, development and financing of low-carbon technologies and the removal of regulatory barriers to decentralized energy.

Our aim is that by 2025, London will be a model low-carbon city for Europe and the world. We will do this by drastically reducing use of energy in buildings, by decentralizing the way in which energy is supplied, by cutting carbon emissions from transport and from other major producers of carbon emissions – the waste and the water industries.

Behavioural change by Londoners is vital. There is no need to reduce quality of life, but there is a need to make important changes in the way we all behave – how we use energy and water, how we insulate our homes, how we travel around, what goods we buy and how we recycle our waste.

WHO SHOULD SAVE HOW MUCH?

The Climate Change Action Plan, published by the Mayor of London, aims to reduce London's CO_2 emissions below the national target. The plan sets out measurements in all sectors, that span from energy-efficient household appliances to avoiding inefficient heating and cooling of commercial buildings as well as behavioural changes. However, the plan currently projects that only 60 per cent of the necessary CO_2 emission reduction can be achieved through the measures outlined in the document and further action on national and European levels will be necessary to achieve the goals.

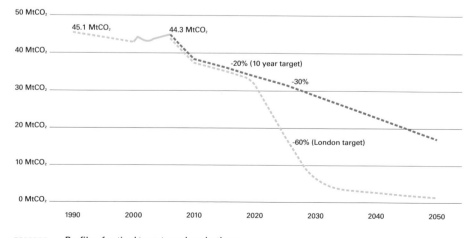

Profile of natinal targets and aspirations

Proposed London reductions to achieve 450ppm stabilization

What Mechanisms Do We Need

The first is planning. The 'London Plan', first published in 2004, is the corner-stone of our climate-change policies, integrating all the other strategies. It is the strategic development plan for London and a powerful legal framework, guiding public and particularly private investment decisions. All borough development plans will, over time, be brought into general conformity with it. In a 'plan-led' system, that means all the planning decisions for new or refurbished buildings in London must be consistent with the London Plan.

At its simplest, the London Plan is about sustainable land use and trans-portation. There are two big ideas. The first is to accommodate London's rapidly rising employment and population – projected to grow by a million over the next two decades – within the London boundary, without building on green spaces. This will involve co-locating new development in London with much-improved and expanded public transport. This is in direct contrast to the post-war policy of exporting London's population and jobs to New and Expanded Towns, beyond the Green Belt and to redevelop inner London at lower densities.

The second big idea is to redress the historic imbalance in wealth and opportunity between West London and East London, where the loss of industry and port activities over decades has contributed to the area's high level of multi-ple deprivation. In particular, this means the sustainable development of the London Thames Gateway, where about a dozen square kilometres of brownfield development land can accommodate 100,000 more homes and a huge increase in jobs. As part of this, the Olympic site in the lower Lea Valley is a vital catalyst for change, helping to bring life and prosperity back to East London and change the image of the whole area.

The London Plan proposes a more compact and higher-density city – reversing the urban sprawl symptomatic of developed cities worldwide – with mixed-use and socially balanced communities, combining housing with offices, shops, leisure and entertainment, healthcare facilities, schools and colleges. It aims to produce nearly double the number of new homes in London anually, compared with 2000, which include a balance of market, social and intermediate housing and homes. The Plan stipulates that 50 per cent of new homes should be 'affordable', of which 70 per cent should be social rented and 30 per cent inter-mediate homes. The Plan also requires homes of different sizes to accommodate families with children as well as singles or couples. This will result in more socially balanced and inclusive communities and easy access to facilities, all reducing the need to travel, especially by car, and encouraging the use of public transport, walking and cycling.

Surface transport is responsible for 22 per cent of London carbon emissions. We have focused on changing the way Londoners travel by offering attractive alternatives to the car. The fastest and most cost-effective option was the comprehensive improvement in the bus network, increasing the bus fleet from 6,500 to over 8,000 vehicles, with more bus routes, more night buses and with safety addressed by dedicated police and CCTV. The introduction of the Oyster Card and a greater number of bus lanes, rigorously enforced, has improved the speed and reliability of services. Overall, the number of bus journeys has gone up by about 40 per cent since 2000.

At the same time, we embarked on the longer-term improvements to London's underground and rail networks, helped by the government giving the

URBAN EYE
The 500,000 CCTV cameras dispersed throughout London provide surveillance to secure safety.

mayor the power of prudential borrowing, which has enabled an investment programme of up to GB£10 billion (US$20 billion). This has allowed us to initiate schemes, particularly in the Thames Gateway. Work on the East London Line extension is due to be completed in 2011, while work on the rest of the overland system, linking and enhancing the orbital rail lines around inner London is also proceeding. The Docklands Light Railway, which began life as a low-capacity link from the City to Canary Wharf, is expanding into a major public transport network. Together with Crossrail, these schemes represent a huge increase in public transport capacity in London, opening up the Thames Gateway and inner-London development opportunities. At the same time, the public-private partnership is beginning to deliver real improvements to the underground system.

I consistently supported Ken Livingstone's determination to introduce the Congestion Charge scheme in the face of determined media opposition – and salute his courage in doing so. The scheme has met its objectives of cutting the number of vehicles entering the zone, reducing congestion and pollution and incentivizing clean-fuel vehicles. The scheme reduced CO_2 emissions by 16 per cent as well as cutting nitrogen oxides and particulate emissions.[10]

The mayor and I have worked closely with New York City politicians and the New York City Business Partnership on their proposals for road pricing in Manhattan and we have helped to convince critics that the proposed Manhattan scheme would be a major benefit to our great sister city.

The current central and western zones of London are a starting point. Longer term we will be looking to road pricing over the whole city, incentivizing demand for low-carbon vehicles and fuels, through a sophisticated system of road pricing based on emission levels.

The combination of London Plan policies – investment in buses and other forms of public transport, pricing policies that allow under-16s and under-18s in full-time education, together with over-60s, to travel free, and the Congestion Charge – have led to the fastest shift out of the car to other – more environmentally friendly, modes than has been achieved in any other large conurbation. Since 2001, there has been a 5 per cent shift from the car to more sustainable modes of transport, mainly the bus, ver the whole of greater London. This is only the beginning. Modal shift must continue.

Another major initiative is the introduction of the London Low Emission Zone in February 2008. The aim of the zone is to deter the most polluting vehicles entering London. These are mainly the older heavy goods vehicles, buses and coaches, large vans and other heavy vehicles. Those that do not meet the standard are heavily fined. Other measures to cut CO_2 emissions from vehicles, set out in the Action Plan, include continuing to improve alternatives to the car and promoting their use by marketing, better information and demand management. Simply driving vehicles efficiently can reduce fuel consumption by 5 to 10 per cent. Promoting lower-carbon vehicles and fuels by, for example, buying the most fuel-efficient vehicles in their class can make a significant impact.

Longer term, the choice between power and fuel options needs to be guided by carbon pricing. We are leading by example in our own fleets of buses and operational vehicles, promoting low-carbon vehicles and fuels, piloting new technologies. We have acquired 6 diesel/electric hybrid buses as the technology matures. All London's buses were at Euro 2 standard by the end of 2005 and fitted with particulate filters. New types of motor power such as plug-in hybrid electric and hydrogen fuel cell are being explored. We have piloted 3 hydrogen buses as part of the CUTE programme since 2004 and will introduce 10 more hydrogen buses by 2010. Substantial reductions in carbon emissions can be achieved by fuel-efficient driving – accelerating and decelerating slowly, keeping within speed-limits and maintaining proper tyre pressures.

Dealing with the CO_2 emissions of surface transport is a major issue, but buildings are the big producers of greenhouse gases, contributing 71 per cent of London's carbon emissions with 38 per cent coming from homes. The London Plan was ahead of its time. Its policies on sustainable design and construction of new and refurbished buildings laid the foundations for more detailed Supplementary Planning Guidance, which go way beyond government targets, setting out the essential goals expected of all developments and the more aspirational 'preferred' targets.

One of the positive forces in London is that the private sector is willing to work with us and tackle climate change. Not surprisingly, developers and the construction industry want visible fairness and equity. They want the rules and regulations to be robust over time, strongly and clearly expressed and legally enforceable. That is what the London Plan seeks to do.

The London Plan and its Further Alterations aim to reduce London's CO_2 by minimizing emissions from all sectors – domestic, commercial, industry and transport – and this will be under constant review to raise standards and targets. The main mantra in our climate-change policies is to make buildings low or even zero carbon, balanced electrically and thermally. This means:

– Energy-efficient design, including orientation, selection of materials, optimizing solar benefits, use of green roofs and walls and sustainable urban drainage;
– Decentralized electricity generation, mainly through combined cooling, heat and power systems (CCHP), where possible networked together to form a linked series of district and neighbourhood schemes;
– A proportion of energy requirements to be met from on-site renewable sources, which will be raised over time.[11]

The science behind decentralized energy is simple. Globally, centralized power generation is the main source of CO_2 emissions. Furthermore, it is highly inefficient in its use of resources. Coal, gas and nuclear power stations waste about 70 per cent of their primary energy as heat and lose another 9 per cent in distribution. In contrast, generating and supplying power locally, close to where people live and work, means heat can be used to warm and cool buildings and is, inherently, much more efficient. The Carbon Scenarios report for London shows the CCHP approach is the most cost-effective way of delivering CO_2 reductions in London.[12]

Decentralized energy is, therefore, key to reducing London's greenhouse-gas emissions and adapting to future temperatures. It represents the new paradigm for energy, which can operate from domestic scale micro-generation up to neighbourhood systems, networked together. Decentralized energy is ideal for dense urban areas like London and for other cities in the UK and worldwide. It not only cuts carbon emissions but also offers more security of supply and complements the grid-based systems, which are vulnerable to blackouts.

CCHP systems work most efficiently when they cover a mix of land uses that need heat, power and cooling at different times of day. Extending existing schemes to nearby areas improves their efficiency, while new schemes should be designed so they can be extended. All systems should be capable of being networked together, so as much as possible will operate on the local distribution grid and off the national grid. But government must help. As things stand, generators of decentralized energy cannot trade with the national grid on the same equal terms as they can in many countries. They receive a tiny fraction of the retail price for electricity exported to the grid but pay the full retail price for any imports. Decentralized energy needs a reasonable approach if it is to fulfil its potential in London and other urban areas. This includes fair payment for exported electricity and the removal of the other regulatory barriers. At present, the regulations are preventing the energy revolution, which will be as dramatic as – and analogous to – the mobile-phone revolution in telecommunications.

The London Plan and its alterations are beginning to have a significant effect, as the development frameworks and planning applications for major development schemes now include CCHP. But planning cannot do it alone. The London Development Agency (LDA) is leading by example. It is one of the four functional bodies, set up by the 1999 Act, and acts as the GLA's development arm. It is able to buy and sell land and initiate development. In this capacity, it is incorporating decentralized energy into all its specifications for development projects and its participation in the zero energy Gallions Park scheme.

One of the primary aims of the London Plan Alterations and the Climate Change Action Plan is to change the way energy is generated and supplied. The challenge for London is to achieve this rapidly and at a scale that will make a difference by going with the grain of the private sector. Business has said the public sector must give them the confidence to accelerate their commitment through political leadership and public action.

The London Climate Change Agency was set up in 2005 to reinforce the planning policies by catalysing the markets for CCHP, renewable fuels and ESCos. It is a 'show by doing' organization, designed to tackle coordination failure and to work across institutional barriers with the big carbon-emitting sectors – energy, waste, water and transport. To advance this, it has taken a minority stake in a new kind of public-private venture, the London Energy Services Company or ESCo, with EDF Energy. ESCos can design, finance, install and manage decentralized energy systems for new and existing developments. They can enter into partnerships with boroughs and other public as well as private interests. The government recognizes that ESCos offer a useful model to facilitate the implementation of decentralized energy systems.

The agency is undertaking a series of flagship, high-profile projects, including fitting solar panels to the roof of City Hall, and is working on a whole range of projects with developers in the private sector, together with the promotion of private sector ESCos. Parallel with promoting decentralized energy, the agency is developing renewable energy sources, including wind, solar, tide, bio-fuels and fuel cells. One renewable source it is developing is the has the potential to supply a large proportion of London's energy needs from local resources.

As long ago as 1969, Jane Jacobs looked at city waste streams as mines of raw materials for new manufacturing industries, for construction and to produce compost for agriculture.[13] However, most of London's municipal waste still goes to landfill, with another 20 per cent incinerated. Where waste cannot be recycled, we are promoting the production of energy from waste, not through conventional mass-burn incinerators, which are just small and inefficient power stations, with high CO_2 emissions, but through the emerging technologies of anaerobic digestion, pyrolysis and gasification, which are both more efficient and have low carbon emissions. These technologies make bio or synthetic gas – good for powering CCHP systems and from which hydrogen can be extracted – or liquid fuels, suitable for vehicles. This represents a fundamental change in the way London deals with its municipal and commercial waste streams, with an increasing proportion processed by new technologies on a larger number – more than 200 – of smaller local treatment sites.

The potential scale of the contribution to cutting London's carbon emissions is tremendous. The biological and residual waste London currently sends to landfill could provide the electricity for 1.2 million homes or heat for 375,000.[14] Similarly we need to make full use of sewage as a potential source of renewable energy.

Planning and housing powers are about new buildings, but they also influence how existing buildings are managed and modernized. Planning powers, together with the government's code for sustainable housing, harmonized with building regulations will set the standards for how people adapt their homes and workplaces, but we do not have any specific powers over the existing stock of buildings. That is why other initiatives in the Climate Change Action Plan look at how to cut emissions from existing commercial, public and domestic buildings. The emissions from commercial and public-sector buildings is 33 per cent of all CO_2 emissions in London, and about 15 million tonnes annually. The Green Organisations Programme focuses on three key areas. The Better Buildings Partnership works with and incentivizes the large commercial landlords to upgrade their buildings, especially during routine refurbishment. The Green Organisations Badging Scheme works with tenants in the public and private sectors to reduce emissions through staff behaviour and operational changes to achieve a clear set of targets. The third initiative is a lobbying campaign to develop and deliver these programmes.

Londoners' homes contribute 38 per cent of London's CO_2 emissions. The Green Homes Programme includes subsidies for loft and cavity insulation, together with an awareness campaign and a one-stop shop on implementing energy-saving measures. There is a Concierge Service, which provides energy audits and installation management, customized for the 'able-to-pay' sector. Many Londoners want to be part of the solution and these are measures they can rally round. MORI polls show Londoners want to do the right thing, but they need it to be made easy for them.

London should take the lead in a more community or neighbourhood approach. There are a number of similarities between our current priority of cutting greenhouse-gas emissions and the way the Clean Air Act operated in the 1950s. That gave local authorities the power to declare smoke-free zones, with new fires, cookers and boilers largely funded by grants. A Low Carbon Act would empower local authorities to designate low-carbon zones and nominate an ESCo to sort out the measures needed to cut carbon emissions from each building to a defined minimum standard and create markets for more extensive energy effiency and micro-generation for those who wish to go further. The ESCo would then fund the work with the costs met from long-term savings shared with the householders, resulting in both low emissions and low fuel bills. Other benefits include economies of scale from a rolling programme of works and the transformation of energy suppliers into ESCos, as suggested by the Energy Review. This process would put communities and local government in the driving seat, but what we need is legislation to empower local authorities to take a proactive approach.

Connecting World Cities

But London and other cities are not islands. They are linked by intricate economic, social and cultural ties with one another, and to their hinterlands. They cannot wall themselves off and tackle climate change on their own. Cities concentrate economic activities and wealth creation in both the developed and the developing world. In everything we have done on sustainable development and tackling climate change we have learned from other cities – Curitiba, Stockholm, Toronto, Trondheim, Singapore and Woking to name but a few. It is often the smaller cities that can innovate and test concepts, but it is in large cities that huge reductions in emissions can be achieved.

Large cities across the world need to build wider and stronger links with one another. It was for this reason that the mayor and I convened the Large Cities Leadership Group summit in October 2005 and created the C20 initiative, which rapidly became the C40. Its aim is to develop long-term international collaboration among large cities in order to implement carbon-emissions reduction programmes, act as champions and stimulate business and national government action. At the first summit, it was agreed that city governments must lead by example, with measurable outcomes, and they should use their procurement clout to drive down the cost and promote development of products and services cutting CO_2 emissions.

The newly announced Clinton Climate Initiative will act as C40's implementation partner, working with partner cities to reduce energy use and cut carbon emissions by:
– Creating a purchasing consortium to lower prices for energy-saving products and promote new technologies;
– Mobilizing the best experts for technical assistance;
– Creating and employing common measurement tools.

The second C40 summit in May 2007 in New York, hosted by Mayor Michael R. Bloomberg, was attended by mayors and delegations from 33 of the world's largest and most influential cities. It witnessed the launch the first of the procurement packages – the Energy Efficiency Buildings Retrofit programme – developed by the Clinton Climate Initiative to bring together four of the world's largest Energy Service Companies with five of the world's largest banks and 16 of the world's largest cities. The programme offers building owners an audit of energy use and emissions, with recommendations of how to reduce them, a comprehensive discount for goods and services to achieve the reductions and financing to pay for the works, reimbursed through energy savings and underwritten by the banks.

The GLA and its functional bodies run 900 buildings and are eligible for the programme. Typical savings of about 20–50 per cent per building could mean cutting London's emissions by 1 per cent. The programme can be expanded to include other buildings in the public and commercial sectors as well as other cities. The summit in New York showed what could be achieved by cities working together as world leaders are making slow progress on a successor to Kyoto.

RECYCLING FOR THE FUTURE

Throughout the London boroughs there is a wide range of council initiatives to stimulate and facilitate the recycling of domestic waste, including glass (separated by colour), paper, plastic and metal. Many boroughs now also run pick-up schemes for organic waste and repair and subsequent reuse of domestic appliances such as fridges.

Looking Back to the Future

In the nineteenth century, London piloted the concept of the industrial megacity and spread it worldwide. We therefore have a special responsibility in the twenty-first century to test-drive the corollary concept of the 'sustainable world city', by rolling back our carbon emissions and helping other cities to do the same.

There is a sense of historical *déjà vu*. In the nineteenth century municipal enterprise invested in energy, water and waste infrastructure. In the twentieth century much of this was centralized and taken out of local control. Now the need to cut greenhouse-gas emissions through energy efficiency and greening the energy supply – especially through neighbourhood power generation and waste management – means we must go local again. Governments must put cities back in the driving seat so they can reinvent municipal enterprise through partnerships with the private sector.

The wheel comes full circle. Cities really are centre stage in the fight to save our planet for future generations – and, after years in limbo, London is leading the pack.

SUSTAINABLE CITIES

Guy Battle

HOW TO FLUSH A TOILET WITHOUT WATER?

With the United Nations predicting a doubling of the population of slum dwellers over the next 30 years, creative measures are needed to cope with the scarcity of water. Almost half the water consumption in the average house in Mexico City is used by toilets, while half of the population in Caracas receives water from municipal authorities only twice a week. The 'dry toilet' developed by Marjetica Potrč and Liyat Esakov in the *barrios* of Caracas presents a case study for replication, either inside or outside the house.

Cities are centres for the generation of knowledge and the exchange of wealth, for cultural growth and scientific achievement. While they offer many social and economic benefits, however, the cost they generate to our environment is often too great to ignore: urbanization is linked to resource depletion, increased waste and pollution, and the reduction of species.

In 2006, the World Wildlife Fund published its second 'Living Planet' report – a comprehensive survey of how mankind is using (and abusing) Earth. This survey covers every nation in the world, comparing data on issues such as water usage, energy consumption and waste management. Its conclusions are startling: currently, we are making use of the world's resources to the extreme – materials, space and water are rapidly being exhausted, and the Earth's ability to effectively absorb our waste and pollution is diminishing at great pace. If we keep living the way we do, our planet will soon run dry and it may become too hot and polluted to inhabit. However, beneath these conclusions lies a more worrying issue.

The 'Living Planet' report, which assesses the performance of countries based on their 'greenness', uses the ecological footprint indicator – measured in global hectares per person. This measure records the amount of resources (as land units) required by an individual in to support his or her life. In accepting that we have only one world, we must also accept that everyone deserves an equal share of its resources; this means that everyone should be entitled to 0.013 global square kilometres per person. If this was our target, the report states, the West would have to reduce its footprint by 80 per cent to allow those in the developing world to improve their current living standards. Needless to say, this is an unlikely scenario.

The 'Living Planet' demonstrates that the present model for urban living is fundamentally flawed. A new model is needed that is not based on the idea that the environment is an endless pool of resources, or a bottomless pit into which we can dump all our waste. If every nation in the world used as many resources as the highest polluters, at least three new planets would be needed to support our current lifestyles. Unless we all move to Mars, this is physically impossible.

A New Urban Model

It is clear that any future urban model must be sustainable at heart. Economies must thrive and people should have the right to earn a prosperous, comfortable and happy living. However, whether this can be achieved without causing environmental

The dump on the far-eastern edge of Mexico City's Iztapalapa (opposite) serves as an informal recycling centre with residents hand-sorting rubbish and re-using materials discarded by the rich for their self-built housing. As developed cities struggle to inspire their residents to 'go green', the informal sector constitutes the most environmentally advanced with regards to housing and transport. In Shanghai alone, there is an estimated 9 million bicycles, or roughly one for every two residents (right). In many cities of the developing world provide high sustainable forms of recycling and transport which should be abandoned as cities like Shanghai, right, face rapid growth and expansion.

disruption is something that is yet to be established. If we are to make up for past failures, future cities will have to be significantly better, or what has become known as Planet Positive. This will involve four key changes for cities: producing more energy than they need; becoming net carbon absorbers; collecting and processing waste within city limits; collecting and cleaning recycled water.

All this should happen in parallel to the creation of wealth and the promotion of social well-being and individual health. A sustainable city would find an optimum balance between fulfilling these needs and respecting the environment, ensuring that both present and future generations can rely on a system that will allow them and the environment to flourish symbiotically in the long term.

Beyond Short-Term Solutions

Our cities are centres of technological innovation, where we surround ourselves with technological advancement. But high-tech buildings, cars, mobile phones, clothes, etc. tend to be only a reflection of the short-sighted pleasure-seeking nature of western civilization, purely based on our status-driven society. While gadgets seem to generate the development and use of new technologies, the places where we live (our homes) and the utilities that serve them (our infrastructure) are ignored.

The infrastructure of the cities we live in was built by our ancestors and most existing infrastructure is old, creaking and inefficient. Much of London, one of the most affluent cities in the world, still uses sewers built more than150 years ago and these are now showing cracks. London's water system still uses lead piping in places and the rail network is in need of significant restructuring. So this is the reason why our sewage plants, which collect and produce methane gas, are not integrated in our power-supply stations or our gas-supply systems. And that is why our water-supply systems are still unable to collect and recycle rainwater and why London still is under drought conditions.

It is clear that as cities have developed, we have been rushed to implement short-term infrastructure solutions – investment decisions are still taken for immediate savings rather than long-term gain. Instead of applying light-rail solutions, we build more roads; instead of constructing tunnels, we raise flyovers; instead of turning to renewable energy sources, we invest in fire power stations. Chicago is a good example of this. The famous 'El' is a popular tourist attraction but also a noisy, polluting and dust-generating urban travel solution. This transit system was implemented as a quick fix 100 years ago, in an attempt to bring the city's transport standards a step closer to those of New York. It was, however, a bad solution, which has led to long-lasting difficulties. The developing world has a chance to learn from mistakes such as these and to concentrate on creating a better, more adaptable future. We have the opportunity to make a fresh start and base our decisions on gains, using new technologies to create a better future. New green technologies that are offering more sustainable futures include combined heat and power using gas from sewage digestion; the gasification of waste and distribution of gas utilizing existing gas networks to supply existing natural gas customers (thus replacing fossil fuels); city-wide geothermal systems using ground temperature on a seasonal basis; fuel-cell technologies using gas packaged from sewage units on a building-by-building basis, and building-integrated wind-turbine technology.

People Power

Sustainable issues cannot and will not be fixed by technology alone. We live in a throw-away society where waste and social exhaustion are the norm. We need other solutions that bind people together in common goals and understanding. Mexico City and Mumbai are two of the world's largest and most polluted cities, yet in both the amount of waste each person produces is less than anywhere in Europe. Why? Because recycling is a valuable business there – a way of life for millions of people.

The informal sector is not a counterfeit economy; it is a fluid, vibrant and successful economy that generates a significant percentage of Mexico City's wealth and economic activity. This is because waste has value; in a sense, the waste of the affluent feeds the poor. Despite this, authorities both here and in Mumbai talk about 'cleaning up the squats' due to a misconception that the poor are living off the rich without contributing to society. Often these communities are 'off-grid' (i.e. the people live without mains electricity or mains water). Such is the case with a large segment of the population in Caracas and the rest of Venezuela, where there is no official power or

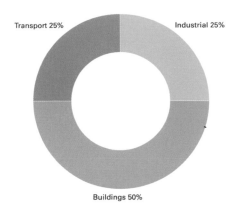

GLOBAL ENERGY USE

Lighting, heating, air-conditioning and other forms of electricity-based appliances consume over half the world's energy, with a further quarter consumed by vehicles and other forms of transport. Therefore, cities consume about 75 per cent of world energy and contribute an equivalent amount to global pollution.

CAR TRADING?

There are an estimated 400 private cars per 1,000 people in Mexico City's Federal District, a proportion that drops by almost half in the greater Metropolitan area. For the wealthy, private cars constitute a primary means of access through the city's low-rise sprawl, with bicycle usage an all but non-existent form of transport due to a lack of cycle lanes and persisting insecurity.

water provision in many communities because people have been denied access to it.

Beyond the social inequalities, community-based recycling should be seen as a key element in a symbiotic process: the rich have the means to consume and the poor utilize what is left of these purchases, resulting in an integrated waste-management strategy. There are other reasons why these seemingly unsustainable communities should be supported. Their 'social fabric' and organized nature may have emerged from lack of resources and tense living conditions, but they nevertheless have the capacity to generate improvements from the inside. Community-based architecture generates sustainable solutions such as the community dung hole, the community gardens and the community toilet.

The dry toilet in Caracas is a great example of such sustainable projects. In the capital of Venezuela, 60 per cent of the population are *barrio* or slum residents, and water supply to the slums is scarce. Some residents connect their water and sewage system to the municipal grid but this does not provide long-term solutions to a large-scale problem, and could result in devastating consequences, such as drying up water resources. Toilets are an essential component in a house and require vast quantities of water. The dry toilet in the Barrio La Vega was intended to put an end to the cries of the people by radically reducing the consumption of water and providing long-term water waste management solutions. By promoting individual empowerment and transferring knowledge from institutions to the people, the dry toilet constitutes a metaphor for self-sustainable solutions. Completed in 2003, it contains a mechanism that separates urine and faeces for compost. The dry toilet is a project by Marjetica Potrč in collaboration with Israeli architect Liyat Esakov under a programme developed by Alfredo Brillembourg and Hubert Klumpner. If people in places such as the Barrio La Vega did not have rules by which they lived their lives, or if they did not cooperate with local services, there would be no community.

People in the West have much to learn – we need to re-create our cities and implement similar interlocking and symbiotic systems and processes that will ultimately result in no waste, no carbon and zero-Earth-impact. Current market trends are encouraging developing countries to adopt low-carbon technologies that will enable them to achieve western living standards without the added carbon cost. These market trends allow companies to invest in low-carbon solutions in the developing world, saving carbon and creating carbon credits which may be bought back into the EU market to enable companies to achieve their own reduction targets.

There has been much criticism over non-regulated projects such as the planting of trees and land-filling. Although justified, these criticisms should not detract from the bigger picture. If we do not find a way to encourage developing countries to adopt the latest carbon technologies, which often cost more, they will use the same poorly performing technologies as we once did in the West because they are generally the cheapest. Carbon equation allows technology to be transferred as a benefit to all. The decisions we make now will set the parameters for the future. This is a long-term process. The children of our grandchildren will probably not be able to witness these results, but we can at least agree on certain points:

– The city is the battleground – sustainability will be won and lost within its limits;
– The urban models that the developed world has used to grow rich are flawed – they are failing us and already failing the developing world;
– We must make a paradigm shift – we must not only change light bulbs, but also change our mode of transport and way of thinking;

— It is no longer acceptable to talk in percentage reductions or neutrality – we must talk about net positive impacts – we must go Planet Positive.

Carbon is the New Gold

Green is the new way of living; sustainable social solutions are our goal. Furthermore, it seems that this phenomenon is reaching into the very commercial depths of our society. There is a broad range of companies that spent years ignoring the issue that are now ready to convert in the race to go green. Striking examples include BP with their recent 'Beyond Petroleum' addition to their brand name; British company M&S with their statement 'Plan A because there is no plan B'; and Wal Mart with their 'company-wide emphasis on sustainability extending to (our) environmental footprint to engage associates, suppliers, communities and customers'.

Politicians are getting in on the act too. In the UK, leading up to recent local elections, an amazing and somewhat comical contest was witnessed between the three main political parties, all competing for the 'greenest' agenda. The Conservative Party used to talk about creating 'clear blue water' between it and its rivals. Labour has gone a step further by using terms such as 'clean green water'. This shift in policy is a reflection of the fact that government rarely leads but usually follows public opinion, and this opinion has changed. Latest surveys show that 25 per cent of people now consider the environment as the single most important issue facing the world today.

This is not an issue that will go away, and our cities must respond, the will of the people demands it. Being aware of the fact that, to some extent, we could be in danger of green wash spin, we must not lose sight of our end goal: to create long-term sustainable solutions that can eventually be exported to those who need it most – China, India, South America and beyond.

In all of this, it seems that we have a new currency: green is the new cool, carbon is the new gold. The Kyoto Protocol has fundamentally changed the way we think about the environment. Before it people did the right thing because a few of them wanted to; now people do the right thing because many of them can make money from it. Carbon has put a value on energy savings, not only in terms of monetary wealth but also in terms of brand worth. Suddenly we are not only legislated to save our planet, we are also incentivized to do so because it creates wealth. Carbon has unlocked the value equation in our society; everything we do can be measured in terms of global-warming impact. Buildings and transportation together make up approximately 70 per cent of the world's CO_2 emissions, and it is in our cities that the vast majority of buildings exist. It is, therefore, inconceivable that urban designers, the architects of our new social structure, do not take this into account. In the future our cities will need to be carbon-free and dense with carbon-negative buildings. As a result, we will see new systems to incentivize savings: carbon credits for recycling plastic bottles/paper/cans/glass; carbon quotas issued at birth (you pay if you exceed them); carbon community programmes; online carbon auctions.

Rather than proposals, these are initiatives that are already being implemented. ProLogis Park in Pineham, Northampton, for example, is the world's first carbon-negative building, or, to use the new vocabulary, the first to be 'Planet Positive'. The development of the 55,000-square-metre distribution centre's new premises involves: increased air tightness; 15 per cent more skylights and thus reduced artificial lighting requirements; a combined heat and power unit that basically provides the centre's own power plant; and green energy is supplied from a solar wall providing energy for the storage building. Each material's carbon footprint measures the energy use

China has recently surpassed the United States as the world's biggest carbon dioxide emitter and is developing renewable technologies (opposite) expected to supply 10 per cent of its energy needs by 2020. Meanwhile, the Beddington Zero Energy Development (below) is the UK's largest eco-village with heating requirements around 10 per cent of a typical home.

SANDMARTIN WAY

from cradle (e.g. for steel mining iron ore), site (e.g. transportation by heavy goods vehicles and erection), use during the building lifetime (e.g. maintenance), and finally to grave (end-of-life recycling). The total carbon footprint includes mechanical and electrical fit-out, as well as the fuel and electricity required to manufacture, deliver and construct the building, creating a complete reflection of the building's carbon impact at day one of operation.

The project is unprecedented, engaging all suppliers to understand and reduce their carbon footprints for the benefit of the end user. Furthermore, the desire for suppliers to maintain customer loyalty encourages a focus on carbon management and sustainability with a view to enhancing their future business. This approach sets a logical route for sustainable cities. As such, when the retail sector asks how to achieve its ambitious emission-reduction targets, our advice should always be to use their influence and buying power to effect change throughout their entire supply chain.

Beyond the Niche

Sustainable developments remain elusive and as difficult to predict as ever – there is no one definition or methodology. However, we can establish that our present models are flawed since they do not present an acceptable blueprint for growth in the world's developing nations. The new model must find a balance between the needs of individuals, society, the economy and the environment. We cannot continue to abuse the planet as if it is a never-ending source of materials or sink for our waste. It is finite and we must necessarily change our ways.

New advances in technology will present us with new hope and new horizons in finding a solution. Technology alone will not provide us with a way out and we must look for new social patterns. It is here that the West has the most to learn from those it is supposed to be trying to help, in its unique implementation of social cooperatives. Carbon will eventually be recognized as the redistributor of wealth – those who pollute more will have to pay accordingly and those who do not pollute will be able to sell their credits. Carbon will become the new leveller. We have but one planet, we are but one people, sharing the same air, water, earth and sunlight. Sustainability must become a generally accepted way of life rather than a mere niche focus of a few.

A TAXONOMY OF TOWERS

Alejandro Zaera-Polo

FEELING THE POWER

The 88-storey Jin Mao Tower in the Pudong Financial District of Shanghai was designed by the Chicago office of Skidmore, Owings and Merrill. The tallest building in the People's Republic of China at the time of its realization, it is set to be overtaken by the Shanghai World Financial Centre by Kohn Pedersen Fox. Mega-projects such as these constitute an increasing proportion of the revenues of American architectural offices, with commissions in Asia estimated at 40 per cent of their total income.

After a two-decade lapse that coincides almost exactly with the lifespan of the World Trade Center in Manhattan, high-rise building is back in vogue. The World Trade Center, finished in 1972 – one year before the Sears Tower in Chicago – was completed as the 1973 oil crisis unfolded, pausing the race for taller buildings by instilling doubts about the solidity of an oil-based economy. Their demise, which took place in an economy driven by information, seems to have convinced everyone again of the charisma that tall buildings command. A few global websites are now devoted to following the growing array of high-rise buildings and to discussing and admiring their technical prowess. According to Emporis, one of these websites, 40 per cent of the high-rise buildings – buildings above 12 storeys – on Earth have been built since 2000, and around 8 per cent of the world's stock of tall buildings is under construction right now. The most high-rise-intensive city in the world – Benidorm, Spain – already has one high-rise building for every 180 inhabitants; there is even a high-rise cemetery, the Memorial Necrópole Ecumênica III, in Santos, Brazil.

The fascination is not just with the renewed importance of urban charisma, the glamour of high-life, the breathtaking views, the feeling of power from living with cutting-edge technology and humming gadgets, and even the vertigo caused by buildings swaying in the wind. There is also the inevitable trend towards the densification of existing urban centres, as the planet's human population flocks irreversibly towards urban cores. The superiority of the 'culture of congestion' and the green credentials of the lift core as an alternative to the gas-guzzling six-lane motorway are becoming universally accepted facts. Beyond their renewed aesthetic hipness, tall buildings offer a high-density model for distributing population on the planet that helps preserve the green belt from the ever-expanding suburb and has a smaller land and ecological footprint.

Once the preserve of the very rich and powerful inhabitants of the world financial centres, skyscrapers in some cities are becoming a sort of vernacular typology engaging the middle class, no longer the outcome of land shortage or urban speculation, as in the classic examples of Manhattan, Hong Kong and Singapore. Examples of this democratization of the skyscraper can be found everywhere, from London to Kuala Lumpur, Moscow to Panama, Dubai to Madrid. This building type has stopped being an expensive extravagance and is now a serious investment and development vehicle. The success of high-rise, mixed-use complexes like Roppongi Hills in Tokyo, The Arch in Kowloon, Tower Place in Seoul and Kanyon in Istanbul is being noticed

by international developers as an example of urban development quality and plentiful profit to be replicated as often as circumstances allow. Globalization has brought high-rises a customer base on an unprecedented scale.

One of the reasons for the democratization of building height has been a substantial development of related building technologies: materials with higher strength and faster construction technologies, in steel and concrete, high-efficiency curtain-wall systems with superior insulation and solar filtering values, intelligent vertical transportation systems with higher lifting capacities, more efficient energy plants running on renewable sources. The efficiency of high-rises is now substantially greater than it was in 1973, and this is making the construction and maintenance of high-rise buildings affordable for a widening spectrum of customers. In current urbanization, skyscrapers have ceased to be specially crafted products for the rich and powerful and are becoming a mass-product. There has been a huge growth of high-rise residential buildings in particular. As opposed to the post-war high-rise residential construction, which was the result of enlightened politics and urbanism mostly for low-income populations, new high-rise residential building is driven by market demand. The commercialization of the type has also brought a higher level of industrialization in the making of tall buildings.

The building industry's answer to the inherent complexity of the high-rise typology and the scale of its economies has been to break down the project into different problems to be resolved by different experts. The typical high-rise today is designed first by well-established market ratios administered by real-estate specialists: population ratios, facade-to-core depths, floor-plate sizes, planning grids, floor-to-floor heights, net-to-gross ratios and facade ratios form the first level of constraint. Safety regulations and lift capacities, interpreted by vertical transportation and fire consultants, add more constraints. Environmental regulations, channelled into the project through mechanical and electrical engineers, constrain the skin design to achieve certain daylight and insulation values and solar-gain ratios. Finally, the local construction industry's speed and skills and the price of commodities filtered through the structural consultants or contractors determine what kind of structure – and therefore massing – the project may acquire.

The ruthless force of these economies has usually 'designed' most of the building by the time architects get involved, relegating their role to the design of the skin (usually with contributions by facade consultants), lobby and toilets. To illustrate the force of these constraints, it is sufficient to calculate the cost per year of one lift in a 50-storey office building in a generic global city: every rentable square metre of floor plate will have a market value of, for example, US$750 per year. A standard lift shaft will have a surface per floor of 9 square metres. If we make the calculation of 9 square metres x 50 floors x US$750, we get costs of US$337,500 per year. Given that the total floor plate will usually be restricted by planning constraints, the elimination of one lift by an architect or fire consultant will produce revenues for the developer of over US$1 million in three years.

The only possibility of preventing these forces from controlling design comes when the project requires the delivery of an image to brand a corporation, city or developer. In the best-case scenario, the architect is empowered by formalizing an envelope that will be attractive to potential customers, create brand value for the occupier or seduce local planning committees and politicians to allow higher floor/area ratios. The taller the structure, the more relevant this factor becomes. The skyscraper is still the paradigmatic urban form, and in very competitive or politically sensitive situations its brand value becomes so critical that it can actually change a few standard building equations and produce an entirely different sort of economy. The recent history of the type is not short of examples in which the involvement of a particular architect has been able to subvert customary economics.

We are now witnessing an unprecedented number of high-profile design competitions in which attention-seeking clients are commissioning well-known architects to produce spectacular buildings that defy all conventions, including budgetary ones. But 'the current mania for flamboyant skyscrapers has been a mixed blessing for architecture. While it has yielded a stunning outburst of creativity, it has also created an atmosphere in which novelty is often prized over innovation. It is as if the architects were dog owners parading their poodles in front of a frivolous audience.'[1] This is *New York Times* critic Nicolai Ouroussoff writing about the latest examples of this global quest for the flamboyant skyscraper: the competitions for the Gazprom City in St Petersburg for Russian energy giant Gazprom and the Phare Tower in La Défense, Paris.

The question here is how to distinguish innovation from novelty, particularly within the double standard that rules contemporary high-rise projects. These projects are subject either to ruthless efficiencies that constrain possibilities to the repetition of verified models, or they fall into the economy of the brand image, in which everything is possible and the desired novelty can direct choices without drawing any significant links to the typological phylum. Those projects that, because of their profile, would allow the benchmark to slide further are often misused in producing weird and spectacular high-rises full of contingent gestures that fail to open the market to meaningful experimentation. This is one of the reasons that these projects – as opposed to, for instance, museums – have remained in the hands of large commercial firms and beyond the reach of more speculative architects, who have systematically either failed to understand or chosen to ignore the underlying economies at play in this typology.

To work effectively in this evolving market, we need to develop the typological knowledge that could reactivate the synergies across the divides in which the industry has split the high-rise project. The creation of new relationships between efficiency and expression will allow us to grow beyond the wave of vacuous expressionism that has captured the most interesting high-rise commissions and voided them of true innovation, which cannot ignore the context of given technology and marketplace fundamentals; the real opportunities for invention lie in the engagement and the problematization of those seemingly neutral parameters that regulate the typology.

A City of Exceptions

The extraordinary increase in high-rise construction opens up an opportunity for considering its possibilities as an urban typology. High-rise fever is putting unprecedented pressure on urban cores to accommodate new skyscrapers, often forcing city leaders to rethink their planning policies. The key question is whether the high-rise buildings still remain extravagant and unique – objects whose proliferation creates a city of exceptions, a city shaped by the sum of individual initiatives – or whether its population has grown so large that it has become an integral part of the urban fabric and therefore requires a more sophisticated policy than just limiting heights. What should be the nature of that policy? A location of landmarks in strategic points to construct new views? A design guideline on the character or environmental performance of tall buildings? The delimitation of zones with unlimited height? A policy of

CROWNING ACHIEVEMENT

The 2006 competition-winning design by
Thom Mayne of Morphosis for Phare Tower, or
lighthouse, in Paris is crowned by wind turbines
which combine with other innovative and sustainable technologies to significantly reduce the
building's energy needs. At 300 metres, Phare
Tower will be almost as tall as the Eiffel Tower.

Floor Area Ratio (FAR) allocation related to public transport capacity and daylight thresholds? Many policies are already under development in different cities across the world, and it is interesting to notice that the attitude towards high-rise buildings has deep cultural roots.

The relationship between high-rise buildings and cities is a complex one, and is strongly tinged with local flavour. In the United States, downtown has been traditionally linked to high-density and high-rise buildings, primarily dedicated to workspace. The distribution of high-rises follows a mono-functional pattern radiating from a centre, usually one of financial activities. In Europe, where the closest precedents of skyscrapers are church towers and other representations of power, high-rises have been generally perceived as anti-urban and exiled to special precincts away from the centre. La Défense in Paris and Canary Wharf in London are good examples of this trend. Asian cities have located their high-rises less idiosyncratically, as punctual intensifications of the fabric. High-rises have become a more continuous distribution usually related to transport-infrastructure capacity and location. The Asian models have enthusiastically adopted the residential high-rise as an inner-city land use in contrast to the mono-functional models in the United States (except New York City) and in European central business districts.

Tokyo provides probably the best example of the coupling of transportation infrastructure and high-rises. The main stations on the Yamanote Line have concentrated clusters of high density and skyscrapers; such clusters replicate, graph-like, the patterns of accessibility in the inner-city core. There is no central business district or high-rise ghetto but instead a distribution of high-density clusters where transportation conditions are optimal. Seoul, Kuala Lumpur and Shanghai (although paradoxically Pudong replicates the European model of a high-rise ghetto) present similar approaches to urban policy for high-rises – not characterized as forming a precinct, but rather as exemplifying standard rules. The skyscraper clusters are the result of the intersection of FARs, transport capacities and the casting of shadows. There is no *a priori* formal consistency or delimitation. Skyscrapers appear where there is a coincidence of four factors: sufficient transport infrastructure, a high FAR, sufficient land to justify the concentration of a large built floor area, and sufficient distance to neighbouring buildings to ensure required daylighting. The local tendency to build tall projects by a riverfront or along main infrastructural lines allows for both accessibility and shadow buffers. The recent redevelopments of remaining tracts of land in central Tokyo (Shinagawa or Shiodome) and the development of riverfront locations in Seoul, such as AIG's complex in Yeouido, Jamsil and Mokdong's Richensia and Hyperion complexes, confirm the vitality of this model.

In contrast, London, which has undergone a massive transformation of its core during the last decade, is addressing the enormous current pressure to densify by delimiting a high-rise cluster formed around Tower 42 (currently London's tallest building). The planning envelope follows a sort of Gaussian curve – taller at the centre and fading towards the edges. In addition, an area of exclusion is formed by seven view corridors for St Paul's, London Bridge and Big Ben. Most interestingly, in London there is no FAR assignment by a city plan as there is in most other European cities: floor-plate allowance is at the discretion of the local planning authorities, and developers are required to build up their case, submitting environmental, transport and daylight-impact reports. Aesthetics feature prominently in the assessment of proposals to the extent that a more 'iconic' proposal will have an advantage in the planning-permission application process. All this confirms London as the world's

FORM AND POWER

The competition for a high-rise tower to house the headquarters of Gazprom at the heart of the historic centre of St Petersburg in Russia raised a furious debate about the relationship between form, function and power. The competion entries by Herzog & de Meuron (top), Studio Daniel Libeskind (bottom), Office for Metropolitan Architecture (opposite, top), Jean Nouvel (opposite, middle) and competition winner RMJM (opposite, bottom).

most picturesque city in terms of high-rise policy. Barcelona has a similar 'City Beautiful' approach, in which high-rises (which usually end up being headquarters for public utilities like water, gas and telephone) are essentially ornaments aimed at producing vistas or orientation points in an otherwise relatively low skyline. A flamboyant design, like Jean Nouvel's Torre Agbar or EMBT's Gas Natural Tower, is therefore critical to the success of any tall project.

The approach to the questions of location, height and design cannot be more different in the European capitals and in the Asian metropolises: in Europe, high-rises are still treated as monuments, extravagances that used to be paid for by the king or the Church and now are paid for and exploited by private corporations but approved by public agencies, placed as landmarks in strategic locations and required to have iconic designs. In the current European debate on skyscrapers, a struggle exists between the pressure on urban centres to accommodate a normalization of higher densities, and larger buildings with their monumental character; this struggle may generate interesting opportunities to invest tall buildings with iconic content but also to develop adequate prototypes for local urban milieus.

In Asia and, for the most part, America, the skyscraper is a more mundane endeavour treated with a certain indifference about design. If, in the European case, skyscrapers are still 'avant-garde' and are determined by vistas and relationships to the existing skyline, in Asia and America they are more integral to the urban fabric and will be determined largely by technical and financial matters (generic urban-planning rules, infrastructural capacity, FAR allocation, disaster-prevention planning, daylight rights, environmental impacts, etc.). In most cases, the iconicity of the proposal will be secondary to these more quantitative assessments.

There are monumental exceptions to these rules: the Petronas Towers in Kuala Lumpur, Burj Dubai, Taipei 101 in Taipei and the Jin-Mao Tower in Shanghai take the monumental, extravagant approach predominant in Europe, while Canary Wharf creates a more generic high-rise fabric. There is no easy conclusion or universal prescription, and what is adequate for an economy and culture like Barcelona's may be totally wrong for London's, which faces a much higher pressure to densify the city. It seems unlikely that the 'iconic' approach to the skyscrapers will be able to evolve the typology, generate knowledge to frame the future engagement of high-rise buildings with urban fabrics, and avoid the emphasis on novelty for its own sake. But it is also true that if there is no further ambition in these projects but to satisfy commercial interests, it is unlikely that the enormous energy that propels them will be able to evolve new urban models. Without a more deliberate connection between the efficiencies of high-rise buildings and their expression, developing an urban policy for them will be difficult.

The Icon and the Type

The growing popularity of the skyscraper and its progressive industrialization have evolved the high-rise phylum substantially in the last decade. There is an increasingly complex body of efficiencies, differentiated in terms of location, use and scales, that regulates the relationship between the structural, programmatic and environmental drivers both within the building's configuration and in its engagement with the urban landscape. This evolved high-rise phylum is now ripe to be projected into an engine of design that could produce real typological and expressive innovation.

The traditional high-rise building from the second half of the twentieth century was primarily determined by the extrusion of a floor plate and a structural grid.

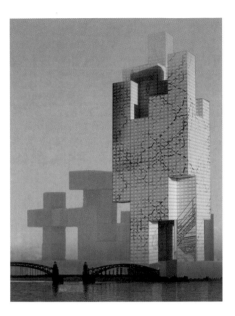

Squares, circles, slabs, Hs, Ls or Ys were the basic plan choices. Gone were Eliel Saarinen, Raymond Hood or Hugh Ferriss's attempts to derive high-rise form from the constraints of shadows and the need for daylighting, William Van Alen's efforts to invest the skyscraper with a representational charge, and even Robert Le Ricolais or Richard Buckminster Fuller's attempts to shape the building in response to diagonal forces. Fazlur Khan's experiments with diagrids and tapering spires were isolated and extravagant experiments in an industry in which the efficiency of the grid was a real advantage. In the 1960s and 1970s skyscrapers had been conceptually liberated from the city, and their form was meant to respond only to internal efficiencies of construction technology and programme. Only at the end of the 1980s did the representational drive reappear in a series of image-driven high-rises that offered the type again as a centre-city agent.

Increasing pressure from the market is now forcing planners and designers to provide towers with more compelling and crafted images than those of the mere repetitive extrusions. Very often, this added layer of expression is produced by the mere treatment of the envelope with unusual materials or patterns, by playing with balconies in residential towers, or by slight deformations of the facade in office buildings. An elaborated or a decorated skin is probably the most economical device that can provide an aura in high-rise design. In some sections of Shanghai and Guangzhou, fields of towers are designed simply as extrusions of an optimized footprint but are then given a variety of *tempiettos*, *pagodas* and so on, aimed at individuating them. They are effective as far as the market is concerned, but, unlike Hugh Ferriss's setbacks for daylight and Louis Sullivan's ornamented ceramic panels for fire-protection, they are detached from real efficiency in the tall-building typology. They demonstrate a paradigmatic outcome of the negative side of the industrialization of the high-rise, in which expression has become an alternative detached from functional and constructive concerns. The expressive layer is not alien to the history of the type, but the tension between expression and efficiencies has never been greater. Early twentieth-century tall buildings in America were often given sophisticated, intricate silhouettes that expressed appropriately the ambitious enterprise of building high-rises and differentiated their presence on the skyline. The skylines of cities like Prague, Moscow or Cairo reveal a level of crafting of such structures that exemplifies the mystique of tall buildings and the consciousness of profile, even if tall buildings then were exclusively driven by the goal of monumentality.

The current trend towards profiled high-rises is often at odds with the economic and functional forces ruling the office and residential high-rise economies. This is a potentially generative conflict between the increasingly demanding requests of developers and planners to produce dramatic tall buildings and increasingly precise market demands – particular dimensions of facade-to-core, specific facade and fenestration ratios, market-driven population ratios, compliance with certain models of structural efficiency and procurement systems. As the high-rise becomes an industrial product, the typology becomes increasingly optimized and constrained.

In most European cities and increasingly in cities in America and Asia, it is unlikely that developers will present authorities with an extruded form without any formal complexity for fear that planners and potential tenants will dismiss such projects as banal. In many cities, particularly in the Eurozone, extravagant projects help developers get through planning-permission applications, increase the FAR of the site and eventually attract higher income for the building. Within this process, market parameters are subverted and owners relinquish some efficiencies in order to

HIGH PROFILE

The form of the twenty-first century skyscraper is increasingly defined by extravagant profiles and innovative volumes, such as those modelled in the structural ingenuity of OMA's 2002 CCTV in Beijing (above) and FOA's competition entry for Ground Zero in New York's Lower Manhattan designed in 2004 (right).

maximize their revenues. The case of Norman Foster's 30 St Mary Axe (Swiss Re) in the City of London is interesting in this respect: because of its unique geometry, it is the first tall building to obtain planning permission in the City for decades. Swiss Re, the commissioner, has gained enormous exposure because of this building which, on the other hand, has failed to attract subtenants to fill the substantial portion of the building that the owner does not need. Swiss Re has recently sold the building at a sum that allegedly delivered a profit of around GB£250 million (US$500 million). German property firm IVG Immobilien and UK investment firm Evans Randall bought the building.

In London there is a flood of profiled skyscrapers that, because of their idiosyncratic forms, have been immediately given nicknames: The Gherkin (Foster's 30 St Mary Axe), The Shard (Renzo Piano's tower in the City), Helter-Skelter (Kohn Pedersen Fox's Bishopsgate Tower) and Handset (a Rafael Viñoly design), among them. In New York, where simple extrusions were the norm, the World Trade Center's unapologetic simplicity is being replaced by the more complex profiles of buildings like the Freedom Tower and Foster's Hearst Tower.

Some projects are trying to manipulate to dramatic effect some of the constraints that high-rise buildings impose on geometry to escape conventional extrusions and produce bold images. Some of the best examples among these idiosyncratic towers, many designed by Norman Foster, are using structural or functional efficiencies to generate their extravagant profiles. Foster has argued for the round and tapering profile of his 30 St Mary Axe in London on the grounds that it liberates views around it and decreases wind at street level and its scale in the skyline. His Hearst Tower uses the diagrid that provides extra stability against lateral forces as an argument to produce a profiled volume. His Russia Tower, with a Y-shaped up-tapering plan, is justified on the grounds of structural efficiency and programmatic flexibility.

An alternative path of experimentation is represented by those towers that address local iconographies not as expressions but as efficiencies, as crucial elements of contemporary skyscrapers. Pelli's Petronas Towers, SOM's Burj Dubai and its Jin Mao Tower in Pudong, and C. Y. Lee's Taipei 101 have attempted to distil images that resonate with local cultural figurations, using the rotated squares of Asian Muslim towers (in the case of Petronas), the desert flower (Burj Dubai) and the tiered pagodas repetition of older Chinese architecture (Jin Mao Tower). Taipei 101 is filled with symbolism. Its eight distinctive sections create the impression of a bamboo stalk but actually represent gold ingots used in ancient China as royal currency. Each of its eight sections has eight floors – the number eight sounds like 'earn fortune' in Chinese; four circles on each side of the building near the base represent coins. There is no question that iconography is integral to high-rise buildings. Those who did not take it into consideration have sometimes been forced to do so: Kohn Pedersen Fox's Shanghai Hills World Financial Center, now under construction, which once featured a round hole at its tower top, suffered a last-minute redesign to present a square. The circle recalled the Japanese flag and, since it was owned by the Japanese Mori Corporation, its image had to be changed to avoid offending the locals.

In the best examples, the designers have sought a resonance between local iconographies and certain building efficiencies. Petronas offers an increased facade ratio by striating the skin of the building, while Burj Dubai's desert flower provides a pure geometrical basis for using three tapering buttresses as structural ribs, in much the same way as Foster's Russia Tower. Both buildings are built using reinforced concrete, relatively new in buildings of this height, and both step back towards the top to lower the centre of gravity in response to the added weight of concrete. This architecture explores the efficiencies of its technology to produce an idiosyncratic profile that expresses its construction method.

The sheer scale of some of these buildings is in itself one of the new parameters in the high-rise world, since it is almost impossible to resolve it with a minimal geometry if one is to avoid being relatively inefficient. The need to go beyond the simple extrusion to create very large, tall structures was realized first by SOM's Sears Tower (1974) in Chicago; it was explored further by I. M. Pei's Bank of China (1990), built in Hong Kong, another early example of structural expressionism. OMA's Togok and CCTV projects – designed, according to its patent description as 'an alternative to the traditional diagram of the super-high-rise' and to 'avoid the isolation of the traditional high-rise' – are excursions into the unprecedented scale of some contemporary high-rise projects. My firm's, Foreign Office Architects, own Bundle Tower™ project – carried out for the Max Protech exhibition 'A New World Trade Center', started as an attempt to develop a structural concept for a new generation of super-high-rise buildings but, in a curious turn of events, ended up resonating with the 'United We Stand' motto – was another attempt to turn the fragmentation of volumes that becomes almost unavoidable in projects above 300,000 square metres into a structural advantage that enables an alternative vertical transportation system, allowing the different towers to share the cores of its neighbours by linking them with a system of sky lobbies.

It is precisely in the correlation of emerging tower efficiencies and local specificities of the high-rise population with the tower's capacity to generate alternative expressions that we can find true innovation, rather than one-off, iconic extravagances. In this investigation, the resonance between technical problems and local iconographies, as in Petronas or Burj Dubai, is an interesting additional vernacular trait of differentiation in the increasingly urban character of the type, as opposed to a global replication of the same models.

GLOBAL REACH
Jean Nouvel's design of Torre Agbar for the Barcelona-based water company features environmentally friendly light emitting diodes (LEDs) as well as temperature sensors that regulate the building's glass blinds. The icon is inspired by the shape of a geyser of water shooting into the air.

The Vernacular High-Rise

The high-rise type lies at the crossroads between the global processes of densification shaping contemporary urban development and the protocols and iconographies that define local cultural specificities. As a type that requires a substantial level of investment, the high-rise is often linked to global economic processes, foreign investment and migrant populations, presenting an ideal battleground for global trends and local uses. Particularly since the global success of the high-rise residential building – a relatively recent phenomenon – the high-rise population has become increasingly differentiated, producing vernacular varieties that do not always conform exactly to global trends. As prime real estate, centrally located and not entirely suitable for certain lifestyles, these inner-city residential high-rises are often filled with expatriates and cosmopolitan locals who tend to be temporary inhabitants. But even with a certain 'international' standard expected from this type of development, very specific design expectations arise from the local communities owning a controlling market share. Although many developers on these projects are corporations or investors with multinational portfolios seeking to profit from rising property prices, they need to carefully consider the specificities of the local market. Recent examples like the Tower Palace development in Seoul (built by Samsung on the site where OMA's Togok Towers were to go), The Arch in Kowloon (built by Sun Hung Kai Properties) and Tokyo's Roppongi Hills (built by the Mori Corporation) have become phenomenal real-estate successes that everybody is trying to replicate, and a proof of the vitality of the inner-city residential high-rise typology, particularly in South-east Asia.

There are many similarities among these projects, but there are also several differences that account for the specificities of each market. The Korean building, for example, features considerably larger units, as well as conservatories, while the other two rely on more conventional fenestration patterns – the Japanese example is still based on a tatami grid, while the Chinese model features the traditional facade articulation typical of Hong Kong that provides external walls for almost all rooms. The high-rise as a vernacular species may resonate with local iconographies and symbols, but its primary field of diversification occurs on a more subtle level, by complying with a number of parameters that embody local specificities of lifestyle, trade protocols, cultural preferences and climatic conditions.

An analysis of the floor plates of the global stock of high-rise building demonstrates that this type is no longer just a western export but is increasingly developing local varieties of such strength that in some cases they are spreading back towards the original epicentres of the type. For example, some of the condominiums now in Seattle, Miami or the London Docklands incorporate Asian traits, such as increased facade ratios and exterior toilets, as developers learn from Asian markets or target Asian investors. Contemporary high-rise residential floor plates across the globe have become radiographies of cultural hybridization and the synthesis of local variations. The scale of the units, level of provision and the position of the toilets in the plan (next to or away from the facade, en-suite or collective), the provision of service areas within the apartments and the level of differentiation between the private and public areas of the dwelling, are often indicative of domestic protocols in western, Middle-Eastern and Asian populations. Instead of focusing on the iconic nature of high-rise buildings, a comparative, quantitative or topological analysis of the different parameters of residential organizations could become an extraordinary instrument for producing a deeper understanding of these processes of simultaneous vernacularization and hybridization of high-rise life. What follows is an attempt to map this battlefield between transnational trends and vernacular variations, setting up a global frame of reference to identify variations, tendencies and innovations, abandoning the utopian models of novelty, to be able to trace, like craftsmen, the high-rise phylum.

But there are other processes that have a global reach. The dramatic shift of the typology towards the residential is increasing the use of building technologies that provide better acoustic insulation and less wind deflection. Given that residential use does not require the amplitude of spaces needed for offices, reinforced concrete wall construction is rapidly gaining market share among high-rise builders and is even starting to reverse the trend towards large spans in office buildings. The rapid increase in global steel prices is decisively contributing to this technological shift. New concrete additives allow unprecedented speed of construction for a technology that a few years ago would not have been considered – because of programme constraints – for buildings higher than 25 floors. Current developments in high-strength concrete technology also allow increasing capacity to reach heights previously restricted to those resulting from steel technology. In fact, Burj Dubai, soon to be the tallest inhabited building in the world and a pioneer in many ways, is using reinforced concrete for its 150-plus storey structure. In South Korea, the local industry has developed a technology for residential high-rises based on mass-construction, slip-formed reinforced concrete, the optimal use of which runs now at 24 floors (it was 16 only six years ago).

As height becomes a desirable commodity, there is a growing disparity in the rental values on different building levels. In a commercial high-rise, lower levels are desirable because of their proximity to the street (for retail or high-density uses like trading floors). Upper levels are desirable because of the views and diminishing acoustic intrusion. In residential high-rise buildings, as the value per square metre increases with the floor level, it is common to have fewer, larger apartments, where buyers with higher purchasing capacity will aim. Following this logic, there seems to be an unexploited potential to design sectional differentiation in high-rise buildings rather than follow the direct extrusion of floor plates.

Another global tendency is towards a less artificially controlled environment, due to the increase in global energy prices. Also in South Korea, where there is a real industry of tall residential buildings, the facade ratio has been constantly increasing over the last 20 years, coming closer and closer to Hong Kong levels, even with a much higher average of surface per unit. Under-floor heating, winter gardens and cross-ventilation are part of a local standard that in the current energy market is likely to be exported soon. What is more important, the optimization reached by the building industry in the use of slip-formed reinforced concrete for high-rise residential will change the landscape of high-rise technology once dominated by steel construction.

All these developments depart from the original western high-rise tradition, which is based on an artificially maintained environment, and expensive and techno-logically complex systems. Glass and steel construction, a technology transferred from ship building and railway construction, and once exclusive to high-rise building, is rapidly losing market share to the more earthbound concrete technology. The wider impact of these construction technologies, both in appearance and in typology, remains to be seen.

As a relatively complex technical enterprise, the design of a high-rise building is subject to precise calculation – probably more than any other building type. These calculations are made to estimate the level of service needed to provide for its different systems – for example, the total population that the lift core is supposed to serve at peak times and the length of elevator waiting times, the population that the air-conditioning system is intended to serve, or the dimensioning of toilets and fire escapes. Space is scarce and needs to be accounted for carefully, and this level of accountability is what enables us to quantify its multiple performances as a technical and cultural phenomenon and generate the knowledge that will enable us to criticize the contemporary stock of high-rise typologies, not as a series of novel occurrences but as a particularly intriguing species in constant evolution – one that diversifies geographically in response to climate, topography and cultural protocols. What follows here is a list of indexes that may allow us to map out the geographical or cultural diversification of high-rise typologies to generate a frame of references that will enable us to criticize and develop the current typologies, to ground innovation and avoid mere novelty.

Certain population standards are compulsory by building laws, such as the population for which a fire-escape system is designed, but most of the time the esti-mation of populations will vary across the different systems in a high-rise building to provide different standards. It may be that the overall population for the vertical transportation system is based on 12 square metres per person, but for the air-renewal rate that figure is enhanced to 10 square metres per person and the toilets downgraded to 14 square metres per person. It may also be that population density varies across the section of the building, reaching 7 square metres per person in the lower floors to accommodate trading floors and other population-intensive uses, while decreasing to 14 square metres per person at higher levels. These decisions may sometimes trigger arguments to set the specifications that will be affected by local work cultures and social uses. When one is calculating the lift or air-renewal capacity of a high-rise facility in some European countries, for example, it is acceptable to decrease the population by 12 per cent to account for daily vacancies that reflect local working culture and the type of work done in these buildings. But will these conditions apply elsewhere, for example in South Korea?

The specification of an office building's toilet-block population has similar social implications. The number of toilet units will be given by a locally established ratio in respect to a population that will typically oscillate around a standard guideline. However, when that overall number must be split into male and female populations, the situation becomes more politically charged. If we follow workplace statistics, it is unlikely that the female population in a high-rise building today will reach 40 per cent of the total, no matter where we are. But should we design our buildings to meet the current statistics or should we aim for a more politically correct 50-50 ratio? If we do, it is likely that the male block would be undersupplied for the present workplace market. The solution is often to dimension for 60-50 or 60-60 to match all requirements. This comes at a price: two extra toilet cubicles will consume approximately 4 square metres of floor-plate area. Following the same rough calcula-tion as before, in a 50-storey tower in a generic global city this will mean a loss of US$150,000 per year in rent. This is the price of political correctness.

In commercial buildings, the consideration of the planning grids is also important for the design of the building fenestration and for interior organization. For example, a lawyer's office in the UK and most of the Commonwealth states will require cellular offices to be 3 metres wide, while an American lawyer will consume a minimum of 3.6 metres of facade. In locations like London or New York City, where firms on both sides of the Atlantic share the available space, the decision to choose the

FORM FOLLOWS MONEY
Like many other commerical developments
of the 1980s and 1990s, the shape of Canary
Wharf's containers for finance and business
have created a landscape of 'groundscrapers'
and stunted skyscrapers that create a one-
dimensional urban experience.

facade quantity is an important one and will affect the planning grids of the building and the rhythm of fenestration, which is inevitably linked to the subdivision possibilities of the floor plate. The decision on the module of the planning grid is linked to the density of the population that will inhabit the building and the density of occupation patterns, and types of activity.

The facade ratio is one of the most powerful tools to analyse the evolution of high-rise typologies and their geographical diversification, and to be used as a design engine. Since the facade of a high-rise building is one of the most expensive elements, cost consultants use a ratio comparing the surface of facade to the floor area. This parameter has been employed for decades by developers and quantity surveyors to analyse the financial implications of a design, and by mechanical engineers to estimate energy requirements. If the ratio is high, it means greater expenses; if it is low, daylight and ventilation may need to be artificially supplied. It is therefore a parameter that connects financial implications with environmental qualities, often involving cultural specificities and technical specifications.

Parameters such as the surface-to-volume and the window ratios, traditionally used to calculate energy requirements and to specify the composition of the facade, become indicative of the increasing differentiation of high-rise residential types in their global reach. If we compare these ratios for residential high-rises across different geographies, we see the differentiation generated by cultural, climatic and construction factors. In a prototypical high-rise development in Dubai, for example, the average facade ratio would be around 0.45 square metres per indoor square metre, in London 0.5 square metres per square metre, in Miami 0.55 square metres per square metre, in Seoul 0.6 square metres per square metre, in Kuala Lumpur 0.75 square metres per square metre, and in Hong Kong 0.85 square metres per square metre.[2] The manipulation of these parameters offers the possibility of playing with a spectrum of culturally specific possibilities.

The implications of this diversification in a typology that is generally considered global are interesting: in America and the Middle East, a high level of mechanically controlled environment in a home is acceptable, while the further we move towards South-east Asia, the more common the requirement for all rooms to have direct contact with outside air. In the western models, residential units rely heavily on full air-conditioning, while in South-east Asian prototypes, natural ventilation and under-floor heating are standard, even when air-conditioning equipment is installed.

The argument for this radical increase in the facade ratio in South-east Asia is often based on the humid climate, but it is more likely the result of certain living patterns that Asian cultures are not prepared to sacrifice, even in a high-rise building. Local cooking rituals have developed certain types of kitchen organization, with dry and wet areas; complex systems of service access and entrances into service areas exist within apartments of a certain standard; a particular bathing culture while being able to see daylight and views is possibly fuelling some expensivecharacteristics of the Asian residential high-rise such as the systematic location of bathrooms on the facade of the building, as opposed to the western models, where the bathrooms and kitchens tend to be internal and are therefore artificially ventilated and lit. Kuala Lumpur and Hong Kong are certainly very humid, and when the air-conditioning is turned off there may be problems, but there is no reason to think that Seoul or Beijing need very different residential structures than those in Manhattan, Chicago or San Francisco.

The impact of this requirement not only affects the quality of interior spaces, daylight and topological organization of the plan; it also radically affects the

appearance of the tower: low facade ratios usually generate more simple and slender forms, while higher facade ratios generate larger floor dimensions and a more geometrically complex envelope, establishing crucial relationships between the aesthetics of the tower and its performance as a domestic environment.

The floor-plate size is a critical parameter in the design of a high-rise and possibly the one that may affect its profile most drastically. Variations in floor-plate sizes may have crucial impact in the rent values of an office building and on the efficiency of the vertical circulation system. They are also closely linked to a location, be it a city or a sector of a city.

In residential buildings, the floor plate is primarily related to the facade ratio and the scale of the units. In a high-rise building, the combination of unit size and a certain residential typology usually determines the floor plate to a substantial degree. In commercial buildings, the size of the floor plate is set by the scale of leases in a certain office market rather than by climatic and environmental factors as common in the residential high-rises, since it is understood that high-rise office space is fully air-conditioned and artificially lit. For example, most of the commercial floor plates in cities in emerging economies, such as those of Guangzhou, Shanghai or Kuala Lumpur, tend to require very large floor plates, even in inner-city locations, since a substantial part of those markets is driven by back-office operations. In more established financial centres, such as London, New York, Singapore or Tokyo, where the offices have a more representative purpose, the pressure towards very large floor plates is smaller although, given the size of the tenant populations, it is unlikely that floor plates below 1,500 square metres will be considered commercially adequate.

SKYLINE DEBATE

Rafael Viñoly's 'Walkie Talkie' skyscraper (left) in the City of London is one of a new generation of highly idiosyncratic skyscrapers, designed by signature architects, which will transform the city's skyline.

Another parameter that remains closely related to the floor plate is the facade-to-core dimension. This reveals opposing global tendencies in the residential and the commercial markets, showing a growing typological differentiation within the high-rise species. As we have already seen, the residential high-rise shows a tendency towards a higher level of relationship between inside and outside, seeking views, daylight and natural ventilation. This tendency of the market is towards narrower bays and facade-to-core distance. In commercial buildings, this dimension is tending to increase in most markets, despite the green calls for increased daylighting and ventilation, because it is seen to improve the flexibility of the space. With the exception of countries like Germany or the Netherlands, where the local daylight and ventilation regulations force offices to remain shallow, most of the commercial high-rise floor plates aim at bays at least 10.5 metres deep, but it is now common for this type of building to aim for 12 to 15 metres deep because of the flexibility that size offers in accommodating different organizations with a more or less cellular or dense space. It is interesting to analyse this parameter in the context of the growing hybrid high-rise typologies, which combine residential and tertiary functions such as work-live or officetel. The facade-to-core dimension is obviously an index of the degree of connection between the inside and the outside, and the level of artificiality of the environment. Like the facade ratio, facade-to-core depth is closely related with energy consumption: more daylight and natural ventilation are the result of a smaller acade-to-core dimension, but it usually involves more heat loss and more solar gains in terms of conditioning the space. And the balance between daylighting, heating and cooling, and air renewal is not a simple equation. Neither are the experiential and cultural implications of the relationship between inside and outside, natural and artificial.

All these parameters, often ignored when discussing the merits and demerits of high-rise projects, constitute the material grain of the contemporary high-rise phylum and provide a potential frame to discuss the way projects are in fact evolved specimens of this growing population. Many of these parameters have been extracted from technical indexes traditionally used by developers, quantity surveyors and engineering consultants to analyse the performance of a design, but that have so far been absent from any public debate on high-rise buildings. They are technical indexes, and yet they are loaded with political arguments and cultural questions. To problematize them may be the design engine that will generate true innovation. They offer dimensions of a possible map whereby we could start understanding the new possibilities of the high-rise building.

First published in Harvard Design Magazine, *Spring/Summer 2007, no. 26.*

NTIONS

FROM THEORY INTO PRACTICE

Sarah Ichioka

This chapter discusses 20 innovative urban projects in the six Urban Age cities. Collectively, they offer design responses to many of the social and economic conditions explored elsewhere in this book, representing various intersections of the Urban Age themes: Labour Markets and Workplaces, Mobility and Transport, Housing and Urban Neighbourhoods, and Public Life and Urban Space – categories that frequently overlap and merge given the complex nature of cities. The projects were selected to reflect a diversity of architectural and planning approaches, management structures and physical forms, ranging broadly in scale from the single building to an urban quarter, as well as integrated systems such as transport networks spreading across an entire city. All are recently realized rather than speculative projects, and as real-world entities they necessarily contain elements that attract criticism as well as praise. The projects selected share the quality of retro-fitting in that they are interventions within the pre-existing urban fabric (there are no New Towns here), with the majority reinterpreting or reanimating older structures in the historic centres of their respective cities. Most include elements that promote the efficient use of environmental resources and many include facilities intended to be shared by a diverse range of users.

A project's green credentials were an important criteria in evaluating which projects to include. Hearst Tower is New York City's first commercial building to earn a Gold Rating standards set by the United States Green Building Council. In Shanghai, extensive environmental remediation by Shanghai's municipal government facilitated the redevelopment along 53 kilometres of the Suzhou Creek.

Selected public transport systems are included for socially integrating disparate groups through the innovative reduction of private car use. Berlin boasts Germany's largest tram network, which connects with and supplements the city's metro and rail routes. Car-sharing companies such as GreenWheels allow access to private, compact cars on the occasions they are needed. Also in Berlin, the Call-a-Bike pilot scheme encompasses a special fleet of bikes distributed across the city. The bikes can be hired and returned at all major urban intersections via a telephone call.

London's Congestion Charge scheme imposes a daily charge for driving or parking a vehicle on public roads within a designated central zone on weekdays between 7 a.m. and 6 p.m. The scheme has reduced congestion within the zone by an average of 21 per cent compared with pre-charging levels, and profits from the charge have been ploughed back into public-transport provision and public-space improvements. Some projects intervene at key nodes or corridors within urban-transport systems. In Johannesburg, the Faraday Station Precinct provides an integrated transport node for a population long under-provisioned. The Metrobús rapid transit project along Mexico City's primary north-south route builds upon a tradition of successful similar projects in other rapidly developing cities such as Bogotá, Colombia. Travel times have been halved since its fleet of articulated buses replaced the assortment of privately-run minibuses and buses that previously crowded this corridor.

In a significant number of these interventions, cultural facilities are drivers of regeneration and sociability. The conversion of the monumental Bankside Power Station into the new Tate Modern gallery has helped to regenerate long-neglected Southwark, London. On the south bank of Shanghai's Suzhou Creek, 50 Moganshan Lu – a complex of old factories and workshops from the 1930s – hosts artists' studios as well as internationally visible galleries and art dealers. La Fábrica de Artes y Oficios de Oriente (FARO) is a cultural centre in Iztapalapa, a populous and socially deprived zone on Mexico City's eastern edges. The building's original programme was altered after local officials re-appropriated the site for a progressive community arts centre.

In other cases, public buildings have been dramatically reinvented for emerging civic ideas or aspirations. In Berlin, the GDR-era Palast der Republik was temporarily revived through a broad spectrum of cultural programmes. The Constitution Hill precinct in Johannesburg is a more sober and ceremonial space. The Constitutional Court, South Africa's first major new post-apartheid government building, is erected on the site of a notorious apartheid-era prison.

Other projects creatively re-inhabit older typologies at a more modest scale to meet the changing demands of their constituent urban populations. In New York City, the city government and community groups have sought to accommodate a resurging school-age population through the creative reuse of existing buildings, and investment in smaller, specialized schools.

Some of the study projects provide public spaces for recreation and relief within dense urban environments. Yan'an Zhong Lu Park is located in the heart of Shanghai, acting as a green belt between two motorways and surrounding buildings. Meanwhile, the Badeschiff, an outdoor swimming pool suspended in the east harbour of the Spree, allows Berliners to swim 'in' an otherwise polluted river.

Other projects aid the retention of diverse economic activities and communities that might otherwise be pushed out from homogenizing city centres. Around 1,000 years old and covering more than 4 acres, Borough Market is central London's sole remaining wholesale food market, diversified in recent years to include a 'fine-food' retail component. Greenpoint Manufacturing and Design Center is New York City's only not-for-profit industrial developer, acting as an incubator and support system for small and medium-sized light manufacturers and artisans. South Africa's largest public-private housing partnership to date produced the Brickfields Social Housing project in Newtown, offering flats for rental to both government-subsidized and market-rate tenants.

If the Urban Age themes and issues are often daunting or thrillingly grand in their scale, the projects selected for reflection and commendation here tend to be more modest and subtle interventions within broader urban systems and their respective urban conditions. As an ensemble, these projects suggest that a fine-grained, nimble, locally embedded approach – more than the massive scale of an Olympic site or the *tabula rasa* of a satellite town – offers architects and planners the opportunity to create projects that are truly of and for their cities.

SKYSCRAPERS RECONSIDERED

HEARST TOWER, NEW YORK CITY

The Hearst Corporation's gleaming new 46-storey tower rises above the 6-storey limestone facade of the International Magazine Building in Manhattan's Columbus Circle neighbourhood, where the media company has been based since 1928. From its initial design, commissioned by William Randolph Hearst, the building was structurally reinforced to support a tower, but remained low-rise until 2006, when Norman Foster's stainless steel-clad, diagonal grid building opened. The 79,500-square-metre tower contains offices and social amenities for the Hearst Corporation's 2,000-plus employees previously scattered across 10 Manhattan locations. Its facilities include a fully equiped television studio, laboratory and test kitchens, and a fitness centre. The Hearst Tower is most notable for its environmentally friendly technical innovations. Foster's design employs a diagonal grid construction system (left) eliminating the need for horizontal steel beams, thus saving about 20 per cent of the material needed. It also gives the building its distinctive facade, comprised of a series of four-storey triangles. Foster's design includes as few internal walls as possible in order to maximize natural light. The building's windows are treated with a 'low-E' coating that admits sunlight but blocks heat. The tower is New York City's first commercial building to earn a Gold Rating under the Leadership in Energy and Environmental Design (LEED) standards set by the United States Green Building Council. Its green qualifications include the use of locally sourced, recycled materials and a bundle of technological and programmatic efficiencies that allow the building to use 26 per cent less energy than a building that minimally complies with New York State and City's energy codes. About 85 per cent of the original International Magazine Building structure was recycled for future use. Energy efficiency measures include sensors to adjust the amount of artificial light on each floor according to outdoor conditions, while additional motion sensors switch off lights and computers when a room is vacant. The building's high-efficiency heating and air-conditioning equipment uses outside air for cooling and ventilation nine months of the year (see page 417). The green ethos extends to small details of the office fittings: the walls are coated with low-vapour paints; floor and ceiling tiles are manufactured with recycled content; the furniture is formaldehyde-free; and appliances are high-efficiency. The tower's roof has been designed to collect rainwater, reducing the

amount of water dumped into the city's sewer
system during rainfall by 25 per cent. This
collected rainwater is used to replace water
lost to evaporation in the office air-conditioning
system, to irrigate plants and trees inside and
outside the building. The recycled rainwater
also animates 'Icefall', a 3-storey water feature
(bottom middle) in the building's 12 to 20 metre
high atrium lobby, serving to humidify and chill
this space as necessary. This central area,
enclosed by the four floors of the original facade,
contains an upper level with the corporation's
employee cafeteria (top right), exhibition
space and auditorium, accessed by escalators
embedded in the Icefall feature.

Client: Hearst Corporation
Architect: Foster + Partners
Associate Architect: Adamson Associates
Interior Architect: Gensler
Development Manager: Tishman Speyer
Consultants: WSP Cantor Seinuk, Flack & Kurtz,
George Sexton
Opened: 2006

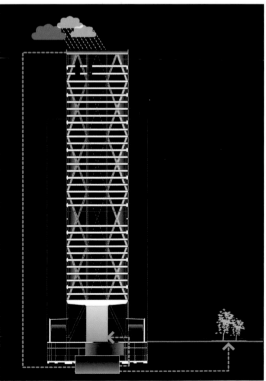

COMMUNITY BUILDING

GREENPOINT MANUFACTURING & DESIGN CENTER, NEW YORK CITY

Active since the late 1980s (and formally established in 1992), the Greenpoint Manufacturing and Design Center (GMDC) is New York City's only not-for-profit industrial developer. GMDC – which is guided by a mix of social welfare and market forces – acts as an incubator and support system for displaced small- and medium-sized light manufacturers, artisans and designers forced to compete with residential, commercial and IT uses across New York City's rapidly changing neighbourhoods. Primary production districts of Manhattan, formerly home to printing, garment and food industries, have in the last several decades turned over to majority residential and retail occupation, while manufacturing areas in the outlying boroughs such as Long Island City, the area between the Manhattan and Brooklyn bridges and Fort Green have also been converted to residential and office uses. The Center argues that New York should retain manufacturing uses within its urban core to maintain a diverse economic base, and in particular to afford opportunities for economic advancement to less-skilled workers. GMDC buys, renovates and manages neglected industrial buildings. It guarantees loans for working capital, lobbies for pro-industrial manufacturing policies and shares its expertise with other communities looking to undertake similar economic development strategies. The organization has returned five buildings in North Brooklyn – including its flagship building at 1155 Manhattan Avenue in Greenpoint (bottom right), a historically working-class neighbourhood of Hispanic, Irish and Polish immigrants – to active manufacturing uses, providing flexible and affordable work spaces for small- and medium-sized businesses. Properties that had earlier incarnations as a bowling alley or rope factory now house 100-odd businesses including a cluster of specialist wood- and metalworkers. Demand for its spaces is high, but the organization has pursued policies of very selective tenant admission, preferring to focus on a number of key industries. Initially subsidized by grants from the private sector and community-development foundations, the Center is now financially self-sufficient. In 2002, the organization set a new precedent by installing New York City's largest commercial solar-power system on the roofs of two of its buildings (top left). This 115-kilowatt system, covering an area of more than 1,000 square metres, collects solar energy with photovoltaic panels, and stores excess energy in zinc

bromide batteries for later use. The solar initiative was funded through a public-private partnership. The interior layouts of the GMDC buildings provide flexible and well-ventilated environments for the production of light industry long associated with the Greenpoint/Williamsburg community (far right).

Refurbishment: Greenpoint Manufacturing and Design Center Local Development Corporation
First building fully tenanted: 1996

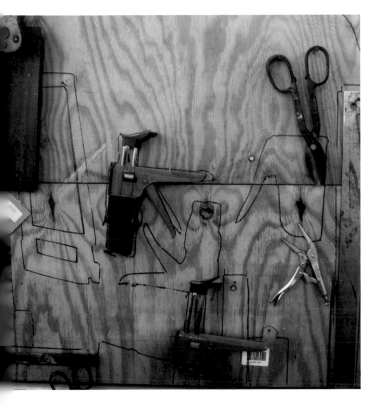

BRONX CHARTER SCHOOL FOR THE ARTS, NEW YORK CITY

New York City seeks to provide enough facilities to meet the demands of a resurging school-age population, often through the creative reuse of existing buildings and – under Mayor Michael Bloomberg and a reorganized Department of Education – smaller, specialized schools. While the city's school-aged population shrank in the 1970s, causing the abandonment of a range of school buildings, it is now growing again, causing overcrowding within existing schools and creating demand for new structures. The Department of Education responded by shedding the restrictive and outdated building regulations and, along with it, a reputation for corruption and bureaucracy. Although the majority of the schools planned in the city will be large-scale new buildings, a significant proportion of them reuse industrial or commercial buildings. Mayor Bloomberg's educational policy encourages the development of smaller charter schools, publicly funded institutions that operate independently from standard school regulations. Offering innovative teaching methods and agreed academic standards, charter schools can be well-suited to small urban sites, although the recycling of older buildings for school use poses challenging health and safety concerns. Likewise, the densely built locations of many of the sites also mean less space for sports and assembly facilities. The Bronx Charter School for the Arts was established by the not-for-profit developer, Civic Builders, and a group of parents, teachers and local residents in response to the lack of quality education in Hunts Point, an industrial neighbourhood of the South Bronx. New educational facilities failed to keep pace with the area's growth, as significant improvements in its housing stock and cultural amenities were not matched by investment in schools that were not performing well. The primary school was granted its charter from New York State in 2002, one of the few grass roots organizations to gain charter approval. Housed in a 2,200-square-metre refurbished sausage factory and distribution warehouse that opened in 2005, its nearly 300 pupils are overwhelmingly Latino or African American, almost half of them living locally. The building, by Weisz + Yoes Architecture, incorporates a light-filled gallery and community event spaces as well as classrooms and staff areas. The building presents a colourful tiled facade to its industrial surroundings and its performance spaces face out on to the street, offering a signpost of the community's participation.

MILLENNIUM HIGH SCHOOL , NEW YORK CITY

On the other side of the city, Millennium High School, designed by HLW International LLP, occupies three floors of a refurbished skyscraper in Lower Manhattan (top middle). Founded in 2002 with a grant from New Visions for Public Schools, with money donated by Bill and Melinda Gates, the Carnegie Corporation and the Open Society Institute, the school provides a liberal arts academic programme in partnership with the YMCA of Greater New York. A core stairway (bottom right) unifies the three floors, surrounded by ample informal break-out space for student meetings, meals and activities. The location of Millennium High School, only a few blocks from Ground Zero, was a deliberate move to inject new life into a depressed Lower Manhattan; the school gives priorities to pupils who live south of Houston Street.

Client: Civic Builders and Bronx Charter School for the Arts
Architect: Weisz + Yoes Architecture
Consultants: Buro Happold and Jim Conti Lighting Design
Opened: 2005

Client: Millennium High School
Architect: HLW International LLP
Consultant: Fielding/Nair International
Opened: 2002

CULTURAL RENEWAL

50 MOGANSHAN LU, SHANGHAI

Many contributors to and players in Shanghai's vibrant contemporary art industries cluster in old warehouses along Suzhou Creek, to the north of the city centre. Located on the creek's south bank, 50 Moganshan Lu, a complex of old textile factories and workshops dating from the 1930s onwards, now hosts artists' studios as well as design and production firms (see pages 428–9). There are also independent galleries and contemporary art dealers, including the internationally visible Eastlink, ShanghART Gallery and the BizArt Art Center (the latter two organizations both established by European expatriates – a recent, but growing, trend). Moganshan Lu, or Chunming Art Industrial Park, as the Shanghai Municipal Economic Committee dubbed the quarter in 2004, is one of the most recent sites for creative activities displaced from neighbouring buildings by a series of successive demolitions as part of the city's efforts to modernize its building stock. The area around 50 Moganshan Lu is already crowded with new high-rise towers (see page 429, top). The creative cluster here has gained prominence in the public eye, due in part to the rapidly expanding market for contemporary Chinese art and this particular complex's visibility on the international art and tourist circuits. It is now preserved as the core of a wider redevelopment scheme, indicating a newfound appreciation by Shanghai's government and development agents for the value of older buildings as creative incubators.

SUZHOU CREEK REHABILITATION, SHANGHAI

Suzhou Creek, which runs through northern Shanghai, is recovering from environmental degradation following an extensive clean-up project initiated by the municipal government and sponsored by the Asian Development Bank. Historically, the Creek served as a key shipping channel from the coast into central China, and formed the official boundary between the Japanese Concession and the International Settlement. The pollution of the Creek reached its nadir in the 1970s and 1980s, during the industrial expansion of Shanghai's economy, when the Creek was used as a thoroughfare for waste-transporting barges and a receptacle for sewage effluent from surrounding neighbourhoods. The 53-kilometre stretch of the stream that runs through Shanghai had become fetid, black and choked with algae. Beginning in the mid 1990s, the Shanghai Suzhou Creek Rehabilitation Construction Company implemented a series of restoration measures, including the erection of a waste-water collection and treatment plant, control gates from feeder canals, closure or move of polluting factories, mechanical oxygenation of the water and the construction of a modern solid-waste transfer station in the city's Jing'an district, which is landscaped to look like a park. Improvements to water quality became visible in 1999. A second phase of the project saw the redevelopment of sections of the Creek's banks with landscaped promenades and parks (following the enforced relocation of previous occupants from their riverside homes and working wharves). The green recreational spaces along the banks were designed and developed in sections by a variety of international and Chinese firms. A number of historic creek-side buildings, including warehouses once slated for demolition, have now been protected and house various art galleries and workshops. Large stretches of the Creek's banks, on the other hand, remain undeveloped, traversed by small bridges and separated by low walls from adjacent roads, footpaths and disparate residential and industrial neighbourhoods. The restoration project is ongoing; the Shanghai Water Authority aims to make the river inhabitable for fish and other aquatic life by 2010.

Client: Asian Development Bank
Designer/Engineer: Shanghai Suzhou Creek Rehabilitation Construction Company
Phase I completed: 2005; Phase II: ongoing

GREENING THE CITY

YAN'AN ZHONG LU PARK, SHANGHAI

In parallel with national policies to encourage private car use and a rapid rate of 'modernizing' construction projects in China's urban centres, Shanghai's fabric has accommodated numerous new roads and overpasses over the last decade. Yan'an Zhong Lu Park is located in the heart of Shanghai, at the intersection of three districts – Huangpu, Luwan and Jing'an – and at the crossing of the city's two primary arterial motorways: the east-west Yan'an Lu with the north-south motorway (see page 434). Acting as a green cushion between these intersecting elevated, multi-lane motorways and the surrounding high-rise buildings, Yan'an Zhong Lu Park improves air quality, and relieves some of the pressures of central Shanghai's extreme structural density, providing public spaces for the recreation of city-centre residents with limited personal space within their own homes. Canadian landscape architects Williams, Asselin, Ackaoui & Associates divided the 210,000-square-metre park area into thematic sections, each with a distinct set of design guidelines and intended programmes. The park's wooded and open meadows, arranged around a central body of water, are punctuated by squares dedicated to specific leisure activities, including T'ai Chi, basketball, nature walks and picnics. The park – commissioned by the Shanghai Greenery Management Bureau – opened to the public in 2001.

Architect/ Designer: Williams, Asselim, Askaoui & Associates
Client: Shanghai Greenery Management Bureau
Completed: 2001

NEW LIFE IN THE CITY

BANKSIDE, LONDON

The transformation of the Bankside area of London from a forgotten backwater to one of the most intensively used and internationally-known areas south of the River Thames reflects London's potential for unplanned adaptation. There is no formal planning document for the regeneration of an area characterized by dark alleyways, a fragmented urban fabric and criss-crossing Victorian viaducts. Rather, Bankside's regeneration was due to the coincidence of initiatives – many of them disconnected in policy terms – spurred on by the dynamic yet isolated planning department of the London Borough of Southwark. The regeneration was initiated in the early 1990s in parallel with the construction of the Jubilee Line extension of the London Underground, an investment that created a much-needed link from central London north of the Thames to a zone previously underserved by public transport. Two new tube stations at Southwark and London Bridge have given access to a largely under-developed zone, geographically well-located near the job markets in the City of London and Westminster, yielding the potential for a latent housing market. The bold decision by the Tate Gallery's trustees to create a new museum – Tate Modern – inside the Bankside Power Station (opened in 2000 and attracting 5 million visitors a year) has done more to shift London's cultural epicentre than any government-based policy initiative since the 1970s, with the Norman Foster-designed Millennium footbridge (bottom left) providing a new means of pedestrian access and a contemporary link across the river to St Paul's Cathedral from the public promenade in front of Tate Modern. Building on the success of Tate Modern in establishing an identity for and increasing pedestrian use of Bankside, a series of office, commercial and housing developers have invested heavily in the wider area with new construction (far right) and refurbishment of nineteenth-century industrial and residential buildings. Southwark Borough Council has also promoted design-led public space projects for the area, and the long-established Borough Market has been transformed into one of London's most frequented high-end food markets, surrounded by a cluster of intensely used bars, pubs and restaurants.

TATE MODERN, LONDON

Herzog & de Meuron's conversion of Giles Gilbert Scott's monumental Bankside Power Station to house Britain's national collection of international modern and contemporary art maintains much of the formal integrity of the original structure, built between 1947 and 1963, and closed in the early 1980s. Retained components include the iconic tower, topped with a light installation by artist Michael Craig-Martin, and the 155-metre-long, 35-metre-tall Turbine Hall, which has hosted a series of large-scale specially commissioned art installations. Prompted in part by an overwhelming number of visitors and a desire to expand its gallery spaces to accommodate new art forms, in 2007 the Tate obtained planning permission for a building extension, also to be designed by Herzog & de Meuron, scheduled to open in 2012. Although the Tate has arguably been the strongest single factor in putting Bankside on the mental and tourist map of central London, the area hosts a complex, historically-layered network of other cultural institutions and attractions, including a cathedral (London's first Gothic church, Southwark Cathedral), a prison (Clink Prison), a Shakespearean theatre (the Globe) and historic ships.

Client: Tate Gallery
Architect: Herzog & de Meuron
Consultant: Arup
Opened: 2000

BOROUGH MARKET, LONDON

Located an easy walk's distance to the east of Tate Modern, Borough Market offers a prime example of how the area has reinvented its rich cultural legacy for contemporary users. Around 1,000 years old and covering more than 1.6 hectares, Borough Market is central London's sole remaining wholesale and retail food market. The market, which began during the Roman occupation, was formalized by Royal Charter in 1550 and moved to its current location in 1754. The wholesale market, traditionally focused on vegetables and fruits and operating every weekday morning, was diversified in 1998 to incorporate a fine food retail component, which has expanded several times since then to meet enthusiastic demand. In parallel with the repaving of local roads and pavements and the provision of new street furniture by the Borough of Southwark, the market has undertaken its own physical renovation (funded by the sale of several adjacent properties) including the recon-struction of the market's frontage along Stoney Street, showcasing a piece of the Victorian-era cast-iron portico, recycled from the renovation of another historic central London site, the old Covent Garden Market. Seen in the context of community groups' and local planners' long-term regeneration strategies and the responsive interest by private-sector partners, Borough Market's fine-grained approach of community involvement complements the headline-drawing appeal of its neighbour, Tate Modern, in engaging both embedded communities and new visitors to Bankside's diverse cultural offer-ings. Registered as a charity in 1999, the market manages an extensive range of community programmes including local business advice, food-related training, and childcare for working parents, and the activation of adjacent small shop fronts in market ownership. It won a Single Regeneration Bid for Challenge Funding to create the London's Larder Partnership Board, which oversees these community initiatives.

Client: Trustees of the Borough Market
Architect: Greig & Stephenson Architects
Refurbished facilities opened: 2004

TAMING THE CAR

CONGESTION CHARGE, LONDON

Since the reinstatement of a city-wide governing body and the appointment of London's first directly elected mayor in 2000, the city has followed a broad policy of rebalancing the distribution of its central city between private vehicles, public transport and pedestrians. The much debated Congestion Charge scheme has formed the core of this policy, complemented by strategic reinvestments in the city's public transport services and selected public spaces. Congestion charging was first formally proposed by Transport for London (TfL) in 2001, confirmed by Mayor Ken Livingstone in 2002, and implemented in central London in February 2003. The scheme imposes a daily charge for driving or parking a vehicle on public roads between 7 a.m. and 6 p.m. within a designated oval shaped, 22-square-kilometre central London zone, Monday to Friday (excluding public holidays). The scheme is enforced by a sophisticated system of computer-linked licence-plate recognition cameras operated and monitored by TfL (far right); the charge may be paid in person at local agents, via mobile phone or on the Internet. The zone takes in the historic centre of the capital and its major cultural and financial institutions and is marked on streets and signposts throughout the zone (left). It is an interesting example of road-pricing theory, usually the territory of free-market economists, implemented by a generally left-leaning local government. Following the general success of the scheme – despite continued opposition from central London businesses claiming a negative effect on their trade – the charge was increased from GB£5 (US$10) to GB£8 (US$16) in 2005 with a westward expansion implemented in early 2007. The scheme has reduced car use within the zone by an average of 21 per cent compared with pre-charging levels during peak hours, and significantly reduced congestion in general. Profits from the Congestion Charge are ploughed back into public-transport provision and public-space improvements. Bus ridership has increased significantly, a growth met by increased and more reliable services as well as the introduction of new stock. Road surface has been redistributed from private car use to dedicated bus and cycle lanes, and in 2002 the mayor launched a programme to create or upgrade 100 of the city's public spaces to enhance the value of London's existing network of open space and demonstrate how new and revitalized public spaces can improve an individual's quality of life and community vitality.

TRAFALGAR SQUARE, LONDON

The early and prominent transformation of
Trafalgar Square (far right), one of London's
most iconic spaces, returned to pedestrian use
through the elimination of vehicular traffic along
its North Terrace edge at the forecourt of the
National Gallery (bottom left), and the accompanying extensive re-routing of traffic along its
southern edges. A grand staircase for pedestrians replaced five lanes of traffic. The scheme –
part of Foster + Partners' GB£50 million (US$
102 million) World Squares for All masterplan
for the Mayor of London Transport for London –
reopened to the public in July 2003. Historically
a site of gathering and protest, the square's
pedestrianized northern side has become a key
location for concerts and public performances,
and latterly provoked new controversy with the
rotating sculpture programme for its Fourth
Plinth, most recently occupied by artist Mark
Quinn's sculpture of the nude, pregnant, physically impaired artist Alison Lapper (top left).

Congestion Charge Client and Operator:
Transport for London, Mayor of London
Phase I: 2003; Extension: 2007

Trafalgar Square Redevelopment Client:
Transport for London, Mayor of London
Architect: Fosters + Partners
Consultants : Atkins Design Environment and
Engineering, Davis Langdon & Everest, Peter
Walker and Partners, Speirs & Major
Completed: 2003

REACHING THE EDGE

FARO DE ORIENTE, MEXICO CITY

La Fábrica de Artes y Oficios, FARO de Oriente ('the arts and crafts factory' or 'lighthouse of the east') is a cultural centre located in Iztapalapa, a populous and amenity-deprived zone on Mexico City's eastern edge. FARO serves a large catchment area (Iztapalapa, Ciudad Nezahualcóyotl, Chimalhuacán and the surrounding urbanized zone) comprising some 5.5 million inhabitants, yet poorly served by infrastructure of any sort. Mexico City's galleries, performance venues, schools and libraries cluster along a central spine, running from the historic centre in the north through Chapultepec Park and terminating at the National University in the south, leaving peripheral communities like Iztapalapa underserved by cultural resources. Iztapalapa has further struggled with a stigma of violence, and its poverty is such that the area hosts a street market for items of rubbish reclaimed from a nearby dump. FARO sits in the south-west corner of a part of Iztapalapa originally intended as an ecological reserve, but later given over to residential development. The building was initially designed to house a government office, but its programme was altered by its architect, Alberto Kalach/Taller de Arquitectura X, after local government officials re-appropriated the building as a progressive community arts centre. It opened in that capacity in 2000. The shape of the building is intended to evoke the shape of a boat in the now-dusty basin of the drained Lake Texcoco. To address relatively unstable site conditions, Kalach designed the building around a concrete base that supports a lightweight steel structure above it. At ground level, workshops open off a central corridor, with criss-crossing stairs leading to gallery, office and library spaces above (see page 449). The 1,500-square-metre building sits within a larger development area of some 16,000 square metres, which contains an adjacent garden and terrace. The building's long, narrow shape (bottom left) is encircled at its southern end by a raked mound of earth, accessed through cast-concrete tubular tunnels enclosing an outdoor amphitheatre space. FARO's operators consider its programming just as important as the physical container. The building houses a school of arts and crafts for the local community, studios, a gallery for established international artists as well as local producers, a library and performance spaces for dance, music and theatre. Large open-air concerts held at the FARO, during which community volunteers effectively oversee the peaceful conduct of thousands,

including local gang members, add to the eclectic mix. The products of some arts workshops are sold for a profit, giving their creators an alternative income stream. The centre, managed with significant community input, has become a focal point for the discussion of local matters, and a cultural platform from which Iztapalapa's citizens can project a diverse range of positive messages to the rest of Mexico City.

Client and Operator: La Fábrica de Artes y Oficios
Architect: Alberto Kalach/Taller de Arquitectura
Renovation completed: 2000

METROBÚS, MEXICO CITY

Mexico City's governor launched the Metrobús rapid transit system partly to address pollution in the city, by providing a more efficient and reliable alternative to increasing car ownership. Mexico City's predominance of low-capacity vehicles, including private cars, taxis and minibuses, generates significant transport problems. Although private transport accounts for only 19 per cent of metropolitan journeys, it contributes 95 per cent of vehicles occupying road surfaces. Additionally, the city's dispersed form – the result of sprawl during the 1970s and 1980s – creates a large number of long daily journeys across the metropolitan road network beyond Mexico City's existing underground system. Metrobús builds upon a tradition of successful bus rapid transit projects in other rapidly developing cities such as Curitiba, Brazil and Bogotá, Colombia. Promoted as a cheaper alternative to rail-based public transport, rapid bus transport systems (BRT) generally feature physically separate bus lanes with priority, integration with other modes of transport at key nodes, quick boarding and disembarking systems through the pre-boarding collection of fares and often raised platforms and doors (bottom left), and rationalization of licensing and management of bus operators. Metrobús's 80 articulated buses, powered by low-emission engines, serve 34 stations along Avenida de Insurgentes, the city's main north-south route. Service covers 19.4 kilometres along a dedicated bus lane, providing inter-modal connections with six of the city's underground lines. Fares are paid exclusively by smartcard at turnstiles for separate bus platforms. Metrobús carries more than 250,000 passengers each day. Travel times along the corridor have been halved since its fleet of articulated buses replaced the assort-ment of privately run minibuses and buses that previously crowded this corridor. A parallel cycle route was also constructed to the west of the Metrobús route, although use to date has proven far less successful than cycle routes along BRT corridors in, for example, Bogotá. Both the Metrobús and cycling facilities lack adequate funding to operate at maximum efficiency, and face difficulties in competing with the trend towards private car ownership. Despite this, newly elected Mayor Marcelo Ebrard has recently committed funds to extend its service area with new lines.

Client and Operator: Government of Mexico City
Phase I completed: 2005; Phase II: ongoing

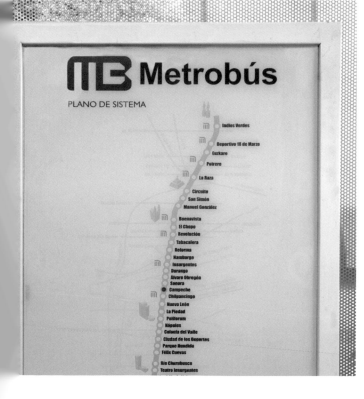

BUILDING FOR JUSTICE

CONSTITUTION HILL, JOHANNESBURG

Constitution Hill lies at the intersection of three distinctive neighbourhoods in central Johannesburg: dense, mostly residential Hillbrow to the east, mostly commercial Braamfontein to its west, and green, wealthy Parktown. It is built on the site of the infamous Old Fort prison complex dating from the early 1900s (see pages 454–5). Hundreds of thousands of people, including Mahatma Gandhi and Nelson Mandela, were jailed there before the prison was closed in 1983. In 1997 the Constitutional Court's judges chose the Old Fort for the site of a new building; the following year Urban Solutions and OMM Design Workshop won the international competition to design and build the new Court. The three-storey Constitutional Court takes up 8,178 square metres on the eastern side of the Constitution Hill complex. Primarily constructed of timber, concrete, steel, glass and black slate, the court's core contains the 400,000-volume constitutional law library, administrative offices, judges' conference and meeting rooms, and private chambers facing on to a private garden. Wrapped around this core are the court chambers, interpreters' booths, foyer, auditorium, exhibition space, and four towers with viewing decks (far right). The court's main outdoor public spaces are Constitution Square and the Great African Steps, which connect the square to the ramparts of the Old Fort. The 'We the People' wall along the length of the square records Constitution Hill's visitors' comments, including those of former prisoners. A public football field and basketball court are located beneath the building. The complex retains three of the Old Fort's main prison buildings. The court chamber and Constitution Square occupy the site of the demolished Awaiting Trial Block. The new building still has four of the block's original stairwells and reuses its bricks for the court chamber walls. Bricks from the old prison buildings were used for the construction of the court and the Great African Steps (see page 454); bars from the Awaiting Trial Block are used as sunshades in the open spaces of the judicial chamber. The architecture of the court is overtly symbolic, making many visual references to democratic principles and the South African constitution. The typeface of the entrance wall was designed by Garth Walker to reflect vernacular lettering styles of signage in South Africa. The foyer of the court contains slanting columns, covered in mosaic, that are intended to evoke the trees that traditionally sheltered legal

deliberations in African villages. The roof's concrete beams are inscribed with the words 'human dignity, equality and freedom' in the handwriting of each of the judges who held office during the court's construction. The double-height wooden door to the foyer is covered with words and sign-language symbols representing the 27 constitutional rights. The court also houses one of South Africa's major public art collections, assembled under the supervision of Justice Albie Sachs. In addition to the court, the 95,000-square-metre, publicly-owned Constitution Hill complex houses a series of state institutions supporting constitutional democracy, 36,000 square metres of commercial space, improved transport and circulation infra-structure including underground parking bays, bus and taxi holding and drop-off facilities – secured by CCTV and 24-hour security – and upgraded peripheral roads and internal streets. The complex also includes a visitor information and exhibition centre, heritage buildings reno-vated to house museums and related tourism activities, approximately 200 rental residential units, community facilities and public open spaces. In the north-west corner, the old Queen Victoria Hospital and adjacent nurses' home have been refitted as luxury apartments. In 2003, the Gauteng provincial government created the Blue IQ Investment Holdings as a development agency to devise financing mechanisms and strategies to deliver 11 targeted urban mega-projects, including Constitution Hill. The complex cost an initial 700 million rand (ca. US$100 million), of which 492 million rand (ca. US$70 million) was public-sector money from Blue IQ and the Department of Justice. These funds were intended to spur an equivalent amount by the private sector.

Client: Johannesburg Development Agency for the City of Johannesburg
Architects: Urban Solutions and OMM Design Workshop
Constitutional Court opened: 2004

FARADAY MARKET AND TRANSPORT INTERCHANGE, JOHANNESBURG

The Faraday Station precinct, designed by
Albonica Sack Mzumara Architects & Urban
Designers with MMA Architects for and with
the City of Johannesburg and the Johannesburg
Development Agency, provides an integrated
transport node for a population and location
long under-provisioned by the city's social and
physical infrastructure. The precinct, which
opened in 2003, incorporates taxi ranks for long-
distance and local minibuses atop an existing
commuter rail system. The precinct is also
notable for providing safer, more formalized
facilities for traditional *muti* healers and herb
sellers. The Market and Transport Interchange
form a focused area within the larger 900 by
450 metre Faraday Precinct in an industrial area
to the south-east of the central business district
(5 minutes walking distance) and near to the M2
motorway, identified by government planners
as a 'zone of transition'. Formerly housing light
industrial, commercial and offices, this area is
increasingly occupied by low-income families
illegally sub-letting portions of office buildings
and open lots cleared for minibus taxis. A new,
shaded inter-modal transport node integrates
local and long-distance taxi ranks with a pre-
existing underground station. The old Faraday
railway station was a port of entry for miners
commuting from rural areas to the 'gold reef'
of Johannesburg. The newly rationalized taxi
rank is located at the site's southernmost edge,
closest to the M2 motorway and other roads
connecting to outlying areas of the city. A
formalized herb market for traditional *muti*
healers is complemented by consulting rooms
for these healers housed in converted former
office buildings. Some stakeholders disapprove
of the formalization and implied legitimization
of the traditional healers' trading of plants and
animals that may be endangered species.
The complex has also struggled to balance the
desires to accommodate local informal traders
and to generate substantial income from formal
tenants of the market. The intervention included
streetscape improvements (resurfacing, lighting, landscaping, and relocation of a range of
retail units) to the area's two main pedestrian
zones, Eloff and Von Wielligh Streets, which lead
from north to south to and from Johannesburg's
central business district. The design of the
complex includes an extensive programme
of public, craft-based artwork. Albonica Sack
Mzumara and MMA consulted a cross-discipli-
nary team including economists, health experts,

urban designers and community facilitators. They conducted an extensive series of stakeholder consultations with groups including taxi drivers and *muti* practitioners. The market and taxi ranks are administered by the Metropolitan Trading Company (MTC), an independent agency that manages all such facilities in the inner city. The precinct's rationalization of informal activities and integration with formal activities directly addresses two key elements of the City of Johannesburg's City Centre Plan: firstly, how to formalize and manage the large, informal minibus taxi industry, and secondly, how to formalize and manage less-organized street commerce in a series of organized markets distributed throughout the city (far right). The precinct is a key example of the City of Johannesburg's efforts to regenerate its inner city through strategic public-sector investments – primarily in infrastructure – intended to leverage private sector reinvestment in the central area. The project is also addressing the fact that so many of Johannesburg's working-class population must spend large portions of their day commuting from home (in outer townships or rural areas) to work in city centres (as a legacy of apartheid spatial planning and of a long history of a migrant worker-based economy). The design team has emphasized its intention to create an 'extroverted' node, in contrast with other such transport hubs constructed in Johannesburg around the same time.

Client: Johannesburg Development Agency for the City of Johannesburg
Design Team: Albonica Sack Mzumara Architects & Urban Designers, with MMA Architects
Opened: 2003

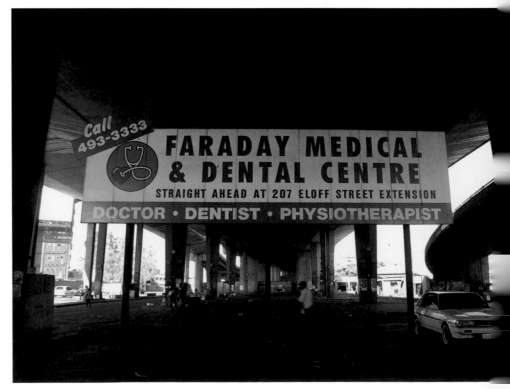

BRICKFIELDS, JOHANNESBURG

South Africa's largest public-private housing partnership to date produced the Brickfields project in Newtown, central Johannesburg, offering flats for rent to both subsidized and market-rate tenants. Brickfields is the first high-rise housing development in Johannesburg's inner city since the 1970s, a period that has otherwise seen the area abandoned by businesses, redlined by banks and informally occupied in overcrowded and often dangerous conditions. Designed by a group of architects led by the firm Savage + Dodd, Brickfields was opened by President Thabo Mbeki in August 2005, and subsequently won a UN HABITAT award. Brickfields was developed, owned and managed by the Johannesburg Housing Company, a not-for-profit urban-development company founded in 1995. It was the company's first high-rise construction venture and its largest single investment. The project was financed through a joint venture between the Gauteng housing department, the Gauteng Partnership Fund and a number of private companies. The 97.8 million-rand (ca. US$14 million) project forms a key part of the City of Johannesburg's Newtown urban-regeneration scheme, which has brought more than 1,600 new residents into this area of Johannesburg. It is a pilot of South Africa's Presidential Job Summit Programme, which aims to create jobs through urban-regeneration projects. Brickfields has also been praised for breaking 'redlining', the process by which financers shun property in areas seen as a risky investment, a decision that has depressed Johannesburg's inner city. The development comprises 742 units of one- to three-bedroom flats in a perimeter-block configuration that mixes high- and low-rise buildings comprising three- and four-storey walk-ups and nine-storey tower blocks (see page 463, bottom right), arranged around central parking courtyards. Retail units face out on to the perimeter streets. The flats cater for a range of incomes: 40 per cent of them are available to people who qualify for a rent subsidy (they pay rent at 20 per cent less than market rates). The rest are available at market rents. Units for one of the three distinct precincts within the larger development – the Brickfields Social Housing Project 'Precinct D+E' – were 90 per cent full within a month of opening, suggesting a high demand for this type of development. Johannesburg has struggled to accommodate the waves of new migrants seeking economic opportunities within its boundaries. Some of the poor newcomers

'JO'BURG MAN' by
ARLENE AMALER-RAVIV & DALE YUDELMAN

choose to live close to their jobs, although under grim circumstances, but the majority of them live in informal or subsidized detached homes at the far edges of the city – facing long and expensive commutes, and creating a sprawling and racially segregated urban landscape. Critics of the project argue that many residents of Johannesburg would prefer to buy their own free-standing house rather than rent a flat. Others suggest that developers have been allowed to convert city-centre office buildings into luxury flats with inadequate attention to the need for low-income housing in this area of the city. The project was built on land provided by the local government, previously an illegal rubbish tip beginning to be occupied by informal settlements. The Brickfields area emerged as a dormitory for the mining industry in the later part of the nineteenth century and was a multi-cultural and multiracial slum area by 1890, containing immigrants from Europe, China and India, along with Cape Malays and local Africans. The area saw previous incarnations as a brick factory and abattoir, before lying vacant for a number of years. Brickfields' new residents are majority black but racially diverse, and a mix of professionals and blue-collar workers. Residents benefit from the location's proximity to city-centre offices, the Metromall taxi rank and the Mandela Bridge. However, they must also contend with the possible dangers of the nearby degraded Hillbrow neighbourhood, where many buildings are overcrowded, lack basic services and are threatened by organized crime.

Client: Johannesburg Housing Company
Design team (for D+E Precincts): Architect Joint Venture Architects consisting of Savage + Dodd Architects, Fee & Challis Architecture and Makhene and Associates, GAPP Architects & Urban Designers
Opened: 2005

INTEGRATED MOBILITY

METRO, TRAM, CALL-A-BIKE AND
CAR SHARING, BERLIN

Like many other German cities, post-unification
Berlin has benefited from a sustained
programme of investment into its transport
infrastructure. The city's transport system offers
a wide and well-integrated variety of modal
choices. The Berlin Transportation Company
(BVG) website serves as a key portal for the
network, providing real-time information about
the core transport services of metro, buses
and trams alongside information about other
modes, such as private taxi companies and
ferries. Berlin's route-based network of multiple-
passenger modes is complemented by a
number of schemes that allow individual users
to borrow single-occupancy vehicles on
demand, including cars and bicycles. Berlin
boasts Germany's largest tram network, which
comprises nearly 190 kilometres of track and
almost 800 tram stops, carrying 560,000 passengers each day. Improved since 1994 through an
extensive modernization programme initiated
by the State of Berlin, the city's trams are praised
for their frequency, reliability and wide coverage, which connects with and supplements the
city's U-Bahn (metro) and S-Bahn (rail) routes.
Together with a system of dedicated buses, the
trams form the BVG's 'MetroNetz' – its core city
network. The tram's accessibility at street grade
and the close-knit distribution of its stops
throughout the city make the iconic yellow
carriages an appealing option for residents and
visitors alike, while fully integrating people with
limited mobility (wheelchair users, the elderly
and parents with baby buggies). The network
consists of many different types of tram
carriages, enabling it to navigate streets of
varied widths. A pilot Call-a-Bike scheme run
by Deutsche Bahn AG allows customers to use
a special fleet of bikes (see page 467) distributed
across Berlin (as well as Frankfurt, Cologne,
Munich and Stuttgart, with other German cities
to follow). The CallBikes can be hired and
returned throughout the central city via a
telephone call; users pay a small fee over the
phone by registering their credit or debit card.
Each bike is equipped with an electronic lock,
opened by numeric code, with a light that
signals whether or not the bike is available for
hire. Car-sharing companies, such as the
Berlin-based GreenWheels, allow their members
access to private, compacts cars whenever they
need one. Members pay a monthly fee, and
thereafter only the hourly or daily charges for
the period they 'check out' one of the company

cars. Sharing schemes are well-suited to German cities because their comprehensive public transport systems mean that people only occasionally need to use a car. In some cases German car-sharing companies have directly joined efforts with urban public transport systems; for example, GreenWheels waives its monthly fee for customers with yearly bus and train travel cards. Some research posits that 1 shared car can replace between 4 and 10 private cars. GreenWheels has 50 'check-out' parking lots throughout Berlin; convenience of access is key to car-sharing schemes' ability to compete with private ownership. Originally marketed as environmentally friendly, alternative lifestyle schemes, most car-sharing companies now emphasize cost-saving benefits to their customers. The schemes still struggle to make a profit, and StattAuto – GreenWheel's previous incarnation – found that while it signed up plenty of members, not enough of them were actually using its cars.

Call-A-Bike Client and Operator: Deutsche Bahn AG
Launched: 2002

Car Sharing Client and Operator: Greenwheels GmbH
Launched: 2005 (its precursor, StattAuto, was founded in 1988)

REDEFINING PUBLIC SPACE

BADESCHIFF AUF DER SPREE, BERLIN

Berlin's surplus of often underused and relatively inexpensive spaces has famously enabled a wide variety of public space interventions and animations that many other European capitals would be hard-pressed to accommodate in their city centres. One such intervention, originally devised by an interdisciplinary team of artists and architects as a mobile facility for an arts competition, found a permanent location in the East Harbour of the River Spree. The Badeschiff ('swimming ship') is an outdoor swimming pool inside a recycled river-cargo container, suspended from the river bank (top left). The 32 by 8 metre pool, filled with slightly heated fresh water, allows Berliners to swim 'in' a river that is otherwise too polluted to allow this sort of recreation. In the winter the structure is covered with a translucent membrane and heated to become a sauna and relaxation lounge (far right). The Badeschiff, open to the public since 2004, can be understood as part of a recent broader trend in European cities from Paris to London to Berlin to create facilities that allow citizens and visitors to enjoy seasonal recreation in the heart of the city, and to renew leisure-based relationships to their bodies of water, often through the creation of 'city beaches'. Indeed, the pool now forms one component of the Arena cultural complex, which also contains theatre and concert venues and a bar.

Client: Urban Art Projects
Designers: AMP Arquitectors with Gil Wilk and artist Susanne Lorenz
Opened: 2004

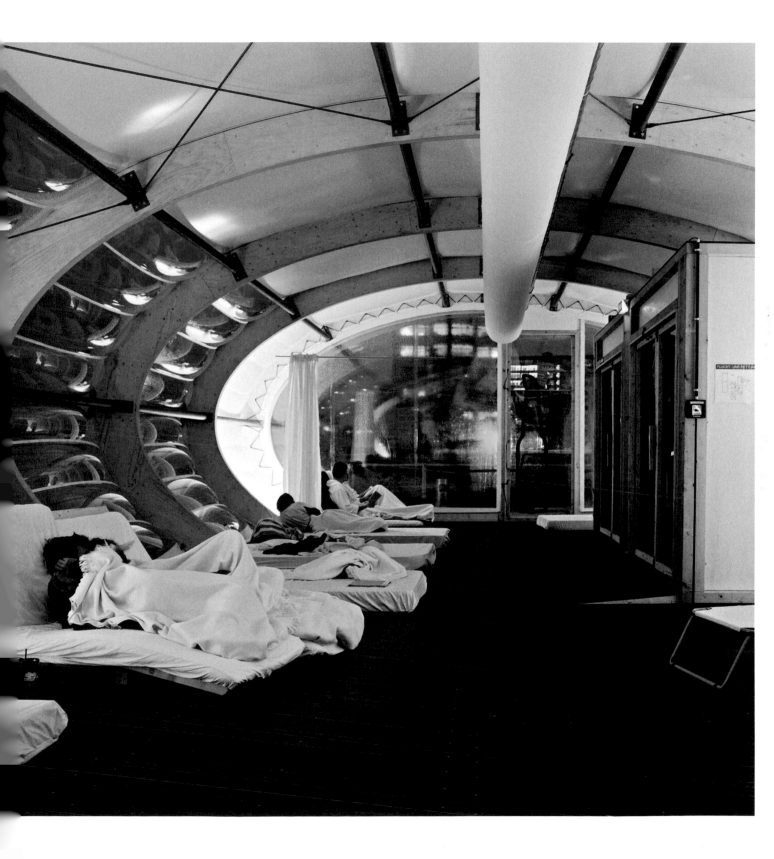

VOLKSPALAST, BERLIN

The Volkspalast was a temporary project that
animated and re-imagined a GDR-era building
through participative performances and
installations. The Palast der Republik (Palace of
the Republic) housed the GDR parliament, along
with significant cultural and leisure facilities.
The building was abandoned in 1990 due to
asbestos contamination, after a mere 14 years
of occupation. The removal of the offending
asbestos left the building a large, disused space.
It was slated for demolition on the recommenda-
tion of an expert panel and the vote of the
German parliament in 2002. The palace became
the object of intense debate, with some wanting
its demolition and replacement by the reconstruction of a Prussian castle that once stood
on the site, and others seeking to refurbish the
existing structure. A temporary palace utilization
association, comprising a coalition of architects,
curators and other interested citizens, formed
in 2003, proposed a programme. In 2004, the
structure was given over to a series of cultural
activities, coordinated by the Volkspalast
('people's palace') project. Re-imagining the
palace as a cultural centre for contemporary
users and needs, the Volkspalast project provided a framework for a broad spectrum of cultural
programmes, including art installations, theatre,
dance and musical performances, lectures and
many other events. Despite the success of this
project in attracting public participation and
encouraging debate about the future of the
structure, the demolition of the above-ground
components of the palace has proceeded as
planned, with clearance completed in mid 2007.
However, the redevelopment of the area will
not commence until 2012 at the earliest, due
to budget constraints; the future of the site
remains contested.

Design: Urban Catalyst (2002); Zwischen
PalastNutzung (2003–2004); Volkspalast
(2004–2005)
Launched: 2004

AN AGENDA FOR THE URBAN AGE

Bruce Katz, Andy Altman and Julie Wagner

The 'urban age'. A simple, clear, unqualified phrase. An incontrovertible statement of fact. In 2007, the population living in the world's cities – some 3.2 billion souls –constituted the majority of the world's population.[2] *Ipso facto*, we live in an urban age.[1]

Yet 'urban age' is more than just a description of what is; it is a vision of what can be, if we imagine it, will it and deliver it. There is simply no parallel effort underway in the world today that takes cities as the organizing units for the new global order and declares boldly that we have much to learn from each other across nations, across continents, across cultures.

We make the following propositions. First, the twenty-first century will be the urban age, where an ever-growing majority of the world's population will live in cities. This urban age is happening at a dizzying pace and with a scale, diversity, complexity and level of connectivity that challenges traditional paradigms and renders many conventional tools and practices obsolete. This great urbanization explodes the very notion of 'city', given the vast physical expanses where a growing portion of people and businesses now congregate. The urban age positions these conurbations as the vehicles for addressing the major challenges facing the world today: extending economic prosperity, promoting environmental sustainability and reducing poverty.

This leads to our second point: in the face of rapid, unrelenting, unsettling change, cities lack a coherent roadmap to realize the promise of the urban age. Our visits to and inquiries about five global cities – New York, Shanghai, London, Mexico City and Johannesburg – and the sixth city Berlin, have revealed the stresses and strains that many cities face as they grapple with accelerated growth, demographic change and economic restructuring. Although each of these cities has shown a remarkable ability to innovate and experiment, our primary conclusion is that there are broad disconnects between urban change on the one hand and urban policy and practice on the other. These disconnects are magnified at national and multinational levels, where specialized and one-dimensional policies dominate. As a result, the promise of cities is systematically undermined.

Thus, we call for an urban agenda that matches the pace and intensity of the urban age. This agenda will embrace the goals of competitive, sustainable and inclusive cities and, equally important, commit to pursuing and delivering these objectives in tandem. This will require wholesale change in how people – practitioners, policymakers and researchers – conduct their business. It will necessitate programmes and

LINKING THE PHYSICAL TO THE SOCIAL

By analyzing the urban conditions of six world
cities, the Urban Age has identified key trends in
a period of fast urbanization, which challenge
the next generation of urban developments.
The Ponti tower in downtown Johannesburg –
a white middle-class housing project taken over
by illegal black African immigrants – epitomizes
the tensions and opportunities of the twenty-
first-century city.

policies that drive integrative, multidimensional thinking and action. It will extol the role of the physical, emphasizing the importance of building cities that are adaptive and resilient, and advance broader objectives. It will reinvent urban politics to advance the new urban paradigm. And it will require multinational corporations to be grounded in 'place' and become strong partners for change.

Make no mistake, the stakes are high: the path of development in many cities around the world is simply not sustainable socially or environmentally or politically – nor, ultimately, economically.

The Twenty-First Century will be the Urban Age

Our world is undergoing a period of change and transformation that is unprecedented in ancient or modern times. The world population grew in leaps and bounds throughout the twentieth century – from 1.7 billion in 1900 to 2.5 billion in 1950 to 6.5 billion in 2000 – and is projected to expand by another 2.6 billion people in the next 50 years.[3] Globalization has opened and integrated markets and restructured the economies of both developed and developing countries. The volume and value of global trade have increased exponentially in recent decades, rising 118 per cent and 161 per cent respectively since 1990 alone.[4] The industrial revolution in the developing world has rewired the circuitry of global markets almost overnight: China's manufacturing exports alone have jumped from 1 per cent to 7 per cent of the global total since 1980.[5]

Over the past two decades, some two and a half billion people in China, India, eastern Europe and the former Soviet Union have discarded economic isolationism and entered a global labour market.[6] Technological innovation has shrunk the world, reducing the cost of transmitting information to virtually nothing. Internet users in developing countries could constitute more than half the world total within five years if current trends persist.[7] The metaphor, popularized by Tom Friedman, is that the world is now flat.

But population and economic activity are not uniformly distributed across the globe. Rather people have settled and the economy is organized in a discontinuous, non-linear fashion. The world, to borrow a phrase from Richard Florida, is 'spiky' and each spike represents a city in which the world's economy and population is disproportionately concentrated.[8] Globalization and technological innovation, rather than flattening the world spatially, is physically rooting itself in dense spatial arrangements of people and firms, transportation and housing, ports and facilities. The new world order is an urban order.

This urban age has five central characteristics. First is scale and size: the world's urban population today is over three billion people – the same size as the world's total population in 1960.[9] There are now 400 cities with populations of more than one million people, when a century ago there were only 16.[10]

In recent decades, we have grown a network of megacities; 23 cities with more than 10 million people now comprise 5 per cent of the world's population.[11] Greater Mumbai's population is now larger than the population of Norway and Sweden combined; likewise, Greater São Paulo's population is now roughly equal to Australia's.[12] With even more growth projected in developing countries, the urban population of Africa will exceed the total population of Europe by 2030.[13] As cities have grown in people, they have stretched outwards, consuming vast expanses of land and covering enormous distances. Over a 70-year period, the New York metropolis, for example, expanded over 1,300 per cent and now covers more than 19,000 square kilometres.[14]

Secondly, speed and velocity define the urban age. In 1950, 29 per cent of the world's population lived in cities. By 1990, the share had risen to 43 per cent. Now, as stated before, passed 50 per cent in 2007. And, by 2030, it will surpass 60 per cent of the world's population.[15] Since 1950, the world's urban population has almost quadrupled in size.[16] Between 2005 and 2030, it is expected to increase at an average annual rate of close to 2 per cent – almost twice the growth rate of the world's population. If current trends persist, the world's urban population will surpass five billion sometime around 2030.[17]

Third, urban growth is being fuelled by new levels of mobility and migration of diverse populations, within and across nations. Hundreds of millions of rural residents in China, Brazil, India and elsewhere are moving in droves to cities. These rural-to-urban migrants are pulled by the tantalizing prospect of jobs and opportunity, driven by the harsh realities of rural life and, particularly in Africa, displaced by horrific wars and civil conflicts.

Tens of millions of people are also on the move across national borders. Today, international migrants comprise 3 per cent of the world's population and they are settling in a growing number of countries.[18] Between 1960 and 2005, the number of countries hosting more than 500,000 migrants grew from 30 to 64.[19] Immigration has fuelled urbanization in developed countries. In the United States, for example, cities grew during the 1990s almost exclusively because of the influx of Hispanic and Asian populations. In Berlin, over 13 per cent of the population are immigrants.[20]

Fourth, urban expansion has created new conurbations of staggering complexity. In one respect, cities are playing their traditional roles as the great levellers of people from radically disparate walks of life – of foreign born and native born, of rural migrants and urban residents, of rich and poor, of traditional and modern cultures. In the twenty-first century, cities also represent an uneasy coexistence between the global and the local – of high-rise office towers and dilapidated slums, of the formal and informal economy, of educated elites and impoverished residents, of global chains and indigenous firms. The divisions between these phenomena are not stark: there are often symbiotic and synergistic relationships – between the formal and informal economy, for example – which are multilayered and evolving.

Finally, the urban age is characterized by an unprecedented level of connectivity, between and among people, firms and places. Transnational migration connects countries of origin and immigrant-rich cities, as people, money and ideas flow back and forth. In 2004, immigrants around the globe sent US$226 billion in remittances back to their home countries – an astonishing one per cent of global GDP.[21] Across nations, tight linkages are being forged between cities with similar industry clusters: financial centres like London and Tokyo; technology centres like San Jose and Bangalore; or trading centres like Rotterdam and Singapore. Even within nations, countries like Germany are taking this reality of urban connectivity to its logical conclusion and creating a network of interlinked cities, connected, and soon to be even more connected, by modern rail and technology.

These five qualities of urbanization – scale, speed, diversity, complexity and connectivity – place cities at the centre of the global economy, global challenges and, ultimately, global solutions.

Can the world extend the promise of economic prosperity and integrated markets and productive labour? Today, the path to prosperity runs directly through cities. As UN-HABITAT has bluntly stated: 'Cities make countries rich. Countries that are highly urbanized have higher incomes, more stable economies, stronger institutions and are better able to withstand the volatility of the global economy than those with less urbanized populations.'[22]

Can the world address the environmental crisis of global warming and climate change? Rapid urbanization has, no doubt, exacerbated environmental pressures. Yet cities offer the best promise of developing in ways that are environmentally sound and energy efficient; objectives that, as a major report to the British government recently concluded, are prerequisites to global prosperity.[23]

Can the world win the global fight against poverty? Incredibly, 998 million people now live in disease-spreading slums characterized by inadequate housing, unsafe drinking water and open sewer and sanitation systems.[24] Yet cities offer the promise of ultimately connecting hundreds of millions of workers to the expanding job opportunities offered by the global economy.

Economic Prosperity, Environmental Sustainability, Social Inclusivity

In an urban age, the battles to achieve the highest aspirations of the twenty-first century and beyond will be fought – and won or lost – in our cities. Yet moving from the general to the specific, from aggregate global statistics to the experiences of individual cities, the general observations can be summarized as follows:

- There is a sharp disconnect between the challenges of the urban age and our current set of urban solutions.
- There is a disconnect between policies intended to promote economic growth, policies designed to advance environmental sustainability and policies aimed at reducing poverty.
- There is a disconnect between the complexity of challenges and the narrow responses that dominate urban policy.
- There is a disconnect between the artificial geography of government, and the real footprint of the economy and environment.

In the twenty-first century, markets are moving quickly to reshape and remake urban places. Yet urban policy and urban governance appears stuck somewhere in the twentieth century. The lag between transformational change and governmental action is immense.

So, how do we design and implement an urban agenda that matches the pace and intensity of the urban age? The goals of the urban agenda – competitive cities, sustainable cities, inclusive cities – are not at issue. The trinity of economy, environment and equity is substantively warranted, morally imperative and widely accepted. Each of the cities that we visited is pursuing these three objectives to a greater or lesser degree. Yet, as we have seen, these cities are often putting these elements into practice mechanistically, at the wrong scale, in hermetically sealed policies labelled 'transportation', 'education', 'housing', 'economic development' or even 'environmental protection'.

Cities are complex and interdependent. As such, they require multidimensional, integrated and holistic interventions. This century's urban agenda needs to be about delivery as much as aspiration. It is an agenda that must empower people, with more integrated and transformative programmes and policies, through a heightened awareness of the physical 'place', with a realignment of politics and an infusion of new partners.

We first need to focus on the people who deliver the urban agenda. Imagine networks of city builders who cut across disciplines, programmes, practices and professions. These city builders will perfect new ways of 'reading' cities, deploy new metrics and measures to diagnose city assets and ailments, and gauge city progress. They will be fluent in multiple city 'languages' – such as architecture, demographics, engineering, economics and sociology – and be cognizant of theory and practice. Modern society has deified specialists and technicians who interpret and strive to fix discrete problems such as traffic congestion or slum housing.

If cities are to succeed, we must build a generation of generalists who see the connections between challenges and who work to devise and implement policies that advance multiple objectives simultaneously. Our academies and universities must become central agents in furthering this ambition, breaking down artificial divisions between separate schools, professions curricula, departments and self-defeating academic fiefdoms. And we must find institutional vehicles that can deliver continuous, multidisciplinary learning – so that professional evolution can respond to new challenges and changing demands.

We should encourage city builders like Richard Baron, the premiere affordable housing developer in the United States. He is using the production of mixed-income housing in America's poorest neighbourhoods as a catalyst for modernizing and improving neighbourhood schools. The result is not just quality, distinctive housing but, more importantly, a neighbourhood school that works, and is showing sharp improvements in student performance. In Richard Baron's mind, a 'housing developer' cannot just build shelter to be successful; he or she must engage on those things that directly lift people out of poverty – education, skills training and transportation.

To create more Richard Barons, we need to arm city builders with programmes and policies that champion integration and holistic thinking. If housing is going to be a platform for opportunity, then housing policies must connect with education, childcare, transportation and policies. If transportation is going to promote mobility and advance sustainability, then transportation policies need to expand choices and embrace dense, transit-rich corridors of mixed residential, retail and employment uses. If employment growth is going to benefit low-income workers, than economic development policies need to include workforce development as a central feature.

Making linkages and connections between policies must be the norm not the exception, reinforced by incentives and new structures and systems. We must, borrowing from the law enforcement's adoption of 'community policing', focus on the 'co-production of solutions' across disciplines and professions. The vertical, silo-driven bureaucracies of the past century need to be laid horizontal. In many respects, closing the divide between related but separately administered policies is as important as bridging the partisan and ideological divides that characterize so many countries and undermine urban success.

In all we do, we need to extol the role of place and the physical. As Ricky Burdett has eloquently reminded us, linking the physical to the human and the social is a vehicle to achieve broader city goals. Centuries of city building have shown the value of an urban form that is resilient, adaptive to changing demands, conducive to retro-fitting and recycling. How we grow physically, in essence affects whether we grow economically, sustainably and inclusively.

We see today that what makes cities vital in the twenty-first century are those very attributes of urbanism – what Saskia Sassen calls 'cityness'– that we destroyed in the twentieth century.[25] Complexity. Density. Diversity of people and cultures. The convergence of the physical environment at multiple scales. The messy intersection of activities. A variance of distinctive designs. The layering of the old and the new. These are the physical elements that advance competitive, sustainable and inclusive cities.

The right physical interventions can truly have a seismic, transformative impact on markets, the environment and human potential. This can happen at multiple levels, from the micro to the macro, from the retro-fitting of small, older properties to meet new residential demands, to large-scale interventions that have the power to realign the physical landscape of cities in ways that advance the opportunities of a new century: Johannesburg 2010, the Football World Cup; Shanghai 2010, the World Expo; London 2012, the Olympics.

As we extend the notion of transformative interventions, we need to find new languages and methodologies to capture the complex reality of cities. The twentieth-century notion of measuring density, for example, fails to reflect the wide range of economic, residential and social activities that are simultaneously underway in all parts of the city. Cities are not black and white, but shades of grey, increasingly blurring the line between the working world and the living world, informal and formal activities.

The deficit of language becomes even more apparent as we strive to understand cities in the developing world. Participants in the Shanghai, Mexico City and Johannesburg forums all argued forcefully that the emerging Asian, Latin American and African urbanism is distinct from the experiences of Europe and the United States. With transnational discourse on global cities set to increase, a heightened awareness is required of how cultural distinctions manifest differently in the physical, social and economic landscape.

To achieve policy reforms, we need to reinvent the politics of the urban, by which we mean the extent to which national and multinational leaders feel any pressure to meaningfully understand and respond to cities.

In the end, cities are just cities. They act within the context of constitutional and statutory law, set by higher levels of government. A city focuses on its immigrants but cannot control immigration laws. A city focuses on reducing income disparities, but does not have the tools to close the gap between wages and prices. A city focuses on environmental sustainability, but generally lacks the power to catalyse market change through regulatory interventions. Yet cities do not just need smart national policies to succeed. The opposite is also true. National prosperity is now completely dependent on the ability of cities to reach their full potential.

So nations need to respect cities, revalue them and put 'urban' realities at the heart of national decisions. For some countries, such as the United Kingdom, this will entail 'letting go' of national power and giving cities more flexibility to adapt to demographic and economic change. For countries like the United States it will require the national government to take more responsibility for issues over which cities have little control – wages and incomes. All nations (or states or provinces) must right size the administrative geography of local and metropolitan government – or empower accountable entities with regional remits and powers, so that challenges that cross borders can be addressed cleanly and clearly. All nations must make integration easy and compartmentalization difficult. And all nations, particularly the United States, must do what it takes – through new tools, incentives and regulations, ambitious goals and objectives – to help cities grow in ways that address global warming and climate change.

Nations, in short, need an urban agenda themselves, given the economy-, environment- and people-shaping power of cities. The evolution of British urban policy over the past decade is one model to assess, as ultimately is Germany's Chancellor Merkel's more explicit commitment to an integrated, environmentally sensitive urban agenda. In a global world, of course, nation states are no longer the final arbiter of city futures. Supranational institutions ranging from the United Nations to the World Bank have enormous impact on cities and the people who live there, for better or for worse.

These institutions, and many others, have principally viewed poverty as a rural phenomenon, to be tackled and overcome with targeted initiatives. The international community, therefore, has lacked a cohesive framework for thinking about and acting in cities. For the most part, these institutions relegate cities to the sidelines of decision-making or ineffectual sub-bureaucracies, treating them as just one more supplicant for aid or constituency to be mollified. The lack of spatial focus in these institutions, the lack of integrative thinking and action, must end. As the Clinton Global Initiative on climate change recognizes, cities are the vehicles to combat global warming.[26] And as the Millennium Development Goals should recognize, cities must be the vehicles to eradicate a planet of slums.

Cities must move to the forefront of national and supranational agendas and priorities. This will require a quantum leap in international commitments to urban infrastructure and development. It will require a holistic, integrated approach to the deployment of these resources. And it will require a palpable lift in leadership. An annual World Summit on Cities with presidents and prime ministers and the heads of major corporations and philanthropies? The time is long past due.

One final avenue for action: the urban age cannot be delivered by government alone; it requires new partners in the private sector. Cities do not just make nations rich: they make corporations rich. And, it is in the self-interest, the shareholder interest, of corporations to advance a full vision of prosperity of cities.

Thus, transnational corporations, the glue of global cities, have significant roles to play: becoming champions for market principles like transparency, accountability, innovation and empiricism; devising new ways of amassing and deploying private capital to accelerate the building of housing and infrastructure; and collaborating to extend the sharing of practices and innovations across cities and nations.

What Next?

In the end, an 'urban age' is a clarion call – a wake-up message. If cities are the organizing units of the new global order, then a broad range of policies and practices at the city, national and supranational levels need to be overhauled, reordered and integrated around new spatial realities and paradigms.

This Urban Age initiative telegraphs where we as city builders need to go:
– We need to break down the barriers between specialized and self-referential disciplines, professions and bureaucracies.
– We need to share innovations across networks of urban researchers, practitioners and policymakers, across the developing and developed worlds.
– We need to build cities that are prosperous, sustainable and inclusive.

The urban age has meaning and import far beyond those few of us who observe cities or build cities or govern cities. This is truly a call to this generation to build a different world of urban opportunity and possibility. An urban age requires that we act – with vision, imagination and confidence. Will we seize the possibilities?

owing pages

KING AT CITIES

massive structural and economic changes
g experienced by the citizens of the world's
al cities have a dramatic impact on the lives
ver 2 billion city dwellers, such as those
g in this housing block in downtown
nnesburg.

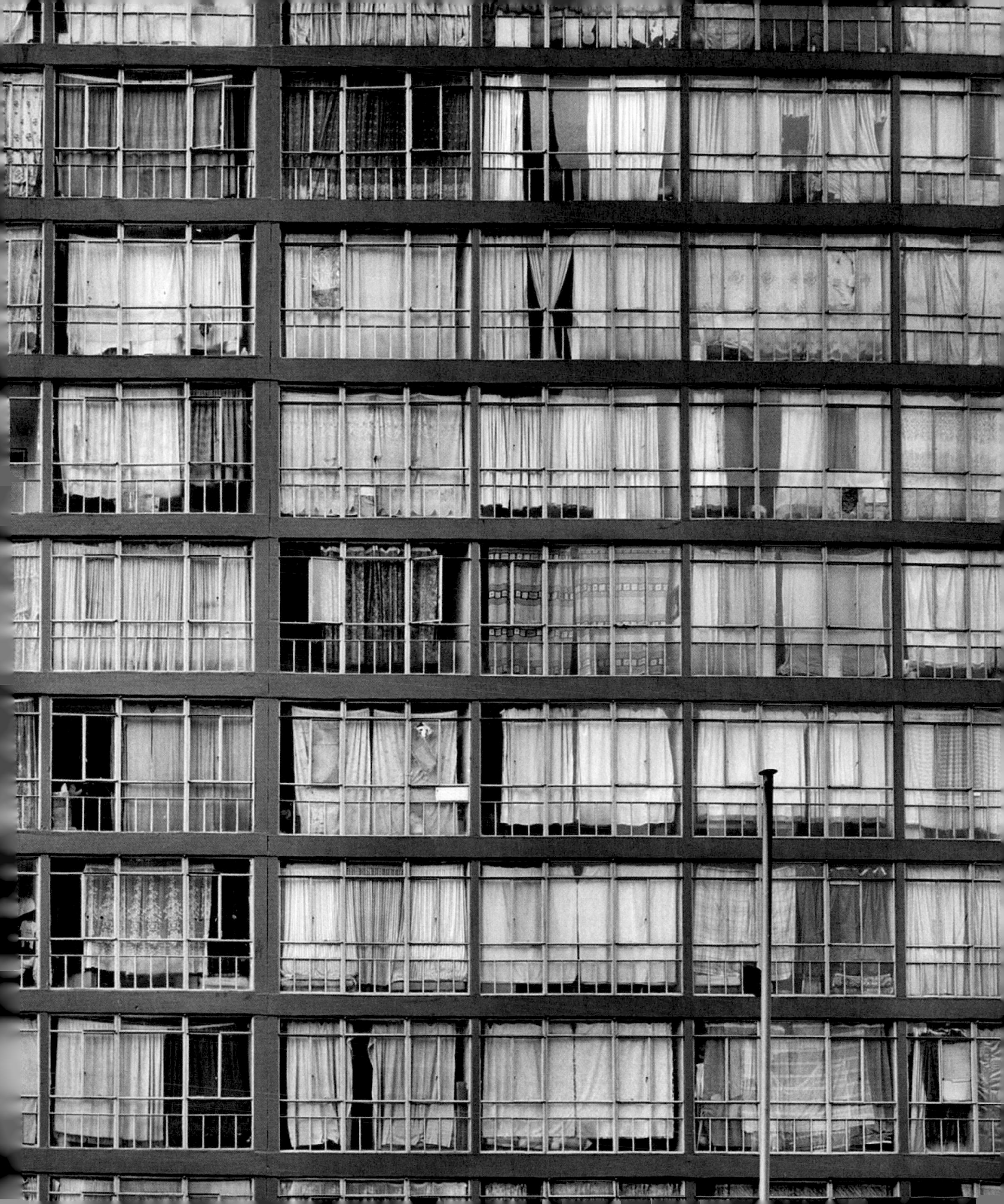

URBAN AGE GLOSSARY

Excerpts from Urban Age conferences

Architecture

Architecture has a role in the manufacturing of identity in urban contexts and the unique ability to make something visible long before it has actually happened. Architecture creates a sense of what a city is like. It is what we use to identify a city.
Deyan Sudjic

The intriguing thing about London is its vast repertoire of forms that are currently used in an incredibly virtuoso manner, in ways that they were never intended to be used. That is where I find the absolute brilliance of this city. Maybe more than 90 per cent of the accommodation in borough housing is used for entirely different purposes from those for which it was conceived.
Rem Koolhaas

Design to me is the imaginative manipulation of the physical fabric of cities, landscapes, buildings, in between spaces, environments, interiors and products to accommodate people in a sustainable way over time. I say design, as an active term, rather than buildings or architecture, because both buildings and architecture on their own are inert.
Frank Duffy

Architecture performs as an edification mechanism which empowers citizens: allows communities to have a sense of cohesion and allows disparate parts of communities to find some sense of direction within the idea of a city.
David Adjaye

I look to architects to be the animators and problem solvers in a very holistic way and I don't know whether all of them are capable of being that, but urban design is about interdisciplinary teams of people working together.
Nicky Gavron

Cityness

Urban agglomerations are very often seen as lacking the features, quality and sense of what we think of as cities. Yet urbanity is perhaps too charged a term, charged with a western sense of cosmopolitanism of what public space is or should be. Instead, cityness suggests the possibility that there are kinds of urbanity that do not fit with this large body of urbanism developed in the West.
Saskia Sassen

If we cannot produce new theory, and I agree it is not easy, we can at least find new words. I noticed how Saskia Sassen introduced the word 'cityness' and how that word, even if it is pretty ungainly,

has immediately been picked up … If we find new words we can hope to produce a framework of understanding. Without a framework, any means of instrumentality are futile.
Rem Koolhaas

Charm is not enough. Buildings do not do anything on their own. There has to be an idea of what that charm is for in this highly competitive twenty-first-century world, and that needs to connect to economic survival and development through the generation of powerful world-beating ideas … not just to copy outmoded twentieth-century models, nor to rely upon the lovely historical fabric of the old city, but to reinvent the idea of what a city is for.
Frank Duffy

City-Regions

In terms of social outcomes, what really matters in London, and in any city of its complexity at the macrolevel, is the successful economic development of the broader city-region. This functional region is interconnected in ways that go beyond the understanding of most individual actors living in it.
Ian Gordon

My view is that the Executive Commission for Metropolitan

Coordination is a very promising beginning towards regional governance in Mexico City. Given that the metropolitan population is roughly equally divided between the federal district and the state, having the governor and the mayor as co-equal partners is a good form of organization. It is also very important given the power of the national government over state and local matters. Historically and currently to have a mechanism that involves these three parties, implemented by their own governments, is the best way to address a range of metropolitan problems. No other city that I know of has such an institution capable of working on metropolitan issues.
Gerald Frug

A regional urbanization process is replacing old ideas that cities are not simply growing through suburbanization and sprawl but in a very different way. They are hiving off new cities. We get multicentric, polycentric, networked city-regions forming, and so the Mexico City region is the one that is 37 million.
Edward Soja

Community

Schools of design – as well as schools of business, law, social work, public administration – have an eighteenth- and nineteenth-century academic form to deal with twenty-first century problems. It is impossible to find graduate students who have a broad enough background to deal with the multiplicity of Urban Age issues … how all these things get interwoven in building new communities is absolutely critical. We have people who approach problems one-dimensionally, designers who understand nothing about finance and school systems that are isolated from the political process in neighbourhoods.
Richard Baron

We need to change the bourgeois point of view and begin to see the city from the point of view of poor people, the majority of the people that live in cities today. For poor people, community is essential; they need to aggregate in order not to be powerless, to create change.
Max Bond Jr

Not enough attention has been given to the mechanisms to ensure that any new community that we are creating, e.g. through re-zoning, is inclusive from its beginning in terms of income and race.
Shaun Donovan

Traditionally the centre of a community is its most important place. In my view, the boundaries and borders are the city's most socially important places. Culture gets made at the edges between difference, that's how we create bonding.
Richard Sennett

Contestations centre not only on the right to reside in the city, but also on actively shaping its future in accordance with people's needs and values.
Caroline Kihato

Density

We have a challenge to provide, in those neighbourhoods where we can grow, enough density to ensure affordability. Enough density to leverage open public space. Enough density to provide vitality and vibrancy of neighbourhoods, while respecting the built fabric of adjacent communities.
Amanda M. Burden

Research at the LSE shows that certain parts of London, rich and poor, are able to deliver density. In fact, the street grids of many areas are currently supporting relatively high density levels.
Tony Travers

Where concentration predominates over dispersal, half of Shanghai's population lives in an area smaller than 5 per

cent of its total land surface.
Miguel Kanai

In Shanghai, rapid suburban sprawl has not relieved the conditions of overcrowding in the centre. This could be solved by changing the land-use regulations that generate overly accelerated development and artificially low densities in inner-ring suburbs. We are trying to improve unusually low densities by focusing on small and mixed streets, a local market, open-air theatres for the local community and the overall revitalization of local culture.
Yue Wu

The European city model is based on two policies: avoiding the formation of social, cultural and functional ghettos; and creating and defending public space so that everybody can use them. No single activity can take full control of what is public. These two policies depend on the precondition of density.
Joan Clos

Economic Development

Civility means that the diversity of urban life becomes a source of mutual strength rather than a source of estrangement and civic bitterness. In the past this issue has been framed in terms of ethnicity or culture. In the current period of inequality, it needs to be increasingly framed in economic terms.
Richard Sennett

By the year 2050, Shanghai's economic size will be 12 times bigger, an amount equal to the product of the whole of China in the year 2000. Policies by Shanghai's government are designed to channel this growth so as to make Shanghai an advanced manufacturing centre, a centre of trade and transport, and an international finance centre. Its current weaknesses are the relatively low level of international connectivity of the city, the glass ceilings that small

and medium enterprises face to growth and the limited participation that civil society has as a stakeholder in the economic development process.
Qiyu Tu

Many Alexandrian business owners lacked formal certification to enable them to access wider markets. Most businesses had limited access to a broader set of ideas that would enable them to upgrade to more profitable activities. Strategic focus was placed on enabling those who already had some momentum to raise profitability and expand their business: they might then employ long-term unemployed and youths.
Miriam Altman

China's demographic context, economic dynamics and pro-urbanization policies provide the background of Shanghai's hyper-growth, translating into hyper-density not only of population and structures, but also of ideas and styles … the job for Shanghai planners is to integrate all these differences.
Siegfried Zhiqiang Wu

We need twenty-first-century organizational structures, we need new models for our agencies to deal with innovative funding, with the fact that there are stakeholder groups, that the systems that were once seen as independent are now highly interactive.
Robert E. Paaswell

Equality

I think that in every city, but particularly cities in the developing world, urban design can be an extremely powerful tool to construct equality and integration. Even if we do not have income equality, we can aspire to construct equality in the distribution of quality of life so that the public good prevails over private interests. Just to mention a

local example: if the hundreds of miles of New York's waterfront were used for public space rather than private land, a lot of equality would be created.
Enrique Peñalosa

Modern transport is what collapses the distances between two points – it needs to be available to all equally.
Hermann Knoflacher

The transition from a state-organized urban working system to a market-driven labour market produces severe forms of inequalities and exclusion. The former needs a complex institutional framework for a sustainable economic and social development, including access to educational facilities and healthcare institutions.
Miguel Kanai

Global City

For researchers and policymakers, I think one of the critical strategies is to disaggregate the global economy into the multiple highly specialized circuits that compose it, from the many highly specialized financial systems to the small and semi-formal international real-estate markets that immigrants set up. Two things then happen. First, you can actually study the very slippery concept of the 'global'. More importantly, you can locate your city on many global circuits and detect the links and strategic geographies that connect it to a whole bunch of other cities.
Saskia Sassen

The global city is a central location for production and a transnational marketplace for high-quality, knowledge-based services.
Dieter Läpple

How does one understand the impact of their global-city status on the power of these cities? More precisely, what is the role of the city government in becoming

a global city? There is little doubt that government officials promote their global-city status. But none of them can easily control such a development, let alone rethink or redirect city policy away from such a goal.
Gerald Frug

Globalization

About globalization, Mexico City does not have the instruments to make a real change in public policy about economic development, technology, education or telecommunications. The city is not at the table about those decisions because traditionally, all the decisions about economic policy are Federal, without local participation. So we are spectators.
Marcelo Ebrard

The defining feature of contemporary African urbanism is the *slum*. What is underestimated is the extent to which major African cities attract, in their own ways, certain forms of colonial and now global capital. That such forms of capital are for the most part predatory is without doubt. But isn't this what, at least partly, globalization is all about – that is, a set of processes that are refracted, splintered and cracked?
Achille Mbembe

Global businesses operate very differently from a decade ago. I am deeply impressed by the impact that information technologies have had on every aspect of work. Assumptions of co-location and synchrony no longer correspond with the realities of these businesses. We need a radical change from the assumptions on which the architecture of cities in the nineteenth and twentieth centuries was based. We have to be inventive in the way we design, deliver and manage buildings. The workplace needs to be prepared for mobility, volatility, permeability and complementarity of the big and the

small, what is internal to the firm and what is not.
Frank Duffy

Shanghai has always been an open city, ready to seize opportunities and allow its citizens to display their talent and creativity. This competitive tradition underlies its dynamic and progressive nature – an entrepreneurial spirit that sets it apart from other Chinese cities. But, as with any city that occupies a strategic global position, its future lies not only in the hands of its architects and policymakers, but in the national policy for growth and redevelopment.
Zheng Shiling

No matter how much the world's cities operate as part of a single global system, acquiring the same kind of landmarks, museums, airports, motorways, and subject to the same quack remedies of tax incentives and marketing programmes, the understanding of how different and distinct they are remains.
Deyan Sudjic

Governance

Who is a stakeholder? Which corporations and interest groups are entitled to participate in urban governance? Who is included in the concept of community? It's important to recognize that there's no uncontroversial answer to any of these questions. In the UK, urban decision-making seems to rest above all on a single word, a word repeated so often on every page in every report that it is, quite frankly, overwhelming. That word is: partnership.
Gerald Frug

We need to create Metropolitan institutions, not Metropolitan government (which is different). Institutions with budget and public responsibility.
Marcelo Ebrard

The scale of urbanization, with its new vast geography of commuter sheds and supplier networks and labour and housing markets, is outstripping the structure and the administrative geography of city government.
Bruce Katz

The management of complexity in places where rights, knowledge and education now rightly have been allowed to give a voice to neighbourhoods and individuals means that the task of governing cities is more complex than ever before. Citywide interests conflict with the most local of interests and it clearly takes the legitimacy of city leaders to bring about change. Examples such as Bogotá's cycle ways, Washington's renaissance, New York's control of its education system or London's Congestion Charge would not have come to fruition without the legitimacy of ballot boxes.
Tony Travers

I look at citizens as nuclear power. Properly channelled and harnessed, nuclear power can power the city, otherwise it can destroy it.
Anthony Williams

Housing

A house is not just a house; it is far more. A house involves land, water, electricity, and a whole range of issues that have to come together. Each one is a separate department in the city and unless you can bring them all together as a single team, you will never provide a fully serviced urban environment.
Julian Baskin

In China, the state had a standard for individual living space of 10 square metres per person within a room. All facilities, including bathrooms and kitchens, were meant to be communal and not the personal space of individuals. As recently as last year, this standard was changed. It has been raised to a little over 23 square metres per person and that includes various facilities. The measuring unit is now the apartment rather than the room. What it means, of course, is that we are leading more private lives rather than a completely public life. This increase in personal space changes not only how we live but also how we think about urban issues. The role of housing in relation to community, neighbourhood and city is tied to the notion of urban fabric – that is to say housing as fabric. In opposition to the kind of monumental architecture or the architecture of monumentality, the architecture of fabric is an architecture, or urbanism, of democracy.
Yung Ho Chang

The drive for the regeneration of Elephant & Castle began in 1998, after the experiences of Bankside, Tate Modern, and Peckham in Southwark. The original plan had an energetic programme for people to move out of poverty into employment. The borough, which has a very large percentage of subsidized (council) housing, has to face up to the alarming correlation between education achievement and housing tenure. My hope is that the current initiative will also be directly linked to the social problems that we find in the area, rather than turned into a purely physical approach that believes it can reduce and resolve these problems.
Fred Manson

Informality

Informality can not be approached as a specific form of 'lawlessness', but we have to understand urban informality as mode of development, as metropolitan urbanization under the condition of globalization. Informality means not a given state but a process of continuous

shifting between deformalization and reformalization. The informal economy should not be read as social disorganization or anarchy; it has its own institutions and forms of regulation. Its settlements are also working places with basic needs for shelter, living, spaces of inclusion and interpersonal integration.
Dieter Läpple

The informal economy is not equivalent to the illegal or underground economy. But then why do these activities fall outside of regulatory frameworks? On the one hand, there is an old informal economy, particularly in the global south. But there is also a new informal economy that is part of the most advanced forms of contemporary capitalis. The old informal economy and the survival strategies that we know so well in Latin America may look similar, but we must make an analytical distinction between the two. The new informal economy exists in the global south; in Mexico City, Mumbai and Buenos Aires, in the intersections between high-power professionals who inhabit the buildings of the corporate centres and the street vendors peddling their foods outside.
Saskia Sassen

There is a frequently occurring and erroneous belief that one size-fits-all policies can be applied to the entire informal sector.
José Castillo

Cities are built on commerce which goes all the way back to essentially informal economy. It is the soul of the city … we are in a world now where you go from one city to another, and beyond the airport, beyond the road system, more and more cities are looking more alike. The informal economy is important because it distinguishes that city.
Anthony Williams

Labour Markets

Urban manufacturing is the 'silent partner' in the urban economy supporting other key sectors, such as the creative, cultural and healthcare industries; it serves as a gateway to social integration by providing important employment opportunities with low entry barriers for people with different cultural backgrounds and qualifications.
Dieter Läpple

The scale of economic development in Shanghai can be characterized by its massive labour force. The total number of employees was 8.13 million in 2003, more than double the labour force in New York or London and larger than Tokyo's. More than half of these workers are employed in the service sector but more than a third work in labour-intensive manufacturing industries. Growth at the top has meant an increase in international workers. Shanghai's labour market provides opportunities for low-skill workers and this is a key element to explain the attraction of a 'floating population' of 5 million people to the city.
Yuemin Ning

The informal economy, if it's pushed right, has people actually engaged in their own business. Fundamental economics will tell you that if you support that economy, you are more likely to create wealth than taking me from running my own business to working as wage labourer somewhere else.
Anthony Williams

Part of the problem has to do with overemphasizing the service sector and falling into a post-industrial trap and completely ignoring the manufacturing sector, the industrial sector; assuming that the trend in the world today is that the big cities of the world are completely losing manufacturing and therefore it

should never enter into the picture.
Dieter Läpple

The distinction of manufacturing versus services is a historically changing one that has gone through a revolution over the past 15 years. A lot of specialized services today depend on manufacturing. Architects, real-estate developers, and designer provide services actually dependent on manufacturing.
Saskia Sassen

There may be new jobs generated and new forms of value added in high-end employment related to forward and backward linkages among productive sectors, but are these the types of jobs and spillovers that can address basic employment needs in a declining industrial locale like Mexico City, where informal-sector work is the lifeblood for most families and formal employment levels are down? … Without new investments in job training or educational capital, it is unreasonable to expect that these new investments will translate into new forms of employment.
Miguel Kanai

My theory is that the new workplace will probably not need new forms, but the new dynamics of work will simply infiltrate existing forms of the city, exactly because they are new and therefore have a more creative ability to interpret and less need to convert. In a sense they will be both condemned and privileged to use existing substance.
Rem Koolhaas

Migration

The conflicts between city residents and in-migrants, or peasant workers, could assume larger and deeper proportions in the future given the increasing volume of rural migration to cities. The Shanghai Municipal Government's policies to educate and train in-migrants

and to regularize their situation have reduced conflict and furthered social integration. But the reform of the household registration system, which prevents in-migrants from becoming residents, is still pending. As the former reduces the psychological gap between city-residents and in-migrants, the latter would eliminate an institutional wall against cohesion. If these two strategies can be achieved, we will make a large step towards a harmonious society.
Guixin Wang

Migrant networks play a critical role in providing a safety net for members without money, work or shelter. But few of these initiatives actively engage or demand inclusion in decision-making processes shaping the future of the city.
Caroline Kihato

The shrinking ability of the globalized city to benefit the vast marginal zones of exclusion has turned Mexico City's metropolitan zone into the main region expelling Mexican migrants to the United States.
Néstor Canclini

The Mexican diaspora continues to transform the very physical nature of the North American city – primarily in California – challenging the rigidity of its incriminatory zoning policies by engendering an interest in flexible, inclusive and temporal urbanism.
Teddy Cruz

Governance imagines 'stakeholders' being 'at the table', working with city officials and others to formulate policy through consensus. It's unimaginable that representatives of global business enterprises will be excluded from such a meeting. It's quite imaginable, on the other hand, that there will be no one there from the floating population, the informal economy, or representing the poor newcomers who have recently immigrated from another country.
Gerald Frug

Mobility

Johannesburg is founded on mobility. Since the discovery of gold in the nineteenth century, the city has attracted labourers, entrepreneurs and industrialists hoping for a better life. As a place where strangers have always converged, the city is the site of continuous contestations over who belongs in the city and to whom the city belongs.
Caroline Kihato

What was once actively planned under apartheid is often reproduced and compounded in ongoing, usually unintended ways. One of the major commitments of the African National Congress government was to build some two million low-cost, subsidized houses within 10 years. We have got close to doing that, but in order to meet the budget and to develop these dwellings, they were built where land was cheap on the far peripheries of the city. Therefore, mobility injustice has deepened, unintentionally, in the post-apartheid era.
Jeremy Cronin

A rigid zoning approach, which separates uses and dedicates large proportions of land – particularly for new developments – to discrete residential, office, industrial or service uses, will have a huge impact on mobility requirements. Over the last 10 years, the daily distance travelled by Shanghai residents has increased by 50 per cent.
Hermann Knoflacher

The result of treating informal as problematic comes at a high social cost. People move to cities to improve quality of life. However, since the informal settlements are outside the plans and the law, citizens have limited access to education and other opportunities, resulting in lower social mobility.
Geetam Tiwari

Developers, and the financial institutions that support them, fall into default positions very easily. They do not realize that the office of today is not a stable building type because, especially in cities like London, neither synchrony nor co-location are necessary conditions of work any longer. This does not mean that people are going to work from home all the time, but they are going to be much more mobile, using many settings, in many different ways, in many different places.
Gerald Frug

Neighbourhoods

Have large-scale regeneration projects forgotten about the wider city? These bundles of public and private activities are powerful instruments that have excluded entire parts of the city and its people. Therefore, I think these projects need to be embedded in a larger socio-economic master plan that would also bring about benefits to the neighbourhoods and to those people who are not included.
Dieter Läpple

New York City is indeed built out to its edges and yet it is now undergoing unprecedented immigration and population growth. This is a tremendous challenge to those of us in charge of planning this city. We must find places to channel this growth, while preserving neighbourhood character.
Amanda M. Burden

We have 16 local governments in Mexico City, but they don't have accountability in real terms with neighbourhoods or citizens, and they do not represent the citizens. A very important reform is needed. We need to guarantee that all citizens can evaluate the services

we provide, and that the results will be published.
Marcelo Ebrard

Are Shanghai elites really eager to produce inclusivity in their city? What new identity formation springs from rapidly changing spaces? What is the meaning of community or neighbourliness in a fluid society like this? We know by experience that it is more advantageous to govern by consent than by coercion.
Sophie Body-Gendrot

Part of the story in Washington, New York and London is about having a strong vision for the city and a strong framework within which participation and debate can occur. Otherwise it boils down to parochial interests. Every neighbourhood says 'I love the vision for the city – just not in my neighbourhood do I want density'. Cities are coming out of an era where planning was too timid and afraid of big visions because they resulted in catastrophic effects. Now you are seeing a balancing between vision and participation.
Andy Altman

Other cities have a higher proportion of people from ethnic-minority backgrounds but no city has more different cultural communities … one of the things we're doing since London government came in is to make sure that those cultures are able to celebrate their distinctiveness; so more and more festivals, more and more restaurants, more and more different kinds of experiences.
Nicky Gavron

Planning

Today's planner has an arsenal of technological tools – from lighting to bridging and tunnelling, to materials for buildings – which urbanists even a hun-

dred years ago could not begin to imagine: we have more resources to use, but we don't use them very creatively.
Richard Sennett

London is almost unique in being geographically defined by a 40-mile-wide green belt surrounding Greater London, an area where you cannot build anything. The major underlying challenge, and theme for urban development debates, is that London will have to contain its long-term growth within that boundary of the Green Belt.
Anthony Mayer

The growth of future cities depends upon how well we are able to plan for the 'unplanned'. The generic theme evolving from Asia, Latin America and Africa is that as cities expand, the 'informal' grows faster than the 'formal'. Thus plans will need paradigmatic change to deal with the heterogeneous housing and mobility needs of growing populations. We will have to plan for activities that cannot be well-defined and predicted, which is better than turning a blind eye to the future.
Geetam Tiwari

Planning and bold visions are back again. Planning is emerging from the coma that it has been in since urban renewal. After those failures and the reactions to those failures, planning suffered a crisis of confidence in the profession, and planners thought: do we really have something to say about the city? Are we trying to do too much? Can we accomplish all these things? Are we listening enough to what people want? But now, cities are again looking at physical planning as a way of re-imagining their futures, as way of mobilizing actions and as way of empowerment.
Andy Altman

Contemporary Chinese urbanism is not based on the individualistic freedom of

capitalism but rather on a system of effective cooperation. At the risk of sounding politically backward, we can put people together and find an agent intelligent enough to plan scientifically, rather than by the aggregation of individual desires focused on acquiring and occupying bigger spaces, wider ocean or park views and more happiness.
Qingyun Ma

For half of the public planning and public policy questions, you have to put yourself out there: close, face to face, eye to eye, spend a lot of time on the street, convince communities you know every street, every block, every house, that you really care, that you really hear their concerns, and as your plans go through the public process that you modify them to reflect what you have heard and little by little you achieve a consensus.
Amanda M. Burden

Public Space

Public space and cosmopolitanism are foundational elements of any city. They have, however, been constructed in deeply western ways. In Shanghai, many interventions seem to be destabilizing these western concepts. Quingyun Ma argues that the Chinese city does not need public space because it makes public spaces that we might think of as private; bus shelters at night become a public space where people set up their tables to play cards. Clearly the notion of public space developed out of a western European context might not help us read a city such as Shanghai, or perhaps even Mexico City, in ways that are useful. We need to strip our concept of the city from the overcharged meanings it currently has.
Saskia Sassen

New York and London, in their endeavours to revitalize former derelict spaces, have progressively defined which users

they envision will use future embellished spaces that look public but in fact are subject to control: either from private security guards (i.e. waterfronts, commercial malls), or from publicly hired security employees (semi-public parks), or by police officers.
Sophie Body-Gendrot

We dream of a new European city where you can walk instead of taking the car, where the places for work, play and living are at a walking distance in a 'pedestrianized' city. If we are dense enough, we can pay for the construction, control and maintenance of public space. We can avoid the conditions that create ghettos, people can talk to each other, and the city then becomes a place for encounters between different cultures, different ideas, different opportunities.
Joan Clos

Now while we agonize over public space in our western sector, ironically in poor developing cities such as Lagos, public space is absolutely not an issue and I would say that public space is a dominant experience of city. Every square metre of the city is used most intensely for private life and public life. There is almost a merging of the two. I have never with my own eyes seen a larger intensity of urban interaction than in these really poor conditions.
Rem Koolhaas

One type of public space that has emerged since 1994 is understandably that which commemorates the struggle against apartheid. Symbolic buildings and public spaces have been built as sites for the presence of occluded histories and the mobilizing of collected bodies. Perhaps it is always like this when urban space is conceived as grand political gesture but surely, I would ask, it should now be layered with the multiple registers of public life, of selling of exchanging, of celebrating, of playing if it is

going to fulfil the revolutionary potential which it commemorates.
Lindsay Bremner

Playing with the words that Lindsay mentioned, actually in one of the papers it says 'making public life', in the second it says 'making public space', and I would shift those words and say making life public and making space public or, as Bruno Latour would say, making things public. We have to imagine that the construction of public space has a wider sense of urgency beyond the duality of the park or the plaza.
José Castillo

Public transport constitutes a major element of 'public space'. The time spent on commuting to work, changing modes or operators, constitutes a major experience of urbanity in Johannesburg.
Mpeththi Morojole

Retro-fitting

All cities that currently exist are going to have to recycle their city spaces and their buildings.
Anne Power

Ambiguity is something that happens over time and in living urban public spaces. This is why the architecture in these spaces is so important: the physical forms have the capacity to mutate.
Richard Sennett

Many who live in Shanghai are very interested in the preservation of the old city and its spaces, but when you look at Xian Ti Di you see a shell of a neighbourhood and a preservation of physical space but no preservation of social infrastructure; losing the surroundings, the community is disappearing and being moved away.
James Ferrer

Risk

Architecture can never be passive and there is a strong intolerance for our profession when we don't have any answers and, perhaps worst, when we don't even claim any answers.
Rem Koolhaas

Architects in London are having a great time now, but in a sense they are playing with fire. The architectural metaphor of the 'zip' to reconnect the tissue of the city looks very good on a sketch. However, when expanded to the scale that we are talking about, it runs the risk of actually backfiring.
Ricky Burdett

Scale

Every project is a mega-project in comparison to developed countries. Different languages, ideas, styles, materials and even a different attitude towards the implementation of projects is what we deal with every day.
Siegfried Zhiqiang Wu

Traditionally cities depended on the division of labour. Human-scale settlements were planned for places where everything from small-scale transactions to wholesale business activities could occur.
Geetam Tiwari

Shanghai's ambition is to once again become a world-class centre of finance, commerce, trade and shipping. It has developed master plans covering over 800 square kilometres in the city to accommodate this growth. About 20 million square metres of housing, offices and other activities are expected to be built every year. This equates to the addition of a city the size of Shanghai in 1949, every two years.
Zheng Shiling

Security

Public space embodies a sense of belonging to the wider political community through an architecture of sympathy, it conveys a sense of safety in the crowd.
Sophie Body-Gendrot

Policymakers seem to be oblivious of the positive impact of street vendors on the social life of a city. The availability of work options on the street provides a positive outlet for employment to a large section of the population that is poor but has entrepreneurial skills. Their presence makes streets relatively crime-free and safer for women, children and older people.
Geetam Tiwari

There is a persistent emphasis on the problem of public space and crime and how a certain type of public space generates criminality. It is not only because we create dark environments that people are more easily mugged. If you generate an environment that does not show respect for human dignity, the whole social organization, the state, will not have enough legitimacy. People will not obey the law and people will not denounce those who break the law simply because they will not identify with the social organization.
Enrique Peñalosa

The police are in the middle ground fighting crime, committing crimes and being over-violent. There is not a fall-back position where the society fights crime.
Helena Maria Gasparian

There is an issue that safety and security are not simply up to the police. There is an element of civility that is required within society and an element of informal control required by society if we are going to create a safe city and a safe world. Obviously this requires some kind of regulatory framework: it can't be completely informal – to allow everyone to do what they want and expect that it's going to sort itself out into some kind of organized chaos – but it also needs a common vision of citizens of what they expect the city to look like.
Evan Rice

Social Cohesion

Gated communities and boom neighbourhoods with high walls dominate the South African landscape, over-responding to crime-prevention challenges and undermining social cohesion at the neighbourhood scale. In fact they enforce the converse effect of creating unsafe spaces.
Ruby Mathang

When we think about densification we need to coordinate questions of density with questions of open space. Density in itself can be quite oppressive without a clear strategy for the development of open space.
Darren Walker

Inclusion fundamentally means the recognition of the presence of others. In this context, the meaning of bonding is not limited to participating to achieve an end but it rather represents the real identification with others in the city.
Richard Sennett

That urban violence is used as an excuse to refuse to live together and enclosures reinforce segregation cannot be ignored. Such attitudes are lethal to cities.
Sophie Body-Gendrot

Social Justice

We see incentives in zoning policy and the links between additional density and the creation of affordable housing as a bedrock way of fighting the potential increased segregation from rising real-estate values.
Shaun Donovan

New York City does work, but it could work a lot better. For the money we invest in our health system, we don't need the infant mortality rates we see in Harlem and other parts of the city; for the amounts that we invest in transport, we don't need our subway system lingering on the edge of collapse; for the money that we invest in housing, we shouldn't have housing of 20-year lives and 30-year mortgages.
Ronald Shiffman

New settlements outside cities are highly energy intensive and socially segregating; they simply cannot go on being funded.
Anne Power

Speed

The speed of urbanization is confounding efforts to maintain the special qualities of cities. Architecture becomes same-ness instead of fine 'grain-ness'; economic speculation outstrips true demand; bold visions are quickly rendered obsolete by rapid change; and processes to engage and empower people in local decisions are eroded.
Bruce Katz

If you want people to move up the social ladder quickly then you need speed. If I do not have a new apartment to move into, the person who wants to buy my apartment has to wait. It is only when I vacate that they can move in. When they vacate, someone else will move in. That is what makes society work well.
Zhang Xin

Two years ago we implemented an urban-development policy that confers tighter controls to the urban-planning authority. We call it 'double decrease, double increase' because it decreases the

means and pace of development and provides the potential to increase the urban character and green areas of the city. This policy slowed the speed of development in Shanghai and provoked a large reaction from developers, leading to noticeable rises in the price of housing, challenging the balance between policies for better urban space and controls to stabilize the market.
Jiang Wu

In both China and India, the two fast-growing mega-economies of the future, the spread of urbanization is taking place along the growth of the informal sector. Since India's independence, we have been doing a lot of planning and making grand master plans but have ended up building roads where there is nothing designed for pedestrians, really nothing designed for bicycles. We have six-lane motorways with standards copied from American or British motorway capacity manuals, but if you notice how the road is being used, the reality is very different. The pedestrians and bicycles that occupy the road are captive users, people without choices. We, as designers, may keep blaming people who do not know how to be on the road, but their reality remains the same.
Geetam Tiwari

Sustainability

To plan a sustainable future we need to think through the linkages between housing, open space and transport infrastructure, otherwise you have people working in silos and isolated projects. The suburban train that is planned to run from the northern area of the Federal District into the State of Mexico is an opportunity to connect the city and the larger region; not just a transport policy but also a land-use policy.
Andy Altman

There is much we can do about the environment, not just locally, but together with other cities. We can form procurement alliances across nations to reduce the cost of environmentally friendly technologies, we can exchange things and work together more economically.
Nicky Gavron

We are essentially accepting the neoliberal global economic agenda when we think of cities as reactive mechanisms. We talk easily about the availability to walk to your job, but on the other hand wider environmental issues are ignored. A small but not trivial example: to send a kiwi fruit from New Zealand to London emits five times the weight of the fruit in greenhouse gases.
Michael Sorkin

The urban-policy framework is limited in its capacity to link public transport to other urban interventions. A case in point is Metrobús, a financially and operatively sustainable project that has also been able to diminish the emission of pollutants. Oddly enough, the project has not been synergized as an architectural element regenerating the city nor as a democratizing element for the city.
Clara Salazar Cruz

The duality between the global city and the insecure local city of the fringes may become the main obstacle for Mexico City to be imagined as an attractive location by those that bind global networks and for the city to reach a more balanced and sustainable development.
Néstor Canclini

Unless planning and urban-renewal strategies acknowledge the transient nature of life in the city – and provide incentives for mobile populations to belong to city life and perceive it as belonging to them – their sustainability and effectiveness will be undermined.
Caroline Kihato

Transport

If we want to deal with traffic safety we have to treat it like a public-health issue where you don't depend on people doing the right thing on their own. People will make mistakes, so we have to make a forgiving infrastructure.
Geetam Tiwari

The dilemma is that if we try to improve the mobility of our city, we induce more people to drive cars; if we do not, mounting congestion makes our city unliveable. From 1986 to 2004, the area serviced by underground lines increased by 50 per cent but the average trip length remained the same at about 13 minutes. This is an advantage of improved mobility that critics of transport planning in Shanghai do not see.
Xiaohong Chen

Despite huge investment in its transport system – over US$40 billion in the last decade – New York suffers from a flawed system of governance where the budget of the Mass Transit Authority is determined hundreds of miles away in the state capital of New York – resulting in poor strategic coordination.
Ricky Burdett

One possible contribution to respond to the increasing demands on mass transport is to change the way we conceive stations. To think of the transportation terminal as an object, an ascetic monument not connected to the social and commercial tissues of the city, misses the opportunity to explore contemporary forms of transportation space.
Alejandro Zaera-Polo

The deep problem of transport in our metropolis is rooted in the predominance of low-capacity vehicles. Interestingly, we find 50,000 utility vehicles, minivans and minibuses that constitute the majority of trips. In addition to the 160,000 taxis in the agglom-

eration, we must also count the half a million vehicles used for the transport of goods and messenger services. These units make an intensive use of road space and, given the fragmentary corporate organization of the sector, they are also highly inefficient.
Bernardo Navarro Benitez

When we talk about the safety of an area, and seek community support and the involvement of residents, when we want them to be the 'eyes on the street' that organically generate a sense of security, they cannot do that if their eyes and ears are clogged, if the public space that surrounds them is obliterated by cars.
Hermann Knoflacher

Urban Economy

Our primary challenge in contemporary Johannesburg is how to boost delivery and at the same time achieve better quality living environments, sustainable human settlements, quality neighbourhoods and quality houses that will be identified, or at least recognized, by the owners as an asset; and not just by the owners but by the industry too, so that a person who owns a house can use that house to participate in the economy of this country.
Uhuru Nene

Urban Form

We need a vision for the future – explicit social, economic and cultural goals. Transport improvements must be consistent with other urban dynamics and interventions on the city.
Clara Salazar Cruz

Not only are we asked, as designers, to provide forms that have to be amenable to housing, retail, office space, but also to a mixture, and preferably several iter-

ations of this mixture over an extended period of time. So if one formula does not work, another could. All of that has to be done while providing an identity or an immediate character that precedes and survives their use, their occupation.
Hashim Sarkis

The informal is not identifiable as a pattern or morphology, but nonetheless manufactures the material reality of urban form. It is an alliance of transformative ingenuity and the tactical mobilization of resources, produced from conditions of need and in the almost complete absence of centralization.
Rem Koolhaas

Urban designers in a time of turbulent social and technological change can and indeed must be prepared to use design to accelerate cultural and organizational change, using persuasion as well as imagination to bridge the social and the physical. Urban design can be strengthened and its relevance ratified only by its being part of a wider process of cultural, operational and economic revitalization, a condition that is even more relevant at the urban scale than in individual buildings.
Frank Duffy

Urbanization

The complexity of urbanization mocks dominant conventions of urban policy: one-dimensional, compartmentalized, driven by specialized professions, often incoherent and even contradictory.
Bruce Katz

The word 'gentrification' that only a decade ago had a very negative connotation has now become frankly positive, with urban life reduced to four sectors: film screenings, music, shopping and fashion. We have therefore seen a kind of systematic laundering of authentic conditions in urban life in the name of

those four categories.
Rem Koolhaas

A city is an *à la carte* menu – that is what makes it different from a village which offers so much less in the way of choice. A positive vision of urbanity has to be based on ensuring that more and more customers can afford to make the choice.
Deyan Sudjic

CONFERENCE PARTICIPANTS

URBAN AGE CONFERENCE PARTICIPANTS
2005–2006

Josef Ackermann, Chairman of Group Executive Committee, Deutsche Bank
Brigitte Adam, Federal Office for Building and Regional Planning, Bonn
David Adjaye, Principal, Adjaye Associates, London
Taffy Adler, CEO, Johannesburg Housing Company
Gerd-Axel Ahrens, Professor for Transport and Infrastructure Planning, TU Dresden
Omar Akbar, Director, Bauhaus Dessau Foundation
Monica Albonico, Albonico & Sack, Architects & Urban Designers, Johannesburg
Simon, Allford, Partner, Allford Hall Monaghan Morris, London
Bob Allies, Partner, Allies and Morrison, London
Ashley Ally, CEO, Izingwe, Johannesburg
Will Alsop, Chairman, Alsop Design, London
Andy Altman, former Planning Director, Washington DC
Miriam Altman, Human Sciences Research Council of South Africa
Julio Amezcua, Founder, Estudio AT103, Mexico City
Donald Anderson, Leader, Edinburgh City Council
Manuel Arango Arias, President, Grupo Concord, Mexico City
Anton Arendse, Director of Policy Planning, Department of Housing, Gauteng
Stephan Articus, Director, German Association of Cities
Joanna Averley, Deputy Chief Executive, CABE, London
George Azariah-Moreno, LSE
Karel Bakker, Professor, Department of Architecture, University of Pretoria
Peter Barber, Peter Barber Architects, London
Richard Baron, McCormack Baron & Associates, St Louis
Julian Baskin, CEO, Alexandra Renewal Project, Johannesburg
Stephen Bates, Principal, Sergison Bates, London
Donald Bates, Lab Architecture Studio, London
Guy Battle, Battle McCarthy, London
Alex Bax, Mayor's Office, Greater London Authority
Robert Beauregard, Professor of Urban Studies, New School University, New York
Keith Beavon, University of Pretoria
Terence Bendixson, Independent Transport Commission, University of Southampton
Pablo Benlliure, Planning Department, Mexico City
Deidre Berger, Director, The American Jewish Committee, Berlin
Knut Bergmann, Office of the Federal President of Germany, Berlin
Ann Bernstein, Founding Director, Center for Development and Enterprise, Johannesburg
Joe Berridge, Partner, Urban Strategies, Toronto
Lael Bethlehem, Director, Johannesburg Development Agency
Robert Beyer, Broker Fisher Brothers, New York
Timon Beyes, University of St Gallen
Wieslaw Bielawski, Deputy Mayor of the City of Gdansk
Peter Bishop, Director, Design for London
Ian Blair, Commissioner, Metropolitan Police, London
Ulrich Blum, Institut für Wirtschaftsforschung, Halle
Paul Boateng, British High Commission in South Africa
Harald Bodenschatz, University of Technology, Berlin
Sophie Body-Gendrot, Director, Center for Urban Studies, Sorbonne, Paris
Norbert Bogendörfer, MDSE Mitteldeutsche Sanierungs, Berlin
Andreas Bohm, Liberal Party, Berlin
Max Bond, Max Bond Architects, New York
Matthew Bonning-Snook, Development Executive, Helical Bar, London

Elsabe Booyens, Deputy Director, Head of Marketing, City of Johannesburg
Andrew Boraine, Chair, South Africa Cities Network
Werner Borrmann, Executive Director, A.T. Kearney GmbH, Berlin
Michael Bose, Technical University, Hamburg-Harburg
Alfonso Botha, CEO, Urban Ocean, Johannesburg
Klaus Brake, Professor for Urban and Regional Development, Berlin
Doug Branson, Branson Coates Architecture, London
Benita Braun-Feldweg, GF bfstudio-architekten, Berlin
Ingrld Breckner, HafenCity University, Hamburg
Eckhardt Bremer, Solicitor, Hogan & Hartson Raue LLP, Berlin
Lindsay Bremner, Chair, Architecture Program Temple University, Philadelphia
Alfredo Brillembourg, Director, Caracas Urban Think Tank
Oliver Brinkmann, Deutsche Bank AG, Shanghai
Lynn Broadbent, Secretary, Royal Society of Arts in the US, New York
Patricia Brown, Chief Executive, Central London Partnership
Peter Brown, Chief Operating Officer, Transport for London
Colin Brown, Director of Corporate Affairs, Deutsche Bank Africa Foundation
George Brugmans, Director, Architecture Biennale Rotterdam
Cesar Buenrostro Hernández, Government of the Federal District, Mexico City
Lucy Bullivant, Architectural critic, London
Amanda M. Burden, Chair, City Planning Commission Planning Department, New York City
Ricky Burdett, Director, Urban Age, LSE
Wilhelm Bürklin, Member of the Board, Bundesverband Deutscher Banken, Berlin
Hans-Joachim Bürkner, Research Institute for Regional Development and Structural Planning, Berlin
Kim Burnett, Programme Officer, The Surdna Foundation, New York
Marie Burns, Director, Burns + Nice, London
Friedrich Busmann, Curator, 1200 Jahre, Halle
Joan Busquets, Professor, Barcelona GSD, Harvard University, Cambridge, MA
Nazira Cachalia, Economic Development Unit, Johannesburg
Xavier Calderon, Mexico City
Tina Di Carlo, Curator MoMA, New York
Matthew Carmona, Head, Bartlett School of Planning, University College, London
André Odenbreit Carvalho, Brazilian Embassy, London
Héctor Castillo Berthier, Universidad Nacional Autónoma de México
Laura Itzel Castillo Juárez, Secretary for Urban Design and the Environment, Government of the Federal District, Mexico City
José Manuel Castillo Olea, Universidad Iberoamericana, School of Architecture, Mexico City
Yung Ho Chang, Head of Department of Architecture, MIT, Cambridge, MA
Weishu Chen, Vice Chairman, Shanghai Industrial Investment Co.
Christina Chen, British Consulate-General, Shanghai
Wei Chen, Shanghai Economy Studies, Shanghai Academy of Social Sciences
Xiaohong Chen, School of Transportation Engineering, Tongji University, Shanghai
Xiangming Chen, Dean, Center of Urban and Global Studies at Trinity College, Hartford, CT
David Chou-Shulin, Partner, OUM, Shanghai
Thomas Chow, Director, SURV, Shanghai
Kees Christiaanse, Partner, KCAP Architects and Planners, Rotterdam
Susan Christopherson, Professor City and Regional Planning

Department, Cornell University, Ithaca, NY
Annie Chung, Senior Architect, Arup
Dominic Church, CABE, London
Joan Clos, former Mayor of the City of Barcelona; Minister of Energy, Trade and Tourism of the Spanish Government
Nigel Coates, Professor of Architecture, Royal College of Art, London
Henry Cobb, Pei Cobb Freed and Partners, New York
Job Cohen, Mayor of the City of Amsterdam
Hans-Jürgen Commerell, Direktor Aedes Architekturforum, Berlin
John Connorton, Hawkins Delafield & Wood, New York
Cas Coovadia, Managing Director, The Banking Association of South Africa
José Luis Cortés Delgado, Department of Architecture, Universidad Iberoamericana, Mexico City
René Coulomb Bosc, Professor, Universidad Autónoma Metropolitana, Mexico City
Jeremy Cronin, Deputy Secretary General, South African Communist Party
Teddy Cruz, Professor, University of California, San Diego
Sarah Curtis, Professor, Department of Geography, Queen Mary, University of London
Andre Czegledy, Anthropology Department, University of the Witwatersrand, Johannesburg
Markus Dahmen, Head Public Sector Germany, Deutsche Bank AG
Howard Davies, Director, LSE
Wendy Davis, Director, Women's Design Service, London
Diane Davis, Associate Dean, School of Architecture and Planning, MIT, Cambridge, MA
Henry Davis, Metrópoli 2025, Mexico City
Craig Davis Arzac, SEDESOL, Federal Government, Mexico City
Xavier De Souza-Briggs, Associate Professor of Sociology and Urban Planning, MIT, Cambridge, MA
Isabel Dedring, Director Policy Unit, Transport for London
Dave DeGroot, World Bank, Pretoria Office
Johannes Dell, Albert Speer and Partner, Shanghai
Gabor Demszky, Mayor of the City of Budapest
Bernhard M. Deppisch, Director, Deutsche Bank AG
Klaus Deutsch, Senior Economist, DB Research, Deutsche Bank AG
Patrick Diamond, Director, Policy Network, London
Oscar Edmundo Diaz, Director, Por el País que Queremos Foundation, Bogota
Alessandra DiGiusto, Deutsche Bank, Americas Foundation, New York
Harry Dimitriou, Bartlett School of Planning, University College London
Heather Dodd, Partner, Savage Dodd Architects, Johannesburg
Marta Döhler-Behzadi, Office for Urban Projects, Leipzig
Shanfeng Dong, Senior Urban Designer, Arup, Shanghai
Shaun Donovan, Commissioner, Department of Housing Preservation and Development, New York City
Mathias Döpfner, Axel Springer Verlag AG, Berlin
Frank Duffy, Principal, DEGW, London
Marcelo Ebrard, Mayor of Mexico City Federal District
Roberto Eibenschutz, former Director of Planning, Government of the Federal District, Mexico City
Franziska Eichstädt-Bohlig, Green Party, Berlin
Harald Eisenach, Member ExCo, German MidCaps Deutsche Bank AG
Peter Eisenman, Eisenman Architects, New York
John Ellis, Director of Urban Design, Solomon ETC, San Francisco
Alejandro Encinas, former Mayor of Mexico City Federal District
Lutz Engelke, CEO, Triad, Berlin

City of Johannesburg
Anthony Mayer, Chief Executive Greater, London Authority
Sithole Mbanga, CEO, South African Cities Network, Johannesburg
Siyabonga Mbanjwa, Regional Development Manager, Old Mutual Properties, Johannesburg
Achille Mbembe, Professor in History and Politics, WISER, University of the Witwatersrand, Joahnnesburg
Rory McGowan, Director, Arup, Beijing
Rocky McKnight, Corporate Relations Manager, LSE
Deborah McKoy, Director, Center on Cities and Schools, University of California, Berkeley
Donald McNeill, Professor, Department of Geography, King's College London
Markus Mehlin, German Aerospace Center, Berlin
Florian Meinel, Wissenschaftszentrum, Berlin
Maria Dora Victoriana Mejia Marulanda, Ambassador of Colombia, Berlin
Magali Menant, Delegation of German Industry and Commerce, Shanghai
Angela Merkel, Chancellor, Federal Republic of Germany
Ulrich Meyer-Höllings, Managing Director, HKLM Europe
Lothar Meyer-Mertel, Manager, City-Marketing, Halle
Niq Mhlope, Novelist, Johannesburg
Arturo Mier y Terán, Housing Improvement Programme, Colegio de Arquitectos, Mexico City
Ishmael Mkhabela, Community Development Association, Johannesburg
John Mollenkopf, Department of Political Science, CUNY, New York
Harvey Molotch, Professor of Sociology, New York University
Barbara Molsen, Director, Radio Programme MDR, Leipzig
Rowan Moore, Director, The Architecture Foundation, London
Maria Moreno, Department of Architecture, University of California, Berkeley
Mphethi Morojele, Director MMA Architects, Johannesburg
Graham Morrison, Allies and Morrison, London
Bruno Moser, Research Associate, Urban Age, LSE
Edgar Most, Deutsche Bank AG
Mohsen Mostafavi, Dean School of Architecture, Cornell University, Ithaca, NY
Fanuel Motsepe, Director, Motsepe Architects Pty Ltd, Johannesburg
Eric Motshwane, Chair, Johannesburg Regional Taxi Council
Matthias Muffert, Architekt bfstudio-architekten Gbr, Berlin
Meike Müller, mc-quadrat, Berlin
Julia Müller, Centre for Urban Regeneration, Görlitz
Thomas Müller-Bahlke, Director, Franckesche Stiftungen, Halle
Alfred Munkenbeck, Munkenbeck + Marshall Architects, London
Peter Murray, Chair, Wordsearch, London
Bernardo Navarro Benitez, Professor, Universidad Autónoma Metropolitana, Mexico City
Jo Negrini, London Borough of Lambeth
David Nelson, Deputy Chairman, Foster + Partners, London
Uhuru Nene, Executive Director, Housing, City of Johannesburg
Dick Netzer, Wagner School of Public Service, New York University
Christian Neuhaus, Society & Technology Research Group, DaimlerChrysler AG
Yuemin Ning, Professor of Urban Geography, East China Normal University, Shanghai
Seana Nkhahle, National Programme Coordinator, South African Cities Network
Peter Noetzel, Mayor of the City of Bottrop
Lindiwe Nonceba Sisulu, Minister of Housing, South Africa
Loyiso Nongxa, Vice Chancellor, University of the Witwatersrand, Johannesburg
Catherine Seavitt Nordenson, Catherine Seavitt Studio, New York
Guy Nordenson, Professor of Structural Engineering, Princeton University
Enrique Norten, TEN Arquitectos, New York
Leonard Novy, Project Manager, Bertelsmann Foundation, Gütersloh
Johannes Novy, Columbia University, New York
Wolfgang Nowak, Managing Director, AHS
Nkele Ntingane, Speaker of Council, City of Johannesburg
Sarah Nuttall, Senior Researcher, WISER, University of the Witwatersrand, Johannesburg
Ralf Oberdorfer, Mayor, City of Plauen
Nicola Oddati, Deputy Mayor of the City of Naples
Michael O'Donovan, Human Sciences Research Council of South Africa
Nicholas Olsberg, Canadian Centre for Architecture, Montreal
Giles Omezi, Architect, Allies and Morrison, London
Mark Oranje, Head of Department of Urban and Regional Planning, University of Pretoria
Iliana Ortega-Alcazar, Researcher, Urban Age, LSE
Enrique Ortíz Flores, President, Habitat International Coalition, Mexico City
Jo Osae-Addo, Architect, JADDO Studio, Johannesburg
Franz Oswald, Professor of Architecture and Urbanism, ETH Zurich
Philipp Oswalt, Shrinking Cities, Berlin
Robert E. Paaswell, Director, Institute for Urban Systems, The City College of New York
Rosalind Paaswell, Vice-President, National Development Council, New York
Maria Edith Pacheco Gomez, Colegio de México, Mexico City
Adrián Pandal, Director, Fundación del Centro Histórico, Mexico City
Xiaokui Pang, Project Manager, KfW Bankengruppe, Beijing
Eric Parry, Principal, Eric Parry Architects, London
PS Pasricha, Director General, Maharashtra State Police, Mumbai
Pankaj Patel, Patel Taylor Architects, London
Joachim Paulick, Mayor of City of Görlitz,, Federal Republic of Germany
Wolfgang Peiner, Department of Finance, City of Hamburg
Enrique Peña Nieto, Governor of the State of Mexico
Enrique Peñalosa, former Mayor of Bogotá
Xizhe Peng, Dean and Professor School of Social Policy and Public Policy, Fudan University, Shanghai
Manuel Perló Cohen, Universidad Nacional Autónoma de México, Mexico City
Deike Peters, Graduate Research Program Berlin-New York, University of Technology, Berlin
Nikolai Petersen, Head of Programmes, Goethe Insitut, Johannesburg
Karen Phillips, former Commissioner New York City Planning Department, New York
Volker Pietsch, District Administrator, Landkreis Sangerhausen, Sachsen-Anhalt
Elke Plate, Senate Department for Urban Development, Berlin
Ben Plowden, Managing Director, Group Communications, Transport for London
John Polak, Director of Centre for Transport Studies, Imperial College, London
Lee Polisano, President, Kohn Pederson Fox, London
Lone Poulsen, School of Architecture and Planning, University of the Witwatersrand, Johannesburg
Georgina Pozo Rivas, Planning Secretariat, Government of the State of Mexico
Anne Power, Profesor of Social Policy, LSE
Emilio Pradilla-Cobos, Professor, Universidad Autónoma Metropolitana, Mexico City
Sunand Prasad, Penoyre and Prasad, London
Jason Prior, EDAW, London
Pamela Puchalski, Projects Coordinator, Urban Age, LSE
Dirk Punk-Jakobsen, Head, Transport, Building and Urban Development Unit, Chancellor's Office, Berlin
Steven Purcell, Council Leader, Glasgow City Council
Bruce M. Ramer, Board member, AHS
Hector Ramos, Vice President, Deutsche Bank Americas Foundation, Mexico City
Klaus-Peter Rauen, Curator, 1200 Jahre, Halle
Richard Ravitch, Principal, Ravitch, Rice & Company, New York
Elias Redstone, Curator, Architecture Foundation, London
Graeme Reid, Director, Urban Skywalkers, Johannesburg
Yuan Ren, Center for Urban and Regional Development Studies, Fudan University, Shanghai
Nicolas Retsinas, Director, Joint Center for Housing Studies, Harvard University, Cambridge, MA
Eric Reynolds, Managing Director, Urban Space Management, London
Stefan Richter, Triad, Berlin
Charles Rifkind, Partner, Rifkind Levy Partnership, London
Kristien Ring, Director, German Architecture Centre, Berlin
Bernardo Riojas Achutegui President, Desarrolladora Metropolitana, Mexico City
Philipp Rode, Executive Director, Urban Age, LSE
Jonathan Rose, Principal, Jonathan Rose Companies, New York
Daniel Rose, President and CEO, Rose Associates, New York
Jeremy Rose, Partner, Mashabane Rose Architects, Johannesburg
Markus Rosenthal, Rosenthal Relations, Berlin
Bridget Rosewell, Chief Economist, Greater London Authority
John Ross Director, Economic and Business Policy, Greater London Authority
Wolfgang Roters, Director, Museum für Architektur und Ingenieurkunst NRW
Richard Rubens, Columbia University, New York
Margot Rubin, Researcher, CUBES, University of the Witwatersrand, Johannesburg
David Rudlin, Director, Urbed, Manchester
Antònia Sabartés, Director International Relations, Barcelona City Council
Michael Sachs, Policy Planning and Evaluation, Gauteng Provincial Government
Susan Saegert, Professor of Sociology, Graduate Center, CUNY, New York
Yehuda Safran, Professor of Architecture, Columbia University, New York
Heinz Sahner, Professor of Sociology, Martin Luther University,Halle-Wittenberg
Roland Sahr, Vice President, CIB Global Banking, Deutsche Bank AG
Ayse Saktanber, Professor of Sociology, Middle East Technical University, Ankara
Clara Salazar Cruz, Colegio de México, Mexico City
Robert Salkeld, Senior Consultant, URS Corporation Ltd, London
Jenny Saltiel Cohen, Secretary for Economic Development, Government of the Federal District, Mexico City
Claudia Samlenski, Embassy of the Republic of South-Africa, Berlin
Javier Sánchez, Higuera & Sánchez, Mexico City
R. F. Sandenbergh, Dean of the Faculty of Engineering, Built Environment and Information Technology, University of Pretoria
Robert Sander, Scientist, German Institute of Urban Affairs, Berlin
Georgina Sandoval, Casa y Ciudad AC, Mexico City
Lino Santacruz, Embassy of Mexico, Berlin
Hashim Sarkis, Aga Khan Professor of Landscape Architecture & Urbanism, Harvard University, Cambridge, MA
Saskia Sassen, Centennial Visiting Professor, LSE and Professor, Committee on Global Thought, Columbia University, New York
Vishwas Satgar, Executive Director, Co-operative and Policy Alternative Centre (COPAC), Yeoville
Stephan Sattler, *Focus Magazin*, Board Member, AHS
Christoph Sattler, Sattler & Sattler, Berlin
Matthias Sauerbruch, Sauerbruch Hutton Architects, Berlin
Deborah Saunt, DSDHA, London
Rosemary Scanlon, Real Estate Institute, New York University
Frank Schade, Mayor of the City of Blankenburg
Michael Schädlich, Director, Institute for Economic Development, Halle
Rudolf Schäfer, Dean of the Department of Architecture, Environment and Society, Berlin Technical University
Sandro Schaffner, Landscape Architect, Grupo de Diseño Urbano (GDU), Mexico City
Carolin Scheffler, Producer, Hoferichter & Jacobs, Berlin
Mario Schjetnan, Founder, Grupo de Diseño Urbano, Mexico City
Oliver Schmidt, Executive Director, Center for Metropolitan Studies, TU Berlin
Martha Schteingart, Colegio de México, Mexico City
Nicola Schüller, Institute for Urban Design, ETH Zurich
Angelika Schulz, German Aerospace Centre, Berlin
Gunnar Folke Schuppert, Professor of Governance Social Science Research Centre, Berlin
Alex Schwartz, Milano Graduate School, New School, New York
Martha Schwartz, President Martha Schwartz Inc, Boston
Christoph Schwöbel, Eberhard Karls Universität, Tübingen
Peter Schwinger, Researcher, Urban Age, LSE
Elliot Sclar, Professor of Urban Planning and Public Affairs, Columbia University, New York
Rashid Seedat, Director, Corporate Planning Unit, City of Johannesburg
Lisa Seftel, Government Department for Public Transport, Gauteng Province
Peter Seifert, Mayor, City of Chemnitz
Liuz Felipe Seixas Correa, Ambassador, Brazilian Embassy, Berlin
Richard Sennett, Profesor of Sociology, LSE, London and MIT, Cambridge, MA
Nicholas Serota, Director, Tate, London
Narcís Serra, former Mayor of Barcelona, President Fundació CIDOB, Barcelona
Jose Serra, Governor of São Paulo
Adi Shamir, Executive Director, Van Alen Institute, New York
Bob Shead, British Consulate-General, Shanghai
Claudia Sheinbaum Pardo, Secretary of the Environment, Government of the Federal District, Mexico City
Wang Shi, Chair, China Vanke Co Ltd, Shenzhen City
Ron Shiffman, Graduate Center for Planning and the Environment, Pratt Institute, New York
Ullrich Sierau Department of Urban Planning, City of Dortmund
Thomas Sieverts, Architect, KAT, Bonn
Richard Simmons, Chief Executive, CABE, London
Audrey Singer, The Brookings Institution, Washington DC
Heidi Sinning, Professor, University of Applied Sciences, Erfurt
Joshua Sirefman, Director, Economic Development and Rebuilding, City of New York
Edward Skloot, Executive Director, The Surdna Foundation, New York
Dan Smit, Development Consultant, Johannesburg
Sylvia Smith, Fox and Fowle Architects, New York
Edgard Soja, Professor, LSE, London and University of California, Los Angeles
Elena Solis, Universidad Iberoamericana, Mexico City
René Solis Brun, Metrópoli 2025, Mexico City
Hussein Solomon, University of Pretoria
Rainer Sontowski, Federal Ministry of the Environment, Berlin
Michael Sorkin, Michael Sorkin Studio, New York
Werner Spec, Mayor of the City of Ludwigsburg
Albert Speer, Albert Speer & Partner, Frankfurt am Main
Saidee Springall, Principal, arquitectura 911sc, Mexico City
David Stark, Columbia University, New York
Dietmar Steiner, Director, Vienna Architecture Centre
Richard Stemmler, Technical University Berlin
Gus Stewart, Director, Research and Project Development Division, LSE
Hans Stimmann, former Director of the Department for City Planning, Berlin
Ulf Stötzel, Mayor of the City of Siegen
Michael Storper, Centennial Professor of Economic Geography, LSE

Norbert Streitz, Senior Scientist and Strategic Adviser, Fraunhofer IPSI, Berlin
Ning Su, Institute of World Economy, Shanghai Academy of Social Sciences
Deyan Sudjic, Director, Design Museum, London
Jürg Sulzer, Professor for Urban Redevelopment, Technical University of Dresden
Stuart Suna, President, Silvercup Studios, Berlin
Alan Suna, CEO, Silvercup Studios, Berlin
Nicole Surchat Vial, Director, Urbanistes sans Frontières, Geneva
Graeme Sutherland, Director, Adams and Sutherland, London
Pierre Swanepoel, Urban Designer, studio MAS architects, Johannesburg
Robert Tavernor, Director, Cities Programme, LSE
Andrew Taylor, Shalom Baranes Associates, New York
Marilyn Taylor, Partner, Skidmore Owings and Merrill, New York
Eduardo Terrazas, Terrazas Arquitectos Urbanistas, Mexico City
Oscar Terrazas, Profesor, Universidad Autónoma Metropolitana, Mexico City
Joachim Thiel, Scientist, HafenCity University, Hamburg
Freddy Thielemans, Mayor of the City of Brussels
Philip Thomas, Consul-General, British Embassy, New York
Ian Thomas, Chief Superintendent for Southwark, Southwark Borough Police, London
Ciko Thomas, CEO, Johannesburg City Auto
Victoria Thornton, Founding Director, Open House, London
Julia Thrift, Director, CABE Space, London
Geetam Tiwari, Chair and Associate Professor, TRIPP, Civil Engineering Department, Indian Institute of Technology, Delhi
Wolfgang Tiefensee, Minister for Transport, Building and City Planning, German Federal Government
Richard Tomlinson, School of Architecture and Planning, University of the Witwatersrand, Johannesburg
Fran Tonkiss, Cities Programme, LSE
Thorsten Tonndorf, Senate Department for City Development, Berlin
Steve Topham, Managing Director, International Organization Development South Africa
Hartmut H. Topp, Professor for Transport Planning, Technical University of Kaiserslautern
Michèle Tranda-Pittion, Swiss Federal Institute of Technology, Lausanne
Tony Travers, Director, Greater London Group, LSE
Alexander Trog, Patron, Johann Wolfgang Goethe University, Frankfurt
Shin-pei Tsay, Director of Marketing, Project for Public Spaces, New York
Qiyu Tu, Shanghai Academy of Social Sciences
Jürgen Turek, Managing Director, Center for Applied Policy Research, Munich
Derek Turner, Managing Director Street Management, Transport for London
Sebastian Turner, Scholz + Friends AG, Berlin; Board Member AHS
Günther Uhlig, Karlsruhe University
Florian Urban, Center for Metropolitan Studies, Technical University, Berlin
Arnulfo Valdivia Machuca, International Relations, Governor of the State of Mexico
Lawrence Vale, Ford Professor of Urban & Environmental Planning, MIT, Cambridge, MA
Sue Valentine, Director, Media Program, Open Society Foundation, Johannesburg
Ahmedi Vawda, Deputy Director-General, National Department of Housing, South Africa
Eduardo Vega López, Government of Mexico City
America Vera-Zavala, Attac Sweden; Board Member AHS
Savvas Verdis, Cities Programme, LSE
Francisco Vidal Luna, Municipal Planning Secretary, City of São Paulo
Rafael Viñoly, Rafael Vinoly Architects, New York
Francois Viruly, School of Construction Economics and Management, University of the Witwatersrand, Johannesburg
Marc Vlessing, Director, Pocket, London
Hortensia Völkers, Director, Kulturstiftung des Bundes, Halle
Wolfgang von Eckartsberg, Managing Director, Deutsche Bank AG
Tessen von Heydebreck, Deutsche Bank AG and Board Member, AHS
Hilmar von Lojewski, Senate Department for Urban Development, Berlin
Herrman Freiherr von Richthofen, Barclays Capital
Julie Wagner, Assistant, Brookings Institution, Washington DC
Olly Wainwright, Urban Designer, Greater London Authority
Darren Walker, Vice-President, Rockefeller Foundation, New York
Norbert Walter, Deutsche Bank AG
Frank Wang, Project Architect, SURV, Shanghai
Hongxia Wang, Centre for Urban and Regional Studies, Shanghai Academy of Social Sciences
Guixin Wang, Center for Urban and Regional Development Studies, Fudan University, Shanghai
Hong Xia Wang, Centre for Urban & Regional Studies, Shanghai

Academy of Social Sciences
Beate Weber, Mayor of City of Heidelberg
Josef Weber, Chief Urban Planner, City of Halle
Stefan Weber, Deputy Chairman of the Board, Sächsische Aufbaubank
Ute Weiland, Coordinator LSE-AHS, AHS
Ronald Weichert, Deputy Head Press Department Germany, Deutsche Bank AG
George Weidenfeld, Board Member, AHS
Ursula Weidenfeld, Der Tagesspiegel
Franz Weigt, University Potsdam
Carl Weisbrod, former President, New York Downtown Alliance
Dorothee Wenner, Director, Talent Campus, International Film Festival, Berlin
Mike West, Managing Director, Head of Communications, Asia Pacific Deutsche Bank AG
Paul White, Executive Director Transportation Alternatives, New York City
Sarah Whiting, Associate Professor of Architecture Graduate School of Design, Harvard University, Cambridge, MA
Gerhard Widder, Mayor, City of Mannheim
Irene Wiese von Ofen, Director Executive Board, EUROPAN, Germany
Axel Wiesener, Deutsche Bank AG
Anthony Williams, former Mayor of Washington DC
Stuart Wilson, Centre for Applied Legal Studies, University of the Witwatersrand, Johannesburg
Murray Winckler, CEO Deutsche Bank SA & Head of Global Markets, Deutsche Bank SA
Alexander Winkler, Vice President Global Banking, Deutsche Bank AG
Stephen Witherford, Director, Witherford Watson Mann Architects, London
Josef Wolf, Director, Department of Public Works, Schwerin
Michael Wolffsohn, Gartenstadt Atlantic, Berlin
Petra Wollenberg, Insitute for Urban Design, ETH Zurich
Karen Wong, Managing Director, Adjaye Associates, London
Sarah Worthington, Deputy Director, LSE
Klaus Wowereit, Mayor of the City of Berlin
Thomas Wright, Executive Vice President, Regional Plan Association, New York
Jiang Wu, Deputy Director, Shanghai Municipal Urban Planning Bureau
Yue Wu Chief Planner, Planning Bureau of Pudong, Shanghai
Gerd Würdemann, Federal Office for Building and Regional Planning, Bonn
Paul Wygers, Urban Solutions Architects and Urban Designers, Johannesburg
Kathryn Wylde, President and CEO, The Partnership for New York City
Zhang Xin, Co-CEO, Soho China, Beijing
Peikun Yang, Doctoral Supervisor, Tongji University, Shanghai
Robert Yaro, President, Regional Plan Association, New York
Sauw Yim, CIB Divisional Functions, Deutsche Bank
Yonnie Yiu, National Sales Manager, Haworth, Shanghai
Guillermo Ysusi Farfán, Planning Department, Government of the Federal District, Mexico City
Alejandro Zaera-Polo, Architect, Foreign Office Architects, London
Mirko Zardini, Director, Canadian Centre for Architecture, Montreal
Gang Zeng, School of Resources and Environmental Science, East China Normal University
Nicola Zeuner, Friedrich-Ebert-Foundation, Berlin
Lee Zhang, Managing Director, Global Banking, Deutsche Bank, China
Jiwen Zhang, Vice President, China Vanke Co Ltd, Shenzhen
Shiling Zheng, Architecture Urban Planning Commission of Shanghai Municipal Government
Siegfried Zhiqiang Wu, Dean and Professor, College of Architecture and Urban Planning, Tongji University, Shanghai
Rose Zhu, Director and CEO, Deutsche Bank in China
Xiaofeng Zhu, Architect, Scenic Architecture, Shanghai
Dajian Zhu, Professor of Economics and Sustainable Development, Harvard University, Cambridge, MA, and Tongji University, Shanghai
Peter Zlonicky, Urban Planner and Architect, Büro für Stadtplanung und Stadtforschung, Munich
Roger Zogolovitch, Director, AZ Urban Studio, London
Sharon Zukin, Professor of Sociology Brooklyn College, CUNY, New York
Xuejin Zuo, Institute of Economics, Shanghai Academy of Social Sciences

URBAN AGE TEAM

Urban Age Board
Ricky Burdett, *Director, Urban Age, LSE*
Philipp Rode, *Executive Director, Urban Age, LSE*
Ute Weiland, *Coordinator, AHS-LSE, AHS*
Wolfgang Nowak, *Managing Director, AHS*
Bruce Katz, *Vice President & Director, Metropolitan Policy Progam, Brookings Institution, Washington DC*
Andy Altman, *Planning Director 1999 to 2004, Washington DC*

Advisory Board
Richard Sennett (Co-chair), *Professor of Sociology, LSE & MIT*
Deyan Sudjic (Co-chair), *Director, Design Museum, London*
David Adjaye, *Architect, Adjaye Associates, London*
Sophie Body-Gendrot, *Director, Center for Urban Studies, Sorbonne, Paris*
Amanda M. Burden, *Chair, City Planning Commission and Director, Department of City Planning, New York City*
Yung Ho Chang, *Head of Department of Architecture, MIT, Cambridge, MA*
Xiangming Chen, *Founding Dean and Director, Center for Urban and Global Studies, Trinity College, Hartford, CT*
Joan Clos, *Mayor of Barcelona 1997 to 2006, from 2006 Minister of Industry, Tourism and Trade, Spain*
Frank Duffy, *Architect, DEGW, London*
Gerald Frug, *Louis D. Brandeis Professor of Law, Harvard University, Cambridge, MA*
Niall Hobhouse, *Governor, LSE and member of Urban Age Steering Committee*
Gareth Jones, *Senior Lecturer in Development Geography, LSE*
Hermann Knoflacher, *Professor of Transport Planning and Traffic Engineering, Vienna University of Technology*
Rem Koolhaas, *Architect, Office for Metropolitan Architecture, Rotterdam*
Dieter Läpple, *Professor of Urban & Regional Economics, HafenCity University, Hamburg*
Murray Low, *Lecturer in Human Geography, LSE*
Guy Nordenson, *Professor of Structural Engineering, Princeton University and Engineer, Guy Nordenson and Associates*
Enrique Peñalosa, *former Mayor of Bogotá*
Anne Power, *Professor of Social Policy, LSE*
Hashim Sarkis, *Aga Khan Professor of Landscape Architecture & Urbanism, Harvard University, Cambridge, MA*
Saskia Sassen, *Centennial Visiting Professor, LSE and Professor, Committee on Global Thought, Columbia University, New York*
Edward Soja, *Professor, LSE and University of California, Los Angeles*
Michael Storper, *Centennial Professor of Economic Geography, LSE*
Geetam Tiwari, *Chair and Associate Professor, TRIPP, Civil Engineering Department, Indian Institute of Technology, Delhi*
Tony Travers, *Director, Greater London Group, LSE*
Lawrence Vale, *Ford Professor of Urban & Environmental Planning, MIT, Cambridge, MA*
Anthony Williams, *former Mayor, Washington DC*
Alejandro Zaera-Polo, *Architect, Foreign Office Architects, London*
Siegfried Zhiqiang Wu, *Dean and Professor, College of Architecture and Urban Planning, Tongji University, Shanghai*

Executive Group
Ricky Burdett, *Director, Urban Age, LSE*
Philipp Rode, *Executive Director, Urban Age, LSE*
Ute Weiland, *Coordinator, AHS-LSE, AHS*

Staff London School of Economics and Political Science/Urban Age, Cities Programme
Pamela Puchalski, *Projects Coordinator*
Miguel Kanai, *Project Researcher*
Bruno Moser, *Research Associate*
Sarah Ichioka, *Research Associate*
Emily Cruz, *Publications Manager*
Mira Krusteff, *Programme Assistant*
Adam Kaasa, *Programme Assistant*
Iliana Ortega-Alcazar, *Researcher*
Peter Schwinger, *Researcher*
Richard Simpson, *Researcher*

**Staff Alfred Herrhausen Society,
The International Forum of Deutsche Bank**
Jessica Barthel, *Project Manager*
Christiane Timmerhaus, *Events & Publications Manager*
Sonja Ecker, *Project Manager*

BOOK CONTRIBUTORS

Guy Battle is a founding partner of Battle McCarthy Consulting Engineers. He is an environmental and building services engineer specializing in the design of environmentally responsive buildings, Visiting Professor at the Illinois Institute of Technology and has worked with the AA, the RCA and the Bartlett.

Sophie Body-Gendrot is a Professor of Political Science and of American studies, Director of the Center of Urban Studies at Université-Sorbonne-Paris IV and a CNRS researcher. She chaired a European network on the dynamics of violence in 18 European countries and was the editor of the French *Review of American Studies*.

Lindsay Bremner is Chair of Architecture at Temple University in Philadelphia. Formerly Chair of Architecture at the University of the Witwatersrand in Johannesburg and Visiting Professor at MIT, Lindsay has written and lectured extensively on the transformation of Johannesburg since the end of apartheid.

Ricky Burdett is Director of the Urban Age Programme and Centennial Professor in Architecture and Urbanism at the LSE, and founding director of the LSE Cities Programme. His latest appointment is as Chief Adviser on Architecture and Urbanism for the Olympic Delivery Authority. He was Director of the 2006 Architecture Biennale in Venice and chairman of the Jury for the 2007 Mies van der Rohe Prize.

Néstor Canclini is Director of the Urban Culture Studies Program at Universidad Autónoma Metropolitana in Mexico. He was Professor at Austin, Duke, Stanford, Barcelona, Buenos Aires and São Paulo universities. Awarded the Guggenheim scholarship, the Premio Casa de las Américas and the Book Award of Latin American Studies Association for *Hybrid Cultures*.

José Castillo is the principal and co-founder of arquitectura 911sc in Mexico City. He is a Professor at the University of Pennsylvania's School of Design and the Universidad Iberoamericana. He curated *Mexico City: The Space of Potentiality*, at the 2006 Venice Architecture Biennale and *Peripheral Landscapes* at the 2007 Rotterdam Biennale.

Xiangming Chen is founding Dean and Director of the new Center for Urban and Global Studies and the Paul E. Raether Distinguished Professor of Sociology and International Studies at Trinity College in Hartford, CT, as well as Distinguished Professor in the School of Social Development and Public Policy at Fudan University, Shanghai.

Joan Clos was Mayor of Barcelona from 1997 to 2006, and recently appointed as Minister of Industry, Tourism and Trade in the Spanish Government. During his mandate, he was the president of Educating Cities, the United Nations Advisory Committee of Local Authorities, the Association of Major Metropolises and vice-president of United Cities and Local Authorities.

Frank Duffy co-founded DEGW, a multi-disciplinary 'space planning' firm in London in 1973. Duffy chairs the BBC's Architecture Design and Workplace Advisory Council and the Stratford City Design Review Panel. President of the RIBA (1993–1995), Duffy was awarded a CBE in 1997 and the British Council for Offices President's Award in 2004.

Franziska Eichstädt-Bohlig is a Member of Parliament of Berlin, Chair of the Green Parliamentary Group and has been a member of the German Green Party since 1993. She studied Architecture and Urban Buildings at the Technical-University of Berlin and worked in Berlin's regional planning department. She was Member of the German Parliament 1994–2005.

Susan Fainstein is a Professor at Harvard University Graduate School of Design. She previously taught at Columbia and Rutgers Universities. She focuses on comparative urban public policy, planning theory, and urban redevelopment. She is the recipient of the 2004 Distinguished Educator Award of the Association of Collegiate Schools of Planning.

Gerald Frug is the Louis D. Brandeis Professor of Law at Harvard Law School and Visiting Professor at the LSE. He worked as a Special Assistant to the Chairman of the Equal Employment Opportunity Commission, in Washington DC, and as Health Services Administrator of the City of New York. He previously taught at the University of Pennsylvania Law School.

Nicky Gavron has been laying the foundations for sustainable development in London for more than three decades. As Deputy Mayor of London since 2000, she has led in shaping the London Plan and on climate change she is overseeing the implementation of much of the Climate Change Action Plan.

Jacques Herzog and Pierre de Meuron established their office in 1978 and received the Pritzker Architecture Prize 2001 and the RIBA Royal Gold Medal 2007. Herzog and de Meuron teach at Harvard University (since 1994) and at the Swiss Federal Institute of Technology Zürich (since 1999). In 2002 they co-founded the ETH Studio Basel – Contemporary City Institute.

Sarah Ichioka was recently Consultant Curator for the *Global Cities* exhibition at Tate Modern, London. She helped develop the tenth Venice Architecture Biennale and co-edited the catalogue. She was a founding Urban Age Research Associate, holding an MSc in City Design and Social Science from the LSE and a BA from Yale University. She is now Deputy Director of the London Festival of Architecture.

Miguel Kanai is an Argentine-Japanese urbanist interested in the relationship between economic restructuring and the social and spatial transformations of cities. He holds a BA in Integrated Human Studies from Kyoto University and an MA in Urban Policy Analysis from the New School for Social Research. He was a founding Project Researcher with the Urban Age.

Bruce Katz is Vice President at the Brookings Institution and founding Director of the Brookings Metropolitan Policy Program. He received the prestigious Heinz Award in Public Policy in 2006 and is a Visiting Professor of Social Policy at the LSE. Katz served as Chief of Staff to Henry G. Cisneros, and as staff director of the Senate Subcommittee on Housing and Urban Affairs.

Caroline Kihato is a Research Fellow at the University of South Africa in Pretoria. Her main research areas are urbanization and migration. She has worked as a Policy Analyst at the Development Bank of Southern Africa, as Senior Lecturer, Researcher in Architecture and Planning and Project Manager for the Centre for Policy Studies in Johannesburg.

Hermann Knoflacher is Professor in Transport Planning and Traffic Engineering at the University of Technology in Vienna. He founded the Institute of Transport Science, and advised the Austrian Minister of Transport for eight years. Since 1972, he has taught at the University of Technology in Vienna with visiting Professorships at universities in Europe, Japan and in the United States.

Rem Koolhaas founded Office for Metropolitan Architecture in 1975 together with Elia and Zoe Zenghelis and Madelon Vriesendorp. He graduated from the Architectural Association in London and in 1978 published *Delirious New York, a Retroactive Manifesto for Manhattan*. Rem Koolhaas is a Professor at Harvard University where he leads the Project on the City.

Dieter Läpple is Professor and Director of the Institute for Urban and Regional Economics and Sociology at the HafenCity University Hamburg. He has worked as Lecturer and Visiting Professor in Berlin, Amsterdam, Paris, Aix-en-Provence/Marseille and Leiden. He is a member of the German Academy for Urban and Regional Planning.

Bruno Moser studied architecture at the ETH in Zurich. He worked for several architectural practices before joining the Cities Programme at LSE and subsequently the research unit led by Ricky Burdett. He worked as a research fellow on density studies in London and the Urban Age Cities, the Venice Architecture Biennale and the *Global*

Cities exhibition at Tate Modern, London. He recently joined Foster + Partners as an urban designer.

Wolfgang Nowak is Managing Director of the Alfred Herrhausen Society, the International Forum of Deutsche Bank. He has held various senior positions in Germany's state and federal governments, France's Centre national de la recherche scientifique in Paris and UNESCO. A former State Secretary, Wolfgang was Director-General for Political Analysis and Planning at the German Federal Chancellery from 1999 to 2002.

Enrique Peñalosa has worked in government, academia and the public sector. As Mayor of Bogotá, Colombia, between 1998 and 2001, he led a profound transformation of the city. He became visiting scholar at New York University, returned to Colombian politics in 2004 and is currently running once again for mayor of Bogotá.

Anne Power is Professor of Social Policy at the LSE. In 1997, she became Deputy Director of LSE's Centre for the Analysis of Social Exclusion (CASE). She is a member of the UK government's Neighbourhood, Cities and Regions Analysis Panel, the Sustainable Development Commission, and is a visiting fellow at the Brookings Institution.

Philipp Rode is Executive Director of Urban Age and Associate of the Cities Programme at the London School of Economics. As researcher and consultant he is involved in interdisciplinary projects on urban governance, transport, city planning and urban design. He was awarded the Schinkel Urban Design Prize in 2000.

Saskia Sassen is now at Columbia University's Committee on Global Thought, after a decade at the University of Chicago and London School of Economics. Her most recent books are *Territory, Authority, Rights: From Medieval to Global Assemblages* (Princeton, NJ, 2006), *A Sociology of Globalization* (New York, 2007) and one of UNESCO's Encyclopedia of Life Support Systems (EOLSS) (Oxford, www.eolss.net).

Richard Sennett is a Professor of Sociology at the LSE and Bemis Professor of Social Sciences at MIT. His research interests include the relationship between urban design and urban society, urban family patterns, the history of cities and the changing nature of work. He is a fellow of the American Academy of Arts and Sciences, the Royal Society of Literature, the Royal Society of the Arts, and the Academia Europea.

Edward Soja is Distinguished Professor of Urban Planning at UCLA and Centennial Professor of Sociology at LSE. His interests have focused on making connections between the spatial disciplines of geography, architecture

and urban and regional studies, and in promoting a critical spatial perspective in the social sciences and humanities.

Deyan Sudjic is Director of the Design Museum in London. Previously, Sudjic was Dean of the Faculty of Art, Architecture and Design at Kingston University, *The Observer* design and architecture writer and Director of the Venice Architecture Biennale in 2002. He was Editor of *Domus*, Founding Editor of *Blueprint* magazine and was made an OBE in 2000.

Geetam Tiwari is Chair and Associate Professor for Transport Planning Transportation Research and Injury Prevention Programme (TRIPP), Indian Institute of Technology Delhi, India. Her professional experience lies in the areas of transport planning, traffic engineering and safety and she has taught at the Indian Institute of Technology in Delhi since 1990.

Tony Travers is Director of the Greater London Group, a research centre at the London School of Economics. He is also Expenditure Adviser to the House of Commons Select Committee on Education and Skills, a Senior Associate at the King's Fund and a member of the Arts Council of England's Touring Panel.

Julie Wagner, a Non-Resident Senior Fellow with the Brookings Institution, is a trained city planner with an expertise in land use planning, public involvement, and land use conflict resolution. She served as the Deputy Planning Director, Long Range Planning for Washington DC. Wagner holds an MA in City Planning from MIT.

Alejandro Zaera-Polo studied at the ETS of Architecture in Madrid and received an MARCHII degree from Harvard Graduate school of Design in 1991. Together with Farshid Moussavi he founded Foreign Office Architects in 1992. Zaera-Polo is currently the Dean of the Berlage Institute and lectures at several architectural schools around the world.

CREDITS

PHOTO CREDITS IN ALPHABETICAL ORDER OF PHOTOGRAPHER

AP: 79
Architecture and Urbanism Unit, Greater London Authority: 144
Arena: 476 and 477
Artist's impression Pudong: 114
David Baltzer ZENIT: 470, 471
Olivo Barbieri: 106–7
Gabriele Basilico: 72–3
Richard Berenholtz: 82–3
Peter Bialobrzeski / Laif, Camera Press, London: 15, 113
Marcus Bredt: 220, 221 bottom, 222 bottom, 228, 229, 464, 465, 466, 467 top
Lindsay Bremner: 196 top, 201 bottom, 205, 206, 207, 211
Alfredo Brillembourg and Hubert Klumpner / U-TT 2003: 387, and U-TT 2006: 311
Adam Broomberg and Oliver Chanarin: 49, 212–3, 475, 482–3
The Bruner Foundation: 100
Richard Bryant: 13, 152–3, 335 top and middle
Dante Busquets: 40–1, 46, 115, 127, 130–1, 166, 167 top, 177, 181, 185, 283 top, 295 top right, 323, 325, 344, 350 bottom, 390, 446, 447, 448, 449, 450, 451
José Castillo: 178
Mara Catalan: 74, 75, 84, 90 top, 414, 415, 416, 418, 419, 420, 421, 424, 425
City of New York: 12
CITYSCAPE: 373
Richard Davies: 158
Oscar Diaz: 309 top left
Philipp Ebeling: 138, 143, 149, 331, 365, 369, 385, 392, 436, 437, 438, 439, 440, 441, 442, 443, 444, 445
Karl Fjellstrom, ITDP: 309 top right
Foreign Office Architects: 402 right
Studio Foster + Partners: 423 bottom right
Chris Gascoigne: 335 bottom
Getty Images: 380
Francisco Gómez Sosa: 361
David Gregor: 353
Werner Hausmann: 327 bottom
Jason Hawkes: 136–7
Herzog & de Meuron: 400 top
Jackie Hobbs: 456
Loanna Hoffmann: 295 top left, 321
Jen-Hui Huang, Kingston University MA Design: 407
Jeffrey Inaba: 98
Francesco Jodice: 341
Hilary Koob-Sassen: 278–9
Rem Koolhaas: 322 top
Ian Lambot: 327 top
Michael Latz + Partner: 156 top
Armin Linke: 16
Liu Liqun/CORBIS: 303 middle
Jackson Lowen: 108, 109 top, 119, 128, 426, 427, 428, 429, 431, 432, 433, 434, 435
Urban Age, LSE: 20
Alex MacLean – Landslides: 97
Magnum: 357 middle
Morphosis: 398
Bruno Moser: 350 top
Jan Mun: 422, 423
Bernd Noack: 217
Jean Nouvel: 401 middle
OMA: 143, 401 top, 402 left

Peter Oswalt: 101
Christa Panick: 156 bottom
Carlos F. Pardo: 309 bottom right
Scott Peterman: 175
Pamela Puchalski: 38, 90 bottom, 227, 389
Ryan Pyle: 37, 55, 109 bottom, 120, 123, 124, 277, 283 bottom, 285, 292 bottom, 343, 388, 393, 430
Larry Racioppo: 89, 91
Reuters/CORBIS: 303 bottom
RMJM: 401 bottom
Philipp Rode: 34, 171, 179, 204, 286, 322 bottom, 357 bottom
Hugh Rooney; Eye Ubiquitous/CORBIS: 303 top
Paolo Rosselli: 45, 182, 164–5, 172–3
Art Rothfuss III: 317
Anja Schlamann: 17, 221 top, 222 top, 223, 467 bottom left and right
Norbert Shoerner: 297
Giovanna Silva: 308, 309 bottom left, 312
Skidmore, Owings and Merrill LLP: 395
Ezra Stoller / Exto / Arcaid: 334
Studio Daniel Libeskind: 400 bottom
Guy Tillim: 14, 194–5
John Tran: 139, 150
Sze Tsung Leong, Courtesy Yossi Milo Gallery, NYC: 116–17, 295 bottom left
Jean-Michel Turpin/CORBIS: 357 top
Tuca Vieira: 187, 190, 349
Rafael Viñoly: 408
Graeme Williams: 196 bottom, 197 top, 201 top, 202, 208–9, 215, 452, 453, 454, 455, 457, 458, 459, 460, 461, 462, 463
Adam Wiseman: 86–7, 94–5, 165 bottom, 291, 299, 357 middle
Nigel Young / Foster + Partners: 295 bottom right
Alejandro Zaera-Polo: 151

CREDITS FOR MAPS AND GRAPHICS AND DATA SOURCE REFERENCES IN PAGE ORDER

Unless stated otherwise, all maps and graphics have been produced by the Urban Age project at the London School of Economics and Political Science.
The references below indicate:
Page number: subject of map or graphics – and the data source.

18: London Green Belt – LSE, GIS calculations.
23: Urbanization – United Nations Department of Economic and Social Affairs Population Division, 'World Urbanization Prospects: The 2005 Revision'.
23: City growth – United Nations Department of Economic and Social Affairs Population Division, 'World Urbanization Prospects: The 2005 Revision'; H. Clydesdale, 'Shanghai Chronology', 2006, http://www.askasia.org/students/downloads/Shanghai_Chronology.pdf; *Tales of Old China, All About Shanghai and Environs, A Standard Guide Book*, chapter 4, 'Population', 1934, Shanghai http://www.talesofoldchina.com/library/all.cfm; Berliner Senatsverwaltung für Stadtentwicklung, 'Prognosergebnisse für Berlin', http://www.stadtentwicklung.berlin.de/planen/bevoelkerungsprognose/de/prognose_berlin/bezirke.shtml; R. Tomlinson, 'Impacts of HIV/AIDS at the Local Level in South Africa', Report commissioned by the Urban Management Programme of UN HABITAT,

http://www.wits.ac.za/depts/wcs/cubes/docs/CUBESHousing Seminar_13March2007_Tomlinson.ppt#256,1; Demographia, 'Demographia World Urban Areas: Population Projections 2007 and 2015', http://www.demographia.com/db-worldua2015.pdf; Greater London Authority, 'Greater London Demographic Review 2005', http://www.london.gov.uk/gla/publications/factsandfigures/dmag-briefing2006-35.pdf; New York City Department of City Planning, 'Population Division: Appendix Table 5-3 Total and Foreign born population New York Metropolitan Region by subregion and county 1900-2000', http://www.nyc.gov/html/dcp/html/census/nny_appendix.shtml; P. R. Lankao, 'Are we missing the point? Particularities of urbanization, sustainability and carbon emissions in Latin American cities', *Environment and Urbanization*, vol.19, no. 1, 2007, pp. 159-75.
24–5: Human footprint – Center for International Earth Science Information Network (CIESIN), 'Human Footprint', 2002, http://www.ciesin.columbia.edu/wild_areas/#.
26–7 and **28–9**: Cities over 1 million, scaled by size; population growth per hour, top 25 cities – LSE calculations based upon UN data from United Nations Department of Economic and Social Affairs Population Division, 'World Urbanization Prospects: The 2005 Revision'.
30–1: Air traffic – G. Lasnier, 'World Air Traffic Flowchart based upon International Civil Aviation Organization and WorldSat International Inc., http://www.esri.com/mapmuseum/mapbook_gallery/volume19/transportation7.html.
56–7, 58 and **60**: Million-plus city-regions 1825–2000; Percentage of the world's urban population 1950–2030; The world's largest city regions 1950, 1985, 2005 – United Nations Department of Economic and Social Affairs Population Division, 'World Urbanization Prospects: The 2005 Revision'.
63: Continental zones of macro-regional urbanization – R. Florida, 'The New Megalopolis; Our focus on cities is wrong. Growth and innovation come from new urban corridors', *Newsweek International Edition*, Special Report, 2006; M. Dear and G. Leclerc, *Postborder City: Cultural Spaces of Bajalta California* (London/New York, 2003); US Census Bureau, '2005 Data Profiles', http://factfinder.census.gov/servlet/ADPTable?_bm=y&-geo_id=16000US3651000&-qr_name=ACS_2005_EST_G00_DP3&-ds_name=ACS_2005_EST_G00_&-_lang=en&-_sse=on.
76: NYC key data – US Census Bureau, '2005 Data Profiles'. http://factfinder.census.gov/servlet/ADPTable?_bm=y&-geo_id=16000US3651000&-qr_name=ACS_2005_EST_G00_DP3&-ds_name=ACS_2005_EST_G00_&-_lang=en&-_sse=on, 2005; Prudential Douglas Elliman Real Estate, 'Manhattan, Market Overview: A Quarterly Survey of Manhattan Co-op and Condo Sales 2007', http://www.prudentialelliman.com/NYCPhotos/retail_reports/mmo2q07.pdf; New Yorker for Parks, 2003; New York University, Office of Public Affairs, Press Release: 'New Report Looks at Renaissance of NYC, Mass Transit System', 6 October 2005, http://www.nyu.edu/public.affairs/releases/detail/773; New York State Department of Labour, 'NAICS based Industry Employment and Wages, Census of Employment and Wages, 2005; New York Official Marketing and Tourism Website, 'NYC Statistics', http://www.nycvisit.com/content/index.cfm?pagePkey=57; City of New York Police Department, http://www.nyc.gov/html/nypd/html/pct/cspdf.html, 2007; New York City Department of City Planning, 'Population Division: Appendix Table 5-3 Total and Foreign born population New York Metropolitan Region by subregion and county 1900-2000',

http://www.nyc.gov/html/dcp/html/census/nny_appendix.shtml; 'For parking space, the price is right at $225,000, *the New York Times* 12 July 2007, http://www.nytimes.com/2007/07/12/us/12parking.html?ex=1185422400&en=ff2f5d16570882a0&ei=5070.
77: New York City map – United States Census Bureau, Population Division, Decennial Programs Coordination Branch, 'United States Census 2000'
110: Shanghai key data – X. Chen, this publication; T. Luard, 'Shanghai ends reign of the bicycle', http://news.bbc.co.uk/1/hi/world/asia-pacific/3303655.stm BBC; *Shanghai Statistical Year book*, 2003 and 2006; *Yearbook of China Transport and Communication, 1997-2004*; National Bureau of Statistics of China,'China 5th Population Census Data', 2000; UBS, 'Prices and Earnings: A comparison of purchasing power around the globe' (Zurich, 2006): H. Clydesdale, 'Shanghai Chronology', 2006, Asia Society, http://www.askasia.org/students/downloads/Shanghai_Chronology.pdf; United Nations Department of Economic and Social Affairs Population Division, 'World Urbanization Prospects, The 2005 Revision', http://www.un.org/esa/population/unpop.htm.
111: Shanghai map – National Bureau of Statistics of China, 'China 5th Population Census Data', 2000.
140: London key data: Greater London Authority, 'GLA Population and Household Forecasts based on the First Results from the 2001 Census, SDS Technical Report Twenty-three', 2003, http://mayor.london.gov.uk/mayor/planning/docs/tr23_population_forecasts_01_census.pdf National Statistics and Greater London Authority, 'Focus on London', 2007 http://www.statistics.gov.uk/downloads/theme_compendia/fol2007/Focus_on_London_2007.pdf; Communities and Local Government, 'Generalised Land Use Database Statistics for England 2005', http://www.communities.gov.uk/index.asp?id=1146084; Transport for London, 'Central London Congestion Charging: Impacts monitoring Fifth Annual Report', 2007, http://www.tfl.gov.uk/assets/downloads/fifth-annual-impacts-monitoring-report-2007-07-07.pdf; M. McCahill and C. Norris, 'Working Paper No. 6 CCTV in London in the Urban Eye', 2002, http://www.urbaneye.net/results/ue_wp6.pdf; Office of National Statistics: housing, including 'Tenure of dwellings: Regional Trends 38', www.statistics.gov.uk, data from 2003; Land Registry, 'House Price Index January 2007' and 'Average Regional House Prices', Housing Finance, Council of Mortgage Lenders and DCLG website cited by York.ac.uk; 'London Employment Projections, Briefing Note by Duncan Melville', Greater London Authority Economics, 2005; Office for National Statistics General Register Office for Scotland, Northern Ireland Statistics and Research Agency, 'Foreign born population as percentage of all residents by London Borough 2001', 2001 Census; C. Hall, 'Greater London Demographic Review 2005, DMAG Briefing 2006/35 December 2006', GLA London Centre for Housing Policy; 'The UK Housing Review 2004/2005', 2005, York, http://www.york.ac.uk/res/ukhr/ukhr0405/compendium.htm; Mayor of London, 'Housing in London: the London housing strategy evidence base 2005', 2005, http://www.london.gov.uk/mayor/housing/evidencebase/fulldocument.pdf; Official Website of BAA, '10 year record only 05 data source', 2005, http://www.baa.co.uk/assets/B2CPortal/Static%20Files/10_YEAR_RECORD_ONLY_05.xls; Department of Transport and National Statistics,' Road Casualties Great Britain', 2004, London; Mayor of London, http://mayor.london.gov.uk/mayor/planning/docs/tr23_population_forecasts_01_census.pdf.
141: London map – Office for National Statistics, 'UK Census 2001'.
146: London commuting map – Office for National Statistics, '2001 Census: Special Workplace Statistics (England, Wales and Northern Ireland)', ed. C.o.I.D.E.a.R. ESRC/JISC Census Programme, 2001, University of Leeds.
147: High speed rail diagram – LSE.
151: Olympics location 2012 – LSE.
168: Mexico City key data – P. R. Lankao, 'Are we missing the point? Particularities of urbanization, sustainability and carbon emissions in Latin America', *Environment and Urbanization,* vol. 19, no. 1, pp. 159–75; United Nations Department of Economic and Social Affairs Population Division, 'World Urbanization Prospects: The 2005 Revision', 2005, http://www.un.org/esa/population/unpop.htm; Instituto Nacional de Estadística, Geografía e Informática (INEGI): 'Población por Entidad Federativa', 2006; INEGI, 'Cuaderno Estadístico de la Zona Metropolitana de la Ciudad de Mexico', 2005; INEGI, 'Estadisticas del Medio Ambiente del Distrito Federal y Zona Metropolitana 2002', Aguascalientes, 2005, p. 10; INEGI, 'Síntesis de Resultados. Zona Metropolitana de la Ciudad de México. XII Censo General de Población y Vivienda 2000', Aguascalientes, 2004, pp. 88-9; INEGI, 'Anuario Stadístico Distrito Federal', 2006; P. M. Ward, *Mexico City* (Chichester/New York, 1998) second and revised edition; P. Connolly, 'Uncontrolled settlement and self-build: what kind of solution? The Mexico City case', in P. Ward (ed), *Self-help housing: a critique* (London/Mansell, 1982), pp. 141–74; EMBARQ, 'The WRI Center for Transport and the Environment: Mexico City on the Move', http://embarq.wri.org/documentupload/EMBARQ_MexCity_english.pdf; B.N. Benitez, 'Congestion at the limits? Mexico City Growth at the Limit?' (London, 2006); UN HABITAT, 'An essential option for the urban poor in developing countries', 2003, http://ww2.unhabitat.org/programmes/housingpolicy/documents/HS-695.pdf; G. Garza, *La Ciudad de Mexico en el fin del segundo millenio* (Mexico City, 2000); Secretaria de Transporte y Vialidad (SETRAVI), 'Programa Integral de Transporte y Vialidad 2001-2006', http://www.setravi.df.gob.mx/programas/pitv.pdf; Secretariat of Transport, Mexico DF, 2005; United Nations Department of Economic and Social Affairs Population Division, 'World Urbanization Prospects: The 2005 Revision', 2005, http://esa.un.org/unpp/; G. Frug, this publication; http://www.senado.gob.mx/sgsp/gaceta/index2.php?sesion=2005/06/22/1&documento=36; http://www.inegi.gob.mx/inegi/contenidos/espanol/prensa/Boletines/Boletin/Comunicados/Especiales/2000/Agosto/cp_103.pdf.
169: Mexico City / State diagram – Instituto Nacional de Estadística Geografía e Informática 2000, supplied by Desarrolladora Metropolitana SA.
198: Johannesburg key data – Francois Viruly; Official website of the City of Johannesburg, 'Joburg Statistics', http://www.joburg.org.za/stats/pop_group.stm; Statistics of South Africa, 'Census 2001', http://www.statssa.gov.za/census01; South Africa Police Services, 'Crime in the RSA for April to March 2001/2002 to 2006/2007; Area: Johannesburg', 2007, http://www.saps.gov.za/statistics/reports/crimestats/2007/_pdf/province/gauteng/johannesburg/johannesburg_area_total.pdf; S. Burrows and C. Harris, 'South African Health infor: violence', Chapter 4, 'Johannesburg', 2003, http://www.sahealthinfo.org.za/violence/2003chapter4a.pdf; City of Johannesburg, 'City Development Plan 2001/2002' 2002, http://www.johannesburgnews.co.za/budget_2001/develop_plan/dev_overview.html; http://www.statssa.gov.za/publications/P0441/P04413rdQuarter2006.pdf; Johannesburg Development Agency, 'Randburg Economic Revitalisation Study', 2004, http://www.jda.co.za/randburg/docs/economic_impact.stm.
199: Johannesburg map – Statistics of South Africa, 'Census 2001', http://www.statssa.gov.za/census01.
206: Apartheid city diagram – LSE.
224: Berlin key data – Berliner Senatsverwaltung für Stadtentwicklung, 'Prognosergebnisse für Berlin', http://www.stadtentwicklung.berlin.de/planen/bevoelkerungsprognose/de/prognose_berlin/bezirke.shtml, 2007; Statistisches Landesamt Berlin,'Berlin in Figures 2005', http://www.statistik-berlin.de/aktuell/berlinzahlen/berlin-fbe.pdf; Berliner Senatsverwaltung für Stadtentwicklung, 'Berlin Housing Market, report 2005', http://www.stadtentwicklung.berlin.de/wohnen/wohnungsmarktbericht/pdf/wohnungsmarktbericht_summary_2005.pdf; Statistisches Bundesamt Deutschland, 'Lebenserwartung der Menschen in Deutschland steigt weiter an', http://www.destatis.de/jetspeed/portal/cms/Sites/destatis/Internet/DE/Presse/pm/2006/10/PD06__443__12621,templateId=renderPrint.psml; Deutsche Bank Research, 'Current Issues: Berlin Property market: Heavily mortgaging the future', http://www.dbresearch.de/PROD/DBR_INTERNET_EN-PROD/PROD0000000000185434.pdf; Amt für Statistiken Berlin Brandenburg, 'Arbeitsmarktstatistiken', http://www.statistik-berlin-brandenburg.de; Berliner Verkehrsbetriebe (BVG), 'BVG Zahlenspiege', 2006.
225: Berlin map – Berliner Senatsverwaltung für Stadtentwicklung.
230–1: Berlin maps – Berliner Senatsverwaltung für Stadtentwicklung, 2007, Hilmar von Lojewski, and Taklis Sgouros.
232: Urban unemployment / employment levels – 'Unemployment rates in German cities' – IAB 2003/05, calculations Dieter Läpple, HCU, Institute for Urban and Regional Economics, S. Kröger.
233: Employment levels – 'Changes in the employment figures of German Cities 1997–2004', IAB 2003/05, calculations Dieter Läpple, HCU, Institute for Urban and Regional Economics, S. Kröger.
234: Urban migration trends – 'Tendencies towards a reurbanization – Population development' – IAB 2003/05, calculations Dieter Läpple, HCU, Institute for Urban and Regional Economics, S. Kröger.
237: Manufacturing and services – 'Employment in advanced produced services' – IAB 2003/05, calculations Dieter Läpple, HCU, Institute for Urban and Regional Economics, A. Kaiser.
238: Germany's urban hierarchy – 'Hierarchy profile of the urban system 1939, 1970 and 1995', after H. Blotevogel, *The German Metropolitan System*, 2002, HCU, Institute for Urban and Regional Economics.
241: Locating dynamic sectors – 'Ranking of location quotients among West German metropolitan regions (engineering and architecture)' – IAB 2003/05, calculations Dieter Läpple, HCU, Institute for Urban and Regional Economics, A. Kaiser; 'Ranking of location quotients among West German metropolitan region (consulting and accountancy) – IAB 2003/05, calculations Dieter Läpple, HCU, Institute for Urban and Regional Economics, A. Kaiser; Ranking of location quotients among West German metropolitan region (advertising) – IAB 2003/05, calculations Dieter Läpple, HCU, Institute for Urban and Regional Economics, A. Kaiser.
242: Global economic supremacy – after H. Blotevogel, *The German Metropolitan System*, 2002, HCU, Institute for Urban and Regional Economics, D. Lapple / S.Kröger
246–7: All graphics: Atelierworks.
246/252: Population density – Berliner Senatsverwaltung für Stadtentwicklung, http://www.stadtentwicklung.berlin.de/; Office for National Statistics, http://www.statistics.gov.uk/; US Census Bureau, http://factfinder.census.gov/home/saff/main.html?_lang=en, 2005; Instituto Nacional de Estadistica Geografía e Informática (INEGI), 'Estadisticas del Medio Ambiente del Distrito Federal y Zona Metropolitana 2002', Aguascalientes, 2005; National Bureau of Statistics of China, 'China 5th Population Census Data', 2000; City of Johannesburg Official Website 2005, http://www.joburg-archive.co.za/city_vision/idp2005/waterpolicyp63-93a.pdf.
247: Income levels – UBS, *Prices and Earnings: A comparison of purchasing power around the globe* (Zurich, 2006), pp. 40–7.
247: Murder rates – City of New York Police Department, http://www.nyc.gov/html/nypd/html/pct/cspdf.html, 2005; *Shanghai Statistical Yearbook,* 2006; Metropolitan Police, 'Financial Year 2006-2007 Summary', http://www.met.police.uk/crimestatistics/2007/2006_07_yend.xls; Instituto Nacional de Estadística Geografía e Informática (INEGI), 'Estadisticas del Medio Ambiente del Distrito Federal y Zona Metropolitana 2002', Aguascalientes, 2005; South Africa Police Services, 'Crime in the RSA for April to March 2001/2002 to 2006/2007; Area: Johannesburg', http://www.saps.gov.za/statistics/reports/crimestats/2007/_pdf/province/gauteng/johannesburg/johannesburg_area_total.pdf, 2007; Statistisches Landesamt Berlin, 'Rechtspflege und Öffentliche Sicherheit: Polizeilich bekanntgewordene Straftaten, aufgeklärte Straftaten und Tatverdächtige in Berlin 2005', http://www.statistik-berlin.de/framesets/berl.htm, 2005.
247: Water consumption – G. Battle, 'Mobility and Sustainable Community', Urban Age Conference Mexico City, 2006; Official Website of Shanghai Municipality, 'Shanghai Snapshots', http://www.shanghai.gov.cn/shanghai/node8059/node8302/node8385/index.html, 2007; (US FedStats, 1990); New York City Department of Environmental Protection, 'History of Drought and Water Consumption', http://www.nyc.gov/html/dep/html/droughthist.html, 2007; Ofwat, 'Security of supply, leakage and water efficiency, 2005–6 report', http://www.ofwat.gov.uk/aptrix/ofwat/publish.nsf/Content/navigation-ofwat-faqs-statistics, 2006; National Bureau of Statistics of China, '12-3 Water Supply and Water Use', *China Statistical Yearbook,* 2005, http://www.stats.gov.cn/tjsj/ndsj/2005/indexeh.htm; Berliner Wasserbetriebe,'Wasserabsatz: Die Daten seit 1992', 2007, http://www.bwb.de/deutsch/trinkwasser/wasserverbrauch.html; (City of Johannesburg, 2005)
248: Employment by sector – Statistisches Landesamt Berlin, 'Berlin in Figures 2005', http://www.statistik-berlin.de/aktuell/berlinzahlen/berlin-fbe.pdf; 'Statistics of South Africa, Census 2001', http://www.statssa.gov.za/census01; Office for National Statistics, 'Labour Market', 2004; INEGI, 'Anuario Stadistico Distrito Federal 2006'; New York State Department of Labour, 'NAICS based Industry Employment and Wages, Census of Employment and Wages', 2005; *Shanghai Statistical Yearbook*, 2006.
250: Berliner Senatsverwaltung für Stadtentwicklung, 2005; Office for National Statistics, 'UK Census 2001'; United States Census Bureau, Population Division, Decennial Programs Coordination Branch, 'United States Census 2000'; Instituto Nacional de Estadistica Geografia e informatica 2000, supplied by Desarrolladora Metropolitana SA; Bureau of Statistics of China, 'China 5th Population Census Data', 2000.
254: Social disadvantage – Berliner Senatsverwaltung für Stadtentwicklung, http://www.stadtentwicklung.berling.de/kontakt/index_en.shtl, 2005; Office for National Statistics, 'UK Census 2001'; United States Census Bureau, Population Division, Decennial Programs Coordination Branch, 'United States Census 2000'; Instituto Nacional de Estadistica Geografia e informatica 2000, supplied by Desarrolladora Metropolitana SA [DeMet]; National Bureau of Statistics of China, 'China 5th Population Census Data', 2000; Statistics of South Africa, 'Census 2001', http://www.statssa.gov.za/census01.
256: Living with children – National Bureau of Statistics of China, 'China 5th Population Census Data', 2000; United States Census Bureau, Population Division, Decennial Programs Coordination Branch, 'United States Census 2000'; Office for National Statistics, 'UK Census 2001'; Statistics South Africa, 'Census 2001',http://www.statssa.gov.za/; Berliner Senatsverwaltung für Stadtentwicklung, 2005.
258: Finding work/ unemployment – National Bureau of Statistics of China, 'China 5th Population Census Data', 2000; United States Census Bureau, Population Division, Decennial Programs Coordination Branch, 'United States Census 2000'; Office for National Statistics, 'UK Census 2001'; Statistics South Africa, 'Census 2001',http://www.statssa.gov.za/; Berliner Senatsverwaltung für Stadtentwicklung, 2005.

260: Rail-based public transport network in layers of urbanized area, rail, intercity rail and subway network – Berliner Senatsverwaltung für Stadtentwicklung, 2005; Instituto Nacional de Estadistica Geografía e Informática, 2000, supplied by Desarrolladora Metropolitana SA; Office for National Statistics, 'UK Census 2001'; Transport for London, http://www.tfl.gov.uk publications from various years; Shanghai City Transport Planning Institute, '3rd Comprehensive Transport Survey', 2005; United States Census Bureau, Population Division, Decennial Programs Coordination Branch, 'United States Census 2000'; Metropolitan Transportation Authority, State of New York, http://www.mta.info/nyct/ publications from various years; New York Metropolitan Transportation Council, NYMTC online, http://www.nymtc.org/;Statistics of South Africa, 'Census 2001', http://www.statssa.gov.za/census01.

262: Modal split – Transport for London, 2006; Berliner Senatsverwaltung für Stadtentwicklung, 'Passenger Traffic by mode of transport and purpose of journey', http://www.stadten-twicklung.berlin.de/verkehr/verkehr_in_zahlen/download/en_s_ 018.pdf; Statistics of South Africa, 'Census 2001', http://www.statssa.gov.za/census01; EMBARQ, 'The WRI Center for Transport and the Environment: Mexico City on the Move', http://embarq.wri.org/documentupload/EMBARQ_MexCity_ english.pdf; Shanghai City Transport Planning Institute, '3rd Comprehensive Transport Survey', 2005; US Census Bureau, '2005 Data Profiles', http://factfinder.census.gov/servlet/ADPTable?_bm=y&-geo_id=16000US3651000&-qr_name=ACS_2005_EST_G00_DP3&-ds_name=ACS_2005_EST_G00_&-_lang=en&-_sse=o.

262: Car ownership – *Shanghai Statistical Yearbook*, 2006; EMBARQ, 'The WRI Center for Transport and the Environment: Mexico City on the Move', http://embarq.wri.org/documentu-pload/EMBARQ_MexCity_english.pdf; New York Metropolitan Transportation Council, NYMTC online, http://www.nymtc.org/; Department for Transportation (DfT), United Kingdom, http://www.dft.gov.uk/ various publications; South African Department for Transport, http://www.transport.gov.za/, 2006; Statistisches Landesamt Berlin, http://www.statistik-berlin.de/framesets/berl.htm; Amt für Statistic Berlin-Brandendurg, http://www.statistik-berlln-brandenburg.do/.

262: Road fatality rates – Statistisches Bundesamt Deutschland, 'Lebenserwartung der Menschen in Deutschland steigt weiter an', http://www.destatis.de/jetspeed/portal/cms/Sites/destatis/Interne t/DE/Presse/pm/2006/10/PD06__443__12621,templateId=render Print.psml; Department of Transport and National Statistics, 'Road Casualties Great Britain 2005, Annual Report', London; S. Burrows and C. Harris, 'South African Health infor: violence', Chapter 4 'Johannesburg', http://www.sahealthinfo.org.za/vio-lence/2003chapter4a.pdf; EMBARQ, 'The WRI Center for Transport and the Environment, 'Mexico City on the Move', http://embarq.wri.org/documentupload/EMBARQ_MexCity_ english.pdf; New York State Department of Motor Vehicles, 'Summary of New York City Motor Vehicle Accidents', http://www.nydmv.state.ny.us/Statistics/2005_NYC.pdf; *Shanghai Statistical Yearbook*, 2006. **264**: Diversity in New York and London – United States Census Bureau, Population Division, Decennial Programs Coordination Branch, 'United States Census 2000'; Office for National Statistics, 'UK Census 2001'.

254: Diversity in New York – United States Census Bureau, Population Division, Decennial Programs Coordination Branch, 'United States Census 2000'.

266–7: Urban Grain – LSE.

268–73: QuickBird satellite images – © DigitalGlobe distributed with exclusive right for Europe by Telespazio.

301: MXC DF/State diagram – Instituto Nacional de Estadística Geografía e Informática 2000, supplied by Desarolladora Metropolitana SA.

335: Office typology sketches – Frank Duffy.

374: London flood plain – Environment Agency, 'Maps, Flood Maps', 2007,http://maps.environment-agency.gov.uk/wiyby/mapController.

376: CO_2 emissions – Greater London Authority, 'Action Today to Protect Tomorrow, The Mayor's Climate Change Action Plan', 2007.

378: CO_2 trajectories – Greater London Authority, 'Action Today to Protect Tomorrow, The Mayor's Climate Change Action Plan', 2007.

391: Global energy use (50 per cent buildings) – G. Battle, 'Mobility and Sustainable Community', Urban Age Conference Mexico City, 2006.

NOTES

CITIES/THE URBANIZATION OF THE WORLD

1 It would have been noticed that the world became predominantly urban much earlier if, for example, a consistent definition of cities was adopted worldwide based on population densities, land uses, sources of income and cultural norms – rather than maintaining country-specific administrative demarcations that are often arbitrarily drawn.
2 See P. Hall, *The World Cities* (London, 1966) and J. Friedmann and G. Wolff, 'World City Formation: An Agenda for Research and Action', in *Journal of Urban and Regional Research* (6), 1982, pp. 309–44.
3 P. Taylor and R. Lang have listed 50 terms used to conceptualize new metropolitan forms and another 50 describing inter-metropolitan functional relations. See P. Taylor and R. Lang, 'The Shock of the New: 100 concepts describing recent urban change', in *Environment and Planning A*, vol. 36, no. 6, 2004, pp. 951–58.
4 See A. Scott (ed.), *Global City regions: Trends, Theory, Prospects* (New York, 2001).
5 An interesting statistic is that almost 25 per cent of the cities on this list are national capitals. Looked at in another way, nearly all but the smallest countries have their capital cities on the list, suggesting a general trend for capital cities to have grown especially rapidly over the past few decades. This can be explained in part by the concentration of institutional, political, police and military power and control, offering at least the impression of greater safety and stability.
6 According to an updated online listing of the 'principal agglomerations of the world' compiled by Thomas Brinkhoff, there were 438 million-plus city regions and 25 mega-cities as of early 2006. See T. Brinkhoff, *The Principal Agglomerations of the World*, http://www.citypopulation.de (accessed 28 January 2006).
7 As Caroline Kihato reminds us in her essay in this volume, African urbanism raises many challenges to western concepts of cities and urban development, challenges that will have to be dealt with as the new urban majority becomes increasingly centred in the developing world.
8 A. Chen, 'Urbanization in China and the case of Fujian Province', in *Modern China*, vol. 32, no.1, 2006, pp. 99–130.
9 J. Friedmann, *China's Urban Transition* (Minneapolis, MN, 2005), p. 39.
10 R. Florida, 'The New Megalopolis; Our focus on cities is wrong. Growth and innovation come from new urban corridors', in *Newsweek* International Edition, 3 July 2006, Special Report.
11 M. Dear and G. Leclerc, *Postborder City: Cultural Spaces of Bajalta California* (New York, 2003).
12 B. J. Godfrey, 'Revisiting Rio de Janeiro and São Paulo', in *Geographical Review*, vol. 89, no. 1, 1999, pp. 94–121.
13 D. Silberfaden, Latitud 33°41'S, Latitud 59°41'W', in the presentation of Argentine at the tenth Architecture Biennale Venice.
14 Source: T. Brinkhoff, *The Principal Agglomerations of the World*, http://www.citypopulation.de, 28 January 2006.
15 E. Soja, *Postmetropolis: Critical Studies of Cities and Regions* (Oxford/ Cambridge, MA, 2000).
16 See for instance M. Porter, 'The Competitive Advantage of the Inner City', in *Harvard Business Review*, vol. 73, no. 3, May–June 1995, pp. 55–71 and M. Porter, 'Location, Competition and Economic Development: Local Clusters in a Global Economy', in *Economic Development Quarterly*, vol. 14, no. 1, February 2000, pp. 15–34; M. Storper, *The Regional World: Territorial Development in a Global Economy* (New York, 1997); M. Storper and A. J. Venables, 'Buzz: face-to-face contact and the urban economy', in *Journal of Economic Geography*, vol. 4 , no. 4, 2004,

pp. 351–370; R. Florida, *The rise of the creative class: and how it's transforming work, leisure, community and everyday life* (New York, 2002); and E. Soja, 'Writing the city spatially', in *City*, vol. 7, no. 3, 2003, pp. 269–281.
17 S. Sassen (ed), *Global Networks, Linked Cities* (New York, 2002); P. Taylor, *World city network: a global urban analysis* (New York, 2003).
18 Particularly useful in understanding these multiple scales of global urbanization is the hybrid (if awkward-sounding) notion of glocalization. This neologism focuses attention on the regions in between the macro and the micro, the global and the local, tying together these multiple scales and highlighting the spatial interplay of the general and the particular, endogenous and exogenous effects. See for example E. Swyngedouw, 'Neither global nor local: "Glocalization" and the politics of scale', in K. R. Cox (ed), S*paces of globalization* (New York / London, 1997), pp. 137–66.
19 M. Davis, *Planet of Slums* (London / New York, 2006).
20 P. Oswalt (ed), *Shrinking Cities* (Ostfildern-Ruit, 2005).
21 D. Sudjic, *The 100 Mile City* (London, 1992).
22 E. Soja, *Postmetropolis: Critical Studies of Cities and Regions* (Oxford / Cambridge, MA, 2000).
23 M. Pastor *et al*, *Regions that Work: How Cities and Suburbs Can Grow Together* (Minneapolis, 2000).
24 D. Chavez and B. Goldfrank (eds), *The Left in the City: Participatory Local Governments in Latin America* (London, 2004).
25 See also R. Burdett and M. Kanai, 'City-building in an age of global urban transformation', in *Cities: Architecture and Society* (Venice, 2006), pp. 3–23.
26 R. Koolhaas, 'On working cities', in *Cities: Architecture and Society* (Venice, 2006), p. 74.

NEW YORK/BEHIND THE BOOM

1 S. Roberts, 'Census Figures Show Scant Improvement in City Poverty Rate', *New York Times*, 30 August 2006.
2 M. Levitan, 'Poverty in New York City, 2005', Community Service Society, New York, September 2006, p. 2.
3 A. S. Sorkin, 'Dealbook; Goldman's Season to Reward and Shock', *New York Times*, 17 December 2006.
4 A. Beveridge, 'Four Trends that Shape the City's Political Landscape', *Gotham Gazette*, 25 May 2005.
5 'A Home for All New Yorkers: Housing First! 2005 Policy Update', Housing First, August 2005, www.housingfirst.net, p. 1.
6 Ibid., p. 5.
7 Once a unit left the affordable-housing pool, it did not revert to its previous status even if a high-income occupant moved out.
8 There is considerable debate concerning whether Giuliani's policies deserved the credit for improved public safety.
9 See S. Sassen, *The Global City* (2nd edition, Princeton, NJ, 2001).
10 See S. S. Fainstein, *The City Builders*, (revised edition, Lawrence, KS, 2001).
11 L. Currid, 'New York as a global creative hub: a competitive analysis of four theories on world cities', *Economic Development Quarterly*, 20 (4), November 2006, p. 341.
12 S. Sassen and F. Roost, 'The City: Strategic Site for the Global Entertainment Industry', in R. D. Judd and S. S. Fainstein (eds), *The Tourist City* (New Haven, CT, 1999), pp. 143–54.
13 NYC & Co., press release, 8 September 2006.
14 S. Fainstein and J. C. Powers, 'Tourism and New York's Ethnic Diversity: An Underutilized Resource?', in J. Rath (ed), *Tourism, Ethnic Diversity and the City* (London, 2007).
15 C. V. Bagli, 'Megadeal: Inside a New York Real Estate Coup', *New York Times*, 31 December 2006.

16 A. S. Beveridge, 'Segregation and Isolation: NYC 1910–2000', http://www1.socialexplorer.com/pub/demography/poppattern-snyc1910-2000/Segregation.asp, 2006.
17 'PlanNYC2030'--http://www.nyc.gov/html/planyc2030/html/plan/land_housing.shtml (accessed April 24, 2007).

SHANGHAI/THE URBAN LABORATORY

1 Reported by F. Balfour, 'Shanghai Rising', *Business Week* (19 February 2007), p. 53.
2 W. Qi and Z. Xiao, 'The Historical Background and Contemporary Implications of the Establishment of Shanghai's Central City Position in Modern China', in Xiaomin Feng (ed), *A Collection of Modern Shanghai Studies* (Shanghai, 2005), p. 13.
3 S. Lei, Q. Ge, and Y. Min, *Shanghai Ren Da Zhihui* (*The Smart Shanghainese*) (Beijing, 2004), p. 6.
4 These figures were calculated from *China Statistical Yearbook 2005* and *Shanghai Statistical Yearbook 2005*, respectively.
5 M. South, 'Urbanites head for new life in suburbs', *China Daily*, 3 July 2006; reprinted and accessed on Asian Development Bank Institute (ADBI) website at http://www.adbi.org/e-newsline/index.html.
6 See F. Balfour, 'Shanghai Rising', *Business Week* (19 February 2007), p. 54.
7 Mayor Han Zheng's speech at the twelfth Annual Asia Leadership Forum, November 2003; reported by China Xihua News Agency (5 December 2003).

SHANGHAI/CHINA'S NEW REVOLUTION

1 X. Chen, *As Borders Bend: Transnational Spaces on the Pacific Rim* (Lanham, MD, 2005).
2 'China gets the postgraduate blues', *Asia Times* online; reprinted and accessed on the Asian Development Bank Institute (ADBI) website at http://www.adbi.org/e-newsline/index.html (13 February 2007).
3 J. Ng, 'Privatized housing impedes cooling efforts', *Asia Times* online (6 July 2006); reprinted and accessed on the Asian Development Bank Institute (ADBI) website at http://www.adbi.org/e-newsline/index.html.
4 Industry Overview, 'Real estate: cooling the fires', *China Economic Review* (August 2006); accessed on http://chinaeconomicreview.com/subscriber/articledetail/1397.html.
5 Reported in *China Daily* (12 June 2006); reprinted and accessed on the Asian Development Bank Institute (ADBI) website at http://www.adbi.org/e-newsline/index.html.
6 *People's Daily* online (13 April 2005) and *China Daily* online (18 August 2006); reprinted and accessed on the Asian Development Bank Institute (ADBI) website at http://www.adbi.org/e-newsline/index.html.

LONDON/TOWARDS A EUROPE OF CITIES

1 Published by the Department of the Environment in 1977.
2 T. Travers, *The Politics of Local Government Finance* (London, 1987).
3 Urban Task Force (1999).
4 BURA, *Local Government, New Localism and Delivery of Regeneration* (London, 2006).
5 BURA, *Local Government, New Localism and Delivery of Regeneration* (London, 2006).
6 DCLG, *Strong and prosperous communities The Local Government White Paper*, Cm 6939, (London, 2006).

JOHANNESBURG/RECOVERING FROM APARTHEID

1 C. Chipkin, *Johannesburg Style. Architecture and Society 1880s–1960s* (Cape Town, 1993).
2 C. W. De Kiewiet, *A History of South Africa Social and Economic* (Oxford, 1966).
3 *The Times*, weekly edition (January 1936) in C. Chipkin, op cit, p. 105.
4 C. Rogerson, 'Image Enhancement and Local Economic Development in Johannesburg', in *Urban Forum*, vol. 7, issue 2 (1996), p. 141
5 G. Agamben, Homo Sacer. *Sovereign Power and Bare Life*, translated by D. Heller-Roazen (Stanford, CA,1998).
6 D. Dewar and R. Uytenbogaardt, *South African Cities: A Manifesto for Change* (Cape Town, 1991), p. 77.
7 The Regional and Town Planning Report of 1944 in A. Mabin and D. Smit, 'Reconstructing South Africa's Cities? The Making of Urban Planning 1900-2000', *Planning Perspectives*, 12 (1997) pp. 193-223.
8 Its economy today is dominated by four sectors: financial and business services (35 per cent of GDP); retail and wholesale trade (18 per cent); manufacturing (16 per cent); and community and social services (13 per cent).
9 Alexandra came into existence in 1914 as a freehold suburb for the white working class. When it failed to attract this market, its properties were sold to black buyers. It remained the only black township north of the city centre throughout the apartheid years.
10 Between 1982 and 1994, 17 of the 65 top 100 national public companies located in Johannesburg moved from downtown to decentralized locations. Similarly, of 104 top national business enterprises located in Johannesburg in 1994, only 27 per cent were located in the city centre. Of the top 10 retail companies with their head offices in Johannesburg, only two remain in the city centre today. See R. Tomlinson et al, Johannesburg Inner City Strategic Development Framework: Economic Analysis (Johannesburg, 1995).
11 A. Mbembe, 'Aesthetics of Superfluity', in *Public Culture*, vol. 16, issue 3 (2004), p. 402.
12 L. Segal, J. Pelo and P. Rampa, 'Asicamtheni Magents Let's Talk Magents. Youth Attitudes Towards Crime', in *Crime and Conflict*

JOHANNESBURG/AFRICAN URBANISM

1 Mathare is Nairobi's poorest slum, created in the 1970s as a result of rural migration to the city.
2 Excerpts from the lyrics and interviews of hip-hop artists featured in 'Kilio Cha Haki – a cry for justice.
3 B. Bakare-Yusuf and J. Wheates, 'Ojuelegba: The sacred profanities of a West African crossroad', in T. Fayola and S. J. Salm (eds), *Urbanisation and African Cultures* (Durham, 2005), p. 324.
4 A. Mbembe and S. Nuttal, 'Writing the world from an African metropolis', *Public Culture*, vol. 16, issue 3, p. 353.
5 Idem.
6 A. M. Simone, *For the city yet to come, Changing Urban Life in Four African Cities* (Durham, 2004).
7 *Idem*, p. 4.
8 B. Bakare-Yusuf and J. Weates, op cit, p. 329.
9 I am aware that in using this illustration it may be read by some as feeding into African's exoticism. However, I do this because it is necessary to locate urban experiences within lived realities.
10 P. Chatterjee, *The Politics of the Governed: Reflections on Popular Politics in Most of the World* (Delhi, 2004), p. 4.
11 M. Mamdani, *Citizen and Subject* (Cape Town, 1996), p. 9.
12 G. W. F. Hegel, *The Philosophy of History*, trans. J. Sibree (New York, 1956), p. 99.
13 Mamdani, op cit.

BERLIN/THE GERMAN SYSTEM

1 See H. Häußermann, 'Desintegration durch Stadtpolitik?', in *Aus Politik und Zeitgeschehen. Beilage zur Wochenzeitung Das Parlament*, 40/41 2006.
2 See C. Hannemann and D. Läpple, 'Zwischen Reurbanisierung, Suburbanisierung und Schrumpfung. Ökonomische Perspektiven der Stadtentwicklung in West und Ost', in *Kommune*, 5/04, pp. V–X.
3 Workplace centrality = the relationship of employees with the work place compared to the living place (author's translation). H. P. Gatzweiler et al., 'Herausforderungen deutscher Städte und Stadtregionen. Ergebnisse aus der Laufenden Raum- und Stadtbeobachtung des BBR zur Entwicklung der Städte und Stadtregionen in Deutschland', *BBR-Online-Publikation*, no. 8, 2006, Bundesamt für Bauwesen und Raumordnung, Bonn.
4 See P. Veltz,'The Rationale for a Resurgence in the Major Cities of Advanced Economies'. Paper presented at the Leverhulme International Symposium, London School of Economics, 19–21 April 2004.
5 E. L. Glaeser, 'Why Economists Still Like Cities', in *City Journal*, vol. 6, no. 2, p. 73.
6 Idem, p. 74
7 See Velz, op cit., p. 5.
8 See for instance S. Sassen, *Losing Control? Sovereignty in an Age of Globalization* (New York, 1996); S. Sassen, *Cities in a World Economy* (Thousand Oaks, CA, 2000, new updated edition, originally published in 1994); S. Sassen, *The Global City. New York, London, Tokyo* (Princeton, NJ, 2001, new updated edition, originally published in 1991).
9 S. Sassen, 2001, p. XXII.
10 For discussions on German metropolitan regions see, among others, H. Blotevogel 2000, ; BBR – Bundesamt für Bauwesen und Raumordnung (ed.), *Die großräumigen Verflechtungen deutscher Metropolregionen. Informationen zur Raumentwicklung*, vol. 6/, 2005; and H. J. Kujath, 'Leistungsfähigkeit von Metropolregionen in der Wissensökonomie. Die institutionentheoretische Sicht', Working Paper, Erkner, Leipnitz-Institut für Regionalforschung und Strukturplanung, 2006, http://www.irs-net.de/download/ wp wissenoekonomie.pdf, p. 1 (accessed November 2006), author's translation.
11 This process of metropolization is taken up by political institutions. The Conference of German Ministers for Spatial Planning (Minister-konferenz für Raumordnung – MKRO) has formally established the so called 'European Metropolitan Regions'. 1995 in a first step the following six metropolitan regions were nominated as 'European Metropolitan Regions' (EMR): Berlin/Brandenburg, Hamburg, Munich, Rhine-Maine, Rhine-Ruhr and Stuttgart. In a further decision in 1997 the MKRO has integrated the metropolitan region Halle/Leipzig, Dresden and Chemniz, the so called 'Halle/Leipzip –Saxony triangle', as potential seventh EMR. In 2005 this list was complemented by the integration of city regions of Nuremberg, Hannover-Braunschweig-Göttingen, Rhine-Neckar and Bremen-Oldenburg as (potential) 'European Metropolitan Regions'. In June 2006 it adopted the new concept of spatial development 'Growth and Innovation' and made hereby clear, that the process of metropolization should be further strengthened.
12 H. Plessner, *Die verspätete Nation* (Frankfurt, 2001).
13 H. Blotevogel, 'Städtesystem und Metropolregionen', in K. Friedrich, B. Hahn and H. Popp (eds), *Nationalatlas Bundesrepublik Deutschland – Dörfer und Städte*, (Munich, 2004) pp. 40–43.
14 See Blotevogel, op. cit., p. 41 and further.
15 P. A. Hall, and D. Soskice (eds), *Varieties of Capitalism. The Institutional Foundations of Comparative Advantage* (Oxford, 2001) and C. Hay, 'Common trajectories, variable paces, divergent outcomes? Models of European capitalism under conditions of complex economic interdependence', in *Review of International Political Economy*, vol. 11, no. 1, pp. 232–62.
16 See W. Abelshauser, *Deutsche Wirtschaftsgeschichte seit 1945* (Munich, 2004), pp. 28–59.
17 W. Abelshauser, *Kulturkampf. Der deutsche Weg in die Neue Wirtschaft und die amerikanische Herausforderung* (Berlin, 2003), p. 53.
18 Abelshauser 2003, p. 93, author's translation.
19 Idem.
20 The two following sections build on reflections I developed together with J. Thiel in two papers on advanced producer services in the German metropolitan regions. D. Läpple and J. Thiel, 'Unternehmensorientierte Dienstleistungen in westdeutschen Großstadtregionen. Hamburg im Vergleich', in *Hamburg in Zahlen. Zeitschrift des Statistischen Landesamtes der Freien und Hansestadt Hamburg*, vol. 53, no. 3 / 4, pp. 41 52; D. Läpple and J. Thiel, 'Advanced Producer Services in the German Metropolitan Regions: Towards a Dynamic Understanding of the Spatial Pattern of Service-Manufacturing Links', Updated version of a paper presented at the VIII annual RESER-conference, Berlin, 8–10 October 1998 at the Technical University Hamburg-Harburg.
21 See B. Reissert, G. Schmid and S. Jahn, 'Mehr Arbeitsplätze durch Dienstleistungen? Ein Vergleich der Beschäftigtigungs-entwicklung in den Ballungsregionen der Bundesrepublik Deutschland', WZB discussion paper FS I 89-14 (Wissenschafts-zentrum Berlin für Sozialforschung), Berlin, and F.J. Bade, 'Regionale Beschäftigungsentwicklung und produktionsorientierte Dienstleistungen', in DIW, special issue 143 (Berlin, 1987).
22 D. Darthe and G. Schmid, *Urbane Beschäftigungsdynamik., Berlin im Standortvergleich mit Ballungsregionen* (Berlin 2001), p. 60, author's translation.
23 See Läpple/Thiel 1999 and 2000.
24 K. Yamamura and W. Streeck (eds), *The End of Diversity? Prospects for German and Japanese Capitalism* (Ithaca ,2003).
25 Veltz, op. cit., p. 2.
26 Thereby we are able to identify both intra- and interregional specialization. If the location quotient for a region is one, it means that the proportion of an economic branch in the region is equivalent to the average of the whole observed region. Values over one mean an over-average stocking and values under one indicate an under-average stocking. An increase of the quotient of a region can only occur 'at the expense' of others. Thanks to A. Kaiser for carrying out the data processing work for the calculation of the location quotients.
27 J. Thiel, *Creativity And Space: Labour And The Restructuring Of The German Advertising Industry* (Aldershot , 2005).
28 Kujath, op cit..
29 See among other sources BBR – Bundesamt für Bauwesen und Raumordnung (ed.), *Die großräumigen Verflechtungen deutscher Metropolregionen. Informationen zur Raumentwicklung*, vol. 6/, 2005.
30 C. Fischer et al., 'Rhein-Main als polyzentrische Metropolregion. Zur Geographie der Standortnetze von wissensintensiven Dienstleistungsunternehmen', in *Informationen zur Raumentwicklungt*, vol. 7, 2005, p. 442
31 M. Hoyler, 'Transnationale Organisationsstrukturen, vernetzte Städte: ein Ansatz zur Analyse zur Analyse der globalen Verflechtung von Metropolregionen',in *Informationen zur Raumentwicklung*, vol. 7, 2005, p. 437.
32 Fischer et al., op. cit., p. 442 and further.

ISSUES/THE PARTICULAR AND THE GENERIC

1 The 2003 Italy blackout was a serious power outage that affected the entire country, except Sardinia, as well as part of Switzerland. It was the most severe black-out in Italy in 20 years. Initial reports from Italy's electricity supplier, ENEL stated that the power line that supplied electricity to Italy from Switzerland was damaged by storms. The blackout coincided with the annual overnight White Night Carnival in Rome.

ISSUES/THE DEATH AND THE LIFE OF THE URBAN OFFICE

1 W. J. Mitchell, *City of Bits, Space, Place and the Infobahn* (Cambridge, MA, 1995).
2 H. Loyrette, 'Chicago: A French View', in John Zukowsky, *Chicago Architecture 1872—1922 Birth of a Metropolis* (Munich, 1988).
3 C. Willis, *Form Follows Finance: Skyscrapers and Skylines in New York and Chicago* (New York, 1995).
4 Carried out by DEGW using Time Utilization Surveys (TUS), a technique for measuring workplace occupancy over time.
5 A similar transition from Europe to the United States in the 1930s is described with characteristic hubris in Le Corbusier, *When the Cathedrals Were White* (London, 1947).
6 Kurd K. Alsleben, *Neue Technik der Mobiliaordnung im Büroraum*, (Quickborn, 1960).
7 F. B. Gilbreth, *Motion Study* (New York, 1911).
8 A. Harrison, P. Wheeler and C. Whitehead, *The Distributed Workplace* (London, 2004).

ISSUES/CONFRONTING FEAR

1 Z. Bauman, *Globalization: The Human Consequences* (Cambridge, MA, 1998).
2 C. Robin, *Fear: History of a Political idea* (Oxford, 2004).
3 I. Loader and N. Walker, 'Necessary Virtues: the Legitimate Place of the State in the Production of Security', in B. Dupont and J. Woods (eds), *Democracy, Society and the Governance of Security* (Cambridge, MA, 2006).
4 N. Mandelstam, *Hope Against Hope* (New York, 1970/99), p. 42.
5 R. Beauregard, 'Urbanism's Spaces: The Case of the World Trade Center', in R. Garbaye, J. Carre and S. Body-Gendrot (eds), *The Privatization of the City in Historical and Contemporary Perspective* (London, forthcoming).
6 S. Body-Gendrot and P. Spierenburg (eds), *The Civilization of Violence in Europe. Historical and Contemporary Perspectives* (New York, 2007).
7 D. Campbell, *Writing security. United States Foreign Policy and the Politics of Identity* (Minneapolis, 1998), Chapter IX; pp. 1–2.
8 D. Lyon, *Surveillance after September 11* (Oxford, 2003), p. 4.
9 R. Beauregard, 'Urbanism's Spaces: The Case of the World Trade Center' in R. Garbaye, J. Carre and S. Body-Gendrot (eds), *The Privatization of the City in Historical and Contemporary Perspective'* (London, 2007).
10 R. Rogers, A. Power, *Cities for a Small Country* (London, 2000).
11 N. Elias, *The Civilizing Process* (Oxford, 1978).
12 S. Body-Gendrot, *The Social Control of Cities? A Comparative Perspective* (Oxford, 2000).
13 Ian Blair, in a discussion at the Urban Age Berlin summit (November 2006), unpublished.
14 See note 13.
15 S. Zukin, *The Culture of Cities* (Oxford, 1995), p. 259.
16 R. Sennett, *Flesh and Stone. The Body and the City in Western Civilization* (London, 1994); G. Martinotti, 'A City for Whom? Transient and Public Life in the Second-Generation Metropolis', in R. Beauregard and S. Body-Gendrot (eds), *The Urban Moment* (Thousand Oaks, CA, 1999).
17 M. Ricard, 'Un urbaniste au service des projets', in *Urbanisme* (30 February 2007).
18 S. Sassen, presentation at the Urban Age conference in Mexico City (February 2006).
19 R. Sennett, *Uses of Disorder: Personal Identity and City Life* (London, 1996); Z. Bauman, *op. cit.*, pp. 46–47.

ISSUES/AT HOME IN THE CITY

1 This text is based on a lecture in Cambridge in March 2006 for the Environment on the Edge UN HABITAT series and it draws on my earlier work in *EastEnders*, *Cities for A Small Country*, *Boom or Abandonment*, *Jigsaw Cities* and *A Framework for Housing in the Thames Gateway*. It also draws on URBED, London Development Research, The Mayor's Plan for London, Urban Age

Berlin and Halle, Shrinking Cities.
2 Newcastle upon Tyne and Stoke-on-Trent are medium-sized cities with approximately a quarter of a million residents each that are respectively located in the north-east and Midlands regions of England. With a density of less than 2,500 people per square kilometre, they are much less densely inhabited than cities of comparable size on the European continent.
3 The Thames Gateway is a 60-kilometre-long corridor stretching along both sides of the River Thames between East London and the Thames Estuary. Some 2.4 million people live in this area, which contains multiple brownfield sites. The UK government has designated the Thames Gateway, an area with some of the most deprived wards in the country, a national priority for urban regeneration and growth.

ISSUES/TOWARDS A CARBON NEUTRAL LONDON

1 N. Gavron, J. Jacometti and Lord Oxburgh, *Megacities – a key to a sustainable future*, (Tokyo, 2006).
2 P. Droege, *Renewable Energy and the City, Encyclopedia of Energy*, Vol. 5 (2004), p. 301.
3 J. Hansen *et al, Climate Change and Trace Gases, Philosophical Transactions of the Royal Society* (London, 2007).
4 The Environmental Effectiveness of London (London, 2005).
5 D. Foy and R. Healy, 'Cities are the Answer', (4 April 2007).
6 'Greater London Authority Act', 1999, Part II – 'General Functions and Procedure'.
7 The London Plan, Spatial Development Strategy for Greater London (, 2004)
8 At the time of writing, the Greater London Authority Act was at a late stage in its Parliamentary progress.
9 'Action Today to Protect Tomorrow, The Mayor's Climate Change Action Pla'n (London, 2007).
10 'Central London Congestion Charging Impacts Monitoring – Fourth Annual Report ' (London, 2006).
11 'The London Plan 2004' set this at 10 per cent, raised to 20 per cent in the 'Further Alterations', subject to an Examination in Public at the time of writing.
12 'London Carbon Scenarios to 2026' (London, November 2006).
13 Jane Jacobs, *The Economy of Cities* (New York, 1969).
14 'Climate Change Action Plan' (London,2007).

A TAXONOMY OF TOWERS

1 'Towers to transform skylines of Paris and St. Petersburg', *the New York Times* (4 December 2006).
2 Data from Foreign Office Architect's high-rise unit.

POSITIONS/AN AGENDA FOR THE URBAN AGE

1 This text was originally written for and presented at the Urban Age Conference in Berlin, on 10 November 2006.
2 'State of the World's Cities 2006/7: 'The Millennium Development Goals and Urban Sustainability', United Nations Human Settlements Programme (2006).
3 United Nations, 'World Population Prospects: The 2004 Revision', available at http://esa.un.org/unpp/.
4 World Trade Organization, 'Table II-1: World merchandise exports, production and gross domestic product, 1951–05', available at http://www.wto.org/english/res_e/statis_e/its2006_e/section2_e/ii01.xls.
5 J. Quinlan, 'Who's Ahead in Global Manufacturing Exports?', *The Globalist* (September 2005), available at http://www.theglobalist.com/StoryId.aspx?StoryId=4763.
6 T. Palley, 'The Global Labor Threat' (29 September 2005), http://www.tompaine.com/articles/2005/09/29/the_global_labor_threat.php.
7 'Measuring Globalization', *Foreign Policy* 141 (March/April 2004), p. 54.
8 R. Florida, 'The World is Spiky', *Atlantic Monthly* 296 (3) (2005), p. 48.
9 United Nations, 'World Population Prospects: The 2004 Revision'.
10 B. Cohen, 'Urban Growth in Developing Countries: A Review of Current Trends and a Caution Regarding Existing Forecasts', *World Development* 32 (1) (2004), p. 24.
11 United Nations, 'State of the World's Cities'.
12 Ibid.
13 Ibid.
14 Regional Plan Association, www.rpa.org.
15 United Nations Secretariat, Population Division of the Department of Economic and Social Affairs, *World Population Prospects: The 2004 Revision* and *World Urbanization Prospects: The 2003 Revision*, available at http://esa.un.org/unpp (October 2006).
16 United Nations, 'State of the World's Cities'.
17 Ibid.

18 United Nations Population Division, *World Migrant Stock: The 2005 Revision*, available at http://esa.un.org/migration.
19 A. L. Beath, 'Migration', in I. Goldin and K. Reinert (eds), *Globalization for Development* (Washington DC, 2006).
20 M. Rediske, 'Integration and Immigration in Berlin', statement for the Bologna Conference on Immigration (March 2004).
21 United Nations, 'International Migration 2006', available at http://www.un.org/esa/population/publications/2006Migration_Chart/2006IttMig_chart.htm.
22 A. Tibaijuka, Under-Secretary-General of the United Nations and Executive Director, UN-HABITAT, 'Cities Magnets of Hope: The Executive Director's message on the occasion of World Habitat Day', available at http://www.unhabitat.org/downloads/docs/3761_24967_WHD%20ED%20Message.pdf.
23 'Stern Review on the Economics of Climate Change', available at http://www.hm-treasury.gov.uk/independent_reviews/stern__review_economics_climate_change/stern_review_report.cfm.
24 UN-HABITAT 2005, Global Urban Observatory, Urban Indicators Programme, Phase III.
25 S. Sassen, 'Cityness in the Urban Age', *Urban Age Bulletin 2* (Autumn 2005), p. 5.
26 William J. Clinton Foundation, Clinton Climate Initiative C40 Cities, http://www.clintonfoundation.org/cf-pgm-cci-home.htm.

INDEX

Phaidon Press Ltd
Regent's Wharf
All Saints Street
London N1 9PA

Phaidon Press Inc.
180 Varick Street
New York, NY 10014

www.phaidon.com

First published 2007
© 2007 Phaidon Press Limited

ISBN 978 0 7148 4820 4
A CIP catalogue record for this book is available
from the British Library.

All rights reserved. No part of this publication
may be reproduced, stored in a retrieval system
or transmitted, in any form or by any means,
electronic, mechanical, photocopying,
recording or otherwise, without the prior
written permission of Phaidon Press Limited.

City Profiles and Mapping by Bruno Moser
Designed by Quentin Newark and
Paola Faoro, Atelierworks

Printed in China

The editors, Ricky Burdett and Deyan Sudjic,
would like to thank Gerrie van Noord and
Pamela Puchalski for their editorial coordination,
and Miguel Kanai and Philipp Rode for their
research assistance. They would also like to
thank Josef Ackermann, Chairman of the
Board of the Alfred Herrhausen Society, The
International Forum of Deutsche Bank and
Wolfgang Nowak, Director of the Alfred
Herrhausen Society, for their support of and
enthusiasm for the Urban Age project. In
addition they would like to acknowledge the
commitment of fellow urbanists who have
contributed to the Urban Age conferences
and to this book, and to Richard Sennett for
developing the original concept for an international investigation on cities.